MONT
BONNE
NUIT
BELLE HOUGUE
MADO
BOULEY BAY
HAUTES CROIX
LE CÂTEL
ROZEL BAY
LE COUPERON
JARDIN D'OLIVET
TRINITY
TRINITY MANOR
LES CÂTEAUX
DIÉLAMENT
MANOR
ROZEL MANOR
ST CATHERINE'S
BREAKWATER
MACPELA CEMETERY
ST MARTIN
ST CATHERINE'S BAY
ANNEVILLE
T HELIER
ST SAVIOUR
LA HOUGUE BIE
MONT ORGUEIL CASTLE
MONT À L'ABBÉ
GOREY
QUEEN'S VALLEY
T TOWER
GALLOWS
HILL
HIGHLANDS
LE CÂTILLON
GAS
WORKS
PRISON
LE FAUX BIE
GROUVILLE
VICTORIA COLLEGE
LE GRAND DOUET
1781
LONGUEVILLE MANOR
GROUVILLE BAY
T HELIER
CROIX DE LA
BATAILLE
LE MONT
DE LA VILLE
BAGOT
CHAPELLE DES PAS
RUE DE CRÈVE-CŒUR
SAMARÈS MANOR
LA COLLETTE
ST CLEMENT
LA ROCQUE
ROCQUEBERG
PLATTE ROCQUE
1781
LA MOTTE
SEYMOUR TOWER
ICHO TOWER

BALLEINE'S HISTORY OF JERSEY

View across St Aubin's Bay

'Bishop Wilberforce of Winchester came to dine at Belle Vue ... Walked to the flagstaff with Canon Woodford, the Vicar of Leeds, and me; they said it was the loveliest view they had ever looked upon.' From Sir John Le Couteur's diary of 5 August 1870

BALLEINE'S HISTORY OF JERSEY

REVISED AND ENLARGED BY

MARGUERITE SYVRET

AND

JOAN STEVENS

PHILLIMORE

First published by
Staples Press Ltd.,
Kettering, Northamptonshire
1950

1981 and 1998 editions published by
PHILLIMORE & CO. LTD.
Shopwyke Manor Barn, Chichester, West Sussex

for

Société Jersiaise,
7 Pier Road, St Helier, Jersey

Reprinted 2001

ISBN 1 86077 065 7

Printed and bound in Great Britain by
BUTLER AND TANNER LTD.
London and Frome

Contents

'A rugged isle, but a good nurse of noble youths;
and for myself I can see nought beside sweeter
than a man's own country.'

Homer. *Odyssey IX*

(Quoted by Poingdestre, in Greek, on the title page of his Caesarea.*)*

This revision of the original book
by G. R. Balleine is respectfully
dedicated to his memory

List of Monochrome Illustrations

List of Colour Illustrations

Frontispiece: View across St Aubin's Bay

Foreword to the 1981 Edition

BY

HIS EXCELLENCY GENERAL SIR PETER WHITELEY, G.C.B., O.B.E.
(LIEUTENANT-GOVERNOR OF JERSEY)

Unless one is disposed to agree with Carlyle that 'History is a distillation of rumour' the search for fact and reason in order to establish the integrity and dignity of recorded history must be a primary aim of the historian.

The History of the Island of Jersey as originally completed by Balleine, a deeply researched and scholarly work, was , as he was the first to admit, incomplete for many reasons, not the least being the lack of contemporary records which to fill important chapters of events. In many instances the aid of folk lore had been called in to fill the gap and to explain some of Jersey's charming idiosyncrasies.

In the 30 years which have elapsed since the original publication Joan Stevens and Marguerite Syvret have, by their diligent researches, brought in many new sources with which to verify and complement the existing work. They have moreover produced an up-to-date, expanded and eminently readable book which nevertheless retains most of the character of Balleine's original history.

To all who cherish Jersey and its people, its history, social structure, customs and traditions, and who wish for a deeper understanding of its unique constitutional position, I confidently commend this new definitive history of our Island, whether it be for historical research or simply enjoyable reading.

Foreword to the 1998 Edition

BY

MARIE-LOUISE BACKHURST
PRESIDENT OF THE SOCIÉTÉ JERSIAISE

The Société Jersiaise is delighted and proud to be associated with the reprinting by Phillimore and Company Limited of Balleine's History of Jersey. As the only comprehensive book on Jersey it has been out of print for several years although still much in demand. It was decided to reprint with corrections and with additions to the final chapter relating to the modern finance industry contributed by Mr. Colin Powell to whom we are most grateful. We have to acknowledge, also, financial support from the Education Committee of the States of Jersey.

Written in the inimitable style of the Reverend George Balleine, Miss Marguerite Syvret and Mrs. Joan Stevens, it covers the fascinating history of a small Island struggling to maintain its status as a peculiar of the English Crown. Faced with continual threats to its political and economic survival Jersey slowly found prosperity with a diverse range of activities: the trade in knitted goods, the cod fisheries on the Grand Banks of Newfoundland and, later, around the Gaspé Peninsula, extensive trade around the world and the consequent growth of shipbuilding, the export of early potatoes and the Jersey cow, tourism and, more recently, the finance industry.

Mr. Balleine's History was first published in 1950 and, in the late 1970s, it was decided that a revised and much expanded version was desirable. Marguerite Syvret and Joan Stevens, both local historians with a wide range of interests, undertook the task. Their careful research resulted in an excellent book with full textual references, something omitted in the original version, an invaluable aid to future historians. Marguerite's knowledge of Jersey's links with Canada and Joan's of architectural and social history gave the book new dimensions.

Highly readable and accessible to both the general reader and as a grounding for the student interested in the search for more detail, I strongly recommend this book to all who care for Jersey, its past, present and future.

Acknowledgements

We are most grateful to many friends and colleagues who have helped us, and would like to mention in particular; Miss J. Arthur, Messrs P. Bisson, S. W. Bisson, R. Cox, P. Crill (Deputy Bailiff), L. Dethan, T. Dorey, Raymond Falle, Mrs. M. Finlaison, Professor J. Le Patourel, Mrs. F. Le Sueur, Sir Robert Marett, Mr. R. Mayne, the late Professor C. McBurney, Professor A. Messervy, Mrs. M. Mimmack, Dr. A. E. Mourant, Dr. J. N. Myres, Dr. Rosemary Ommer, Messrs. V. Palmer, H. Perrée, A. Podger, the late Mr. C. G. Stevens and Senator R. Vibert.

Also the staff at the Museum of La Société Jersiaise, the Honorary Secretary Mrs. W. Macready, the Librarian, Mrs. V. Ainsworth and her helpers, Mr. J. G. Speer and Mr. R. Long of the Publications Committee. We have also consulted the officers of the States and Judicial Greffe, the Chamber of Commerce and the Methodist Archives. We have corresponded with Garter King of Arms and the Huguenot Society of London.

We are very grateful to the States Education and Tourism Committees for their encouragement and financial support.

We thank Richard Le Sueur for most of the line drawings and the maps, and most particularly Mr. Maurice Richardson, then President of La Société, who as an expert photographer has co-operated with us by taking many of the photographs used to illustrate the book, and by making copies for our use of existing prints and pictures. Photographs taken by others all carry their own acknowledgements.

Jersey
1981

MARGUERITE SYVRET
JOAN STEVENS

In a book such as this some errors inevitably slipped past the keen eyes of the two authors in 1981. Every effort has been made to correct them for this edition and, in a few appropriate cases, the authors' views have been reinterpreted and their speculations modified in line with eventual outcomes. Only the final chapter, covering recent events crucial to the island's development, has been amplified, with the help of Mr. G. C. Powell to whom the Société expresses its thanks.

The lengthy and laborious task of renumbering the magnificent index has been painstakingly carried out by Mrs. E. M. Bois, and Mrs. M. N. Mimmack has worked with equal thoroughness on checking the main text and the nineteen pages of sources, notes and references.

Finally, thanks are expressed to the States' Education Committee and to an anonymous donor for the financial help which has enabled this edition to be published.

Société Jersiaise
1998

ROGER LONG
Publications Committee

Preface

'Happy is the country that has no history'. Jersey is a fortunate and happy island, yet, for so small a place, it has a long, well documented and often tempestuous history, resulting mainly from its strategic position between two erstwhile enemies. If so often in earlier times the Jerseyman appears to be cantankerous, it is perhaps because the *doléances* of the poor and the quarrels of the rich are more often recorded than the pleasanter annals of everyday life.

The late G. R. Balleine, in his foreword to the original edition of this book, pointed out the uniqueness of Jersey. Although its history has run parallel with the sister Bailiwick of Guernsey, students find a fascination in noting the differences between these very similar communities.

At the time when Mr. Balleine was collecting material for his work, the authoritative histories available for study were Poingdestre, whose *Caesarea* had been published by the Société Jersiaise, Le Geyt, Falle and Le Quesne, all long out of print. The 19th century saw a spate of guide books of varying quality, perhaps the most reliable being that of the Plees. There were also some specialized books such as Hoskins' *Charles II in the Channel Islands* and Quayle's *Agriculture in Jersey*. Writing in the *Annual Bulletin* of the Société Jersiaise in 1941, during the dark days of the Occupation, Mr. Balleine stressed the need for far more research to be undertaken: 'Homes and Furniture, Dress and Ornaments, Food and Cooking, Sports and Amusements, Health and Disease, Crime and Punishment, Books and Education, Folklore and Superstition, Religion and Morals, Trade and Travel, Immigration and Emigration. When those investigations have been carried right through the centuries, then, and not till then, will it be possible for someone to write a real history of Jersey'.

Meanwhile Mr. Balleine was busy collecting material from all available sources within the Island: from the archives of the States, the Royal Court and the Ecclesiastical Court, from the Public Library and, above all, from the Library of the Société Jersiaise with its valuable collection of rare books and its priceless store of manuscript material and ancient documents, of which he was custodian for many years. From this research and from material gleaned while in England came the *Biographical Dictionary of Jersey* and the popular but scholarly *History of Jersey*, published in 1950.

Since that time, as the bibliography on page 293 will show, a great many books, many of them excellent, have been written on varied aspects of island history, but for years no definitive history of Jersey has been available for purchase. The Société Jersiaise deemed it to be part of its responsibility to good learning, to the community and to the coming generation to fill this gap and to provide a history for residents, for informed visitors to the Island and for the schools. It was hard to decide whether to start *de novo*, or whether to reprint the original work by Balleine. His work was far too good to be shelved, and none of us felt that we could equal, let alone excel it. So it was decided, with the consent of the owner of the copyright, to revise and greatly expand it to include the result of recent research, which has added to our knowledge since 1950, and to cover the post-war period up till 1980. We have also added many illustrations, mostly the work of members of La Société, and have included a list of sources for the guidance of students of our history.

The study of local history is no longer frowned upon by academics; for it is seen to be the seed from which grows the national tree. So the history of Jersey is an important study in its own right as well as furnishing a microcosm of the whole. It is the story of a people who, since 1066, have been in a unique position geographically, politically, and ecclesiastically, a position that has shaped their destiny and over and over again, a people friendly, hardworking, thrifty, independent and proud, proud of their island heritage and, above all, proud of their special relationship with the Crown of England, as descended from the Dukedom of Normandy.

It is with these feelings in mind that we offer to the public a book which is a tribute to the memory of G. R. Balleine and is indeed mainly his work, trusting it will commend itself to all those who seek for further knowledge of the Island and to those who, as we do, love Jersey.

Chapter One

THE STONE AGE TO THE GAULS

Look unto the rock whence ye are hewn, and to the hole of the pit whence ye are digged.–Isaiah, Chapter 15

THIS BOOK IS THE STORY of man in Jersey, and so it must stretch backward in time to the earliest evidence of his presence.

Jersey was not always an island, but was joined to the continent on several occasions during the period of the earliest men. So also was Britain. We know this quite certainly from the evidence of animal remains, including those of small specialised invertebrates such as snails and freshwater organisms.

The rock we call Jersey then looked over a wide grassy plain, through which flowed the waters of the Seine and other rivers emptying into the Atlantic. From the high cliffs of Jersey, as we know it, men could look across this plain, swept by the chill wind from the northern ice-sheets, to the hill tops of the Pierres de Lecq (often called the Paternosters) and of the other more northerly Channel Islands.

The first evidence of man belongs to the Old Stone Age. Palaeolithic man left traces of his occupation in La Cotte de St Brelade and La Cotte à la Chèvre.[1] The former is an extremely important site which has been excavated intermittently from 1910 to 1978. It offers evidence of human occupation in two phases over a total period of some 80,000 years, and in this fact lies its international importance, as well as the unique nature of some of the finds. La Cotte à la Chèvre, hollowed out when the sea-level, at 18 metres,[2] was higher than today, contained deposits which were excavated early in this century, when numerous stone implements were found, but few traces of animal life. Two caves at Belle Hougue,[3] in Trinity parish, were probably never occupied by man, but are important because of the fossil animal bones found there. Some of the fossil shells from the cave indicate a warmer climate. The deposits belong to the last warm interval before the last Ice Age and are contemporary with the eight-metre raised beach. Particularly interesting are the bones of the red deer found there, which are those of a very small variant, *Cervus elaphus jerseyensis*,[4] apparently evolved through genetic isolation leading to inbreeding. A similar phenomenon has been observed on other islands at this period, notably in the Mediterranean. There were, however, no human remains whatever found in these caves, and the Island is believed to have been uninhabited at that time, that is to say approximately between 130,000 and 75,000 years before the present.

La Cotte is a cave with two phases of occupation, each sub-divided into many sub-levels, representing two widely separated eras of occupation. It was hollowed out by marine action at some period prior to the penultimate or Rissian Glaciation. As mentioned above, Jersey became an island during the temperate interglacial periods, when the water, locked up in the great northern ice-sheets, melted and returned to the sea; it was during glacial times that the Channel Islands and Britain itself were joined to the French mainland. It was then only that human occupation took

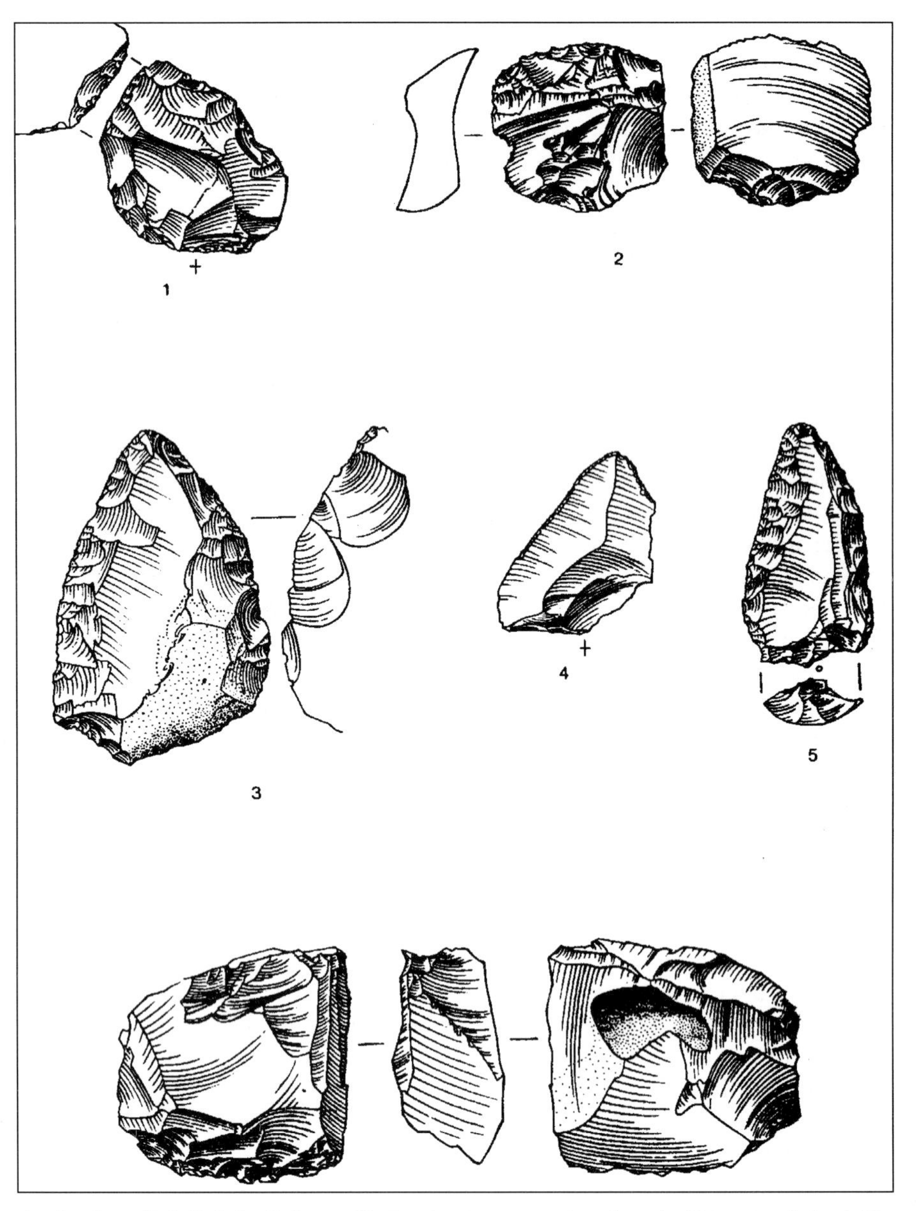

1 *La Cotte de St Brelade. Tools suitable for planning or scraping, from the University of Cambridge excavations. Some 130,000 years b.p. Except for no. 3, all are made by retouch on flakes and show the very extensive trimming characteristic of tools from layer A of the site.*

place, together with the presence of a rich glacial fauna which included such striking extinct species as the woolly rhinoceros and the arctic mammoth.

The evidence of the high sea levels offered by the so-called 'raised beaches' forms, nevertheless, a useful framework in which to subdivide the different periods of occupation. The latest and lowest of these beaches, recognisable throughout the Channel Islands and, under favourable conditions, in many areas of the world, reached a height of some five to eight metres above present mean sea-level. An earlier level is at 18 metres, and before that a still older one in the order of 30 metres. Between each of these the sea fell anything up to 100 metres below the present mean sea level.[5]

The earliest reliably dated human occupation is that found in the lower stage at La Cotte de St Brelade.[6] Physical readings assign it to a date of some 250,000 years ago. During the subsequent eight metre high sea level a part of the deposit was removed by the sea which laid down instead typical beach shingle. When the sea withdrew, as the ice-sheets of the last glaciation advanced, the second human occupation occurred with similar traces of severe arctic cold. Five hand axes, which have been found loose at various places, are probably derived from deposits of the earlier of these two periods. They could therefore belong to a very late phase of the so-called Acheulian Period. They are of moderate workmanship, small and cordiform in outline, and are made of sea-rolled nodules of flint, while other implements are of Breton sandstone. Geological research shows that the submerged plain between Jersey and the French mainland had flint-bearing deposits now far under the sea. These would have been accessible to the inhabitants, but gradually became less available as the sea level rose. As a result the hunters were obliged to fall back on less suitable materials, some of which could be obtained locally, while some were almost certainly imported from Brittany where actual ancient quarry sites, yielding similar materials and tools of the same form, have recently been identified.

Pollen analysis has been carried out in various levels in the cave. A peaty deposit at the base of the later settlement provides evidence of ten types of tree, twenty-three of herbs and five ferns, all characteristic of the end of the last temperate (interglacial) period. Further pollen samples, obtained from the lower settlement, provide evidence of an arctic flora typical of the penultimate glaciation, and yet other samples in an intermediate position confirm this general dating.

Perhaps the most dramatic of all discoveries was made in 1910,[7] when 13 human teeth, in a good state of preservation, were found in the later occupation level. They were those of a young person of Neanderthal stock, the precursor of *Homo sapiens*. The complete rhinoceros and elephant skulls, found at the much lower level (penultimate glacial date) in 1970, are of equal importance. The manner in which separate piles of skull and other bones were found strongly suggests that some preparation of the meat was undertaken after the animals' death. The marked impact fractures of many of the skulls may indicate that the animals were driven over the edge of a cliff, perhaps into the cave itself.

The mammoth hunters of La Cotte finally abandoned the cave some 50,000 years ago at a time when the accumulated deposits had reached within a few feet of the roof, so that the cave was no longer habitable. No certain traces of upper Palaeolithic man, who left his magnificent cave paintings on the mainland of France, have been detected and it is only recently that rare traces of his presence have been recognised in Brittany.

Scattered over the Island in various localities flint-chipping floors have also been identified, but an archaeological study of these shows that they are much later in date and belong to the post-glacial period. The flint for these may have been brought from the mainland, since we know that boats were already being made at that time, or they may have been obtained from natural erratics in the eight-metre beach, or indeed their makers may simply have walked over still dry land. These tools are suggestive of the mesolithic hunters, and, if this is so, there is a possibility that Jersey was inhabited continuously throughout these early ages.

After stormy weather peat beds and tree stumps are revealed below the beach sand in various bays, notably St Ouen's Bay. These again indicate a period of union with the continental mainland, or at least a much larger island of Jersey than at present. The predominant species among the trees were oak, beech, hazel and alder, and stumps seen from time to time denote trees of considerable size. At earliest this forest can be dated at 5,000 B.C.[8]

In about 4,000 B.C. neolithic colonists arrived, coming across Europe and up the western seaboard. They were dolichocephalic, small and comparatively civilised, making finely worked flint implements and also bows; as is proved by the many flint arrow-heads unearthed in Jersey. But most interesting of all, they were a settled people, in contrast to the nomadic Palaeolithic man, and they discovered the advantage of growing crops and domesticating animals for food, instead of relying on hunting, with the chance fruit or root to vary their diet. In fact neolithic man was the first farmer. He learnt to grind corn to make meal, and stone querns used for this purpose are found on archaeological sites. He built huts, or perhaps true houses, made baskets, cloth and pottery. Those who settled on the Minquiers reef[9] were seal hunters, so must also have

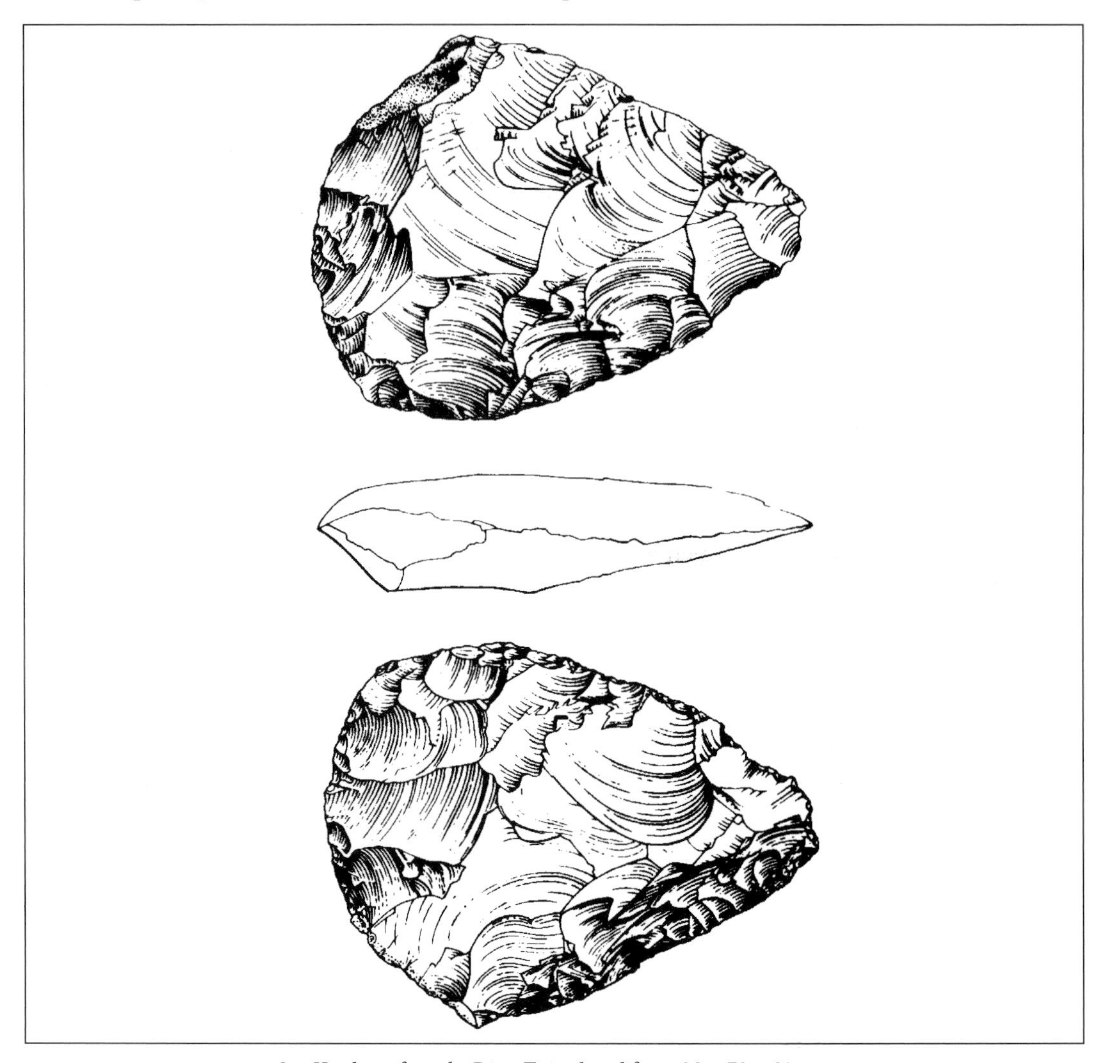

2 *Hand axe from the Dicq. Twisted cordiform, 98 x 72 x 21mm.*

built boats. There was trade, as is shown by implements brought from afar, and particularly by the eight 'jadeite' axes of advanced workmanship, probably emanating from the Alps via Brittany.[10] Other axes are made of Grand Pressigny flint, Indre et Loire and Plussulien dolomite, and fibrolite from Brittany. These apparently warlike tools were almost certainly used principally for felling trees, working with wood and hunting small animals. 'Cup markings' on some stone monuments may be a first step towards a form of written communication.[11]

Jersey is rich in dolmens, the tombs of Stone-Age man. The word is Breton and means *dol*, a table, and *men,* a stone. In their simplest form they consist of two upright stones with a capstone laid across them. They are often erroneously referred to as Druids' temples, but they pre-date the Druids (of whom there is no clear evidence in Jersey) by many centuries. There are seven major dolmens, Faldouet in St Martin, Mont Ubé in St Clement, Les Monts Grantez in St Ouen, Le Couperon in St Martin, two in First Tower Park and one now buried in the peat beneath the Gas Works site in town. But the most outstanding example is La Hougue Bie[12] in Grouville, where a mound 13 metres high covers a spectacular example of a neolithic passage grave. Pottery was found within and the bones of eight persons, three of them women. There used to be many more of what are locally called *pouquelayes*, for Poingdestre, writing in 1682, speaks of 'half a hundred'. One (perhaps two) stood on Le Mont de la Ville above the town and was discovered in 1785. It obstructed the levelling of a military parade ground and was given to the then Governor, Marshal Conway, who had taken a great interest in its discovery. He conveyed it to his home, Park Place, near Henley, where it may still be seen.[13] The frequent occurrence of the word *hougue* (a mound) and *pouquelaye* (a dolmen) in documents and in place names is evidence of the many monuments which have at some time existed.

The tombs, dating from about 4,000 B.C., may have been erected for important people only, such as tribal chiefs, and they presuppose a population able to drag the immense blocks of stone from distant beaches and other sites, to erect these monuments and then to cover them with earth. At La Hougue Bie, for instance, there are 69 large stones, some weighing about 30 ton, brought uphill from considerable distances. It has even been suggested, perhaps fancifully, that this is the origin of the name *La Rue Crève-Coeur* (Heartbreak Road) which leads to La Hougue Bie across the spine of the Grouville Hills.

The fair number of menhirs, or standing stones, are clearly man's work; often they are not of the stone of the locality in which they are found, and on excavation they are seen to have 'trig stones' to support them at their base. Many have been moved or broken up for building material. Whether they were intended for worship or for some ritualistic purpose, we do not know.

Jersey remained inhabited by the neolithic peoples for about 1,300 years, a period long enough to leave time for developments which cannot be traced in detail. It is known that early in this period England and Northern France were invaded by the Beaker folk, warlike tribes named from a distinctive type of drinking vessel which they used. Fragments of 16 of their beakers, as well as many sherds, have been found in the Island, 12 of them in the passage grave at First Tower, which must therefore have been an important tomb; only four have been found elsewhere.

The Bronze Age is sometimes thought of as a new type of civilisation, but it was not so in Jersey. When wandering smiths of the metal-workers' craft reached our shores some of the rich no doubt invested in this wonderful new metal; but the mass of the people continued to use flint or stone implements. One particularly important chief brought to the island the magnificent torque, owned by La Société Jersiaise, which workmen found in 1889 when digging foundations for a house in St Helier.[14] It is composed of 140 centimetres of gold, twisted into a four-flanged spiral bar. It weighs 746 grammes and is of Irish origin: similar, but smaller, torques have been found in Wales, England, Brittany and Normandy. None can say to whom it belonged nor exactly whence it came. Nor can we be sure of its purpose, but it must surely have been some sort

3 *The gold torque, before repair done by the British Museum. Drawn from an early photograph. Bronze-Age.*

of human adornment. Evidence of the Bronze Age is present in Jersey, and some hoards of implements have been found. The most notable collection was one of 110 items, unearthed in 1976,[15] consisting of a pottery jar containing weapons, mostly spears and swords, perhaps the stock in trade of an itinerant smith as mentioned above. This hoard was found in St Lawrence, but it is possible that Jersey's acid soil has destroyed much Bronze-Age material, which would otherwise have been more plentiful.

Life for the inhabitants was not always peaceful. The cracked sling-stone found inside the Iron-Age village at the Pinnacle, and arrow-heads with their tips broken suggest that on some occasion there was a severe assault here. In another village site at Blanches Banques was found a cooking pot, still upright and half filled with limpet shells, suggesting that the inhabitants had had to flee for their lives and had never returned. But of inter-tribal wars we know nothing; a

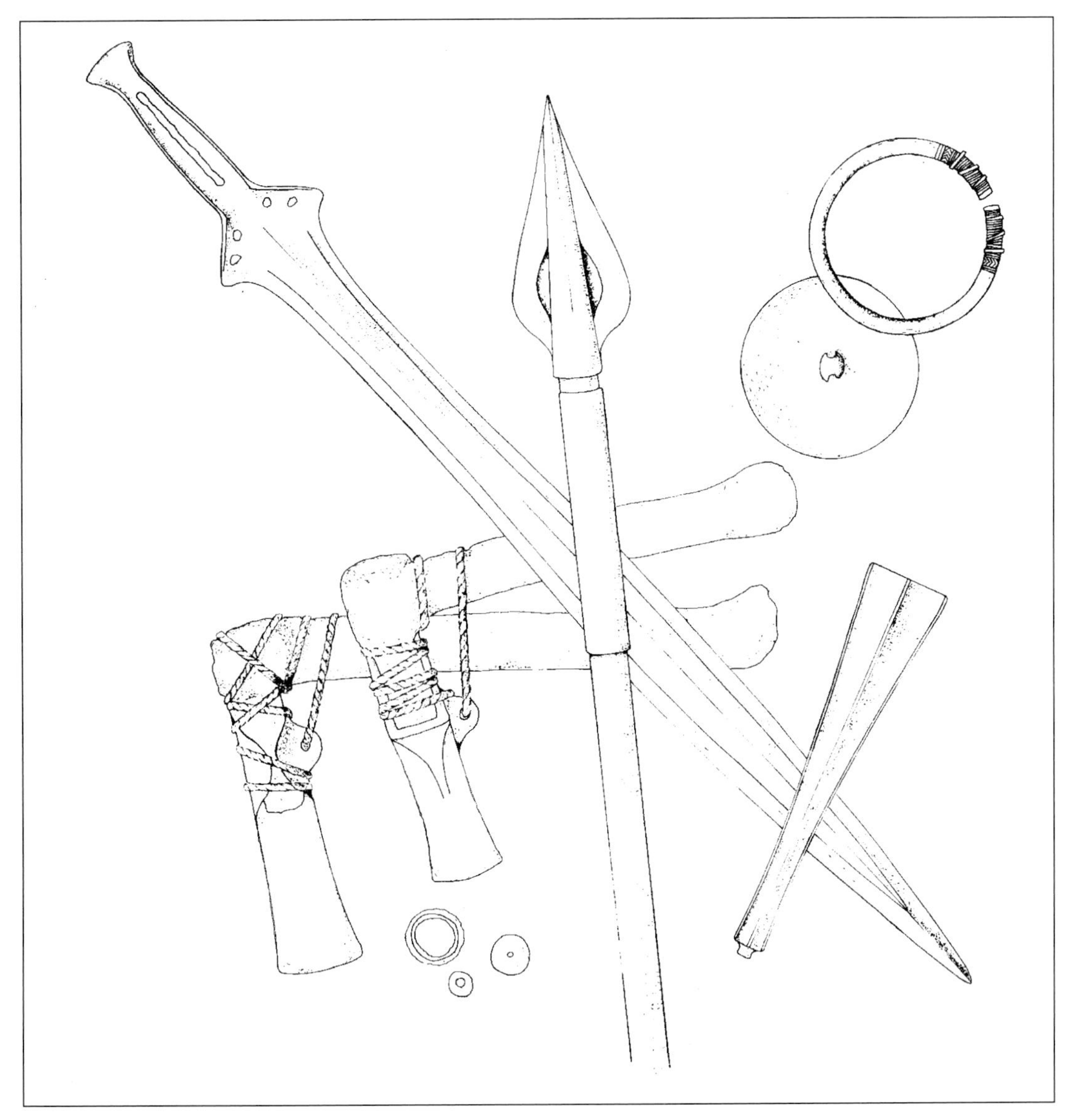

4 *An artist's impression of items from the late Bronze-Age hoard discovered in St Lawrence in 1976.* c.*1,000 B.C.*

pity, as one would greatly like to know more of these swarthy folk, who must be the ancestors of some of our present-day population.

But a time of great change and further invasion was looming. In the forests of Central Europe the tribes were again stirring, and wave after wave of tall, fair-haired, blue-eyed warriors began to pour up the Danube, across France and up to Normandy and Brittany, though they had not yet assumed these names. These were the Iron-Age Celts, or Gauls, who enter history in about 800 B.C.

At intervals in the story of man, some discovery has been so fundamental as to alter the future of the world. One was that fire could warm us and cook our food, perhaps the greatest discovery of all and the one which to a great extent separates man from the apes. Another was the motive power of the wheel; another, centuries later, was the printing press. The Celts, in their

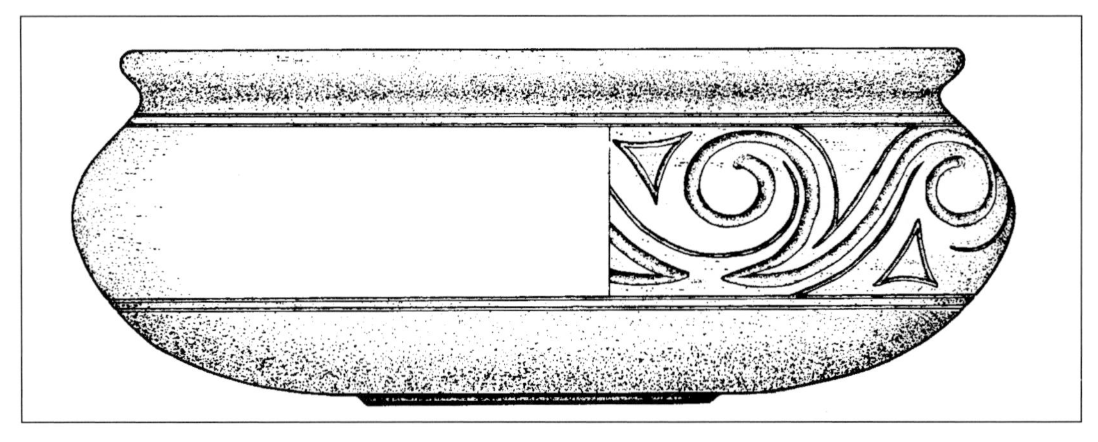

5 *Early Iron Age bowl, La Téne culture, dated 3rd century B.C. Diameter at lip 26cm. Uncovered during a rescue excavation in Broad Street, St Helier.*

time, were irresistible, as they had discovered iron, which gave them weapons that were invincible; they also introduced into Western Europe and domesticated the horse, and this made them mobile. About 300 B.C. one of these tribes, the Coriosolites, conquered the Cotentin (the peninsula due east of the islands) and subjugated that part of Normandy and apparently the off-shore island of Jersey also. It is questionable whether they came to Jersey permanently or temporarily, but in either case, with their superior strength, they would have conquered the indigenous population. Intermarriage, the inevitable result of a conquest, would further have established their dominance.[16]

These Iron-Age men came of a race new to these latitudes: they had a culture, language and religion that were all foreign. They brought with them a more advanced degree of civilisation, and in France (though not in Jersey) they have left inscriptions which cannot as yet be interpreted. They loved music, particularly the harp; with iron saws, hammers and nails they built timber houses; with bill-hooks, axes and spades they brought the land under cultivation; they controlled preying animals and grew wheat, barley, oats and rye, as well as beans; but they fed principally on meat and drank a form of barley beer. They had oak ships with skin sails, clumsy to handle, but so strong that the Romans found it impossible to sink them. Their government was autocratic, with the Chief supreme in his tribe, and the father in his family, with power of life and death. It is interesting to speculate whether it was the power of iron, in implements of war and peace, which made them so belligerent. Which was cause and which effect? We can only surmise to what extent they affected life in Jersey.

Each tribal chief coined his own money. The Greeks had established a colony at Marseilles, which used Philip of Macedon's coins with the head of Apollo on one side and on the reverse Philip's chariot winning the Olympic crown. These were copied and adapted, and thousands of examples, with their striking designs, have been dug up in Jersey on several sites, notably La Marquanderie in St Brelade, Le Câtel at Rozel and Le Câtillon at Grouville. They vary from near copies to almost unrecognisable stylisations. They can be closely dated to 53-50 B.C. and are of copper/tin/silver alloy. Our examples come from the Coriosolites and appear to be the accumulated wealth of Gauls fleeing from the advancing Romans and taking refuge in this remote island, which they thought might offer some security for their life's capital savings.[17]

A striking feature in the life of these Gauls was their bloodthirsty religion. The Romans declared that no race on earth was so fantastically religious. Their white-robed, college-trained priesthood of Druids, with a 20 years' noviciate, was the powerful unifying bond between the tribes.

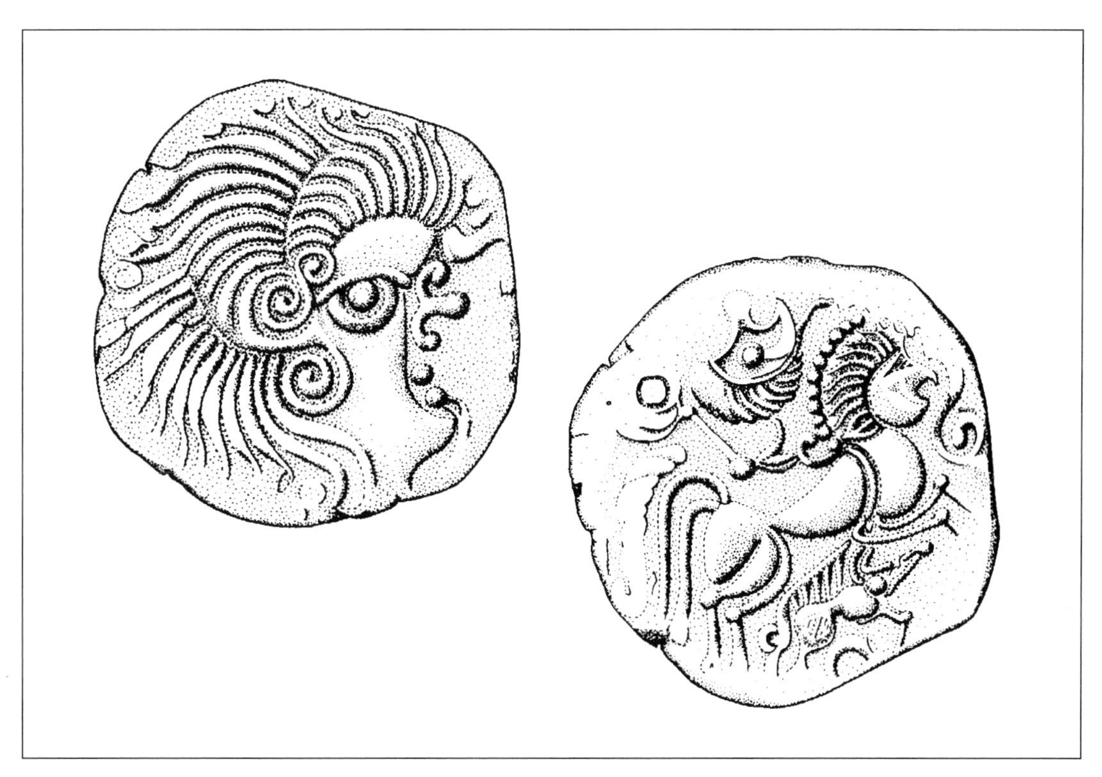

6 *Obverse and reverse of a typical coin from the Armorican hoards, 1st century B.C.*

The Druids had no temples, but built altars in the open air, on hill tops or in sacred groves. To the old worship of the Earth Mother almost universal in prehistoric times (two images of her survive in Guernsey), they added a sky-god, whom they made her husband, and a host of nature deities, such as Borvo, god of the hot springs, Vosegus, god of the forests, and Taranis, god of thunder.[18] And they worshipped them with human sacrifices, who were burnt alive. The old customs could not survive against this fierce, fanatical faith, and no more dolmens were built. In a couple of generations the descendants of the dolmen builders had forgotten their old ways, and presumably the Island, like the mainland, adopted the gods of the Gauls.

Many descriptions of these Gauls have come down to us from classical texts. Strabo, a Greek historian and geographer of the 1st century A.D., tells us that the race was

> madly fond of war, high-spirited and quick to battle, but otherwise straightforward and not of evil character ... To the frankness and high-spiritedness of their temperament must be added the traits of childish boastfulness and love of decoration. They wear ornaments of gold, torques on their necks and bracelets on their arms and wrists, while people of high rank wear dyed garments besprinkled with gold.[19]

Today modern archaeological discoveries are deepening our knowledge of the Celtic race to which they belonged, and whose influence was felt throughout Europe from the borders of Scythia[20] to the western shores of Brittany and Ireland. The dominance of these Celtic people lasted for five centuries, but in 56 B.C. they in their turn were conquered by the Romans.

Chapter Two

FROM JULIUS CAESAR TO WILLIAM LONGSWORD, 56 B.C. TO A.D. 931

This darkness in our affairs which useth to deterre others, hath wrought ye contrary effect in mee, by instigating mee to a more exact search in ye Threasury of Antiquity.– Poingdestre, *Caesarea*

CAESAR'S CAMPAIGN IN GAUL began in 58 B.C. and is recorded in *De Bello Gallico.* In two years the Romans reached the Channel, his general, Sabinus, defeated the Venelli, a tribe in what is now the Cotentin, and destroyed the fleet of the Veneti, who gave their name to Vannes and were the most powerful tribe in Armor, which meant 'the country of the sea' and was the ancient name of Brittany. Despite an occasional revolt, Gaul remained for the next five centuries a prosperous Roman province.

There is at present no definite evidence of a Roman occupation of Jersey, though it is hard to see why the Island should have escaped. It would have been a simple matter for a detachment of the 7th or 10th legions campaigning in that area in 56 B.C. to absorb the islands visible from the French coast, though it is possible that a cohort, stationed at Valognes and later at Coutances, and a Roman naval station at Alderney were considered adequate to protect the islands and maintain law and order. Even in the 20th century they have presented a challenge to a force in control in Normandy.

Later writers have attributed various sites to the Romans: Caesar's fort at Mont Orgueil, Caesar's wall at Rozel, Caesar's camp at Les Câteaux; this latter one bears evidence that its Roman origin is not impossible.[1] Also many Roman coins have been found, from those mentioned by Poingdestre in 1682 to a group discovered on the north coast at Ile Agois,[2] an Iron-Age eremetic settlement. However these could be no more than proof of trade existing between the Island and the continental mainland. Roman officials came over, collected taxes and heard cases, but otherwise apparently left the islanders to their own devices. As yet no definite trace of Roman building has been found in the Island bar a small Celtic shrine in the Roman style at the Pinnacle Rock.[3] Roman work was solid and did not perish easily. When one thinks of the innumerable Roman forts, Roman villas and Roman inscriptions unearthed both in England and Normandy, the situation is very surprising. Is it that we have failed so far to recognise the evidence? It is still hoped that modern archaeologists may find traces of a Roman presence in Jersey.

Augustus, Caesar's successor, divided Gaul into four provinces, and Jersey became part of Lugdunensis (Lyonnaise) with distant headquarters at Lyons. But it is too soon to speak of *Jersey.* What did the Romans call the Island? As the empire grew, they published route lists to guide officials on their journeys, and the most famous of these, the Antonine Itinerary, was drawn up some time after A.D. 284. It lists '... the islands in the sea between Gaul and Britain'. The ship passes *Vecta,* which is the Isle of Wight, and eventually reaches *Uxantis* which is Ushant. Next on the list after *Vecta* are *Riduna*, *Sarnia* and *Caesarea.* Many writers refuse to believe that these are the Channel Islands, as they claim that the ship would have sailed straight on until she met the Scillies; but it is a considerable distance from the Scillies to Ushant, and Roman sailors, who had no compasses, liked to keep the shore in view. By steering south-west from the Isle of Wight, they would soon sight some of the Channel Islands and then be able to hug the Breton coast on their way westwards; so it is possible that the old antiquaries[4] were right when they equated *Riduna* with Alderney, *Sarnia* with Guernsey (or more probably Sark, with *Lesia* for Guernsey) and *Caesarea* with Jersey, as these were consecutive on the list. On the other hand we also find *Andium* on this list, and from other sources we know that Jersey was known as *Andium*, *Agna*, *Augia*, and other variants, and it would hardly have been given two names in the same list. It has been suggested that the Minquiers were *Caesarea*; at low tide this reef covers an area larger than Jersey, so the passing sailor may have thought this the biggest land mass and given it the name of the emperor. The area of the Minquiers, covered with turf and vegetation, was probably still considerable in Roman times and may have supported a permanent population. However, the name *Caesarea* has been so firmly rooted in popular imagination (as is *Sarnia* for Guernsey), from the time of Camden, that it will probably always be attributed to Jersey, rightly or wrongly. In whatever way we consider and study the names on the Itinerary, they do not represent a consecutive journey. Did the geographer stop at some of the islands and set out again in a different direction, or was he afterwards told that he had omitted some islands? We shall never know.[5]

Few Roman officials may have set foot in Jersey, and then only as visitors, but the fact that it now formed part of the Empire had an enormous influence on the population. The tremendous prestige of Rome led to rapid romanisation. The Gaulish language died, as to speak it was to proclaim oneself a barbarian. To be civilised one had to speak vernacular Latin, while scholars studied the written forms and also Roman law, the justest law in the world. The Gaulish religion became blended with the Roman but, as Roman law forbade sacrifice, the Druids, the priestly class, were deprived of their most spectacular ceremony, and, with their dourly conservative outlook, they rapidly lost their influence as civilisation spread among the Gauls. Meanwhile Rome had learnt the value of a tactful hyphen, and Gaulish gods were endowed with a Roman surname. Altars were dedicated to Belenus-Apollo, Tutates-Mars and Ogmios-Hercules. The religion of the Gauls survived in this form until the coming of Christianity.[6]

At about this time there was, in what was to be Normandy, a reaction in conservative circles in favour of the older religious rites, a final flicker of faith from a dying religion. In lonely places, far from human habitation, tiny stone shrines were erected to local deities. One may picture little groups of devotees making a pilgrimage to the Pinnacle Rock in the far north-west of the Island, bearing offerings to the shrine of some god whom everyone else had forgotten.

Roman coins circulated everywhere in the Empire, and amongst those found in Jersey are some of Mark Antony (43 B.C.), of Justinian (A.D. 527) and of Commodus (A.D. 181), the latter helping to date the building already mentioned at the Pinnacle. Two small pottery bowls from this shrine are likely to have been in use as late as the 4th century A.D., suggesting that it existed for two hundred years or more. One from the Ile Agois is of the 3rd century A.D. Roman pottery, when it is found, is dated at the peak of the coin finds, surely no coincidence.[7]

However our greatest debt to Rome is undoubtedly our language and our legal system, later modified by the Normans. Gradually, during the Gallo-Roman period, the Celtic tongue was superseded by Latin; not the classical forms of Cicero, but the vernacular speech of the Roman soldiers. Their slang word for 'head' (*testa*, a tile) developed into *tête*, while the classical *caput* gave us *chef* and the fusion of three verbs (*vadere*, *ambulare* and *ire*) resulted in the complicated conjugation of the French verb *aller*, to go, giving us the Jersey Norman French *j'vais*, *j'allons* and *j'ithai*. Over the years the language developed from Vulgar Latin to medieval and modern French. With its separate insular development, Jersey French still retains ancient forms like *tchaie*, to fall, and *oui*, to hear, now virtually obsolete in standard French.[8]

When Rome adopted Christianity, the use of Latin in the churches and their schools also served to reinforce its acceptance by the people. While rural areas remained pagan, vigorous churches had been founded in the towns, and, in the anarchy which followed the collapse of Rome, the bishops remained the only officials with any authority. Gibbon declared that the century from Vespasian to Marcus Aurelius (A.D. 69-180) was the happiest mankind has known. It was the period of the *Pax Romana*, when the legions held the frontiers and kept the barbarians at bay; no civilian might carry arms, and the people were able to devote their energies to the arts of peace. But in the 3rd century life grew less comfortable, and Rome suffered from internecine quarrels.

And from the forests of Germany warlike tribes were gazing greedily at the lands across the Rhine, and tribe after tribe crossed the river. At first they were driven back; but, when Clovis and his Franks defeated the Roman general Syagrius in A.D. 486, he and his tribesmen became masters of most of Gaul. Like Constantine before him, Clovis had sworn to adopt Christianity, the religion of his wife, Clothilde, if he defeated his enemies in battle. In 496 he was baptised, and the bishops of Roman Gaul were quick to make him their ally. The Pope acknowledged him as a son, the Roman Emperor made him a Consul, and he took over the running of Gaul, now renamed Francia, without greatly altering the language, religion or pattern of administration set up by the Romans. Such are the ancient origins of our language and legal system. When Clovis died in 511, his kingdom was divided between his sons, and Jersey became part of the kingdom of Neustria, the north-western section of the Frankish kingdom, and presumably paid taxes to the Merovingian kings in Paris, the new capital.

It is not, however, certain who were the first Christians to set foot in Jersey, but they may have been fugitive Britons. To understand how this happened we must look rather far afield. The part of Gaul which suffered most from barbarians was Armorica, now Brittany; once it had been romanised with Roman roads, towns and a Latin-speaking population. Procopius, a contemporary, wrote, 'No other district was so completely pillaged and depopulated'. Meanwhile across the Channel in Britain the same kind of thing was happening. Savage Anglo-Saxon pagans were breaking in from the east and streams of Christian refugees were pouring into Devon and Cornwall (then known as West Wales), till the land could no longer hold them. Then news arrived that Armorica was empty, and wave after wave of Christian Britons crossed over and settled there, taking with them their British language, customs, religion and even their own bishops and clergy. The inundation was so complete that the name Armorica was forgotten, and the district became Brittany,[9] the people Bretons. The Latin language disappeared and was replaced by the Celtic tongue, which these people had brought with them. The Gauls, as we have seen, were of Celtic origin and in Brittany they readily readopted the language with its Celtic forms still found today in Breton inscriptions. The Breton/Britons also brought their own legends of the Arthurian cycle with their tales of sorcerers and magic potions. These are now closely associated with the forest of Brocélande, south-west of Rennes, and were first recorded in French by our own poet Wace.[10] It may well be that, while the Jerseyman's love of litigation derives from Rome or the Normans, his folklore and belief in magic influences are Celtic in origin. The first missionaries we learn of had Celtic names: St Samson, who gave his name to a parish in Guernsey and is remembered in Jersey place names; St Magloire, identified with St Mannelier, and St Brelade. There is today a hamlet near Dol in Brittany called St Broladre whose patron saint is St Brendan, but the association of this navigator-saint with Brittany seems to date from the 15th and 16th centuries and it is now thought that Brelade is a variant of Branwalader.[11]

One of the waves of this invasion was in fact led by St Samson, Bishop of Dol. His party landed near St Malo, so must have passed within sight of Jersey and Guernsey. Since they were seeking new homes, it is likely that they stopped to investigate, and almost certainly some of them settled here. In the nearly contemporary *Life of St Samson*, we are told how, after the conquest of Brittany, a dispute arose about the headship of a clan. St Samson supported the claim of a lad named Judual, 'so he set out for Lesia and Angia, islands in the sea, and, as the inhabitants were well known to him, they all came with Judual to Brittany, and God gave them to victory'. From other writings we know that Lesia was now the name of Guernsey and Angia or Andium of Jersey, and, if St Samson was so well known in the islands that he could raise an army there, many of the inhabitants must have been Britons who had sailed with him from Fowey. Again, *The Life of St Marculf* speaks of 'Agna, an island off the Breton coast',[12] and *The Life of St Wandrille* tells how Charlemagne sent an envoy, St Gervold, who may have given his name to Grouville, 'to an island called Angia, which Breton people inhabit'.[13]

So somewhere about 525 Jersey was occupied by some of St Samson's Christian Bretons. They did not take full possession, as their brethren did in Brittany, for it seems that French, not Breton, remained the language of the people, and there are few, if any, Celtic place names in the Island. They may have seized the estates and servants of Gallo-Roman and Frankish aristocrats; for their Christianity was not of a very exalted kind. The *Life of St Samson* describes Piro, the abbot under whom he trained, as an 'eminent and holy priest', yet tells, without a hint that the writer regarded it as shocking, how 'one night in a stupid intoxication he fell into a deep pit and was dragged out dying'. But the priests, even if some of them were drunkards, built small, simple chapels and conducted services. And so the islanders probably made their first acquaintance with Christianity.

If one wonders why the Franks allowed the Bretons to conquer part of their territory, the answer is that Clovis was dead and his four sons were busy quarrelling with one another, so that they had no time to protect outlying portions of the inheritance left them by their father.

But what of St Helier, who is said to have been the first missionary in the Island? In the 6th century the hermit movement was in full swing. The Christianity of the Gaulish cities had become flabby, and a reaction had set in. Hundreds of enthusiasts were taking a vow of total abstinence from luxury, and the islets along the Breton coast were dotted with hermit caves; so it is perfectly possible that a hermit lived on the rock near where Elizabeth Castle now stands, and where the little 12th-century oratory was later erected.[14] Helier was, it seems, established there by 543, and, even if little is known for certain about him, he gave his name to what has always been the centre of population in the island, in itself a testimony to his existence. To what extent was he an evangelist, living his solitary life on a distant rock, cut off by the tide for half of the time? We are told that he was a healer, for he cured a lame man named Anquetil; according to Poingdestre, he was 'wont to delude pirates' by showing false lights, in fact a 'goodie' wrecker. And Saxon pirates it was who murdered him, traditionally, in 555.

However, a hermit was not a missionary, for his religion was intensely self-centred, his whole ambition being to find a place where he could be alone with God. So Helier (Helibertus) may not have had a great deal to do with the conversion of the Island.

The Life of St Marculf, the founder of the monastery of Nanteuil in the Cotentin, who died in 558, tells how he and his friend Romard, feeling a need for solitude, crossed to Agna (Jersey), for what would now be called a retreat.[15] Here they found 'a very religious man named Helibertus, who was disciplining his body with extremely rigorous privations. They practised with him the contemplative life and the severest penitence'. This was the period when Saxons were raiding the south of England, and a fleet approached the Island, causing panic among the islanders. Marculf encouraged them to resist, and their victory was attributed to his prayers. There is nothing incredible in this.

Six hundred years later a book called *The Passion of St Helier* was written. Many of the details given here appear also in posthumously written lives of other saints. In this account Helier is murdered, not by Saxons, but by Vandals operating from North Africa, and his body is said to have been wafted to Holland. The details given in this Passion are referred to as '*une légende peu sûre*' by the Bollandists, Jesuits who specialise in a study of the lives of the saints. It may be noted, however, that Bréville on the Normandy coast opposite to Jersey also has a church dedicated to St Helier, and the belief is that his body was washed ashore there. This is not impossible, as the strong currents round the Écréhous do tend to carry the bodies of persons drowned in Jersey to that part of the French coast. A wooden carved statue of St Helier, modelled on a larger stone monument to the Saint in the churchyard at Bréville, now stands above the north porch inside St Helier's church in Jersey.

It is interesting to note, however, that St Helier, who is commemorated in Jersey on 16 July, does not appear in the Roman Calendar of Martyrs and was not added in Coutances until the 18th century. St Hilaire, who has given his name to villages in Normandy and Brittany and who is commemorated on 14 January, is a fourth-century Bishop of Poitiers.

To return to fact as opposed to what may be embroidered legend, we do know that St Samson founded a monastery at Dol and died there in 565. He was succeeded by his cousin, St Magloire, better known in Jersey as St Mannelier, who after three years retired with 62 of his monks to Sark, where he formed an important monastery. He is said to have visited Jersey, which is quite feasible, as the journey from Sark to Grève de Lecq is not long. He is reputed to have been much interested in education and may well have wanted to visit other religious centres in Jersey and to expand his missionary activities. Indeed a small daughter-house may well have existed at or near the parish church of St Mary, which, already in 1042, was known as St Mary of the Burnt Monastery, and where there is an extremely early priest's tombstone (now built into the west wall of the church).[16]

The conversion of the people was probably a slow process. In the Cotentin the country folk clung for years to their pagan ways, and so it would have been in Jersey. But the zeal of the Celtic monks and their clear-cut picture of the contrast between heaven and hell gradually won the day. The old altars were deserted and more and more people knelt in the little chapels of Christ.

But the church established by the expatriate Britons in Brittany was a schismatic one. When the Britons swept over the land, they brought their own bishops with them, entirely ignoring the Archbishop of Tours, whose province they were invading. At first they had no fixed dioceses; they were abbots in episcopal orders travelling around performing episcopal functions and they kept Easter on a different day from the rest of Christendom.[17] They tonsured their priests in a different fashion and horrified the French bishops by permitting women to aid them in their religious ceremonies.

In 577 the Island received an unexpected visitor. Praetextatus, Archbishop of Rouen, became entangled in a conspiracy to dethrone the Frankish king. Gregory of Tours, who was one of his judges, says, in his *History of the Franks*, 'When he tried to escape by night he was cruelly beaten and banished to an island over against Coutances'. Historians agree that this must have been Jersey. His exile lasted for seven years, and the presence in the Island for so long a time of an energetic archbishop must have left its mark on the local church. Whether it was he who secured the transference of the islands from the diocese of Dol to that of Coutances no one can say, but Romacarus, Bishop of Coutances, who was a friend of Praetextatus, is reported to have attached '*définitivement et officiellement toutes les îles de la Manche à l'évêché de Coutances*'.[18]

For the next two centuries our history is almost a blank, which is unfortunate, for this is the time when our parishes may have been formed. Doubtless they evolved over the years and to begin with would have been but the area surrounding the parish church, itself likely to have been a megalithic centre of population for centuries; a parish boundary would be created automatically at a natural feature, such as a stream, and in some cases it might have faded out in a marsh that could neither be forded nor cultivated. By Norman times the parish boundaries were firmly fixed and have not changed, bar *minutiae*, in the intervening millennium. However, Jean Poingdestre, writing in the mid-17th century in his *Lois et Coutumes de l'Ile de Jersey*, notes that there was less confusion about these boundaries when solemn processions at least once a year beat the bounds '*par tous les confins de la paroisse*', especially where these were disputed by neighbouring parishes, than in his day when they had to rely on conjecture, presumption and the recently introduced *dîmes et terriers*. Incidentally he remarks that title deeds make it easier to define the limits of the fiefs. Over the years slight errors have crept into maps showing parish boundaries, and in 1980 a determined effort was made to arrive at a correct version in preparation for a new Ordnance Survey map of Jersey.

The original boundaries probably became stabilised with the introduction of the tithe system derived from the Old Testament. Every tenth sheaf of corn was given to the church. This was at first voluntary, but was made compulsory by Charlemagne in 779. It then became necessary to define which estates paid tithes to which churches. A great many of the country churches in Western Europe were founded by landowners, who treated them as private possessions, took the revenues and appointed and paid a priest. Gradually the bishops were able to convert the right of appointing the priest into the right of presenting a candidate to them for institution (the system of patronage); but when the reforming movement of the 11th and 12th centuries tried to secure the revenues for the church, these were often given to monasteries rather than to the priest for his maintenance. In such cases the monastery had an obligation to provide for the priest; but the monastic life rather than the parish ministry was considered the greater good, and such provision was often inadequate.

While the parish system in England, France and the islands may have a common origin, in England it has been eroded by the counties, evolved from Saxon shires, and by regional reorganisation, and in France by the secular reforms of Napoleon. In Jersey it has retained its original character as an ecclesiastical parish which is also a municipal unit of considerable significance locally. The Ecclesiastical and Parish Assemblies overlap in their functions, and the office of Constable has developed into one of major importance in the Island, its holder being the secular head of the parish with a voice in the States Assembly. He is neither the *comes stabuli* (keeper of the horse), which denoted high military rank in France, nor the village 'constable', who was responsible for law and order in England until the introduction of a paid police force. The first known reference to a Constable in Jersey is in 1462.[19] He is helped in his duties by centeniers and vingteniers. These too in their origin may have affinities with similar officers in England and France, but over the centuries have developed into a unique body of men. Originally they may have been responsible for a hundred or twenty houses, hence the term *vingtaine* to denote a division of the parish.[20] Now they represent steps in the parish hierarchy leading from Constable's Officer to Constable. The centeniers still act as honorary police within the parish.

We hear nothing of Jersey in Charlemagne's reign except that *The Chronicle of Fontenelle Abbey* records that in about 802 he sent his abbot, 'the abbot Gerald, in peril of the sea, but suddenly snatched therefrom by the aid of the Holy Father (St Wandrille), on a mission to an island called Angia which Bretons inhabit. It is adjacent to the territory of Coutances, and was ruled by a chief named Anouvarith'.[21] This mission may have been one of Charlemagne's efforts to bring Brittany into line with the rest of his empire, but we hear nothing more about it. It is only mentioned because the abbot attributed his escape from shipwreck to the fact that he prayed to St Wandrille, and the story was recorded among the miracles attributed to that saint, a fortunate circumstance for us.

Even Charlemagne succeeded in establishing only a nominal suzerainty over Brittany, which then included the Cotentin and the Islands. There was constant revolt and, after his death (in 814), a Breton of unknown origin, called Nominoé, Count of Vannes, was made Duke of Brittany in 826 by the emperor, Louis le Débonnaire. Nominoé seems to have been the founder of Breton unity. When Louis died in 840, the new Duke refused to collaborate with his successor, Charles le Chauve, and, when peace was made in 846, Brittany was given her independence. Nominoé's son, Erispoé, carried on the dynasty. In 819 Louis le Débonnaire had ordered the Breton church to abandon Celtic rites, but, in 846, Nominoé reconstituted the dioceses of Brittany into seven bishoprics with Dol as the metropolitan church, and thus cut off the Breton church from the main current of ecclesiastical life in Europe. For several centuries there was conflict between the bishoprics of Dol and Tours.[22] There is some doubt as to whether at this period Jersey was attached to Dol or Coutances. In either case the situation must have had some effect on church life in the island.

But Jersey people had little time to think about this. The ninth century was the most troublous in the Island's history. It was the century of the Viking raids. From about the year 800 sea robbers began to descend on the Channel from behind the mists of the unknown north. Scandinavians they were, probably from Denmark, though this is not certain. Every summer their long ships, propelled by oars and sails, spread rapine, fire and slaughter on every hand. Neither England, France nor Brittany had a fleet able to check them. Jersey must have been plundered again and again, and its simple houses and chapels went up in flames. As we have seen, St Mary's parish became St Mary of the Burnt Monastery. Even the prehistoric tombs were rifled for buried treasure, which accounts for the fact that, when opened in modern times, little but broken pottery was discovered in them.

It is now that we begin to find our earliest place names, Norse names, given by these pirates as they sailed around our coasts. L'Etacq in St Ouen, which in old documents is spelt L'Estak, is the Norse word *stakkr*, meaning a high rock. It is repeated again and again on the coasts, L'Etacquerel in Trinity, Etacquerel at St Ouen, the north and south Etacs off Grouville, the Gros Etacs off La Rocque and Etoc, one of the Ecréhous. *Holmr*, the Norse word for an islet, has given us Jethou, Lihou, Brecqhou, Écréhous and a number of rocks called Le Houmet. Gorey, when first mentioned, is spelt Gorroic, Gorryk and Gourroic, which reminds one of the Norse settlement of Gourock in Scotland. The burial mounds, which the Vikings marked down for treasure hunts, they called *haugrs*, a word which later ages softened into '*hougue*', giving La Hougue Bie, La Hougue Boëte, La Hougue Dirvault and others. The Norse word *ey*, an island, gave us the final syllable in Jersey, Guernsey, Alderney and Chausey. It must have been Norsemen who coined the word '*Jersey*', but the meaning of the first syllable is still in doubt. One suggestion is that it is the Frisian word *gers*, meaning grass, which would make Jersey 'the grassy isle'; an alternative is the Norwegian personal name *Geirr*: a pirate may have seized the island when it came to be known as Geirr's Ey. Similarly it has been suggested that Guernsey is Gutrin's Ey, or Varin's Ey. Another possibility for Jersey is Jarl's Island, or Earl's Island after some Norse nobleman. It will be seen that '*ey*' was the suffix for large islands, '*ou*' for the smaller islets nearby. It also seems likely that some local family names, like Hacquoil, Vibert and Vautier, are derived from personal Norse names. A study of any Scandinavian telephone directory encourages such speculation. Finally comes the possibility that Jersey is a corruption of Caesar's Ey, which would vindicate the 'Caesarea' theory.[23]

However, though these raiders left names behind, they left little else. Wace, the 12th-century Jersey-born poet,[24] speaks of the utter devastation they caused:

En Auremen, en Guernsei,
En Sairc, en Erim, en Gersi.

Dupont, the French historian, thinks that during these raids most of the Breton landowners fled to the mainland.

As the century progressed, the raiders grew bolder and bolder. In 850 they wintered on the Seine. In 885 they sailed up the river and besieged Paris, till they were bought off. The raids now became a regular invasion; the Norsemen had come to stay. Just as even King Alfred had been compelled in 878 to surrender half England to the Danes by the Treaty of Wedmore, so Charles the Simple of France purchased peace in 911, by the Treaty of Saint-Clair-sur-Epte, surrendering to Rollo, the pirate chief who held Rouen and half the province which became known as Normandy, the Normans' Land. At first Rollo's dominion did not extend further west than the river Dives; and, though he later acquired the Bessin, the district round Bayeux, he never secured the Cotentin nor the Channel Islands. These were won by his son, William Longsword.

Chapter Three

WHEN JERSEY WAS RULED BY NORMANS, 931-1204

I looked. Aside the dust cloud rolled
The Master seemed the Builder too.
Upspringing from the ruined Old
I saw the New.–Whittier

IN 925, ROLLO, who was then at least eighty, handed over the government of his duchy to his son, William Longsword, who soon had to show his mettle. In 930, with the help of Norsemen from the Loire, he overran Brittany; but the Bretons rallied and, on Michaelmas Day 931, they massacred their conquerors and invaded Normandy,[1] hoping to recover Bayeux. The Young Duke completely crushed them and annexed l'Avranchin, le Cotentin and the Channel Islands, fixing the Norman-Breton frontier along the river Couesnon. However, although this date is a landmark in Channel Island history as marking our first association with the Duke of Normandy, William's troubles were by no means over. Whereas the area around Rouen was fast becoming French-speaking and christianised, the Cotentin was still Norse-speaking and less civilised. It had, at an earlier date, been overrun by Saxons, who were joined by Vikings, probably Danes. Count Riulph of Brittany tried to drive a wedge between the Norse-speaking and French-speaking elements in the Dukedom, and in 933 marched as far as Rouen before William Longsword decided to take action and routed the Bretons once more.

For the next 273 years Jersey came under Norman or Angevin rule. The Battle of Hastings, or Senlac, comes almost exactly halfway through this period; from Rollo to King John, who lost Normandy, there were 14 Dukes, and of them William the Conqueror was the seventh. So the Dukes of Normandy, who were more often than not joint rulers of England and Normandy, and indeed for a time of the Angevin Empire and Aquitaine, ruled Jersey for 135 years before the Conquest and for 138 years after it.

For this period our knowledge is still scanty. Normandy is poor in old historical documents, as its towns and castles were so often ravaged. Many of the records perished during the Hundred Years War, the Huguenot Wars and the French Revolution. A large number of those that survived were lost in the allied bombardments of the Second World War. A notable contribution to our knowledge, however, is the *Cartulaire des Iles Normandes*, containing the text of 365 documents, spanning a period from 1025-1698. The original documents disappeared in flames in 1945; they have in a sense been saved by this publication. From it and some other sources it is possible to make some assessment of the situation. The *Cartulaire*, however, records mainly donations and other details relevant to the Norman abbeys which held possessions in the islands. It therefore throws more light on ecclesiastical than on secular matters and is largely concerned with the revenues these parent abbeys could extract from the unfortunate islanders, who never saw abbot or bishop on their soil, but who had to subscribe in one form or another to incomes which left Jersey, and for which they can have seen little benefit.

The settlement of the Normans must have made enormous changes in these islands, so close to and so clearly visible from the continental mainland. The new inhabitants of Normandy found Jersey devastated by the ever-frequent Scandinavian raids. It is believed that the Cotentin, particularly the northern part, had almost been reduced to a desert,[3] and the islands, which were even more exposed, must have suffered just as severely. But, while stress is laid on the ravages of the Norsemen, their more civilised accomplishments are often overlooked. They were skilled sailors and boat-builders, competent farmers and merchants trading widely throughout Europe. A number of words in Norman-French connected with ships and the sea are of Scandinavian origin, as are the terms *bel* (farmyard), and *haûgard* (stack yard) still used in Jersey contracts. It was in the interest of the new rulers to encourage agriculture, the basis of a prosperous community, and this they did. It was largely in the fields of navigation, agriculture and commerce overseas that the islands were to make a name for themselves in later centuries.

William Longsword reserved a large amount of land for himself, the royal fief. He must have sent men over to colonise his outlying possessions and establish civilised government. It was probably in the 11th century that fiefs were first granted by the King/Duke to those whom he wished to reward and those with whom he wished to ingratiate himself. A fief is a grant of land from King to Commoner (often an ecclesiastical establishment) on which certain dues, in kind and labour, had to be paid. The tenants, however, retained the freehold of the land, subject to their paying taxes and providing services.

Among the earliest fief holders were the de Carterets, who held larger and more valuable estates near Carteret in Normandy, but also received land in Jersey,[4] and there were many others like them. The fiefs have so changed over the years that their history and their boundaries cannot be recorded with certainty. They did not necessarily observe parish boundaries, though both would take an obvious feature, such as a stream, as a perimeter. Local people thus found themselves '*tenants*' (holders of land) under a new overlord, Jersey being part and parcel of Normandy. There is, however, no evidence of slavery or serfdom.

The Jersey character and indeed the appearance of some Jerseymen are so intensely Norman, that it is evident that the Norman immigration must have been a large one. Go to a Norman town and you will see people who could be the brothers of friends at home; go to a Breton town and you will not be so reminded of home. The predominantly dolichocephalic head of the Norman is recognised, but seldom the brachycephalic head of the Breton among those whose families have been in the island and intermarried for many generations. Although some are short and dark, the tall fair Jerseyman is by no means unknown, witness to the Viking infiltration. Similarly you will find many names familiar in Jersey on memorials and in cemeteries in Normandy, some appearing in records of the Conquest and others perhaps connected with later refugees.

The Normans proved themselves to be most adaptable; like the Franks before them, they determined to become as civilised as those they had conquered; not that they themselves were barbarians, as recent work on the Viking inheritance has shown. Their northern language, often referred to as Danish,[5] disappeared, and they adopted the Romance language being spoken in their new lands, a French derived from medieval Latin,[6] still spoken in Normandy today and, in a slightly different form, in Jersey. The two variants have many characteristics in common; for example the sound *ai* replaces the French *oi*, as in *trais* (trois) and *naire* or *naithe* for *noire*. Although many of the rocks around Jersey have Norse names, given them by marauding pirates before the settlement of Normandy, inland place-names are generally French.

Every Norman was a born sailor and a born lawyer, taking delight in legal forms and subtleties, hence perhaps the well-known litigiousness of the Jerseyman. Step by step there came into existence that great code of laws, still the basis of Jersey law, although in modern times the criminal law is similar to that of Britain. The *Coutumier*, compiled at an unknown date late in the 13th century, was a codifying of these laws, but for three centuries before that every Norman had regarded the law with respect. Professor Le Patourel has pointed out that during the

Anglo-Norman period the judicial administration was largely Norman-inspired, while in Normandy itself it provided much of the substance of the *Coutume de Normandie*. The Exchequers and ecclesiastical law also had a similar basis and origin.

One relic of those early days remains in the *Clameur de Haro*. If a man thought he was wronged, he had only to raise this cry, and the aggressor was bound to desist until the case had been tried in Court. The cry is: '*Haro, haro, à l'aide mon Prince, on me fait tort*'. (Haro, Haro, help me, my Prince, I am being wronged.) It is questionable whether the Haro refers to Rollo, the first Duke of Normandy (*ha, Rou*'), or is just a general cry for help. In either case, it is a dramatic ritual of great antiquity which offers immediate redress. By calling on the Duke, founder of the Norman state, and as such the fount of all justice, the injured person goes to the highest authority known to him. The *clameur* may be raised rightly, *à bon droit* or wrongly, *à tort*, and in the latter case the person appealing will be fined. In early medieval times the *clameur* was restricted to criminal matters such as burglary, homicide, arson or any pressing peril. By the mid-17th century it had become confined, in Jersey, to cases of interference with real property and remains so to this day. It must be raised on the site of the alleged wrong, and immediately before witnesses. Changes in the use of this interesting procedure were doubtless gradual and evolved over the years. The *clameur* is still raised occasionally.[7]

The fervour with which these erstwhile pirates developed a respect for the law is matched by their enthusiasm for religion. As pagans they had burned churches and massacred monks; but when they adopted Christianity, they showed the zeal of all converts; from this stems the beauty of their early cathedrals, glorious hymns of praise in stone, never to be excelled. Jersey, being very small and very poor, could not boast any such church building, except perhaps the abbey on the Islet (later the site of Elizabeth Castle), scant as is our evidence for it.[8] This does show, as one would expect round-headed arches, from which our typical Jersey round arch, to be discussed later, is clearly derived.[9]

In the 50 years before the conquest of England 26 great abbeys were founded in Normandy and innumerable priories and smaller foundations, a record without parallel. In Jersey small chapels, of which we have only vague knowledge, had often been burnt by raiders and rebuilt. In 12 instances a parish church began its evolution. It is known that St Mary and St Martin had churches before 1042, and presumably Grouville, as the former is called 'St Martin the Old'.[10] It seems more than likely that all 12 existed in some form at this period, even if proof has not always survived. It would be surprising if St Lawrence, at least, did not exist as a Christian site long before this, judging from the incised stones built into the east wall and other evidence.[11] The stones date from the ninth and 10th centuries, and similar stones may be seen in the fabric of St Mary, St Peter and St Ouen.

The construction of our parish churches (and Guernsey's are very similar) is curious and more interesting than a casual glance might suggest. There is a marked similarity between the 12 buildings, more so than would normally be found in any comparable area. They are aisleless cruciform in original plan, and none has a western tower, but all have a central crossing supporting a tower in four cases, and a spire (a later addition) in the remaining eight. If there were ever apses, all trace of them has gone, and in many cases the transepts have been swallowed up in later additions, which have given the church two parallel naves, and, in the case of St Peter and St Ouen, three naves. The roofs are pointed barrel vaults in stone, steeply sloping on the outside. All now have a covering of slate or tile, but the written records do not tell us if the stone roof was originally uncovered, though Ecclesiastical Assemblies report instances of tile, slate and thatch being ordered for roof repairs. Stone roofs of a somewhat similar construction are also found on guard houses and forts, on at least one colombier and even on some pig sties,[12] and it may be that the Jerseyman had an inherited skill in such construction.

Here we may mention the spurious dates so often attributed to our parish churches, said to have emanated from *Le Livre Noir de Coutances*. These dates, such as 1111 for St Brelade, first appeared in an almanac of 1792. *Le Livre Noir* was the official register of the diocese of Coutances, of which we formed part, and it was compiled in 1251. In 1898 La Société Jersiaise took the step of visiting Coutances to examine the original and report thereon. They found that the *Livre Noir* contained no such dates, but that they had been added in a modern handwriting. The source of these dates is unknown, but in most cases proof can be found that the church in question existed far earlier than the date ascribed to it; for example St Martin, already recorded in 1042, was given as 1116.

Such far-reaching restoration of parish churches took place toward the middle of the 19th century that one must conclude that by then the buildings were in sore need of repair; an early picture postcard of St John's shows the spire supporting a sizeable bush growing out of the masonry.

The dedications of the churches are of great interest, but only two appear to be of Celtic origin; St Brelade and St Ouen (a Gaulish name akin to Owen), the latter being a seventh-century bishop of Rouen. Of the others St Clement was probably a first-century Roman Christian who became Pope, St Martin a bishop of Tours, St Lawrence a martyr and St Helier a hermit and martyr with local connections. The other five dedications are derived from the New Testament, though surprisingly none of the four evangelists is represented, St John being dedicated to the Baptist. It has been noted that Celtic dedications in the islands tend to be near the coast, while the more orthodox biblical ones are inland.

Nothing is known of the first Rectors, but when the churches themselves or their advowsons were given to one of the great Norman abbeys (St Mary and St Martin were given to Cerisy),[13] the Rector would have been appointed by the parent abbey, which gave him powerful backing in any disputes. However this also drained wealth from the Island in the form of tithes.[14] One may well wonder what were the practicalities of getting this tithe wheat over to the appropriate abbey, in good condition, and who took it. Official documents do not recount the human difficulties with which people had to contend.

Of the early Dukes only one, as far as we know, ever set foot in Jersey. In 1029 Robert I, the Conqueror's father, planned the first eruption of Normandy into English history. Edward the Atheling, who later was known as Edward the Confessor, was a refugee at his court, while Canute the Dane sat on the English throne. Robert gathered a fleet to oust the usurper and make Edward king; but when they came within sight of the Sussex coast a great tempest arose and, to quote Wace, 'they could neither land nor return to Normandy, so they came to the island of Gersui, which is close to the Cotentin where Normandy comes to an end'. There they spent long weary days waiting in great discomfort for favourable winds and tides. William of Jumièges, a contemporary chronicler, on whom Wace relied for some of his material,[15] adds 'they were detained many days, and when contrary winds continued and the Duke saw he had no chance of crossing the Channel, he turned the prows of his ships around and disembarked at Mont-St-Michel.'

At this period Mont-St-Michel appears in many contexts. In 1167/8 Philippe de Carteret, with the consent of his wife Nicolaa, his son Renaud and his nephew William, gave to the Abbey of Mont-St-Michel the church of St Ouen with its appurtenances, the Chapel of St Mary and a neighbouring dwelling, and gifts of straw, oats, a cloak, a pair of boots, basins, a cloth and candles, in exchange for which a member of his family was to be received into the Abbey as a monk.[16] A quarter of a century after Robert's visit, a more disreputable member of the ducal family arrived. In 1055, Mauger, Archbishop of Rouen, the Conqueror's uncle, whose life, even in those lax days, had become a public scandal, was deposed by the Papal legate at the Council of

Lisieux and banished by his nephew to the Channel Islands. Here, according to Wace, he continued his unseemly life, crossing from island to island and begetting many children. On one of these journeys he fell overboard and was drowned. He was reputed to practise black magic and to keep a private devil named Toret.

When the Conqueror sailed for Hastings in 1066, did any Jerseymen go with him? Wace tells us how his father saw the fleet gathered at Saint-Valéry-sur-Somme and counted the number of the ships, but he does not say that he sailed in them, nor does he quote his father as a witness when he describes the battle. In his list of those who fought at Hastings, he mentions Onfrai and Maugier de Carteret and tells us that Maugier was newly knighted; Domesday Book shows us that he was rewarded with estates in Somerset. Either or both of these men may have come from Carteret in the Cotentin. One would expect that, if a Jersey contingent had helped to win the victory, Wace, the Jerseyman, would have mentioned the fact, though it must be remembered that his account was not contemporary. However if those mentioned were absentee landlords, owning more valuable estates on the mainland, no one would have thought of them as being Jerseymen. It does seem that Onfroi kept the ancestral lands in Normandy and probably those in Jersey, as his son Renaud held both the Carteret and the St Ouen fiefs.[17] Some local names like Mallet and Le Gresley were represented in the Conqueror's army, though they may not at that time have had branches settled in Jersey. Gaulthier (Walter) Giffard is said to have provided 100 men and 30 ships, and the pilot for Pevensey is reported as coming from the Cotentin.[18]

William was crowned at Westminster, but this did not make Jersey a part of the kingdom of England, for it remained a cantlet of Normandy. The Island formed part of the duchy in all respects, in its currency, in the administration of justice and in the interests which continental landowners had there. For a long time to come the religious centre remained at Coutances. The political centre was the Court, which was itinerant, as medieval rulers were constantly moving about in their domains. In fact everything went on as before. When the Conqueror died in 1087, all connection with England, frail as it was, was broken, and Jersey saw 60 years of constantly changing rulers; for William bequeathed Normandy to his eldest son Robert and England to his second son William Rufus. But Robert was in need of money, so he sold or pledged (it is not certain which) the Cotentin and the islands for £3,000 to this third brother Henry, who assumed the title of Count of the Cotentin. The brothers were always quarrelling, and in 1091 Robert recaptured the Cotentin. Five years later Rufus defeated Robert and gave it back to Henry. In 1100, at the death of Rufus, Henry became King of England and restored the Cotentin to Robert. In 1106 he overthrew his brother and made himself Duke of Normandy.

One of the earliest of our charters, telling us anything of a personal nature, is that of 1135 when Philippe de Carteret, grandson of Onfroi, 'moved by the counsel of evil men', tried to recover some land which his father had given to the monks of Mont-St-Michel. Later he relented in the presence of his mother Lucia, and his younger brothers Geffroi and Onfroi. To this gift he then added '*duas plateas terre in Gerseio extra curiam suam*', that is two plots of land in Jersey outside his courtyard. This would seem to suggest that by then the de Carterets were established in the Island, though it does not prove that they were normally resident. However their choice of the English allegiance in 1204, which lost them their larger territories near Carteret, would lead one to suppose that they were well-established here by 1200 at least. By another charter Renaud gave the Abbey the tithes of St Ouen and an acre of land on which to build a barn to receive them.'[19]

When Stephen was Duke things were even more anarchic than in England, and Geoffrey of Anjou, who had married Henry I's daughter, and was the founder of the Plantagenet dynasty, swallowed Normandy bit by bit 'as if it were an artichoke'.[20] In 1144 he captured Rouen and was accepted as Duke. Six years later he resigned the duchy to his son, Henry, who, after Stephen's death, became Henry II. In the middle of the 12th century the Abbey of St Helier was founded[21] on the islet on which Elizabeth Castle now stands by William Fitz Hamon, a knight of some importance at Court, who later became Seneschal of Nantes and then of Brittany. It remained with its monastic buildings clustered around it in the lee of the rock on which the castle keep was built, standing there until it was blown up by a bomb in 1651.[22] Henry granted to the Abbey the Town Mill, St Helier's Marsh and the patronage of Trinity church, while other benefactors gave pieces of land. But the new foundation came to an ignominious end as a result of an ecclesiastical quarrel. The St Helier's monks were Victorines, a sub-Order of the Augustinians, whose beliefs were based on the work of St Victor of Paris (1096-1141).[23] But the Augustinians were at this time split into two rival factions; the Jersey monks belonged to one party, the monks of the abbey of Notre-Dame at Cherbourg to another. Between the two abbeys such unseemly bickering arose, that in 1175 the King and the Archbishop of Rouen made St Helier's abbey a mere dependency of Cherbourg 'that there might be one flock and one shepherd'.

The great church survived all these vicissitudes. The abbey appears in the *Cartulaire* as '*Abbotis Sti Elerii*' in 1172 and 1185, as '*monasterium Beati Elerii*', *c.*1179, '*ecclesia Sti Elerii de insula Gereseio*' in 1180, and '*domus Sti Elerii de Insulis*' in 1185. After it became but a priory, it was still an important property owner, maintaining buildings on the islet and on the mainland. By 1205 it appears as '*prioratus Ste Elerii*'. It escaped the dissolution of the Alien Priories in 1413, and priests were still living there in 1515, when two men forcibly entered the garden of the Prieuré de l'Islet and stole some apples and pears, destroying the fruit trees and to the detriment of Maistre Hyou Pole, the Prior. The priory was finally suppressed in 1540.[24]

Wace belongs to this reign, the earliest famous Jerseyman known to us. In the 12th century there was a remarkable outburst of Norman-French literature. A leisured class had grown up, eager for knowledge and entertainment, not in Latin, but in their own language, as the Englishman was two centuries later when he welcomed Chaucer. A group of writers began to cater for this need, in prose and verse; Wace was one of them. He tells us that he was a Jerseyman, '*En l'isle de Gersui fu nez*', educated at Caen and ordained, but we hear little of his clerical duties. He records that he earned his bread by writing romances. After producing several minor poems, he settled down to his great work, *Le Roman de Brut*, based on Geoffrey of Monmouth's *History of the Kings of Britain*. In 16,000 lines he describes how, after the fall of Troy, Brutus, the grandson of Aeneas, sailed into Britain and founded London to be a second Troy. He narrates the story of King Lear and his daughters, and King Arthur and the Round Table. Indeed the Round Table appear for the first time in Wace. This poem won him the patronage of Henry II, who, on his tours through Normandy, frequently stayed at Caen. He gave Wace a canonry at Bayeux and commissioned him to write the history of the Dukes of Normandy. So he began the *Roman de Rou*, another immense poem, which among other things sheds much light on the invasion of England. But Wace was no hustler. Fourteen years later the King asked for the poem, but finding it still unfinished, he not unreasonably transferred the commission to Wace's rival, Benoît de Sainte-Maure. We get our last glimpse of the old poet in his lodgings at Bayeux, a soured and disappointed man. His fingers are frozen and he cannot afford a fire, he throws down his pen and leaves his poem unfinished. 'Let any who will, finish it.' But before he gave it up, it too had reached more than 16,000 lines. When referring for historical details to Wace, we must always bear in mind that he was writing at a later date than the events he recorded and for a patron whom he was in duty bound to flatter. The same caution must be observed in consulting other chroniclers of his time.[25]

At last in 1180 we find the Rolls of the Norman Exchequer, our first official information as to how Jersey was administered. The island was divided into three Ministeria. They were called de Gorroic, de Groceio and de Crapoudoit. Gorroic is one of the old spellings for Gorey and evidently refers to a district of which Gorey was the centre. Groceio possibly has something to do with the de Gruchy family, perhaps the part of the Island in which they held land and where even to this day the names Gruchy and de Gruchy are most often found. It is reasonable to suppose, from these names, that these three Ministeria divided the Island into three parts of four parishes each, that of Gorroic covering St Martin, St Saviour, Grouville and St Clement, Groceio covering St John, Trinity, St Lawrence and St Helier, and Crapoudoit covering St Brelade, St Peter, St Mary and St Ouen, with the likelihood that the St Peter's valley stream was called Crapedoit (the brook of the toads) and that it divided the central from the western ministerium.[26]

Three local landowners had bought the right to collect the Duke's taxes. Richard Godel had paid £140 for that privilege in Groceio, Richard Burnouf the same sum for Crapoudoit, and Gilbert de la Hougue £160 for Gorroic. A fact that emerges from these figures is that, if these three men found it worth their while to pay between them £440 for this right, a sum equivalent to many thousands of pounds in our money, Jersey cannot have been at that time a poverty-stricken wilderness.

They not only collected the Duke's revenue, they also administered the Duke's justice. Below them were the seigneurial courts, dealing with petty cases, though we do not actually know at what date these courts became operative. Many books of their proceedings have survived, but few before 1600, though ownership of land at St Ouen is mentioned in a charter of 1135. Above them were the Assizes, held periodically by Justices from Normandy. The Roll does not give these functionaries a name, but it seems likely that they were called ministers. They had to walk warily. In 1180 each of them was fined for exceeding his powers: Godel and La Hougue for dealing with cases of maiming, Burnouf for using ordeal by hot iron without the Justices' consent. Ordeal by battle was also employed in Jersey, for Richard Norman owed 30 shillings in connection with his duel. Another fact that transpires from what is mainly a financial document is that the Island already had a Dean, the local representative of the Bishop of Coutances; for it is noted that Robert Merlin, the Dean, owed the Duke £12. Surprisingly too, Jersey had a money-lender, a fact which implies a certain amount of commercial activity, for Robert, son of Vital, paid a fine to prevent the goods of his dead brother being confiscated as those of a usurer.

When Richard the Lionheart became Duke and King in 1189, he made his younger brother, John, Count of Mortain, a dignity which carried with it the rule of the Cotentin and its islands. Jersey never had a more irreligious ruler, yet curiously enough the only trace of his government that survives is two gifts to monasteries. In 1198 Hugh de Gornaco founded the Abbey of Bellozanne, in the pays de Bray, north-east of Rouen. He must have been a good beggar, for he obtained a subscription from John of land in St Helier sufficient to bring in £20 a year. This grant gave its name to the hill still called Mont à l'Abbé and to the Bellozanne valley that lies behind. By another charter he gave the advowson of St Lawrence church to the Abbey of Blanchelands.[27]

In 1199 John succeeded his brother on the throne and handed over the Channel Islands to Pierre de Préaux, one of six brothers who all held responsible positions under Richard and John. He too was an endower of monasteries, and, among other gifts in 1203, he granted to the Abbey of Valricher 'the island of Escréhou to build there a church in honour of God and the Blessed Mary'. In 1309 a prior was living there with one monk and a servant, and they lit a lantern nightly. The grant was for the building of a church for the salvation of the soul of the King as well as for himself and all his relatives. At the general suppression of all Alien Priories this establishment disappeared and the monks returned to Valricher, though it was still being mentioned by name in a 15th-century '*rentier*' when Guillaume de Lomey owed a gold crown '*por la capelle et mason*' in a list of dues to Notre Dame de Escrehoy en Gierrsey'.[28] After the suppression, the King's Receiver took these dues, which are again mentioned in the *Extentes* of 1528, 1607, 1668 and 1749, though a light was no longer maintained to assist lost mariners. The chapel, of which fragments remain, was 10ft. 3ins. broad and 16ft. 6ins. long; there were two windows in the eastern end, almost certainly round topped, and one at the eastern end of the south wall, with a rough, simple piscina in the south wall. The monk's dwelling, a priory, was built as a prolongation of the chapel.

But now a crisis was approaching. Richard's death had raised the problem as to who was the rightful heir. John was accepted by Normandy and England; but Anjou, Maine and Brittany acknowledged Arthur, the son of John's elder brother; and across the border Philippe Auguste, the shrewdest statesman in Europe, was watching the course of events, determined to be king of all France. In 1202 he invaded Normandy as a supporter of Arthur. John, by a dash across the border, took Arthur prisoner and then the lad disappeared. The official story was that he had broken his neck while trying to escape, but everyone believed that he had been murdered by his uncle's orders. The horror caused by this crime immensely strengthened Philippe's hand. One by one the castles of Normandy opened their gates to him, John fled from Rouen, almost alone and took ship for England. He really was John Lackland, Jean Sans Terre. When in March 1204 Château Gaillard, the new fort that was thought to be impregnable, surrendered with its English garrison, Falaise, Bayeux and Caen opened their gates. Three months later Rouen capitulated and this brought the war to an end. Normandy now became part of the kingdom of France.

The French historian, Dupont, claims that Pierre de Préaux was governor of Rouen and headed the signatories of capitulation, having being promised extensive lands by Philippe-Auguste. When the French king failed to keep his promise, Pierre de Préaux abandoned him and returned to support John, thus giving to England in 1206 the Channel Islands of which he was also Governor. A more cogent reason for the islands not being lost with Normandy seems to be that as yet the French had no fleet with which to protect them, while the English not only had a strong naval force, but were anxious to preserve the islands as an important staging post on the route to Gascony.[29]

Nevertheless it seems that for a time the fate of the islands hung in the balance. There was some confused fighting, about which we know nothing. The uncertainty of the times is revealed in some of the material published by La Société Jersiaise in 1879 under the title *Documents historiques relatifs aux Iles de la Manche* and taken from the Archives of the Public Record Office (1199-1244). A charter of 1216[30] shows that John gave to his 'well-beloved and faithful' Guillaume de Préaux all the land that had belonged to Guillaume de Lanvalaye and to Raoul of Rochester and, if by chance he were unable to guarantee these lands, John would give in their place either the island of Jersey or £300 worth of land in England, provided the requisite services were rendered by Guillaume.

At the Assize of 1309 it was stated: 'The King of France twice ejected Lord John, the King, from these islands, and occupied them as annexed to the Duchy, and John by armed force twice reconquered them'. At first John seems to have regarded the islands as lost, for when that picturesque ruffian, Eustace the Monk,[31] a renegade monk who had turned pirate, entered his service, the first task he gave him was to harry the Channel Islands; he did this so thoroughly that we are told 'nought was left to burn', and in September 1205 he returned to Sandwich with the spoil. By 1207, however, matters were sufficiently stabilised for Hasculf de Suligny to be sent to Jersey as Warden, with a strong force of galleys, knights and sergeants, to establish his authority. All political communication with Rouen now ceased, and a new system of administration had to be created.

Chapter Four

THE GROWTH OF NATIONALISM, 1204-1328

The land we from our fathers had in trust,
And to our children will transmit or die.–Wordsworth

IN THE 18TH CENTURY JOHN was regarded as Jersey's great benefactor, and indeed the late Lord Coutanche, in recent years, with a twinkle in his eye, always referred to him as 'good King John'. Falle, in his *History*, wrote:

> No sooner was he apprised of the hazards the island ran of being overpowered, he, not thinking it enough to send over necessary succours, hastened himself in person to animate the people and to keep up their courage by his presence. He instituted a Royal Court in Jersey and Guernsey. He gave us a body of *Constitutions* which have been the foundation of all our franchises to this day, and may not improperly be called our *Magna Charta*.[1]

But much information has come to light since Falle wrote. The late Sir Thomas Duffus Hardy, sometime Keeper of the Record Office, published an itinerary of King John, which traces the King's movements day by day and leaves no possible room for a visit to the Channel Islands at this time.

The *Constitutions of King John*, so often spoken of, and accepted by Falle as genuine, is a concept (one cannot say a document, as none exists) with a curious history.[2] There is reason to think that belief in its existence arose thus: 400 years after John, Sir John Peyton, a newly-arrived Governor, asked Thomas Olivier, Rector of St Helier, to give him a short account of the Island's constitution. So the Rector took three clauses out of the report of a Guernsey enquiry into the laws of the islands. This was not a charter, but an *ex parte* statement by Guernseymen in the reign of Henry II of what they believed had been done in John's reign with the King's sanction. To this Olivier added 15 clauses from a petition sent 100 years later to Edward III, which says not a word about John, but merely pleads for the retention of certain ancient customs. There was no deception about this. The Rector gave the 17th-century Governor exactly what he wanted, a concise summary of the special privileges that the islands were accustomed to claim. However, because the first clause was one of those taken from the report to Henry III which begins, 'Constitutions constituted by our Lord, King John, after the loss of Normandy', it was assumed later that all the 18 clauses were in fact a charter granted by John.[3]

In all probability John personally had nothing to do with Jersey's constitution, but our liberties and customs had existed long before this time. They are referred to in 1218 by Henry III:

> It is not our intention to institute new assizes in the islands at present, but it is our will that the assizes which were observed there in the time of King Henry our grandfather, King Richard our uncle, and of the Lord King John our father, should be observed there now.[4]

Nevertheless the so-called *Constitutions* were accepted as genuine by the Royal Commissioners in 1860.

As it was in John's reign that Normandy was lost, those responsible for the good government of the island had a problem, and a form of insular government gradually developed. Ultimately all authority was in the hands of de Suligny, the Warden, but he must have been mainly occupied with problems of defence. It has recently been suggested that the stone vaulted roofs of our parish churches replaced wood or thatch at this period as a means of defence against burning in raids. De Suligny confiscated the estates of all suspected of pro-French sympathies, including those of his own grandson, Thomas Paynel. Silvestre de Furnet lost Rozel; Morville, Anneville and Craqueville all changed hands. Even with seigneurs who had remained loyal he took no risks. Every family of any importance had to surrender one of its sons as a hostage. Ralph Gallichan was entrusted to the Prior of St Albans, Guillaume Malet to the Abbot of Gloucester, Jean de Ste Croix to the Mayor of Lincoln, Gervaise Becquet to the Sheriff of Gloucestershire. Scores of unfortunate young Jerseymen were scattered over England, and most of them did not get home until eight years later. Even Renaud de Carteret of St Ouen, who had defended the island before de Suligny arrived, and for John's sake had sacrificed his estates in Normandy, had to give up his eldest son, Philippe. This was a most effective way of ensuring loyalty from the islanders; for who will not promise support in exchange for his son's life?[5]

Jersey no longer lay snugly in the middle of the King's dominions, with England on one side and Normandy on the other. It had become a frontier outpost within sight of the enemy. So Suligny built a castle on the spot nearest to France. This was at Gorey, but it did not spring up at once in all its glory, nor at first did it bear the name of Mont Orgueil (Mount Pride). Much of the fortress we see today dates from Tudor and Stuart times. But the ancient keep on the edge of the cliff, which is now partly hidden by later fortifications, is Suligny's work, and he probably surrounded it with an outer wall as a first line of defence.[6]

Meanwhile it was essential to keep the islanders in a good temper and Suligny took care not to provoke a conflict with the Church. The local clergy felt no affection for the king of France, but they would probably have been loyal to their bishop and would have resisted any attempt to transfer them to an English diocese. So for another 300 years Jersey was allowed to remain part of the diocese of Coutances, and the Norman abbeys were still permitted to appoint Rectors and collect their dues, although at times restrictions were placed on these activities by the English kings, particularly in time of war. A relevant edict came from the King in 1295, when he ordered that the clergy

> and anyone else suspected of treachery, who dally near the shore in the Isles at places where enemies could to some extent be sheltered, be completely removed from such places to avoid risks of this kind. We bid you to have such clergy and others remaining in such places ... removed. If they are not suspect, then you may allow the clergy reasonable sustenance from their own property in those places, converting the rest of their property in full to the safety and defence of the isles.[7]

It may be noted that all the priories were near the shore, except in St Peter. The above quotation may explain why the assumed site of the Prieuré de Lecq, at Ville Bagot, is far removed from the fief de la Chapelle on the beach at Grève de Lecq, where one might have expected to find it.

No attempt was made to introduce English law and, as mentioned earlier, some aspects of Norman law remain in force today. However, the three administrative districts, mentioned in the last chapter, were abolished, and the whole of Jersey brought under one central control.

The Jurats now come to the fore as the most important group of officials in the islands, 12 for Jersey, 12 for Guernsey, seven for Alderney and six for Sark. Their origin poses many problems, particularly as the word itself is not unique to the islands. Just as 'constable' (*connétable*) and 'bailiff' (*bailli*) have different connotations in England, France and the islands, so 'jurat' has no exact parallel elsewhere, and their function is more clearly expressed by the French title '*Juré-Justicier*'. The idea of 12 men acting as coroners or jurors is very old, and it has been suggested that the nearest equivalent to the early jurats were the *échevins* whom the Visigoth judges called to their assistance as assessors and colleagues. They were selected from freemen and appointed for life. A similar group functioned in France in the Middle Ages. We also find jurats in south coast towns in England and in the cities of Gascony and Aquitaine. In Romney Marsh, where special recognition for ship service was given to the Cinque Ports, sworn men or jurats were elected as early as 1250 by the commonalty to enforce contributions of land-holders within the Marsh towards the maintenance of sea-walls and water courses. In medieval Southampton we find the terms bailiff, constable, échevin and jurat used in a special context: here the function of the four market jurats was to enforce the statutes controlling the quality of fish, meat, poultry and bread. Bayonne, Bordeaux and La Rochelle had jurats elected yearly and jealous of the privileges granted them by Plantagenet kings anxious for their support.[8]

When the King's court was mobile and travelled through England and France, often headed by the King himself, and bearing the rolls of the law, its authority in the Island was delegated to the King's representative, and the local jurats would seem to have been restricted to preparatory work in anticipation of the visit of Justices in Eyre, who held assizes. Although the creation of the office of jurat has been attributed to King John, because it is defined in the so called *Constitutions* (an inquest in 1248 stated that John instituted 12 sworn coroners, *coronatores jurates*, to keep the peace and rights pertaining to the Crown), it seems more likely that this office had existed at a far earlier period, but that its scope was enlarged by circumstances when ties with Normandy were severed temporarily or permanently. The islanders were later to protest that it had existed from time immemorial, which suggests a logical development from a system of elders elected at an early stage in the Island's history.

Two factors seem to have contributed to the extension of the Jurats' powers: the long rule of the unpopular and absentee warden, Otho de Grandison[9] and the phasing out of the Justices in Eyre. Absence of the Warden gave more scope to the Bailiff, who by then was usually an islander; any attempt to usurp his powers was resisted by jurats and seigneurs alike, who were men of substance likely to be losers if there were maladministration in England. When the eyre became moribund and the *justiciers* ceased to visit the Island, in spite of requests from the islanders, it would seem that the *juré* took on the added rôle of '*justicier*'. But, as Professor Le Patourel has said, 'the problem of the origin of the jurats is one of the most baffling in all the medieval history of the islands'.

It is only since the reforms of 1948 that Jurats have been chosen by an electoral college. Formerly they were chosen by the King's officials and the *Optimates* or large landowners, and later by popular franchise. What is certain is that from small beginnings and weekly meetings in what came to be called the Royal Court, they developed into the governing body of the island, later calling on the Constables and Rectors to assist them in the States' Assembly.[10] Today, though they no longer legislate in the States, their office is still considered as one of the highest distinctions to which an islander may aspire.

In 1212 Eustace the Monk made his second raid. He had deserted John and gone over to Philippe with five of the King's galleys, and was rewarded with the gift of the Channel Islands. He swooped down on them, but this time with less success. Jersey and Guernsey repelled him, but he succeeded in occupying Sark, where he left his uncle with a garrison. The career of this colourful personage is fully dealt with by Wendy Stevenson in an article on 'England, France and the Channel Islands, 1204-1259'.[11]

To revert to the claim that John really did pay a visit to Jersey in 1213. There is no proof of this bar the testimony of Matthew of Paris (*c.*1200-1259).[12] He tells us that John had summoned

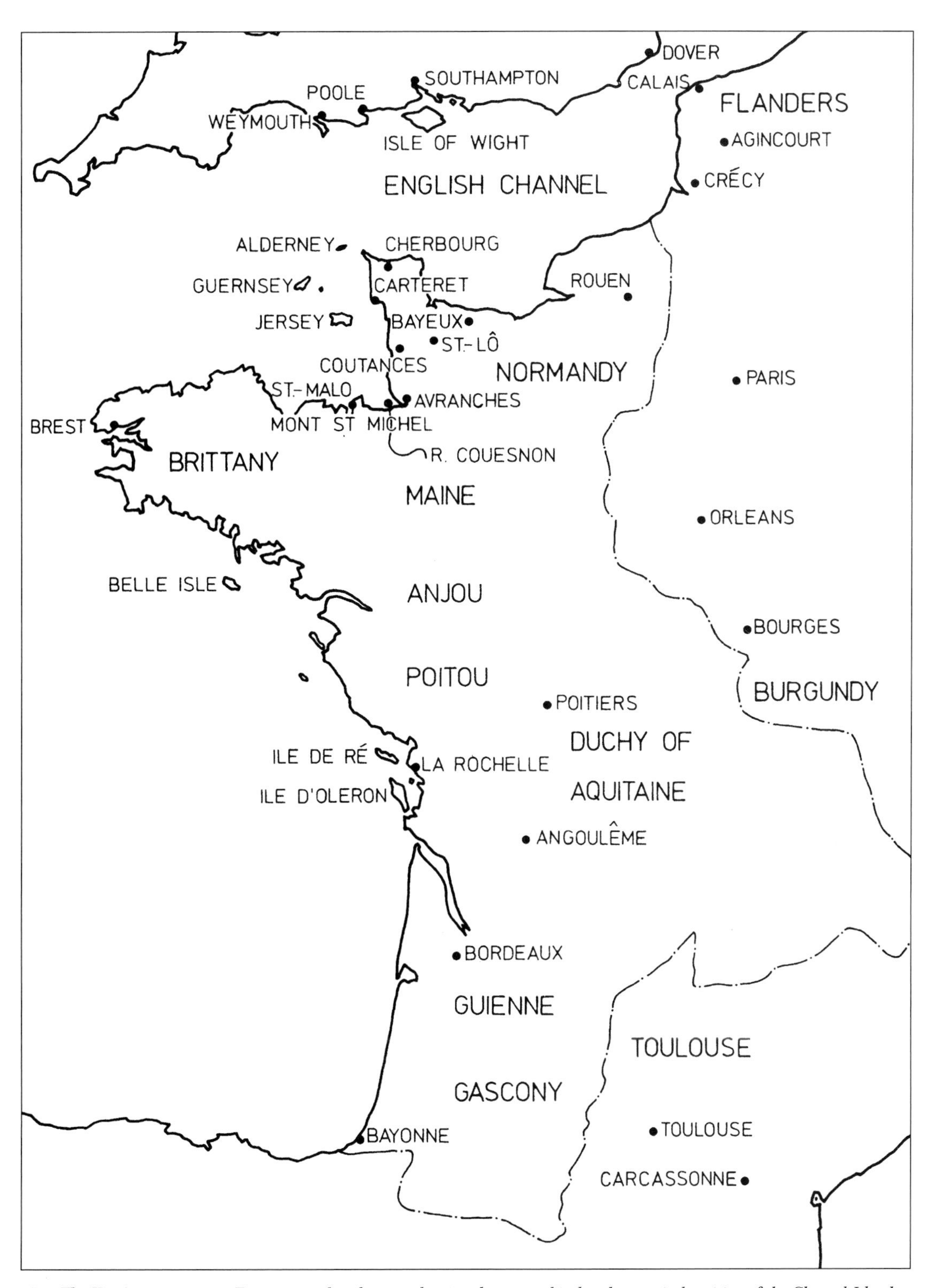

7 *The King's possessions in France in medieval times, showing the geographical and strategical position of the Channel Islands.*

his barons to Portsmouth for an invasion of Poitou, but they refused to embark until he paid them the money they had spent in arming their tenants. John as usual was bankrupt, so to force their hands he set sail with his household thinking they were bound to follow. But they packed up their tents and went home. Matthew of Paris then continues: 'After three days John came to the isle of Geserie. But when he saw he was deserted, he was forced to return to England'. It will be seen that this does not actually state that he landed, and perhaps he only came within sight of the Island.

It may have been these events which stirred up Philippe d'Aubigny, the new Warden (1212-1224, 1232-1234), to attack Sark, which was formally entrusted to him in 1214. With a force of Jerseymen he recovered the island and sent the pirate's little army of occupation as prisoners to Winchester. Next month the King wrote to the Island: 'We return you many thanks for your faithful service to vindicate our honour. We also send you back your hostages, because we have full confidence in your fidelity'.[13]

But we have not heard the last of Eustace the Monk. *Magna Carta* did not bring peace between the King and his barons; the Barons' war began, and they appealed to France for help; d'Aubigny, ever loyal to the King, went to England to support him and, during his absence from Jersey, Eustace took revenge. 'In 1215', wrote the Prior of Dunstable,[14] 'Eustace the Monk, a powerful pirate, seized the islands on behalf of the French.' In May 1216 he convoyed to England an army of 12,000 knights, and John's cause seemed hopelessly lost, when a surfeit of peaches and new cider relieved England of the worst of her kings. Medical opinion suggests that he may have died of acute appendicitis.

The nine-year-old boy, Henry III, inherited the throne, and the barons returned to their allegiance. When Eustace tried to bring reinforcements from France, his ship was captured by d'Aubigny, who beheaded him on his own deck; so peace was made. The eighth clause of the so-called *Constitutions* ran: 'Concerning the Isles. The Lord Louis shall send letters to the brethren of Eustace the Monk ordering them to give these back to the Lord Henry of England, and if they surrender them not, the Lord Louis shall compel them to do so'. The Lord Louis was Louis VIII, son of Philippe Auguste of France. Apparently the brethren made no resistance.

While d'Aubigny was Warden, steps were taken to retain in Jersey the *fouage* (the tax paid on each house or hearth). In 1219 he was bidden to take for the use of the King the *fouage* in the islands according to the custom of Normandy. This document was signed by the Bishop of Winchester and by '*Notre chef justicier*'. An inquest was also held into the loyalty of the chief landowners, and the result was another large crop of confiscations. As a result of this and of previous upheavals, the de Carterets seem to have been the only one of the important Norman families to retain their estates. A new aristocracy arose, drawn largely from royal officials, but they soon ceased to think of themselves as Englishmen, and spoke of 'the customs and privileges of our ancestors', as though their families had been settled in the Island for centuries. Yet even after this great purge the authorities remained suspicious. In 1223 the rule was made that any landowner who spent more than a week in Normandy would have his estates confiscated.[15]

The feudal system based on the granting of fiefs, common in most parts of Europe in the Middle Ages and introduced ready-made into England by the Normans (though perhaps grafted on to a somewhat similar mode of government already in existence), was firmly established in Jersey, and many aspects of it survived into the present century.[16]

A fief was an area of land granted by an overlord to an abbey or an individual in exchange for certain duties and obligations. The Seigneur of the fief did not own the freehold, but held rights over those who lived on his fief, even if they themselves were freeholders. These duties varied enormously from fief to fief: 'Blancs esperons' required a gift of spurs, Câtelet a chaplet of roses, Diélament a fat ewe, to be paid to the Seigneur when his eldest son married, and Lecq certain duties if the eldest son died. More commonly the obligations were connected with defence, and gradually domestic duties accrued, such as carting the Seigneur's hay and vraic (seaweed), cleaning his colombier (dovecot), and repairing parts of his mill. In medieval times the system was one of reciprocal benefit, as the Seigneur recognised an obligation to protect his 'tenants', to have justice meted out to them in his court, to provide a mill where they could grind their own corn, even if he did exact payment of some sheaves for his work. The early seigneurial court rolls shows justice tempered with mercy, but from about 1600 new ideas, political and religious, crept in, and the whole medieval structure was doomed. Gradually the court of the fief became a means whereby the Seigneur could exact dues and fines, and it fell in public esteem, as it was no longer democratic or even just. It has been questioned whether the smallest fiefs, often sub-fiefs, actually held their own courts. Judging from the surviving books of court rolls, some of which concerned only a dozen or less households, it would seem that most of them did.[17] They all elected their own officials, Senechal, Prévôt, Sergent and Greffier, just as did their larger neighbours. It must sometimes have been hard to find enough tenants to hold all these posts. A few of the larger fiefs, the '*fiefs nobles*', had the right to gallows and to hang offending tenants thereon, but they did not have *haute justice*, that is the right to condemn them; this could be done only by the Royal Court.

From the State Papers of Henry's reign we can gather a few more particulars. The strengthening of Gorey Castle was going on vigorously. There are orders for shiploads of timber to be sent from the King's forests and for cross-bows and other munitions to be shipped from the Tower of London. While in 1226 the 'baillis' of Southampton were ordered to send five loads of lead to Jersey and Guernsey for the repair of their castle.[18]

Like all medieval communities Jersey had its share of lepers. There was a leper house dedicated to St Nicolas, situated at La Croix or Le Carrefour St Nicolas in St Peter, and another on Mont St Nicolas, opposite Gorey Castle, to which the King gave a donation.[19]

Fishing was at this time the chief industry of the island. In pre-Reformation days, with the emphasis on fasting, the demand for fish was enormous, and this was the only commodity that Jersey could export on a large scale. Not only was the trade in conger and mackerel profitable for the islanders, it also produced revenue for the Crown. There were strict regulations about the export of fish outside the King's dominions, fixed seasons during which herring and mackerel might be caught and fixed places, *esperqueries*, where alone conger might be dried and salted. The word *esperquerie*, preserved in place names in Sark and Guernsey, is generally thought to be derived from the method used for drying conger by erecting stakes ('*perques*' or poles) on which a net was slung to hold the fish while it dried. Salt for the preservation of the fish had to be obtained from Gascony, so Jersey boats plied backwards and forwards in the Bay of Biscay carrying salt and fish, long before the great expansion to the Newfoundland banks. The word *esperquerie* is peculiar to the Channel Islands and is usually expressed in Latin documents as *espercaria*, but a reference in the rolls of Gascony, dated 1253, speaks of *piscarias nostras*, suggesting an analogy, perhaps erroneous, with *pêcherie*.[20] The right of '*éperquerie*' was often farmed out to the seigneurs, and in 1274 Regnaud de Carteret was required to show by what right (*quo warranto*) he had established an *esperquerie* '*in portu du Stako*' (l'Etacq).[21] The fish trade was evidently regarded as being one of vital importance.

Towards the end of Henry's reign, Edward, Prince of Wales, later Edward I, was put in charge of the islands with the title Lord of the Isles (*Dominus Insularum*); he had two bailiffs under him, one in Jersey and one in Guernsey. When he became King he transferred the Lordship of the Isles to his friend, Otho de Grandison. This was only one of the gifts that were showered upon this knight, and, though he held the Lordship for more than fifty years, he was an old man of nearly ninety when he paid his first visit to Jersey. He was a gallant and faithful servant of the

Crown. Three times he was sent to quell disturbances in Gascony, seven times he was Edward's ambassador at the Papal Court, and for six years he was absent on a crusade. These world-wide duties forced him to leave the islands to subordinates, who, when he was abroad, had to apply for instructions to his English lawyers. Their main anxiety was to obtain funds for their employer, whose expenses were high but whose family estates were small. Jersey naturally objected to being bled to pay the debts of a Burgundian knight whom they had never seen. A stream of protests poured into Westminster[22] and the organising of these petitions welded the islanders into a united opposition to the English government.

It is from this period that the role of Bailiff in the islands begins to assume importance, as a counterpart to the Wardens, who were later replaced by Captains and Governors, and were more often than not absent from their charge. The Bailiff, usually an islander, spearheaded the attack against any encroachment on or eroding of ancient privileges. Mr F. de L. Bois, formerly Deputy-Bailiff, writes thus of the origin of this important office, whose holder is still the chief citizen of the island, presiding over the Royal Court and over the States Assembly;

> In due time, the Warden appointed Bailiffs for the Islands to whom he delegated part of his functions. The Dukes of Normandy, before and after they had succeeded to the Crown of England, had had bailiffs in all parts of their domains. The Close Rolls of the 13th century contain letters addressed to the Bailiffs of Jersey and Guernsey. Other letters are addressed to the Warden and his bailiffs and charge them with various duties, and it is therefore natural that the title of Bailiff should come into permanent use. However, it is not until the end of the century that one is able to trace a succession of Bailiffs of Jersey and of Guernsey, Bailiffs whose functions were peculiar to the Channel Islands.[23]

Edward I and Philippe of France were both anxious for peace, but they could not restrain the pugnacity of their subjects, and at this point in island history a crisis threw all other troubles into the shade. A rumour ran through the Cinque Ports that a Norman ship had sailed down the Channel with dead dogs and dead Englishmen dangling from the yards. Dover sent a challenge to the Normans to come and fight it out. The fleets met off Brittany and the English were completely victorious. The French were roused to reprisals, one of which was a savage raid on the Channel Islands, under Jean d'Harcourt and Mathieu de Montmorency; the devastation was appalling. A Jersey petition declared:[24] 'The body of our Lord (the consecrated host) was there cut down with swords and spat upon. The images were cut down and roasted without food. The chalices were destroyed and taken away. The women and girls were killed, 1,500 in number …' (All writers have queried the reference to the images.) 'The houses were burnt and the corn, so the people have nought to eat. Their money and all their other chattels were carried off: Of the chasubles and the vestments they made strappings for horses, and when the horses had served them they hamstrung them.' Another petition to the King said, 'The mills that you had in the isle were burnt together with all our goods. Your Bailiffs wish to make us rebuild them, but Sir, we have nothing to do it with'.

This stirred the King to action. Gorey Castle had been strengthened with a tower and wall, and troops and munitions were hurried over.[25] But this had roused opposition. Jersey resented the breaking up of the fishermen's boats to provide for a palisade round the Castle; it resented the commandeering of provisions to feed the increased garrison. When Parliament met in 1298 Westminster was bombarded with complaints against Otho's officials, so the King ordered an Eyre. Justices in Eyre were sent to the Island 'to hear and give amends for any complaint that should be brought by any against any'.[26] The accused officials had two lines of defence. They pleaded that, though the islanders demanded to be judged by their own customs, no one could discover what those customs were. English law was fast becoming an exact science, but Jersey law was still a tangle of uncodified tradition and the officials declared that, whenever the islanders wanted anything, they always declared that it had been their right 'from time immemorial'. But Otho's second safeguard was the surest. His influence was so great that, whenever an enquiry was ordered, he always arranged for one of his followers to sit on the Commission. In this Eyre the Chief Justice, the Prior of Wenlock, was one of the many Swiss relatives for whom Otho had found posts in England. He was Otho's Attorney when he was abroad and was actually the man who had appointed the accused officials. His colleague was also a man who owed his position to Otho and had served under him in Gascony. From such a Commission the protesting islanders could hope for little redress, but its proceedings throw many sidelights on life in the islands.

On St Clement's Day 1299 the Justices rode from the Castle to the town with a clattering escort of knights. In the Royal Court, a large wooden shed on the site of the present Court room, all the officials of the Island were gathered, Bailiff, Jurats, Seigneurs and 72 jurors, six of them acting in each of the 12 parishes, whose duty was to present the criminals. There was an immense agenda and the meetings lasted for six weeks. The complaints against officials were quickly dismissed and in every case the complainant was fined for bringing a frivolous accusation. Then came a long series of civil cases, enlivened by an incident when the Greffier (the clerk of the Court) was accused of incorrectly entering a suit in the rolls. The Jurats avowed it was correct, and the complainant, Richard Horman, was sent to gaol for contempt of court. Some of the alleged assaults took place on the foreshore (*in refluctu maris*) and the place where the crime occurred is usually stated.

Then came the criminal charges. It was an age of violence, and 184 of these cases were for violent assault. One man had been bitten in the face; another had had his hair set on fire with a candle, one had been felled with an axe, another had had his head broken with a pitcher. Vraicing and ormering seem to have given rise to constant quarrels, and among the prisoners was a pugnacious leper given to breaking windows and rolling people in the mud.

The clergy were by no means all men of peace, for Emma Balleine complained that Guillaume Chastelain, the chaplain at the Castle, had wounded a man with his sword. Geoffrey de Carteret, who later became Dean, was fined for beating Thomasia de la Hougue and dragging her from her house by the hair, for breaking a window in another house and stealing a green overcoat, for beating a farmer in his cart until blood flowed and assaulting the Vicomte's servant although he raised the *Clameur de Haro.*

And there was the strange story of Robert de Cumberwell, Rector of St Brelade. He had had a long standing feud with the prior of Wenlock, who had seized a boat of his in Guernsey, when the Prior was Bailiff there. In 1297 he had been appointed Rector of St Ouen, but the Prior, as Otho's attorney, had forbidden his institution and 'inhumanely bound him in prison and in chains'. The King, however, had ordered his release and had given him the Rectorship of St Brelade. Up to this point he had been winning, but now he put himself hopelessly in the wrong. At the Assize it was stated that 'with certain unknown malefactors, his adherents, he had gone to Castle Cornet in Guernsey, climbed the walls, broken the doors and windows and assaulted the Prior by force of arms, grievously injuring him'. He was summoned but could not be found and we hear no more of him.

The worst offender was Sire Drogo de Barentin, Seigneur of Rozel, a typical bad seigneur of the period. He hunted over his neighbour's corn, encroached on his neighbour's property and sent out his retainers to capture women in the neighbourhood. They had captured the wife of Viel Vasset in the presence of her husband and carried her to Drogo's house, who had wrought his will on her. Another evening they captured the daughter of Pierre Renaud, and, on another occasion, their victim was Collette Brisebarre. He sent his retainers to Thomas Malzard's house, where they broke down the doors, burst open his chests and killed the dog. When Malzard went to complain to the Bailiff, they dragged him out of Court, beat him and broke his arms.

But it was not easy to punish a man like Drogo. Trial by Jury, an old Norman custom, had long been the law in Jersey. The Grand Coutumier ordered that, when there was a dispute as to facts, 24 neighbours of the accused should decide whether he was guilty. This was known as *enquête du pays* or *grande enquête* and the jury consisted of eight men from the parish in which the offence had taken place and eight from each of the neighbouring parishes.[27] This was an admirable rule except when the delinquent was a powerful seigneur who terrorised the whole district. In every case Drogo demanded the *enquête du pays* and a jury composed of his own tenants brought in a verdict of 'not guilty'. But his crimes had been so flagrant that the Justices could not ignore them. He was put 'at the King's mercy' and had to pay 300 *livres tournois* to obtain pardon.

Misdemeanours of many kinds were brought before the Court. A warrener had beaten a lad for trapping larks for roasting, though larks were not game birds and therefore free to all. Two boys had climbed the Castle walls to steal the King's pigeons. Some butchers had sold sheep carcasses without their heads; were they trying to palm off dog's flesh as mutton? And among these cases we hear the first rumble of what was to grow into a great storm. For a long time in England there had been friction between the ecclesiastical and civil courts. In Jersey the position was aggravated by the fact that the Bishop's court was at Coutances, so that the King's subjects were being summoned out of the King's dominions to be tried by a foreign court. The Dean's Summoner was arraigned for citing four persons to Coutances. When he could not be found, his property was confiscated. Even after the Reformation, when both courts sat in Jersey, there was conflict for many years between the rival authorities.

Next the justices drew from their leather bag a bundle of writs *quo warranto*, and this was a shock for the Seigneurs. They found themselves called upon to explain by what warrant they claimed rights they had always taken for granted: the right to impound stray beasts, which in

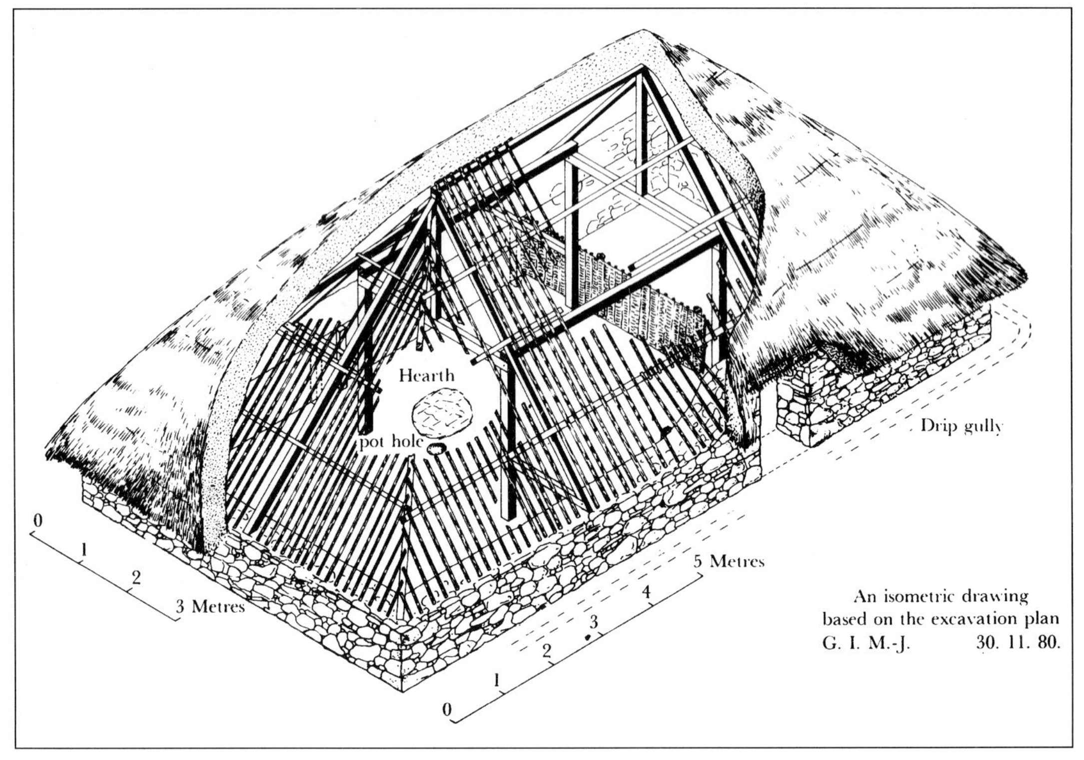

8 *Reconstruction of 13th-century house excavated in Old Street in 1974 and 1979.*

England belonged to the King, the right to hunt over their own land, whereas the King's advocate claimed that hunting was a royal sport, which could be indulged in only by the King's express permission, and the right to wreckage washed ashore on their fiefs, which in England was the King's property. In this context it is interesting to note that in 1174 Henry II had abolished the right of wreck in England, Poitou and Gascony in the belief that it led to the abuse of 'wrecking', but had made an exception of Brittany, where many Breton lords relied upon the profit from wrecks to boost their incomes.[28]

In the *Cartulaire* there is an interesting sidelight on the right of wreckage. In 1254, replying to a letter from the Bailiff of Jersey, Henry III stated that the monks of Mont-St-Michel were entitled to wreckage, excepting 'gold, unworked silk, uncut scarlet cloth and new scarlet mantles' throughout their Jersey lands, including Noirmont, which had been exchanged by the King for Alderney. The Seigneur of St Ouen was challenged to show by what right he kept private gallows, the Seigneur of Samarès by what right he hunted rabbits on the Town Hill. No Jersey seigneur was strong enough to emulate Earl Warenne in England, lay his sword on the table and say: 'here is my warrant'. But those writs aroused much resentment and, with a possible war with France looming on the horizon, the Government shrank from testing too hard the seigneurs' loyalty, and this side of the enquiry was dropped.

Until the end of Edward I's reign, Assizes were held every three years and thereafter more irregularly and less frequently. It was still possible for a group of English judges to administer Norman law; the language would not have presented difficulties, as the affairs were conducted in Latin and in any case French was still widely spoken by English officials and in educated circles until the time of Chaucer. But whatever their aims or difficulties, the King's purse was still the matter uppermost in the judges' minds, and by modern standards their findings were a travesty of justice.[29]

In 1307 Edward I was succeeded by his son Edward II, the Poltroon. This made little difference to Jersey, for Otho remained in control, and his agents continued the ruthless squeeze. The new King was showered with fresh petitions from the Island and in 1309 another Assize was held. This time the visiting justices were the Constable of Carisbrooke Castle and John de Fresingfeld, an experienced lawyer from Dublin. The *quo warranto* writs were pressed home more stringently. The Seigneurs of St Ouen, Samarés, Augrés, Trinity, Vinchelez, Mélèches and Rozel were closely cross-examined as to their seigneurial rights 'to which none of them answered, save that they and their forbears had ever been wont to enjoy these'. The Seigneur of Mélèches 'returned the writs badly mutilated and torn as if in contempt'. The matter was referred at last to Westminster, where, after many adjournments, it was eventually dropped. But this controversy threw the very men, who would otherwise have been strongly pro-English, even more wholeheartedly into opposition to Westminster.

Then came a further extension of the *quo warranto*. The whole community was challenged to show its right to elect 12 Jurats, 'who arrogate to themselves the functions of the King's judges'. They answered, 'we have had this right from time immemorial'.[30] They were then asked by what law they claimed to be governed, the law of England, of Normandy, or by special customs of their own? They answered 'By the law of Normandy', and referred the Justices to the *Summa of Malcael* 'where the Norman laws are well embodied'. This is probably a reference to the *Grand Coutumier*; if so, their reply preserves the name of the compiler of *the Coutumier*.[31] But they added, and this is a clause that caused much trouble later, 'except that we have certain customs used in this island from time immemorial'. This matter too was eventually referred to Westminster for decision, where, after many delays, it was allowed to be forgotten.

There was the usual conglomeration of civil and criminal cases; millers put in the pillory for using false measures, a man fined for cutting off the tail of a lady's ass, a curious dispute about a burial at St Brelade, where the Rector had come with a band of parishioners at dawn to the house of Ralph de Grapedoit and 'carried off the corpse of Emma de Grapedoit, though the wife of Ralph raised the *clameur de haro*'. But the main features of this Assize were the struggle between the civil and ecclesiastical courts and the difficulties caused by a slump in the value of French money.

In the rough days that followed the barbarian invasions, the clergy had managed to make their persons sacrosanct, and no lay court could touch them, for they were responsible to the Bishop, alone. In lawless days this had been a useful privilege, but it had become an anachronism. The civil courts had now established their own tradition of justice, yet the bishops still claimed the right to decide in all cases in which 'clerics' were concerned; this meant not only priests, but sub-deacons and acolytes, even vergers and grave-diggers. This was particularly obnoxious in Jersey, where trial at Coutances meant also imprisonment in a foreign gaol. Otho, who was *persona grata* at the Papal Court, had obtained from the Pope in 1308 an order stopping this, and the King had written thus to the Bailiff: 'We command you to proclaim in full court and in such other places as seem expedient to you, that no one under pain of forfeiture of lands shall cause anyone to be cited before the Bishop for matters of which the cognizance belongs to ourselves'. But neither Pope nor King could persuade the militant Bishop of Coutances nor Pierre Faleyse, the equally militant Dean of Jersey, to surrender one jot of what they considered their rights. When the Bailiff read the King's proclamation, Faleyse summoned him to appear before the Bishop for attacking the authority of the church. Not only did he continue to keep his Summoners busy committing drunkards, fornicators, usurers and blasphemers to the Bishop's prison, as though no proclamation had been issued, but he even summoned the Captain of the Castle and the King's Advocate to appear at Coutances.[32]

When the Justices arrived, they had to deal with this defiance. Thirty-three persons were arrested for 'causing subjects of the King to be summoned out of the realm'. The Prior of Bonne Nuit was fined 20 *livres* for 'falsely publishing that the Bishop would send 80 men at arms to seize the King's justices and take them to prison at Coutances. And this he could not deny'.

The clergy and their leading lay supporters held a meeting at St Helier's Rectory and decided to throw down the gauntlet. Early next morning, while the Justices were in session, the Dean arrived with a great crowd of clerics and demanded in the name of the Bishop the release of the clerics arrested in Guernsey, no matter what charge lay against them, and declared that the Bailiff's proclamation was a breach of the church's liberties. Though the Justices told him that the proclamation was made by the King's order, the Dean refused to accept this answer and said that a Papal decretal laid down that all pleas (presumably those in which clerics were concerned) belonged wholly to the church, and that any who denied this would incur the Greater Excommunication. The Justices pointed out that the King had ever had cognizance of all trespasses by whomsoever committed, save those concerning wills and marriages; but the Dean four times admonished them to have the proclamation withdrawn. Though the Justices repeatedly informed him that the proclamation was issued by the King, he first gave notice in general terms that all responsible for it were excommunicated, and then proceeded to excommunicate the Justices by name. This he did in open court,[33] and charged the whole population of the island not to obey them on pain of excommunication. The Justices at once passed sentence of imprisonment on him and arrested him, but the clerics who accompanied him 'violently rescued him from prison'. The church, for the moment, proved too strong for the state. As soon as the Justices left, the whole system revived and the Dean's Summoners continued to deport all kinds of transgressors to Coutances.

The Assize also had to deal with a problem which we shall meet again later,[34] the fall in the value of French money. Jersey used coins struck at the mint in Tours. Rents and debts were reckoned in *livres tournois*, *sols* and *deniers* but the *livre* had slumped to a third of its nominal value. Could Otho's debtors, who owed money for fines or mill rents or dues, pay in 'weak' coins, or must they pay three *livres* for one? The debtors claimed that they had brought the specified amount, and that it was not their fault if the value had fallen; but they were told that their debts must be paid in 'strong' not 'weak' money. The Assize had to deal with more complaints on this score than on any other. Here is one example: Jourdain de la Hougue complained that he was amerced at the last Assize in the sum of 14 *sols*, which he paid, but now the Prevot was demanding 28 *sols* to make up the value in 'strong' money. The matter was referred to the King in Council and the plaintiffs were told to appear at Westminster 'one to sue for all'. But they lost their case; the Council decided that all debts must be paid in 'strong' money, and Jersey had one more grievance against the English Government.

On the money making side the Justices were as efficient as usual. No question, however trivial, was left uninvestigated, if it could provide an excuse for another amercement. Had someone moved turf from the King's common? What had happened to some tallow that had been washed ashore, part of which had been eaten by dogs? Clemencia La Bastarde had been hanged eight years before, but what had happened to a pan which she had possessed? Horman, a coiner, had been boiled alive, and what had happened to his chattels? Whole parishes were amerced; a house in St Ouen had been broken open and the culprits not discovered, so everyone in the parish was amerced. A robbery on the sands near the town had not been reported to the Bailiff, so all St Helier was amerced. A baby had been left in a cradle and its head gnawed by a dog and, because no inquest was held, all St Saviour was amerced. The Justices finally amerced the 72 jurors very heavily for 'many concealments of their verdicts'.

It is hardly surprising that petitions again began to pour into Westminster complaining that many of the amercements had been illegal, and adding, 'we cannot have right because Sir Otho's attorneys always seek to be justices'. This last complaint was recognised as reasonable and the King ordered that henceforth no one connected with the Island government should sit on an assize.

In these troublous times documents sent to the islands from France or England were apt to get lost. In 1212 a letter from the Bishop of Coutances to Philippe d'Aubigny and the King's bailiffs in the Isles stated that he had seen Henry II's charters about the foundation of Cherbourg Abbey, but that he was sending copies only, owing to the constant threat of loss at sea (*propter pericula in mari frequenter imminentia*).[35] In 1279 some deeds were lost on their way to Westminster; so the King gave a seal to the islands so that documents might be sealed locally. It bore the royal arms, the leopard/lions of England, and the inscription: '*S. Ballivie Insularum. pro. rege. anglie*' (seal of the Bailiwick of the Isles for the King of England). In making this gift the King recognised that '... our men of the aforesaid islands have oft-times hitherto suffered divers losses and no small perils sometimes at sea through shipwrecks, sometimes on land by robberies and other hazards of the road ...'. A few years later two separate seals were struck, one for each Bailiwick. Needless to say the present seal used by the Bailiff is not the original, far too precious to be used daily, but a copy made in 1931.[36] It is also interesting to note that even during the Occupation the imprint of this seal travelled to England on Red Cross messages sent from the islands and authenticated by this means.

When these seals were originally presented, the men on the spot had ingenious ways of turning attempted reforms to their own advantage. Otho's bailiffs began to use these to give the King's authority to their own illegal acts. In 1327 Jerseymen complained that 'whereas no new laws should be made without the King's consent', the Bailiffs were extorting money by merely sealing orders and then 'imprisoning us in the Castle if we refuse to pay'.[37]

A new Assize was ordered. This time two of the three Justices were men with a stake in the Island: Sir Nicolas de Chesney held the fiefs of Pinel and Morville; Sir Jean de Carteret was a brother of the seigneur of St Ouen. Now the offending officials were smitten hip and thigh. The Constable of Castle Cornet was hanged, the Constable of Gorey fled for his life. Other functionaries were heavily fined, and many vergées[38] of sequestered lands restored to their owners. But Otho reminded the King that he only held the island revenues for life, that after his death they would revert to the Crown and that the judges were seriously diminishing the future revenue of the Exchequer. So Edward 'had the records brought before him and found that the Commissioners had issued orders to the King's disherison; whereat he was much displeased and revoked the judgments of the Commission, and ordered Otho to resume all the lands and tenements'.

This brought the islands to the verge of revolt. In 1321, when Otho's nephew arrived in Guernsey as sub-warden, he was thrown into prison, and this drew Otho from his Swiss castle. The old man, now nearing 90, arrived on 1 June 1323, but his presence did not mend matters. In 1324 a petition declared: 'If the Justices did right, Sir Otho would be expelled from the isles'. Yet another Assize became necessary. This time the work was entrusted to that formidable old judge, Henry Spigurnel, who had not hesitated to condemn Piers Gaveston, the King's favourite. But, before the Assize opened, Otho returned to Switzerland. Spigurnel is chiefly remembered by his '*Ordinances for the good of the Isle*'[39] which for centuries were read aloud in court every Michaelmas: the *Cour de Cattel* (which dealt with chattels and criminals), the *Cour des Dettes* and the *Cour des Transgressions* were to meet weekly and the *Cour d'Heritage* fortnightly. The verdict of seven jurats was to be decisive. Except in case of abnormal difficulty no litigant was to be kept waiting more than a month for his verdict. Advocates must swear never to prolong litigation by frivolous objections. Every landowner was to be responsible for repairing the roads around his own property and millers must measure corn and flour in their customers' presence. No weights or measures must be used until they had been tested and sealed by the Bailiff and two Jurats. Four beer-tasters in each parish must visit every tavern and sample every cask of beer, wine and cider, once when it had been broached, once when it was half full and once when it was nearly empty. This sounds like an occupational health hazard.

Two subsidiary Courts were added later: the *Cour du Billet* and the *Cour du Samedi*, which, despite its name, met on other days as well as Saturday and now meets regularly on a Friday. In the lower Courts the Bailiff and two Jurats form a quorum. Appeals from their decision lie to the Full Court at which seven Jurats must be present. In addition to its judicial powers, the Court had, until 1771, power to issue Ordinances which had the force of laws. Further developments in the history of the Royal Court will be discussed as they occur.

In 1327 Edward II was deposed, and in the following year old Sir Otho died and a new regime began. But Otho's long reign had left a lasting mark on Jersey. Fifty years of struggle against oppression had created in the Island a political consciousness, a sense of solidarity, that had been unknown before. The constant organising of petitions and the sending of deputations to Westminster had taught Jerseymen to act together. Common grievances had welded seigneurs and tenants into a united people whose rallying cry was always to be: 'Those who rule us must maintain the ancient customs of our island'.[40]

Chapter Five

THE HUNDRED YEARS' WAR: FIRST STAGE, 1331-1376

It is always easy to begin a war, but very difficult to stop one.–Sallust

THE ACCESSION OF EDWARD III was a serious matter for Jersey, for unfortunately he had, on paper, a plausible claim to the French throne. The last three kings of France had left no sons, and Edward, through his mother, Ysabelle of France, was a grandson of Philip IV. No woman had ever sat on the French throne, but it was by no means clear that the inheritance could not pass through the female line. Edward, the late King's nephew, was certainly a nearer relation than the other claimant, Philip of Valois, who was only the late King's cousin. This is the kind of case over which lawyers love to wrangle; but, as a matter of practical politics, Edward's claim was weak. Edward's mother raised a mild protest, but Philip was crowned without question.

For the first 10 years of his reign Edward was too busy fighting the Scots to press his claim on France, and life in Jersey went on as usual with the constitutional struggle continuing. In 1331 the detested Judges in Eyre paid a last visit which led to an extraordinary incident. Before the Justices arrived, 23 men met in St Helier's Priory on the Islet and bound themselves by a tremendous oath to resist to the death any interference with the ancient liberties of the Island.[1] They were a curious group. The leader was a Basque merchant, Pierre Bernard de Pynsole, from Bayonne, who bought fish from the local fishermen and farmed some of the monastic revenues; with him was another Basque, a wine merchant, Laurens du Galars or de Gaillard who had just bought the post of Warden, and two French monks from Mont-St-Michel. No doubt these foreigners had a vested interest in the Island's immemorial privileges and feared that the justices might curtail some of their sources of profit. Only two Jersey seigneurs joined this cabal. But when the justices landed in Guernsey, the conspirators met them with 500 men, shouting that the King had no right to change their customs, and that they would defend them with their blood.

'Then', says the Assize Roll of 1331,

> when the Justices refused to sanction the customs without consulting the King, they rose up with bitter words and swore recklessly that, though they hazarded life and limb, they would not surrender their customs. And divers unknown persons backed them up by shouting "Yea, yea, yea," insulting the King, terrorizing the people and endangering the lives of the justices. The Vicomte was bidden to arrest them, and later they appeared before the justices, and, being questioned, they demanded trial by jury. The jurors declared them not guilty, and then were discharged.

The justices refused to accept their verdict, and, when they reached Jersey, ordered a retrial. One appeared and made his submission, but then comes one of those tantalising gaps so trying to the patience of the historian. The Assize Roll ends and no other document available carries on the story.[2]

In many respects this Assize was similar to others. The thorny question of the ancient customs and the *quo warranto* writs were left to the King to decide. There was the usual trouble about the Ecclesiastical Court. A curious case was that of a priest, Roger de Castillon. Some years before the Lieutenant-Bailiff had been riding home with a naked sword under his arm, and Roger had met him and playfully ('as friend with friend', says the Roll) pulled the sword away. But in so doing he severed a vein and his friend bled to death. For this he had been brought before Spigurnel's Assize and released as a cleric. He next spent three years in the Bishop's prison at Coutances and then escaped by purgation, that is by swearing his innocence and having his oath confirmed by 11 other clergy. The justices found him living in the Island and had him re-arrested, but the Dean forced them to accept the Bishop's acquittal as final.

While this Assize was in progress, two other Commissioners were at work, sent 'to inform themselves of the true value of the emoluments pertaining to the King'. The *Extente* which they compiled has been called the Jersey Domesday Book: it is the foundation of much of our knowledge and the source from which so much flows that it has rendered the year 1331 one of the most frequently quoted in our history. It was written in Latin and in 1876 was translated into French by La Société Jersiaise, the first of a stream of learned works to pour from their doors.[3] This *Extente* is not a complete survey of the Island, as it deals only with money and services due to the King, but from its pages it is possible to glean many interesting facts. The hearth tax helps to assess the population of the Island; for every house had to pay a shilling and 1,865 shillings were collected. However, as certain people who owed special services were exempt from this tax, there must have been at least 2,000 houses in the Island. And, if one allows an average of six persons to a house {by no means an excessive figure in those days of large families), the population cannot have been less than 12,000. These figures also reveal the comparative size of the parishes: the highest come from St Ouen, St Saviour, St Martin, Trinity and Grouville. Next comes St Helier, which, though always the legislative centre, was not of great commercial significance for hundreds of years after this, partly for lack of harbour facilities. St Mary, then as now, had the smallest population.

Four years later Jersey had a taste of what was soon to be its fate. England was not yet at war with France, but away in Scotland David Bruce, the young Scots king, had been driven by the English from his throne. He fled to France and with Philip's connivance collected a fleet in various French ports. Two proclamations of Edward III tell what then happened. In December 1336 he wrote, 'David Bruce, with other Scots and their adherents, has attacked Jersey and Guernsey, inhumanly commiting arson, murder and divers other atrocities'. In May he sent a very important order.

> Because we are informed that the Scots are planning to perpetrate similar crimes in the islands a second time, we order Thomas de Ferrers (the Warden) to levy and array all men capable of bearing arms, and to form them into companies of thousands, hundreds and twenties, and to lead them well-armed and arrayed for the defence of the islands.[4]

This is the first time we hear of any organised defensive army and it is generally taken to be the origin of the Jersey Militia, albeit in embryonic form. Doubtless there had been some kind of 'home guard' before this. The appearance of 'hundreds' and 'twenties' cannot be unconnected with the 'centeniers' and 'vingteniers' in our parochial system, although these are now purely civil appointments.

Lists made at this time show that the greater part of the garrison were natives of the Island. Among the archers, cross-bowmen and other men-at-arms one finds many names extant today, more than six hundred years later. A random list taken as illustration shows in the choice of Christian names a preponderantly Norman or Plantagenet allegiance: John Amy, Stephen Bertram, Philippe Falle, Robert Godel, Roger Horman, Collas Laffoley, Richard Le Cras, John Messervy, Philippe Nicolle, Richard Norman, Richard Pallot and John Syvret.

Bruce's raid was one of a score of incidents that made war inevitable. In November 1337 Edward broke off negotiations, and the Hundred Years' War began, though this did not mean a century of uninterrupted fighting. There were truces, some of which lasted for several years. But from 1337 to 1453 England and France were at war, and for most of that time Jersey was the outermost bastion of the King's domain, exposed to constant attacks.

The first was made in 1338 by Béhuchet, an Admiral of France, of whom Ferrers wrote: 'On the morrow after the Annunciation he invaded the island with a great host, and burnt every blade of corn and all the houses'. (*In crastino Annuncionis beatae Marie anno XI Nicholus Bahuchet alias Behuchet, Admirallus Francie intravit cum magno exercitu in Insula de Jersey et combussit omnia blada et domos et alia bona in dicta insula devastavit.*)[5] How widespread the devastation was can be seen in the loss sustained by one abbey, that of Montvilliers. In Grouville, St Mary, St Helier and St Ouen all its tithe corn was burnt, and in St Peter only a twelfth remained. Behuchet then besieged the Castle for at least six months; for in September Jean de Barentin, Seigneur of Rozel, was slain while leading a sortie, though the French failed to capture it and eventually withdrew. Behuchet then sailed to Guernsey, where he captured the whole island, including Castle Cornet, and also Alderney and Sark. Jersey alone kept the banner of St George flying from the Castle keep.

The French king transferred the islands to his son Jean, who passed them on to Robert Bertrand, Seigneur of Bricquebec in Normandy. In March 1339 he invaded Jersey. 'On St Gregory's day', said a Jersey petition,

> Sire Robert Bertrand, Marshal of France, with a multitude of barons and notables to the number of about 8,000, arrived in 17 Genoese galleys and 35 ships of Normandy. They landed and summoned us to parley. So two of their chief officers and two of ours met half way between the hosts. They promised, if we would surrender the Castle, to restore our lands and liberties, and that the French king would confirm whatever franchises we desired.

This was a cunning bid to win over the Jersey nationalists, for up to now English kings had declined to ratify these. The petition continued:

> To this we made answer that, while ten men were alive in it, the Castle would not surrender. Whereupon they returned to their ships and sent to reconnoitre the Castle by land and sea. This they did many times, but, thanks be to God, they saw every side so well prepared for defence, that they returned to their fleet. On the Monday following they made a foray and burnt many houses and mills, carrying off much plunder. But some of our men sailed forth from the Castle and fell upon the raiders and slew forty or more. On the Tuesday Bertrand and his fleet sailed for Normandy.

But this was not the only raid, for another petition[6] declared: 'The island hath been destroyed and burnt three times this year'. It cannot have been a healthy place in which to live.

These raids reveal a disquieting fact: the existence of a pro-French party among some of the leading islanders. Jurat Payn, who had helped the invaders, fled to Normandy. The Seigneur of Samarès, who was Vicomte, also had his manor confiscated and was compensated by the French with lands in the Cotentin that had belonged to Renaud de Carteret.[7] The long struggle for local rights had made men like these become anti-English.

It was probably about this time that Grosnez Castle was built. It belongs to the bow-and-arrow age, before the invention of fire-arms. It was merely a moat, a gatehouse and a wall protecting the landward side of a high and rugged promontory, where islanders in the west could find refuge for themselves and their cattle during hit-and-run raids. A small party could hold this wall against raiders pressed for time, but the castle would not have withstood a siege, as it had no water supply. It is noteworthy that a tiny inlet facing west is named *Le Creux au Français*. The castle never had a garrison and has no recorded history. The first time that it is

9 *Piscina at St Mary, 1342.*

10 *Font at Grouville, 15th century.*

TREASURES OF CHURCH AND HOME

11 *Coffee pot by Pierre Amiraux,* c.*1770.*

12 *Pewter jug by J. de Ste Croix,* c.*1730.*

mentioned by name in any surviving record is in a 16th-century map,[8] where it is marked as 'the ruined castle of Grosnez'.

In 1340 the Battle of Sluys gave Edward command of the sea, and he avenged Jersey by hanging Béhuchet from his own masthead.[9] In the same year the French were ousted from Guernsey, though Castle Cornet on its little islet still flaunted the lilies of France. Then the Truce of Espléchin brought to a close the first phase of the Hundred Years' War, leaving each side in possession of what it had won. During this breathing space Jersey gained what it had been wanting for years, the confirmation of its customs. In 1341, Edward III, prompted no doubt by the offer the French king had made, and by the importance of keeping the islanders loyal, issued the most important of all the charters granted to the Island:

> Considering how faithfully the beloved men of our isles have ever maintained their loyalty toward the King of England, and how much they have suffered in defence of their islands, and of our rights and honour, we concede for ourselves and our heirs, that they hold and retain all privileges, liberties, immunities and customs granted by our forbears or of other legal competency, and that they enjoy them freely without molestation by ourselves, our heirs or officers.[10]

This charter has never been revoked by any succeeding monarch.

In 1342 war flared up again, and Sir Thomas of Hampton, who had bought the Wardenship, made an attempt to recapture Castle Cornet. He took with him a large contingent of Jerseymen, and the siege lasted for three years; but, before it was over, Jersey's loyalty had been strained almost to breaking point by the high-handed tyranny of Henry de la More, Sir Thomas' Lieutenant. He was a man with a shady past, who had been outlawed in England for embezzlement, but had obtained the King's pardon. In Jersey he destroyed all the goodwill that the King had won by his charter. In 1342 a letter from the King states: 'The men of Jersey have shown that Henry de la More detains divers sums of money, victuals, garniture and goods, which they brought to the Castle for safety'.[11] This suggests that there must have been yet another threat of invasion. The King ordered 'all money, victuals etc so brought, to be delivered without delay'.

But this did not end the trouble. In January 1345 when the King was crossing to France, a boat-load of Jerseymen intercepted his ship in the Gulf of Morbihan, boarded her and presented a petition.[12] This declared: 'Many good people have been killed on the Island. De la More hath burnt many houses and robbed many of their goods, and imprisoned many.' Another petition complained: 'He hath now killed by treachery Guillaume du Mont and two others with him'. This implies a rising of some kind. Thomas Hampton then came to support his Lieutenant and the petition continues: 'Sir Thomas, when he came to Portsmouth, enlisted 150 bad characters who rob and kill Jerseymen by night ...' At Southampton, Hampton collected another 150 men to cause further mischief in Jersey. '... The island is without assizes, so evil-doers cannot be punished'; the messengers prayed for instant redress.

The rule of Thomas de Hampton evidently developed into a reign of terror. Even such well-tried patriots as Renaud de Carteret, Seigneur of St Ouen, and his uncle Geoffroi, the Dean, took advantage of a temporary truce and escaped to Normandy. In 1343 Commissioners came from England[14] to report on the dissensions between the Warden and the islanders 'whereby divers evils have happened, and it is feared that greater evils will ensue'. They were ordered to enquire

> who started the dissensions who conspired among themselves and with the enemy; who left the island without licence and sent their wives and children to Normandy, and why; who have risen against the King and scorn the King's officers; by whom were the houses called *loges* erected on account of war, thrown down and burnt.

These documents reveal a picture of an island in sullen revolt, a revolt which from time to time broke out into actual fighting. The Commission evidently reported unfavourably on Thomas of

Hampton and de la More, for both were recalled, and Thomas Ferrers, a former Warden, sent back to the Islands. He continued the siege of Castle Cornet for another two years. Then the government decided to end this menace in the Channel. They sent an overwhelming force, which stormed the Castle with scaling ladders, and the French lost their last foothold on the islands.

The following year Edward landed at St Vaast-la-Hougue in the Cotentin and began the campaign over the succession of Brittany, which led to the victory of Crécy in 1346, and the capture of Calais. The claws of France seemed to have been clipped.

A new peril was approaching, the plague that later ages have named the Black Death. It arose in China, reached Europe in Genoese trading vessels and spread through the West like wildfire. No cure was known. A French eyewitness wrote, 'Nothing checks it, neither heat nor cold, nor the healthiest surroundings. When it strikes a house, scarce one inmate escapes. The dead outnumber the living and towns are depopulated. A thousand houses are boarded up'. Walsingham's statement that only a tenth of the population of Europe survived is certainly an exaggeration, but most modern historians accept Froissart's estimate that 'a third of the world's population perished'.

In Normandy the ravages of the plague were exceptionally deadly. No taxes could be gathered, say the Exchequer Accounts, 'because there hath fallen on the land so great a mortality'. In Rouen in four months 100,000 corpses were buried; and Jersey did not escape. The local records are scanty, but, of the 10 parishes whose lists of clergy go back to that date, only two Rectors survived. The King wrote: 'By reason of the mortality among the fishing folk which has been so great, our fishing rents cannot be obtained without the excessive oppression of the fishermen who are left.'[15] The Black Death and the French massacres must have brought the Island's population far below the figure of 12,000 suggested as a minimum for the hearth tax of some seventeen years before.

The Black Death also swept over England, and this had, indirectly, a lasting effect upon Jersey. Ever since the Norman Conquest Norman-French, so closely allied to Jersey-French, had been the language of polite society in England, the language of the Court, of the Law and of the schools. In the towns even the poorest people tended to be bilingual, while Anglo-Saxon developing into English remained the tongue of rustics. After the Black Death communication was more difficult, for gradually French was less used and Latin was reserved for the Church. The *Extente* for 1331 was in Latin, but the next so far discovered, that for 1528, was in English and showed that then as now the visiting officials had much difficulty with Jersey names. Chaucer's writings encouraged, for the first time, the use of English as an acceptable literary medium. When, a century later, Caxton introduced printed books, English as a written language replaced Norman-French in England.

More than half the clergy had died and their places were taken by hastily ordained peasant priests, who knew no French. The children of the barons were brought up by English-speaking servants from whom they learnt to speak English, and the war encouraged the feeling that it was unpatriotic to speak French, the language of the enemy. The result was that in one generation England became English-speaking. Hitherto Jersey and England had spoken the same language and officials had had little difficulty in understanding one another. Now for most Jerseymen English was as unknown as Sanskrit, and this remained true for some time to come.

The years which followed the Black Death were bad years for France. Jean le Bon, King of France (1350-1364) had serious financial problems in his country and, while still grappling with them, was taken prisoner at Poitiers by the Black Prince. His son was kept in England as a hostage, but broke parole and escaped. Jean offered himself as a prisoner again and is credited with saying: 'If honesty were banished from the world, it ought to be found still in the hearts and mouths of kings'.

The kingless kingdom fell into anarchy and a revolutionary government was set up in Paris. A peasant rising burnt the nobles' castles. But internal troubles for France meant quieter times in Jersey, especially as an English army now held the Cotentin. But, if this gave the Island a sense of security, it had a rude awakening. In 1356 the French recaptured Castle Cornet, and, when the news reached Jersey, a force was raised under Regnaud de Carteret of St Ouen, Raoul Lemprière, the Bailiff, and Richard de St Martin, Seigneur of Trinity. What followed is told in the Close Rolls.[16]

> After bitter conflict they took prisoner the French Captain of the Castle, who ransomed himself for 80,000 *moutons* (a French florin stamped with a lamb), and, though they might have kept these florins for their own expenses, they released the Captain free of ransom in return for the surrender of the Castle.

We might have expected Guernsey to be grateful, but the Jerseymen then did something which Guernsey could not forgive: they executed a Guernseyman as a traitor. 'Guillaume Le Feyvre was slain as a traitor by the common counsel of the armed men.' The Guernsey Court ordered the arrest of those responsible for the execution, but de Carteret and Lemprière stood by their men.

> Though they were not at the killing nor consenting thereto, considering that those impeached were in no wise to blame, they told the Court that they were as much to blame as any of those impeached. Whereupon the Bailiff and Jurats of Guernsey recorded that they were guilty of the death, and adjudged them to the King's prison to be detained till justice was done.

The Warden managed to get their trial transferred to the Privy Council, and obtained a writ of *supersedeas*, superseding all proceedings against them. But the dead man's widow, Nicolaa, was either very loyal or very vindictive. She went to London and, like the widow in the parable, gave the King no rest until she obtained an order to the Warden to proceed with the trial. Feeling now was very bitter, and the Guernsey Jurats threatened to resign if justice was not done. For two years the unfortunate Jerseymen waited in a Guernsey dungeon, until at last in 1359 they obtained the King's pardon 'in regard to the arduous task they had performed in recovering the island and the castle'.

Meanwhile Edward was engaged in a futile campaign in France, in which neither side won any decisive victory. When, in 1360, the Treaty of Brétigny established an 18 months' truce, which, it was hoped, would lead to a 'perpetual peace', one of its clauses made the French abandon all claim to the Channel Islands.[17]

During this pause Rozel Manor passed to the Lemprières. It had belonged to the de Barentins, one of the leading families of the Island, if not the most noted for their mercy, but Philippe de Barentin, the Seigneur at this time, was a colourless person. An old manuscript tells this story:

> One day the wife of Philippe de Barentin said to her sons, "Jehannet de St Martin has called me an adultress. Avenge this insult on your mother. Such slanderers ought to have their tongues torn out."

The sons, in fury, laid an ambush and set a boy to whistle a warning, and when de St Martin drew nigh they seized him and tore out his tongue. It is said that the Croix de Jehannet was erected in memory of this crime on the spot where it was perpetrated. This may well have been the cross at Augrès Manor, the home of the Jersey Wildlife Preservation Trust but we cannot be sure of this.[18] The sons fled to Normandy where one was arrested and hanged. As de Barentin's other son never returned to Jersey, he sold Rozel to Raoul Lemprière, the Bailiff, and went to live in England. His relations did their utmost to prevent the sale, even declaring he was a leper, and so, by Norman law, incapable of transacting legal business. But this could not be proved, as Philippe had left the Island, and so Lemprière was allowed to take possession of Rozel and other manors. At the same time Guillaume Payn bought Samarès from de Barentin.

The 'perpetual peace' promised by the Treaty of Brétigny proved a vain illusion. Before long Jersey's thatched roofs were again going up in flames. The first raider was Owen, or Ifan, of Wales, son of a Welsh princeling[19] whom Edward had slain. He had entered the service of the French king, who had provided him with 600 men-at-arms to raise a revolt in Wales. In 1372 he sent a bombastic challenge to Edward, saying, 'I am coming to recover the throne of my ancestors', but he got no further than Guernsey. While waiting for reinforcements, he landed in the island and drove the garrison into Castle Cornet. 'Then', according to Froissart, 'there was great slaughter. The French burnt and wasted the whole island and put men and women to ransom. They then entered Jersey and burnt and wasted there also. After this they laid siege to Castle Cornet'. But sieges of Castle Cornet had a way of dragging on for years, and the French king needed troops. So Owen was recalled'.[20] The Jerseymen then petitioned the King for protection.[21] This was promised, and the Keeper of Gorey Castle, Edmund Rose, applied himself to the matter of defence. Though he obtained little support, it is recorded that the Sheriffs of Southampton and Portsmouth had been instructed by the King to hold ships in readiness for transporting men and munitions, should they be necessary.[22]

The following year, however, brought a more formidable foe. The war had thrown up on the French side a really great commander, Bertrand du Guesclin, a small Breton squire, who, by his courage, coolness and constant success, above all by his skill in siegecraft, storming in a few days castles that were deemed to be impregnable, had risen to be Constable of France. In five years he stripped England of almost all her continental possessions. In 1373 he was besieging Brest, and the English commander agreed to surrender, if he was not relieved within a month. But the Black Dog of Brittany was not the man to keep his troops idle, and one of Owen's captains suggested that he should try his luck in Jersey. So he sailed from Hennebont in four captured ships, with the Duke of Bourbon and 2,000 men-at-arms, and 600 bowmen 'at great peril to their lives, for the ships were far from seaworthy'.[23] On landing the Duke marched against Grosnez Castle, which he captured without difficulty, and du Guesclin turned to the far more formidable problem of Gorey. 'The Constable', we read,

> surrounded the castle and made many assaults, but those within defended it valorously, and of the storm-troops they wounded and slew not a few. So, seeing that he could not force an entrance thuswise, he sent for picks and matlocks. The besieged did their duty staunchly, hurling down rocks and casks full of earth on the sappers' heads, while the cross-bowmen poured arrows from every loophole.

But eventually a section of the walls collapsed and the defenders retreated to the Keep and held a Council of War. Edmund Rose, the Captain, had been recalled to London to take command of a new warship presented to the King by the City, and William of Asthorp, his successor, had only just arrived. The Bailiff and Jurats had taken refuge in the Castle, and now, when they saw most of it, including the wall, in the enemy's hands, they insisted that Asthorp should do what the garrison of Brest had done, make a pact to surrender, if not relieved within a fixed time, and Du Guesclin was glad to come to terms. His ladders were too short to scale the Keep and his sappers had reported that the foundations were exceptionally hard; moreover he had no time for a siege, for he was due back in Brest before the month was up. So he gave them till Michaelmas, and they agreed, paid a ransom and surrendered hostages. 'And', said the standard bearer of the Duke of Bourbon, 'the islemen promised to be good and loyal subjects of the King of France; and Messire Jehan de Hangest and Thiebaut, his brother, were left to guard the island for the King'.[24] The Castle was relieved by the Admiral of the Fleet on 2 September and so was free from the promise to surrender.[25] But the garrison was severely reprimanded and the chief blame fell on Jean de St Martin, the Bailiff. He was imprisoned, first on the spot and then in the Tower of London. But 'on being interrogated in the presence of the Council, when every point had been considered, the Council, pronounced him wholly guiltless of treason' and restored him to his post.[26]

The Castle was now held for the King, but the rest of the Island still lay at du Guesclin's mercy. Three years later, when the Pope sent two cardinals to arrange a truce, Edward complained to them:

> Du Guesclin, with whom our liege men of Jersey agreed to pay ransom for one year only, which ransom was paid in full, and later to pay another fixed ransom for one year only, has again compelled them by harsh imprisonments, burning to death, to pledge themselves to pay yet a further year's ransom.[27]

The Receiver's accounts for these last two years declare that the full quota could not be sent 'because of the frequent raids in the islands and destruction of houses and mills.'[28]Jersey was paying dearly for her allegiance to England.

Chapter Six

THE HUNDRED YEARS' WAR: SECOND STAGE, 1377-1453

What can war but endless war still breed?–Milton

IN 1377 KING EDWARD DIED, and in 1380 the King of France and du Guesclin followed him to the grave; the war then languished. In each country a child of 11 came to the throne with uncles as Regents, whose incompetence made any spirited foreign policy on either side impossible. In England, so long as Richard II (the Redeless) was king, peasant revolts, Lollard agitation and court jealousies stopped any large scale campaign for regaining the lost provinces: but hostilities continued and, with conflicting evidence from chroniclers, raids and rumours of raids, it is difficult to disentangle Jersey's part in the struggle. France and Castile renewed their alliance, first formed in 1345, and agreed that, since England was using the islands as a base for raids on Brittany, they should be entirely depopulated, every house destroyed and every tree cut down and nothing left but a blackened desert.[1] Jean de Vienne, one of the signatories of the renewed treaty and a famous French admiral, was sent to implement these orders, but he did not carry out the threatened devastation.

Sir Hugh de Calveley, who had been appointed Warden in 1376, re-arrested the Bailiff, de St Martin, for treason and kept him in close confinement in the Castle for more than four years. His wife crossed to England to plead his cause and, when nothing came of this, he made his escape and threw himself on the mercy of the King. In January 1387 his case was investigated, and he was found 'entirely innocent of treason' but was not restored to his Bailiffship on this second occasion.[2]

Although Jersey was free from raids for the rest of the reign, ecclesiastical matters now began to give trouble; for, just as the Hundred Years' War was leaving its imprint on the islands, so they could not fail to feel the repercussions of the Great Schism in the western Church which occurred in 1378.[3] This not only raised questions of conscience and religious allegiance, but also stimulated rival national interests at a time when the consciousness of nationhood was eroding the medieval belief in a universal order. On the death of Pope Gregory XI in 1378 there had been a disputed election in Rome, when 13 cardinals had declared the election of Urban VI invalid, and had enthroned a new Pope, Clement VII. The Catholic world was confronted with the problem of deciding which was the true successor to St Peter. France supported Clement, but England favoured Urban; this put Jersey in a most awkward position. The Bishop of Coutances was an ardent Clementine, and most of the Rectors, nominees of the French abbeys, followed his lead. But Calveley, the Warden, a somewhat reluctant Urbanite, was under orders to show little mercy to Clementines in Jersey. He banished the Dean as an 'adherent of the anti-Pope' and closed the Ecclesiastical Court. An Urbanite bishop of Nantes named Pierre, who could not obtain possession of his own see, because a Clementine was installed there, was brought to Jersey as 'Administrator of that part of the Coutances diocese that remains loyal to the Roman Church'. He remained in charge of the Jersey church for 12 years.[4] At a later date Calveley led an unsuccessful armed Crusade to slay all Clementines in Europe.

Meanwhile in England political spirit was running high and blood was beginning to flow. The Merciless Parliament executed many of the King's friends; 11 years later the King, Richard II, took his revenge and the leaders of the Merciless Parliament were condemned to death, among them Sir John Cobham, an old man of over eighty who had withdrawn from the world into a Carthusian monastery; he was dragged out and sentenced to be hanged, drawn and quartered, but, because of his age, his sentence was reduced to imprisonment for life, and he became the first of the long roll of distinguished men imprisoned in Gorey Castle.[5] He was released later, when Richard fell.

The King was now eager for peace with France at any price, and to seal it he agreed to marry Isabella, the pathetic little seven-year-old daughter of the King of France, Charles VI. But his father-in-law kept pressing demands upon him; Richard consented to give up Cherbourg and Brest, and then Charles instructed his ambassador to claim the surrender of the Channel Islands as an integral part of Normandy. But, before a decision could be reached on this point, the whole situation had changed; the King seems in his later years to have been somewhat unbalanced, and his freakish tyrannies convinced his subjects that no man's life or liberty were safe. When his banished cousin, Henry of Lancaster (later to be Henry IV of England) landed in the West Country, he was hailed as a liberator. Richard was captured in Wales, brought to London and handed over to Drogo de Barentin,[6] great-nephew of the Seigneur of Rozel, who had just succeeded Dick Whittington as Mayor of London. To the Londoners Henry said: 'My lords and friends, here is King Richard. I deliver him into your custody. I beg you do with him as you will.' This was tantamount to a request for murder, but de Barentin took him to his private house and the next day to the Tower. Here Richard was forced to sign a deed of abdication, confessing himself 'insufficient and useless'. No one except his gaolers ever saw him alive again.

When Henry IV, known as Bolinbroke, seized the throne, he at once renewed the charters by which his predecessors had confirmed the privileges of Jersey.[7] He also showed his determination to stamp out the Clementine clergy. In March 1400 he bade the Bailiff pay attention to the fact that all jurisdiction had been withdrawn from that 'son of treason', the schismatic Bishop of Coutances. In May he wrote again ordering all clergy to appear in person before the Privy Council (*devant la Chancellerie d'Angleterre*) on pain of losing their benefices.[8] In spite of the risk of being trapped by the breaking of a truce, pilgrimages from Jersey to Rome were encouraged. Already in 1220 we have a record that the 'faithful men of the island' were requested by Henry III to give help to Philippe d'Aubigny, the Warden, who was planning a pilgrimage. Now it was the turn of the islanders themselves. A contract of January 1400 shows that Vincent Dupont was selling his property in order to go 'on the holy voyage'.[9]

The new King, however, was so obviously a usurper that he soon found the throne no easy place to occupy. If Richard were dead, the rightful heir was the young Earl of March, who was descended from the second son of Edward III. For many years rumours were current that Richard had escaped, and spasmodic rising to re-enthrone him were constantly occurring. One of these apparently extended to the islands, for in June 1403 orders were sent to the Warden to take steps to 'suppress the revolt'.

In July 1403 the French war suddenly flared up again. Though it was obviously still a period of truce, a fleet of English freebooters were plundering merchant vessels off the Breton coast, so Jean de Penhouet, Admiral of Brittany, sailed in pursuit and captured 40 prizes. Flushed with victory the Bretons raided Jersey, where, so the Constable of Calais declared, 'contrary to the truce, they fired the houses, took prisoners and booty and laid the island under a contribution of great and intolerable sums of money as acts of reprisal, thus punishing the innocent for the guilty'.[10]

In the autumn of 1406 there was another raid. Castile and France were still allied against England,[11] and Pero Nino, a Castilian corsair, was cruising down the Channel when he was joined by six Harfleur whalers, also prowling for prizes. This use of the word 'whaler' is interesting, particularly as we find the same word in use in a St Ouen's Manor document dated 1409. It tells how one Thiebaut Dupont and others from Brittany were held up through bad weather on the fief of Michel le Feyvre, seigneur of Vinchelez, who was claiming wreckage. Theirs was a small whale-boat from Quimper (*un petit balegnier de Kempercorentyn*) and the cargo included bolts of cloth and other wares. This seems to imply that men from our neighbouring coasts were already sailing far out into the Atlantic, although in modern French the word *baleinière* is sometimes extended to include boats shaped like whalers.

To return to the men of Harfleur. Their captains reported to Nino: 'Near here is a fertile English island Jarrasuy the Great. Only three or four thousand men dwell therein. Had'st thou troops to conquer it thou could'st win a goodly ransom'.[12] At Harfleur, a notorious pirate centre, Nino met the Breton knight, Hector de Pontbriant, a typical knight-errant of the period who could handle a ship in a fight as skilfully as a horse. He was convoying a fleet of salt ships to protect them against Jersey privateers and he readily fell in with the scheme for a raid on Jersey.

But this was too tough a task for sailors alone to tackle; heavily-armed troops were needed. So they sailed to St Malo where a threatened English attack had drawn together a large force. Jersey was unpopular there, for Jersey privateers often blockaded the roadstead, and many St Malo sailors were prisoners of war in the Island. In spite of opposition from the commandant, the corsairs quickly secured a thousand men-at-arms and a number of light-armed troops and archers. They crossed in the salt boats and, on 7 October, landed on the islet where the Abbey stood.

A historian is always at the mercy of his authorities; on some events he can say little, because few records survive; on others he can write at length because an eyewitness happens to have left a full description. Nino's raid was by no means the worst that Jersey endured, but it is the one about which we know most, because Nino's standard-bearer, Diaz de Gamez, left a graphic pen-picture of the event.

At dawn on the day following the landing, Nino drew up his army on the sands, while 3,000 Jerseymen, under the Receiver,[13] watched from the shore. The invaders advanced slowly under cover of a wall of linked shields, which protected them from arrows. The Jerseymen opened battle with a charge of 200 horse: but a deadly volley from the French archers threw them into confusion. The first line then charged: the Jerseymen 'fought right sturdily! But the Castilians defended their line so well that, though most reluctantly, the islanders were forced to retire'. But the charge of the second line broke the invaders ranks.

> Dropping their spears they grasped swords and axes, and joined in a fierce rough-and-tumble. Then you could see helm severed from breast-plate, and armplates and greaves hacked off. Some grappled with daggers drawn and blood flowed in torrents. Such steadfast courage did both sides show, that all would have been slain, had not Nino observed a white flag with St George's Cross, which, though many a standard had been battered down, still remained upright. So he called to Pontbriant: "While yon flag flies, they will never own themselves defeated. Let us go and capture it". With 50 men-at-arms they wheeled out of the mêlée to where the banner stood. The colour party were doughty knights and the fight was hard, but in the first assault the Receiver was slain. I saw him lying at my feet. Then the Jerseymen began to flee; but the French were so fatigued that they could not pursue.

So Nino withdrew to the islet and held a council of war.

He learnt from prisoners that the Jerseymen had a 'villa' two leagues away, 'wherein they left their goods, their wives and children', and that it was 'encircled with stockades and deep moats

ARCHAEOLOGICAL SITES

I *Le Pinacle. Wild thrift adorns the site of a Celtic shrine. (Photo: David Fry)*

II *La Cotte, St Brelade.*

III *Le Castel de Lecq, St Mary.*

FIELD, ROCK AND COASTAL PATTERNS

IV The north coast.

V La Rocco Tower and St Ouen's Bay. (Photo: R. Long)

PRE-REFORMATION CROSSES

VI *Framing cow and calf at St Mary, an unchanging pattern.*

VII *At Les Augrès, Trinity, and placed above a 16th-century arch.*

VIII *Modernisation at La Fosse, Trinity.*

IX *Preservation at Le Rât, St Lawrence.*

X *Dating by documentation, La Petite Genée, St John, 1539.*

EARLY VERNACULAR ARCHITECTURE

filled with water'; that 'never had Frenchman or Englishman set foot therein', that 'they had a law never to yield it either to friend or foe, and that all must die ere they suffer it to be taken'. This villa has caused endless perplexity to local historians. It cannot be St Helier which is close to the islet and never had a moat, nor can it be Gorey Castle where the garrison was English. It is probably the earthwork at Trinity known as Chastel Sedement, which is roughly two leagues from town. It enclosed almost ten acres and therefore it could shelter several thousand refugees and their cattle; it also had a moat that could be filled by diverting water from a neighbouring spring. Since the women and children would probably have been provided with huts and shelters, it was possible to speak of it as a 'villa', or place of quasi-permanent residence.[14] Even at that period it may have been a very ancient defensive position, and certainly Poingdestre, writing in 1681, thought it was of Roman origin. Part of the earth bank on the north survives and is known as 'Caesar'.

The day after this action Nino crossed the Island towards this camp of refuge. 'He sent ahead light-armed troops to fire the countryside. Everywhere houses, gardens, crops were soon all ablaze, a piteous sight, for the folk who dwell there are Christians! … Then came a gentleman in herald's tabard, asking for the Spanish captain. He bent his knee and said, "The people of this island throw themselves on your mercy. You have beaten them in battle. For the love of the Queen of Castile,[15] who was born in England, have pity". The Captain replied, "Bid those who sent you choose five of their leaders to parley with me". When they came he said, "You know that, whenever the English fleet sets out to war with Spain, it calls here and obtains victuals and recruits. Therefore ye are the enemies of Castile. Moreover these islands belong to Brittany; but your forbears in the naughtiness of their hearts rebelled and made themselves English. Therefore do homage to me in the name of the Lord of Castile. Otherwise ye and your land shall be put to fire and sword".'

But Nino's captains had reconnoitred the camp and realised that its capture would be costly; and they heard of four other castles that they had not seen (probably Gorey, Grosnez and the earthworks at Rozel and Grève de Lecq). Their losses on the previous day had shown that Jerseymen were sturdy fighters, and an English fleet was known to be at sea. So they forced Nino to reduce his terms, and a bargain was struck by which Jersey agreed to pay a ransom of 10,000 gold crowns, to release all French prisoners and to pay for the next 10 years a tribute of 12 lances, 12 axes, 12 bows and 12 trumpets.

> They handed over part of the crowns, and for the rest gave as sureties the four richest men in the Island, and Nino carried them away. Meanwhile the sailors from the salt ships had driven to the shore a great booty of flocks, horses, cows and chattels, and loaded them on their ships. Then they continued their voyage.

The hostages were sent to St Malo with a safe-conduct signed by Pontbriant, but the Captain of the town refused to recognise this and threw them into prison. 'In time of war none but the King can give a safe-conduct', they said; but de Pontbriant and his men broke open the gaol and rescued their precious hostages and carried them to Brest. 'Here merchants of Brittany came to Pero and he handed them over the hostages, and they gave him what remained unpaid of the 10,000 crowns. He divided the money very fairly between the Bretons, the Normans and his own men'. Nevertheless three years later there was a lawsuit before the Parlement de Paris when the Harfleur corsairs sued de Pontbriant for their share of the ransom.

The rest of the reign of Henry IV was uneventful in Jersey. The war simmered down; the French king went mad, thought he was made of glass and shrieked if anyone came near him lest he should get chipped. The English king was smitten with a disease, which many thought was leprosy. However, when Henry V came to the throne in 1412, young and full of ambition, the old lethargy vanished. To 'busy giddy minds with foreign quarrels'[16] was his cure for internal troubles. He renewed his claim to the French crown and prepared to invade France. This claim was later strengthened when he married the French king's daughter.

His first move was to attack the alien priories. This was not the first time they had been confiscated by English kings, for it was their habit when at war with France to prevent church revenue leaving the Island. These were first seized by Edward I in 1285. In 1337 Edward III confiscated the church estates and let out priories at his pleasure for 23 years. He restored the estates in 1361. They were again sequestered in Richard II's reign, but some were restored by Henry IV, and Parliament complained that, though Richard II had ordered that 'no Frenchman should enjoy any benefice within this realm, Frenchmen yet occupy many benefices and bear out of the realm great treasure'.[17] This was especially true of Jersey where nine-tenths of the tithes went to abbeys in Normandy, which also owned a great amount of land in the Island.

So in 1413 Parliament ordered all property of foreign ecclesiastics to be handed over to the Crown. This meant great changes in the Island. Six priories, if we include St Pierre du Désert, which continued for some time,[18] the others being St Clement, Ste Marie de Bonne Nuit, Ste Marie des Écréhous, Ste Marie de Lecq and St Michel de Noirmont, were suppressed and fell into ruins, though the Priory of the Islet was spared. It is doubtful whether St Blaise was a priory, but the name had a particular significance for the island, as he was the patron saint of weavers and wool-combers. According to tradition 'the worthy Bishop Blaise, who came from Jersey', was responsible for introducing these arts to the weavers of Halifax in Yorkshire.[19]

All the tithe that had been paid to the abbeys was now paid to the Crown and never reverted to the Church. It is often assumed that Henry VIII was responsible for suppressing the alien priories at the Reformation, but this had already been done in most cases a century before by his great-grandmother's first husband. The income from Bonne Nuit, St Clement and Ste Marie de Lecq was used later by Henry VI as part of the endowment of Eton College of which he was founder.

Similar moves had been made by earlier sovereigns to seize priories in England, and this sheds light on the appointment of William de Marchia as Rector of St Mary in 1298,[20] the wording being:

> after the presentation of William de Spissa to St Sampson in Guernsey, and Nicholas de Cumberwell to Trinity in Jersey ... the like of Master William de Marchia to the church of St Mary Mosterars (of the Burnt Monastery) Gereseye in the same diocese in the King's gift by reason of the lands of the island of the Abbot of St Sauveur-le-Vicomte being in his hands.

The advowson of both St Mary and St Martin had been given to Cerisy Abbey in 1042,[21] but later grants show gifts to St-Sauveur-le-Vicomte.[22] De Marchia was Bishop of Bath and Wells in 1293 and may rank as the most important Rector ever to be appointed to such a small Jersey parish, though it is doubtful if he ever set foot in Jersey.

But more exciting than the harassing of the monks were the young king's military exploits. In 1415 came the dashing campaign, which began with the capture of Harfleur and ended with the annihilation of the French feudal army at Agincourt. In 1417 town by town and castle by castle, a large part of Normandy was conquered, and in 1418 the King's brother, the Duke of Gloucester, reduced the Cotentin. In January 1419 Rouen opened its gates, and by the end of that year all Normandy except Mont-Saint-Michel had become an English province.[23] Jersey seemed as safe again as it had been in the days of the Conqueror.

In all this fighting the Island had played its part. At the siege of Cherbourg in 1418 every boat in the island was called out to help the blockade.[24] Jerseymen too had their rewards: John Lemprière, Seigneur of Rozel, was granted the manor of La Haye de Barneville on the opposite coast within sight of his manor windows 'to have and to hold in return for one pole-axe to be delivered every St John's day.' On similar terms Jean de St Martin received the fief of Sartilly.[25] France, distracted by civil strife, could make no stand against Henry, and the Burgundian faction accepted him as Regent of the mad king and as heir to the throne. In 1420 he entered Paris in triumph. Jersey was no longer an outpost, for the war had passed far from its shores.

In 1417 the Council of Constance had made strenuous efforts to end the Great Schism. It persuaded one of the rival Popes to resign and deposed the other; the deposed Pope refused to submit and carried on the struggle, but both England and France accepted the new Pope, Benedict XIII, and so ecclesiastical peace was restored to Jersey. When Henry summoned the Bishops of Normandy to Rouen to do him homage, the Bishop of Coutances was one of the very few who obeyed and as a reward the Channel Islands were restored to his jurisdiction.[26]

One sign of the increasing safety of travel, when no actual war was being waged, was the revival of pilgrimages. Licences were granted to various ports of England for captains of vessels to carry devout persons, being the King's subjects, to St James' shrine, provided that those pilgrims would first swear 'not to take anything prejudicial to England, nor to reveal any of its secrets, nor carry with them more gold or silver than would be sufficient for their reasonable expense'—an interesting early example of exchange control. In 1428, 60 pilgrims from Jersey went to northern Spain to visit the shrine of St James (St Jacques de Compostelle). The shrine remained for the next hundred years a favourite pilgrimage for Jersey folk. The scallop shell on an alcove in St Saviour's church may indicate that George Lemprière, who was Constable in 1464, had visited the shrine.[27] There is also a fine piece of church plate at St Brelade, a silver-gilt dish of Spanish workmanship, said to date from about 1450; its decoration of scallop shells in the centre may also have a similar connection.[28]

The Island was now prospering and the danger of raids 'seemed to have passed'. Jerseymen serving in France brought back loot from sacked cities, and constant visits of the King's ships provided a ready market for corn, fish and butter. Nor did foreign trade suffer, for it was possible to buy safe-conducts from the Admirals on either side.[29] These lasted for three months and were always honourably observed.

One way in which Jersey spent its wealth was in church enlargement, and many additions and improvements were made to the parish churches in this period.[30] Thus at St Helier and St Saviour the whole crossing was rebuilt on a bigger scale to carry the present tall square towers. North and south chancels were added on both sides of the eastern limb of Grouville, north and south aisles to the nave at St Ouen, north naves to St Brelade and St Lawrence and south naves to St Martin and St Peter. Most of the chancels were similarly extended, the south chancel of St Mary being dated 1342. The effect of these developments was often to absorb or replace the original transepts, so that eventually the ground plan became more or less rectangular and only the central tower and crossing remained to show that the church had originally been cruciform. At St Brelade the added north nave and chancel extended to the full length of the north transept, but its north/south gable was left standing separately between them. But it was more usual in such cases, as at St Mary and St Martin, for the east/west roof of the added nave and chancel to be carried across the site of the old transept which was thus completely absorbed by them. It is interesting that at St Lawrence the very stylish Hamptonne chapel, added north of the chancel in 1524, which partly absorbed the north transept, not only retained its north/south gable, but was itself roofed in a series of additional north/south gables, a most unusual feature evidently intended to suggest further transepts east of the original one. But it is worth noting that, in spite of the increased prosperity to which the expansion of the churches bears witness, nearly all the exteriors were roofed with heavy barrel vaults of rubble stone, evidently as the best form of fire precaution against the ever present danger of French raids. Guernsey, whose churches are less uniform than ours, was not in acute danger, as it lies on a direct shipping route from the English possessions in southern France, and was therefore a very important port of call; also it had deeper waters around it and therefore better harbour facilities than we had. A raiding party might well have wished to make sure of reducing Jersey and establishing a base there, before moving on to conquer Guernsey, a richer island in medieval times.

Building was also going on in the 14th and 15th centuries at Mont Orgueil Castle. The first recorded use of this title for Gorey Castle is in the Ordinances issued in 1462 by the Lieutenant of the Comte de Maulevrier for the defence of the Castle;[31] but tradition has it that Thomas, Duke of Clarence, a brother of Henry V, while engaged in the wars in Normandy, paid a visit to Jersey and, struck with the strength and beauty of the Castle, conferred this name upon it. For a century almost every Warden had added something to it, and it now included all the area that it covers today. But soon the advent of cannon would make drastic alterations necessary.

Excavations on building sites in the town are producing valuable information about domestic life in medieval Jersey. A very few of our oldest farmhouses may date from this period, but the eternal raids of the previous century can have left few domestic properties standing, particularly as they would all have had thatched roofs. It seems likely that stone was always our building medium; the evidence for a 12th-century house in the Parade shows some stone foundations. If wood-framed houses had been built, as in Normandy and Brittany, there surely would have been some evidence for them.

Henry V and his father-in-law, the poor old madman who had reigned so long over France, both died in 1422, and Henry VI, an infant-in-arms was proclaimed King of England and France. For 13 years his uncle, the Duke of Bedford, was Protector, an honest, able man, coping with a desperately difficult situation. The south of France remained loyal to the mad king's son, Charles, and in the northern provinces most of the people resented the English rule and a strong resistance movement sprang up, hundreds of peasants taking to the woods and waging guerilla warfare. For the first time Frenchmen began to feel themselves a nation, and the colour of Charles' domestic livery became the badge of the new nationalism.

In 1429 Bedford was faced with an adversary such as no English commander had ever met before. Jeanne d'Arc, a peasant girl of 17, appeared in white armour at the head of the French forces. She inspired such fervour in her troops that they became invincible. She escorted Charles to be crowned in Rheims in the heart of Bedford's territory. To the English the only explanation of her success was witchcraft, but even when she was captured and burned, her soul, like John Brown's, went marching on. City by city France was liberated and at last came the turn of Normandy. In a single year from August 1449 to August 1450 the whole province was freed, and three years later the Hundred Years' War was over. Of all her possessions in France England retained only Calais.[32]

Had it not been for St Joan, the subsequent history of Jersey might have been very different. She unquestionably saved the islands from becoming part of France. If Henry V's dream had come true and England and France had been united into a single kingdom, France, with its larger population and much greater wealth, must inevitably have become the predominant partner. The Court would have moved from Westminster to Paris, and Henry's successors would have been far more French than English. England would have shrunk into an outlying province of the French king's dominions and French-speaking Jersey, lying within a French bay, would certainly have become French. Indeed there may well have been a movement to become united with France.[33]

Though most of the Jersey priories were now falling into ruins, towards the end of the war the priory on the islet took on a new lease of life. The Abbey of the Vow at Cherbourg had been burned down when the city was sacked, so the monks migrated to their daughter house in Jersey.

The great abbey of St-Sauveur-le-Vicomte had also been destroyed, and this community too found shelter on the islet. The advent of all these monks must have made it a busy religious centre, and it was perhaps at this time that an effort was made, with a certain amount of success, to make a pilgrimage centre of the little chapel called the Hermitage.

In the closing years of the conflict England entirely lost the command of the sea. When John Nanfan, of whom more anon, was made Warden in 1452, he had to pay 250 crowns to the French admiral for a safe-conduct, before he could cross the Channel. He arrived with a strange retinue: Richard Joyner, grocer of London, John Wyndham, haberdasher of London, John Barret, mercer of London, John Duff, hooper of Bristol, William More, tailor of Fleet Street, Thomas Baferley, fishmonger of London, John Fryth, goldsmith of London, William Bettys, glover of London and a number of other tradesmen.[35] What they hoped to do in Jersey is not related, though we learn from the Patent Rolls of 1456 that 'William Bettys, citizen and glover of London … staying in the company of John Nanfan, warden and governor-general of the isles of Geresey and Guernesey' was granted protection while engaged on the 'safe-keeping and victualling of the Castle of Cornet in the Isle of Guernesey'.

The war ended, as it had begun, with a raid on Jersey. In Nanfan's first report to the Council he wrote: 'The island was overrun, before my coming here, by the King's adversaries right piteously' and he added that he had had to pay £1,000 out of his own pocket to the Captain of Cherbourg and St-Sauveur-le-Vicomte 'for the salvation of the lives of the hostages of Jersey, who were in their ward in peril of death'.[36]

Chapter Seven

THE WARS OF THE ROSES, 1455-1484

Now for the bare-picked bone of majesty
Doth dogged war bristle his angry crest,
And snarleth on the gentle eyes of peace.
Shakespeare, *King John*

TWO YEARS AFTER the French war ceased, the Wars of the Roses began. To many this period is a blur, battles fought for no principle, leaders changing from side to side, kings throned and dethroned, 30 ignominious years of treachery and treason. Yet in Jersey its reactions were important.

At first it looked as though the islands might keep out of the struggle. It mattered not to Jersey whether Percys or Nevilles held the whip hand in Yorkshire, nor whether in Oxfordshire Lovels or de Veres were in the ascendant, for John Nanfan, the Warden, had links with both camps. He was a Cornishman, a veteran soldier with a fine record who for 40 years had been a loyal servant of the House of Lancaster. He had fought under Henry V at Agincourt and done 30 years' continuous service in the French War. He had been Constable of Cardiff Castle, Sheriff and MP for Worcestershire, forester of Glamorgan and still held a position at court as squire of the Body to the King. But he also had ties that bound him closely to the Earl of Warwick, leader of the Yorkist faction. He had first gone to France as a retainer of the Earl; for years he had worn the Warwick badge of the ragged staff, and the Earl had made him a guardian of his infant son.[1]

For eight years he managed to keep his islands out of the fighting, and both sides seem to have trusted him. When the Yorkists seized power after the first battle of St Albans, they renewed his appointment. When the Lancastrians gained the upper hand, he was again reappointed. When Warwick set Edward IV on the throne, he retained Nanfan as Warden. These details of his career are important, because the problem will arise as to whether he later turned traitor.

Before long the unrest in England made itself felt in Jersey, and, when war-fever spreads abroad, it is hard to keep heads cool. Jersey was rife with family feuds and, if one seigneur called himself Yorkist, another would proclaim himself Lancastrian, far removed as the conflict must have seemed to them. Also, the Earl of Warwick was now Lord of the Isles. During these years Nanfan could not remain continuously in Jersey, as his court duties and his Cornish tin mines often took him to England; when absent he left Otys Colin as his Lieutenant. Otys was a Yorkist, but the powerful family of de St Martin were Lancastrians. In 1456 Jannequin de St Martin showed the Court wounds in his thigh caused by 'soldiers of Colin who calls himself Lieutenant of The Castle', and the Court placed him under the King's protection. A few weeks later Jannequin's mother reappeared before the Court pleading for three other of her sons whom Colin had imprisoned in the Castle. The Jurats ordered him to bring them before the Court if he had a charge against them, but he promptly sent them to Castle Cornet, outside the Court's jurisdiction. Here for nearly two years they 'suffered grievous bodily harm for lack of food in a dungeon'. In 1458 there was a hollow reconciliation between Lancastrians and Yorkists; the Queen and the Duke of York walked hand in hand to St Paul's and the de St Martins were released and returned to Jersey. But the peace soon ended. In 1460 the Battle of Ludlow gave the Red Rose the victory for the moment, Warwick lost the Lordship of the Isles and Guillaume de St Martin became Attorney-General with his brother Raullet as Comptroller.[2]

One night early in 1461 Mont Orgueil was surprised by a French force under Jean Carbonnel, cousin and standard-bearer of Pierre de Brézé, Comte de Maulevrier. The Count was one of the most remarkable men of the period, a poet whose rondels are still printed in French anthologies, a statesman who had for years been Charles VII's right-hand man, a soldier who had fought from boyhood to drive the English out of France. When Normandy was liberated he had been made Grand Seneschal of the Duchy. He was also a nephew of René, Duke of Anjou, and so first cousin of Marguerite of Anjou, Henry VI's strong-minded Queen, who was the heart and soul of the Lancastrian cause.

Maulevrier's raid was undoubtedly planned to help his indomitable cousin, and it is highly probable that she was privy to it. Her cause was declining fast; Warwick had returned from exile and set Edward IV, the Yorkist claimant, on the throne, and Henry and Marguerite had fled to Yorkshire. A letter from Maulevrier to the French King has survived, warning him to be careful how he corresponded with Marguerite, 'for if a letter should be intercepted, she would be put to death; her own party, if they knew her intention, would join with others to slay her'.[3] Evidently she and Maulevrier were planning something which even her own followers would regard as unpardonable treason. She was probably urging her cousin to seize the Channel Islands to provide a refuge for the Royal family, should they be driven from England, and had promised to persuade her husband to make Maulevrier Lord of the Isles. To most Englishmen this would have had only one interpretation, that the French-born Queen was betraying the islands to France.

Was Nanfan in the plot? Later writers assume that he was. Falle wrote, 'The English commander, who was of the Lancastrian faction and a creature of the Queen, had secret orders to deliver the Castle up'. N.V.L. Rybot claimed, 'The Lancastrian Warden treacherously surrendered the Castle'.[4] This is not impossible. Nanfan's position at Court must have brought him into touch with Marguerite, and she had the knack of winning the devotion of every man who came near her. If she ordered him, in the King's name, to hand over the Castle to her cousin, who was going to help the King recover his throne, he might have found it hard to disobey. But as a matter of fact no early authority ever accused Nanfan of treason. His English estates were not confiscated and an enquiry of 1531 said that he lost the Castle 'through negligence'.[5] The Jersey Chronicler, who wrote in about 1580, merely repeated the charge, '... he was criminally negligent and careless'. Strange things happen in civil wars, but it seems surprising that such a fine old soldier, who had spent his life fighting the French, would suddenly betray an English castle to the enemy.

It was believed at the time that the Castle had been betrayed and that someone had left a postern open and plied the guards with drink; the person accused was not Nanfan, but Guillaume de St Martin, the Attorney-General, who, as we have seen, had been imprisoned by the Yorkists in Castle Cornet. 'That false traitor, Guillaume de St Martin', said Renaud Lempriére later,[6] 'sold us like meat on a butcher's stall'. The *Extente* of 1528 records that the de St Martin property had been forfeited 'by reason of treason in selling the King's Castle'.

One question remains: the French held the island for seven years, but how much of it did they occupy? For the next hundred years we shall have the help of *Les Chroniques de Jersey*, an invaluable book, written by someone closely in touch with the de Carteret family. It is in the main extremely accurate,[7] but one of its statements about this French occupation is demonstrably untrue. 'They seized', it says,

> the Seigneur of Samarès and other well-to-do men in the neighbourhood of the Castle, but they could never conquer the six western parishes. They dared not pass the town of St Helier, for Philippe de Carteret, Seigneur of St Ouen, raised a force and resisted them so stoutly all the time they held the Castle, that oft he skirmished with them even under the Castle walls.

This statement may just conceivably have been true in the closing months of the occupation, but for most of the seven years it is contradicted by plain facts. The islet on which the Priory stood is west of the town, yet the monks complained to Louis XI that since the Isle had been reduced to his allegiance, those who governed in his name had seized their revenue and forced them to beg for a living, and the King ordered the Bailiff to see that their endowments were restored.[8] St Mary is much further west, yet a contract of 1513 records that the father of Denys Le Cornu 'when the French conquered the Island, went to England and would not take the oath of allegiance; so they took his fief into their hands'. St Peter is also far to the west, but the Prior of St Peter's complained to Louis that Maulevrier's officers had filled his priory with secular persons.[9] De Carteret himself must have made his submission, for, as we shall see in a moment, when one of Warwick's men landed in St Ouen's Bay, he handed him over to the French, and at Whitsuntide 1463 the Lady of St Ouen was dining at the Castle with the French commander and his wife.[10] The whole Island evidently accepted the inevitable and, for the next seven years, all Jersey once more became a part of Normandy. Nicolas Morin, the Bailiff, whose family had provided Jurats for many generations, continued to hold his Courts all through the occupation, but now he was forced to sign documents as 'Bailiff under the high and mighty Lord, the Count of Maulevrier, Lord of the Isles'. Nor was he considered a traitor when the French were expelled. Though replaced as Bailiff, he retained his seat on the bench of Jurats until his death.

Maulevrier had hardly secured Jersey when his position at home became precarious. Charles VII died and Louis XI, who had always hated his father, made a clean sweep of all the old King's ministers; Maulevrier was thrown into prison. Then Louis changed his mind. Civil war kept England from being a danger to France and Louis' policy was to keep the war blazing across the Channel. But at the moment the Yorkists seemed to be winning, so he offered Maulevrier his freedom, if he would raise a force to go and help Marguerite; this he accepted.

Jersey historians, including Le Quesne and Nicolle, assert that in the autumn of 1462 Maulevrier visited Jersey. This statement is based on two authentic documents: some garrison orders, dated 'Mont Orgueil, 22 October', and his Ordinances for the government of the island,[11] 'given at our Castle of Mont Orgueil on the 3rd day of November'. But he sailed with Marguerite for Northumbria on 9 October, so could not have been signing documents at Gorey some three weeks later. The explanation must be that he signed both documents in Normandy, before the expedition started, and that the dates were added when the proclamations were made at the Castle. Apart from this there is no evidence that he ever set foot in Jersey.

In October, by his orders, a Commission of six held an Assize in the Island. A deputation of clergy and notables presented a petition asking that they might be governed 'as of old by the custom of Normandy with certain exceptions which were granted some time ago in writing'. These matters were 'investigated by the persons holding the Assize, who made certain corrections and additions with the consent of the deputation'. The result was the charter known as *The Ordinances of Maulevrier*. This was a definite bid to make the new régime popular. As in another occupation, centuries later, the aim was to create a good impression of clemency at the onset. All existing institutions were confirmed and approved, the only outstanding alteration being that in future Jurats were to be chosen by the Bailiff, Jurats, Rectors and Constables. This Assembly was the embryo of our present day States. It originated, at an unknown time before 1524, from the Royal Court. The Jurats' functions were extended to legislative as well as judicial work and they called on the Rectors and Constables to represent the parishes. The word '*Etats*', corresponding to a similar use in France, may perhaps date from Maulevrier. In its origin it stood for the three 'estates' in Jersey: bench, church and parish.

One useful suggestion was for the establishment of a public register for all transfers of property.[12] The request of the deputation that a Saturday market, which Carbonnel had moved to Gorey for the convenience of the garrison, should be restored to St Helier, was referred to Maulevrier for decision ... ('Monseigneur shall be informed thereof ...') a strong hint that the Ordinances were not issued personally by the Count.

From now on the Castle was to be known as Mont Orgueil. Was the name a compliment paid by the brother of Henry V? There is no proof of this. Was it perhaps a local sobriquet coined in reference to the arrogant pride of those who guarded the frightening prison, or was it the poetic invention of some Frenchman? Whatever the origin of the name, the garrison orders mentioned above were issued for 'Mont Orgueil', the Ordinances were given 'at our Castle of Mont Orgueil', and, when Carbonnel sailed to join Maulevrier in England, his successor, Guillaume, was appointed 'Lieutenant-General and Governor of the Castle of Mont Orgueil'. A curious entry in a Patent Roll of 1292 mentions 'the chaplain and chapel of St Mary, Orgoil [sic] Castle, Guernsey'. Was Jersey intended? Possibly not, as in Guernsey legend has it that the moated Chateau des Marais, built in the 11th century, was originally known as le Château d'Orgueil.[13]

In 1463 Carbonnel's cousin, Guillaume, was in command. His first task was to nip in the bud a plot to recapture the Castle. In August he arrested Renaud Lemprière, seigneur of Rozel, and Thomas le Hardy, Rector of St Martin. The evidence at their trial throws many sidelights on life in the Island. Renaud, a man of 45, had a young Dorsetshire wife, Katherine Camel, an extraordinarily plucky girl of 22, and two young children. The rest of the family consisted of Renaud's 15-year-old niece, who waited at table and helped her aunt with the babies, and Renaud's illegitimate son, Jean, known as 'the bastard of Rozel', who was old enough to drink with the men, but not too old to be thrashed by his father if he was late for supper. Every day began with Mass in the manor chapel and on Sundays the household attended Mass and Vespers at St Martin's church. As a Jurat Lemprière rode into town twice a week to the Court, but his main interest lay at home. He kept open house, and even the most unwelcome caller was expected to stay for dinner. He took pride in his gardens and in showing them to visitors and he was a keen fisherman. For his younger guests he had a fives court in his barn,[14] preferring a quiet game of chess himself. Fives was evidently a popular game, as there was another court at St Martin's tavern.

Thomas Le Hardy was the elderly Rector of St Martin. It is sometimes said that on the eve of the Reformation the Church was staffed by ignorant peasant priests. But Le Hardy was Seigneur of Méléches and one of the leading men of the Island.[15] The evidence at his trial shows him riding about the parish on his mule, saying Mass, now at the Manor, now at the Castle and now in the parish church. His household consisted of his curate, a boy cousin whom he was educating, and a man and boy who looked after them. He too, in a modest way, kept open house. Friends who came to church dropped into the Rectory for a mazer of beer after the service. A knowledge of English was evidently spreading among the island gentry; Le Hardy spoke it easily, and Lemprière of Rozel and de Carteret of St Ouen both had English wives. Other facts which emerge are that the oyster beds at Gorey were already being exploited;[16] the fair at St Lawrence, on St Lawrence's day, was a rowdy island festival, and the fraternities were important institutions. On the Feast of the Assumption the Marshal of the Castle[17] gave a dinner to the Fraternity of Our Lady.

The account of the trial reads like a detective story. We have most of the evidence, but some early pages were missing at the time when the article on Maulevrier was written in 1924. Since then pages 14-18 have been seen and transcribed,[18] though the record of the preliminary hearing has still not been found. The depositions may have been sent to a higher authority for a verdict, so we do not know the final outcome of the trial. The story told is this: towards the end of 1462 one of Warwick's boats from Calais, where he was now Captain, landed a foraging party in St Ouen's Bay and a young man named John Hareford was taken prisoner. De Carteret, instead of smuggling him to Guernsey, which should not have been difficult, for communication between the islands was still open, handed him over to Carbonnel, who imprisoned him in Mont Orgueil. He was evidently a man of breeding, for in the Castle he dined at the Governor's table and later, when released on parole, was a frequent visitor to St Ouen's Manor and Rozel, where Katherine Lemprière believed his story that he knew her father in England. There is little doubt that Carbonnel employed him as a spy. As an English prisoner he would be welcome in pro-English families and be able to report on their attitude to the new régime.

Lemprière was evidently considered a possible source of danger, so a trap was set to arouse the sympathy of his young wife. The Governor insisted that her husband must bring her to the Castle for dinner, and there Hareford was introduced to her as a friend of her father, but his ankles were fettered. He asked her to persuade the Governor to have his chains removed, and, when he consented, she herself helped to unshackle him. He then came often to the manor, playing fives, helping with the harvest and going fishing with the seigneur.

Hareford declared in his evidence that Le Hardy had sounded him at confession as to whether he would help to drive out the French and that Lemprière had offered him 100 crowns to leave the sally-port open and had shown him a letter from Guernsey promising 60 men to help in the attack. Le Hardy and Lemprière denied all Hareford's allegations. For a day and a half Katherine faced a gruelling cross-examination, swearing, 'as she hoped for paradise', that Hareford's stories were lies. Nevertheless the statements of witnesses leave a strong suspicion that the plot was a real one. But, if so, it came to nothing, and the French, who were evidently doing their utmost to conciliate the Island, may have considered it so futile that after a few months they decided to pardon the prisoners. It is generally stated that Lemprière died five years later in an assault on the Castle, though some writers incline to the opinion that he did not survive till then.

Le Hardy, however, appears to have lost his estates, for a little later one of the de St Martins appears as seigneur of Mélèches.

When Jean Carbonnel returned from his raid on the north of England, he found himself in an awkward position. Civil war broke out in France and Maulevrier died in the fighting. Normandy for a short time became an independent duchy, but Louis XI reconquered it and its Duke, Charles of France, had to fly. Carbonnel, an enthusiast for a free Normandy, remained loyal to the Duke with the result that he had against him not only the King of England but also the King of France. But the Castle, now armed with culverins and cannon,[20] was considered impregnable — '*uno castello inexpugnabile!*' the Milanese ambassador called it — and the Duke sent in large supplies of provisions and gunpowder.

It is possibly to this period that the Chronicler's story of the resistance of the western parishes belongs. Carbonnel's hold on distant parts of the Island may have weakened and de Carteret become known as a resistance leader. Carbonnel ordered his arrest. 'One day,' says the Chronicler,

> the seigneur of St Ouen went to his pond to fish, and the French came furtively along the beach, hoping to catch him unawares. The seigneur, however, saw them and sprang to the saddle. But ere he could reach the crest of the hill, another troop appeared, spurring to cut him off. So he swerved towards the Val de la Charrière and reaching a sunken lane, where it is 18 feet deep and 22 feet wide, he made his horse leap it, and racing for Les Landes made his escape. But ere he came to his Manor gates his horse dropped dead beneath him, whereat he grieved greatly and caused it to be buried in his garden for the good service it had done.

The feat is not impossible. Experts say that it would be easier for the horse to jump in these circumstances than to stop suddenly, while some years ago bones of a horse, identified as being some hundreds of years old, were found near the Manor entrance.[21]

In 1468 Richard Harliston,[22] a Yorkist Vice-Admiral, paid a secret visit to Jersey. He came with some of his ships to Guernsey 'and was minded', says the Chronicler, 'to visit Jersey privily by night'. He landed at Plémont and made his way through the darkness to St Ouen's Manor.

The seigneur received him gladly, and they agreed that he should go back to Guernsey and return with all speed, while the seigneur recruited as many men as possible. De Carteret kept their plans secret, merely warning his people to be alert when the call should come. When Harliston had all in trim he landed his troops in the dark and led them to the manor. The seigneur mustered his people and they marched stealthily along the north coast, and so well did they do their duty that, ere day dawned, they were camped before the Castle, encircling it at every side'. Harliston's ships blockaded it by sea. He subsequently became the first Governor appointed solely for Jersey as opposed to a Gardien des Iles.

The siege lasted for 19 weeks, but provisions ran short and Carbonnel began to build a boat to secure fresh supplies 'knowing that the besiegers would hear the carpenters' hammers, they built a second boat in full view, and while some hammered on one boat, others hammered on the other' . In this way they finished the real boat while the dummy was only half built, hoping by this ruse to go undetected. But a Jerseyman working inside the walls fired an arrow by night into the besieger's lines with a letter revealing the trick, and the shore was watched so closely that, as soon as the boat was launched, it was captured.[23]

The Duke of Normandy managed to do something for his one remaining fortress. A St Malo boat, the *Jehanette*, ran the blockade with reinforcements of archers, biscuits, dried cod and cider, to say nothing of casks of dragon's blood[24] as medicine and plasters called *dei gratia.* This enabled Carbonnel to hold out for two months longer, but then he had to surrender. The garrison marched out with the honours of war, and then, 'Sir Richard and the seigneur of St Ouen's and the leading men of the Island entered the Castle with great joy and placed the King's banners on every tower'.[25]

Edward IV now confirmed all Jersey's ancient franchises 'and, bearing in mind with what constancy and courage the community has proved loyal to us and our forefathers, and how many perils and losses they have borne in reducing our Castle of Mont Orgill' (the English government here adopts the French name) he granted an extraordinary award, freedom from pontages, pavages, murages, carriages, fossages and other similar charges in all the cities of England.[26] It makes a magnificently impressive piece of Latin, but meant little to Jersey farmers who were not accustomed to roam about England paying bridge tolls, baggage tolls or tolls for road repairs. However, the clause recognizing the loyalty of Jerseymen and the dangers and losses they had suffered was well-earned and appreciated.

Just as things seemed to be settling down the civil war broke out again with redoubled fury. Warwick quarrelled with King Edward and swung over from the white rose to the red. So the wily Louis arranged a reconciliation between him and Queen Marguerite. Warwick invaded England, Edward fled and poor Henry VI was brought out of the Tower and set on the throne again. Geoffrey Walsh, seigneur of St Germain, the largest landowner in Jersey, mustered his tenants and led them to England to support the Kingmaker. At first all went well, but in March 1471 Edward returned. The armies met at Barnet where Warwick was killed and Walsh fell with his leader. Those of the unfortunate Jerseymen who escaped alive from the battle, made their way to Southampton, hoping to seize a ship, but they were hanged as traitors, though some survived.[27]

Two things remain to be mentioned: the foundation of the grammar school of St Mannelier and the famous Bull of Neutrality. Jean Hue became Rector of St Saviour in the year of the French invasion. His register, recording mainly burials, although incomplete, is far the oldest church register to survive. Its present whereabouts is unknown, but it was printed in full by de la Croix.[28] This register gives little glimpses of church life at this period. There were four fraternities in the parish of which many parishioners were members, St Saviour, St Catherine and two of St Nicolas. Absence from a fraternity meant a fine of two quarts of good wine.[29] North of the church stood the Hôtel-Dieu, an almshouse for the poor. A candle was kept perpetually burning before the great crucifix; the lamp before the image of our Lady of Pity was never allowed to go out. Among recent gifts was an image of St Sebastian, patron saint of bowmen. Hue himself had made donations, but his greatest benefaction was his grammar school.

A mile and a half from his church stood the little chapel of St Magloire, the apostle of Sark, whom Jerseymen called St Mannelier. As was often the case with such chapels, the priest took on the rôle of educating the boys of the neighbourhood. Hue inherited a field adjoining this chapel, and in 1477 he wrote to Harliston offering to build a school there and endow it, if legal difficulties connected with the law of mortmain could be overcome, that is the law which forbade anyone to leave property to something that would never die. The Royal Court accepted this gift[30] and the King exempted it from mortmain. The Bishop of Coutances issued a Pastoral urging the faithful to keep the building in repair for ever, and the school was built. It was to be entirely free. Winter and summer lessons were to last from 6 a.m. to 6 p.m. and it was to be a grammar school, which meant in those days a school for the teaching of Latin grammar. We shall hear more of this school in the next chapter.

Throughout the Hundred Years' War the church had tried many times to stop the bloodshed. Now at last one successful move was made to bring permanent relief to the islands. In 1480 Edward IV and Louis XI agreed that if there were war between England and France, the islands should be regarded as neutral. In the following year Pope Sixtus IV enforced the agreement with a Bull, though he may have been confirming an existing state of affairs.[31] He declared that he had learnt with horror that sons of iniquity were wont to land, burn houses and goods, carry off crops and cattle and murder the inhabitants, throwing them into the sea. He pronounced 'sentence of anathema and eternal damnation with confiscation of goods' on all who should commit such crimes on the islands 'or within sight of them as far as human eye can reach'. The cities and castles of all who should disobey this Bull were placed under an interdict, whether they were Kings, Archbishops, Dukes or Counts, and all their vassals freed from their oath of fealty.

It is curious that the actual document, dated 27 February 1480, lists towns where the text is to be affixed to church doors in England, Brittany and St Peter Port in Guernsey, but not in Jersey. According to Monseigneur Bernard Jacqueline, this suggests that the pirates were English and Breton, rather than Norman, and Dupont states that the execution of the Bull was entrusted to the Archbishop of Canterbury and to the Bishop of Salisbury, and was to be posted on the doors of their two cathedrals as well as on the churches of Nantes, Léon, Tréguier and St Peter Port, no mention being made of the Cotentin or St Helier. This does not necessarily mean that Jersey was excluded, but that at the time, as the neutrality of the islands was important for the trade between Gascony and England, the harbour in Guernsey was on the direct route between the two and was superior to any that existed then in Jersey. Dupont quoting from de la Croix, bases his information on an *inspeximus* of Henry VIII, dated 12 May 1513. A copy of this document with an attractively illuminated initial letter has recently been acquired by La Société Jersiaise.

In 1487 knowledge of this papal interdiction was extended to various Norman ports. This privilege of neutrality lasted for more than 200 years and Jersey seamen continued to enjoy its advantages until it was annulled by William III in 1689. This is not to say that the islands were thenceforth completely free from raids or their ships from molestation on the high seas, but it did give them grounds for claiming redress if the neutrality was violated.

Even after the Reformation Queen Elizabeth, when confirming the privileges of Jersey, admitted that in time of war merchants of all nations, aliens as well as natives, friends and foes, could without impediment frequent the islands to escape storms or for the purpose of commerce and depart without molestation and remain in safety so long as the islands remained in sight. So, despite the papal fury with Elizabeth, the terms were still observed to the great advantage of both Jersey and England.[32]

Chapter Eight

EARLY TUDOR DAYS, 1483-1547

A people weary of dynastic politics, and set on the new pursuit of money making.–Stubbs

EDWARD IV DIED, and his little son had reigned for only ten weeks or so when he was murdered, but whether by his uncle, who thus became Richard III, or exactly when and in what circumstances is a question over which historians are at variance. However the Red Rose party was not dead and it found a leader in Henry Tudor, Earl of Richmond, who liked to think himself a Lancastrian, because his grandfather had married Henry V's widow, Katherine of France.[1] He was living in Brittany, but in October 1483 he sailed to Poole to try to win the crown. But 'the greatest wind that ever was' scattered his little fleet, his supporters' rising petered out and he could not land. Local tradition declares that he took refuge in Jersey; a monument in Westminster Abbey, erected in 1732 to the memory of Admiral Sir Thomas Le Hardy (1666-1732), asserts that his ancestor, Clement Le Hardy[2]

> had the office of Bailiff conferred on him by Henry VII as a reward for the important service rendered him, after the disappointment he met with in his first attempt on England, when, being separated from his fleet by a storm, he landed privately in Jersey, intending to stay there till he could obtain leave from the French king to come into his dominions. He was sheltered at the house of the said Clement, who protected him and conveyed him to Normandy at the hazard of his life, notwithstanding that a proclamation for apprehending the earl had been published in the island.

This story is late, but not improbable. On his way from Poole to Normandy Henry would pass near Jersey and might well have thought it wise to make sure of Louis XI's intentions before venturing within his reach. If, however, he landed in Jersey, it must have been a secret visit, for Harliston was still Governor and a whole-hearted Yorkist. Moreover it is true that Le Hardy, a man of no special prominence, was made Bailiff as soon as Henry became King.

Harliston had now been Governor for 15 years and was popular in the Island. According to the Chronicler,[3] 'He comported himself so wisely and well that he gained the goodwill of all. He never met a boy with a bow without giving him money to buy arrows; so every Saturday the lads took their bows and waited as he rode into town, to get the largesse he scattered'. Unlike many Governors, he was not constantly disappearing to England. He made Trinity Manor his home and married his only daughter Margaret to young Philippe de Carteret of St Ouen's. He strengthened Mont Orgueil by building the Harliston Tower[4] which commands the main entrance, with walls of immense strength and a platform for cannon on the roof; to provide material he pulled down the old Manor of St Helier, or de la Motte (not to be confused with La Maison de Téhy on the north of the road: until recently these two names have been thought to apply to one house not two).[5] The old manor had been the home of the traitor de St Martin. Harliston gave his son-in-law leave to convert St Ouen's Manor into a castle 'with towers, loopholes, bulwarkes, gates, moats and drawbridges, with artillery for its defence'. This he did, of course, in the King's name.[6]

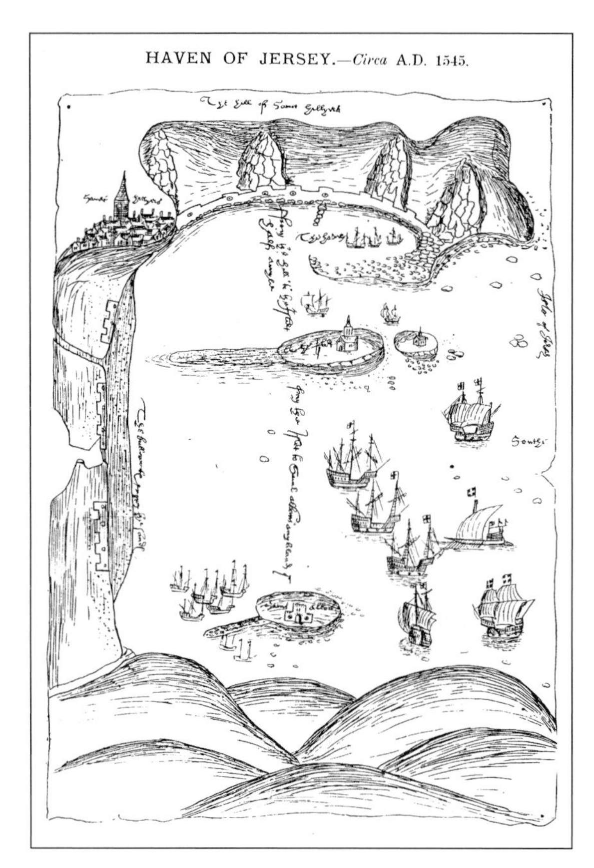

13 *Haven of Jersey, map of 1545 showing 'saint albans'.*

ST AUBIN'S BAY

14 *Vraicing at low tide at St Aubin's Fort, by Edmund Blampied. 'A peece for eternity.' (Poingdestre)*

This work, however, can hardly have begun when there came another upheaval. In 1485 Henry Tudor again invaded England, this time with success. Richard III, after a very short reign, was killed at Bosworth, and the Welshman became Henry VII, a king by conquest. But the White Rose party did not yet lose heart. In the 11-year-old Earl of Warwick[7] they still had an heir to the crown, and Harliston, staunch old Yorkist that he was, resolved to hold Jersey for the boy. But the local seigneurs were not ready to fight for a cause that seemed hopelessly dead. Edmund Weston,[8] one of Harliston's officers, who had married Lemprière's widow and was living at Rozel Manor, slipped over to England to report what was happening. He acted so promptly that only 15 days after Bosworth he received a commission from Henry to reduce Jersey, and he felt so sure of support that he took back with him only 25 soldiers. Nor was he disappointed. Harliston withdrew behind the Castle walls, and again Mont Orgueil was besieged, this time with Harliston inside. He held out for some months, but his party had no fleet and he was forced to surrender. He received 'a general pardon and restitution of possessions'. But, as an unrepentant Yorkist, he took part the next year in Lambert Simnel's rising and eight years later he landed at Deal to fight for Perkin Warbeck. He died in exile in Burgundy.[9]

The Governorship of Jersey was given to two young men, Matthew Baker and David Philippe, the latter being Governor of Guernsey in 1503, but spending most of his time in England, seeking and gaining preferment. They had been the King's companions in exile, and Matthew Baker now took up his duties. The Chronicler describes him as 'extremely peevish, malicious and terribly vindictive'.[10] He was certainly tactless and high-handed. He infuriated the seigneurs by making them produce their title-deeds; he enraged the tenants of the crown lands by increasing and even doubling their rents. A torrent of protests poured in to the Privy Council, and in all these appeals de Carteret was spokesman for the Island. Baker naturally resented this, especially as his chief opponent was Harliston's son-in-law, so he determined to destroy him.

Here is the story as told by the Chronicler. In 1494 Baker forged a letter in de Carteret's name to some nobles in Normandy, in which he offered to betray Mont Orgueil to the French. He had this dropped in a lane down which he rode every Saturday on his way to town. When he saw it, he bade one of his men pick it up opened it and read it. He then rode to the Court, where de Carteret was sitting as one of the Jurats, and charged him with treason. De Carteret naturally denied all knowledge of the letter, so Baker resorted to a procedure that had become almost obsolete. In earlier days, when evidence was conflicting, judges ordered the Ordeal by Battle; this was an appeal to the supernatural. Each party swore that he had spoken the truth and then they fought with clubs and it was assumed that God would not allow a perjurer to win. A Lateran Council in 1215 had forbidden the clergy to countenance this test and so had virtually abolished it, for it was nothing if not a religious ceremony. However it still lingered on in the statute-book. Le Boutillier, who had picked up the letter, threw down his gauntlet and offered to prove before God that de Carteret had lied. De Carteret objected that Le Boutillier was a criminal whom he had saved from the gallows, and that he could not be expected to fight such a man. But party feeling ran strong, and Le Hardy, the Red Rose Bailiff, allowed the Ordeal, refused bail and committed both men to the Castle until the day of the battle which was fixed for 10 August, St Lawrence's Day.

Le Boutillier, a hefty ruffian, was fed like a fighting cock, while de Carteret was kept in a dark cell on bread and water. To make the result doubly sure, hidden trenches were dug on the combat ground in order to trip De Carteret. One thing more was essential. The de Carterets' loyalty was proverbial and Philippe had friends at Court, made when he was appearing before Council in the Island's suits. So Baker felt he must cross the Channel to tell his version of the story before any appeal could arrive from Jersey, and to stop this he forbade any boat to leave the Island.

But Margaret, de Carteret's wife, was a worthy daughter of Harliston. Three days before her husband's arrest she had given birth to a baby. Which of her supposed family of 20 sons and one daughter this child was, we do not know; it can hardly have been the twenty-first, as the Chronicler says, for we know that her fifth son was born in 1480, so she could barely have had the twenty-first by 1494. Her husband is known to have died shortly after 1500. However that may be, she arose from bed and persuaded a fisherman to row her to Guernsey. Here Jurat de Beauvoir, whose mother had come from Vinchelez de Bas in St Ouen, took her in his own sloop. It was now a race between Margaret and Baker as to who would reach the King first, and Baker had several hours start. As they entered Poole harbour they saw him, but Margaret's luck held, as a hail-storm forced him to seek shelter and she was able to land unobserved. On reaching Sheen, where the King was staying, she found Bishop Fox[11] of Durham, who took her into the King's presence and pleaded her cause so effectively that Henry at once signed an order forbidding the trial by combat and reserving the case for judgment by the Council. Fox took the precaution of getting this sealed with the Great Seal, and, as Margaret came down the palace steps, she met Baker who had just, arrived, 'whereat', says the Chronicler, 'he was greatly surprised'.

It was still a race against time, for the feast of St Lawrence was only a few days off, but Margaret found a boat in Southampton and arrived home on St Lawrence's Eve. She at once presented the King's order to the Bailiff, whom Baker had appointed as his Lieutenant-Governor,[12] and he had to obey. When de Carteret's case was heard before the Council his character was cleared. But the Chronicler was mistaken when he said that 'Baker was expelled from the office in ignominy, so that he died in poverty bereft of his possessions'. He was transferred from Jersey, but he retained the King's confidence, for he was twice sent as Ambassador to France and once to the King of the Romans. Later we meet him as 'Keeper of Paradise, Purgatory and Hell', which sounds a tall order, but these were Jocular terms for three of the floors in Westminster Hall.[13]

Meanwhile the Chronicler records with glee the fate of Clement Le Hardy. A Spanish ship, laden with wine, was wrecked off La Corbière, and the sands were strewn with puncheons. The seigneurs whose fiefs touched St Ouen's Bay had a rich haul of wreckage, and the great hall in de Carteret's manor was well-nigh filled with wine-tuns. The Bailiff, as Lieutenant-Governor, had charge of the Crown fiefs and he was tempted to keep some of the wine for himself. For this, Baker, before his removal from office, had him thrown into a dungeon, 'and there', gloats the Chronicler, 'at last he died covered with lice and vermin'.

After Baker's dismissal two orders in Council curtailed the Governor's powers.[14] He was no longer allowed to nominate Bailiff, Dean, Vicomte or Attorney-General, or to interfere in any way with the administration of justice. He lost the right to arrest or imprison except for treason, and then the case must be at once reported to the King. Disputes between Governor and Jurats must be referred to the Council and no subject of the King must be hindered from leaving the Island for England. The duties of a Jurat were also more clearly defined: he must never fail to be present in Court when summoned, unless he provided another Jurat to replace him. All judgments must be signed in a register kept for that purpose and no Jurat had power to pardon a criminal. The Island's seal must never be used unless seven Jurats were present. Since brewers, bakers and taverners had to be licensed by the Court, no member of these trades might sit on the bench; Jurats who presided at elections must not try to influence the votes. Ten clauses dealt with the Castle; one of these abolished the annual St George's Day pilgrimage to the chapel in the Middle Ward, lest some day the great crowds might overpower the garrison. However the habit of visiting the Castle on Easter Monday was a popular island custom until well into the 19th century.[15]

The next Governor, Thomas Overy,[16] was a Southampton merchant who had been three times elected mayor of that city. The experiment of having a merchant, instead of a soldier as

Governor, seems to have been successful. According to the Chronicler, he found marvellous favour with all. He did much to increase the commerce of the Island by inducing French and English merchants to visit it, so that thanks to him in a short time it became opulent'. He died in office and his coffin was much later found in St George's Chapel.[17]

Now that Normandy was a foreign country, it was obviously undesirable that Jersey should be under a foreign Bishop. Indeed one is amazed that this situation had been allowed to continue for so long, with the islands owing allegiance to a King in England, but ecclesiastical loyalty to a Bishop in Coutances. So in 1496 Henry obtained from that most bribable of Popes, Alexander Borgia, a Bull transferring the islands from Coutances to Salisbury, and three years later another Bull altering this to Winchester.[18] In 1501 Richard Le Haguais was instituted at Winchester to the Rectorship of St Brelade, but he was a prudent man and took care to be instituted by the Bishop of Coutances also.[19] Apart from this one institution the Bulls appear to have remained a dead letter. The islands were far from Winchester, but close and profitable to Coutances, and Bishop Fox was far too busy a statesman to take time to assert his authority. For another 50 years the Bishops of Coutances continued to confirm, ordain, institute and act in every way as undisputed Bishops of the islands, though no record has been found of a Bishop actually visiting Jersey.

Meanwhile a group of Jerseymen had obtained important positions in the household of Prince Arthur, the nine-year-old Prince of Wales. The religious education of the boy was entrusted to Jean Neel, a Jerseyman who had been Master of Arundel College; Thomas de St Martin, seigneur of Trinity, was Premier-Usher and Edward de Carteret Gentleman-Carver. If Prince Arthur had lived to be King, these men would probably have risen to high positions, but Arthur died before his father.[20]

Neel, however, made one handsome benefaction to the Island. With his friend Vincent Téhy, a St Helier's man who had become Mayor of Southampton, he increased the endowment of St Mannelier and founded a second grammar school in 1496 for the western parishes. This was attached to an old chapel dedicated to St Anastase[21] in a lane leading down to St Peter's valley still named le Mont de l'École. Both schools lasted until the middle of the 19th century, and today their endowments are used for scholarships to Victoria College.[22] Although both St Mannelier and St Anastase had their shortcomings and vicissitudes, they remained the centres of learning in the Island for 400 years.

In 1502 a fire in Morier Lane[23] had disastrous results for future historians. At an inquest held in 1532, 12 old men testified that 'about thirty years back a house in St Helier belonging to Thomas Lemprière, the Bailiff, was accidentally destroyed by fire and in it were the privileges, confirmations, ancient rolls, records and registers of the island, and these were burnt with the house'. It has also been suggested that the burning was because of feared contamination during an outbreak of plague.

The next Governor was Sir Hugh Vaughan, a Welsh tailor's son whom Henry had come to know when they were boys in Wales. He was a strikingly handsome man and at tournaments no one could unseat him; but our Chronicler gives him a very unsavoury reputation. He admits that he was 'a marvellous fine horseman, very gallant and courtly', but goes on to say that …

> he gave himself up to wenching (*paillardise et dissolution*) and became so lecherous that he would rape young girls by force, so that they dared not walk in the lanes alone for fear of him. Furthermore, if he claimed an estate, he would send for the title-deeds and tear off the seals. He belaboured first one, then another, so violently that they were often in danger of death.

Official documents confirm these charges; 'where it speaks of the ravishing certain girls', said a jury in 1531, 'it is received beyond doubt as true'. The same jurors reported: 'The Captain … in order to extort the goods of L'Evesque and Pipon *meurdyt* them [beat them black and blue] so as

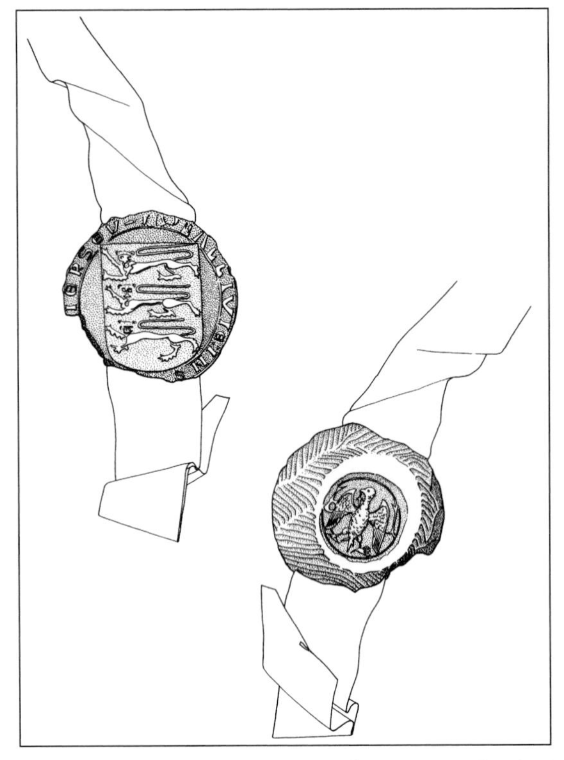

15 *Seal of Thomas Lemprière, Bailiff 1495-1513. The Island arms are on the obverse and were granted in 1279.*

to cause their death'.[24] In a petition to the Council in 1529 the parishioners of St Martin complained that they had lost the endowment of a weekly Mass because Vaughan had imprisoned the chaplain until he gave up a letter of foundation, which he had then torn into bits. The name of the chaplain was Sire Guille Vaultre.[25] It is perhaps surprising to find this same Hugh Vaughan creating an obit, *meu en devotion* for a Mass to be celebrated for the souls of himself and his family, in 1519.

In 1513, however, the Governor's conduct had become so outrageous that Lemprière crossed to Westminster to complain. But in spite of the new rule that a Bailiff could only be removed by the King, Vaughan dismissed him and appointed Helier de Carteret, a son of the seigneur of St Ouen, in his place. The young Henry VIII, who had succeeded his father, was more interested in sport than in business, and Vaughan hoped that this irregularity would pass unnoticed. The Council, however, sent two Commissioners in 1515 to investigate the unrest in Jersey, but 'through the influence of the seigneur of St Ouen, all was hushed up'. Their report was a skilful bit of whitewashing and left Vaughan master of the Island.

But then he quarrelled with the de Carterets. Drouet Lemprière, who had married de Carteret's sister, Mabel (the only daughter of the famous family of 21 children), inherited Trinity Manor. But Vaughan claimed it as forfeit to the Crown because 60 years before, Lemprière's uncle, de St Martin, had sided with the French, and he ignored the fact that the King's pardon had been granted. At the time the Court was sitting at Grouville[26] as plague was raging in town. When Vaughan saw that de Carteret, as Bailiff, was going to give judgment against him, the Chronicler reports:

> he put his hand to his sword, shouting "Deny me the verdict and I will thrust this up to the hilt through your belly". Whereupon the Bailiff sprang to his feet, ordered the doors to be opened, and grasping Sir Hugh's wrist firmly, told him that if he moved he would be a dead man. Then the people rushed in and in open court he discharged Lemprière from this action.

Vaughan retorted that he would have him dismissed 'though it cost him his last shirt'. De Carteret then took the offensive and summoned Vaughan before the Council for interfering with the administration of justice. At first he was wonderfully successful. The Chronicler describes him as 'very handsome, fascinating and extremely eloquent, good-humoured, large-hearted and invariably cheerful'. He attracted the notice of the young King by his skill with cross-bow and arquebus, and obtained a place in the Royal Household as Sewer of the Chamber.[27] (The Sewer's duty was to arrange the seating of the guests.) In December 1521 the King confirmed his appointment as Bailiff, and in March 1522 granted him the fief of St Germain, in St Lawrence's parish, which was a nasty blow for Vaughan, for it diverted the rents and dues from this fairly large fief from his pocket to de Carteret's.

Vaughan, however, pinned his faith on Wolsey, who was now at the zenith of his power. 'The Cardinal', wrote the Venetian ambassador, 'is really King.' But the insolent grandeur of his household ate up a lot of money, and everyone knew that he was not unwilling to accept gifts. In the Record Office is a long letter about de Carteret's case in which Vaughan says he is sending the Cardinal 500 gallons of wine and that there is more to follow. So whenever the case came up, Wolsey, the Chancellor, quietly adjourned it until the next session. In this way he managed to drag the case on for nearly twelve years, and Lieutenant-Bailiffs had to carry on in Helier's absence.

Eventually de Carteret lost patience. On the closing day of the term, when his counsel rose in the Star Chamber and Wolsey as usual called the next case, de Carteret shouted, 'I demand justice'.

> The Cardinal pretended to be deaf and passed on to the other suit, but the Bailiff cried again at the top of his voice, "I demand justice". He made such a noise that the Cardinal could no longer feign deafness and said, "Justice? If you had justice, you would be punished as a man who had wrought much ill to his country". The Bailiff replied, "You charge me with things you cannot prove". The Cardinal rose in a rage and said, "Did you ever hear such insolence? We can guess how he lords it in his own land, if he is so malapert here". And he called for the Keeper of the Fleet Prison. The Bailiff answered boldly, "Before you send me there, I pray you tell me why? Is it for demanding justice? You have kept me waiting in this city for years and I have not had a hearing. You have cut off my livelihood. My money is spent. I am a poor gentleman with his wife and children. Have I not cause to protest?" Everyone marvelled that he spoke so stoutly. The Cardinal suspended the sitting in great fury.

There are, however, reasons for thinking that de Carteret was a man of ungovernable temper and not always as just and disinterested as the Chronicler would have us believe.

But Wolsey's arrogance had made many enemies and his fall was close at hand. That night the Duke of Norfolk sent for de Carteret and, striking him on the shoulder, said, 'You are a real man. Be not uneasy about funds. If you have need of £500 draw on me'. On the opening day of the Michaelmas Term 1529 Wolsey was arrested and de Carteret was allowed to return to Jersey and resume his duties as Bailiff. The Island then made strenuous efforts to get rid of Vaughan. The Council was bombarded with petitions and a new Commission was sent to make enquiries.[28] This unearthed flagrant misdoings. Vaughan was drawing wages for 54 soldiers, but could only produce eighteen. The contents of the Castle store-room tallied exactly with the ledger, but it had all been borrowed after the Commission had landed and was to be restored to the owners as soon as they had left. Cases were cited in which men had died of thrashings which he had given them. After such a Report he had to be removed.

In 1524 we meet with the earliest surviving Act of the States, a regulation about foreign sailors 'issued by the Captain, Jurats and States of the isle'. However, the name *Etats* for a governmental assembly had already appeared in 1497,[29] when the security of the endowments of the Grammar schools was guaranteed 'by the consent of all the States' (*les Etats*). This body had been gaining influence very gradually and although originally all authority had lain with the Royal Court, the Jurats, when resisting Grandison,[30] had begun to strengthen their protests by stating that they spoke in the name 'of the Community of the Isle', though they never disclosed how this community voiced its opinions. Later, when the custom arose for the Jurats from time to time to invite the Rectors and Constables, to advise the Court' (*Conseiller la Justice*), this was at first purely an act of courtesy, but before long it came to be expected as a right. By the reign of Henry VIII the States met pretty frequently, but still in a purely consultative capacity. In 1526 the Rector of St Mary, Sire Nicolas Despetits, was fined 'for failing to attend to give counsel to the Court on the matter of the hearth tax.'[31]

It is in this period that we find the earliest date so far recorded for a private dwelling. This was in 1539 and refers to a very small cottage at St John, La Petite Genée. It is a single cell with sleeping rooms in the roof and has one ground floor hearth. We also know that another was built in 1532 somewhere near Morel Farm, and this was to be 24 feet long, 14 feet wide and eight feet high in stone.[32] These details may be taken as indicative of moderate houses of the period.

In 1536 Sir Edward Seymour became Governor. He was the King's brother-in-law, for his ill-fated sister Jane had become Henry's third queen. He was far too busy a man to pay much attention to Jersey, and his Lieutenants were not popular. The first, Robert Raymond, had to cope in 1540 with a terrible outbreak of plague. All markets, fairs and public assemblies were closed; those who nursed the sick had to wear a red cross on their shoulders, infected houses had to have a white cross painted on their doors. No one exposed to infection might attend church and beggars might not wander from parish to parish on pain of the whipping-post. Merchants might not hawk their wares from door to door.[33]

In spite of this crisis Jerseymen became more and more quarrelsome. The Jurats quarrelled with the Bailiff and refused to work with him, and both alike quarrelled with the Lieutenant-Governor, Raymond. So in 1541 Seymour, who had now become Earl of Hertford, replaced him by Henry Cornish, the King's godson.

Seymour also wrote to the Jurats:

> Whereas it hath pleased the King's Majesty to summon his High Court of Parliament, I, minding the redress of such things as do derogate the commonwealth of the isle, have thought good to require you to elect two of the discreetest and most experienced in the State, and to send the same hither that they may be admitted Burgesses for the isle.[34]

The Council, which had just granted an MP to Calais, evidently planned to give two seats in Parliament to Jersey. This letter was translated into French and sent to each of the parishes, but no further steps were taken. The Parliament of 1542 contained no members for Jersey, nor have any subsequent Parliaments, although a small number of Jerseymen have sat in Parliament, in the Lords or as member for some English constituency. Commenting on the situation in 1542 Mr. Bois writes:

> As the day on which the letter was presented to the States was the day on or before which the persons elected were required to arrive in London, it was impossible to comply with the Governor's requirements, and it is thus unsafe to conjecture on what action the States would have taken if it had been possible to do so.

The relationship of Jersey to Parliament has been raised on many occasions since that date.

Cornish's main work was fortification. Henry's tortuous foreign policy was bringing the country daily nearer to a war with France, and Jersey was far from ready to repel an attack.

Mont Orgueil still relied for defence mainly on bows and arrows, and a large section of the outer wall had collapsed. Cornish repaired this and began to add a new Keep to the Castle, the mighty Somerset Tower (so called because by the time it was finished Hertford had become Duke of Somerset). This was built in an attempt to dominate with its guns the dangerous hill opposite. Cornish also built in 1542 a squat one-storied tower on the islet of St Aubin and laid plans for a companion fort on the islet of St Helier. But all this cost money, and increased taxation merely increased discontent. In January 1546 Hertford wrote:

> I am informed that divers of the inhabitants, neither regarding their duties of allegiance nor yet their own safeguard, do show themselves rather like brute beasts than men, refusing to contribute according to their rates to such charges as from time to time have been thought requisite. I, not a little marvelling at their folly and obstinacy, nevertheless charge you to tax how much each parish is to bear, and, in case any person obstinately refuse the accomplishment thereof, to commit them to strict ward, there to remain till they have paid the taxation.[35]

The great creative surge of the Renaissance which followed the fall of Constantinople in 1452 is seldom mentioned by Jersey historians, yet it was to have a profound influence on island life. At a later date we were to share to some extent the common heritage of Europe in the revival of classical forms of architecture and new attitudes of learning, but most important was the modern spirit of scientific enquiry which replaced the authoritarian teaching of the medieval Church. The discovery made by Copernicus that the earth revolved round the sun, the Portuguese exploration of the African coast, the voyages of Columbus and the circumnavigation of the globe were to open the way for a great expansion in foreign trade in the 16th and 17th centuries, encouraged by a rising secular demand for exotic luxuries. Jersey was to play her full part in this new and larger world. Meanwhile these new attitudes had led to the Reformation and this too had an enormous influence on Jersey.

Chapter Nine

THE REFORMATION, 1547-1558

A Change was coming upon the world, the meaning and direction of which even still is hidden from us … The paths trodden by the footsteps of ages were broken up … The faith and the life of ten centuries were dissolving like a dream.–Froude, *History of England*

TO UNDERSTAND the radical revolution which was now to remodel the whole of the life of the Island, we must glance at events in the outside world. In Wittenberg, an obscure little Saxon university, it was the custom, if someone wished to challenge his fellow-students to debate, to nail the thesis he meant to defend on the door of the Castle church. In 1517, Martin Luther, a young theological lecturer, nailed there a denial of the efficacy of Indulgences, which were being hawked throughout Europe, for the rebuilding of St Peter's at Rome. Nothing could seem less likely to have any repercussion in Jersey, yet it stirred up a storm that swept across half Europe and whose reverberations are still felt throughout the Christian world.

The Reformation, as this hurricane was called, was due mainly to three causes. For more than a century there had been a cry for Church reform. The Church was riddled with abuses; its endowments were sold as investments, as stocks and shares are today. A man would buy a prebend for his son, or a headship of a nunnery for his daughter; a King's bastard might be abbot of half a dozen abbeys, and court officials were paid by giving them bishoprics and canonries. Thomas de Soulemont, the King's Latin secretary, was Dean of Jersey from 1534 to 1541, but during that time he never once set foot in the Island, though he kept in close touch with Jersey affairs which might be to his benefit.[1] John Carvenal, Chaplain to the Queen of Scotland, who was Henry VIII's sister, was given the Priory of St Helier. He continued to live in Edinburgh, but took strenuous steps to make his tenants pay their rents regularly. Of the four Bishops of Coutances who had oversight of the Church in Jersey for the first half of the century, one was a Cardinal and lived in Rome, as did the next while writing the obscenest comedies of the period. His two successors were courtiers at the French king's palace, who never entered their diocese. The most loyal of Catholics might well cry out for some drastic reform.[2]

But apart from disgust at these scandals, a rationalistic spirit was astir. The capture of Constantinople by the Turks had driven Greek scholars westward, and a passion for Greek studies had swept through the universities. But Greek literature was pagan and Greek minds moved in regions uncharted by Church fathers. Everywhere critics were asserting that legends long accepted as history were not fact but fiction; relics long revered as genuine were exposed as impostures; writings on which great dogmas had been based were said to be forgeries. Even in out of the way places like Jersey men's minds were becoming unsettled.

The Reformation would possibly have remained a purely negative movement, had it not been reinforced by a new type of religious experience. There was plenty of genuine piety still alive in Europe, and some were trying to put fresh life into the old ceremonies. Pilgrimages and processions were multiplying and men flocked in thousands to any shrine that held out a hope of pardon. In about 1515 Richard Mabon, Dean of Jersey, made the long pilgrimage to Jerusalem and, after his return, built or added to the chapels on La Hougue Bie, with the oratory 'en manière d'un sépulture semblable ou viron au St Sépulture de Jérusalem'. This latter he made into a place of pilgrimage profitable to himself.[3] It seems likely that the name Jerusalem may have referred to some edifice on the mound before Mabon's building, as there is mention of '*hospitalibus Iheros*' (a Jerusalem hospital or hospice) in wills of 1495 and 1496.[4] Jerusalem was a natural name to choose, being 'the city on a hill, whither the tribes went up'.

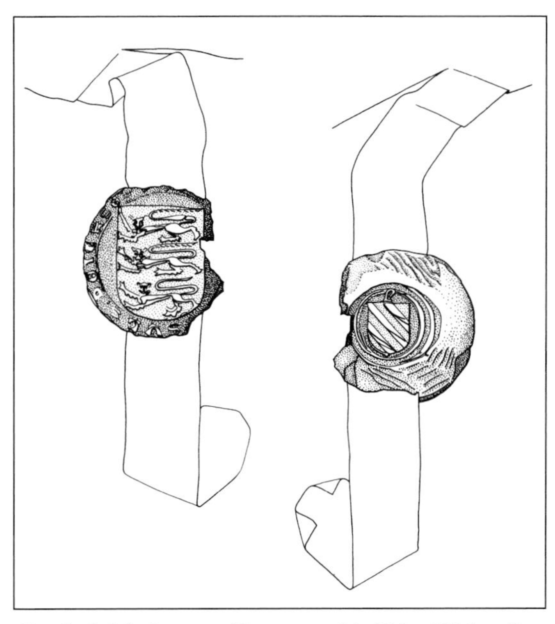

16 *Seal of the Deanery of Jersey, as used by Richard Mabon, Dean (intermittently) 1500-1542.*

Others, however, like Luther, began to draw from St Paul's Epistles a new concept of salvation, not as a prize to be worked for, but as a gift to be received. 'We are saved', they said, 'not by pious observances, but by faith alone; not by the love we show, but by the love we trust. Cast yourself in simple faith directly at the feet of Christ. Give up trying to earn salvation and trust Him to save you'.[5] This doctrine, which received the name of Justification by Faith, seems to have emerged simultaneously in several different quarters. Jacques le Fèvre, a Frenchman (1455-1537), taught it in his *Commentary* five years before Luther. It sounded so refreshingly simple that thousands gave it a trial and declared that it worked. A new power came into their lives which they were eager to share with others.

To Luther's surprise his thesis attacking one definite abuse proved to be the spark that set ablaze all those explosive elements. The printing presses broadcast copies of the thesis and these started debates which shook the medieval church to its foundations. The Reformation reached Jersey, however, not from Germany but from France. The French Reform Movement, in its early days, was wholly religious; Jacques Le Fèvre, its first leader, was a quiet, devout old scholar, who made no attacks on the Church, but hoped to see it reform itself from within. In 1523 he printed a French translation of the New Testament. The Bishop of Meaux invited him to his diocese, and groups of wool-carders and fullers began to meet in private to read the Bible together. Soon they noticed the difference between their own church and that of the first century and began to long for a religion more on New Testament lines.[6]

But the news from Germany had startled the Sorbonne, which was originally founded as the Theological Faculty of the University of Paris. It awoke and grew vigilant. It ordered Le Fèvre's French Testament to be burned and all found reading it to be imprisoned. In 1523 the first victims were burned at Meaux and Paris; by 1526 burnings were general and grew even more barbarous. To prevent the martyrs from testifying before they died, their tongues were torn out with hot irons; in some cases they were suspended by pulleys and dipped in and out of the flames to prolong their agony. Under pressure from this persecution a fanatical fighting spirit awoke in the French reformers. Like the left-wing followers of St Francis, they attacked the Pope and the wealth and abuses of the Catholic Church. The wilder among them began to smash off the heads of statues of saints; this led to fresh burnings and to yet further outrages. It is a point to remember that the Protestantism that eventually captured Jersey was not the comparatively mild variety that was spreading through England, but the stern, militant, uncompromising Protestantism of France, where all who belonged to the 'New Religion' thought of themselves as soldiers engaged in a life and death struggle with the Devil.

The movement was driven underground and public preaching became impossible, but the new ideas spread unceasingly. By 1528 they were already causing alarm in Normandy. That year a layman was burned at Rouen, another at Coutances and three women at Avranches. In 1531 the University of Caen was declared by its Warden to be 'wholly infected with the venom of heresy'. Some of the Normandy priests were accepting the new teaching. In 1534 one was burned at Rouen and three more at Alençon. The propaganda went on perpetually; pedlars hawked New Testaments from fair to fair and had controversial tracts hidden under lace and ribbons. Placards appeared at street corners denouncing the doctrine of the Mass as cannibalism.[7]

There was more intercourse then than now between Jersey and Normandy, and the new ideas soon began to filter into the Island. Many people owned boats and took their wives to shop at Guibray and Lessay fairs. When they crossed to Carteret with cargoes of corn, some of them brought back copies of the forbidden literature. It is not unlikely that colporteurs paid visits to Jersey, but we hear nothing of this movement as it was all underground; it must have been very thorough, for, as soon as a change in Government withdrew the support of the secular arm, the old church system collapsed like a house of cards.

In 1547 Henry VIII died and was succeeded by his son, Edward VI, a serious, delicate small boy of nine. Hertford, his uncle, who was still Governor of Jersey, now became Duke of Somerset and Protector of the Kingdom. During Henry's lifetime he had lain low in matters of religion, but now he showed himself to be a militant anti-Catholic. His first attempt was to repeal all the old laws against heresy. Then he launched a big attack on the practice of masses for the dead, an easy target, for even those who believed in praying for the dead had begun to doubt the value of prayers which could be purchased. In November 1547 the Chantries Act sequestered all chantry chapels and all endowments for masses.[8]

Small chapels abounded in Jersey and by no means all were chantries. In St Martin's parish, for example, there were St Catherine's, which gave its name to St Catherine's Bay, St Agatha's, St Julien's, St Stephen's, St Médard's, St Barbara's, St Margaret's and the lonely chapel of St Mary on the Écréhous. Trinity had the chapels of Notre-Dame, St Symphorian, St Maur and St Cosme. Hardly a parish was without some, and the suppression threw a large number of priests out of work, but it did not leave them penniless, for the Court was ordered to 'appoint convenient pensions' for them.[9] Many of the chapels were turned into cottages: the sale of a house called La Chapelle de St Maurice is recorded in 1552, and a similar instance refers to the chapel of St Cosme.[10] Human bones have been found on the sites of some of these chapels: La Chapelle de la Madeleine at St Helier, de St Thomas at Longueville and de Ste Catherine at St Martin.[11]

Obits were endowments left for a mass to be said on the anniversary of the donor's death, or that of some relative whose memory he wished to preserve and whose soul he wished to save. The number of these was considerable, but impossible to ascertain accurately; there are 31 recorded for Trinity, 15 for Grouville, for example. Twenty years earlier neglect of these masses would have filled the island with horror; it would have meant leaving one's mother, or someone else dear to one, helpless as they suffered the pangs of Purgatory. Now, so thoroughly had the underground movement done its work, that these obits were swept away apparently without protest, and at this time were being sold by the dozen.

Already in 1545 parishes were starting to sell them, anticipating the royal edict to dispose of all emblems of popery. In the case of St Saviour, it is admitted that long before this Nicolas de Soulemont had paid by this means for the purchase and delivery of a '*pièce d'artillerie*' for the garrison of the parish and the defence of the island; so St Saviour at least had a parish gun some years before St Peter where our only surviving example is dated 1551.[12] Documents have survived for St Martin[13] and St Clement,[14] where a *rente* was due for maintaining four wax candles in the future, a duty that, had they known it, was not to last for many more years. In St Helier a bronze gun was bought as well as other pieces of artillery in iron, hacquebuttes, powder, bows, arrows and other munitions.

Documents signed by Cornish, the Lieutenant-Governor, and Charles Mabson, Rector of St Martin, show continuing sales of 'obits, masses, freries, terres et chapelles', sold for the King under the Commission appointed in 1548/9; a decade later, in 1559, the Procureur of St Helier,[15] Jean Le Moigne, recalls that two years previously he sold four cabots of wheat rente,[16] part of a larger sum, which Guille Gosselin, the purchaser, used for the re-edification of the windows in the church. One assumes that this is for replacements of windows that had been smashed 10 years before, an important piece of evidence.[17]

Even more surprising was the ease with which the parish fraternities were suppressed, on the grounds that part of their funds had been left to provide masses for deceased members. At St Martin there were fraternities of the blessed Sacrament, the Crucifix, St Catherine and St Nicolas; St Peter had some dedicated to Notre-Dame, St Nicholas and the Crucifix; St Brelade to the Crucifix, Notre-Dame and St Brelade; every parish had them, but they were now disbanded and their properties seized.[18] Jersey often showed that it could protest with vigour against injustice; at this very moment it was clamouring loudly against some of Cornish's actions, and indeed he was recalled soon after the French had succeeded in landing at Bouley Bay in 1549. If this great spoliation of the Fraternities could take place without expostulation, it can only mean that the membership had dwindled to such a point that no one greatly cared what happened to them.[19]

In July 1548 Royal Injunctions arrived ordering the destruction of every object of superstition.[20] Jersey was once as full of wayside crosses as Brittany, though with us they took the form of a simple tall granite cross with short cross members morticed into a heavy base, usually octagonal; we do not appear to have had the elaborate carved crucifixes of the Continent. Dozens of place names preserve their memory: La Route ès Croix, les Hautes Croix, la Croix à la Dame, la Croix Demades, la Croix Hastain, la Croix de Bois, la Croix de Harène, la Croix Morin, la Croix Varin. A few bases and fewer fragments and top segments remain as testimony. So few have survived that one wonders whether many of them recorded in place names were not in wood as was the one at Five Oaks.[21] Crucifix smashing had been a regular feature in France, and when this order arrived the crosses were smashed, it seems without much reluctance. This destruction of symbols that a few years before had been saluted by everyman doffing his hat and bowing, is another proof of the amazing success of the new way of thinking.

The Rectors themselves seem to have favoured the Reform movements, but they felt that the Island needed education in theology, so they took steps to import some French Protestant theologians. An Act of the States of August 1548 runs:

> For the food and maintenance of Maistre Martin Langeoys and Maistre Thomas Johanne, all the Rectors and Jurats of the Island have deliberated and each voluntarily contributed to them a quarter of wheat to be given to them next Michaelmas for their maintenance for the coming year, to preach to the people the pure and sincere word of God according to the Bible. And the Bailiff gave two quarters of wheat for the same purpose.

Langeoys was naturalised a year later.[22] Maistre, or Master, signifies that he was a Master of Arts. In due course Langeoys became Rector of St Saviour, and Johanne of St Helier; Soler, a Spaniard and ex-Benedictine monk, was appointed Rector of St Clement.

In January 1549 the Act of Uniformity swept away the Latin services and ordered Cranmer's first Prayer Book to be used in every church in the King's dominions. The old services were apparently at once discontinued, for a year later the Council thanked the Island 'for embracing His Majesty's laws in the Order of Divine Service'. But what took their place? An English book would have been as unintelligible to many as was the Latin, but the French translation 'for the use of the churches of Calais, Guisnes, Jersey and Guernsey' was not issued until April 1550. Most of the Rectors probably used the only French Prayer book available to them, the book of *Prières Ecclésiastiques* compiled by Calvin for the Reformers in France.

How did the clergy react to these changes? Two Rectors, Le Roy of St Saviour and Dolbel of St Clement, refused to conform and were deprived of their livings. Three, Mabson of St Helier, Bertram of St Brelade and Payn of St Ouen, embraced the Reformed faith with enthusiasm. When in 1549 marriage for the clergy was legalised, many of them married a wife of good family, another sign of the swing of public opinion; for to Roman Catholics a priest's wife would have been merely a concubine. The other Rectors seem to have acquiesced in the inevitable.

This same year the long threatened blow from France fell. On 20 July Henry II was assuring the English ambassador that his love for England made war entirely unthinkable; on the following day an expedition sailed and seized Sark. On the 31st it attacked Guernsey, but was repulsed by ships in the harbour. So it sailed for Jersey and landed in Bouley Bay. The Militia met it at Jardin d'Olivet and, after a stiff fight, in which Jurat Helier de la Rocque, the Lieutenant-Bailiff, was killed, the French were routed and retired to St Malo with their dead and wounded. A report to the Privy Council said, 'We have heard out of France that one vessel there brought at least three score gentlemen to be buried'. But for the next nine years the French held Sark and were a constant menace to Jersey.

Cornish's term of office was now drawing to a close. Within the boy king's council there were bitter rivalries, for Somerset's Protectorate of England had not been a success. Froude's verdict is, 'The magnificent weakness of his character had aimed at achievements beyond his ability. He had attempted the work of a giant with the strength of a woman'. One rumour spread by his enemies was that he meant to carry off the King to Jersey to have him wholly in his power. In October 1549 Somerset was sent to the Tower and Sir Hugh Poulet was commissioned to go to Jersey[23] to investigate complaints that had been coming up against Somerset's officials. He arrived on Christmas Eve, summoned the Court to meet him at the Castle and, after three weeks' enquiry, dismissed Cornish and returned to England with his report.

In March 1550 Poulet was appointed Governor for life, and founded a dynasty that ruled the Island for three generations. The Poulets were a Somerset family which had early thrown in its lot with the Reformation and Sir Hugh continued Cornish's work of purging the Island of popery, though strangely enough the rights of the Bishop of Coutances were still respected. However, as Jersey had by then embraced Protestantism with fervour, this suggests that the Bishop did not concern himself unduly with what was happening in the remoter parts of his diocese. 'The King's pleasure is', wrote the Council, 'that the Bishop shall be permitted to have like jurisdiction in the isle as he and his predecessors have had heretofore, in all things not repugnant to the King's orders.'[24] With all forms of popery being so very repugnant to the King's orders, one may wonder how anyone's conscience was at rest.

'Poulet', writes the Chronicler with apparent satisfaction, 'was bidden to pull down all idols, and extirpate, oust and abolish all idolatry and superstition.' In England this policy caused two rebellions, in France it led to nine years of civil war, but in Jersey only one or two voices were raised against it. In 1550 Jean Ahier, a priest, was fined 'for contradicting the word of God and upholding the superstitions of Rome'. In 1552 another priest had 'to confess publikly in St Martin's church that he did wrong when he caused a tumult and protested, while the word of God was being preached'. In 1553 Pierre Fallu was imprisoned because he allowed his wife to take rosaries with her to St Peter's, and it was the husband who was punished. But these were voices crying in the wilderness, for the victory of Protestantism was complete. The only question was, would it be the Protestantism of England or of France?

Sir Hugh's main work was in fortifications. Before he left home he secured some of the Glastonbury lead for Mont Orgueil. We learn this from Privy Council records of 1550 showing that orders had been given for a quantity of lead 'had out of the late monastery of Glastonbury' to be sent to Sir Hugh Paulet 'to be by him employed about His Majesty's Castell of Jersey'. He pressed the building of the central keep that had been begun under Somerset. 'He also', according to the Chronicler, 'strengthened well nigh all the circuit of the walls, repaired and raised the road that entered by the garden gate, and fortified and enlarged the Rochfort tower and divers other parts of the Castle.' He transformed Cornish's St Aubin's Tower[26] into a fort by building bastions round it, and began the fortifications on the Islet of St Helier which eventually grew into Elizabeth Castle. To pay part of the cost of this he sold the church bells,[27] leaving only one for each parish, a transaction which brought in £171. He also 'held many General Parades, and drilled the men hard, for he had been all his life a Captain expert in war'. On one point however he was beaten. His instructions were 'to convey the town of St Helier unto the hill above the same', (that is le Mont de la Ville where Fort Regent now stands) 'which, we be informed, may with little charge be made strong and defensible'.[28] But though the Council wrote to the States, 'We doubt not, you will be persuaded your only surety resteth therein ...', the townsfolk resolutely refused to move from their old homes.

The winds that swept over La Montagne, as they called it, and the lack of water there did not make this proposition attractive to a populace snugly housed on the low ground, backed by farm lands in the north, protected from east winds by the hill and watered by Le Grand Douet and Le Faux Bié which drove their mills. The town bordered the shores of St Aubin's bay where they could fish and collect vraic, and moreover, history had shown them that attacks were nearly always first directed at Mont Orgueil Castle.

Let us pause at this point to consider the architecture of this community, emerging slowly out of medievalism.

The important buildings were the churches, mills and castles, serving soul, body and defence. They were all built of granite with some lime for mortar and the churches and castles doubtless had glass in their windows before it was used in domestic buildings. The houses of the people were likewise built of granite, but with very little lime, which in any case had to be imported or made from burnt shells. A kind of mortar was effected by binding clay with fragments of pottery, straw and animal hair; this was quite effective if it kept dry, but was very apt to fall after heavy rain. There was not a great deal of difference between the houses of rich and poor, and we had no really impressive manor houses, except perhaps St Ouen's, until well into the 17th century. The basic plan was very simple and of two storeys; so few single storey houses of stone have survived which show features that can be dated before say 1700 that one feels they must have been rare. The house consisted of two ground-floor rooms, with two bedrooms and a very small 'cabinet' bedroom above the front entrance. Partitions in most cases were of wood; a pre-1700 house with stone interior partitions is not only rare, but indicates a degree of wealth. The floors downstairs were of clay, with wood on the first floor. The stairs were usually of stone and circular, built within a '*tourelle*' that was semi-circular or square and on the north wall. Most of the houses faced south. Window surrounds were chamfered, that is bevelled, with decorated lintels, the more elaborate the decoration, the earlier the feature. Up till 1700 the main door, on the south, was almost always a round arched one, composed of nine stones; a keystone, two shoulder stones and three supporters on each side. Modest carving appeared, with a date frequently shown on the façade or on the arch keystone. Inside the hearth was again of granite, with massive lintels supported on corbels which projected both inside and outside the building. These corbels were frequently decorated with simple carved devices, and the hearth was always placed in the end gable wall. These early houses are small, low and dark by modern standards, and are often so much altered that their original beauty has been lost for ever.

17 *La Cotte palaeolithic cave during the first excavation in 1910.*

DIGGING UP THE PAST

18 *(left and right) Coin of Posthumus, c.260 A.D. found at l'Ile Agois during excavation. 23 mm diameter max.*

19 *A modern excavation at Les Blanches Banques, late neolithic or early Bronze-Age.*

To return to the reign of Edward VI: in 1552 the Government issued a new Prayer book with a more Protestant flavour. This was translated into French by François Philippe, 'servant of the Lord Chancellor', and sent to Jersey in the spring of 1553. But before it could be used the boy king died, and was succeeded by his elder sister Mary, an embittered Catholic, eager to stamp out Protestantism as thoroughly as had been done in the Spain of her mother, Catherine of Aragon. The religious policy of the last reign was reversed. In Jersey the Latin services were restored, the notoriously Protestant Rectors fled, Bertram to Geneva, Soler to become a daring Protestant pioneer in the Cotentin.[30] Le Roy was restored to St Saviour, Dolbel to St Clement. Priests who had married were severely disciplined, and four were sent to prison on bread and water for refusing to leave their wives.[31] One was threatened with a flogging by the hangman if he held any communication with his wife; another was sentenced to walk with bare feet, holding a lighted candle in front of the cross in the procession in St Helier's church and to remain kneeling in the chancel throughout the Mass. But while in England bishops and working men were being burned at the stake, and even in Guernsey there were three hideous martyrdoms,[32] Jersey escaped any death sentence, thanks to Poulet's masterly skill in keeping the Island out of the limelight. He saw that all the Queen's commands were outwardly obeyed, and by making his brother John, who was still a Catholic, Dean, he was able to check excessive zeal on the part of the church authorities. Perhaps this Vicar-of-Bray attitude was the safest solution.

But the Island did not become Catholic. The Chronicler gives a list of leading men,[33] Seigneurs, Jurats, Constables, 'who would not assist at mass or the superstitions of the Papists whatever terrors were held over their heads, but always found a way to receive the Sacrament in some Reformed Church either at St Lo or elsewhere and all their life upheld the gospel and abode therein'. Then a priest struck a crushing blow against all prospect of a Counter-Reformation. Richard Averty, Proctor of the Dean's Court, had 'grievously oppressed the poor folk, who were faithful to the Reformed religion', but in June 1555 he was arrested for murder. The Act of the Court ran:

> Richard Averty, prisoner on a capital charge, who had tried to escape, but had been seized by prompt pursuit, confessed before the full Court that, on the Wednesday before Pentecost, Marie Belée, domestic servant in his employ, was delivered of a live boy, he alone being present, and that when the child was born he baptized it and deliberately strangled it, and the same evening buried it beneath the hearth in his dwelling, where it was found and disinterred by order of the Court. Therefore he was sentenced to be dragged to the gallows and hanged till he was dead, his body to be left on the gibbet till it should rot away.

The Dean tried hard to save him, throwing a surplice over his head and claiming that he could be tried only by the Ecclesiastical Court, but the Jurats would not give way. When he was tied to the hurdle to be dragged to Gallows Hill,[34] the Dean again vested him in a surplice and dared the authorities to hang him, but it was stripped off at the foot of the scaffold. This crime sent a thrill of horror through the Island, which eventually chilled any hope of a Catholic revival. When an effort was made to restart the Maundy Procession in St Helier, two youths marched in front carrying a dead toad in a gibbet. For this insult to the priesthood in France or England they would have been burned alive. In Jersey they merely had to find bail for good behaviour. Averty's execution caused a long quarrel between the Dean and his brother. Sir Hugh refused to admit for a moment the right of clergy who committed crimes to be tried by their own Court. At last, in November 1558, the Dean set out for England to appeal to the Queen in Council. Off the Corbière they passed an incoming boat. 'What news?', they cried. 'Good news', came the reply, 'Jezebel is dead.' And the Dean, knowing that if Mary were dead his voyage would be in vain, asked to be put ashore.[35]

Chapter Ten

CALVINIST JERSEY

Discipline is to the Church what sinews are to the body.
Preface to the Order of Church Government for the Channel Islands

UNDER ELIZABETH, JERSEY reverted to Protestantism, but Luther gave way to Calvin. This clear-headed Frenchman, exiled to Geneva, where he was pastor of a church, drew up a logical digest of theology in his *Institutio christianae religionis*[1] and knit his followers into a tough, coherent, well-drilled church, able to meet Rome on almost equal terms. He mapped out a complete scheme of government by ministers, elders and deacons, and a chain of democratic church councils: a Consistory for each parish, a Colloquy for each group of parishes, and a national Synod. Calvin's creed and church order were adopted by the French Protestants, who, in the latter part of the 16th century, became known as Huguenots. As religious persecution in France grew more savage under the Guises, a steady flow of refugees, often noted in Jersey parish registers as '*réfugiés de religion*', began to pour into Jersey. Under their influence and for convenience in language Jersey Protestants naturally gravitated toward the French model.

One of the first converts to Calvinism was Amyas Poulet, the Governor's son, who, as Lieutenant to Sir Hugh, often took his father's duties when the latter was sent on important missions abroad. In 1562 Amyas appointed as Rector of the Town Church Guillaume Morise, Seigneur de la Ripaudière, who was a Huguenot minister from Anjou. 'He was the first to organize a real Reformed Church in Jersey and to administer the Lord's Supper in the Temple of St Helier according to the purity of the Gospel.'[2] For the next two centuries Jersey churches were invariably referred to as 'temples'. 'At this Supper', says the Chronicler, 'Amyas Poulet, the Lieutenant-Governor, the Seigneur of St Ouen and most of the leading gentry of the island were present. Afterwards the Seigneur de la Ripaudière ordained elders and deacons, and, with the assent of the Lieutenant and Jurats, formed a Consistory with a good discipline.'

In 1561 Helier de Carteret, the aged Bailiff who had defied Vaughan and Wolsey, died. He was succeeded by Hostes Nicolle, who, despite his Jersey-sounding name, was descended from a Cornishman who had been gentleman-porter of the Castle. He had bought Longueville Manor in 1480 and his descendants had begun to spell their name in the Jersey manner. Hostes is chiefly remembered by the Chronicler's story of his death in 1564:[3]

> There was a poor man whose house adjoined that of the Bailiff. This land the Bailiff coveted. So one day he bade his servants kill two of his finest sheep and carry them to the house of a man who was by trade a butcher. He then roused the Constable and his officers and bade them search the butcher's house, where they found the sheep hanging in his stable. The man was brought into Court and condemned to be hanged that day. As the hangman put the rope round his neck at the door of the Court, the poor man said to the Bailiff, "I summon you to appear within forty days before the just Judge of all to answer for this!" And on the thirty-ninth day Nicolle fell dead by the wayside as he was returning from town.

There is no evidence to confirm or refute this story, but the Chronicler wrote only some 21 years after Nicolle's death.

Throughout Elizabeth's reign relations with France were generally strained. Shortly after her accession news came from Normandy that a French adventurer, named Glatigny,[4] was preparing a raid. Some years later Throckrmorton[5] wrote from Chartres of a plot to surprise the islands. One obvious safeguard was to modernise Mont Orgueil. For 25 years Amyas squeezed money from Elizabeth for this purpose: 'I am much deceived', he wrote, 'considering the depth of the foundation, the height and thickness of the walls, if a greater piece of work hath ever been done for the like sum'.[6] The result was the mighty Somerset tower,[7] completed just before he died, in which altar-stones, used as gun-platforms, bear witness to the time in which it was built.

By 1564 the Calvinist system had established itself throughout Jersey. Each parish had its Consistory; there was a Colloquy for the island; and in June the first united Synod met in Guernsey. But Elizabeth realised that no Calvinist church had room for a Royal Supreme Head. The Island would have to walk warily. The Synod sent Helier de Carteret (1532-1581), seigneur of St Ouen and nephew of the Bailiff of the same name, to London. He pleaded that the islands had always formed part of the diocese of Coutances, where Calvinism was now widespread; that the doctrine of the Reformed churches in Coutances agreed with that established by the Queen's orders in England; that godly ministers from France were using in the Island the form of service permitted in the Huguenot church in London; and that, if this were forbidden, they would return to their own land and the islands would be without ministers. His argument that Coutances was rapidly becoming a Protestant diocese was corroborated a few years later when the Bishop was drummed out of his cathedral city, sitting on an ass with his face towards the tail.[8]

Elizabeth tried to compromise. In 1565 Poulet received orders that the Huguenot prayer book might be used in the Town Church, 'provided that the residue of the parishes continue the Order of Service ordained within this realm', and Cecil added in his own handwriting, 'without any alteration or innovation'.[9] The same attempt was made in Guernsey; but in both islands the rural parishes were firmly wedded to the Huguenot system and ignored the order.

Meanwhile some of the clergy in England had adopted Calvinism, among them John After, who had come to Guernsey as one of a Royal Commission in 1561 and been made Dean by the Governor. A letter in 1564 declared that he had destroyed all the organs and stained-glass windows, had turned the chancel seats to face the pulpit, had abolished Saints' days and administered Communion without a surplice to communicants seated round a table.[10] But his main interest lies in his claim to be acting with the authority of Bishop Horne of Winchester. Apparently someone had unearthed the forgotten Bull of 1500[15] by which the Pope had transferred the islands from Coutances to Winchester. In those early days the Island clergy paid a certain deference to the Bishop; the second and third synods sent him respectful greetings, and the fourth instructed After to lay their resolutions before him. But the Bishop of Coutances did not surrender his rights without a struggle. In 1564, as French ambassador to England, he had seized the opportunity to press for payment of fees owing to him from the islands. The Council wrote in 1565, 'We find his request reasonable', and ordered that his dues be paid. He sent a Proctor to collect them; but Guernsey refused to pay, and the matter went back to the Council. For a time they hesitated; but in 1569 they ordered the islands to be 'separated for ever from the Diocese of Coutances and perpetually united with Winchester'.[12] Bishop Horne then regularised After's position by appointing him Dean of Jersey, Guernsey, Chausey, Alderney and Sark. For the next six years the new Rectors were instituted by the Bishop; but the Calvinist system had no room for deans or bishops, and After gradually lost power, until the only function he retained was that of registrar of wills. This remained the prerogative of the Dean until the Probate (Jersey) Law came into force in 1949.[13]

Meanwhile news came from France in 1580 that the Bishop of Coutances was recruiting an army to recover the island.[14] A report among the State Papers confirms this:

> Advertisement out of Bretaigne of the 29th October. An Italian Commissary and Delegate from the Pope arrived of late at Coutances and held a Synod secretly wherein it was agreed that the clergy of Lower Normandy should defray the money to be employed in some enterprises against the islands of Jersey and Garnesey and should be done in the name of the Pope ... the Bishop of Coutances was the chief doer and protested that he would never leave till he entirely possessed the said islands.

The Bishop hoped for support from the king of France, as the Pope had excommunicated Elizabeth and had called on all Christians to deprive her of her throne. Although a similar papal expedition was fighting in Ireland, the Bishop's plan for the islands never materialised.

To revert to 1568, the Edict of St Maur had banished all Huguenot ministers and forbidden Protestant worship in France under penalty of death. Every day boats brought to the islands fresh refugees, among them distinguished men like Pierre Loiseleur, minister of Bayeux, one of Calvin's students at Geneva, who published an edition of the Greek testament and became chaplain to the Prince of Orange, and Pierre Henry dit Dangy, who became Rector of St Martin and had seen his congregation at Valognes massacred before his eyes.[15] The advent of men like these stimulated anti-Catholic feeling.

The fifth Synod met in Sark in 1570. In the 13th century Sark had been a prosperous little community with its own Prévot and Jurats;[16] but French and piratical raids had depopulated the island, so that for years it had remained uninhabited. In 1549 the French had seized it and fortified it. Later Flemish adventurers had taken the island and presented it to Queen Mary. She had done nothing with it. Helier de Carteret, seeing the danger to Jersey if it were reoccupied by enemies, decided to add this desert island to his domain. In 1565 he secured Letters Patent from Elizabeth whereby she granted the island to him for 50 shillings a year on condition that he keep at least forty men there. He brought colonists, largely recruiting them from his own parish of St Ouen, so that names associated with that parish still survive in Sark today. He built for them 40 houses; these tenements remain and carry with them the right of the owner to a seat in the Chief Pleas, the island parliament. Sark had for so long constituted a menace to shipping, that pirates found the uninhabited island in the midst of the archipelago a most convenient refuge. So to Helier and the authorities, as well as to island seamen, a permanent settlement was clearly advantageous. For his 'temple' in Sark de Carteret secured one of the best of the Huguenot exiles, Cosmo Brevint,[17] who made his parish the model Calvinist community of the islands.

The massacre on St Bartholomew's Day in 1572 brought still more fugitives,[18] among them the famous Huguenot leader, Gabriel, Count of Montgomery with his wife, son and brother. In December he went to England; but a year later he returned to Jersey and gathered the force with which in 1574 he invaded the Cotentin and lost his life. In the same year Poulet brought to Jersey Arthur Wake,[19] who had been deprived of his livings in England because of his outspoken non-conformity. Poulet made him chaplain of Mont Orgueil, where he remained for 18 years. He became prominent in the local Colloquy, whose members' signatures are appended to the first *Discipline* of 1576, and he and these learned Huguenot Divines fixed for years the type of Protestantism that would prevail in Jersey. He was followed in 1595 by Snape, who also played a full part in ecclesiastical matters.[20]

The most important of all the synods was held in Guernsey in 1576.[21] Amyas Poulet, who had just been knighted on his appointment as Ambassador to Paris, delayed his departure to attend it. After three days' debate, this Synod drew up the detailed *Discipline* which finally established Calvinist worship, Calvinist government and Calvinist moral police in every parish. So entirely had the island churches become part of the Huguenot church, that each Colloquy was ordered to send one delegate to the National Synods in France. This last order, however, was omitted from the second *Discipline* drawn up in 1597.

La Police et Discipline Ecclésiastique was now the law which Jersey had to obey, and it affected deeply the lives of the people. There were no non-conformers. Everyone was expected to go to church. The Temple was the centre of parish interests, secular as well as religious. Here after the sermon the latest orders of the court were read out. The Constable announced when vraic might be cut. This was the local name for seaweed which was for manure and could be cut and collected only at certain times of the year and from areas allotted according to one's place of residence. The Constable also announced when cattle might be turned loose, that is *à banon*, to graze on the corn stubble between harvest and seed sowing. Property was transferred by proclaiming the fact in the hearing of the parish, by *Ouïe de paroisse.*[22] These proceedings existed from very early times and were legal until 1842; but contracts, after being passed verbally, were confirmed in writing and sealed by the Royal Court, and the practice of reading them after the church service gradually lapsed after the Reformation. An interesting document of 17 June 1749 shows that when a certain Mr. Edouard Ricard of St Ouen obtained an Order of Justice prohibiting the drying of vraic on his land to the north of le Chemin Public de la Brecquette, and caused this to be read on three successive Sundays, '*à l'issue du Service Divin en audience du Peuple*' in the cemeteries of St Ouen and St Mary, the Constables protested that the inhabitants of their two parishes had enjoyed the right to use the land in question '*de toute ancienneté*', and the Court was summoned to decide the question on the spot and to examine the evidence and titles of the parties concerned in the dispute. The rules governing the '*ouïe de paroisse*' were excellent judged by the customs of the time, and well-suited to a rural economy of people who were not all literate and could seldom get to town to learn the news.

In the churches themselves the religious character of the services had been revolutionised. Rome had called in the aid of the senses, Geneva made its appeal austerely to the mind. The preachers were the fathers of modern oratory. All seats faced the pulpit. Men and women entered the Temple by separate doors and sat on opposite sides, the men retaining their hats which they removed for the prayers, the confession, the psalms, the sacraments and the text of the sermon when announced by the minister, who, in the pulpit, wore a close-fitting cap, *le claque-oreilles*, familiarised in various portraits of Calvin. The most popular feature of the Huguenot service as drawn up by Calvin was the singing of Marot's metrical psalms, set to stirring tunes like the 'Old Hundredth'. In the morning there was a sermon; the afternoon was devoted to catechizing. The Calvinist Catechism was a portentous manual with over four hundred answers in which everyone was drilled; provision was however made for the aged and persons of feeble memory to be admitted to Communion even if they could not learn the Commandments by heart, as long as they knew the gist of these and were devout and of good character. Thus virtually every farmer and fisherman could state precisely what his church believed. There were four Communion Sundays, spaced out evenly over the year: Easter, in accordance with the medieval tradition, and in addition the Sunday after Midsummer's Day, the first Sunday in October and the Sunday after Christmas. Every parishioner who had reached the age of discretion, 'comme de douze ans pour le moins', had to communicate. They wore deep mourning in memory of Christ's death, a custom surviving for a long time in the predominantly black clothing worn on Sundays. A table was set in front of the pulpit with benches round it, and the people sat down in relays 'as this posture agrees best with the original institution'. One of these tables is still preserved at St Mary; it has flaps that increase its size according to need. Another at St Lawrence is still used at the monthly family service.

Of the three grades of officers, the ministers wore full clerical dress, broad white bands and broad-brimmed hat, the elders kept a watchful eye on the morals of their flock, and the deacons or almoners stood with metal collecting pots at the Temple door every Sunday, after the sermon, so that no one left without contributing alms, and none in the parish went hungry. It was the duty of the deacons to distribute these alms on the instruction of the consistory. If need be, they were to go to the wealthier houses to collect corn and other necessities, and, if there was anything left over after they had ministered to the poor of their flock, they might offer alms to strangers. They had publicly to render their accounts on the Communion Sundays, see that none of the poor were forced to beg from door to door, and make sure that the young, who were fit to work, were apprenticed to some trade.

Many of the collecting pots used by the deacons have survived and are prized items, unknown elsewhere. St John's has one in copper, dated 1677, St Aubin's church two silver jugs, locally made and presented in 1750, and at St Brelade there are two later examples in silver as well as some in pewter. It must be emphasised however that no church silver used prior to the Reformation is known to exist, with the possible exception of a chalice at Trinity, which although much damaged appears to have escaped the reformers. De la Croix tells us that a few items were smuggled away to their homes by devout families.[23]

The most striking feature of the Calvinist system was its stress upon discipline. Good laws strictly enforced were considered essential to decent living. The Church's duty was to see that God's law was obeyed. Each elder had to know every family in his vingtaine, 'whether they have household prayers morning and evening, say grace after meals and live in peace and concord'. All misdoings were reported to the parish consistory which met every Sunday after afternoon service. Culprits who were not persuaded to mend their ways were sent before the island colloquy and, if still impenitent, were excommunicated; 'cut off as septic limbs from the body of Christ, as Adam was expelled from Paradise by a flaming sword'. They could no longer enter the Temple or be buried in the churchyard. Anyone who associated with them became himself excommunicate, for, although this extreme punishment was reserved for serious crimes, contempt of court could be rated as one.[24]

Behind the Church stood the Royal Court and the dungeons of Mont Orgueil. It was stated in the *Discipline* that the magistrate held the sword to constrain men to keep God's laws, and the Court accepted this rôle as part of its normal duties. It issued innumerable Acts against sabbath-breaking. Dancing, skittle-playing or gossiping on a Sunday meant a stretch in prison. All who were absent from the quarterly Communion had to sit in the stocks. The Rolls of the Court contain many Acts against swearing:

> Whoever shall swear by the name of God or any of His creatures, by his own soul, his conscience or his faith, or any other oath save one taken in the presence of a judge, for a first offence shall be fined three liards, for a second six liards, for a third he shall be put in the pillory and for a fourth he shall be imprisoned.

In 1588 the Court ordered that if at an all-night party anyone sang 'lascivious songs or told licentious stories', everyone present would be fined 20 sols 'to be levied on the goods of the principle persons present'. One form of party was '*la veille*', originally a gathering of knitters who met in one another's houses during the winter evenings.[25] In 1598 another Act decreed: 'All women and girls are forbidden to go sand-eeling except in the company of their husbands, fathers or employers'.

Overstrict discipline provoked reaction. In 1599 we read: 'Whereas large gangs, masked and carrying clubs, career at night from house to house committing innumerable obscenities and enormities, the police are ordered to arrest all night-revellers, that they may receive exemplary

20 *The Fishermen's chapel and a Celtic dedication.*

A CONTRAST IN ECCLESIASTICAL ARCHITECTURE AT ST BRELADE

21 *Communicare, an ecumenical experiment at Don Farm.*

punishment'. Other Acts speak of raucous howls that made the night hideous, and the habit of seizing farmers' horses to charge through the countryside. In 1619 Katherine Le Sauteur, convicted of joining in night-revels dressed as a man and wearing '*ung haut de chausses*' (breeches), was ordered to sit all through Saturday in the market stocks with the offending garment hung up beside her and again on Sunday in the stocks in St Peter's churchyard.[26]

From this situation it was only a step to witch mania.[27] Those who rebelled against God were deemed to have enlisted under Satan's banner. A wave of devil-worship was sweeping through western Europe and had gained disciples in Jersey. Court records from the beginning are full of witch trials. In the 16th century they dealt severely with witches, and often their prisoners were openly defiant. In 1585 Pasquette Le Vesconte, previously arrested 'for witchcraft and banished for ever from the island', had returned contrary to her sentence and continued her diabolic devices. She confessed that she had entered into partnership with the Devil and by his help 'perpetrated innumerable crimes and homicides'. Jean Mourant, 'having been so forgetful of his salvation as to make a contract with the Devil by mark (a secret sign branded on the flesh) and pact confirmed by gift of one of his members [probably a finger joint], confessed with his mouth his dealings with the devil, and that by this means he had committed infinite crimes'. He was executed.

These and other similar confessions were not extorted by torture nor made with any hope of escaping the gallows. Accused were of both sexes, though women outnumbered men, from all ages from eighteen to eighty and from all ranks of society. Some were rapscallions constantly in trouble with the police; but Marion Corbel left enough property for her heirs to fight a lawsuit over it; Richard Anley, whose wife was convicted, was a large landowner in St Peter and son of the Constable, while Marie Esnouf was a grand-daughter of a former Rector of St John. The Court tempered justice with mercy. Some were banished, others put on probation. Take Marie Tourgis for example:

> It is ordered that she withdraw from bad companions, and be placed in the care of Guillemine Hulvert to obey her in her household rules in the fear of God. If she does not amend, Guillemine shall complain to the Court, which will administer such correction as her faults deserve.

It was not until 10 years later, when Marie was accused of 'many abominable deeds wrought by the diabolic art of witchcraft', and had boasted that she had caused the death of a child, that she was condemned, 'her body to be reduced to ashes'. Even when sentence of death was passed on hardened offenders, Jersey would seem to have been marginally less cruel than Guernsey, where witches were burned alive. In Jersey the sentence was always: 'to be hanged and strangled by the public executioner till death ensues, after that her body to be burned and entirely consumed'.

A strong point in Calvinism was its care for education. It laid stress on Bible-reading, and a school was started in every parish. Parents whose children were irregular in their attendance were disciplined by the Consistory. Schoolmasters were ordered, 'wherever a boy shows signs of promise, to follow up the matter with the Governor and Magistrates, that they may receive support from public funds'. The States ordered that the parish *trésors* be used to send students to Oxford,[28] the Constables to make collections for the same purpose, and, in 1593, the Governor was supporting one boy at university, the Jurats another, the Rectors another, and the parishes two more. In 1596 Laurens Baudains,[29] a farmer from St Martin, presented to the states 18 quarters of 'wheat rente' (the income from a form of Jersey investment in real property) and the mill of Dannemarche[30] to found a college 'for the instruction of youth in grammar, latin, the liberal arts and religion'. In 1591 he obtained Letters Patent from Queen Elizabeth allowing other persons to add to this gift up to two hundred quarters; the States accepted the gift and appointed three regents in succession, but not one of them could make the scheme work.

So in 1611 Baudains changed his plans and secured Letters Patent from James I to found a Trust to send poor boys to be 'trained up in learning and in the study of Divinity in the Universities of Oxford and Cambridge, or either of them', on condition that they returned to 'devote and employ their services and labours in and about the business of the said isle'. This was the Don Baudains, whose governors still administer what are quaintly termed: 'the possessions, goods and chattels given by Laurens Baudains and others for the maintenance of poor scholars for the service of the Isle of Jersey'. Up to the German Occupation the Trust had helped 120 young Jerseymen through a university course, most of them electing to study at Oxford. Since 1940 four students have been assisted by the Don Baudains, three at Oxford and one at Cambridge.[31]

Various items in the accounts of Edward Payn,[32] Constable of St Martin from 1597 to 1616, illustrate the Calvinist régime in Jersey. Money was paid to 'La Vautière (Vautier's wife) for wine for the midsummer Communion '*dix pots de vin à faire la cène du terme St Jean*', to Monsieur Wake for '*la Bible du Temple*', to William Lane for Monsieur le Capitaine (the Governor) to settle the account of Pierre Guille '*pour le temps qu'il estoit à escollier Oxford*'. In March 1591 money was granted to the 'collocq' to help affairs in the city of Geneva, while in 1597 expenses were paid for an elder who had attended the Synod in Guernsey: '*pour les coutages de l'Ancien et le fret du bateau qui fut au sinode de Guernesey au moys d'octobre 1597*'.

Perhaps the most interesting item in these accounts is the payment to Jean Faultrat, member of a prominent Huguenot family, one of whom was later to preach before Charles II in the Town Church. He was sent post-haste to learn the fate of the Spanish Armada on behalf of the States, '*pour cognoistre des nouvelles des Espagnols qui estoient venus en assaillir le Royaume par fait de guerre equipez de plus de vingt navires avecq quatre galiaces vaisseaux monstrueux et grands de quynze tonneaux et des autres...*' As expected the Armada was reported as having been defeated and lost. The Island was taxed for this voyage of enquiry at '*soixante ecus sols*', of which St Martin's share was '*cyncq ezcus sol*' according to '*l'ancyen rast*'. These accounts from '*le trésor publicq*' were signed among others by Ant. Poulett, Laurens Baudayn and Arthur Wake. The last item reminds us of the seafaring activities of Jerseymen, who, like their West Country brethren, were to take full advantage of the maritime expansion of the great Elizabethan era.

Chapter Eleven

NAVIGATORS, KNITTERS AND A NEW REGIME

When Dr. Heylin came into this Island, he found the people more addicted to tillage and husbandry than to manufactures and navigation ... the matter is much altered since the doctor was here.–Falle, *An Account of the Island of Jersey*

FROM THE ELIZABETHAN AGE onwards two industries, whose origins in Jersey are as yet a matter of speculation, were contributing to the Island's prosperity. Strategically placed on the important trade routes from Normandy and Aquitaine to England and from Spain to the Netherlands, the Channel Islands had long had trading links with French, English, Welsh and Irish ports.[1] Cabot discovered Newfoundland in 1497, and tales of its marvellous fisheries quickly spread among seamen. By the 16th century local merchants and sailors would have known of Jacques Cartier's voyages in 1534 and 1535 from St Malo to Gaspé and the St Lawrence in these 'New Found Lands'. Indeed one of Cartier's crew was a Guillaume de Guernezé. Cartier himself found a ship from La Rochelle there ahead of him, and we had long been trading with the Biscayan ports. When in 1582 we find the earliest reference to the Newfoundland trade in the will of Pierre de la Rocque,[2] it must already have been firmly established in the islands. Pierre left his sons equal shares in his ship, 'which is now unloading after her voyage to Newfoundland'. In 1587 a dispute about a cargo of Newfoundland cod was brought before the Royal Court. In 1591 Jean Guillaume was fined three hundred crowns because, on returning from Newfoundland, he had sold his fish at St Malo.[3] By this time Jerseymen were sailing in small boats across the Atlantic every spring, returning in time for the autumn ploughing. This was to be the most important and thriving industry in which the islands indulged, bringing prosperity, employment, goods and fame to our seamen until late in the 19th century. By 1611 the fishing fleet had become so important that St Brelade was allowed to hold its spring Communion earlier than in other churches, so that fishermen might communicate before sailing from St Aubin. Later in the century similar provision was made in St Ouen.[4]

Before St Aubin's harbour was built Jersey vessels wintered at St Malo,[5] but equally important to island trade was the link with the port of Southampton, which had developed from an Anglo-Norman settlement. The burgesses of the port, with their Norman names, French quarter and 'liberties and customs by land and sea', had much in common with the Jersey merchants, many of whom had settled in the town, become burgesses and, increasingly from Tudor times onwards, held office as water-bailiffs, sheriffs and mayors. Among these were men with names later to become famous in Channel Island shipping history. Peter Seale of Jersey took his nephew, Thomas, as apprentice for seven years, was a prominent member of the French church, Godshouse, in the port of Southampton and acted as local agent for 'the flourishing trade of the Seale family in shipping goods between the town and France and Jersey'. He was also a shipowner and traded in linen cloth; for on one occasion he was fined 10 shillings for allowing it to be sold in his house instead of taking it to the Linen Hall. He died in 1654 leaving a large legacy to the town for apprenticing poor children. Later his son made a similar bequest. Peter Janvrin of Jersey married the daughter and heiress of Edward Marcant (Marquand), a Jerseyman who was twice sheriff of Southampton in the reign of Henry VIII. By his marriage Peter became owner of the Star Inn, and a neighbour of Peter Priaulx, a merchant who leased a house from Winchester College and is recorded as being 'a prominent merchant-adventurer, ship-owner and shipwright, and mariner with Channel Island connections'.[6] He took apprentices to learn the merchant's trade and to be employed 'beyound the seas' during their term of service. Janvrin was admitted burgess in 1564 but disburgessed in 1565 for 'colouring' 'fardells of canvas' belonging to John Grosses alias Bisson and brought in a ship belonging to Richard de Carteret. This transaction is thought to concern two bales of canvas known as 'rumbelo' and charged to John Grosses at the ordinary unprivileged rate, but originally entered under Janvrin's name. The burgess's oath read: 'ye shall not colour or beare the name of any foriners or straungers goodes, whereby the king or the towne might lose any customs, brocage, or advantage'. At this time Janvrin was importing canvas and exporting cloth in Channel Island ships. However he was restored to his burgess-ship in 1566 and rose to be sheriff in 1581.[7]

Southampton too had her links with the New World. In 1582 it was the Merchant Adventurers of this port who were the principal signatories to an agreement to finance Sir Humphrey Gilbert's voyage of discovery to Newfoundland, an enterprise of great interest to the Channel Islanders who gathered at the Star. Another meeting place in Southampton was the French-speaking Huguenot church founded by Walloon refugees, who were later joined by Calvinist Normans and Channel Islanders, many of whose names appear in the church registers. They include Pierre Janvrin, recorded in December 1567 as '*un anglais*' admitted to Communion. This Walloon church was supported by contributions from merchants and seamen, and, as late as 1797, Michel Dupré, youngest son of a Rector of St Helier, was appointed curate-in-charge.[8]

Protestant refugees, the port of Southampton and the Jersey merchants were probably contributory factors in the story of Jersey's second major industry, knitting. As early as the 9th century this art, developed from weaving techniques, was known in places as far apart as Norway and North Africa.[9] The Renaissance gave a secular boost to the trade in knitted garments, while the Tudors set a fashion for knitted stockings. It may be no coincidence that Amyas Poulet was gaoler to Mary Queen of Scots; for at her execution she wore

> shoes of Spanishe leather with the roughe side outward, a payre of greene silke garters, her nether stocke of worsted coloured watchett clocked with silver and edged on the topps with silver and next her leggs a paire of Jersey hose white ... thus apparelled she willingly bended her stepps towards the place of execution being gentlie carried out by two of Sir A. Powlett his chiefest gentlemen.[10]

When and how did the inhabitants of Jersey learn to knit? Possibly from Protestant refugees who brought their skills from France, where intricately patterned stockings were a speciality. Some may have seen the elaborately knitted garments brought to Southampton by Venetian traders. Sailors often knitted at sea, and over the years developed the traditional sweaters which varied from port to port and were close-fitting, warm and without fastenings that could get entangled in fishnets. The word 'jersey' was originally used to define a form of knitting. The following note appears in the State Papers of 1596 on 'diversities of wools, yarns etc': 'The spinning of wools are of three sorts: either upon the great wheel, which is called woollen yarn; or upon the small wheel, which is called Guernsey or Jersey yarn, because that manner of spinning was first practised in these isles; or upon the rock which is called worsted' (the latter was first practised in Worsted, co. Norfolk).[11]

As the wool trade moved from Flanders to England and because the staple of Southampton, Jersey was quick to exploit the new market. Documents such as '*les Registres des Merches de Berquail*', at St Ouen[12] and in other parishes bear witness to the extent of sheep-rearing in the Island; but so great was the demand for wool that some had to be imported from Southampton. For a considerable period knitting dominated island life, and there are numerous references to the Jersey stocking trade in State Papers, Actes des Etats, early local histories and contemporary letters.

In 1586 Camden wrote in his *Britannica*: 'The women make a very gainful trade by knitting of hose which we call Jersey stocks [*quae Jersey Stokes vocamus*]'. In 1587 Harrion's *England* speaks of 'women's diversely coloured stockings of silk jersey'. You seldom saw a Jerseywoman without her knitting-needles. She knitted by the fire at night and as she walked through the lanes. It was whispered in Consistories that some even knitted secretly on Sundays. The trade was so profitable that the men also took to knitting, and the States grew nervous lest the land should go out of cultivation. In 1608 the Court decreed:[13] 'During harvest and vraicing season all persons shall stop making stockings and work on the land on pain of imprisonment on bread and water and the confiscation of their work'. This Act was often renewed, but the authorities also recognised the value of the trade and took steps to keep up the quality of the goods. In 1607 all stockings made of two-ply instead of three-ply wool were confiscated. In 1617 inspectors, who included Richard and Edward Dumaresq, were appointed to reinforce the law. In 1624 a petition to Parliament asked for larger supplies of wool, because 'more than a thousand souls have no other means to get their living but by knitting stockings'. The demand seemed infinite. Elie Brevint of Sark tells in his journal[14] how merchants from the islands were given bills of exchange in Coutances which were honoured by gentlemen, merchants, inn-keepers and sailors alike, thus avoiding the risk of their earnings being stolen. So great was the demand that the French came over themselves to buy, if insufficient stockings were exported; some were even taken to Italy, because they wore better than silk stockings which rain and humidity caused to shrink and rot.

Sometimes stockings were smuggled into France, as we learn from the records of the port of Southampton. In 1627 a case was heard before, among others, Alderman Major (Mauger), a Jerseyman and grandfather-in-law of Richard Cromwell. After persistent questioning of reluctant witnesses, it eventually transpired that two Jersey boats, the *Margaret*, part-owned by Abraham Ahier, master mariner, and the *Hopewell*, owned by Richard and Edward Demarrick (sic), (were they the inspectors mentioned above ?) and Nicholas Bailhache, had been taken at sea between the 'rockes called the mekeys [Minquiers] and St Malo'. There were no bills of lading, but the vessels carried Irish leather and consignments of stockings from various Jersey merchants. The *Hopewell* had run up a French flag and changed her name to *la bone esperans*. Aboard were 'about fortye crownes of ffrench money' and 'ffoure letters for the direction and delivery of goods in St Malo', which were hidden in the boat. When the vessels were taken of Cape Frehey (Fréhel), the boarding party had seen these papers 'torne in pieces and swimming in the sea'.[15]

No doubt the French flag in question had replaced the English cross of St George; for how and when the Jersey flag was first used is still unknown, and no early paintings of ships show it. The flag until now flown on ceremonial occasions is a red saltire on a white ground. People tend to think of it as the Irish flag of St Patrick as incorporated in the Union Jack. It is in fact that of the Fitz Gerald family, while the correct Irish flag is a harp on a blue ground with a cross of St George in the first canton.

Carrington Bowles' *Universal Display of the Naval Flags of all nations*, published in 1783, and based on Dutch charts of 1705 and 1720, shows a red saltire on white attributed to 'Ierse'. This has been taken to mean Jersey, while the harp on a blue ground was labelled 'Irlandois'. Someone at some stage must have thought Ierse was Irish, though at that date it would have been written Iersche. Research has shown that this saltire, red on white, was labelled Iersé in French charts back to at least 1757, and it may be argued that we have a good right by prescription to its use. However, because of the confusion with Ireland, the Queen in 1981 allowed the addition of the arms of Jersey, three lion-leopards, surmounted by a simple medieval, or Plantagenet crown, a happy compromise. Guernsey shows a link with the Plantagenets with a sprig of broom above the arms. Henry II was the first Plantagenet and it was his son John who, whether or not he gave us our constitution, was, as Prince and Count of Mortain, Lord of the Isles. We thus mark our attachment to the English Crown.[16]

The ambivalence of Jersey's trade with France is well illustrated in a State Paper dated 11 June 1587, when the arrest of certain French ships was referred to the Attorney-General, the Solicitor-General and the Judge of the Admiralty, who asked the opinion of Sir Amyas Poulet as to the ancient usage. He replied that all merchant strangers had been from time to time received in the Islands of Jersey and Guernsey, free from arrest of lives, ships and goods.

> As to expedience seeing that it is well known what benefit the crowns of England and France receive in time of hostility, by the neutrality of the isles as a place of common vent, their privileges founded on the same should be maintained ´... the islands being weak and only inhabited by poor labourers and fishermen have been freed from invasions by this intercourse of merchandise.

The document then summarises the advantages of this position: the Queen gained a goodly sum yearly by the customs on cloths, kerseys, tin and lead exported thither and by linen and French wines imported thence to England. The inhabitants gained by the money spent among them by merchants, and the profits from petty customs helped the Captains (Governors) of both isles to support their charges which were doubled in time of war. Intelligence was thus gained of the state of affairs in France, 'more full than they ever gain of us'. (State Papers often reveal that intelligence of enemy movements had been brought to England by merchants trading from the islands.) A further reason given was that broad cloths from the west of England found a good market in Normandy and Brittany.

The Poulets continued to rule Jersey until the end of the 16th century. Sir Amyas, who stood high in the Queen's favour, was often summoned to difficult tasks elsewhere. During his absence he at first left the Island in charge of his brother George; then, when his son Anthony came of age in 1583, he made him his Lieutenant. In 1588, when Amyas died, Anthony became Governor. It seems likely that the names Amice and Rachel were introduced into Jersey families through the important Poulets.[17]

Elizabeth's support for the Huguenots brought England more than once to the verge of war with France and revived the old nightmare of a French invasion. But a greater peril arose from Spain. The Spanish Armada passed well to the north of Jersey, though the seigneurs of Vinchelez and Morville are said to have fought a lawsuit over the wreckage of some Spanish ship that was washed ashore at l'Etacq. A dispute between these same parties in 1669 produced an interesting sidelight on the limits of their fiefs, when Philippe Mahaut, then aged 80, declared that in his youth some old people had shown him the ruins of the castle of La Brécquette and trees marking the separation of the fiefs. At certain very low tides, when suitable conditions prevail, attempts are still made to verify this oral tradition.[18] After the Armada the danger from Spain remained. In 1591 a Spanish fleet anchored off St Malo. State papers reveal that assistance was given to France, but 'only to expel the Spaniards from Brittany'.[19]

In face of this danger Anthony Poulet took a drastic decision. His father and grandfather had spent enormous sums on Mont Orgueil, and he had continued the work. His arms may still be seen over the fourth gateway. But in 1593 he decided that all his money had been wasted. The Council wrote thus to the Governor: 'The Castle lieth subject to a mighty hill but 400 feet distant, and so overtopt by it that no man can possibly show his face this side next the hill'. An entirely new castle was needed. Some 45 years before the Council had ordered a fort to be built on the islet of St Helier, but nothing had been done.[20] Anthony now revived this scheme and pressed forward with such zest, that in the next six years the keep and kernel of what we now know as Elizabeth Castle was built, armed and garrisoned. The architect chosen was Paul Ivy, or Eve, a well-known English engineer, who worked in Jersey from 1594. He drew a sketch of what he proposed to build and the start of his work on the islet is recorded in the date incised in the chimney of the Captain's House. Ralegh in a letter to Cecil said he was 'as prayse worthy a worker both for his judgment, invention and industry in saving charges as any man beside'. At least one mason working under him was a Jerseyman, a certain Paul Byson; this is perhaps the earliest record of a named Jersey builder.[21]

In 1600 Sir Anthony died and was succeeded by Sir Walter Ralegh. Soldier and sailor, poet and philosopher, chemist and courtier, historian and explorer, he was Jersey's most distinguished Governor; but the Island saw little of him. On his first visit he stayed a month, during which time he appointed a Queen's Huntsman (*maître des chasses*).[22] Two years later in 1602 he paid another visit for less than a month. He has been credited with the establishment of a land registry, but, although he was present in the States when this reform was adopted and was clearly in favour of such a measure, it had long been under discussion. In 1562 the Commission composed of Hugh Poulet, Richard Worseley, George Poulet and others had recommended a registry, as did the Commissioners Pyne and Napper in 1590. However the details about the form it was to take and what it was to include were given in Ralegh's presence, and it proved to be a most useful measure, since it effectively created a system of registered title to land in the Island.

From time immemorial transactions in land and property have been effected by means of deeds or contracts sworn by the parties before the Royal Court, each '*contrat*' bearing the island seal (usually with the Bailiff's personal seal on the reverse) and the signatures of the Bailiff or his Lieutenant and the sitting Jurats. They are written in French, the earlier examples on vellum, often in beautiful script, with the initial 'A' of the introductory words: '*A tous ceux qui ces présentes lettres verront ou orront*' (to all who these presents shall see or hear) sometimes elaborately decorated: one particular scribe in the 17th century used his talents in colouring it. Once the deed has been enrolled in the Public Registry, the finely inscribed original is of no intrinsic legal value, but a great number have survived in island families, who often possess dozens or even hundreds of these documents. Many of them relate to transactions in *rentes*, a system of charges secured on land, which were used virtually as currency for the purchase and sale of property until the law was reformed at the end of the 19th century.

22 *Decorated initial letter on a contract of 1649.*

In early documents the date is given, not by the calendar but in relation to a saint's day. As the Reformation approached this custom lapsed and sometimes both were given, as for instance in an MS of 1545, dated 2 May, it refers to a *ouïe de paroisse* passed in 1541 on the Sunday after the feast of St Simon and St Jude.

Under Mary Tudor, the style and title of the monarch became very lengthy. A document referring to the Faultrat family includes the wording:

> Helier de Carteret bailli de l'île de Jersey sous nos souverains roi et reine Philippe et Marie par la grâce de Dieu roi et reine d'Angleterre de France de Naples de Jérusalem et d'Irlande, défenseurs de la foi, princes d'Espagne et de Sicile, archducs d'Autriche, ducs de Milan de Bourgogne et de Brabant, comtes de Gascogne Flandres et Tyrol ....[23]

It is now clear that Ralegh was not the first to introduce Jerseymen to Newfoundland cod, though it is possible that he popularised the smoking of Virginian tobacco; yet that seems unlikely in view of his brief presence in the Island. While in England he regularly received papers concerning island affairs. He spoke French, and had served in France with the Huguenots under Montgomery,[24] and, as a West country man, was interested in promoting trade with America. However, the greatest debt we owe him is for the preservation of Mont Orgueil Castle from destruction. This would have been the fate of a castle thought to have outlived its usefulness, had not Ralegh written to Cecil

> to say true, it is a stately fort of great capacity, both as to maintenance and comfort, to all that part of the island next to Normandy, which stands in view thereof; so until I hear further her Majesty's pleasure, I have left at my own charge, some men in it. And if a small matter may defend it, it were a pity to cast it down, having cost Her Majesty's father, brother and sister – without her own charge – 20,000 marks in the erecting.

Ralegh also named the new castle after his royal mistress. In fulsome flattery of the ageing queen, he 'presumed to christen it Fort Isabella Bellissima' (Elizabeth the most beautiful).[25]

When James I came to the throne in 1603, Ralegh was enmeshed in the tangle of plots that ushered in the new reign. He was implicated in Cobham's scheme to place Lady Arabella Stuart on the throne. At his trial he was accused of conspiring 'to deprive the King of his Government, to raise seditions within the realm; to bring the Roman superstitions and to provide foreign enemies to invade the Kingdom'. It was alleged that Cobham was to bring money from Spain to the isle of Jersey and find Sir Walter Ralegh 'for the distribution of the aforesaid crowns as the occasion of discontent of the subjects should give cause'. In August 1603 Ralegh lost his Governorship to Sir John Peyton, a tough Elizabethan veteran, who had been Captain of the Tower where Ralegh was to spend over ten years under sentence of death.[26]

Under the new Governor, to whom Prayer Book rubrics were as peremptory as army regulations, ecclesiastical questions came to the fore once more. King James hated Presbyterianism, but for the moment left the islands undisturbed: 'We will and order that our Isles shall quietly enjoy their liberty in the use of the ecclesiastical discipline there now established'.[27] In 1604, however, the battle with Peyton began. The parishioners of St John chose Daniel Brevint, son of the minister of Sark, as their Rector, and the Rector of St Lawrence duly ordained him by the laying on of hands. This ignored the Governor's right of presentation, and he appealed to the Council, who were loth to challenge the system which the King had confirmed. Next year Peyton again appealed to the Council to abolish 'Presbyterianism and popular jurisdiction in the Church', but they still took no action.

Now, however, Peyton was helped by a movement within the Island. Jerseymen took pride in their Calvinistic Creed, but widespread revolt was brewing against the Calvinistic discipline. More and more church censures were ignored, and the Colloquy appealed to Peyton: 'A church can no more exist without governance than a wherry without a rudder, yet the minds of the people are imbued with the notion that there is no church jurisdiction among us, many refusing to appear when summoned'. This was a confession that the existing system of church courts had broken down. Peyton's answer was a snub: 'My advice to you is that you walk humbly before your lay brethren, so as you may be reverenced'.[28]

Peyton then hired a man to collect the signatures of malcontents in every parish with the intention of preparing a petition asking for a change in the ecclesiastical system. In 1613 he went a step further. When St Peter's living fell vacant, he appointed Elie Messervy as Rector.[29] Messervy was the first student whom the Don Baudains had sent to Oxford and there he had received episcopal ordination. The Colloquy refused to admit him until he had signed the *Book of Church Order*, and they summoned a Synod to discuss the matter. Peyton forbade the Synod to meet. This brought matters to a crisis. The Council, where Laud was now the moving spirit, ordered both parties, 'those that embrace the present ecclesiastical government as well as those that dislike it', to send 'able and sufficient persons' to Westminster to argue the matter before them. Peyton sent Messervy himself and the Attorney-General, Maret; the Colloquy sent George Poulet, the Bailiff, and four of the leading Rectors. As for St Peter's, the Council ordered that Mr Messervy be admitted to his benefice peaceably. Locally the matter was settled by a compromise. The Colloquy gave him the right hand of fellowship after he had agreed to continue to use the Huguenot prayer book. The larger question was held over until the visit of the Royal Commissioners, Sir Edward Conway and Sir William Bird, in 1617.[30]

As a result of their report the Council wrote: 'For the better government of the ecclesiastical charge, it is ordered that a Dean be elected. His Majesty giving leave to the States *pro hac vice* to nominate three of the most grave and learned ministers there, out of whom His Majesty may choose one'.[31] Now there was a vast hurly-burly behind the scenes. In the Library at Lambeth Palace are two sets of canons proposed by the island clergy.[32] Both retain Presbyterian ordination and the Huguenot prayer book. Both accept the idea of a leader to preside at church councils, but neither uses the title 'Dean'. One calls him 'president', the other suggests that at each biennial Synod a moderator should be elected with an adjoint, '*l'un d'une île et l'autre de l'autre*', and this would appear to be for one Synod only. Meanwhile crazy notions were disquieting the Island. When in 1618 a comet appeared for 22 nights 'with a tail like a bunch of rods' (*l'étoile portait comme une barbe*), many felt that their worst fears were justified. One Sunday the spires of St Peter's and St Martin's were struck by lightning which was thought to be a sign of God's wrath, because his people were forsaking the true faith.[33] Opinion was so divided that the States hesitated to make the three nominations; so the Council had to act on its own authority. One of the original deputations had been David Bandinel, Rector of St Brelade, an Italian Protestant (one of the State Papers refers to him as Spanish), who had come to Jersey at the end of the reign of Elizabeth, a man of outstanding ability, but by no means free from guile. He had evidently made a good impression on the Council as a delegate, and his wife's father, William Stallenge, a silkworm enthusiast who had interested the King in his hobby, may have put in a word for his son-in-law. At all events he was appointed Dean in 1620.[34]

The King gave him 23 instructions 'signed by our Royal hand'. Of these the most important were: '*The Book of Discipline* shall be of no validity, neither shall any lay Elders claim jurisdiction in ecclesiastical causes'. 'All hereafter admitted to a parochial church shall be ordained by some Bishop; but Ministers already admitted shall retain their places, so as they be willing to conform to the Service now observed'. '*The Book of Common Prayer*, translated into French, shall be used in the Public Services; but forbearance shall be shown in the use of the surplice, the Cross in baptism and the reading of the Apocrypha.' 'In every parish two of the discreeter sort shall be chosen, who shall be called churchwardens [the title *surveillant* being used in Jersey and never the French term *marguillier*] to see that the churches are kept in repair and to provide all things necessary for the service.' 'The Dean shall every year visit the churches to inform himself of decays in churches, churchyards and houses of ministers or church offices.' 'The Dean shall have probate of testaments of all that die in the Island.' The King granted him for his stipend 'all tithes of corn or grain within the parish of St Saviour', a grant said to be worth 300 crowns a year.[35]

The appointment of this dark-skinned foreigner was far from popular. Calvinists taunted him with temporising when sent as a delegate to England to uphold their cause. No one was ever allowed to forget that he was not a Jerseyman. Years afterwards Sir Philippe de Carteret would still refer to him in official documents as 'one Bandinel, an alien'.

Few sessions of the States have been as stormy as that on 15 April 1620, when he was sworn in.[36] There was uproar when he handed his Patent to the Governor instead of to the Bailiff, more uproar as to whether he should be allowed to wear his hat. Jurats spoke with their hats on, and Bandinel tried to do the same, but the Bailiff refused to hear him unless he spoke bare-headed. Two Rectors, Samuel de la Place of St Mary and Daniel Brevint of St John, rose and protested that they would never acknowledge him as Dean, 'that the word Dean was not in Scripture, and that they had signed another Discipline'. When Bandinel presented a letter from the Council ordering the States to pay his expenses in England, this was the last straw. They replied: 'We think it hard to be called to bear the charges he was at for his preferment. We think we should not bear the charges of one not chosen by ourselves, nor liked, being a stranger'.

But he was sworn in, and began at once to enforce the Anglican system. When de la Place of St Mary 'uttered irreverent speeches against the *Book of Common Prayer*', Bandinel deprived him of his living and he went to Guernsey,[37] where Presbyterianism survived for another 40 years. When no one could be found to take his place, the Dean himself took charge of St Mary in addition to his own parish of St Brelade. The new French prayer book met with passive resistance from clergy and people. When Brevint died 30 years later, Chevalier, himself a Church officer, wrote approvingly: 'Of all the ministers he was the most loyal to the Reformed religion. He accepted the Prayer Book most against his will. From the first he never used the responses, and set aside all ceremonies and vain repetitions!'.[38] The rubric ordering the Communion to be received kneeling was everywhere ignored, even in the Dean's own churches. A quarter of a century later Heylin called Jerseymen, 'a strange and stubborn generation; and stiffer in the hams than an elephant; such as will neither bow the knee to the name of Jesus, nor kneel to Him in His Sacraments'.[39]

One task remained, the drawing up of the Canons. After many unfraternal sessions the Dean induced the clergy to agree reluctantly to 58, and, in 1623, he crossed to England to lay these before the Council. The Royal Court sent three Jurats to oppose some of these. The Archbishop and two Bishops were appointed to hear the case and they persuaded each side to accept some compromise. The King then affixed his seal, and for more than three hundred years this final draft remained part of the law of Jersey. On the question of Anglicanism versus Presbyterianism they left no loop-hole: 'Whoever shall impugn the government of the Church by Archbishops, Bishops and Deans shall be *ipso facto* excommunicate.' 'It is enjoined unto all sorts of people that they submit themselves to the Divine Service contained in the *Book of Common Prayer*.' 'No man shall be admitted to any benefice who hath not been ordained according to the form used in the Church of England.' Bandinel's powerful personality, backed by the overwhelming resources of the Governor, Council and King, had trampled down all opposition.

Eagleston, in *The Channel Islands under Tudor Government*, writes:

> The effect of the Canons, which still remain in force, was to give the insular church a curious position of semi-independence relative to the diocese of Winchester of which it forms a part and to preserve, in the constitution of the Dean's Court, a fossil relic of the 17th-century movement which aimed at bringing Episcopalians and Presbyterians into one church establishment on the basis of a compromise between the powers of a bishop and those of a Presbyterian synod.[49]

Outwardly Anglicanism triumphed, but for generations Jersey remained Calvinist at heart. In this we may see the seed which flowered more than a century later, when Methodism arrived in the island and was readily accepted by so many.

Chapter Twelve

THE BAILIFFSHIP OF JEAN HÉRAULT, 1615-1626

O world, how apt the poor are to be proud.–Shakespeare, *Twelfth Night*

IT WAS NOT ONLY in church affairs that Peyton proved anti-democratic. In 1606 he had complained to the Council: 'There doth appear in the island some declination of obedience and respect', and had urged that the Court be curbed more strictly by the rules of past Commissioners, and that 'the authority of the States be examined and limited, for this Assembly, for want of true understanding of monarchical obedience doth somewhat incline to popular government'.[1] But he met a foeman worthy of his steel.

Jean Hérault had held some small post in England under Elizabeth and James, and in 1611, 'in consideration of the good service he has rendered and is rendering to the King', he received Letters Patent promising him the office of Bailiff, when it should become vacant. He then had to persuade the aged George Poulet to resign, 'which cost him much money'. But, when the way seemed clear, Peyton claimed that his Letters Patent gave him the right of appointment. It was a case of Letters Patent contradicting Letters Patent, and the case was referred to the Council. Here the King's high doctrine of kingship gave Hérault an easy victory. 'To constitute a Magistrate', wrote James, 'is an act royal inseparable from our Royal Person', and he added, 'Forasmuch as we always intended that a competent pension should be allowed to the Bailiff, we command that 100 marks be paid yearly to Hérault over and above his other emoluments.' This meant that Peyton not only lost his right of nomination, but also 100 marks a year out of his own pocket. The two men became enemies for life.

Hérault was sworn in in 1615. He came of a good Jersey family, whose name may be found in the Extente of 1274. But all his life he was hampered by poverty, and this seems to have created in him an inferiority complex, so that he began madly to magnify his position. He called himself High Bailiff, and assumed the magniloquent title of Monsieur de St Sauveur from a small property that he owned in that parish, probably that now called La Pallotterie,[2] a form of address hitherto limited to the greater seigneurs. He was the first Bailiff to wear red robes like an English judge[3] and he ordered the clergy, in their prayers, to put his name before that of the Governor. He even claimed the title of Governor, asserting that Peyton was only 'Muster Master and Captain of the Troops'. He sent a long memorandum to the Council 'to show that the Bailiff is of greater authority than the Captain', this being the title usually assigned to the senior officer in command of the garrison.[4]

This arrogant claim sprang from his study of the old Norman Coutumiers, which said of the Bailiffs, 'There is no one above them except the Duke in the district committed to their care'. But Bailiffs in the Island had never been front line officials like Bailiffs in the Bessin or the Cotentin. The early Wardens had treated them as servants whom they appointed and dismissed at will.[5] Even when, under the Tudors, the Bailiffs were appointed by the King, it would have been ridiculous to suggest that Ralegh regarded George Poulet as his superior officer. This must have been as obvious to Hérault as it is to us, but his claim was a first move in a campaign to make the Bailiff the real Governor of the Island.

He posed before the Council as the lynx-eyed official in charge of Jersey. He frequently reported Peyton for neglect of duty: 'The Captain is sending his butler to be Master Porter of Elizabeth Castle, an office hitherto held by gentlemen brought up to war. To put there a butler, who only understands serving pots of wine at table, is as bad as sending his pilot to Muscovy'; or again, 'Castle Elizabeth has been abandoned of all its guard save one, who sent on market day to all the taverners to seek his companions'.[6] Peyton in these years of peace had evidently cut down the Castle garrisons to almost vanishing point. He received all the Crown revenues and had to defray all expenses. So the fewer the soldiers on his pay roll, the fatter his own purse. Hérault even went so far as to suggest that the Receiver, Philippe Marett, 'should be bound once a year to render his accounts before your Bailiff'.

Peyton's officers took up the cudgels on his behalf. The Receiver found a malicious pleasure in inventing reasons for withholding Hérault's perquisites, the 20 sous paid for a taverner's licence, or the fee for testing the shopkeeper's scales. But in November 1616 Peyton summoned Hérault before the Council on the charge of 'usurping the office of Governor'. The verdict given in February was almost a complete vindication: 'We acquit the Bailiff of any undutifulness to the King's Majesty or any injustice in the civil government, but not from heat of words, which have unfittingly fallen from him, for which we thought fit to give him a sharp reprehension.' Peyton was ordered to pay Hérault's expenses in London and then the rule was laid down, which became a turning point in Jersey constitutional history: 'We hold it convenient that the charge of the military forces be wholly in the Governor and the care of Justice and Civil affairs in the Bailiff'.[7]

Three times in his career Hérault's conduct was investigated by English authorities and each time the verdict was the same. He was irritable (once he threatened to crop the Denonciateur's ears because of some trivial mistake), tetchy, preposterously vain, but in an age of venality, when even the great Lord Bacon was found guilty of accepting bribes, Hérault remained incorruptible.

But all this friction showed that something was wrong in Jersey. So in April 1617 the Council sent two Royal Commissioners to investigate matters: Sir Edward Conway, a distinguished soldier, who was soon to become President of the Council, and Sir William Bird, an expert on constitutional law. It was no light task to come to a French-speaking island, where the inhabitants used a dialect far more akin to Norman than to Parisian French, where laws and customs were based on obscure local precedents, to be faced with such thorny questions as how to graft the Anglican system on to a Huguenot church, how to harmonise two rival representatives of the King, how to adjust the Norman Coutumiers to modern conditions, how to settle disputes about obscure feudal rights which no English lawyer knew of; yet no one can study their report without admiring their determination to be fair and their sterling common sense. Their verdict in the church dispute we saw in the last chapter. Hérault's character was again vindicated. 'His violence is rather in words to keep up his authority than in act.' His anxiety about the defences was found to be fully justified. 'Neither castles nor island are safe from surprise or conquest.' 'The warding of the castles hath no sufficiency, and a thousand of the militiamen hath no weapons.' The weapons produced were '... exceeding defective. Many of those called bills are bare staves with no iron stall.' 'The men are wholly without order and without knowledge to use their arms effectually.' So the Council ordered the castle garrisons to be largely increased and the militia to be drilled by professional soldiers, and a duty to be levied on wines to provide 'serviceable arms according to modern use'.

But Hérault's claim to be Governor was more than the Commissioners could swallow. On their advice the Council decreed that no one but the Governor had any right to that title, that the

States must obtain his permission before they held a meeting, and that he had the right to veto any decisions that seemed 'prejudicial to His Majesty's service'. On the other hand in Court and States the Bailiff must be given precedence.

The Commissioners wasted several days over Philippe Marett. His case is worth a paragraph because it illustrates what curious creatures some of these island squireens were, proud as turkey-cocks, stubborn as mules, snappish as jungle cubs. Marett had been one of the first lads whom the States had supported at Oxford, had returned to Jersey with Ralegh and then departed to Spain, where, according to Hérault, he was 'brought up in Spanish seminaries and got pernicious maxims'.[8] He was now Peyton's right-hand man and Attorney-General. In 1616, when a case was being tried, a paper was required which was in his possession. The Bailiff sent for him, but though he was only in the market outside, he answered, 'I am busy'. The Court then ordered the Denonciateur to fetch him, but he said, 'Have you got a subpoena?'. Later he stormed into Court with his hat on, shouting, 'Where are my accusers?'. And, when Hérault told him to behave himself, he answered 'in high fashion'. So Hérault asked the Jurats what should be done with him, and when young Philippe de Carteret of St Ouen rose to reply, Marett hurled wild accusations at him. 'You sent assassins to my house by night to cut my throat' (a charge which later he entirely failed to prove before the Commissioners). Such conduct was clearly intolerable, and he was fined 50 crowns and ordered to apologise. When he refused to obey, Hérault suspended him from office and ordered him to appear before the Privy Council. Here his behaviour seems to have been as obstreperous as in Jersey, for the Council committed him to the Gatehouse and deprived him of his Attorney-Generalship. They then ordered him to return to Jersey and carry out his sentence. He reappeared in the Royal Court and was asked if he had come to make his submission. He replied that his case had not yet been tried; but the Bailiff produced a letter from the Secretary of State reporting the Council's judgment. As he still refused to apologise and pay his fine, he was sent to the Castle, Hérault growling, 'You deserve to be put in irons'. This enabled him to describe himself in a petition to the King as 'His Majesty's poor oppressed servant adjudged to be fettered and manacled'. As a matter of fact, so far from being fettered, he was allowed to walk anywhere inside the Castle and even to entertain friends to dinner. The Commissioners with great patience examined all his complaints and decided that his troubles arose wholly from 'his own haughty fashions and insolent behaviour'. He escaped soon afterwards to England.

Other facts emerge incidentally from the Commissioners' Report. The Crown revenues were still received very largely in kind, 870 quarters of wheat, 277 of barley and 941 head of poultry. We learn too that the open field system had now passed away.[9] High banks were now dividing the Island into small rectangles, and the Commissioners note how this would help in its defence, for 'at every forty paces the ground is enclosed like forts with narrow ways to pass'. The earliest mention so far found of a 'clos', or enclosed field,[10] is in Guernsey in 1366, and in Jersey in 1395. In Poingdestre's time the custom was commonplace, and he describes the method of raising hawthorn seedlings for surrounding the fields with thorn hedges. Dry stone walls were also used, but less commonly, and more often on exposed, sandy land, such as the slopes at St Ouen above l'Étacq. Many of these excellent thorn hedges, on high banks, survive to this day.

Up to this point Hérault had won almost every round, but he grew too daring. He had disliked the appointment of a Dean, but had not ventured to resist. However, in 1620, when Bandinel ordered the election of churchwardens, it became clear that they would be sworn in by the new Ecclesiastical Court, and he protested vigorously. 'The temporal power', he wrote, 'hath always administered the oath'. To take from the Bailiff the profit of the seal, given him for life, without his being heard, is very extraordinary.' Expostulation was permissible, but then he overstepped the mark and forbade the elections. This was open defiance of the King's instructions to the Dean. The Council ordered Peyton to see that the elections were held, 'notwithstanding

23 *The dolmen (drawn by G. Heriot,* c.*1790), subsequently removed and given to Marshal Conway. (Photo: F. de L. Bois)*

DIFFERENT ASPECTS OF LE MONT DE LA VILLE

24 *The harbour with the recently-constructed Fort Regent in the background, by J. Young, 1815. (Photo: F. de L. Bois)*

any edict of the Bailiff to the contrary', and Hérault was summoned to Westminster to explain his conduct.[11] Here his temper proved his downfall. 'I was too vehement', he said, 'in my answers to the Lord Chancellor.' He was sent to the Marshalsea, suspended from office, and his duties entrusted to Sir William Parkhurst, 'a gentleman', wrote de Carteret, 'unacquainted with our language, our laws, or our style of proceeding'. But he proved a mere place-hunter, who spent only a few days in Jersey, appointed a Lieutenant-Bailiff, and departed to draw the Bailiff's salary for the next two years.[12]

Hérault was released the same evening, but he had to pledge himself not to leave London, and was kept cooling his heels in Westminster until August 1624. The Council had, not surprisingly, grown tired of Jersey squabbles, and hoped that in his absence the troubled waters might grow calm. But his appointment was for life, and he could not be turned out, unless some serious offence justified his dismissal. So they tried to induce him to resign, offering him a pension of £100 a year, and gilding the pill with the phrase, 'The King having need of his services near his person'. But he demanded a public hearing of the charges against him, and in 1624 his persistence was rewarded, for his case ended in this verdict: 'His Majesty, finding no charge against the Bailiff, and holding it not suitable to remove an officer without sufficient cause, is graciously pleased that Jean Hérault be reintegrated to his office with all perquisites, and that arrears grown due since his sequestration be forthwith paid to him'.

He was nervous about his reception after so long an absence, but he need not have worried. An Act of the States runs: 'Bailiff Hérault having obtained from the King an entire reinstatement, the States assembled to receive him, and a Jurat, a Minister and a Constable were deputed to escort him to his seat as a sign of their joy at seeing him return happily'. But his troubles were not yet over. The Receiver declared that it was impossible to refund his arrears of salary, as the full amount had already been paid to Parkhurst. So in 1625 Hérault returned to England to fight the matter out. He returned unsuccessful at the end of the year and in 1626 he died. It was said in his funeral sermon: 'Though he had faults, as the wisest have, those faults never tarnished his virtues. He never spared himself in the service of his country, striving to maintain its rights and liberties even at his own expense without help or support from anyone'.[13]

Hérault's very foibles, his pig-headedness, his touchiness, his absurd exaggeration of his own dignity, helped to save the Island from a real danger. If he had not been the absurd little fighting cock he was, successive Governors might well have established a military dictatorship, in which retired Generals from England rode roughshod over the Island's liberties. Hérault secured for Jersey the right of self-government.

Chapter Thirteen

THE EVE OF THE CIVIL WARS, 1627-1642

Alas, regardless of their doom,
The little victims play!
No sense have they of ills to come
Nor care beyond today.–Gray

WHEN HÉRAULT DIED three candidates competed for his red robe. Philippe Marett had planned a triumphant return to the island from which he had fled. He had joined the house of the Duke of Buckingham, who ruled England as uncrowned king, and Buckingham had promised him the Bailiffship. But Hérault lived a few weeks too long, for Buckingham's arrogance had aroused such fury that he was threatened with impeachment; and when Conway, who was now Secretary of State,[1] pointed out that Marett could not reappear without the King's pardon, his hopes collapsed. Some urged the claims of Josué de Carteret, Seigneur of Trinity, Hérault's Lieutenant-Bailiff. But the King chose Sir Philippe de Carteret, Seigneur of St Ouen.

He had lost his father when he was 10 and had been a ward of the Crown, but, when he was 17, finding his estates going to rack and ruin, he left Oxford, 'abandoning the studies that he loved more than anything else in the world',[2] and came home to take charge of his property. He soon showed his capabilities. When a Spanish invasion was feared in 1602, and though only 18, he took command of the militia of two parishes. As soon as he came of age he was sworn in as Jurat, and from that time served on every deputation sent by the States to England. In 1617 he was knighted. He had kept aloof from island squabbles and accomplished the remarkable feat of remaining on good terms with both Peyton and Hérault. In the church controversy, though himself a Calvinist, he bowed to the King's wishes.

When he became Bailiff in 1627 he took a wide view of his duties, enlarging Elizabeth Castle, which one would have thought was the Governor's province, and by building the lower ward he more than doubled its size. 'The slothfulness of the labourers', he wrote, 'doth impose on me intolerable pains. I husband the King's money by over-viewing the works daily.'[3] He also had the belfry of the church on the islet pulled down in April 1639, and in the years 1636 to 1638 he caused to be demolished St Germain's Manor in St Lawrence (now Les Saints Germains) and had the stone carted to the islet for the fortifications in the Castle.[4]

The Island was again in danger. Buckingham, whom the King had saved from impeachment, had plunged into war with France, and in 1627 he had seized the island of Ré off La Rochelle, but had been ingloriously defeated by the French commander Toiras. In July the Council was warned that the French king was taking measures to revenge Ré upon Jersey and that 40 ships of great burthen were assembled at St Malo. In 1628 news came that Louis XIII had given Jersey to Toiras as a reward for the capture of Ré.[5]

After much badgering de Carteret got from the Council 200 conscripts, but Jersey did not welcome its defenders. When country authorities had to impress a certain number of men, they naturally freed their districts from some of their rogues and ruffians; respectable farmers strongly objected to having men of this type billeted on them, and de Carteret reported: 'The people murmur and grudge against the soldiers. Disputes are frequent'; but at last he had to confess that the complaints were justified. The men, he said, were 'incorrigible and inefficient', and he asked that they might be recalled. In November, however, he and Peyton wrote urgently to Conway, marking their letter 'Haste! Haste! Haste! Post haste – haste for life', reporting that 100 ships and 80 flat-bottomed hoys were waiting at St Malo for a favourable wind to attack the Island. In March 1629 the Earl of Danby arrived to undertake the defence. In a 'grave and eloquent speech' he assured the States that the King was going to make Jersey 'more impregnable than a wall of brass'.

But his visit is chiefly memorable because we owe to his chaplain, Peter Heylin, the first book ever written on the Channel Islands: *A Survey of the Estate of the two islands. Guernzey and Jarsey with the isles appending.* He found Jersey 'exceedingly pleasant and delightsome', but from a tourist's point of view disappointing. 'The churches are naked of all monuments, not so much as the blazon of an arms permitted for fear of idolatry'; and 'no actions of importance can be heard of in their legends'. So he devoted most of his pages to the Calvinist controversy. He also recorded that 'the souldiers of each regiment are very well arrayed and not unpractised in their Armes, but such as never saw more danger than a Training came to'.[6]

The French war ended in 1629, but the danger from Spain continued and Spanish privateers from Dunkirk were a constant menace, even de Carteret himself having one unpleasant experience. In 1628 he had been returning from England with money, soldiers and stores for the castles (and again one wonders why the Bailiff was undertaking these apparently military duties, though at this period he was also Lieutenant-Governor), when the ship in which he and the Dean were travelling was captured by Dunkirkers. After two months most of the captives were back, penniless, in Dover, but de Carteret was held as a hostage for a Scottish priest who was a prisoner in London, and his ransom was not accepted until the priest was released. This ransom so impoverished him that he seriously thought of entering the service of the Dutch.[7]

But there were worse men afloat than Dunkirkers, Barbary pirates who sold their prisoners in African slave markets. In 1625 the Mayor of Plymouth reported that in 10 days they had captured 27 vessels. In Jersey collections were constantly made to buy back local seamen from slavery. As an example, the brothers and sisters of Richard Dumaresq collected a ransom in order to free him from Barbary. In 1638 the States sent Nicolas Effart to Algiers to find out how many Jerseymen he could discover there. It was no easy task to trace individual slaves in that pirate city, but he returned triumphant with 17 rescued men, including his own brother. The States were so grateful for his efforts that he was decreed free of all militia guard duty, 'et toutes aultres vils services', for the rest of his life.[8]

Peyton died in 1630 and was succeeded by Sir Thomas Jermyn, a courtier who never set foot in Jersey. He appointed as his Lieutenant Captain Francis Rainsford, whose autocratic manner got on everyone's nerves. He ordered St Lawrence's parish to provide a garrison for St Aubin's Fort, and when the Constable asked, 'Why St Lawrence?' Rainsford wrote, 'For this mutinous reply I committed him to the Castle as an example to others. But I was frustrated in my intentions, for most of his parish, with all the Constables and some of the Jurats, came to visit him as a martyr'. De Carteret tried to act as peacemaker and arranged for every parish in turn to provide guards for the Fort. But Rainsford chose this moment to quarrel with him. A sailor was accused of having acted as pilot to an enemy privateer. The evidence against him was weak and de Carteret released him on bail, but Rainsford promptly rearrested him and carried him off to the Castle. De Carteret protested that this was an encroachment on the functions of the Civil Court and this started a violent controversy which had to go before the Council.[9] Eventually, in 1634, Rainsford was recalled.

Jermyn now decided that the best way to restore peace would be to make de Carteret Lieutenant-Governor once again as well as Bailiff. This certainly solved some difficulties, but it created others. Before we look at these, however, let us try to picture life on the Island on the eve of the Civil Wars.

The number of inhabitants was estimated by de Carteret at about 25,000 and these fell into clearly defined groups. At the top of the tree stood the Seigneurs, the squirarchy; their number varied from time to time as fiefs were amalgamated by marriage or divided, but it ranged from about 100 to 130, many of the fiefs being very small indeed, though the holders endeavoured to keep up the dignity of their fiefs by holding their individual courts, at which substantial justice was meted out. To these seigneurs must be added their relations; and seigneurial families, like others, were large: Sir Philippe himself had nine brothers and sisters and 11 children; so with aunts and cousins, this group may have numbered about two thousand. There were subtle distinctions among them and childish disputes about precedence. One fief differed from another in glory, and the Seigneur of Saval was not equal to the Seigneur of Samarès. In 1624 the Seigneur of Diélament preferred to go to prison rather than sit on the bench of Jurats below the Seigneur of Vinchelez de Bas; this may have been because the former owed *Suite de Cour* and the latter did not. But as a class these seigneurs stood apart from the rest of the populace; they were addressed by the names of their fiefs: Monsieur de Méléches, Monsieur de la Trinité and so on, and were spoken of as the *noblesse*, for in Jersey, as in France, nobility began with the *écuyer* (esquire), not as in England with the baron. The seigneurs were well-to-do men, swaggering about in smart clothes, with broad lace collars and rapiers at their sides. A bundle of tradesmen's bills helps us to picture Elie Dumaresq of La Haule in an olive-green suit trimmed with satin ribbons, gold-fringed gloves and sky-blue stockings.[10] When the Seigneur of Trinity died there was a family brawl about his pearl collars, gold chain and silver-hilted sword and about whether the heir who received the clothes was entitled to the gold buttons.

These seigneurs took pride in their gardens. There were peacocks at Trinity and tulips, the latter still a novelty in Western Europe. There were swans at Samarès and at St Ouen, and a good deal of rebuilding was taking place. La Hague Manor was entirely rebuilt in 1634, and Trinity in 1641. In 1637 a west wing was added to Bagot and Longueville was restored. Much of this information and a wealth of further details of life at the time can be gleaned from the Journal of Benjamin La Cloche, Seigneur of Longueville; a quite invaluable document.[11]

Hawking and falconry were favourite sports, and red-legged partridges abounded. Since the Court consisted largely of seigneurs, there were many orders against poaching, and to keep a ferret was a heinous crime; to injure a falcon, even by accident, meant a scourging 'until the blood ran'. Many court orders were flagrant class legislation. One act was passed 'to stop the abuse committed by many of the lower orders who dress in a style unsuited to their station'. Only ladies might wear taffeta or watered silk, and no farmer's wife might wear lace anywhere but in her cap.

However these men were by no means merely sporting squires. The seigneurs of St Ouen, Samarès, La Hague, Diélament and Vinchelez de Bas were all Oxford graduates, and a list has survived of books which Elie Dumaresq of La Haule bought at Guibray Fair. It includes five books of poetry, ranging from du Bartas' epic of the Creation, which suggested to Milton the writing of *Paradise Lost*, to a cynical old satire, *La Grande Malice des Femmes*, four classical authors: Caesar, Pliny, Martial and Herodotus; a digest of Norman law, a treatise on money, d'Aubigny's *Histoire Universelle*, a commentary on the *Book of Revelation*. Crepin's *Martyrs* (the French equivalent of Foxe), Aesop's *Fables* and the *Legend of Faust*. Not a bad selection for a lad who had just kept his twenty-first birthday and indicative of a knowledge of several languages.[12]

Below the seigneurs came the farmers, the backbone of the country, proprietors cultivating their small estates with the help of their families. The farmer had hardly any money, but that did not trouble him, for his house and fields were his own, so he had no rent to pay. He grew

25 *Charles Robin, 1743-1824.*

26 *Marie Bartlet, 1677-1741.*

PIONEERS AND BENEFACTORS

27 *T. B. Davies, 1867-1942.*

28 *Lilian Grandin, 1876-1924.*

enough wheat and rye for a year's supply of home-made bread, grinding his corn at his seigneur's mill and leaving behind a small portion as a fee, usually a twelfth or thirteenth sheaf, a due known as *suite du moulin*. His farm produced milk, eggs, butter, poultry, meat and vegetables. He made cider in his own press from his own apples, the sea provided free vraic for manure and fuel and his bees supplied honey as well as wax for candles. He caught fish from his own boat and salted some for the winter. He also used the livers of conger to extract a crude oil for the hanging lamp known as the *crâsset* (cresset).[13] His wife made most of the clothes for the family with wool from their own sheep spun at home. Thus a farm was almost self-supporting. Things which could not be made at home were paid for on market day with eggs, butter and cider. This was indeed subsistence farming; the modern idea of exchanging produce for money was still in its infancy.

The farmer kept a yoke of oxen to draw his cart and help with ploughing, a custom still prevalent in parts of southern Europe. He kept a cow or two for milk and a few sheep for wool and mutton, which always attracted notice. Camden wrote in 1586: 'Many of their sheep have four horns'. In 1610, when Holland translated Camden into English, he added a note: 'They have six horns, three on each side, one bent towards the nose, another towards the neck, and the third standing upright between the other two'. Such sheep were not unknown in England, for Topsell's *Fourfooted Beasts* (1607), said, 'The rams in England have greater horns than any other rams in the world. Sometimes they have four or six horns'. Evidently they were commoner in Jersey than elsewhere, for Drayton wrote in his *Polyolbion* in 1617:

> Fair Jersey, first of these here scattered in the deep
> Peculiarly that breeds thy double-horned sheep.

Pigs were so numerous that every parish swore in a pig warden (*porcher*) to see that every pig was ringed and to impound the strays. Farmyards were full of fowls and geese, and turkeys are mentioned as early as 1620.[14] But wheat was the farmer's chief crop and in a good year he had a small surplus to export to Normandy, which brought in a little cash to purchase luxuries. Sons who sailed to Newfoundland also brought back a little more and the women earned a good deal by knitting. Yet it was a hard-working life for every member of the family. To Heylin, college don turned courtier, the countryfolk seemed 'very painful and laborious, and by reason of their continual toil, not a little affected by the melancholy surliness incident to ploughmen'.[15]

Artisans formed a very small group, and the Court took care that no rise in their wages should inconvenience their betters. Wool-combers and tailors might not receive more than three sous a day, thatchers three-and-a half sous, masons five, carpenters six, and there was a 10 livres fine for anyone who demanded more. The value of money is only in what it will buy: an account book of the Rector of St Mary[16] helps us to estimate the worth of money at this period: a wild rabbit cost three sous and a pound of butter five. So a tailor worked all day for the price of a rabbit and a mason for the price of a pound of butter.

At the bottom of the social scale was a proletariat of paupers. In Jersey, where the farms were small enough to be worked by the farmer's family, little outside labour was employed, and the lot of the landless man was hard. At the gate of every 'temple' was a box marked *Pour les Pauvres* and each parish had a fund, mostly composed of wheat rentes, or bequests to the church, called La Charité, the proceeds of which went to the poor as did the money collected after every service by the deacons, their collecting pots being of a design perhaps unique to the Island: they are cylindrical, with a handle and locked lid and a protruding slot for coins. The other church fund, *Le Trésor*, used its income for the upkeep of the church and rectory. *La Charité* and *Le Trésor* still retain these ancient names today.[17]

Nothing seemed able to reduce the number of beggars. Heylin was shocked at the way 'children were continually craving alms of every stranger'. In 1618 an attempt to enforce a compulsory poor rate failed, and in 1625 all who begged outside their parish were ordered to be put into the stocks. The unemployed problem proved insoluble.[18]

Normally the island was healthy. 'The air is very wholesome', wrote Camden, 'and the inhabitants are subject to no distempers but fevers, and these in September, which therefore they call *settembres*. For this cause no physicians are found among them.' The Rector's account book, already mentioned, shows that he dosed his parishioners with aloe pills, flowers of sulphur, rhubarb, senna and jalap. In this we may see a continuation of the care of the sick previously undertaken by the priests and monasteries. From time to time the island was swept by appalling visitations of the plague. There was one in 1518 when the Court held its sitting at the house now known as Grouville Court[19] and another in 1626 when the Guernsey and Normandy markets were closed to Jersey goods. In St Brelade, which normally had about nine funerals a year, 130 died in seven months, and the Register is full of entries such as: 'Buried in his garden', 'buried near her house'. Bearers could not be found to carry the bodies to the church yard.

This epidemic involved Bandinel in a new controversy. For six years he had acted as Rector of St Mary as well as St Brelade, but when his son Jacques was ordained, he secured his appointment to St Mary. The parish, however, was sad at having lost de la Place, perhaps because of his medical care, when he resigned from St Mary and went to Guernsey. When Madame Bandinel visited her son and went to church on Sunday, the Constable 'thrust her out with a halberd' on the plea that she might have brought infection from St Brelade, closed the Temple, allowed no more services, and put the Rector into quarantine and forbade visits. On the next Sunday the Dean occupied the pulpit and denounced such conduct as 'more meet for Papists in Mary's day than Protestants'. The Constable reported him for treason, declaring that he had said, 'We are living in a reign worse than Mary's'. The Council took a serious view of this and wrote to the Royal Court. 'The complaints against the Bandinels must be further examined. Take strict examinations of those undutiful speeches alleged to have been uttered.' The Dean had to cross to England before he was finally cleared. It was on his return journey that he was captured by Dunkirkers.[20]

We are now approaching the Civil War, but before the cannon opened fire, Jersey enjoyed 10 peaceful years, the lull before the storm. Sir Philippe, as Lieutenant-Governor, lived at Mont Orgueil Castle with his wife and their 11 children, and here, as King's representative, he maintained a little Vice-Regal court. Distinguished visitors from France and England were frequently entertained: once there arrived from France five Portuguese princesses, waiting for a ship to take them to Holland. On another occasion, the Duke of Vendôme, half-brother of the Queen of England, claimed hospitality when he fled from France to escape a charge of hiring hermits to bewitch Richelieu.[21] A frequent visitor was Sir Philippe's nephew George, son of his favourite brother Elie. He had joined the navy and been given command of the *Lion's Whelps*, little boats especially designed for chasing pirates. In 1640 George married his first cousin, Elizabeth, Sir Philippe's youngest daughter, the wedding taking place at the Castle.

During these quiet years two noteworthy events occurred. In 1632 Sir Philippe was in London: 16 years before he had obtained through Conway a promise from James I of a grant 'for the maintenance at the universities of poor scholars recommended by the States'. Nothing had come of this, so now he approached Laud and found him sympathetic, for Laud knew how half-hearted was Jersey's Anglicanism, and realised that it would help his plans if the island clergy could be trained at Oxford instead of at Saumur. The estate of a London Alderman, the Hobart property in St Lawrence Jewry, had escheated to the Crown in 1635, and this, with the Ridge moiety of the Medmenham lands, was given by the King, persuaded by Laud, in 1636 to endow three fellowships (*socii*) at Oxford. With this windfall he thus redeemed his father's promise. The original deed spoke of three fellowships at Exeter, Pembroke and Jesus, for natives of

Jersey and Guernsey 'and our Royal intention is that after a convenient time the aforesaid Fellows shall return to their respective islands there to serve God'. In 1854 the Oxford University Commission of which François Jeune, as Master of Pembroke, was a member had the Charles I fellowships converted into twice as many scholarships, though for many years the terms of their award were not satisfactorily settled.[22]

In 1638 Mont Orgueil received a prisoner with twice-cropped ears and S.L. (seditious libeller) branded on each cheek. This was William Prynne, an acid little Puritan lawyer, who had set out with his pen to reform the morals of the age. In one of his books, *Histriomastix* which denounced the immorality of the theatre, he had asked how ''... any Christian woman could be so whorishly impudent' as to appear on the stage. Unfortunately a few days before the book was published Charles' French-born queen had appeared in a pastoral play, and this was taken to be an attack on her. Heylin, who since his visit to Jersey had become a Court chaplain, compiled a list of quotations which sent poor Prynne to the pillory with a sentence of imprisonment for life. The orders sent to de Carteret were, 'Suffer none but his keeper to speak with him. Permit him neither pen nor paper and no book but the Bible'. The Castle accounts show £10 12s. spent on irons 'for bars for Mr Prynne's windows' (the cell in which he was kept is shown to visitors to Mont Orgueil). Sir Philippe, however, received him kindly, for he admired his erudition and to some extent sympathised with his Puritan scruples. To Laud's indignation, he obtained an order from the King allowing Prynne considerable liberty inside the Castle walls, and before long he became almost a guest of the de Carteret family. He passed his time in writing verse (no one could call it poetry), and in concocting healing plasters which obtained a wide reputation in the Island. 'I cured hundreds gratis', he said. He dedicated a poem on Mont Orgueil to Sir Philippe 'as a small pledge of my thanks,

> . . . till opportunity
> And better dayes enable me to finde,
> Some other means to pay all that's behinde'.[23]

He sensed, however, that all was not going well among Jerseymen. 'Most have this Norman quality, that never a two of them do really trust one another, and will prove treacherous at any time to their nearest friends and kindred.' For generations family feuds had been poisoning the blood stream of Jersey, and about this time they were festering to a head.

De Carteret had made the fatal mistake of keeping too many of the reins of power in his own hands. Not only was he Bailiff and Lieutenant-Governor and virtually Receiver-General,[24] but his brother Elie was Solicitor-General and his cousin Helier Attorney-General; three cousins and a nephew were Jurats. Of the 12 captains who commanded the Militia, at least seven were de Carterets, two more were nephews and one his sister's husband. Moreover he had secured what his enemies called the 'eternizing' of the de Carteret domination by procuring a promise from the King that, when he died, the next Bailiff should be his brother Elie, and the next his nephew George. Such a concentration of officers in the de Carteret family clan was bound to cause jealousy. Families like the Lemprières and the Dumaresqs resented being shut out from all share in their island's government, they being the other two most wealthy and influential families. But at first they could do little, for Sir Philippe was very firmly in the saddle. His mother was a Poulet and his Poulet cousins could pull strings for him in Whitehall, where his friend Conway was now President of the Council.

But then he made a false move which led to endless trouble. He detested Bandinel, the Dean who had moved to live at Bandinel Farm in St Martin, and was now a fairly close neighbour. The more he saw of him the less he liked him, and he petitioned the Council, unsuccessfully, for a Royal Commission[25] 'to enquire unto the proceedings of David Bandinel, an alien made Dean'.

Eventually he was stung into taking a step which proved indefensible. When the Deanery was revived, the King had endowed it with the great tithes of St Saviour, but de Carteret now claimed these for his own exchequer, on the argument that when Jermyn was made Governor his Patent granted him all the revenues conferred on his predecessor Peyton, and the latter had received the St Saviour's tithes; therefore, he claimed, Jermyn's Patent, which was later than Bandinel's, cancelled the grant to the Dean. This claim entailed another visit to England.

De Carteret found Westminster in no mood to attend to Jersey business, for a revolution was brewing. King Charles had been drilled by his father to believe in the Divine Right of Kings to rule; but the Commons believed in their divine right to discuss grievances. This the King would not tolerate and for 11 years he ruled without a Parliament. But no Parliament meant no taxes, and when Laud tried to impose the Prayer Book on Scotland, a land where ceremonies were more hated than sin, the Scots sprang to arms and poured over the border. The bankrupt King was forced to call a Parliament. This only lasted for three months, but the Scots marched steadily on and, in October 1640, Charles was compelled to call another, the famous Long Parliament, which did not disperse until 1653. Then things began to happen. Charles' chief advisers, Laud and Strafford, were sent to the Tower and a Bill was introduced to extirpate Episcopacy root and branch.

In the midst of this turmoil it is not surprising that Sir Philippe could secure no attention, so he returned to Jersey and summoned Bandinel before the Royal Court, claiming not only the St Saviour's tithes for the future, but the repayment of all that the Dean had received for the last 20 years. But not even his own Jurats would declare a Royal Patent to be waste paper. So de Carteret appealed to the Council and again crossed the Channel, and the end of the tithe dispute can be told briefly. In January 1642 the Council ordered the Vicomte to sequestrate the tithes and hold them until the case was decided. (Were they all paid in kind?; if so, where did the Vicomte store this considerable amount of corn?) The King then fled from London to the north and the Council followed. The Archbishop of York was asked to examine the evidence, and on his advice de Carteret's appeal was dismissed and the Dean's right to the tithes confirmed. But long before the case was settled, both men had become entangled in the ferment of revolutionary London. More than one Jerseyman had come to London to fish in troubled waters. Bandinel was naturally feeling bitter, but he lingered there, hoping that Jersey would have a new Governor and that he might prevent Sir Philippe from being his Lieutenant. But the man who crushed Presbyterianism in Jersey was ill-advised to call attention to his presence in Puritan London. His old opponent, Samuel de la Place, was also in the capital, and he persuaded the Commons to have Bandinel arrested. Prynne says, 'He met with articles of complaint against himself for gross oppressions done as Dean, for which he was committed for two or three months to the Sergeant-at-Arms' custody'.[26]

Three anti de Carteret Jurats now came to Westminster: Michel Lemprière, Seigneur of Diélament, Henri Dumaresq, Seigneur of Samarès, and Abraham Hérault, bringing *A Humble Information of State of His Majesty's Isle of Jersey with part of the Grievances of the inhabitants.*[27] They complained, among other things, that 'Sir Philippe doth entrust with all the chiefest offices those of his own name to get the whole disposing of the Island into his own hands' ...

> he bears sundry offices incompatible in one person, Governor, Bailiff, and Farmer of the King's Revenues ... he procureth the nominations of his own creatures for the Bench of Justice ´... with arbitrary powers he doth commit to prison without order of the Court ... he hath procured from the Lords in Council the alteration of some of our laws without consent of the States.

There were 21 charges in all, some uncomfortably true, and an autocratic pro-Consul might expect short shrift from the men who had impeached Strafford. Things looked black for de Carteret, but the Jurats made a mistake.

One of the first acts of the Long Parliament had been to release Prynne, and he had returned to London in triumph. 'The people rang the bells, yea, they strawed the way with flowers.' The Jurats thought that this Puritan martyr would be the very man to present their petition. But he owed a deep debt of gratitude to Sir Philippe for his kindness when he was in prison and he quietly suppressed the petition and, 'though they used their utmost endeavours and solicited him every day', they could not persuade him to do anything with it. His advocacy of Sir Philippe, in spite of their differing political views, had considerable influence on local events of the time. So they had their petition printed as *A Word left by the Way touching Sir Philip Carteret of Jersey*, and deposited packets of it on the stocks in Cheapside and in other public places, 'desiring any well-affected who should find them to present them to the Houses of Parliament'. Both sides have left accounts of their activities in London, Prynne in his *Lyar Confounded* and the Jurats in their *Pseudomastix*.[28]

When Bandinel was released, he got in touch with Dumaresq, and their efforts became less amateurish. They persuaded the Earl of Strafford to bring their complaint before the House of Lords and it was referred to a Committee; here Prynne undertook de Carteret's defence. Dumaresq[29] and the Dean were asked to show proof that they were commissioned to speak in the name of the Island, and they had to admit that they were acting on their own initiative, whereas Sir Philippe unrolled an Act of the States appointing him their Deputy. Dumaresq was then told to produce witnesses to prove his charges and he had to answer that his witnesses were in Jersey. The Jurats complained that Sir Philippe's 'politic carriage and Mr Prynne's lying commendations' so impressed the Lords that they threatened to commit the petitioners for circulating 'libellous Articles which they could not prove'.

But though de Carteret thus triumphed in the Lords, there was still danger from the Commons, until a letter arrived from Hungerford, Gentleman Porter at Elizabeth Castle, who had made a trip to St Malo to spy out the land. He reported, 'There are come to St Maloes 4,000 soldiers and 8,000 more are expected every day. The Commanders are men of good experience'. As a matter of fact these troops had only been brought there to be shipped to Spain, but everyone knew that Charles' Queen was trying to stir up her sister-in-law, the Queen Regent of France (Anne of Austria) to make some diversion in the King's favour. With this letter in his hand Prynne had no difficulty in persuading both Houses that Jersey was in danger, and in March 1642 Sir Philippe was 'freed from further attendance on Parliament and required to repair forthwith to his charge'.[30]

On 21 April he presided over the States. The minute runs

> Sir Philippe de Carteret, having returned from his voyage to England, declares that the divisions between King and Parliament prevent their obtaining what the States desire, and proposes that they correct internal abuses, and live in peace, which resolution the States acquiesce in.

He showed them the King's Commission, dated 16 February 1642, appointing him Governor during Thomas Jermyn's non-residence. A motion repudiating the charges brought against de Carteret 'in a certain petition presented to Parliament' was carried, though not unanimously; a Public Fast was appointed 'to divert the wrath of God threatened by the divisions in England', and to show their earnestness the Constables were ordered to confiscate the violins of all who fiddled on Sunday.[31]

In September the Dean presented to the Court the Order in Council confirming his possession of the tithes. He walked towards his usual seat (the Court and the States then met in the same building), but the Bailiff forbade him to sit there, stating that he was a criminal on bail, a reference to his arrest by the House of Commons. When this was overruled, de Carteret appealed to the Court for protection. Dumaresq and the Dean had printed a French edition of their pamphlet and circulated it in the Island. Dumaresq denied that the accusations were libellous and pleaded the rule that all disputes between Jurats and Governor must be settled by the Privy Council. The Court avoided the necessity of coming to an awkward decision by accepting this plea.[32]

For the moment the Island was left with nothing to discuss but bad weather. Week after week the rain descended in torrents, and in mid-October most of the harvest was still rotting in the fields, a situation referred to as 'the incompetence of the bad weather' (*l'incompétence du mauvais temps*): a masterly and timeless observation. It was also reported that many houses fell to the ground, so highlighting the danger of stone walls with only clay filling as mortar.[33]

Chapter Fourteen

THE CIVIL WAR BEGINS, 1642-1643

Amor populi praesidium regis. (His people's love is a king's safeguard.)
Motto chosen by Charles I for his gold coins

NO HISTORIAN can tell history precisely to scale, for he is at the mercy of his authorities. An epoch-making event may have to be treated briefly if contemporary records fail, and then may come a decade where one is almost snowed under with documentary evidence. We reach such a period now. Thanks largely to Jean Chevalier, the chatty town vingtenier, who jotted down in his journal[1] all the gossip of the market place, but also to other documents such as *Les Mémoires de la Famille La Cloche*, we know almost as much about the Civil War period as the people who lived through it.

When Charles raised his standard at Nottingham in August 1642, and even in October when the first battle was fought at Edgehill, Sir Philippe hoped to keep his island out of the struggle. Prynne wrote, 'His desire was not to look on the King and Parliament as divided, but united, and he wished to adhere cordially to both without siding against either'. He drew up a lengthy memorial on the state of the defence and the Militia, with recommendations on what needed to be done.[2] Others also hoped to avoid participation in the quarrels of England, and even there, several counties drew up 'county treaties', declaring that they remained loyal both to King and Parliament. Hobbes wrote, 'Few of the common people care much for either of the causes', and de Carteret's opponent Lemprière, as Bailiff in the Commonwealth, saw to it that the privileges and charters of the Island remained untouched.

In Jersey the reasons for neutrality were especially strong. No one had any grievance against the King: he had not in any way interfered with the constitution, he had confirmed the privileges, granted many petitions and presented the Fellowships. The trouble with the English Parliament had nothing to do with Jersey, but, as already observed, war fever is terrifyingly infectious and notoriously hard to control. The rivalry between Lemprière and de Carteret also had a bearing on the situation.

Jerseymen visiting England brought back evil reports of the King, and Brevint's journal probably reveals what many islanders were saying. He declares that Charles was 'plotting to make the English slaves by means of his German cavalry, seizing the common lands to make his private parks, issuing patents for malt, coal, salt, farthings, pins, soap, tobacco, almost everything … and that quintessence of oppression known as Ship Money!'. Religious fears were aroused, for everyone knew that the Queen, Henrietta Maria of France, was a papist and that she was urging Catholics abroad to send troops to help Charles to make himself absolute. Many feared that the triumph of the Queen would bring to Jersey the thumb-screws, the rack and the Inquisition. Some young seigneurs swaggered about with *Vive le Roy* on their hats,[4] but Chevalier says, 'the great majority of the common people ranged themselves on the other side'. Instinctively Jersey sympathised with the English Puritans and the Guernsey Parliamentarians.

Though religious fears were the main cause of the unease, personal spite also played a part. Everyone who had resented anything that Sir Philippe had done during his 15 years in office now made use of the unrest to try to get revenge. Dean Bandinel was a notorious example. He, who had been Laud's protégé and the would-be uprooter of Calvinism, now swung all his craft and energy over to the Puritan side and de Carteret's opponents formed a committee to support Parliament. Its most active members were three Rectors, the Dean, his son Jacques, Rector of St Mary, and Pierre d'Assigny, Rector of St Helier,[5] an eloquent ex-monk, restless, rabid and revengeful. Its backbone was a group of five Jurats, Michel Lemprière, Seigneur of Diélament, a genuine patriot, graduate of Huguenot Saumur and fired with the democratic ideas that lay at the root of Calvinism; Henri Dumaresq, Seigneur of Samarès, who had first quarrelled with Sir Philippe over a militia appointment: 'He laid down his Captain's staff', wrote Prynne, 'in the open field because he could not have his will in disposing of a Lieutenant's place' – but his visit to London had imbued him with the ultra-radical theories then seething in the city, with Abraham Hérault, Benjamin Bisson and François de Carteret, Seigneur of La Hague, who had drifted into this group through a personal squabble with the head of the family. All who followed their lead were known as *Les Bien Affectionnés*.[6] One of their rallying cries was that the church was in danger, because of the Catholic Queen's influence over her husband.

The man who made neutrality impossible was Sir Philippe's nephew, George. On the eve of hostilities he was one of the best known officers in the Navy, and Parliament had offered him the post of Vice-Admiral, but the King had forbidden him to accept. He had come to Jersey, but, 'being impatient of being quiet while his master was in the field, he transported himself to Cornwall to raise a troop of horse'. The Royalists, however, realised that he would be more useful on the sea and gave him the task of supplying them with munitions from France. London ships with cargoes from the East were lumbering up the Channel Londonward, knowing nothing of the war; and, as London was Parliamentarian, they were considered fair spoil. Many of these de Carteret captured and sold in St Malo and with the money bought pikes and powder for Cavalier armies in the west. In January 1643 he called into Jersey and commandeered 'divers hogsheads of ammunition out of the Castle' for the beleaguered garrison at Pendennis.[7] Sir Philippe pleaded that he dared not disobey an order from an officer holding the King's commission, but this was stretching neutrality to breaking point.

On 16 February Parliament ordered the arrest of Sir Philippe. The five Jurats on the Parliamentary committee were commissioned 'to apprehend his person and bring him to Parliament to answer to such crimes as shall be objected against him'. But this was more easily said than done. As Lieutenant-Governor de Carteret was commander of the garrison, and the Cornish and Irish[8] mercenaries in the Castle cared little for Jersey Jurats; so for the moment nothing was done.

Sir Philippe, however, realised that he had crossed the Rubicon. On the day that the order for his arrest was signed, he presented to the States a commission from the King that for a year he had kept up his sleeve. 'Take into custody all the Castles and Forts and deliver not the charge thereof to any without special warrant under Our Hand.' He then tried to make the whole population take an oath to oppose 'all who bear arms against the King on any pretext whatsoever'. But Chevalier reports, 'the generality refused, very few excepted'.

He summoned the States again on 23 March. He knew this meeting would be critical, so he took with him an armed guard. He procured another royal letter in which the King pledged himself to his 'well-beloved and trusty counsellors', the States,

> to preserve the ancient government of the church with their liberties, persons, and estates without any innovation whatsoever; but in case any person (for we have of late had too much experience of like spirits) do reject or attempt to cause others to disobey our Governor or his Deputy, we command you to apprehend such malefactors, and upon any insurrection to subjugate such persons by martial power.

But before this could be read, Lemprière rose, with the order for de Carteret's arrest. Sir Philippe made the perfectly sound constitutional reply: 'The islanders had nothing to do with Parliament, but only with the King in Council', and demanded to see the warrant. Lemprière had brought only a copy, so Sir Philippe adroitly ruled that the States could not concern themselves with copies, that the original document must be placed in the Greffier's hands. Lemprière then tried to leave, but the soldiers at the door with 'halberds pointed at his breast', forced him to remain while the King's letter was read. But his friends had taken steps to ensure his safety, for Dumaresq had called out the militia of St Clement. The men of St Saviour, Lemprière's parish, were marching towards the town. Even St Ouen's was arming. A lad slipped into the Court-room with the news, and de Carteret withdrew with his guard to Elizabeth Castle never to return.[9]

A few days later he called a meeting in the Castle. It was not a session of the States, as all the Rectors and many Jurats and Constables were absent. *Pseudomastix* calls it a conclave of his kindred and adherents. They drew up an address to Parliament, stating that he was 'willing to answer before the King and his Parliament all objections imputed to him', provided that time was given to get the King's permission to hand over the Castles to a Deputy. The address was entrusted to Jean Le Couteur,[10] who was taking money to England to ransom Algerian captives. But in London he was recognised as one of de Carteret's staff and arrested. As a letter found on him was from Sir Philippe to the King, the address was regarded as camouflage and got no further than the Committee for the Safety of the Kingdom.

Meanwhile Osmund Cooke,[11] who had been Prynne's warder at Mont Orgueil, managed to enlist his help. That shrewd lawyer devised a scheme by which all charges against Sir Philippe should be referred to a Royal Commission, which was of course the correct way to deal with Channel Island problems; and he proposed that he himself should be one of the Commission, with Sir Peter Osborne, Lieutenant-Governor of Guernsey, and Nathaniel Darrell. This sounded a well-balanced tribunal, a Puritan, a Royalist and a neutral naval officer, but they all happened to be personal friends of de Carteret and could be relied upon to acquit him. When the King saw Prynne's name, he refused to sign the document and so knocked this ingenious plan on the head.

While waiting for answers from King and Parliament Sir Philippe made overtures to his enemies. He wrote to his cousin François de Carteret, 'I consent to appear before Parliament to answer the charges against me, as soon as I obtain the King's permission to hand over the Castles inviolate. To win peace for our island I offer of my own free will what you tried to procure by force'. The Committee, however, received this offer in silence. They took the line that since a warrant was out for his arrest, he must surrender unconditionally.[12]

There was as yet no open war. The Castle troops came into the town to do their marketing and Sir Philippe's friends went out to visit him. But the townsfolk began to barricade the streets leading to the shore, and to stop this the Castle cannon opened fire on them. But Sir Philippe continued his appeals. On 27 April he wrote to the Royal Court, repudiating the slanders that he was about to turn Papist, to seize the parish guns, to bring in French troops and Irish rebels. He declared that he remained in the Castle only to avoid bloodshed, continuing,

> Seeing that I have lost credit with the people, see to it that you maintain yours. Chastise and stamp out mutiny. Bring to justice all who spread lies against the King. As for the authority I hold, I cannot be deprived of it, save by His Majesty, and by virtue of this I proclaim as public enemies all who call out the Militia without orders from the King's officers.

And he added, 'If the King and His Parliament have disputes, why should we interfere?'.

One day he committed a definite act of war. Some Parliamentarian ships were chasing one of the King's frigates, which ran for refuge under the guns of Elizabeth Castle; he fired on them and drove them off. The pose of neutrality could now no longer be maintained. A few days later he decided to visit his wife (née Anne Dowse[13]); she had remained in Mont Orgueil Castle, bravely holding it for the King when he moved to Elizabeth Castle; by avoiding the town he reached Gorey unchallenged. But when the Committee heard of this they resolved to arrest him on his return. D'Assigny, the excitable Frenchman who was Rector of St Helier, 'urged', according to Chevalier, 'that he must be captured dead or alive'. So they rang the tocsin, beat the drums and summoned the Vingtenier (Chevalier himself) of the Town Vingtaine, who kept the keys of the magazine, to distribute pikes to the soldiers. 'But I knew that this might lead to bloodshed and refused to hand over the keys, though Philippe Le Boutillier threatened me with his sword.' However, de Cartert evaded arrest by sleeping at Mont Orgueil and slipping back to the islet early in the morning when the pickets had gone home.

The Castle now became a rendez-vous for wandering Royalists, a half-way house between Cornwall and St Malo, and those hotheads began to press de Carteret to use his troops against the rebels. But Parliament struck the first blow. Four Parliamentary ships landed sailors in Bouley Bay and arrested some of the leading Royalists who were outside the Castles. At first they were kept on the ships, but they were so seasick that in compassion the captains put them ashore. For a time they were imprisoned in the town, but later they were released on parole.[14] The feeling of the townsfolk was shown by the welcome given to the sailors. 'They lodged them in taverns and houses', says Chevalier, 'and the women took them beds to sleep in. Others took sheets, others counterpanes. Everyone's cry was "What can I do to help?".'

The first actual fighting was on 11 June. This was also market day and the town was full of people. Sir Philippe ordered Laurens Hamptonne, the Viscount,[15] to read a Proclamation in the market offering the King's pardon to all who would lay down their arms, with the exception of the Dean and the Committee. We have two accounts of what happened, that of de Carteret being, 'They sat on horseback in the market with their pistols at the saddle. The Proclamation began, the people flocked to listen, but the rebels caused the bell to be rung and the people dispersed. The townsmen took arms, so the Vicomte and the gentlemen retired hither'. Chevalier's version is,

> When the Vicomte began to read, the English gentlemen, who were new to the island and did not understand our ways, seeing the people running up to listen, took fright and unslung their carbines. The people seeing that fled in panic, upsetting the merchants' stalls, and the English gentlemen hastily returned to the Castle.[16]

They were furious and urged Sir Philippe to attack. 'They cried out on me', he wrote, 'that delays did spoil all. I was fain to give way, persuaded by those who had more experience in martial affairs than I.' He warned the town that in two hours a bombardment would begin and ordered non-combatants to withdraw. Then he opened fire. Fifty balls fell on the house roofs and the church was hit twice. Under cover of this the Royalist officers led out a body of Cornishmen, 'themselves ahorse, colours displayed, drums beating'. Chevalier remarks, 'They thought that the cannonade would have so terrified the people, that they would enter without resistance. But they were mistaken. At the sound of the tocsin the people sprang to arms. Men flocked in from the country and built barricades'. 'The rebels', wrote de Carteret, 'lined the houses and outwalls with musketeers, and drew down two of their field pieces and played on our men who were approaching in the open with no cover.' The south of the town was protected by the town wall (*la muraille de la Ville*), so the attackers wormed their way through the sandhills up the bed of the brook known as the Douet d'Auneville, and launched their attack where the west road entered the town at the point now called Charing Cross.[17] They stormed the Maison Billot, the Dumaresq's big house,[18] but the Rue d'Egypte[19] was protected by a strong barricade. News came that the tide was rising and would soon cut them off from their base, and so their attack ended in an ignominious retreat.

The Committee then took steps to prevent further sorties. 'The day after this action', wrote de Carteret, 'both castles were beset, and continue so surrounded that not a dog can stir out of either, and none have been suffered to venture in.' They were, however, in no real danger, for they could still communicate by sea with St Malo and with one another. 'We have provisions and men enough', he wrote to his wife. His worst worry was when the beer boat was late in arriving.

On 18 June a beggar boy brought to the castle a reply to Sir Philippe's April letter. It began with a long diatribe, drafted by the Dean, and ended with the demand, 'in the name of the people' that he go before Parliament to answer the charges against him. The reply was mainly a bitter attack on Bandinel, whom he likened to a mountebank mouthing on a market stall to sell his quack medicines. 'I hope they may not hopelessly embitter the entrails of our land.' But he made one definite suggestion. He quoted an order of Henry VII which stated: 'If any variance arise betwixt Captain and Jurats, let neither use force against the other, but let both have recourse to the good graces of the King.' And he added, 'In God's name let this order be obeyed'. He proposed a truce, till the King could decide.[20]

There then followed a stream of futile letters. In one he ordered the Lieutenant-Bailiff to arrest the Dean, saying, 'I charge him with high treason'. In another he offered any of his children as hostages, if his opponents would surrender hostages of the same standing. But appeal had been made to the sword, and the sword must decide.

Sickness broke out in the castle. On 29 July Gédéon, Sir Philippe's fourth son, died.[21] A brief truce was arranged and soldiers bore the coffin half way to the shore, where 12 de Carteret tenants met it and carried it to the family grave at St Ouen. On 10 August Sir Philippe himself fell ill, and on the 16th he knew that he was dying. He dictated a note to the Committee, saying, 'Of your Christian charity allow Monsieur La Cloche to minister to me Christian comfort, and permit my poor wife to render to me her last service by closing my eyes'. La Cloche, Rector of St Ouen, was an ardent Royalist, and the Committee suspected a trick. But they granted permission for Sir Philippe's wife, mother and sisters, and one of the other Rectors, to visit him on condition that Captain Lane, the leader of the attack on the town, was surrendered as a hostage. When he was not handed over, Sir Philippe's mother and sisters were turned back. His wife too was at first refused.

On the 23rd the Committee were convinced that he really was dying and granted passes to his mother and sisters. On the following day they escorted from Mont Orgueil his wife and daughter, but by then he was only able to raise his hand to them in a gesture of farewell and he died that day.[22] *Pseudomastix* reports that, 'he gave orders that they should not bury his body till the King had overcome his enemies', and Chevalier confirms this story: 'His widow sent to St Malo for a surgeon to embalm his body, and it was kept unburied according to his dying wish in a leaden coffin'. It was buried at St Ouen 10 months later, when the Royalists had recovered the Island. When the church was restored in 1869 the coffin was opened, and he was seen to have been over six feet tall, unusual at that period, and to have reddish hair.

Hungerford, the Gentleman Porter, assumed command in the castle.[23] The Committee had realised by this time that they knew nothing of siege craft and that the capture was a job for soldiers, so they wrote to Parliament asking for a 'Chief Commander of some eminent quality'. Parliament had appointed the Earl of Warwick as Captain-General of Guernsey and Jersey, but he, as Admiral of the Parliamentary fleet, had no time to attend personally to the islands. So on 6 July he sent Leonard Lydcot, a young Sergeant-Major (in those days this ranked next to a Lieutenant-Colonel). His Jersey mission was such a fiasco that Jersey historians have tended to regard Lydcot as incompetent, though his record in England gives a far different picture. He had already attracted notice as a brilliant cavalry leader, and he became Colonel at the age of 30; and his Regiment of Horse distinguished itself in many Civil War battles. In 1645 he was Commander-in-Chief of the forces round Banbury, and in 1651 he commanded the left wing at Cromwell's great victory at Inverkeithing.

In Jersey, however, he was given an impossible task. Prynne had warned Parliament that 'both castles were so strongly situated that they must have a fleet to block them up by sea, as they would receive by every tide whatever they wanted from France'. But Jurat Hérault's son Jean, with his persuasive tongue, drew such a rosy picture of Jersey's enthusiasm for Parliament, how thousands of armed militiamen only awaited a leader, that Prynne's warnings were disregarded, and Lydcot was allowed to sail with three Captains and three Lieutenants only; he also brought with him his bride, her mother and sister, and his father and brother. He received a warm welcome.[24] Chevalier says that 'the townswomen made ready with the utmost glee, beds, linen, towels, table-cloths, utensils of every kind, and bore them to his lodgings'. They mobbed his six officers, struggling to sew ribbons on their hats. The Royalists were now known as the *Réfractaires* as opposed to the *Bien Affectionnés.*

In August a proclamation was received from the King, offering a pardon to all except Benjamin Bisson, François de Carteret, Henry Dumaresq, David and James Bandinel, if they returned to their allegiance to His Majesty. But on 29 August the States met, nine Jurats, five Rectors and 11 Constables (25 members out of a total of 36 and including those mentioned in the proclamation) and swore in Michel Lemprière as the new Bailiff appointed by the 'two Houses of Parliament'; he then administered the oath to Lydcot as Lieutenant-Governor in the time-honoured form: 'You do swear before God to acknowledge Charles our King as supreme Governor throughout all his Kingdoms'. This was no hypocrisy. The Parliamentary party, even in England, was not yet Republican; it professed to be fighting to deliver the King from the hands of evil counsellors.[25]

Lydcot quickly showed himself to be a man of vigour. Next day he rode to Mont Orgueil and mapped out positions for the trenches. He tightened the investment of Elizabeth Castle, so that no one could slip in or out. Hungerford had to rely for news on his wife's washing line at St Aubin. Three sheets hung out on the line meant 'Good news from England'; one sheet meant 'Bad'. Two sheets with two shirts between them meant that she had no news at all. He also asked her to take a walk along St Aubin's boulevard in the morning so that he could see her through his telescope, '*sa longue veux*' and would know that she was well.[26] Lydcot remounted the guns at the end of the Castle Bridge, strengthened St Aubin's Tower with earthworks and made a tour of the parishes, inspecting the Militia and administering the oath to the inhabitants *en masse* of loyalty to 'the King, the Parliament and the Lieutenant-Governor they have sent'.

Elizabeth Castle kept things lively. Hungerford sent out horsemen on the sands as decoy ducks to tempt the Militia within range of his sharpshooters, and for 10 weeks he bombarded the town with cannon balls. Chevalier noted day by day exactly where each fell. For example:

> September 30. Six balls were fired. One broke the churchyard wall. One entered a house and broke a spinning-wheel by a bed in which four were sleeping. A third rent the roof of a house and fell down the chimney next door. A fourth passed through the roof of a house from end to end. The fifth flew right over the town and the sixth fell in the suburbs.

Here is another of his bombardment pictures:

> October 7. A salvo of twenty guns were fired on market day, when business was at its height. Crowds were gathered from every parish, women who took no part in politics and innocent babes who did not know their right hand from their left. Cannon balls fell like thunderbolts. The terror-stricken crowd threw themselves on the ground, or rushed to take cover in the houses, upsetting the stalls of the haberdashers. The cobblers' tables of shoes were turned topsy-turvy and money scattered on the ground, for everyone knew that cannon balls are no respecters of persons. A Norman was killed as he stood chattering; the ball struck him between the shoulders, came out under his arm and then rebounded from a wall into the belly of a horse.[27]

The town leader was now d'Assigny. The previous Sunday had been the day for the quarterly Communion service, and at the close the militant Rector had called on his congregation to follow him to the brow of the hill to cut turfs for a new redoubt. He distributed spades to the people as they left the church, 'but many even of the "well affected" were shocked by such sabbath-breaking on Communion day'.[28]

Meanwhile from Mont Orgueil the Royal banner was also flying. Lady de Carteret was still in command, but she had with her her nephew Philippe, often known as Philippe de Grouville,[29] George's brother, and he was Colonel; also her son Philippe, now Seigneur of St Ouen and a professional soldier, and Captain Richard Legge. When they saw a siege was inevitable they secured reinforcements from France. With night raids they rounded up most of the cattle in the neighbourhood, and by constant sorties they gave the besiegers an uneasy time, once almost capturing Lydcot himself.

By the end of October enthusiasm for the war was ebbing and Chevalier writes, 'the people were tired of keeping watch and ward'. D'Assigny might crack over their heads the whip of excommunication — 'If you will not give us whole-hearted support. I will sever you from Christ's church' — but he could not rekindle their zeal, and for this there were several reasons. The Militia realised that they too had been given an impossible task. They had proved themselves to be sturdy fighters; they had repulsed the attack on the town and repelled every sally from the castles, but the castles themselves seemed impregnable, and to storm the walls would mean an enormous loss of life; shooting at them was like shooting at a rock, for the guns were too far from their target. So long as supplies could reach them by sea the siege might go on till doomsday. The men had been away from their farms for six months and the women had gathered in the harvest, but ploughing was men's work and they were eager to get home.

The lawlessness that war brings in its train was filling decent people with disgust. Our diarist moans on this score: 'In civil war the fear of God is thrown overboard. Looting, rape and killing are accounted trifles, and oaths are in every mouth. The people abandon themselves to evil, stealing sheep, goats and fowls'. Indeed in his preface Chevalier states that his pictures of life at this period (*comme en un tableaux tiré aux vif*) are drawn so that the reader may be aware of the evils of civil war: lying, slandering — the reign of the devil.[30]

Moreover the leaders themselves were at loggerheads. Friction between Governor and Bailiff was always common in Jersey and in this case it was inevitable. Lydcot was a soldier with a firm belief in the efficacy of military law; Lemprière was a Jerseyman, determined to maintain the island's constitution. Matters were not improved by Lydcot's ignorance of French. Chevalier's view is that 'He rode roughshod over the Royal Court, declaring that the capture of the castles was more urgent than fooling with Jurats', and this is confirmed by a supporter of Lydcot who said, 'The Lieutenant-Governor, seeing that the Court was prejudicial to the safety of the island, forbade Lemprière to hold it any longer till the States was in better order, but he and the rest would not obey. The States assembled contrary to the will of the Lieutenant-Governor'.[31]

The religious situation too had become complicated. There was no longer the clear-cut division between Episcopacy and Calvinism. Parliamentarians had at first been identified with Puritanism, and for the sake of its faith, Jersey had turned a blind eye to much that was obnoxious. 'The most lawless were deemed virtuous because everyone thought that this was a fight for the Religion' (and to a Huguenot 'the Religion' meant Calvinism). But Jersey discovered that Lydcot was 'steeped in the errors of the Independents.' To a Calvinist this was a heresy as dangerous as Popery. Calvinism stood for a strong, united, national church, able to enforce God's laws on public and private life, whereas Independency stood for a multitude of tiny churches where three Christians could form a congregation and 300 would be too many. To Calvinists this was a rending of the seamless robe of Christ.

Other religious novelties, too, were appearing in the Island. Lemprière, the Bailiff, and his brother Nicolas had turned Anabaptist, so had Dumaresq of Samarès. Churchmen like the Bandinels stood aghast, for their church seemed threatened with disruption. Laymen too were disturbed at the prospect of religious anarchy, and began to consider the possibility of making peace with the King.

Bandinel proclaimed a fast for 11 October,[32] 'to pray for the reunion of the King with his kingdom'. A few days later he went to Mont Orgueil on an errand of appeasement, but Lady de Carteret refused to see him. So he smuggled a letter into the Castle, in which, if Chevalier is to be believed, he offered with truly Italian guile to invite the Committee to dinner at St Martin's Rectory, where they would be surprised and taken prisoner. 'But he fell from the frying pan into the fire, for when Lydcot learnt of his visit to the Castle, he sent men to arrest him; but he hid himself so securely that they could not find him.'[33]

Meanwhile the Royalists at St Malo were watching the trend of events. One of them, Etienne La Cloche, the Rector of St Ouen, was starting off to visit the King at Oxford and urged that the time had come to strike, when a letter arrived from Charles appointing Captain George Carteret Bailiff and Lieutenant-Governor, and promising him a thousand men with which to reduce the Island. The King also sent a proclamation, in which he promised to maintain religion as it was in the days of Elizabeth, that is to restore Presbyterianism, and to pardon all who had taken up arms, provided they now laid them down.

La Cloche begged permission to try to recover the Island without bloodshed. On Saturday 28 October he landed after dark in an unguarded creek near Plémont, and on Sunday afternoon he went to his church, where another minister was preaching, and at the close of the service read the Proclamation from the pulpit and 'harangued the parishioners, urging them to obey God and King'. He had hoped to get his parish to rise before the town could move and then call a meeting of the States to hear the King's message. But Lydcot was too quick for him and early the next morning he arrived with troops at the house where La Cloche was staying. The Rector escaped by a back door and eventually found refuge in Mont Orgueil. His *coup d'état* had failed.[34]

Nevertheless everyone was sick of the war. From the trenches round the old castle (*le vieux château* as it came to be called after the building of Elizabeth Castle), the militiamen began to drift home. On 13 November Lydcot called a meeting of the States, and, while they were sitting, news arrived that four of his officers had deserted. The States fell back on Sir Philippe's old idea of neutrality and they sent to the castle to see if some such compromise could be arranged; Lady de Carteret promised a reply by the following Monday. But on Sunday 19 November, without waiting for the promised thousand men, Carteret embarked all the troops he could collect, English, Irish, Scottish, French and landed at Mont Orgueil. Rumours magnified this scratch force into a great army. The next morning the parochial officers of St Martin and Grouville came in to make submission. On Thursday some Royalists landed at St Brelade, strolled out one by one to St Aubin's tower, as though to gossip with the soldiers, and then overpowered them. When he heard a *feu de joie* from the Fort, d'Assigny was supervising the building of new earthworks on the town hill, and he saw boats passing to and fro between the fort and the castle. He rushed down to the town shouting 'Treason'.[35]

Next day Carteret marched into the town, but the streets were empty, for most people kept indoors or had fled into the country. Chevalier tells us that 'the women shed piteous tears. They looked as though they would die of rage, because their hopes had been frustrated'. Or were they just tired of constant changes of government and weary of being expected to adhere first to one and then to the opposite side in a conflict that did not really concern them in their personal lives? Before the civil strife was ended, they were to witness events of an even more dramatic nature.

Chapter Fifteen

SIR GEORGE CARTERET, DICTATOR, 1643-1646

All goes smoothly if men are ready to submit. But the country may resist.–Plato

CARTERET NOW had to stabilise his position. He summoned the States to Trinity church, judging that it was safer there than in the town, where tempers were frayed and the people somewhat hostile. He presented his Letters Patent and was sworn, first as Bailiff and then as Lieutenant-Governor. The States were quite subservient; all supporters of the late régime were in exile or in prison, and the survivors were either returned Royalists or too cowed to resist. Carteret knew, wrote Chevalier, that 'whatever he asked would never be refused so he always called them together; for in this way his orders had more authority with the people'.[1]

He then toured the Island and, at suitable spots, a Bible was laid on a drum and the men were summoned by tens to swear on it fealty to the King. 'Sundry, however, absented themselves, and the common people attached little importance to this oath, because it was obtained by force'. All suspected of disaffection had to find bail, including the women, 'for in the women's gossip gatherings a thousand lies were concocted'. As a sample of the women's spirit Chevalier quotes Debora Alleyn, who was put in the pillory for saying that Sir Philippe ought to be 'boiled in the cauldron of Hell'. Her niece proclaimed, as she stood by the pillory, that her aunt was 'as true a martyr as Christ'.

Carteret soon discovered that the Island would not fight for the King. He planned a raid to recover Guernsey and offered tempting rewards to all who would volunteer; but, says Chevalier, 'Jersey looked on the scheme so coldly that it had to be dropped'. An expedition to reoccupy Sark also miscarried. But finance was his chief trouble. First he confiscated the property of all who had fled, then he demanded a forced loan, and all who refused to pay had soldiers quartered on them. This was a process which could not be repeated too often, so he fell back on privateering. He started with a single, swift sailing galley, built for him at St Malo, which mounted three bronze cannon and carried a crew of thirty-five. Her first prize was only a cargo of faggots, but her next was a brand-new barque laden with leather. This was forthwith armed as a privateer and captured a Yarmouth collier. The process was repeated with every boat taken, till Carteret had in his service a little private fleet.

Technically for the first six months or so his men were pirates pure and simple, liable to be hanged at the yard-arm; for he had no authority to issue Letters of Marque, that is, letters licensing the commander of a privately owned ship to cruise in search of enemy merchant vessels, either as reprisal for injuries suffered or as acts of war. Commissions were issued in England by the Lord High Admiral, and in December 1644 the King regularised Carteret's position by appointing him Vice-Admiral of Jersey with jurisdiction over 'all ships, men, whales, rigs and grampusses'.[2] This incorporated his vessels into the Royal Navy. Chevalier lists some of the prizes brought into St Aubin's Bay: a shipload of beaver hats and snuff meant for Southampton Fair, a cargo of paving stones (doubtless the Swanage so well known in Jersey and found in many a farm kitchen),[3] another of oranges and lemons, another of Guernsey stockings. International law safeguarded merchants by making privateers take every capture back to their port of registration, where an Admiralty Court decided whether it was a 'good and lawful prize'. Later the prize court was to be held at St Aubin, but according to Chevalier de Carteret held his court at Elizabeth Castle. This presented no difficulties; as private speculator he owned the corsairs and as Vice-Admiral of the court every boat was adjudged to him and their cargoes found a ready sale at Fécamp.[5] In this way he not only paid expenses, but laid the foundation of a large personal fortune. However this policy was by no means popular in the Island; few of the crews were local men and they appear to have been an unruly and rowdy lot.

The victualling of Castle Cornet was a source of great annoyance to Carteret. For two years Guernsey had been in the hands of Parliament, but Castle Cornet, on its islet, still held out for the King. Sir Peter Osborne, its gallant commander, kept crying out for provisions: 'My stores are exhausted, and I am like to be lost'. From time to time one of Carteret's boats would run the blockade, but the old cavalier did not think that Jersey was doing enough. 'It shall be your fault if the Castle falls into other hands', he wrote. Carteret resented this and wrote, 'More I cannot do except you oblige yourself to repay the money I have disbursed for you; in case of failing of payment upon the revenues of Guernsey, then your estate in England to be liable for it'. This led to a furious quarrel between the two Governors, but Carteret continued grudgingly to do what he could, while grumbling, 'every tub should stand on its own bottom'.[6]

In January 1645 Sir Thomas Jermyn died and was succeeded as Governor by his son, Sir Henry, a worthless young rake, self-seeking, sleek and pompous, who had established himself as major-domo to the Queen. He reappointed Carteret, who had now been knighted, as his Lieutenant.[7]

Meanwhile Mont Orgueil was full of Parliamentarians who had not escaped in time. Dean Bandinel and his son came to a tragic end. After twelve months' imprisonment news came of Archbishop Laud's execution, and warders said that Carteret meant to hang them as a reprisal; so they decided to escape. Chevalier tells the tale:

> By boring holes close together with a gimlet they brake a plank in the door, which led into a room next to the outer wall. This room had a closet with a narrow window at the top of the battlements. This they squeezed through, and, by the help of a cord and towels knotted together and fastened to a kitchen ladle fixed in a crack in the wall, they climbed down hand over hand. The wall was high and terrifying and the wind was blowing fit to tear the place asunder (*à tout rompre*). Trees were torn up by the roots and one could scarce keep one's feet. At the foot of the wall was a rugged rock, difficult to descend, and below this a steep slope leading to the sea. The son climbed down first, but his rope was too short and he fell on the rocks and injured his limbs. The father came next, but when half way down the rope snapped and he crashed head over heels and broke all his bones. When his son regained consciousness, he was dismayed to see his father in such a plight. Finding a spark of life in him, he covered him with his cloak and fled to hide himself.

The Dean was discovered at dawn and died a few hours later. Jacques was recaptured after three days and taken back to the Castle.[8]

On 18 April, three Royal Commissioners arrived from Paris[9] 'to hear and decide as to treasons committed in Jersey'. They were Henry Janson, Master in Chancery and an Oxford Doctor of Laws, John Nicholas Vaughan, a Welsh lawyer and a Doctor of Laws of Padua, and John Poley, a Suffolk man. Thomas Wright, a strong Royalist, wrote: 'These Commissioners are all young, yet they are very grave. Dr Nicholas is a haughty man, who taketh much on him. We dare not say anything for they have all power in their hands, and if we talk they threaten to put us in prison'.[10] While here they compiled a summary of fiefs and notes on those who held them at the time. The findings of this Commission disappeared under the Parliamentarians so Chevalier's was the only surviving record[11] until a manuscript copy was found in Samarès Manor library in 1924.

For 14 months they held their trials in the Court House, but any bloodthirsty ideas they may have had were effectively curbed by a declaration issued by Parliament:

> The Lords and Commons, looking on the condition of Jersey with much compassion, and with equal indignation on the insolency of its pretended Governor, do hereby declare that, if the said Carteret under any commission shall take the life of any inhabitant adhering to Parliament, they will cause like measure to be offered to prisoners they hold, and for every life that Carteret shall take they will cause three of their prisoners to be executed.[12]

The first Parliamentarian to be tried was Jurat Benjamin Bisson.[13] He 'stoutly based his defence' on the Commission issued by Parliament, which he maintained he was in duty bound to obey. The Court was evidently puzzled as to how to rebut this plea and sent him back to prison where he remained for the next 18 months.

The next prisoner was a surprising one, Etienne La Cloche, the Royalist Rector of St Ouen. Carteret's privateering had roused his righteous indignation. He thundered from his pulpit that Jersey was becoming a pirate's den and that the King ought to be told what was happening. But Carteret, according to Chevalier,

> would not allow ought that he did to be criticized. He and the Commissioners examined him oft, and stinging words were exchanged, after which he was kept without fire or light and friends who brought food were not allowed to speak to him. His wife [14] begged the Commissioners to release him, but they replied that first he must humble himself, and present a petition, which he utterly refused.

The Commissioners soon discovered that Jerseymen were a stubborn race. They kept him in prison for 11 months and then banished him from the Island. 'If he had been willing to eat humble pie', says our diarist, 'they would have fined him and released him. But he insisted that he had done his duty.'

The third prisoner was a sorry scamp, Maximilien Messervy. He had eloped with an heiress of 17, Collette La Cloche,[15] Sir Philippe de Carteret's favourite niece, and married her at St Lo in Normandy. When creditors pressed, he decided that the easiest way to get money was to make it. He became a skilful coiner, and later, when some of his florins were submitted to London goldsmiths, they declared them to be 'the most artful counterfeiting they ever saw'. In 1640 he had been caught passing spurious Spanish pistoles, and it had required all Sir Philippe's influence to save him from the gallows. But he continued in his felonious ways, and, when detected, fled to England where he posed as a Parliamentarian exile. Once more he was caught coining, but, while he was waiting for trial, Parliament was persuaded that his local knowledge would be useful to Lydcot, and released him. When Lydcot fled he remained, trusting perhaps to the fact that his wife was a cousin of Sir George, but this was a vain hope. As a criminal, not a political prisoner, the Commissioners could hang him without fear of reprisals, and they did so without hesitation.

This was the only execution, for Parliament's threat saved the others. But since the Commissioners dared not hang them, they decided to squeeze money out of them. One by one they were given the choice of standing trial for treason, with the unpleasant prospect of being disembowelled alive (for they had heard nothing of the threatened reprisal) or of suing on their knees for pardon and offering to buy it with a fine. 'On consideration', says Chevalier, 'they thought it better to submit': a masterly understatement reflecting an eternal truth, the instinct to survive. Even Jurat Bisson, after 20 months in gaol, decided to plead for mercy, and was fined 8,000 *livres tournois*. The aged Jurat Thomas Lemprière[16] was let off with 2,000 crowns, but to raise this he had to sell his house and his mill. Fines were graded according to means and the rank and file did not escape. Three poor men from St Ouen were each fined 34 crowns. Religious sanctions were added to make their submission more impressive. 'They were ordered to receive communion in the Town Church. An open Bible was laid on the Communion table, and they placed their hands on it. The oath of fealty to the King was read to them, and they signed it before receiving the sacrament.' Although this must seem to us unacceptable, Sir George, faced with the impossible task of maintaining the Island for a penurious and almost defeated king, felt driven to these extremes.

Two stalwarts refused to petition: Jean de Rue[17] and his brother-in-law, Nicolas Le Boutillier; they preferred to remain in prison. But Clement Gallie, Chef Sergent of St Saviour, managed to outwit his judges. He was fined 2,000 crowns, gave bail for this amount and was released in order that he might sell his property to raise it. This he did, then slipped away with the money to St Malo. His sureties proved to be a pauper and a penniless child.[18]

The Commissioners still had to deal with the exiles. Their property had already been confiscated and now they were tried in their absence. First, 13 were found guilty of treason and condemned to be 'suspended in effigy on a gibbet, and, when captured, to be hanged by the executioner'. A board with three crude figures, representing Lemprière, Hérault and Dumaresq, was left swinging on one arm of the gallows, while on the other was a rough sketch of 10, each labelled with his name. At the next session 12 more, including d'Assigny, were sentenced to be hanged when caught, though this time the effigy farce was omitted; a week later the same sentence was passed on 20 more. Jacques Bandinel had escaped trial by dying of his injuries.

Carteret now felt a need to win some popular support. He issued a shrewdly-worded manifesto,[19] saying that Jersey was a part of Normandy, not of England ... our laws and liberties differed from those of the English; and, though subjects of the same King we had never had dealings with the English Parliament, save when necessary to ask permission to import wool from their country. All our charters were authenticated solely with the name of the King as Duke. This was a valid argument in that Jersey was a 'peculiar' of the Crown, but Carteret was brushing aside the theory of the Divine Right of Kings and all the other controversies that had caused the civil strife in England. It was special pleading in the sense that it merely asserted that party squabbles in the English Parliament were no concern of ours. 'Let us remain', he claimed, 'true to our Duke and to our own Constitution.' On 18 March 1646 all heads of houses were summoned to their parish churches where the Manifesto was read aloud and they were ordered to sign. The original copy signed by the parishioners of St Lawrence is still in existence, but Chevalier admitted that the signing proved a fiasco: 'The people's bodies were under control, but their hearts had not been won'.

A spasm of loyalty was awakened by the visit of the young Prince of Wales. On 17 April 1646, an hour before sunset, three ships rounded Noirmont bringing, quite unexpectedly, the King's son, Charles, with about 300 followers. Two months earlier, 'thinking to unboy him', the King had made his 15-year-old heir Commander of the Armies of the West; but he and his generals proved no match for Fairfax and they were squeezed back until the Prince was forced to take refuge in the Isles of Scilly; when even these became unsafe, he made a move to Jersey. Never before had such a motley throng landed in the Island. Earls and ostlers, colonels and cobblers, chaplains and ladies, who described themselves as laundresses, gouty old dodderers like the Earl of Brentford, 'through long-continued, immoderate drinking, much decayed and dozed in his understanding,'[20] and giddy young pages; splendid loyalists who had lost all in the service of their King, and down-and-out scallywags hoping that loyalty might lead to future reward.

29 *Mussels in the Royal Bay of Grouville, Jersey 1980.*

HARVEST OF THE SEA

30 *Cod caught in La Baie des Chaleurs, Canada. (Photo: P. Mckie)*

The Big Four were the Lords of the Council, to whose care the King had entrusted his son: Lord Capel, a cavalier of the finest type, chivalrous, devout, high-minded; Lord Hopton, another man of untarnished honour, the best of the King's generals; Lord Colepepper, an able politician spoilt by a vile temper; and the staunchest of all, Sir Edward Hyde, the future Lord Clarendon, two of whose grand-daughters were to sit on the English throne. At first sight he might seem rather a figure of fun, a fat little man with round baby cheeks and treacle-coloured hair; but he was the wisest statesman left on the King's side, a man of incorruptible honesty, impervious to flattery and bribes, a churchman whose devotion to prayer-book religion was as deep as his loyalty to the King.[21]

It was no light task to find accommodation for such a mob. Fanshaw, the Prince's secretary, and his wife found lodgings in a stocking shop in the market; Colepepper lodged with Chevalier's son, a fact to which we probably owe our knowledge of much that happened. Hyde too found a room in the town. But the Prince himself stayed at Elizabeth Castle, a tall, sallow, Moorish-looking boy with a crooked smile, who had already learnt that perfect courtesy was to help him in many difficulties. Chevalier found him *un prince grandement bénin*. There are several houses which claim the honour of having given hospitality to the Prince; doubtless he visited, and perhaps dined, with some of those who had befriended him, when riding about the country inspecting the defences, or in the pursuit of sport. But we have Chevalier's statement that neither he nor his brother (who accompanied him on his second visit) ever stayed a night anywhere but at the castle.

Chevalier gives us many glimpses of Charles' life in Jersey. He watched him dining in solitary state:

> As he took his seat a kneeling squire presented a silver-gilt dish in which he washed his hands. On his right stood a Doctor of Divinity ready to recite the grace. The silver dishes with which the board was loaded were placed before him, one by one, and when he had chosen, the Gentleman Carver tasted a portion and laid it on the Prince's plate. His drink was brought by a page of about his own age, who tasted the goblet and offered it kneeling on one knee, holding another cup under his chin, lest a drop should be spilt on his clothes.

Then again we see the boy in the Town Church:

> His chair was placed in front of the pulpit with carpets on either side. A small table was set before him with a cushion for his elbow when he knelt. Sweet-scented herbs were scattered round, and the table was strewn with roses. Dr Poley[22] stood at his side to find the psalm for him and to turn in the Bible to the texts which the preacher quoted.

Chevalier's account of the Communion service is interesting liturgically. This was an English service conducted by Royal chaplains, but it wandered widely from the rubrics. The prayer book then in use ordered the churchwardens to put the offertory 'into the Poor Men's box', but our observant vingtenier noted 'a large, empty silver-gilt basin' on the Communion table, Laud's Scottish liturgy ordered the clergy to receive the alms 'in a basin provided for the purpose' which should then be 'humbly presented before the Lord and set on the Lord's table'. The Prince's chaplains, two future bishops and a prebendary, had evidently adopted this Scottish innovation, for Chevalier records that 'a minister presented the basin to the Prince, kneeling on one knee, and the Treasurer laid a handful of silver in it. He then took it to the Lords and Knights, and replaced it on the table'. More surprising is the fact that the communicants did not go up to the table to receive, as had been the custom in Jersey even in Calvinist days, but the clergy carried the sacrament ('the bread cut into long slips') to the people, who remained in their seats, though the Canons of 1640 denounced this as an 'unfitting' custom, and ordered all to 'draw near to receive'.

We see the Prince reviewing the Militia:

> On 29 April Sir George ordered all between 15 and 70 to march by parishes under their captains to the sands to show His Highness what men there were in Jersey. The Prince rode between the ranks and everyone cried, "God save the Prince and the King". He raised his hat and rode to the head of the army, and knighted the Seigneur of St Ouen before them all, waving his sword and striking him on the shoulder and saying, "Arise, Sir Philippe". After sundry manoeuvres the officers knelt on one knee, and the Prince from his horse gave them the back of his hand to kiss. He then made a gift to the troops.

But to distribute largesse a Prince must have money, and his Treasurer had arrived with his strong-box almost empty. He had already borrowed 15,000 pistoles from Carteret, when a rascal arrived from France with a scheme for keeping El Dorado in sight. This Colonel Smyth had the King's permission to establish a mint in Truro, but Parliament's conquest of the west had put an end to that plan. He still, however, had the dies, and he offered to set up a mint in Jersey. Local loyalists could bring in their plate, bullion could be bought in St Malo, and a steady stream of new half crowns would pour into the Prince's exchequer. Furnaces were installed in a house in Trinity, the home of Dr Aaron Guerdain,[23] now called La Guerdainerie; he was a Parliamentary exile, who by a quaint coincidence became later on Cromwell's Master of the Mint. Smyth struck some genuine coins, but it was soon noticed that the Island was being flooded with, in the words of Lord Clarendon, 'naughty money',[24] or of Chevalier 'money of which I do not wish to speak'. These were made of base metal and were traced to the Trinity mint. Smyth's legitimate business was merely a cover for his work as a coiner. To save the Prince's court from scandal, he was allowed to disappear into France. It is a most curious fact that no coin minted at La Guerdainerie has ever been found.

While Charles was dutifully performing the functions expected of him, and between times amusing himself with a sailing boat in the bay, a fierce struggle was in progress for the possession of his person. Englishmen like Capel and Hyde were determined to keep him inside the King's dominions, while his French mother was trying hard to get him to Paris. A rumour had reached her (certainly untrue, but destined to have a sequel) that he had been inveigled into a secret marriage. But Hyde knew that the wily Cardinal Mazarin, who was now virtually the ruler of France, wanted to use the boy as a trump card in his tortuous bargainings with the rival English governments. Moreover the lad's guardians feared the influence of the Queen, an ardent Catholic: if she won him over to her religion this would be worth a score of new battalions to Cromwell.

Hyde wrote: 'He no sooner arrived in Jersey than he received letters from the Queen requiring him to come to Paris'. But his council urged that to fly from his father's realm would create a disastrous impression, and he permitted Capel and Colepepper to go to Paris to try to convince the Queen. Meanwhile there arrived in Jersey the mercurial Lord Digby,[25] eager to kidnap the Prince to lead a rebellion in Ireland. 'He would invite him aboard his frigate for a collation and hoist sails and make no stay till he came to Ireland'. Hyde nipped this in the bud, so Digby rushed off to Paris to persuade the Queen that, once the Prince was in Ireland, the war would be won. But Henrietta Maria was a lady with very winning ways; she talked over Digby and Colepepper, and only Capel remained obdurate and offered to go to Newcastle to lay the facts before the King.

She sent the boy an extract from one of his father's letters: 'I think not Charles safe in Jersey. Send for him with all speed'; to which she added, 'You see the King's command to you and me. I make no doubt you will obey and suddenly. Show yourself a dutiful son'. Hyde, however, knew that the King wrote to the Queen in cipher and that Jermyn did the deciphering, and he suspected that the message had been garbled. He wrote to Jermyn saying that the King had been misinformed if he thought the Island to be in danger, and that the Council felt bound to wait until they heard directly from the King.

For three weeks the Queen hesitated. Then Mazarin sent word that there was a plot in Jersey to sell the Prince to Parliament for 20,000 pistoles. In a panic she sent Colepepper, Jermyn and Digby to bring back her son. They arrived on Saturday 20 June and there was according to Chevalier 'a great conflagration'. 'This begat some wrath and contradiction', wrote Hyde, 'insomuch that the Prince thought it necessary to suspend the debate till the next day.' On Sunday they met again in church. Capel pointed out that the French had not even sent a passport, but the boy settled the question by announcing that he would sail on the Tuesday. On Monday they appealed to him again in vain, 'whereupon', said Hyde, 'every man in his council, Colepepper excepted, besought His Highness that he would give them his pardon if they did not further wait on him'. His departure was delayed till Thursday 25 June by bad weather and Parliamentary ships in the offing. Those of his entourage who urged him not to go to France feared that it would look like a capitulation on the part of the King if the Heir Apparent were to quit His Majesty's dominions, and would be particularly open to criticism were he to place himself in the power of a foreign nation. But he left for Coutainville with Jermyn, Colepepper and most of his court, though Capel, Hyde, Hopton and others remained in Jersey.

Chapter Sixteen

SIR GEORGE VERSUS ALL ENGLAND, 1646-1651

We all thought that one battle would end it, but we were all mistaken.–Baxter

WHEN THE CASTLE EMPTIED, Hyde came to live there, and before long built himself a house.[1] 'We are a handful of honest fellows who love one another heartily. The Governor is most generous and his wife a lady worthy such a husband. We make one very good meal a day, and go to church Wednesdays and Fridays'. These cavaliers of the better sort were staunch Anglicans, and many outdid Hyde in church-going. Chevalier says that Lord Hopton attended service twice daily in the chapel which Carteret had constructed in part of the priory ruins, and paid a chaplain to minister to them. The Roundheads had by no means a monopoly in religion. Here Hyde settled down to write his famous *History of the Great Rebellion* 'in Jersey ink', as Falle reminds his readers.[2]

In September, however, this monastic routine of worship and study was ruffled by rumours from Paris. The court of the Royalist exiles there was bankrupt, the Queen had pawned her last jewel and many a lord with broad acres in England was unable to borrow the price of a dinner. But hope revived when a whisper spread that Jermyn was selling the Channel Islands to France for 200,000 pistoles, and such a bargain was not inconceivable. The King had tried to buy Danish aid by offering Orkney and Shetland. Warning of this possibility reached Hyde from four different sources. So on 19 October 1646 Carteret, Capel, Hopton and Hyde signed Articles of Association:

> We unanimously conclude that the delivery of these islands to the French cannot consist with the duty of an Englishman, and it will be an irreparable dishonour to the Crown, and that the damage will be unspeakable to King and Kingdom. Therefore we resolve by the help of God to the utmost of our power to resist.[3]

Capel hurried to Paris to find out if the report were true. If it were, Carteret would appeal for help to Parliament 'not as an overture of giving up the island to Parliament', but pledging himself to hold it for England 'till His Majesty and his subjects are once more at one'. But Jermyn's schemes came to nothing, possibly because he and Mazarin could not agree on the price. It was notoriously hard to squeeze money out of that old miser.

Meanwhile the Jerseymen who had fled with Lydcot were active in London. Lemprière was one of the trustees for the sale of the King's property, and was said to have been the man who 'brake the King's crown'. Dumaresq was teller at the Mint; Hérault kept in touch with them and, in 1646, together they produced *Pseudo-Mastix, the Lyar's Whipp*, an answer to Prynne's defence of Sir Philippe de Carteret.[4] Other exiles also found work under the new Government in the Office for the sale of the Royal estates; and Dr Aaron Guerdain, as Master of the Mint, was responsible for coining the Commonwealth money.

This group incessantly stirred up Parliament to take steps to recover Jersey. In July 1645 the Commons ordered the Admiralty 'to make immediate plans for its reduction', and again in

September they urged that the plans be submitted speedily. But the report was not presented till March 1646, when the House voted 1,200 men and £2,549. Then the two houses clashed as to who should be commander. Presbyterians and Independents were now eyeing each other like cats and dogs. The Lords appointed Colonel Aldridge, a Presbyterian; the Commons nominated Sir Hardress Waller, an Independent. The dispute dragged on until June when a committee was appointed 'to prepare reasons why the House cannot agree to Colonel Aldridge'. In October the exiles presented a new petition.

In January 1647 the war in England seemed to be over. The King was a prisoner, and Parliament had time to attend to outlying pockets of Royalists like the Isle of Wight and Jersey. Carteret knew that an attack was coming and that there was likely to be a rising in the Island to welcome it. Chevalier, himself a Royalist, confesses again and again that, though Cornish and Irish mercenaries held both castles for the King, most of his fellow islanders were on the other side; official documents confirm this. When Lydcot fled, the King's proclamation admitted that 'Parliament hath seduced the majority of the people from their obedience'; Carteret spoke of 'the rebellion committed by the greater part of the inhabitants':[5] and now Chevalier wrote, 'Sir George knew well that if the enemy landed, most of the people would join hands with them'.

In January Hyde still felt safe. 'There be many fugitives in London, who pretend great power, but they can do nothing. The common people can do no part without the help of the army.' But by March things looked more serious. Hardress Waller had been given 3,000 men and 20 ships. Hyde began to grow anxious: 'We are threatened with the whole power of those who have taken all the King's other dominions': on 3 April he made his will, 'being in a place threatened to be assaulted, and having reason to expect to be called out of this world'.[6]

But at Westminster the invasion plans were not going smoothly, for the refugees, like their fellow Roundheads, were split into two factions, Lemprière, Dumaresq and the main body were working with the Independents, and on 1 May they nominated Rainsborough to command the expedition. This was a good choice; theologically and politically he was an extremist, an Independent and a red-hot Republican, but as a soldier he always got things done. 'You talk of difficulties', he once told the Commons, 'but if you fear difficulties, why was the war begun?' On the 12th the Commons reported that 'all things necessary for reducing Jersey are ready to be embarked', and waited merely for the Lords to confirm Rainsborough's commission.

But another group of refugees, led by old Samuel de La Place, whom Bandinel had ejected from St Mary, and the rampageous Pierre d'Assigny, late Rector of St Helier, all true-blue Presbyterians, bombarded the Lords with petitions protesting that 'if Parliament send to Jersey independent forces, they shall spoil the isle by their tub-preaching and overthrow true religion'. They urged the Lords to revert to their choice of Colonel Aldridge as Commander, 'who hath declared himself a Presbyterian, and speaketh French, a thing absolutely necessary'.[7] This group delayed the expedition until a sudden upheaval in England made its sailing impossible. Now that the war seemed over, Parliament tried to disband the Army, but the Army refused to be disbanded. Rainsborough's men joined the mutiny and he threw in his lot with them. In June the soldiers seized the King, taking him out of the custody of Parliament; in August they marched on London, and Rainsborough's troops occupied Southwark. Amid all this excitement, not surprisingly, Jersey was forgotten. To Chevalier it seemed a miracle: 'God brake their plans and saved us', was his comment.

The Island now had four years' respite and life became almost normal. The States met fortnightly, the Court weekly. Moral transgressors did penance in the Temples, farmers were busy with ploughing and reaping, making black butter[8] and cider. Every spring the fishing fleet still sailed for Newfoundland, though now every captain had to pay a pistole (nearly £1) and every seaman a piece-of-eight (about 22p) in lieu of militia duty. The war hit the stocking trade badly, as no wool could be obtained from England, and when knitters began to use large needles to eke out the local supplies, France refused to buy the goods. The States tried to revive the manufacture of linen 'which had once been a great boon to the island', so every farm was ordered to grow at least ten perch of flax, the quality of which was considered superior to that grown in France. Strenuous efforts were made to solve the pauper problem; Rectors were forbidden to marry 'persons of the lower orders' until they had proved that they could support a family. Carteret presented a house in town, to be used as *une Maison de Correction*[9] where all who begged without a licence from their Constable, or refused to work for a reasonable wage, all able-bodied men found knitting and all habitual drunkards would be confined on bread and water. But the beggars remained a scandal and a public nuisance, and although the States accepted Carteret's gift, they were less enthusiastic when asked to contribute to its maintenance, and according to Chevalier 'received the idea so coldly' that the scheme was eventually dropped.

In 1647 the old Court House in town was pulled down. It was a low, thatched, barn-like building, 'not much to look at', according to Chevalier, and was replaced by a solid granite structure. On the front of it were placed the arms of the King, of the Governor Lord Jermyn, and of Sir George himself, as Lieutenant-Governor and Bailiff. Masons were brought over from St Malo to do the carving.[10]

The war against witches continued, but there was no panic persecution, for each witch was given a fair trial. First the Constable and six *sermentés* (sworn witnesses) had to be convinced of her guilt, and then the Crown officers had to agree to prosecute. The accused had unlimited right to challenge unfriendly jurors, and five votes out of 24 were enough to secure acquittal. Of seven witch trials in 1648, two of the accused were banished, two were discharged with a warning, one was flogged, only two were executed. Marie Esnouf, grand-daughter of a former Rector of St John, was accused of 'having by diabolic spells caused many human beings to die, and others to fall into a decline, and also much cattle'. She strenuously denied her guilt, but more than sixty witnesses appeared against her. At her execution in the Market Place, 'no such crowd had been seen since the Prince came to Jersey; men, women, lads and girls, thronged the churchyard walls and the slopes of the Town Hill'. A fortnight later Marie Grandin paid the same penalty. 'She was accused', says Chevalier, 'of atrocious acts, and from seventy to eighty witnesses gave evidence against her. The "Devil's Mark" was found on her head.'

The trials continue without a break until 1660, and, as late as 1765, an entry in the Trinity parish register suggests that the Rector was having trouble in controlling witch-mania. A woman named Elizabeth Gavey had been found murdered in the public road; the entry in the church register reads:

> ... elle a été trouvée morte le matin 28 jour proche la mare d'ango, à la Ville a l'Evesque, meurtrie par des misérables, superstitieux, l'accusant de sorcellerie qui aprés l'avoir cruellement maltraitée et faite mourir jeterant là son pauvre cadavre. Elle était une pauvre innocente qui était ainsi née et a vescu toute sa vie, une pauvre innocente.

Although Devil-worship as an organised religion was dead by the 18th century, a belief in witchcraft still lingered in Jersey as it did in remote parts of France. *Les mauvais livres* still circulated with their spells and recipes for love philtres. Still there were women of whom their neighbours said in an awed whisper '*elle a du scîn*' (she has the hidden knowledge). An extract from the Minute book of the Ecclesiastical Court for 4 October 1736 reads:

> Marie Godfray, wife of Etienne Machon of St Saviour, for dabbling in the Forbidden Arts and unveiling things that are hidden. The said Godfray has promised to abstain from such practices in future, and moreover to disclose the names of any who approach her for this purpose. Neighbouring parishes are to be informed of this by the reading of this Act of the Court after the Nicene Creed.[11]

Meanwhile in England the King's tragedy was drawing to a close. In November 1647 he escaped from Hampton Court where the army had confined him. He hurried to Southampton Water, expecting to find a boat to take him to Jersey. But something had gone wrong and he was persuaded to cross to the Isle of Wight. Here the garrison of Carisbrooke Castle was only 12 old men, and Hammond, the young Governor, was the nephew of one of Charles' chaplains. The local Royalists hoped to seize the castle with his connivance and hold it until the Hampshire Cavaliers could rally round the King. But Hammond was true to his trust; Charles was received with respect, but, after one attempt to escape, he was not allowed outside the walls.

He remained here for 12 months, presenting the pathetic spectacle of a man of honourable instincts trying to play the twister, plunging into shamelessly dishonest intrigues with Presbyterians, Independents, Catholics, Scots, Irish, promising anything to anybody as he wriggled to get out of his difficulties. Among the Fairfax papers is a report that he had promised that 'Sir George Carteret and other delinquents shall be banished the kingdom for life and their estates sequestered for three years'; a sad reflection considering Sir George's steadfastness.

Meanwhile his faithful friends in Jersey were planning to rescue him. In January 1648 they sent a boat to the Isle of Wight, flying the French flag and pretending to have come from Normandy to sell bacon. By the help of Mrs Wheeler, the King's laundress, they smuggled letters in to Charles concealed inside his shirts.[12] We know no details of the plot, but there must have been considerable correspondence, for Cromwell wrote to Hammond, 'Carteret hath sent three boats from Jersey under the name of Frenchmen to bring the King, if their plot take effect, to Jersey'. But the King apparently turned down these plans, for he still hoped to regain his crown by his own cunning.

That summer Carteret made plans for the invasion of Guernsey. He collected troops and transport, but the scheme broke down through the jealousy of Sir Baldwin Wake, the new Governor of Castle Cornet; yet again Carteret had met a difficult colleague, who feared that Sir George might take Guernsey under his rule. 'He told Sir George', wrote Chevalier, 'that he needed no help from Jersey, and that if he entered Castle Cornet, he must first give up his sword, and he would not be allowed to bring more than six men with him'. So Carteret decided to use force for the reduction of Sark, but 'the floodgates of heaven opened, and Aeolus blew, and Neptune foamed with such angry waves', that this plan too was abandoned.

In December the King was removed to Hurst Castle, which stands in the Solent at the end of a long spit of shingle. Carteret now resolved to make another attempt at rescue. Falle wrote,

> The thing, though hazardous, was not thought absolutely impossible, for, as all ships going to Southampton pass close to this castle, it was presumed that four or five vessels of this island with a sufficient number of chosen hands concealed under hatches might come so near without creating jealousy as to give opportunity to the men to sally forth suddenly and scale the walls.

But before the ships were ready, Charles had been hurried to Windsor, to Westminster and to the block.

On 7 February Captain Skinner brought the news to Jersey, and on 9 February Sir John Poulet, or to quote Chevalier 'collonnel paullet with another english gentleman' told that the King had been beheaded. Sir George could not bring himself to believe such shocking news, until on the 16th it was confirmed by a letter from the Prince's secretary.

Then, though Parliament had abolished the office of King as ' unnecessary, burdensome and dangerous', and had threatened death to any who should speak of the Prince of Wales as King, Carteret ordered the Vicomte[13] to proclaim Prince Charles in the Market Place as 'by right and lawful succession our sole and sovereign lord'. The drums sounded, the trumpets blared and the castle guns thundered. The actual document of this proclamation is owned by the Société Jersiaise.

It bears the signatures of 26 persons, brave men indeed, for they knew not what the future held, nor what might be the result of their public announcement that the beheading was a 'horrible outrage'. Thus it is that the reign of Charles II began in Jersey in 1649 and not in 1660.

The new King was in Holland, but the Dutch government hinted broadly that his presence there was 'inconvenient'. When he joined his mother in Paris, 'his absence was impatiently desired' by the French Regent. He planned to sail for Ireland, where Ormonde's Royalist rising seemed to be making progress, but in September news came that Ormonde was beaten and Blake[14] master of the sea. Of all his dominions, Jersey remained the only safe place of refuge. So on 17 September he arrived, bringing with him his young brother, James, Duke of York, the future James II, 'more to annoy his mother than because prudence required it'. With him came the usual horde of satellites, ranging from the Keeper of the Great Seal to the Bearer of the King's Prayer Book, grooms of the Bedchamber, pages of the Backstairs, ushers, pantlers, secretaries, the Royal barber, the King's tailor 'whose wife in her silks and finery looked more like an army captain', even a jester, a mad little Doctor of Divinity, who amused the King by his antics, earls, barons, knights, colonels, courtiers of every kind and description. All wore deepest mourning in memory of the late King, except Charles who wore 'violet tinged with purple, even the holsters of his pistols were tinged with violet', that being royal mourning. His coach was draped with black and drawn by six black horses. The housing of this multitude was indeed a problem. As before, the King and his immediate staff were quartered in Elizabeth Castle, but every vacant room in the town was filled, and many a nobleman had to be content with a bed in a country farm.

The food problem was solved by proclaiming free trade with France. 'Sir George removed all restrictions on the import of goods and cattle, and the peasants of Normandy and Brittany brought over abundant supplies and the market overflowed with food.' Finance was more difficult. The King had left Paris with 300 pistoles only, and many of his Court had had to walk behind his coach to the sea. They now organised a world-wide campaign of mendicancy. Colepepper went to Russia to try 'to procure the payment of money lent long since to the Emperor by the King's grandfather'. Hyde went to Spain, Brentford to Sweden to beg for subsidies. Others were sent to the German princes and the Italian republics, to Poland, even to Turkey. The results were small. In November Hopton's secretary wrote to the Royalist agent in Holland: 'The King has been forced drastically to reduce the number who dine at court. There remain only a few dishes for the King and the Duke and all the rest are at board wages to be paid when you send us the money'. That same month the Scottish envoy reported. 'The King hath no bread for himself or his servants, and betwixt him and his brother not an English shilling.'

In September Carteret had summoned the States to make a gift to the King, and they voted a levy which produced about £600 sterling,[15] but what was that among so many? Six months later two of the Crown fiefs, Anneville and Avranches, were put up for auction and sold for £2,000. During all this time Charles was not cutting a very impressive figure. Heroic men were risking their lives for him, Ormonde in Ireland and Montrose in the Highlands, while he was shooting rabbits in Jersey and dancing in the castle at night. But what could he do when this was the only place where he could stay in safety? His childhood and boyhood had not equipped him to earn a living, and the same could be said for his followers. The demoralising effect of great poverty and constant wandering from place to place during these formative years had a lasting influence on his character and undermined a temperament, which, in different circumstances, might have given us one of our ablest Kings. His education had, of necessity, been sadly neglected, but of his intelligence, wit and humour, there could be no doubt. Another of his activities while here was the drawing of a map. It is mentioned by Edward Brown in *Travels in divers parts of Europe* (1668): 'In the Chamber of Rareties of the Burgomaster of Leipzig is *The Isle of Jersey* drawn by our King'. When Walpole wrote his *Anecdotes of English Painters* in 1761, it was in the Imperial Library at Vienna.[16] The present whereabouts of this map remains a mystery, but what a find, what a treasure it would be, if only it could be traced.

Of the Jersey houses which claim to have received the King as a guest, Vinchelez de Bas Manor used to show some gloves that the King was said to have left behind, Vinchelez de Haut treasured a gold-headed walking-stick, while Hamptonne pointed to the bedposts from a bed which, supposedly, had been his. But Chevalier's testimony is clear proof that this was not so:[17] 'If any of the island gentry invited the Duke to their house, neither he nor the King ever accepted the invitation, but the Lords of the court used to accept, and the King counted this as a compliment paid to himself'. The story of a visit from a Lord, or of one actually staying in the house, could so easily, as retold over the years, have been translated into a visit from the King in person.

Yet the King's easy-going amiability made him popular. He stood as godfather to Carteret's baby and gave her the name Caroline, which, as Chevalier explains, is 'feminine for Charles'. Laurens Hamptonne was granted leave to rebuild a dovecot, on land which was part of a royal fief. When George Dumaresq,[18] a Parliamentary exile, disgusted at the King's execution, returned to make his peace, Sir George demanded 1,000 crowns for his pardon, but the King granted it for nothing. When Jean Syvret was condemned to death for striking his father, the King pardoned him. When the mad little Doctor of Divinity was turned out of the Town Church for making faces at the people and avenged himself by throwing stones through the window, one of which nearly hit the King on the head, Charles merely gave him a suit of new clothes and sent him back to France. His clemency probably earned him more loyalty than money could have done, and it was all that he had to give.

Elizabeth Castle now began to see a strange ceremony. One of the most interesting forms of faith-healing was the touching for the King's Evil. Both France and England firmly believed that a King's touch could heal scrofula, and the practice was continuous in England from the time of Henry II to Queen Anne; but under Charles II it became no occasional act of mercy, but a political weapon to magnify the sanctity of kingship. After the Restoration the weekly touchings in the Banqueting Hall were one of the sights of London. Ninety thousand sufferers are said to have been touched. In that free-thinking age some of these cures must have been genuine or the practice would surely have been laughed out of court. Jersey saw the King's first experiment as a healer, and it may be noted that such a ceremony had not been suggested on his first visit as a Prince of Wales, but only now that he was an acknowledged, though not sanctified, King. On 4 December, 11 persons came to the castle chapel, and they were certified by doctors as being scrofulous. The King touched them on the breast as they knelt, saying, 'May God heal thee'. 'And all were cured', says Chevalier. The rite was repeated in January and twice in February, and altogether 24 people were said to have been restored to health.

Parliament now appointed the famous Colonel Hutchinson as Governor,[19] but he seems never to have taken up his appointment. His wife reported, 'When Cromwell was made General, he, finding that the Colonel's commission was not taken out, gave a commission for the governorship to one of his own creatures'. All of this, however, did not disturb Elizabeth Castle, though the court there was by no means a happy family. Of Sir Edward Herbert, the Attorney-General, Hyde wrote, 'He lived in perpetual contradiction of other men's opinions'.[20] The same might have been said of most of his companions. The King had to threaten to condemn to death, without hope of mercy, any of his suite convicted of duelling. Some were traitors: Whitelock, a member of Cromwell's council, declared that they knew all the Prince's plans, 'which knowledge they procure by money, whereof the Prince's servants are needy'. And some who were loyal lost heart. 'They are of the opinion', wrote Nicholas[21] 'that the King should go with six or eight persons to Holland and remain there as a private person.' But

31 *La Grande Maison, St John, Jersey, a 'Maison de Terreneuve', 1852.*

CODFISHING ENTERPRISES

32 *Manager's house and stores at L' Anse à Beaufils, Gaspé. (Photo P. Mckie)*

the majority clamoured for action, for they felt that the kingdom would never be recovered if they did nothing, and they were ready to lay down their lives in His Majesty's service, but that, if nothing was done, they would seek their fortunes elsewhere. Moreover inaction was making a bad impression abroad. Byron[22] wrote, 'Foreign princes begin to look on the king as a person so lazy that they think it not safe by contributing to his assistance to irritate potent enemies'.

But the belligerent Royalists were as 'a house divided against itself', one group eager to join Ormonde in Ireland, the other pinning its hopes in Edinburgh. The execution of a Scottish king by an English Parliament had infuriated Scotland. Argyle, the Covenanters' leader, sent Winram to Jersey to offer Charles a loyal welcome if he would accept Presbyterianism, and his mother urged him to do this. Perhaps she felt that, if he had to be a heretic, he might as well choose a heresy that was politically useful. But the Anglicans round him fiercely resented this proposal and Sir John Berkeley wrote: 'Winram will be lucky if he escape with a broken pate. They talk of throwing him over the wall'.[23] Charles, however, was willing to be the defender of whatever faith would defend him. His French grandfather, Henry IV, had said, 'Paris is worth a Mass', and he argued, 'Scots sermons can be stomached, if they will give me Scotland'. Circumstances forced him to abandon Montrose, the flower of his generation, who had said that life held no greater aim for him than 'to do the King, your father, service': his loyalty led to the sacrifice of his life, after he had been sent to stir up the Highlands against the Covenant. On 13 February 1650 Charles left Jersey to meet the Scottish Commissioners at Breda. He was followed by many of his entourage, his horses and clothes having been sent on ahead.

Before he left he made a parting gift to his host. He presented Carteret with a group of islands, with neighbouring islets, called Smith's Isles, off the coast of Virginia. They were not an attractive proposition, and the Captain Smith, whose name they bore,[24] described them as 'a cluster of barren rocks overgrown with sharp whins'. Carteret renamed them New Jersey and sent out a party of emigrants to occupy them, but on their first day at sea they were captured by a Parliamentary privateer. Whitelock writes: '1650 May 14th. A ship of five guns, belonging to Sir George Carteret, bound for Virginia with passengers and goods and tools for planting an island, was taken by Captain Green and brought to the Isle of Wight'. This was the rather ignominious first attempt to found a transatlantic New Jersey.

Charles wanted to leave his young brother, the Duke of York, as Governor, but the post was still held by Jermyn, his mother's major-domo, a heavy man 'full of soup and gold' whose chief characteristic, according to Hyde, was 'kindness for himself'. He offered to surrender his commission for 6,000 pistoles, but the poor young Duke had no such money, so the bargain failed. But the King insisted that the Governorship of Jersey was no sinecure and that Jermyn must take up his office. So on 15 May he arrived at last, with two cooks and 'three silver services for his table, all different'; his secretary was the poet Cowley.[25]

One purpose of his visit was to sell more of the Crown estates for the benefit of the Queen's household, and, incidentally, to pocket £2,000 for himself. This Carteret strongly opposed and wrote urging the King to forbid it. Jermyn then tried to sell the Governorship to Carteret and, as he would not bid, left the island after three weeks in high dudgeon.

Jersey now resumed its normal life once more. The States met regularly, an enlarged assembly, for Carteret summoned the centeniers and often the militia captains. They appointed inspectors to see that leather was properly tanned and rewards were offered for the destruction of stoats.[26] The Rouen ell was made the standard measurement for Jersey. The church was ruffled by a ritual controversy. Dr Henry Byam, Prebendary of Exeter, who is described by

Wood as 'the most eminent preacher of the age', had come to Jersey with the Prince in 1646 and remained as chaplain of the Castle. Under his influence some of the Rectors began to introduce changes that startled their Puritan congregations. He found on a farm, used as pig troughs, the font and piscina that had been in the Town Church and the priory church 'in the days of ignorance when the Mass was celebrated'. They had been cast out of the temples when the light of the gospel appeared. He brought them to the town churchyard, 'a thing which honest folk lamented'; Faultrat the Rector, wanted to put them back in the temple, but was persuaded not to do so.[27]

Faultrat also fell out with his congregation over the Prayer Book responses; for to Jerseymen these offensive little prayers were like a red rag to a bull, and most of the Rectors omitted them. But at the Town Church 'old Dr Byam persuaded Faultrat to use them. The people showed their displeasure by absenting themselves from the Wednesday morning service. They would willingly have attended if Faultrat had been willing to drop the responses; for', says Chevalier, 'you will never force the people of Jersey to make the responses, they will always remain silent' (*tous Jours tins quois*).[27] Faultrat, in true Laudian style, appealed to the States, who ordered 'at least one person from every family to be present every Wednesday under pain of three groats' fine'.[27] We are not told if they were obeyed.

Carteret knew that Cromwell must soon attack the Island, so he began to strengthen his forces with more foreign mercenaries. The castle garrison consisted mainly of Irish, French and Cornish troops. In September 1650, 60 Poles, Swedes and Danes arrived and he ordered the Constables to billet them. These 'Germans', as the local people called them, proved to be a horrid nuisance. 'Of all nations that have come to Jersey the Germans are the worst thieves. The Irish are terrible plunderers, but those rogues surpass them in cunning.'[28] Vegetables, eggs, poultry, vanished from the farms, even sheep and calves, whose skins were found on rocks round the castle. Carteret tried to get rid of these troops by passing them on to Scilly, but Scilly returned them without thanks. In January 1651 he engaged a company of 200 Swiss.

Jersey now became notorious as a nest of pirates, yet few, if any, of these were Jerseymen; for Carteret's privateers were rapscallions of all nations. Of his captains, Skinner, Bowden and Jelf were English, Vandersil, Marrtens and Van Diemen were Dutch, Gernet, Brue and Baudoin French, Hilt and Dessouard Ostenders. Chevalier tells how a Flemish boat put into Jersey to buy Letters of Marque which would enable it to prey on English shipping and how Carteret even sold Letters of Marque to the French Governor of Brest. Yet Jersey was blamed for all their misdeeds. Whitelock, sitting in the Council of State, records with monotonous regularity.

> 21 Feb. Several merchantmen taken off the western coast by Jersey pirates.
>
> 26 Feb. Two Dutchmen laden with salt anchored off Dartmouth. Two Jersey pirates cut their cables and carried them away.
>
> 1 March Jersey pirates very bold on the western coast.
>
> 6 March Several ships taken by pirates of Jersey.
>
> 17 March Jersey pirates take several merchants' ships.
>
> 19 March Letters of piracies committed by those of Jersey.
>
> 17 April Jersey pirates take two boats laden with corn and timber in sight of Portland.
>
> 21 April More prizes taken by Jersey pirates.

Month after month the record goes on. Obviously Cromwell could not allow this to continue.[29]

The first reprisal was a raid on Newfoundland and the capture of 10 Jersey fishing boats there. But this was only by-play. Preparations for reconquering the Island were now resumed in earnest and the task was entrusted to Colonel James Heane, Governor of Weymouth and Commander-in-Chief for Dorset. He began to collect men and supplies, but his plans were interrupted. Charles, who had come to terms with the Scots, invaded England with a Scottish army, and Heane and his men were hurried north to defend London. They fought on 3 September at Worcester, where Charles was utterly defeated. The fugitive king was constantly held up by Heane's preparations, and at Bridport 'the streets were full of redcoats going to embark to Jersey'. When a friend secured a ship for him at Southampton, 'by misfortune she was pressed to transport soldiers to Jersey'. The unfortunate young King was once again forced 'to go on his travels', as he said later, without support, without money and with nowhere to go where he would be welcome. It was by a fortunate chance that he managed to get to France undetected.

On 15 October Heane embarked, 'wind and weather smiling', with his own regiment and six companies of Hardress Waller's Foot, 2,600 men in all, and two troops of horse. Admiral Blake in the *Happy Entrance*, which Carteret had once commanded, was waiting with his fleet to escort them. On the 17th the expedition sailed, with over eighty vessels in all, but the wind drove them back to port as the open boats were getting swamped. They started again on the 19th and anchored off Sark. The next day they appeared in St Ouen's Bay, a treacherous sea to navigate. The surprise was complete, and had they been able to land there would have been no opposition; but the heavy surf left by the gale made landing impossible and the captains of the hired transports refused to run their ships ashore. Sir Philippe de Carteret saw them from his manor and sent a horseman post-haste to the town. The church bells clashed the alarm and the Militia fell in. Sir George sent the Grouville company to patrol the east coast, the St Brelade's company to guard their own bay, and ordered the rest to St Ouen. Then came the first indiscipline. The St Lawrence men marched to Millbrook to defend their own bulwark; by nightfall the other nine companies had joined the castle garrisons at the Blanches Banques.[30] Carteret had about 2,000 men but there was little fight in them. All knew that the Royalist cause had been shattered at Worcester and none could say whether the King was alive or dead. According to Falle, 'some began to cry "What good would sacrificing ourselves do the King now?" ' The fire-ships that Carteret had prepared at St Aubin refused to attack Blake's transports.

All night the militiamen lay in a drenching drizzle. Early on the 21st Heane sent a boat with a white flag bearing a summons to surrender. But Carteret 'knowing that his men would sooner yield than fight', fired on it, and forced it to return. 'This', says a contemporary record among the Clarendon papers,[31]

> almost caused a mutiny. Even those not lacking in loyalty cried out that it was wrong to repulse them without hearing their message. Some called him Man of Blood, who would destroy them by his obstinacy, rather than listen to peace proposals, which willy-nilly he would have to accept, now that the King was defeated!

Blake then brought his ships ashore, and for four hours shots were exchanged: but he saw that the landing would be costly, for the sand dunes gave the defenders ideal cover. So he sailed round to St Brelade's Bay, and Carteret had to follow. Then, using brains to avoid bloodshed, he sent some transports east to St Clement, and others back St Ouen. Carteret had no idea where the blow would fall, his men were worn out with marching and counter-marching, and the rain poured down relentlessly. Blake's warship went on bombarding St Brelade. On the 22nd a Council of War was held on the flagship at 3 a.m. followed by a long prayer meeting. At 5 a.m. a feint was made of landing at St Brelade, and Carteret rushed men to the spot, but then the ships sailed round the Corbière and back to St Ouen. 'When Sir George reviewed his army', we read,[32] 'he was much surprised to find that more than half had drifted away.' This was partly his own fault, for he had neglected the commissariat: the men had eaten the food that they had brought and had gone home for more. Blake had also made a miscalculation. By the time he had doubled the Corbière, he had missed the tide. So he sailed to L'Etacq and Carteret had to follow. He then doubled back to the southern end of the bay, where at sunset Major Harrison joined him with 900 men from Guernsey.

Carteret's troops had now lost two nights' sleep; they were tired, soaked and hungry, and it became more and more difficult to maintain discipline. One section even mutinied and levelled their muskets at him.

The night was 'extraordinarily dark'. At 11 p.m. Heane gave the order to land. The La Pulente[33] gunners could not see the boats, so their fire did little harm. The Guernseymen were the first ashore, shouting 'like Turks'. 'A party of the enemy's horse', wrote one of the men on the flagship, 'charged to the heads of our boats, and there was a fierce encounter, till Colonel Heane and the rest could get to their assistance, who, to give them all possible relief, leaped into the water up to the waist. Whereupon the enemy began to retreat.' The veterans of the New Model Army, fresh from their Worcester victory, were more than a match for the Militia and established themselves on the dunes, waiting for the dawn. When the day broke on the 23rd, Carteret's force had dispersed and he had withdrawn to the castle.

Heane's cavalry reconnoitred the Island and at 2 p.m. he marched to St Aubin. Carteret had converted St Aubin's Tower into a little fort, by surrounding the islet with walls, but it surrendered without firing a shot. 'The Jerseymen in the garrison said they would not bear arms against Parliament, whereupon the English troops escaped in a shallop.' This capture was important, for the guns of Elizabeth Castle could not carry across the bay: now Blake was able to move his fleet into the shelter of St Aubin, and that afternoon Heane occupied the town. By nightfall only the castles remained in Royalist hands.

Heane tackled Mont Orgueil first. The next morning, leaving Waller's men to blockade Elizabeth Castle, he marched his own regiment to Gorey, while Blake moved the fleet to St Catherine's. Sir George had done much to strengthen the old castle; he had built the third gate, with its heavy portcullis and the wall north of the Lower Ward; he had stored provisions for a siege and provided ample ammunition. He had put his brother, Philippe, in command, and given him the help of a professional soldier, the Captain of the Swiss, Major Villers. But Worcester had knocked the heart out of the defenders, for what was the good of fighting for a king whose cause was lost? 'The English Major, whom the King had set there', says the Clarendon manuscript, 'caused the troops to mutiny. They threatened to hand their captain over to the enemy, if he did not capitulate promptly.' Heane offered generous terms; an Act of Oblivion for all done during the war, officers to retain their lands and property; common soldiers to keep their household goods; the garrison to march out with full honours of war, and freedom to go where they pleased. On the 27th the keys were handed over.[34]

Heane's last task was more formidable. Elizabeth Castle had defied Lydcot, and now it was stronger. Carteret had built Fort Charles at the northern tip of the islet and had just added the Windmill Tower. The rocks had been scarped to make them impossible to climb; the crypt of the old priory church was bulging with food and ammunition and Carteret felt reasonably safe. Castle Cornet had kept the King's banner flying for more than nine years and looked like beating the record of Troy. Why should Elizabeth Castle do less?

Heane decided that the reduction of the castle was gunners' work. He built batteries at the end of the bridge, in the churchyard and on the Town Hill, but the distance was just too great for effective fire. His cannon balls reached their mark, but their force was spent, and the chunks they chipped off the walls were easily replaced by turf. So Heane sent to Portsmouth for Parliament's latest weapon. Carteret heard that his enemies were landing 'cannons big as barrels', but he did not believe it. It was however true. Three great mortars were installed at the foot of the Town Hill and the largest took a bomb containing 40 lbs of powder; its third shot landed on the old abbey church crashing through the roof and floor into the crypt below, exploding the castle's store of powder, utterly destroying the abbey and its adjoining houses, causing 40 casualties and scattering to the winds two thirds of Carteret's provisions. It thus destroyed what was perhaps the best piece of ecclesiastical architecture in the Island. We would have no knowledge of the structure, were it not for Hollar's engravings. Although he is not mentioned by Chevalier, the existence of these drawings suggests that the artist accompanied the King to Jersey.[35]

The effect of the explosion was like that of a modern atomic bomb. The soldiers clamoured for surrender and Carteret had to drive them back to their duties with a sword. Numbers deserted during the night; one was caught and hanged, but this did not stop the leak, for, as Chevalier says, 'they feared the bombs more than the hangman's rope'. On 24 November Sir George sent Jean Durel, the future Dean of Windsor,[36] to Paris to report the disaster to the King and to ask for supplies. Durel found Charles literally without a shirt to his back (he had borrowed one from Jermyn) and quite unable to raise funds to revictual the castle. He could only advise Carteret to obtain the best terms he could, for Sir George would never have surrendered without the royal command.

On 5 December negotiations began and lasted for eight days. Sir George was a dexterous bargainer, and he secured for himself extraordinarily favourable conditions. He was to retain his seigneurie of Mélèches and all his other property without compounding. He might remain in the Island, or go to France or to America, and his widowed sisters[37] were also to keep their estates without compounding. But for his friends and supporters he made a rather worse bargain. They had to forfeit two years' income to escape confiscation, though this was lenient compared with what Carteret had done to those who adhered to Parliament. He then had seized all his opponents' property outright.

On 15 December 1651 the garrison marched out, 'ensigns flying, drums beating, matches alight at both ends, bullets in mouth'. This was according to the articles of capitulation. Though recorded, it seems that this ceremonial exodus did not take place.[38] Four days later Castle Cornet also surrendered. Charles was left a vagabond king without the vestige of a kingdom. Sir George joined the French navy and became a Vice-Admiral.

Chapter Seventeen

THE COMMONWEALTH, 1651-1660

There is seldom finality either in victory or defeat.–F. S. Olivier

JERSEY NATURALLY took some time to settle down to the new régime. Some had lost power, others had gained it; the Island was swarming with soldiers and no one could tell what the real situation was. Heane tried hard to be just, but he had trouble with his troops. His own redcoats maintained good discipline, but the men whom Major Harrison had brought from Guernsey got out of hand. Chevalier reports:

> They carried to their ships beds, basins, linen, clothes, whatever they could lay hands on. It was marvellous how they found things that had been buried or built into walls. Colonel Heane forbade looting on pain of death, but to no avail. Some women went to him to complain that their frying-pans had been stolen, whereat he was greatly angered. He sent to the ships to have them recovered, but among such a rabble his orders could not be enforced.[1]

The chief complaint against the redcoats was their treatment of the churches. As Independents they denied that any sanctity could adhere to stone and mortar. To kill what they considered a crass superstition, they deliberately secularised all buildings that had been used for worship. 'They changed the temples into guard rooms and stables, breaking up the pews and burning them; and some, horrible to relate, did not hesitate to use them as latrines. The Town Church became a guard room during the siege of the castle.' Chevalier adds to this account from the Clarendon papers:

> The soldiers burned all the Town Church pews so that not one remained. They began to break up the pulpit and would have destroyed it, had it not been removed. They burned the lectern and smashed the table at which the Lord's Supper was received. And there were scoundrels who even defiled the temple with their dung. Some of them said without shame the Lord's house differed in no wise from any other house, and that every house was a church.

Perhaps in this observation we have an explanation for the total absence in our churches of any old or carved pews or pulpits, such as are found in so many English parish churches.

For six weeks there were no services, as Faultrat had fled to the castle, though occasionally an ensign in a red coat stood up and preached. But later the country Rectors conducted Sunday services in turn, 'while the guard were still feeding their fires with the pews. They showed no reverence for the sermon, for they did not understand the language, but smoked and walked about noisily'. Eventually Heane restored order by himself attending the services, 'though he did not understand French'.[2]

He had difficulties, too, with the returned exiles, who were thirsting for vengeance on their enemies. Many of them had rushed to seize land that had once belonged to their families, even though it had been legally sold. These evictions without authority Heane firmly suppressed, and the exiles complained to Parliament:

> When the island was taken, divers, who had served Parliament, took possession of that which was their own, which their parents had been forced to sell to save their lives, which were threatened, if they did not pay such sums as these bloody tigers demanded. But they were dispossessed by a Council of War.[3]

Heane restored Lemprière to his old position as Bailiff and gave him the task of replacing Carteret's officials with sound Commonwealth men. On 2 February 1652 Lemprière wrote to the Speaker:[4]

> Colonel Heane put the militia at the disposing of Col. Stocall, Cap. Norman and myself. We laboured to place able officers, men who have suffered for the State. I have caused to be elected in each parish a Constable, Centurion [i.e. Centenier], Vingteniers and Sermentés, who for the most part have suffered for the Commonwealth by exile, fine or imprisonment.

Printed slips were brought from England which everyone had to sign: 'I promise to be true and faithful to the Republic of England as at present constituted without King or House of Lords'. It was all very bewildering to the Jerseyman who so recently had promised to be loyal to the King, and one can understand that, as during the Wars of the Roses, he really did not know where he stood, and consequently took the line of least resistance.

Steps were taken to provide for the Island's needs. In December the Council of State ordered: 'As to transportation of wool to Jersey for manufacture of stockings they shall have the same as formerly'. It later decreed: 'Corn of all kinds and any other victuals, except butter, may be exported to Jersey free of customs or stint, likewise 1,000 tods of wool, 400 deckers of leather and 60 firkins of butter yearly'.[5]

Heane's most intricate task was the Royalists' compositions. To redeem their estates they had to pay not more than two and not less than one years' income, but the complicated system of Jersey *rentes* was incomprehensible to an Englishman. Laborious enquiries had to be made concerning every property, with owners wriggling to conceal the value, and Maret, the Receiver-General,[6] storming because he could not get for his department more than Heane and Lemprière considered just. He so notoriously affronted the Bailiff that he was imprisoned in Mont Orgueil until he gave security for better behaviour. The most troublesome case was that of Sir Philippe de Carteret of St Ouen. As one of the garrison of Elizabeth Castle he claimed, by the terms of the surrender, the right to compound,[7] but the exiles asserted that in 1645 his estates had been sequestered by Parliament for his father's rebellion and that in 1650 Parliament had ordered them to be sold for the benefit of those who had been driven from Jersey. They argued that he could not compound for property that was no longer his at the date of the surrender. He went to London to plead his case and indignant petitions followed him. The problem was bandied to and fro for months between the Committee for compounding, the Committee for petitions, the Committee for Relief on Articles of War and the Committee for Raising Money; a sample of the dilly-dallying that destroyed Cromwell's faith in Parliamentary methods. Heane wrote, 'I beg not to be forced to act in breach of my own articles'; but no decision had been reached by the time he was recalled.

One amazing case was that of Josué de Carteret,[8] brother of the Seigneur of Trinity, who was an arrant rascal. He had carried off to Normandy the child heiress of the seigneur of La Hougue Boëte, Jeanne Le Febvre. There the Huguenot ministers refused to marry them without her father's consent so he took her to Sark and married her there. He had posed as a strong Royalist. Chevalier tells us that he:

> became very friendly with Sir George, so that he went at all hours to the Castle, bearing complaints against all and sundry, saying that they were disaffected towards the King. He got many imprisoned and ingratiated himself so successfully with Sir George that he had him made a Jurat. Finding

> himself so firmly set, he deemed he could succeed in anything; so he denounced his father-in-law, hoping to enjoy his property before he died. When thwarted by his fellow Jurats, he appealed to the King, declaring that his father-in-law held for the Parliament.

This was more than Sir George could brook and Josué was sent to the Castle. When Jermyn arrived, he was tried and found guilty of having abducted his wife by force, of suborning persons to bear false witness against his father-in-law, and of accepting bribes. He was still in gaol when Heane arrived, but he then had the astounding impudence to try to pass himself off as a Parliamentary martyr. 'I was often indicted', he said, 'as a traitor to the late King, and was a prisoner thereof, when the isle was taken.' But Jersey knew his record too well and he had to flee.

Meanwhile Lemprière grew alarmed at rumours of changes in the Island's constitution. In that age of revolution no one knew what the wild men of Westminster might be planning. He sent the Speaker a long *Account of the Civil Government of this Island*,[9] 'to dissipate those aspersions, which some beyond the sea, not understanding our laws here, have already endeavoured to cast upon this Government, intending to obtain the setting up of their own conceits'. He also dispatched his nephew, Jacques Stocall, to London, for 'the enlarging of the summary'. On arrival Stocall printed a very rosy *Description of the excellent civil government of Jersey* for distribution among members of Parliament. This was backed by a petition signed by all the Constables, 11 Centeniers, 11 Militia officers and other leading islanders, expressing astonishment at 'rumours that have come from England that some persons have endeavoured to rend in pieces the frame of our government'.

The chief point that they emphasised was the need for more Jurats. Carteret's Royalist Jurats had been dismissed, and of Lydcot's, only two, Dumaresq and Hérault, had survived, and Dumaresq spent most of his time in London, where he was Teller of the Mint. The petitioners spoke of Lemprière as 'a gentleman endowed with rare abilities and virtues', who had 'kept an equal balance of justice betwixt soldiers and islanders', and had 'with dexterity and wisdom made many atonements of differences which have arisen between party and party among the inhabitants'; but they declared that he was 'much discouraged that he cannot fully satisfy the people in the administration of justice' for lack of Jurats to help him.

Immediately after the conquest of the Island in December 1651, the Council had ordered that there should be 'no election of any Jurat till Parliament has taken order therein'. A month later the Commons asked the Council 'to consider what is to be done for the government of Jersey'. In October the Council presented its report. Its chief recommendations were: that the government of the island be in all things restored to its ancient constitution; that Parliament nominate five Commissioners, natives of the isle, to enquire:

> what are the ancient laws and to require obedience thereunto; that all entrusted with public office be annually and freely elected and no longer of continuance for life; that the soldiers in the island be billeted according to the rules of Parliament, and not upon Free Quarter or in private houses as at present; that seeing that pirates and picaroons daily rove about the Island, two small frigates be speedily appointed to go hither.

But in April 1653, before anything had been done, Cromwell sent the Long Parliament packing.

When a new Parliament, Barebone's, assembled, a fresh report recommended in August 1653 that an election for 10 new Jurats be permitted, provided that none be chosen but men who had constantly adhered to Parliament, and that they hold office for two years only. But before this report was approved, the army again dissolved Parliament and Lemprière was left with only Hérault to help him.

Two attempts were made to incorporate Jersey into the English system. In 1652 Parliament had treated it as an English county, and appointed a county committee; the Instrument of

Government, which in 1653 made Cromwell Protector, decreed that in all future Parliaments Jersey should send one member to the House of Commons. Neither of these orders seems to have had any effect. But during the whole of the Commonwealth the States never met.[10] At first there were no Jurats, and Lemprière, as an Anabaptist, refused to summon the Rectors. 'By their turbulence and *brouilleries* [squabbling]', he wrote to the Speaker, 'they have made themselves unworthy of that assembly, and I never intend to call them unless I am commanded.' All of this emphasizes how deeply Jersey may be affected by events in England, in spite of her relative autonomy.

When Carteret fell the church had reverted to Presbyterianism, and the Huguenot service book had replaced the Prayer Book. Josué de la Place, Rector of Trinity,[11] at his appointment 10 years before, had secretly obtained Presbyterian orders in Guernsey, where that system still survived. His brother Jean, Minister of the Huguenot congregations that met in the crypt of Canterbury Cathedral, came to be Rector of St Mary, and Josué ordained another brother to be Rector of St Ouen. The church register records: 'Mons. Pierre de la Place received the laying on of hands in St Ouen's church by his brother Mons. Josué de la Place'. He was instituted in Presbyterian fashion by the Rectors of St Helier and St Martin. The latter was now Pierre d'Assigny, who in Lydcot's time had been the excitable Rector of St Helier.

England was at this time in wild confusion ecclesiastically, and any form of worship was allowed except the prayer book and the Mass. In one parish the minister might be a Presbyterian, in the next an Independent, in the next an Anabaptist. Lawyers became anxious as to whether the marriage registers were being properly kept. So the Barebone's Parliament had ordered all marriages to be performed before a Justice of the Peace. This gave Lemprière an additional task. We now read in the Jersey church registers entries such as these: '16 Dec. 1653. Samuel Le Four and Marguerite Mauger were married in the temple at Grouville; Michel Lemprière, Bailiff, married them according to an order of the English Parliament'; '3 Nov. 1656 Dr Denis Guerdain[12] was married to Mlle Marie Hérault in the New style'. The civil marriage was often followed by a religious ceremony; thus on 3 May 1654 the St Helier's register records: 'Jacques Wittel and Marie Bertram were married. Mons. the Bailiff married them. Afterward the same day Mons. Bonhomme, minister of the parish, married them a second time in church'.

Towards the end of 1654 Cromwell planned an expedition to the West Indies, and Heane's success in landing operations, when he recaptured Jersey, led to his being chosen as second in command. He left at Christmas and fell at the battle of Hispaniola.[13] His place in Jersey was taken by Colonel Robert Gibbon, a truculent soldier with an utter contempt for all civilian officials. The army was now top dog, and he made it clear that the Island was under military rule.

Parliament did however regularise Lemprière's position as Bailiff by new Letters Patent,[14] as his previous ones had been issued in the name of Charles I. An attempt was also made to reconstitute the Court, which now became the Court of His Highness Oliver, Lord Protector of the Commonwealth. This was translated as *L 'Etat*; in modern times no attempt is made to translate the word in its current sense. But it was 'for this time only after the late troubles, wherein things have become much unsettled, in case disaffected persons should get into that trust'. No election was permitted, but Cromwell himself nominated 11 Jerseymen to be sworn in as Jurats.[15]

This did not solve the problem. Hérault, the only surviving member of the old Bench, died. Two of the new Jurats, Philippe Messervy and Jean de Rue, crippled by long imprisonment under Carteret, could seldom attend. Three of the others held important posts elsewhere: Philippe de Carteret of La Hague[16] was Judge-Advocate of the army in Ireland; Nicholas Lemprière was a busy civil servant in London; Aaron Guerdain was Master of the Mint; his brother Denis refused to take the oath, either because he had learned from Quakers to regard oaths as sinful, or

HISTORY IN REPOSE

33 *Primroses on the mound at La Hougue Bie. (Photo: D. Fry)*

34 *Le Rocher Percé, Gaspé, landfall for many Jerseyman. (Photo: P. Mckie)*

because as a staunch Republican he refused to recognise a Protector. The result was that Lemprière still could not secure the seven Jurats without whom no Full Court could be held.

Lemprière and his little team struggled as best they could. The Court met regularly, and Durell, who had examined the Court Rolls, wrote:[17] 'The records were better kept at this time than ever before. The judgments were unexceptionable'. But some of the penalties prescribed by the old *Coutumier* were quaint; for example:

> François Luce, convicted of insults, threats and calumnies, is fined 40 *livres tournois* and ordered to make *amende honorable*, asking pardon of God, His Highness, and the Court and the person wronged, holding the tip of his nose and saying, "In that I have slandered thee, I have lied. The crime is in my own mouth". Which he did forthwith.

Gibbon administered his own justice quite independently. 'He hath bastinadoed', was one complaint, 'and misused to the endangering of their lives, several of the inhabitants, committing them close prisoners without the knowledge of the Jurats, amongst others Mons. Clement Gallie, Constable of St Saviour, and Abraham Becquet, merchant'. These were both wealthy men and prominent Parliamentarians: Gallie had been imprisoned by Carteret and Becquet had been hanged in effigy.[18] Gibbon's deputy, Captain Richard Yeardley, was equally autocratic. Once he imprisoned the Constable of St Brelade and all the parish officials 'for searching a suspected house in that parish in which lived one of his soldiers, for a sheep that had been stolen, as though soldiers' houses were sanctuaries'.

Picaroons (freelance privateers flying the flags of all nations) were now an intolerable nuisance. In Gibbon's first letter after his arrival, he said, 'This bay is infested with small picaroons, so that vessels can hardly look out without danger'.[19] The 12-gun *Cornelian* was sent, but in October her Captain wrote: 'I cannot alone and with so small a vessel, prevent all these pirates'. In November Gibbon complained:

> Ostenders do much infest this coast, and two of our vessels have been taken between this and Guernsey. The Masters came ashore to fetch money to redeem their vessels, one £250 and the other £100; and the pirates came with them under our nose, and we have no power to relieve our friends.

Blake might win great naval victories off the Dutch coast, but it seemed impossible to sweep the Channel of these pestilent little sea-robbers.

One cherished privilege of the Islands, confirmed by many charters, was freedom from press-gang raids. The Commonwealth authorities ignored this. Among the State papers is one that reads:

> In January 1656 the Governor of Guernsey sent out men to press the island, but the inhabitants opposed, and the Bailiff called a Court, which decided that this was contrary to their Privileges. To avoid disturbance the men were sent to Jersey, where, by the assistance of the Governor, they procured twenty.

But the Navy was not content with so meagre a catch and the *Portsmouth* was sent to the islands. In February the Captain reported:

> In obedience to your commands I went to Guernsey, and did my utmost to impress seamen, but received much opposition. The Bailiff called a Court, which resolved not to permit any press, and some took arms and rescued the men I have impressed. On this the Commander advised me to desist, or much mischief would be done. On this I went to Jersey, where I found the Governor very willing to assist, but the inhabitants were not. They forced my men to take a house for security. Had not the Governor assisted me with a party of horse, who had to fire on the people, killing one and wounding several, they would have been destroyed. I only succeeded in pressing fifty men in the two islands.

A later complaint tells how

> some soldiers came to St John, to press one, François Maret, who in a civil manner asked by what order they would press the inhabitants. Whereupon one soldier answered that he would show him his warrant, which was pistolling him through the head. He then fell, with his comrades, on the rest of the company, cutting and slashing them. The Governor made no more enquiry than if the soldiers had killed toads, which indeed was their boast afterwards.

Is this perhaps the earliest record of Jerseymen being called *Crapauds*? The joking sobriquet is still used, while Guernseymen are known as *ânes*.

Even more unpardonable were the bogus impressments staged to extort money. 'Soldiers pretending to have orders to impress persons, seized young people of good families, making believe they would be sent to Jamaica; but, if they would give money they would release them. Their parents chose to part with the money rather than complain'.

Another scandal arose over the compounding for the Royalists' estates. In 1655 five commissioners were appointed to wind up this business and their demands were not excessive. Elie de la Place, the richest man in the Island, was assessed at £110, others had to pay between £60 and £17 and estates worth less than £7 a year were exempt. But everyone resented the way in which Gibbon put the screw on those who could not pay. He billeted soldiers in their houses at free quarters, so that 'often the troopers did eat more than the fines amounted to', while he let it be known that his son would advance the money 'with such horrid extortion, as never was practised among the worst barbarians, to wit 20, 25 and 30% per month'. And to stop complaints to England 'he did prevent any to send letters out of the isle without first bringing them to him to peruse, and he caused all vessels bound for England to be searched for letters'.[21]

Meanwhile Cromwell was using Mont Orgueil as a State prison. First came honest John Lilburne, dauntless defender of the rights of the common people against King, Parliament and Protector. His influence with the soldiers was so great that, though acquitted at the Old Bailey, he was sent to Jersey as Cromwell dared not leave him at large. 'Lilburne', wrote Gibbon, 'remains inflexible, insisting that his liberty must be gained by course of law. He is a trouble here, more than ten men. The garrison give trouble on his account, and I have had to punish divers of them'.

When Lilburne was transferred to Castle Cornet, Robert Overton arrived, one of Cromwell's ablest generals, who had adopted Fifth Monarchy views, and accused Oliver of 'taking the crown from the head of Christ to put it on his own'.[22] He was followed by the Duke of Buckingham, one of the courtiers who had been with the King in Jersey. He had quarrelled with Charles, returned to England and married Fairfax's daughter; but later he became involved in a Royalist plot.[23]

In April 1657 Cromwell allowed an election for three new Jurats. But by this time Gibbon's iron hand had aroused such indignation that two of the three seats were captured by ex-Royalists. Their return was promptly quashed and a new poll ordered, which added two more Lemprières and a Dumaresq to the Bench. 'The eternizing of offices in one family' had been Lemprière's reproach in attacking Sir Philippe de Carteret, but now the list of Jurats contained five of his own close relations, while his nephew was Solicitor-General.[24] Yet in spite of the new recruits, we find the same complaint, that only five Jurats were available.

On 3 September 1658 Cromwell died and was succeeded by his son Richard, a quiet country gentleman with no spark of his father's genius. Jersey accepted his rule, and was perhaps flattered to think that his wife, Dorothy Mauger, now Protectress of England, was the grand-daughter of a Jerseyman.[25] But the army had always kicked against civilian control and resented the fact that Richard had never seen active service. In 1659 it forced him to dissolve his father's latest Parliament, and since a Parliament of some kind was needed to provide them with their pay, they recalled all that was left of the Long Parliament, which Oliver had dismissed six years before. This meant the end of the Protectorate. Richard's Great Seal was solemnly broken in the House of Commons, and he retired to his Hampshire estate.

The restoration of the Long Parliament was hailed with joy in Jersey, for it seemed to offer a chance of getting rid of Gibbon. A group of Jerseymen printed, in 1659, *Twenty-four articles of impeachment against Col Gibbon and Cap Yeardley*. 'You cannot imagine', said this pamphlet, 'how much the dejected spirits of the well-affected in this isle have been revived by the miraculous restoration of the famous Long Parliament ... after their long bondage they hope to be delivered from the yoke of their present oppressors'. The indictment was hardly needed, for Gibbon was recalled to nip in the bud a Royalist rising in Kent, and three days later the appointment was announced of Col. John Mason, an ardent Anabaptist with a taste for the queerer forms of heresy.[26] He began his reign vigorously. 'Though there was neither war nor rumours of war', writes a local diarist[27] 'he made us buy arms, powder, matches, permitting no delay, with threats to those who did not obey. But his power did not last long.' All England was in confusion. The army quarrelled with the restored Parliament and expelled it. The generals bickered, their men mutinied. Half-crazy cranks, political and theological, pranced on extraordinary hobbyhorses. One member of Parliament wrote: 'Chaos was perfection compared with this'. Sober citizens saw that anarchy stared them in the face.

But away in command of the army in Scotland was a strong, taciturn soldier who had always held aloof from politics. 'Old George' Monk used to say that he was trained in Holland, 'where soldiers received orders, but gave none'. He had faithfully served in turn each *de facto* government, Charles, Parliament, Oliver, Richard, then Parliament again. But, now that there was no government left, he felt he must intervene. In January 1660 he marched into England, and resistance crumbled before him. In February he entered London, and on the 29th appointed Colonel Carew Ralegh, Sir Walter's second son, a member of the Rump Parliament, to be Governor of Jersey.

At first Monk had no intention of overthrowing the Republic; but he soon saw that nothing could curb the chaos, but a restoration of the monarchy. He secretly sounded the exiled King and found him reasonable. On Hyde's advice Charles signed the Declaration of Breda, promising a general amnesty, security of tenure for property acquired during the troubles, liberty of conscience, and arrears of pay for the troops. 'About the middle of April' according to a local diarist, 'Captain Hanley came to Jersey in the name of Lord Monk. Then little by little men began to speak of the King, and a Fast was ordered to pray for peace throughout the Realm, without mentioning anything else.'[28]

On 8 May the King was proclaimed in London. On the 11th Lemprière was still presiding over the Jersey Court, but a few days later, remembering that he was still under sentence of death for treason, he and other Commonwealth officials slipped away to Coutainville. Hanley now under Monk's orders easily secured Jersey for the King.[29] When news reached the Island on 2 June that Charles had entered London in triumph, Edouard Hamptonne, the deprived Royalist Vicomte, mounted a stool in the Market Place and, for the second time, Charles was proclaimed King; 'and the cannon fired, muskets went off everywhere; at night bonfires blazed in all the parishes'. Everyone hoped that this would be the end of red-coat rule, and the indecisions in England which made it hard for Jerseymen to know to whom they properly owed their loyalty.[30]

XI *Mont Orgueil. 'To say true it is a stately fort of great capacity', Ralegh.*

HISTORIC CASTLES

XII *Elizabeth Castle. Fort Isabella Bellissima on the Islet of St Helier. So called by Ralegh.*

XIII *Grosnez Castle showing Guernsey. A sketch by Sir John Le Couteur,* c.*1840. (Photo: A. E. Mourant)*

DISTANT ISLES

XIV *Marmoutier, an island at Les Écréhous.*

XV *The lavoir at St Cyr, St John, 1813.*

REFLECTIONS

XVI *A Jersey round tower. Le Hocq. Before 1781.*

XVII *An ocean-going brigantine crossing the bay of Naples; a gouache painting.*

CONTRASTS AT SEA

XVIII *Inshore craft at St Aubin's bay, present day.*

Chapter Eighteen

AFTER THE RESTORATION, 1660-1689

Magnanimity in politics is not seldom the truest wisdom.–Burke

AT THE RESTORATION the Royalists reaped their reward. Eleven years before, in a postscript to a letter of little consequence, Charles had written to Carteret: 'I can never forget the good services you have done to my father and me, and, if God bless me, you shall find I doe remember them to the advantage of you and yours'.[1] This unique and irreplaceable document, now at St Ouen's manor, was saved from probable danger during the German Occupation by the action of the then seigneur's wife, who took it to England, thinking that after their children this was the family's most valued possession.

Now Charles kept his word. Sir George became Vice-Chamberlain of the Royal Household, a post granted to him by Charles while still Prince of Wales,[2] a Privy Councillor and Treasurer of the Navy.[3] He was given manors in Cornwall and Devon to wipe out loans made to the King. Later he was named one of the eight proprietors of Carolina. In March 1664 he received another province in America which still bears the name he gave it: New Jersey. He was a member of the committee of trade and plantations, and in 1670 was one of the six to whom the King granted the Bahamas. He was also one of the original subscribers to the Hudson's Bay Company, of which he was elected Deputy-Governor in 1674.[4]

Two other de Carterets, both named Edouard,[5] had been attached to the King's household all through his exile. One now became Gentleman-Usher to the King and eventually Usher of the Black Rod; the other, the youngest son of the Civil War Sir Philippe, resumed his duties as cup-bearer to Prince James, a post which he had held when the King was in Jersey. In 1663, in acknowledgement of his services, he received a curious gift of '*perquages*'. This has posed a number of as yet unsolved problems by the linking of the word '*perquage*' with the right of sanctuary.[6]

This ancient right existed in many countries, Christian and pagan, including England, Normandy and Scandinavia. In Iceland for example an outlaw, while waiting to go abroad, enjoyed normal rights at three specified farms and on the road to the ship that was to take him abroad; and recently a knocker has been restored to Durham Cathedral upon which 247 people are recorded as knocking for sanctuary between June 1464 and September 1524. In Jersey the malefactor took refuge in a church or cemetery where he was allowed to stay unmolested for nine days. Although the civil power kept him under strict observation, his friends and relations might bring him food. After this period the right was denied him and he was forced to take the oath of abjuration of the Island for ever in the presence of the Bailiff and Jurats. He was then led by the ecclesiastical authorities direct to the sea, any deviation from the prescribed route entailing the forfeiture of his privilege. Two late examples in island records are that of Thomas Le Seelleur, who sought sanctuary at St Martin in 1546, and René Le Hardy who after committing a robbery, fled to the church or cemetery of Trinity in 1558. He claimed sanctuary in the presence of John Poulet, last Catholic Dean of Jersey:[7] this was granted him by the civil authority, but Nicolle concludes, from the wording of the Act of the Ecclesiastical Court, that at this period the civil power was making efforts to restrain this ecclesiastical privilege, which disappeared with the Reformation. After this all accused persons were tried by the civil court; but, until the early years of the 19th century, a prisoner, when first brought before Court, might request to be allowed to leave the Island, *à vuider le pays*, in order to stop further proceedings, and this request was generally granted if the offence did not amount to felony.

Much work has already been done in tracing the perquages given with other 'waste' land to Edouard de Carteret. He sold most of his gift to owners of adjacent fields. Other patches were sold by his sister and nieces up to about 1715, and it is through contracts for these sales of land that it has been possible to trace the routes of most, if not all of them. Except at St Ouen and St Martin they went to the south coast, even from northern parishes where bays like Grève de Lecq, Bonne Nuit and Bouley were closer to the church. The Perquages of St Mary, St John and St Lawrence met together at a point where Tesson chapel now stands, reaching the sea just east of Beaumont. Other parishes may also have merged in this way: Trinity and St Saviour possibly reached the sea by Castle Street, formerly known as Le Perquage. A study of the one at St Peter, which is authenticated, shows how circuitous were the routes taken, though as Poingdestre says, they always followed water courses.

No one denies the existence of the right of sanctuary or of the perquages. The problem lies in relating one to the other. Writing on roads in his *Caesarea* in the 1680s, more than a hundred years after the practice of taking sanctuary had lapsed, Jean Poingdestre defines 'another Way of farre different use called Perquage, of the same breadth as the High Way in Normandy'. Allowing for certain discrepancies in Poingdestre's arithmetic, this was about twenty-four feet, but one had also to remember that the Jersey perch differed from the French.

> These wayes began at every church and by the shortest and most direct line went on to the sea, so that it did commonly pass through boggs and between hills along streams of water. For it had *noe other known use* but to conduct by it such as having committed capital crimes did take sanctuary in those churches; which was then a very ordinary course to doe ... I never heard of such wayes anywhere else ... and soe I think I may place these kind of wayes among the singularities of this island ... although by abolishing of sanctuaries at the Reformation the sayd wayes remained uselesse yet they are still visited yearely in their course; till His Majestie disposed of them by Letters Patent to Sir Edouard de Carteret, who had made conveyance of parcels thereof to those persons who had lands bordering thereon, and by that means quite razed and extinguished them as if they had never been.

Since Poingdestre wrote thus, his theory has been handed down by successive historians, and the tradition maintained that every parish had a '*perquage*' exclusively for the use of '*forbannis*', but there are many anomalies to be ironed out. Poingdestre himself casts doubt on his statement in his *Lois et Coutumes de Jersey*, this time equating the perquage with the King's highway and asking why the widest of roads used by the public for moving troops or for solemn processions should have been reserved for outlaws or indeed belonged to the Church, and suggests that it was a popular error to suppose that they had originally been 'sanctuary' roads. Why, he asks, make roads for criminals when other routes were available?[8]

Poingdestre derives perquage from the Latin *pertica* or the French *perche* used in the measurement of roads. We know from early records that all roads above four feet in width were under royal supervision, hence the term Visite Royale. De Gruchy tells us that Jersey had adopted the Norman custom of classifying roads by width, so that we find them variously called *via regia*, *cheminum regis*, *semita regis*, so ranging from the King's highway to the path or *sentier*. There were also certain rights of way, sometimes across fields such as the *chemin de moulin* and the *chemin des morts*.[9]

To revert to the perquages. Poingdestre suggests that, if they had fallen into disuse, it was because the public had found better ways and so neglected the older roads. In any case, these 'better' ways, by comparison with Don's highways,[10] can have been but tracks of varying widths used by carts or men on horseback. Except on the flat land at St Clement or Grouville, they must have followed for the most part the winding valleys running from north to south of the Island. They did not, it seems, necessarily reach the sea in their parish of origin. Indeed the fact that each parish touches the sea may be for the practicalities of fishing and vraicing, both legally controlled activities with their own close seasons and royal dues.

However folk memory is often a reliable fount of history, and perhaps the solution to the mystery lies in Poingdestre's reference to solemn processions. Anger at the sale of the perquages may have had its roots in memories of wide paths made sacred by earlier religious observances of Feast days and Holy days: one still sees in Breton villages processions making their way to the sea for the blessing of the fishing fleet, and in Catholic countries sacred images are still carried through city streets.

No doubt the clergy used these ancient ways to escort *forbannis* to the sea. That the roads were important is revealed in a document recording a Visite Royale in St Peter in 1645, where, under a sub-heading, encroachments on the perquage are listed.[11] There is a considerable need for further research in this field, particularly as the word *perquage* appears to be unique to the Channel Islands and is used in a different context in Guernsey.[12]

After the Restoration Mont Orgueil remained an important State prison. Five of the late King's judges, who escaped the hangman's rope, were immured there for life: Sir Hardress Waller, who 15 years before had been chosen to recapture Jersey, was reported as being 'desperately ill' on 11 October 1666 and died at Mont Orgueil on 9 February 1667; Dr Gilbert Millington died there before September 1666 and was buried in 'common ground'; Colonel James Temple died at Elizabeth Castle on 17 February 1680 and Henry Smith died there sometime after February 1668. Thomas Wayte was buried at St Saviour on 18 October 1688 and his wife Jeanne on 19 November 1689. General Robert Overton, though not a regicide, was too sturdy a Republican to be left at liberty, and he returned to the cell from which Cromwell's death had released him. He was sent back to England and died on 6 December 1671.[13] There were others too whom the Council thought dangerous, including Colonel Edward Salmon, accused of treason, and Colonel Corbett. Colonel John Lambert was closely confined in Castle Cornet for eight years. In many cases the *Dictionary of National Biography* gives the year of imprisonment in Jersey adding 'date of death unknown'.

All the old Royalist officials resumed their posts in Jersey. Jermyn, now Earl of St Albans, again became Governor and sent his nephew Thomas to be his Lieutenant.[14] Carteret remained for the moment Bailiff, but in 1661 he resigned in favour of Sir Philippe of St Ouen, who, two years later, was succeeded by Sir George's brother, Philippe. The de Carterets were now firmly entrenched as rulers of the Island. In 1663 the King presented a huge silver-gilt mace 'to be carried before the Bailiffs in perpetual memory of their fidelity to his august father and himself'.[15] It is almost identical with the one he gave to the Royal Society which he had founded. It is, on all official occasions, carried before the Bailiff and set before his chair in the Royal Court and States' Chamber, and when taken to church for an official or ceremonial service. On the death of the Sovereign it is draped in black chiffon and laid flat on the table in recognition of the superiority of the spiritual over the temporal power: one of the few occasions when it does not remain upright. The inscription is a proud reminder to Jerseymen of their loyalty to their Sovereign: *Tali haud omnes dignatur honore* (not all doth he deem worthy of such an honour).

The eight surviving Royalist Jurats took up their duties, and an order was issued to fill the vacant seats with men 'of known loyalty'.[16] In the church, d'Assigny was expelled from St Martin and his place taken by Philippe Le Couteur, who, though episcopally ordained, had for nine years been officiating as a Huguenot pastor in France. He was made Dean, and in 1663 he revived the Ecclesiastical Court. Henceforth no infraction of Anglican rubrics was permitted. Two Rectors refused to be reordained and resigned. The Rector of St Saviour was three times summoned for giving the Sacrament to persons who remained standing.[17] Nor did the laity escape: Jean Bichard was cited for saying that to communicate kneeling was idolatry, Simon Lesbirel for calling the Anglican service the Mass. Every Tuesday the Dean's Court dealt with long lists of transgressors. A girl was punished for going to a masquerade in male dress, the Churchwarden of St Mary for neglecting to remove his hat in church. The revised Prayer Book, just issued in England, was translated into French by Jean Durel (1625-1683), a Jerseyman who was minister of the Huguenot chapel in the Savoy, and its use was rigidly enforced.[18] But a change of book did not mean a change of religion; Jersey was still Calvinist at heart.

The most urgent problem in the Island was whether Royalists and Republicans could settle down together, 'that henceforth', in the King's words, 'all notes of discord be utterly abolished among us'. Cavaliers flocked back to Jersey, burning for revenge; but the Restoration had been one of consent not conquest. The King had promised 'that no crime whatsoever committed against us or our Royal father shall ever rise in judgment against any man', the actual regicides excepted; and the pledge had been ratified by the Act of Indemnity and Oblivion. On the strength of this Lemprière returned in November 1660 and, 'though guilty of grave offences', was given back his estate.[19]

For years there was dissatisfaction. The Royalists claimed that they ought to recover the fines they had paid when compounding. Jean Pipon, for example, wrote, 'For my loyalty I was obliged to pay to the late usurper £100 to redeem my estate. I beg an order to be repaid'. On the other hand all Commonwealth men were not as lucky as Lemprière. The Royalist Jurats neglected to register the Act of Indemnity and then pleaded that it did not apply to Jersey. In March 1662 a petition was sent to the Council from some who 'in spite of the Act have had their estates seized for their compliance with Parliament'. In April the English Law Officers ruled that Jersey was expressly named in the Act, and the Bailiff was asked why the estates had not been restored. But the men in power were masters in the art of leaving letters unanswered. Two years later the Council complained that it still awaited a reply. None, however, was sent until February 1665. In May the Council ordered the property to be handed back to the owners; but the King had left London to escape the plague, and the letter was never signed; so nothing was done. In 1668 the petitioners renewed their complaint. Again the Law Officers found in their favour with no result. A third petition in 1669 at last produced the order, 'that a copy of the Act of Oblivion, sealed with the Great Seal, be registered in the Court books to remove all doubts as to whether it extends to the island'.[20] It would be interesting to know if eventually all the dispossessed Roundheads recovered their land.

But the man who really drew the Island together was Louis XIV. In 1666 he declared war on England, and secret agents in Paris reported that his first move would be to attack Jersey. Jermyn was bought out by a pension of £1,000 a year,[21] and the Governorship given to a first-class fighting man, Sir Thomas Morgan.[22] This Welshman had led in the Low Countries a force known as 'the immortal six thousand'; he had fought for Parliament throughout the Civil War and had been Monk's right-hand man in the subjugation of Scotland. The Fairfax correspondence describes him as 'very sharp and peremptory'.

He remodelled the Militia, grouping the parish companies into three regiments and putting the men into scarlet coats[23] like Cromwellian soldiers. He kept them under canvas for long spells of intensive training. In August 1666 a State Paper reports: 'Sir Thomas Morgan has lain in the field every night these six weeks', and again in October we read: 'Sir Thomas has 4,000 foot and

200 horse well equipped. He is camping in the fields resolved to die in defence of the island'. But the threatened invasion never took place, though large forces were gathered at St Malo. In July 1667 peace was proclaimed by the Treaty of Breda.

Like all old Commonwealth soldiers Morgan had no use for civilian officials. With the Court he had constant friction. 'He looked upon us', wrote the Jurats to the Council, 'not as fellow-subjects, but as some conquered people.' 'The Governor's drift', they said, 'is ever to make the Court contemptible.' When they forbade the importation of cider, Morgan had three-score hogshead landed at the gate of Mont Orgueil, not for the garrison, but to be retailed to the neighbouring parishes. When the Constable of St Martin protested, he 'threatened to lay him by the heels'. If a Jurat displeased him, a party of soldiers was promptly quartered in his house.

During his governorship Morgan completed the fortifications of Elizabeth Castle. He found at one end of the islet the castle built by the Poulets and at the other Charles' fort, with a large open space between. This he enclosed with walls. 'He would sit', says Falle, 'whole days on the carriage of a cannon hastening the workmen.' By 1668 he had linked the two strongholds together, making the whole islet into one fortress.

He also built the pier at St Aubin's Fort.[24] There had been until now no decent harbour anywhere in the Island. It seems extraordinary, for a sea-faring community, that ships coming to St Helier could find no better shelter than a broken-down jetty at La Folie until the late 18th century. This was not for want of trying. The great advances made in ship-building under the Tudors and the expansion of commerce overseas meant that Jerseymen were trading in larger vessels. Records from the mid-16th century reveal that attempts were made to remedy the situation. Extracts from the Rolls of the Court show that, in July 1552, fines were being exacted by the Governor to build la Cohue (the Court House) and *le havre neuf*; while in September 1552, one Matthew Le Geyt was condemned to pay 18 *livres tournois* towards the building of this harbour at St Helier.

A map in the British Museum, whose authorship is unknown, but which is thought to date from the reign of Henry VIII in about 1545, is in fact a rough sketch of the whole of St Aubin's Bay. There appears to be a rudimentary jetty and sea-wall at St Helier, which is labelled *le havre*, though havres or havens were not necessarily man-made ports. It shelters a few small sailing vessels. The larger ones are in the roads between the Islet of St Helier (before Elizabeth Castle was erected) and St Aubin's Tower (built between 1542 and 1546). There is another group of small boats in the lee of the Tower.

Dumaresq's *Survey* of 1685[25] makes fascinating reading, as, in his chapter on 'Bays, Roads, Harbours and Landing Places', he takes us round the Island, describing the various anchorages, landmarks, currents and shoals. Of St Brelade he writes:

> It is a sandy bay of about a mile over, but shallow, having in the middle many rocks; but without is good anchorage in seven or eight fathom water, when the sea is very quiet, unless it be upon westerly or southerly winds. At the bottom of it, on the west side, near a church, is a small harbour for boats.

Of Gorey:

> At the other side of the Bay (Grouville) is Mont Orgueil Castle, otherwise called the Old Castle, at the foot of which, on the south side, is the most ancient harbour of all in the island. There is an old and decayed pier, where such small boats as use the neighbouring coast of Normandy do resort.

He is equally uncomplimentary about accommodation in St Helier:

> About half a mile from the Town there was a pier designed and begun at the western point of the Town Hill, called Havre Neuf ... but found inconvenient and so laid aside, as since another at the

> south point of the said hill, called Havre-des-Pas was intended for greater vessels than those it is now fit for which are the St Malo's trade but its entrance is also so narrow and full of rocks that it discourages the bestowing any charges upon it.

However Dumaresq does mention that in addition to St Aubin's Fort, there is 'another place where vessels in summer do unlade for the convenience of the town of St Helier close by Charles' Fort at Elizabeth Castle, where they may come at high water over the beach called the Bridge'.[26] He also mentions a small pier, unfinished, under the castle walls. Finally he describes a shelter for boats under the churchyard of St Helier,

> which with the help of a brook, that comes down there, might (with no great charges) be made fit to secure greater vessels, that would be a great conveniency to the commerce of that town, which is at great charges to bring their merchandise by land from St Aubin, which is above three miles, there being no harbour nearer for vessels of a considerable burthen … .'

Dumaresq's *Survey* remained in manuscript in the archives of the Admiralty until the Napoleonic Wars, when Admiral Philippe d'Auvergne was permitted to make copies of it. But meanwhile attempts to make a pier at St Helier continued. In 1700 the States, through the Lieutenant-Governor, Colonel Collier, asked to be permitted to apply the money raised on the sale of wines and spirits 'to ye building of a small pier at a place called ye Newhaven near ye Town of St Helier and Castle Elizabeth';[27] this suggests that considerable rebuilding was required at *le havre neuf*. Plans were also drawn up in some detail for a quay to extend out to sea as far as a rock opposite the south-west angle of the cemetery wall (then lapped by the sea). The section to the west of the cemetery was to serve as a cattle market, there was to be a narrow stone path outside the cemetery wall, and access to the beach where ships were unloaded. But the money accruing from import duties was insufficient for the building of two harbours and it was the merchants of St Aubin who won the day.

It was in 1669 that the States had obtained permission to levy duties on wines and spirits, part of which was to be used 'to erect a pier at St Aubin for the greater security of the merchants'. Hitherto the larger vessels had had to winter at St Malo. By 1668 merchants had begun to make cellars in the town, as St Aubin was now called, to store their goods. The King's scales, at what is now known as the Old Court House, were already in use to weigh all merchandise landed. But there were delays at the outset and in 1671 Morgan stepped in and offered to do the job himself, if he might build the pier from the Fort, and the States agreed. His hustling spirit soon set men to work. George Ralegh, Deputy Lieutenant-Governor from 1661, wrote in 1675: 'Sir Thomas makes incredible progress with the pier he undertook to build. It is 300 feet long, foundations 41 feet broad and 35 feet broad at the top'.[28] Poingdestre called it 'a piece for eternity if you consider the breadth, materials and workmanship'. It was this harbour that caused St Aubin to grow into a little 'town' where an open-air market was held every Monday for merchants of foreign commodities. The present South Pier at St Aubin was begun in 1754. Originally the houses along the present quay had their own private quays at the bottom of their gardens, and there was only a path four feet wide between the gardens and the sea. Horse traffic at high tide had to climb the steep Rue du Moestre[29] and then go down again to the Boulevard. In December 1789 those who lived in these houses petitioned the States[30] to be allowed to build a public quay at their expense, 30 feet wide with two slips. The petition reveals the names of those who lived along the quay at that date. It was built in 1790, the long gardens in front of the houses showing how much land was reclaimed from the sea. Finally in 1819 the North Pier was added. A stone with the initials of John Janvrin commemorates this.

Meanwhile St Helier had to wait. But when, in 1786, the Chamber of Commerce at last persuaded the States[31] to provide a proper harbour for St Helier the days of St Aubin as the principal port were numbered.

35 *Vraicing at Le Hocq. (Photo: E. F. Guiton)*

SCENES FROM YESTERDAY

36 *Milking with traditional can at the St Ouen's Three Parishes cattle show in 1953. (Photo P. Mckie)*

The harbour problem is still with us as ships grow bigger. Other problems which refuse to go away are already mentioned in Actes des Etats of the 17th and 18th centuries. In 1673 and again in 1704 there are references to damage caused by carts using paths near la Mare au Seigneur (St Ouen's Pond) and to the inadvisability of creating any more roads across the flat land of the bay, which was subject to flooding from the sea. There is also concern about the inroads of the sea in 1673 and 1688, when high tides have made the roads at the Dicq and le Hocq impassable. Floods at Gorey are mentioned in 1789, when the inhabitants of Gorey village complained that the sea had encroached on the sand dunes and had even entered their houses at high tides. This report was lodged *au greffe* while the Committee appointed for the Defence of the Isle was asked to visit the site and report back to the States. In 1979 drainage was laid under the dunes, now the links of the Royal Jersey Golf Club, after similar disastrous floods in the preceding winter.

Housing and land usage are not new problems. In 1673 the States complained that, because so many new houses were being built and so many orchards planted, arable land was fast disappearing, and, unless a stop were put to this, the King's revenue in tithes would be considerably diminished and the Island forced to import corn: this might be difficult for lack of funds, '*le traffic qui nous manque nous oste les moyen d'avoir de l'argent pour en acheter*' — the problem of balance of payments. The States decreed that houses might be built only at St Aubin and Gorey, unless they were surrounded by 20 vergées of arable land. There is even a suggestion in 1695 that an engine for 'making salt water fresh' might be useful at Elizabeth Castle: 'I have ordered the Board to contract the patentes of the salt water engines for two of the said engines to be sent with all possible dispatch to Guernsey and Jersey', wrote Viscount Sydney to Sir John Trenchard.[32] Underwater diving is no new activity. In 1688 one Goodwin Wharton had a patent to dive in Jersey granted by James II. He appears to have been unsuccessful and was involved in a lawsuit with Osmund Cooke. He must however have been a pioneer among marine archaeologists.[33] 'Plus ça change, plus c'est la même chose.'

The urgent problem of what to do with paupers remained. The States tried many expedients. An Act of 1662 recalls that as early as 1630 they had ordained that the children of the poor should be apprenticed to men of substance, while the very young and those too old to work should be maintained by contributions from those who could afford it. The parishes were to be responsible for implementing the law, and anyone who refused to comply was to have his goods forcibly seized and sold in the parish cemetery after the mid-week service. If he had no saleable goods, he was to suffer imprisonment. In 1697 the problem in St Ouen was such that the principals and officers decided that they could provide only '*un écu par an*' towards lodging their poor; the registers contain very lengthy lists of men, women and children 'on the parish'.

Despite the fact that at frequent intervals the States re-enacted their regulations for the care of paupers, the poor they had 'always with them'. Morgan's remedy was characteristically drastic. In 1666 he persuaded the States to seek permission under the Great Seal to export their paupers to Ireland, New England or New Jersey. The State admitted that begging and poverty had increased so much through lack of commerce and the expense and calamity of war that their system of social security had failed, and the problem was out of hand: 'il serait au-dessus de la capacité des autres habitans et hors de toute espérance d'y apporter par des voyes ordinaires le remède requis'.[34] They declared in all sincerity of heart that they were motivated solely by compassion and Christian charity, and they complied with Morgan's suggestion. Fortunately the scheme did not obtain the approval of the Council.

However, despite this ban, records show that throughout the 17th century Jerseymen and women were crossing the Atlantic to settle in America. They came from all classes and must have included paupers taken over as indentured apprentices. The new type of ship developed at the end of the 16th century could stay at sea longer, and the Merchant Adventurers had opened up routes to the West Indies, Virginia and Massachusetts as well as to Newfoundland. The route via Spain, Portugal and the Cape Verde Islands was already well known to Jersey seamen.

In 1631 John Guillam, merchant, and Peter Seale, the elder, of the town and county of Southampton, merchant, made a deposition that the *Hope* (possibly the *Bonne Espérance* mentioned earlier), part owned by John Bailache, the elder, 'of the isle of Jersey, marchaunte', was on her return voyage from Newfoundland, 'surprised and taken together with her lading by a Dunkerke man of war': their claim gives an insight into the cost of fitting out and repairing such ships.[35] The Newfoundland in this context was doubtless New England. By the second half of the 17th century the records in Salem, Massachusetts, abound in Jersey names. The Bailhaches, besides providing Constables for the parish of St Lawrence, one of whom had been the original guarantor for the harbour at St Aubin, had interest in trading from Southampton and in shipbuilding in Massachusetts, whence a thriving triangular trade was already carrying cod from the Newfoundland Banks to the West Indies, Spain and the Mediterranean countries. A contract of 1661 survives between 'John Browne, Nicholas Bailhache and John Balach, merchants of Jersey, and William Stevens ship-builder in Salem, for a new ship 68 feet in length to be built for £3.5s a ton' . John Browne settled in Salem to superintend the trading from that end. In Salem also are recorded the baptism of nine children of John Cabot,[36] 'merchant from the isle of Jersey', the marriage of John Blevin to 'Jane le Marcom (Marquand), a Jersey maid', and the death of John Syvret (alias Savary or Sevret) at Wenham, Massachusetts, in 1742 in his 98th year; almost certainly the Jean Syvret, fils Jean, whose baptism is registered at St Ouen in April 1644.[37]

Janvrins, too, were in New England, among them Daniel ancestor of a long line of Jersey merchants, one of whose descendants has his initials carved on the last arm to be built for St Aubin's harbour. In 1684 Daniel Janvrin was suing Thomas Mudgett of Salisbury, New England, 'for one eight the expense of the maiden voyage of the ship *Daniel and Elizabeth*, built by Mudgett for Janvrin, and in which he retained an eighth interest at the time of sailing from Salem'. In 1681 she was freighted by William Hollingsworth, merchant of Salem, and sailed for Jersey via Bilbao. The crew consisted of 30 men, including three Janvrins, and reached Jersey in 1682. Six months later Janvrin sold his shares in the vessel.[38]

Best known of all the denizens of Salem was Philippe Langlois, born in Trinity and godson of Sir Philippe de Carteret, Seigneur of St Ouen; he changed his name to Philip English when he settled in Salem, inherited the fortune of his father-in-law, Hollingsworth, and began to build ship of his own. Before long he was the richest man on the coast, owned 27 ships, two of which sailed regularly to Jersey from Salem with cargoes of cod, rum, molasses and spermacetti (a fatty substance contained in solution in the heads of spermwhales and from which Jerseymen made candles), returning with French wines and brandy, and Jersey shoes and stockings. At the height of his prosperity he had to flee for his life when he became involved in the witch panic of Salem. English is notorious for having shipped back to New England a number of Jersey boys and girls as indentured apprentices: the girls were hired as domestic servants, the boys as sailors. Copies of their indentures have been preserved in the Essex Institute in Salem. In transporting these children, he was following a common practice, and they were not necessarily ill-treated. Sadder was the fate of the Jersey boy, who, in the 1690s, was with Thomas Pipon when the latter died in Jamaica; he was sold to pay for his master's funeral.[39]

From 1651 onwards there was continual trouble over the Navigation Acts. Parliament ordered that 'No merchandise shall be imported into the Plantations, but in English vessels, under pain of fortfeiture [*sic*]'. Jersey petitioned in vain to send her own boats to America. Many cases resulting from the Act appear in the Rolls of the Court and in the records of the Privy Council. Some owners flouted the Act, some pleaded ignorance, others were fined and lost their cargoes. In 1672/3 a plea was registered at Whitehall from 'Benjamin Dumaresq and others of

His Majestie's subjects in the island of Jersey', who owned the *Hope*, a small vessel of some 30 tons. They claimed that

> before they knew His Majesty's pleasure that they should not trade with America, they freighted the said vessel with manufactures of that island and sent her to Jamaica, where the same was unladed and reladed with logwood and with a small parcel of sugars and indigoes: that by stress of weather having sprung a leak they were forced to New England, where, having refitted the said vessel, they bent their course for England, and meeting with very great storms were forced into the Isle of Wight.

Here the Customs' Officer seized their cargo 'pretending the same to be forfeited for trading with America contrary to the Act of Navigation'.

In March 1676 a complaint was made against Philip English for bringing tobacco from New Jersey in the *Speedwell*, and Customs' Officers were ordered to Jersey to prevent the embezzlement of the cargo'. A further enquiry by the Privy Council shows that the ketch had sailed before the Customs could take action. Towards the end of 1677 Sir Thomas Morgan arrested the *Elizabeth* of Jersey 'for having transgressed the Acts of Parliament relating to Trade and Navigation in coming to that place directly from Boston to New England'. Philip Syvret, Daniel Janvrin and others, 'all His Majesty's subjects and master mariners and others calling themselves owners of the said ship', protested at Whitehall on the 5th and again on 14 December 1677, asking that the *Elizabeth* be not called up to the Exchequer Court in London, 'as they were ready to make proof of passes granted for their voyage to and from New England and would be put to great expense by having to bring the vessel to London'. They pleaded in vain. The case was tried before the Exchequer Court and they lost their ship and cargo. In December 1678 an entry in the Port Books records that £2 2s. 9d. was forfeited to the Crown for a breach of the Act by Daniel Janvrin, '*in nave sua a Jerzy & Newengland*'. There follows a list of the cargo: 'ten loads oaken plankes; two hundred burgendorpe deale, one hundred and halfe oares, twenty-four middle masts, thirty hundred pipe-staves'. Later a broad arrow was put on the *Joanna* of Piscattaway, 'whereof Philip Syvret is master', for taking wines direct from Malaga to Boston. Throughout the 18th century Jersey merchants and master mariners were to protest on many occasions about the restrictions imposed on them by the English Navigation Acts.[40]

Chapter Nineteen

JACOBITES IN JEOPARDY

We were not so dull as not to know how to distinguish betwixt a flagrant Rebellion, that tore up Foundations ... and a Revolution manifestly tending to preserve to us the two most valuable Things in the World, True Religion and Civil Liberty. –Falle, *An Account of the Island of Jersey*

DURING THE CIVIL WARS Jerseymen from both sides had spent time in England and, though they might insist on their right to trade with the French, they knew that their life-line was now securely attached to the other side of the Channel, whichever English King was in power.

In 1677 Jersey faced once more a threat of invasion. England was clamouring for war with France to check the triumphs of Louis XIV in the Low Countries. Morgan wrote in January 1678: 'Merchants from St Malo report great preparations for war. I doubt not they will make an attempt on the island'.[1] In repeated letters marked 'Haste! Haste!' Morgan pleaded for permission to strike a blow at St Malo, before war was declared, by sending fire ships in among the fleet that Louis had mustered there. 'A bonfire', he said, 'might be made of their shipping with little hazzard.' This was intended to have an effect similar to that of Pearl Harbour in the Second World War. Morgan could not know that, by the secret Treaty of Dover, the King of England was receiving a pension from Louis.

Sir George Carteret was now a very great man at Court. 'I have almost brought things to pass', he told Pepys,[2] 'that the King will not be able to whip a cat, but I will be at his tail.' He was also very wealthy: and he did not forget his native land. He planned two benefactions. The first was a reformatory for idlers. Twenty years before when Lieutenant-Governor, he had offered a dwelling to be used as a House of Correction; now he renewed the offer and was warmly thanked by the States, but again the scheme failed to arouse enthusiasm and was eventually dropped.

His next suggestion was to revive the idea, first proposed by Laurens Baudains, of founding a college. He wrote to the States that, 'since nothing is of such great importance to a country as the instruction of its youth', he had set aside 15,000 *livres tournois* to build a college. He promised, if the Island would play its part, to make further contributions and to collect subscriptions from his friends. He secured from the King an annual grant of 2,000 *livres tournois* to be a first charge on the Import duties. A site was chosen not far from the present Victoria College and £31 was spent in levelling it; and that is the last we hear of the matter.[3]

One kindly thought of his did however bear fruit. He heard that Corpus Christi College, Oxford, had some scholarships reserved for Hampshire, and persuaded the King to suggest that one of these should be allotted to the Channel Islands. The King passed on his request through Bishop Morley of Winchester; but Corpus and Hampshire both emphatically rejected the idea. So Morley, one of the most generous of men, who gave away most of the income of his see to charity, decided to found some scholarships himself. Oxford, however, seems to have regarded Jerseymen as barbarians. 'It will be hard', wrote Dean Prideaux, 'to find any College for brutes.' Pembroke did accept, and the bishop founded five scholarships of £10 a year with chambers, three for Jersey, two for Guernsey, the Dean, Bailiff and Jurats to nominate. 'Scholars shall solemnly promise to return to serve the island as preachers, schoolmasters, or otherwise, or pay a forfeit of £200.'[4]

Sir Thomas Morgan died early in 1679 and was succeeded by Sir John Lanier, who had distinguished himself in the English auxiliaries and had served under Monmouth in France.[5] He at once began to quarrel with the States. They had just appealed to the Council against Morgan's high-handedness and received an Order wholly in their favour: 'No Governor shall disturb the inhabitants in the peaceable possession of their privileges'. Lanier demanded to see in writing what those privileges were, and persuaded the Council to rehear the case. The matter was argued at Westminster during several hearings. 'We disputed many months', wrote Sir Edouard de Carteret, the Vicomte and spokesman for the States, 'and Sir John's secretary told me I was a pitiful fellow and a rascal. The last Council day Sir John said in my ear, "Sir Edouard, you and I will decide this business presently", and he took me by the hand and we went to Hyde Park'. The King, however, forbade the duel. But when they returned to Jersey, Lanier had his revenge by vetoing the payment of Sir Edouard's out-of pocket expenses and pulling down his garden wall on the ground that it might be used as a bastion for guns to bombard the Castle. On the main dispute between Governor and States, honours were divided. The States gained some of their points, Lanier beat them on others.[6]

Morgan's death saved Mont Orgueil from destruction. A warrant had been issued for its demolition 'as useless for the defence of the island'. But, on Lanier's appointment, Commissioners came to Jersey, who among other duties inspected the Castles and reported that Mont Orgueil could still be used as barracks; so it was reprieved again, as it had been almost a century earlier by Ralegh.[7]

At Whitehall the Court after the Restoration had become notorious for immorality, but in Jersey people were not allowed to neglect their religious duties.[8] More and more stringent grew the laws against Sabbath-breaking. Heads of houses were fined three groats for every absence of themselves, their family or their servants from either of the Sunday services. At the last stroke of the bell everyone must be in church and remain until after the blessing. Constables must send regular lists of absentees and pay surprise visits during church hours to see if anyone were at home. No one could hold a public office without a certificate from the churchwardens that he was a regular communicant. Some of these certificates still exist in collections of family papers.[9]

Twenty years earlier the King had given Lord Jermyn a written promise that at his death his nephew Thomas should inherit the Governorship. He died in 1684, and Thomas, who was now Baron St Edmundsbury, produced his old warrant and, though his uncle had long ceased to be Governor, his claim was allowed. Lanier was removed to another command and Lord Thomas took his place. He was very unlike his predecessors. Falle praises 'the easiness and affability of his manners'. But he did not stay long, and for the next 20 years was constantly changing his Lieutenants. In the first 10 years he had no less than nine.[10] At that period and for all the next century both Governors and Bailiffs were for most of the time represented in the Island by their Lieutenants. Some never even visited the Island in their charge: their letters of appointment often state, '*bien qu'il ne puisse résider à Jersey*'.

In February 1685 Charles II died, and the States sent his brother James an effusive letter of welcome, praising his 'heroic virtues' and 'the many testimonies of special favour towards this island, from the time it had the honour to enjoy your Royal person to this hour'.[11] Jerseymen were now becoming literary. Within a few years three wrote descriptions of their island. Jurat Jean Poingdestre finished in 1682 his *Caesarea or a Discourse of the Island of Jersey*. In 1685 Philippe Dumaresq presented to James II his *Survey of ye Island of Jersey*. Nine years later Philippe Falle, Rector of St Saviour, published in London the first edition of his *Account of the Isle of Jersey*. From these we gather certain facts which are not mentioned in State Papers.[12]

Falle reckoned the population at 'between fifteen and twenty thousand'; the others agree. Dumaresq, arguing from the hearth tax returns, which showed 3,069 houses, said: 'The number of inhabitants will hardly exceed 15,000'; while Poingdestre calculated from the Militia rolls and the figures for the Easter Communion that 'there are not past 20,000'.

A great change had occurred in the appearance of the Island. A hundred years before it had been a land of open fields. Hedges were almost unknown. While crops were growing, even pigs were tethered to keep them from straying. But once the season of *banon* was proclaimed, everyone's cattle were free to wander where they would. 'About a hundred years since', wrote Poingdestre, 'the land lay almost open with few enclosures; but of late people have applied themselves to make fences.' 'Not', says Falle, 'such fences as in England, but great bulwarks of earth, sometimes ten feet high with thickness answerable to the height, with a hedge of whitethorn on the top'. Between these high embankments meandered narrow lanes, often only four feet wide and heavily shaded by overhanging trees which were kept under control, and still are, by the local system of branchage: every proprietor has to keep his own roadside banks cut, all branches must leave a stipulated clearance to allow loaded farm carts, lorries and other forms of transport to pass. The parochial authorities are responsible for seeing that this is done, and each year the Royal Court inspects a number of roads in two specified parishes, a custom known as *La Visite Royale*. In former days the inspection was made on horseback, the Vicomte armed with his measuring rod.[13] Fines are levied for infringement of these regulations.

All three historical accounts are written in English, the authors believing, doubtless correctly, that people in England should be told about Jersey of which they knew little. The books may not have had a wide circulation locally where the language was predominantly French, but in this context it is well to remember that, in his second edition of 1734, Falle added a paragraph on the language of the Island which to some extent contradicts the statement so often made that English was not spoken before the influx of 'residents' after the Napoleonic wars. So many local men travelled to England as sailors and merchants, held posts in the Civil Service in London or took refuge in England during civil strife; so many English regiments came to the Island, that many more than is sometimes supposed must have been bi-lingual or indeed tri-lingual. To quote Falle:

> Albeit French be our ordinary language, there are few gentlemen, merchants or considerable inhabitants, but speak English tolerably. The better to attain it, they are sent young to England. And among the inferior sort who have not the like means of going abroad, many make a shift to get a good smattering of it in the Island itself. More especially in the town of St Helier, what with this, what with the confluence of the officers and soldiers of the garrison, one hears well-nigh as much English spoken as French. And accordingly the weekly prayers in the Town Church, are one day in French, and another in English.[14]

The three accounts, perhaps Poingdestre most of all, are important primary sources of information, as well as being the first accounts written since *les Chroniques* a hundred years earlier. No other history of Jersey was attempted for more than a century and a half.[15]

All three writers deplore the decay in agriculture. Falle complains that, when Heylin came to the Island in 1629, Jersey not only fed itself, but exported corn to St Malo, whereas now the inhabitants 'must be supplied from England or (in time of peace) from Bretagne in France. They have often gone as far as Dantzig in the Baltic, invited there by the cheapness of the market'. According to Poingdestre the Island imported half the corn it used. One reason for this was the increase in apple-growing, due to a change in drinking habits. Once everyone had drunk mead made from honey, and the Island had buzzed with bees. Now everyone drank cider. Falle estimated that 24,000 hogsheads were made every year, and Poingdestre remarked: 'the whole island is in danger of becoming a continual orchard'. The trend persisted and by 1795 just under 20 per cent of all land area was under orchard, the highest percentage being 36 per cent in St Saviour and the lowest four per cent in St Ouen.

Another contributory cause of the neglect of agriculture was the lure of the sea. Dumaresq bewailed the fact that Jersey owned 'forty vessels with topsails and decks, beside many smaller craft', whereas 20 would be ample for the Island's needs. But the main cause was the stockings, 'that lazy industry', Dumaresq calls it. But it was more profitable to knit than to plough, as today it is to take in guests. 'The greatest part of the inhabitants', writes Poingdestre, 'are knitters. There be many houses where man, wife and children, beginning at the age of five or six, have no other employment, and may be said to make every one a pair of stockings every week; which must according to my account come to more than ten thousand pairs weekly.' These were brought to town on Saturdays and sold to the stocking merchants, who exported them to France, Spain or America.

In his first edition Falle helps to solve one problem which is a constant puzzle to students of Jersey history. All money payments were reckoned in *livres tournois* and all incomes in wheat quarters. But the value of each varied from time to time. When we read, for example, in the *Extente* of 1668, that the Governor's salary was 13,000 *livres tournois* or that the Crown revenue from the Island was 666 quarters, what did that represent in English money? Falle says that in his day the *livre tournois* was worth roughly 1s. 6d. (9p) and the wheat quarter, which went up and down with the price of corn, averaged 80p. Thus a fine of 100 *livres tournois* was about £7 14s. and an income of 100 quarters about £80, though that is only an approximation; it does not indicate the purchasing power, which was far greater than it is now. Falle's comments on the King's revenue, which originally 'made up a pretty estate for the King in so small a country' show that inflation is no new phenomenon: 'now the *livre tournois*, according to which the money-rents were then valued, is fallen so low, that the above said thousand *livres tournois* are brought under one hundred pounds sterling'. Of the *rentes* he writes that they have been so multiplied, 'that 'tis thought there is more wheat due on account every year in this island, than can grow upon the island in two years'. Parish rates are still assessed in 'quarters', but the value of the 'quarters' varies from parish to parish and is fixed at a parochial assembly. A possible change in the rating system is currently under review, and some adjustments have been made in 1980.

Already fine houses were being built, particularly by St Aubin merchants. There are dated stones on several houses along the Bulwarks. A contract of 1682[16] has survived between an owner, Miss Sara Le Sueur, and her master masons, although the exact location of the house is uncertain. The contract states that the house is to be 24 feet long, the gable wall four feet thick, with two hearths therein. The other walls to be 2½ feet thick and 16 feet high. They are 'to place there a rounded doorway'. The number, but not the size, of the windows is stipulated and the price was 14 crowns. The proprietor was to give the Gallichans (her masons) dinner every day, including Sundays, and a pot of cider per man.

In 1685 a new stream of French refugees began to arrive in Jersey following the Revocation of the Edict of Nantes, which 90 years before had granted the Huguenots freedom of worship. When Madame de Maintenon became Louis XIV's morganatic wife, Catholic influence at Court increased, and Louis was persuaded that his duty was to extirpate heresy. First came the *dragonnades*: dragoons in France were quartered on peaceful Protestant homes with permission to behave as badly as they liked. Under pressure of this persecution thousands of Huguenots made outward adhesion to the State religion. Then in October 1685 the King proclaimed that, since all heretics had been converted, the Edict of Nantes could be repealed. All Protestant worship was forbidden, the Huguenot temples were pulled down, their schools closed and their ministers exiled.

Nearly half a million left the country, and of these several thousands found new homes in Jersey, marrying into local families and becoming integrated into island life. From this exodus

CONTRASTS
IN
ARCHITECTURE

37 *Prince's Tower built upon the medieval chapels at La Hougue Bie in* c.*1760. (Photo: F. de L. Bois from a picture by L. Young,* c.*1815)*

38 *The prison at Newgate Street, built in 1811 and demolished in 1976.*

descend many local families such as Girard, Gosselin, de Faye, du Parcq, Gosset, Hemery and Amiraux. There is earlier evidence of silversmiths at work in the Island: a document of 1536[17] speaks of 'Jean Le Porc, argentier, fils Thomas' and in 1540 the same man is referred to as an 'orphevure'.

Of this new influx some were craftsmen, particularly goldsmiths, and to them we owe much of our Jersey silver, locally made and now in great demand, as much for its quality as for its rarity value. Spoons are the most common items and there are few forks; but one also finds tea-pots, coffee pots and a wide variety of mugs, beakers and handsome two-handled cups. The best known item is the Jersey bowl. It is small and shallow, and has two handles, and is believed to have been used originally as a christening bowl. Many items are engraved with arms, initials and sometimes dates.

At this period the Dean's Court was kept busy receiving back those who had lapsed. A typical entry reads:

> 1686 March 13, Paul Alexandre de Goulaine, ecuyer, seigneur de Boisrenaud de l'Évêché de Nantes, Anne Joubert, native de Poitou, of Rennes, Louise de Toury of Sion en Bretagne and Jeanne de l'Espine, widow of Jacques Jandre, sieur de la Guitonnerie de la ville de Vitray, have confessed that, through infirmity of the flesh and the rigours of persecution, they allowed themselves to subscribe to the errors of Rome, for which sin they implore God's pardon and beg the Court to receive them back into the peace of the Church. Their petition is granted on condition that they make public confession of their sin in the Parish Church of St Helier.[18]

These were only the penitent apostates. Most of the newcomers were men and women who had stood firm in their Calvinist creed: and of those we have no register. But we know that many of them founded families that later played a leading part in the life of the Island.

About this time Jersey's smuggling began to attract attention. The English Customs awoke to the fact that the Island was importing far more tobacco than it could possibly smoke. Enterprising merchants were buying it in Southampton, getting a rebate on duty, bringing it to the islands and then landing it on moonless nights in remote Devonshire coves. So in 1681 a Customs' House officer, Lawrence Cole,[19] was sent to Jersey to keep an eye on what went out and came in, and he obtained authority 'to board all vessels coming and going and take account of their loadings'. He was succeeded in 1685 by William Hely, who complained that the whole island was in conspiracy against him and that, whenever he tried to do his duty, he was affronted and beaten and could get no help from Jurats and Constables.[20] The Jersey smugglers defied all efforts to outwit them and ultimately Hely joined them.

Jersey's Republicanism was dead but its Protestantism was lashed wide-awake by tales told by the Huguenots. Moreover it was disturbed by rumours that James was scheming to follow Louis' example and force popery on England. After Monmouth's rebellion he had replaced many army officers by Roman Catholics and recruited in Ireland to treble his troops. Hitherto in Jersey Governors had chosen their own Lieutenants, but James appointed an Irish Catholic, John Legge, and gave him as Deputy another Catholic, Captain Gwilliam. Irish troops were drafted into the garrison and Catholic priests sent as chaplains to the Castles.[21] A rash move in Protestant Jersey.

In the Island as in England there was no open resistance, as the heirs to the throne were Protestant, Mary and Anne, daughters of James' first wife, whose father, Sir Edward Hyde, later Lord Clarendon, had accompanied Charles II to Jersey and there written most of his *History of the Great Rebellion*. Suddenly hope was shattered. James' second wife, Mary of Modena, bore a son, and the heir to the throne was now a boy who would be brought up as a Catholic. Nothing short of a Revolution would save British Protestantism. An invitation was sent to Mary Stuart's husband, William, Stadholder of Holland. He landed on Guy Fawkes' Day 1688, and James fled to France leaving no legal government. On 13 February 1689 William and Mary were proclaimed King and Queen.

Meanwhile in Jersey the States were sitting on thorns. James and his Jesuits had temporarily killed all loyalty to the house of Stuart, though it would be revived later in the wearing of an oak leaf on 29 May,[22] well into the 20th century. This was the anniversary of Charles II's birthday and of his restoration; the oak recalled his escape from Worcester. The Castles were in Catholic hands. Would James try to hold out in Jersey as his brother had done 43 years before? As Louis had declared in his favour would he invite French troops to occupy the Island? The States' records are discreetly silent about this crisis. The only hint comes in an Act of November 1688: 'Considering the dangers threatening in these troublous times, it is ordered that three hundred quintals of biscuits be bought for use in time of need and that the Courts do not sit until further notice, so that no one be withdrawn from guard-duty'.[23]

There was a Jacobite plot. A letter from Jersey among the State Papers declares: 'One Macarthy came from England to Jersey, and there made a party, who promised to deliver the Castles to him if he brought a commission from King James, which he went to Paris to get, and returned.'[24] The organisers were an English priest named Philpot (was this Father Philpot who later became the King's Confessor at St Germain?) and André Simon, Seigneur of Bourg, a St Malo merchant, whose boat, *La Réserve,* was a frequent visitor to Jersey. On 16 December Simon was arrested and lodged in Mont Orgueil. The Court urged Gwilliam to seize Philpot also, but he refused because the priest held a *caveat* signed by James, exempting him from arrest. A fortnight later, however, when it was reported that Philpot had twice tried to leave the Island and that Simon was allowed such freedom that 'the safety of the island was endangered', the Court ignored Gwilliam and ordered Sir Thomas Windham, Captain of the Infantry, to take both men into his own safe-keeping. This was done.

A lady now appeared on the scene. Sarah Archer hired a shallop at St Malo and came to rescue Simon. But her boat was detected in St Clement's Bay and, after a fight in which several men were wounded, her crew was sent to the Castle. In January 1689 a message to the *Orange Gazette* said: 'We have sent Captains Hardy and Allen, gentlemen of this island, to London to prosecute one Bouk, a French papist, and Philpot, an English priest, whom we have imprisoned for traitorously trying to put us into the hands of the French'. In March Lord Jermyn wrote: 'The depositions against Mr du Bourg and Philpot are before the Council'. In April they made a final appearance before the Royal Court and refused to plead. The last we hear of them is in an order to Captain Andrew Cotton: 'The King has directed the two persons, Philpot and Du Bourg, whom you brought from Jersey, to be brought up in the custody of a messenger. You will therefore deliver them to the bearer with any papers relating to the crimes whereof they are accused'.[25]

Philippe Le Geyt,[26] whose commentaries were long the chief authority on Jersey Law, was now Lieutenant-Bailiff. He grappled tactfully with an awkward situation. 'Matters were so managed', he wrote, 'that the inhabitants were admitted to mount guard in the Castle in equal proportions with the soldiers, which secured the fortress against any design to deliver it to the enemy.'

The crisis bred a crop of rumours, and Sir Edouard de Carteret, King James' Cup Bearer, did not escape suspicion. Jurat Jean de la Cloche asserted that he was a Papist and that he was secretly urging militia officers not to resist the French if they landed. This charge gained no credence and de la Cloche was deprived of his Juratship for libel. Later Sir Edouard was appointed Bailiff. The Island was finally made safe by the arrival on 1 April of the Earl of Bath's regiment with his nephew, Sir Bevil Granville, in command. 'At whose coming', says Falle, 'the Papists were disarmed and the island secured for the Prince.'[27]

Chapter Twenty

A TETCHY GENERATION, 1689-1709

Thou wilt quarrel with a man that hath a hair more or less in his head than thou hast.–
Shakespeare, *Romeo and Juliet*

WHEN WILLIAM OF ORANGE became King, England was again drawn into the war with France as an ally of the Dutch in the struggle with Louis XIV. For the next 20 years the very magnitude of the battle which raged from the Netherlands to the Danube, from Gibraltar to Newfoundland, eased the pressure on Jersey. Louis was given no time to think about the Channel Islands.

But this war lost the islands their privilege of neutrality. For two hundred years Pope Sixtus' Bull had been fairly well observed. Poingdestre quotes a French text book on maritime law, *Les Us et Coutumes de la Mer*, which was printed in Rouen in 1671[1] and stated that prizes were adjudged null, if taken on the seas round Jersey and Guernsey, where France and England had agreed, though war rage between them, never to prey on one another, so long as these islands were in sight. In 1678 the States, in a message of gratitude to Charles II for allowing them to use the impôt on wine for the building of a harbour, had expressed the hope that he would not refuse his subjects in the Island freedom to trade in their own vessels with his plantations in Africa, Asia and America, and would confirm their undisputed privileges that 'all merchants, as well as natives as aliens, in peace or war, have liberty of free trade with the island'.[2] William, however, was not the man to tolerate trading with the enemy. In 1689 he issued a proclamation prohibiting 'the importation or retailing of any commodities of the growth and manufacture of France'.[2] The result was to encourage smuggling with France.

An expert on the subject[3] notes that smugglers 'were regarded by perhaps the majority of the nation as men who risked life and liberty itself for the purpose of bringing goods to the poor man's door far more cheaply than grasping governments would permit'. As William pursued his military goal, he exacted more and more money in customs' dues to finance his enterprises. As these levies increased, so did the favourite sport of smuggling on both sides of the Channel. The Jerseyman with his little boat was no exception. When regular trading-vessels stopped, a great field opened for private enterprise.

In 1690 the Council complained:

> The inhabitants are sending ammunition to St Malo. The trade is carried on in the Ecréhous. This traffic is encouraged by the fact that lead is worth in Jersey but twopence or threepence a pound. Upon a signal given, which is the lighting of a fire on the Ecréhous, small vessels belonging to Normandy and Jersey make for that place and drive a trade for lead, powder and other things prohibited by law.[4]

The Lieutenant-Governor was ordered to take steps to stop this; but he, a civilian named Edward Harris,[5] was himself one of the smugglers. In 1691 a report before the Council asserted:

> The French come to the Ecréhous and make great fires, which is the signal for boats to come from Jersey. The Lieutenant-Governor grants passes for these boats. The King's Advocate and the

> Vicomte[6] publicly declared that whoever went about to obstruct the trade with France should have his ears cut off. When Aaron Cabot, a Trinity centenier, stopped a boat going to the Ecréhous, he was ordered by the Court to beg pardon of the Lieutenant-Governor on his knees. On information that a quantity of lead was on a boat going to the Ecréhous, Major Charles Le Hardy, Constable of Grouville, stopped it. For this he was called a dog and a rogue by the Lieutenant-Governor and his commission as Major taken from him. There is an order set up in the Guard House that any boat that has a pass from the Governor should be cleared without search.[6]

The quibble was probably that, since the Ecréhous were part of Jersey, there was nothing illegal in taking goods there. What happened to them after that, no one but a busybody would enquire.

Harris was suspected of worse disloyalty than smuggling. Another State Paper says:

> The Lieutenant-Governor is almost always in bed. He maintains a public commerce with France by vessels which arrive and depart at night. His extreme poverty creates uneasiness, lest he should be corrupted by the French king. Experienced officers of the militia have been displaced to make room for raw youths, because a great deal of money is derived from commissions.

In 1685 he was superseded.

His successor, Colonel Thomas Collier, was a tough professional soldier, veteran of many campaigns, who had hoped for the governorship of New England and was disappointed with his posting to Jersey.[7] However he built himself a house at St Saviour and settled in the Island for the rest of his life. He was puzzled what to do about the smuggling, which was now being carried on almost without concealment. In 1703 Edouard Dumaresq wrote: 'A month ago the Sieur St Paul of St Malo came to my house at 9 p.m. asking me to protect him in buying from me £6,000 worth of tobacco'. Dumaresq handed him over to Collier, but the Frenchman, unabashed, tried to do a deal with him, offering to trade news from St Malo for stockings and tobacco. 'He would leave the news', wrote Collier, 'on any rock I might appoint here.' The truth was that no one regarded the King's prohibition as anything more than a tiresome temporary interference with trade. Even Falle in his first edition in 1694 wrote of the Privilege of Neutrality as though it still existed, though in his second edition in 1734 he was forced to admit: 'Like other antiquated things this privilege seems to have no being now but in books and parchments'.

Smuggling into England was almost as profitable as into France. In 1700 the Customs' Commissioners complained of the 'unlimited practice of the island of Jersey, by the help of their small craft, to run French goods upon the coast of England, notwithstanding all the care that is taken to prevent them'.[8] So the Council ordered every boat leaving Jersey for England to deposit a sum equal to the whole value of her cargo, which would be returned when a certificate was produced that the Customs' duties had been paid. This proved impossible to enforce.

There were however those who realised that trade with England would now be preferable to the commerce which the islands had enjoyed with France and which since the war was 'much impaired by reason of strict prohibition'. In 1691 George Dumaresq, Philip Dauvergne, a number of Englishmen and two Guernseymen petitioned the Council to be allowed to set up a linen and paper manufacture, 'the ground being very proper for sowing and raising hemp, and the people qualified for such work'. A warrant was issued

> to prepare a Bill for the incorporating of a company for carrying on the manufacture of linen and paper within Jersey and Guernsey ... the Company to be incorporated by the name of the Governor and Company of the Royal Corporation of London ... they are to have powers to hold a court in London or Westminster for directing the affairs of the company and the power to elect a sub-committee to meet in London, Jersey and Guernsey.

The petitioners were given power to purchase land etc. not exceeding in value '£1,000 per annum and to make and raise a joint stock of any value whatsoever for the said purpose'. This must surely be one of the earliest attempts to form a Channel Island company and to introduce light industry into the islands. Unfortunately 'upon the complaint of the Governor and assistants of the King and Queen's Corporation for linen manufacture in England against the letters patent', the Council decided not to give permission for the proposed enterprise.[9]

One useful improvement in this period was the building of a prison in the town. Hitherto criminals had been kept at Mont Orgueil, and some of the King's tenants in the eastern parishes of St Martin, Grouville and St Saviour had been forced by the terms of their tenure to guard them, acting as halberdiers on their march to and from the Court. This obligation attached to the property, not the owner, and so passed automatically to a new tenant. The remoteness of the prison was obviously inconvenient, so in 1680 the States asked His Majesty's permission to build a prison in 'some convenient place within the town of St Hilary to be near the Royal Court there'.[10] Work began in 1688 at what is now Charing Cross. This was the only entrance to the Town from the west, and the building straddled the road like a city gate. Carting of material for the work was required from all the inhabitants of the Island, and the Constables were asked to organise this through the parishes and to adjust the rates in due proportion. The first prisoners were lodged in 1693 and the building completed in 1699. By 1749 its condition was parlous, with almost every door and window faulty.[11] Until 1811, when it was demolished, all traffic from the west had to pass under the gloomy tunnel below the gaol. It was replaced by a new prison built in 1811 near the hospital. This was a building of outstanding architectural merit, designed by Captain Victor Prott, R.E., with Amice Norman, a local craftsman, as master carpenter.[12]

Unusual tenants of this second prison have included 13 men from St Ouen, members of the West Regiment of the Militia, who, in May 1891, were sentenced to terms of imprisonment for refusing to obey orders. The Regiment enjoyed the right to lead the Militia on ceremonial occasions, such as the parade held on the sands of St Aubin's Bay to celebrate the Sovereign's Birthday. When deprived of their privilege by an error of command, a group of St Ouennais had stood still and held their ground.[13] During the Second World War a number of respected citizens including Mrs Ivy Forster who, after the war, was to sit in the States as the Island's first lady deputy, were imprisoned for 'crimes' which attracted the attention of the occupying forces. Both groups were treated as heroes by their compatriots. Now it has been found preferable to house prisoners in the country.[14]

Throughout the wars with France Jersey remained undisturbed. Only once did Louis give the Island a fright. In 1692 he allowed an army to gather at La Hougue on the north-east side of the Cotentin peninsula near St-Vaast and dangerously close to Jersey. James II in exile went himself to the Cotentin in a last bid to reclaim his kingdom. Jersey's allegiance, however, was no longer to the Stuarts. The States sent Philippe Falle, the historian and Rector of St Saviour, with Durell, the Solicitor-General, to appeal to King William in person. 'For eighteen months', Falle wrote,

> I constantly attended the Council Board and sometimes the Ordnance, Admiralty and Victualling Office; never ceasing to represent how much it would be for their Majesties' service and the interest of the kingdom to provide for the safety of those islands, until I obtained almost everything I asked; viz: the repair of the barracks which were fallen, so that the soldiers were forced to lie out of the King's garrisons, and thereby left them exposed to the enemy, all manner of warlike stores and provisions wanting in the castles, cannon to be placed round the islands in places lying most open to descent, arms for the militia, light frigates to cruise from time to time about the islands.

Then the danger vanished. In a naval battle off La Hougue, in May 1692, the French fleet was destroyed. James watched British sailors setting fire to his transports and burning them at the water's edge. He could do nothing but disband his army and return to St Germain.[15]

This does not mean that the Island was at peace. After the upheaval of the Commonwealth it was folly to think that life would settle down into the pre-war grooves. Fantastically bitter quarrels were a feature of Jersey life during the reigns of William and Mary and Queen Anne. The Governors were almost always absent. Lord Jermyn paid only two brief visits to the Island during his last 20 years. His successor, Henry Lumley, never came at all. The Bailiffs were almost as bad. Sir Edouard de Carteret spent most of his time in London. After his death no Bailiff was appointed for five years. Then came Sir Charles de Carteret,[16] Gentleman of Queen Anne's Privy Chamber, who, on his rare appearances, proved quite incompetent to deal with the surging unrest.

To illustrate the '*troubles intestins*', a phrase that constantly occurs, we have the letters and papers of Philippe Pipon, Seigneur of Noirmont, Constable of St Brelade and Receiver-General.[17] All his life he was embroiled in furious quarrels with his neighbours. In 1704 Jean Le Couteur, one of his tenants, summoned him for 'wresting a gun out of the hands of the plaintiff's son while he was shooting rabbits on ground which was undoubtedly his own'. This raised an important question: 'Had a seigneur exclusive shooting rights over the tenants' fields?' In the original case the Court found that 'the said seigneur' had a good right to seize upon the said gun provided he, the said seigneur could justify that he had a right of warren upon the ground or a long possession of warren beyond the memory of man'. The judgment was open to question, for, though the fief and seigneurie may have carried right of warren, the seigneur's father, Elie Pipon, had only recently bought, in 1695, the fief and seigneurie of Noirmont from attorneys of Lord George Carteret: it is interesting to note the price he paid: £700 sterling *monnaie d'Angleterre* and £45 for expenses. Le Couteur appealed to the Privy Council and the decision of the Royal Court in favour of Pipon was reversed, instructions being given that the gun was to be restored to the appellant's son.[18] One is constantly surprised at the time taken up by the Privy Council in settling the private affairs of these tetchy Jerseymen. However it is pleasant to record that the Council also heeded the prayers of the poor. In December 1691 a certain Philip de la Cour of St Lawrence was imprisoned for stealing a goose and sheep. He escaped and pleaded with the Council that 'having a poor family to maintain, which had suffered much already', he might be pardoned his offence and be permitted to return home. Pardon was granted accordingly.[19]

Philippe Pipon also embarked on a 14 years' fight with his cousin, Jurat Josué Pipon of La Moye,[20] which began with a trumpery quarrel over tithes. Josué was in the right, but Philippe constantly shouted to the world that his cousin was a thief. Once when they met they drew swords and bystanders had to separate them. A third neighbour, Pierre Seale, ex-Constable of St Brelade, raised the '*Clameur de Haro*' against Pipon, because the latter, when enlarging his house, had encroached on the road to Belle Croute. Seale also complained that he had been attacked by Pipon 'on a Monday when merchants gather on St Aubin's quay to transact business'.

Of wider interest is the opposition to Sir Charles de Carteret, the Bailiff. When he came of age he was faced with a revolt of his tenants at St Ouen against their feudal dues. The *Chefs* of his *Cinquantaines*, whose responsibility it was to see that the tenants in their division of the fief paid their annual dues and carried out their duties to the Seigneur, sued Sir Charles to show 'by what right he claimed annually from each *cinquantaine* a cartload of vraic, the digging of a vergée of land, the cartage of wood and stone for the repair of the manor buildings and manual labour'.[21] The Court appointed a commission of 12, six from each side, to enquire into the matter. They were: Charles Le Hardy, gent., Mr George Marett, Mr Philippe Le Gallais, Mr Raulin Benest, Mr Philippe Falle, Mr Jacques Remon, Mr Elie Le Maistre, Mr Daniel Valpy dit Janvrin, Mr Clement Machon, Mr Jean Le Couteur, Mr Jean Renouf and Mr Thomas Gabourel.[22] The Commission's award shows what seigneurial rights had survived until the 18th century: every tenant must do homage to his seigneur once in a lifetime; tenants must cut and

39 *Mont les Vaux, 1878.*

COMMUNITY SCHOOLS, THE 19TH AND 20TH CENTURIES

40 *Bel Royal, 1974.*

carry the seigneur's hay, every *cinquantaine* must provide annually a four-horse cartload of vraic, dig one vergée of land and supply a man and a cart for repairing the manor and mills; the *chefs* were responsible for collecting all the seigneur's dues; corn grown on the fief must be ground in the manor mill and tenants must provide a guard to escort prisoners from the manor to the gaol and back from the court to the seigneurial gallows. Against this finding the tenants appealed in vain to the Council.

This case stirred up much bad blood in the parish, as the heads of *cinquantaines* sued the tenants for their dues. Tourgis, the greffier of the manorial court, was arrested for handing over to the tenants a confidential paper. The tenants' leader, Simon de Caen, was arrested for accusing Sir Charles of instigating Tourgis to recover the paper 'by subtlety or force'. The Bailiff persuaded the Court to dismiss Tourgis from his post as *lecteur* or clerk to St Ouen's church. The Dean promptly reinstated him, claiming that his court alone had power to dismiss a church official. A battle royal ensued between the two courts, which also had to go before the Privy Council.[23] The dispute reached such a pitch that Sir Charles claimed that all his tenants had forfeited their lands by refusing their feudal dues.

However Sir Charles had to face far more formidable opposition, when a group of Jurats, led by Josué Pipon, complained to the Council that 'he was not well acquainted with the French tongue and a stranger to the laws of the island', that 'he generally resided in England', that the first Lieutenant-Bailiff he appointed, a relation, was 'half the year laid up with gout', while the second was 'struck with a daily palsy and delirium', and when in Court was incapable of preserving order. Sir Charles retorted 'Pipon, a man of unquiet spirit and extremely desirous of power, prevailed on four other Jurats to combine with him in setting up the power of the Jurats, derived from the people, against the power of the Bailiff, derived from the Crown. Having by underhand means procured his brother-in-law to be elected Jurat, he had gotten a majority of the acting Jurats into his combination'.

De Carteret, however, devised a plan to counteract this. In Jersey almost everyone was third or fourth cousin to everyone else, so, whatever case came up, he ruled the opposition Jurats could not sit, because they were related to the plaintiff or defendant. This caused pandemonium. Several times he told the Council that he had been forced to suspend sittings 'by reason of the violent heats of the contending Jurats' that, on one occasion, Pipon did in a seditious manner tell people in a loud speech that they had the privilege of choosing their judges, but the Bailiff was not of their putting in and they ought to desire a deliverance from arbitrary and despotic power'. The Council decided against de Carteret, and 'this blow gave him such a mortal wound that afterwards he lived but a lingering life', and died in 1715.[24] With him ended the direct male line of the de Carterets of St Ouen, who had held the fief from father to son for six hundred years. He was succeeded by John Carteret, Earl Granville. It is interesting to note, from a contract dated 1723, that Carteret's attorneys, instructed to settle Charles' debts, were prepared to commute some of his tenants' feudal dues (they are listed in the contract in considerable detail) in exchange for *un sixtonnier de froment de rente*.[25]

The Rectors were drawn into quarrels, and more than one found himself a prisoner in the new gaol. Clement Le Couteur, who had succeeded his brother as Dean, was at first considered too pacific. When Philippe Falle recovered for the Rectors the right, which the Seigneur of Trinity had usurped, to appoint Regents of the two grammar schools, the Dean did nothing to help; but in 1698 he excommunicated the Constable and Churchwardens of St Peter for refusing to provide wine for the Christmas Communion in addition to the four celebrations ordered by the canons; and he worded his mandate so strongly, that he was sent to prison for 'issuing scandalous statements contrary to their honour and reputation'.[26]

Then followed a long series of clashes between the two courts. In 1704 the Bishop of Winchester appealed to the Council[27] about affairs in Jersey:

> Such hath been the behaviour of the laity toward the clergy that they have frequently assaulted their persons and showed many indignities to them both in private and public. The inferior sort of people frequently throw dust and stones upon the Dean and clergy, while sitting in their Court, which, although it cannot be personally imputed to the Bailiff and Jurats, doth undoubtedly flow from their ill example and daily contempt of the clergy.

There was a complicated controversy with the Queen's Receiver about tithes. Henry V had seized all tithes that were in existence in his day, but the clergy had been allowed to receive the tithe of any land brought under cultivation at a later date. The Rectors now claimed that the Receiver was encroaching on these *dîmes de désert*. The Crown officials resented this. In 1703 the Rector of St Helier was sent to prison for 'uttering many calumnious words against the honour of the Lieutenant-Governor'. In 1706 the Rector of St Ouen also became a tenant of the gaol for having 'in the presence of the Constable and Officers of the Parish, spoken malicious words, tending to prejudice the Queen's interests and the reputation of her officers'.[28]

In the same year there was a trivial dispute about a pew in St John's church. Jean Le Couteur enlarged his pew and obstructed Josué Ahier's view. Ahier complained to the Ecclesiastical Court, which ordered the obstruction to be removed. Le Couteur appealed to the Royal Court which forbade Ahier to disturb him. Ahier protested to the Dean, so the Royal Court sent him to prison for two years. The Dean excommunicated Le Couteur and ordered the excommunication to be read from every pulpit. The Royal Court forbade the Rectors to do this and 'when they persisted' they were fined. Not that pews were to be taken lightly. Well into the 19th century strict protocol was observed in their distribution and tenancy; when one came up for sale high prices were offered for what was obviously a 'status symbol'. A letter to the *Chronique*, dated May 1868, states that the distribution of pews in St Helier's Parish Church had become so embarrassing that it threatened to excite disputes, jealousies and hatred for many long years to come, and suggests a new method of allocation be adopted.[29]

So the bickering went on: clergy versus laity, Jurats versus Bailiff, tenants versus seigneurs, neighbour versus neighbour. Jerseymen were anything but a happy family. However they were not alone in the matter of abuse and slander which was characteristic of the period.

This was the golden age of pamphleteering in England, the age of Swift and Defoe. In 1709 *The Groans of the Inhabitants of Jersey* was published anonymously in London with a French version for use in the Island: *Recueil de quelques Griefs Publics.*[30] It attacked the right of the States to restrict the importation of corn, wine or tobacco, to regulate the building of houses or the planting of orchards, to fix the rate of exchange for foreign coins, to naturalise aliens and to prohibit the barter of stockings for goods instead of money. It denounced at considerable length the fees extorted by Court officials and the method of assessing fines. It declared that farmers had been 'necessitated to leave off husbanding their ground' because of the 'noisome multitude of coneys and pigeons' bred by the seigneurs. This was a very real and justifiable complaint, as only the seigneurs had the right to keep a *colombier* (dove-cot) full of pigeons and a *garenne* (warren) teeming with rabbits, known by the biblical name of coney, for them to shoot, which constituted a festering injustice. The main purpose of the pamphlet was to urge the triennial election of Jurats. Since Jurats were elected for life, it claimed, it often happened that the Court could not sit and cases remained untried, because many of the Jurats were 'ancient and sickly and disturbed with the gout and possessed neither coaches nor chaises'. It was to take over two hundred years before an age limit was set for the office of Jurat, and when Senators replaced them in the States, no age limit was set for their successors in the legislature, although the Jurats themselves had to retire at the age of seventy or at most seventy-five.[31]

The *Recueil* was the only pamphlet printed, for as yet Jersey had no printing press; but others, far more scurrilous were passing from hand to hand in manuscript. The forecast for the future was 'stormy weather ahead'.

Chapter Twenty-one

MERCHANT ADVENTURERS

Trade is the life of an island.–Falle, *An Account of the Island of Jersey*

IT WOULD BE WRONG to assume from the preceding chapter that the Jerseyman was entering the 18th century in a parochial or insular mood. As the power of the Stuarts waned and the *ancien régime* in France tottered towards destruction, belligerence, both personal and national, was a general characteristic of the age. The rise of a middle class of merchants provoked clashes between conservative and progressive elements in Jersey as elsewhere; but these same tetchy Jerseymen were also outward looking. Overseas trade developed enormously, and a powerful merchant class brought to fruition the pioneer trading of earlier centuries.

The letters of Philippe Pipon, written in French or English as the occasion demanded, complement the image created by his lawsuits. In 1693, concerned that stockings were not selling well in England, he asked his agent in Southampton to have them dyed to suit the trade with Spain, and to explore the Lisbon market. He arranged for wine, oil, sugar, raisins, figs, tobacco, 'lymons and China oranges' to be shipped back from Portugal, traded with Bilbao, discussed the price of wheat and pork in Waterford and of wool in Southampton and London.[1] With the same zeal as he showed in pursuing his rights in Jersey, he wrote to his attorney in Carolina and asked his agent to look into his wife's affairs in New York. He had married the widow of Sir George Carteret's younger son,[2] and presumed possession in her name of Little Barnes Island and a mill near Harlem: 'I should be obliged', he wrote, 'to know in what condition the mill and other lands are ... I had only given liberty to Capt. Congrove to cut some firewood upon the island, but Mr Newton has contradicted my leave.'

The Newfoundland fisheries had suffered a certain stagnation during the Commonwealth. Despite a number of Acts under the Stuarts for the protection of English fishermen, the eruption of the French into the colony with their capital at Placentia, and the attacks of Frontenac in 1696 and 1697 had contributed to a falling off in English trade with Newfoundland. Before the fall of Louisberg and Quebec in particular, the fleet of 'sack' boats had been a prey to French and Spanish privateers and Sallee pirates. Often they required armed protection in convoy or to be armed themselves. This may account for the pessimism of the historian, Philippe Dumaresq, who asserted that Jersey had too many ships and was neglecting her agriculture. As, under William III, the tide turned in England's favour, Philippe Pipon's judgement was to prove more accurate. He thought that there were not many vessels in Jersey suitable for the Newfoundland trade, and those who owned them were not prepared to take risks, although great profits might be made if one escaped the dangers of such a voyage. In 1693 he wrote from London to Mr John Seale, merchant in Bilbao: '*Quant est pour les bâtiments à risquer pour terre neuve il n'y a point de propre à Jersey outre que ceux qui ont quelque chose ne veulent rien risquer. Sans doute lorsqu'on en eschappe de ces voyages il y a beaucoup a y profiter*'.[3]

Although links between Jersey and New England and Jersey and Newfoundland had existed for some time, they differed in many respects. Merchants in New England had often settled there and were shore-based. Records show that in 1706 John Janvrin of Jersey married Elizabeth Knight (alias Chevalier) at Dover, New Hampshire, where Janvrin was considered a man of importance and good judgment. In 1707 he was among the prominent citizens who signed an address to the Queen in the name of the Governor.[4] He is thought to have been a brother of Philippe Janvrin, who, in 1721, died on the *Esther* while in quarantine for plague off Noirmont and was originally buried on the Ile au Guerdain, Portelet.[5] On John Janvrin's death, his widow married Joseph Adams, uncle of a future American President.

Apprentices, too, continued to travel from Jersey to New England. In a typical draft indenture of 1741 we learn of Philip Laffoley, bound apprentice for six years to Robert Hooper and his wife of Marblehead, New England. As so many other Jersey youths were to do over the years, he promised that he would 'faithfully serve, their secrets keep, their lawful commands everywhere gladly do'. He was not to marry during the period, nor play cards, nor frequent taverns. He would be taught to read and write and learn arithmetic as far as the rule of three, and would receive in return 'good and wholesome eating, drink, washing, lodging and apparel'. After six years he would receive two new suits besides the old ones, 'one of which if not both to be for the Lord's day'[6]. By mid-century a powerful band of merchants were requesting the Lieutenant-Bailiff that foreigners be prevented from hiring young Jerseymen for the voyage to New England to the detriment of Jersey merchants needing sailors.[7]

The situation in Newfoundland was somewhat different. Various 'plantations' had been made there by French and English, but these had not always been successful. In the early days there was constant rivalry between the nationalities involved: Spanish, Portuguese, Basques, French, New Englanders and West Country men, and possibly too between shore and sedentary fishermen, 'planters' and 'sack' merchants. The latter were merchants with no permanent base in the fisheries, who acted as carriers, collecting in their larger vessels the loads of fish which were to be carried across the Atlantic. 'Sack' is thought to be derived from the sack or wine taken aboard in Spain when the cargo of fish had been delivered, or possibly from '*sec*', which describes the dry, salted fish they carried.

Some Jerseymen may have been early settlers or indentured servants. The initial point of attachment seems to have been Trinity Bay north of the Avalon peninsula, where records show that in 1754 one Thomas de Gruchy was a planter with his wife, son and daughter, and eight English and eight Irish servants. De Quetteville was trading from Harbour Grace between 1750 and 1790, being linked as time went on with Nicholas Fiott.[8] But the majority went out to Newfoundland at this period on a seasonal basis, and the merchants were engaged in the 'sack' trade, and carrying fish on the triangular route to New England, the West Indies and the Mediterranean together with miscellaneous goods collected for the outward journey or from ports of call as they returned to Jersey in the autumn.

These merchants, often younger sons of prominent families and intricately connected by marriage, pursued a pattern of trade already established by the French in the 16th century.[9] The prizes were high, but the risks were great and usually shared among a number of owners who were the *bourgeois* or outfitters, the *armateurs* or suppliers of equipment, the *victualleurs* and sometimes the *maître*. A master might be his own *armateur*. Usually there were no wages, but agreed regulations about the sharing of profits: one third went to the owner, one third to the merchant and one third was to be divided among the crew. On arrival in Newfoundland the men set up temporary stations with wooden staging on which to split and dry the cod, the first captain to arrive being named 'admiral' for that season. The methods for conducting a fishery were established at an early date and are described in the diary of Elie Brevint written in the 17th century. He also mentions that wood and nails were taken from Jersey to make fishing boats, while oars and masts were found *in situ*.[10]

A wealth of material exists in Admiralty protests, diaries, accounts, letter-books and other private papers to fill in the picture of these merchant adventurers who formed so important a part of the Jersey scene in the 18th and 19th centuries. We know the names of many of the *armateurs* and *maîtres*, and sometimes of their crews: Dumaresq, Fiott, Lemprière, Janvrin, Pipon, Robin, Dauvergne, Patriarche, to name but a few. Some were merchants in London, others like Villeneuve and Hemery were Frenchmen recently naturalised; many rose from being captains in the service of *bourgeois* to be owners and *armateurs* themselves; not a few served the Island as Constables and Jurats. They traded from Poole, Southampton and London with places as far apart as Cyprus and Jamaica, Boston and the Baltic. They dealt in many currencies, bartered or accepted bills of exchange, grappled with the complexities of the *livre tournois* and the *livre d'ordre*.[11] At home they built beautiful homes, invested in Government stock, which they called the 'Funds', married well, sent their children to be educated in England;[12] 'to be englished' is the picturesque term used by one writer to describe a daughter's visit to the mainland. They shopped for their wives and friends in London; some even took the waters of Bath[13] or made the grand tour. They gave evidence before the Privy Council and wrote frequent letters, which, happily for the historian, they copied out in careful longhand. It would be impossible in a general history to do justice to all the available material. We must be content with a few relevant examples.

As early as 1625 Pierre Dauvergne set out in the spring for Terre Neuve and, when near the Banks, was taken prisoner by Moorish pirates, who carried him off to Sallee on the Barbary Coast.[14] There he was sold as a slave, tortured and held to ransom. The letters he wrote to his family and friends have been preserved. His uncle and brother, with the Court's permission, realised some of his assets, while a brother-in-law set out for Sallee with the ransom, only to find on arrival that Pierre had died from harsh treatment before the money arrived. So great was the menace of these 'warriors for the Muslim faith', as the Sallee pirates termed themselves, that in 1637 a naval expedition with Captain George Carteret as second in command was sent from England to destroy this pirate fleet and rescue their Christian captives.[15] By 1713 the States noted that certain natives of Jersey had been rescued from the hands of the 'Turks' at an earlier date, so that monies set aside for ransom were to be used instead for the repair of the schools of St Mannelier and St Anastase under the direction of the Rectors of Grouville and St Mary.[15]

A book of protests sworn between 1739 and 1744 before Peter de Ste Croix, notary public, illustrates the complex responsibilities of masters and *armateurs* of the period.[17] On 17 May 1734 Mr Edward Patriarche, a Jerseyman living in London, was informed by the British consul in Cyprus that the brigantine *Seaflower* of Jersey, of 100 tons, had arrived there on a voyage from Dolmetta to Beyroot and that her master, Charles Pinel, had died of plague. The consul had taken possession of the vessel until the owners could be traced. It was not until 1742 that they emerged as Rachel Hardy, M. Lemprière, D. Patriarche, J. Le Hardy, P. Pinel, J. Le Couteur, F. Le Couteur and R. Dumaresq. Was this perhaps the *Seaflower* that features some twenty years later in the diary of Charles Robin?[18] In November 1743, his uncle, Thomas Robin, lodged a protest as master of the brigantine *Philip*. She had sailed from Conception Bay, Newfoundland, with a cargo of 'dry fish, oyle and passengers' and had encountered such heavy seas on her voyage to Jersey that four members of the crew had been swept overboard, three of whom had been drowned; the main mast, the boat and the fireplace had been carried away, the foreyard, topsail and forebeam of the hatch damaged and the decks cleared of all but the foreyard. Finally the vessel reached Jersey and was repaired. By the following March she was ready to sail again. Once more she was delayed by adverse weather conditions, then news came that war had been declared with France, and the new crew refused to sail.

Complicated book-keeping is illustrated in the papers of Pierre Mauger, advocate.[19] £6 sterling is owed to Matthew Mauger by a man who took passage on his ship *Happy Rebecca* from

41 *The* Iris, *showing details of a Jersey owned vessel.*

SKETCHES FROM AN ARTIST'S NOTEBOOK, P. J. OULESS, 1817-1885

42 *Sovereignty at Les Écréhous.*

Canso, Nova Scotia, to Alicante in Spain. Guilleaume Patriarche, *armateur* of the privateer *Duke of Cumberland*, is ordered to pay to the wives and dependants of men who had lost their lives in service on this *corsair* their share of one pistole per head for each of the crew and 10 pistoles *pour le compte des consorts dudit corsair* in accordance with the charter party. In 1712 the sale of *l'Expédition* is prohibited owing to a disagreement between Peter Seale, part owner, and Jean Mauger, representing the others with a stake in her, while in 1741 George and Philippe Robin are forbidden to touch the profits from the sale of the *George and Philippe*, then in St Aubin's harbour, until they have settled their debts to each other.

Some cargoes strike a personal note. In 1758 Noë Le Cras wrote from London to his cousin, Frank Marett, to tell him that he had shipped by the London packet, Philip Le Feuvre, master, 12 Delft flowerpots and roots of globe flower and golden crocus. He also returned Marett's watch, entrusted to Captain Lys for repair in London and to which le Cras had attached 'one of the new fashion steel chains'.

In September 1741 the *Dolphin* of Jersey, Captain Edouard Luce, was taken by a Spanish privateer, carrying 14 guns. The master and charterers were asked for a steep ransom, and, while Edouard Luce, the captain, Samuel Linthorn and Edward Fennell were kept as hostages, two men were deputed to take the cargo to Poole to sell it in order to pay the ransom. A complication arose when the mate, Edward Le Boutillier, sailed the 'snow' (a type of three-masted schooner) direct to Jersey for further consultation with one of her owners, Captain Jacques Lemprière,[20] who was also the ship's husband or agent. When their protest was first recorded in a Bulletin of La Société Jersiaise, the then librarian, Mr A.C. Saunders, wrote: 'We hear nothing more of the dispute and cannot trace the fate of the hostages kept on board the privateer'. Jersey history is like a jigsaw puzzle. Sooner or later a missing piece falls into place. There has recently come to light a comprehensive notebook kept by this same Edouard Luce:[21] *un livre couvert de parchemin* for which in 1739 he paid M. Thomas de Caen £1.15 *livres tournois*. Its record spans the 18th century and gives as good a picture as any of the activities of a Jersey captain who in due course became an *armateur*.

The first section of the book includes accounts, letters and copies of documents covering a period from 1737 to 1745. The accounts begin in 1737 and one is left marvelling at their complexity. Some are entered as pesetas, others as *argent de France*, *pistoles d'Espagne*, *Johannes de Portugal*, *livres sterling*. Loans and bills of exchange are translated into money at various rates. Charles Fauvel owes the sterling equivalent of 5½ piastres lent him at Bilbao. Harbour dues are paid in the same port for Josué Simon; a hat bought from Captain Howard is subtracted from his rent for an old house at St Peter. Thomas Barnaby owes two pounds for Richard Bisson's passage paid by a Le Sauteur to the owners of the *Dolphin*. Among the goods debited to Richard Smith, salmon catcher of Newfoundland, and Ellen his wife, are a hogshead of cider, two pairs of garters, one and a half yards of canvas, one pair of children's stockings, one pound of pepper, two women's petticoats and two pieces of bacon—a mixed cargo indeed. The *bourgeois* owe Luce for 14 *pots* of brandy to be drunk on the voyage from Jersey to Newfoundland, for earnest money and cider in engaging Jean Colas and for money to cover the expenses of a boy Laurens while waiting to settle with the sergeant at the tower (presumably payment for exemption from militia duty). In 1739 a long list of goods, belonging to Edouard Luce and sold in Newfoundland, includes shirts, canvas for sails, Barcelona handkerchiefs, and 15 pairs of shoes. There is a promissory note in which Mons. Jacques Lemprière, junior, [22] engages to pay Capt. Luce £810 for wine bought between 1736 and 1738, and the wages for the voyage, 'on pain of forfeiture of goods and inheritance present and future'. The number of items shipped as cargo is legion: silver pots and gold rings from Spain, green fish, 'spoilt' fish,[23] tobacco, soap, a seaman's chest, rum, molasses, greatcoats, paving stone and oak planks for the store near the boulevard de

St Laurens. There is a dove-tail with the papers of Pierre Mauger as we read an account in which François Marett, gent, Constable of St Lawrence, is debited for an axle delivered to M. Noë Le Cras and Edouard Mauger for use with the parish cannon. Some of the debts are paid in kind, others offset against so many days' labour (the latter in settling his mother's estate). All local sums are in *livres tournois*. A sadder entry in 1743 records that Mons. Philippe de Gruchy, ministre de St Laurens,[24] owes Luce £60 for oil and coal, but this is partly offset against £2.10 *pour des prières à l'enterrement de notre fils, François Edouard, en argent de France*, and £4 from his mother-in-law for the tithe she owed Mons de Gruchy for the same year.

There is a gap in the accounts covering the period of detention in Spain and a suggestion in a letter that Luce has suffered ill-health as a result. It is now his brother Philippe's turn to captain the ship and he, too, is captured by Spaniards. The account book includes a copy of a certificate from Don Bernardo de la Quadra, of the King's army of Spain, stating that he had captured Captain Philippe Luce and 12 sailors on an English brigantine laden with salt for Terre Neuve in May 1743, but had been unable to take her into port for lack of a pilot. He had therefore allowed her to go on her way, but not before taking off her cargo. A letter dated 1744 from Edouard Luce to Mrs Jane Snook of Terre Neuve informs her that goods she had ordered the year before had been captured by the Spaniards from his brother, and replacements were being sent through Mr Jean Janvrin.[25] Luce acknowledged her gift of fish and oil, sent by Captain Fiott, and listed her consignment which included six yards of *indienne* for a dress, six yards of cotton for the lining, four handkerchiefs, two pounds of black tea and one of green, and two pounds of pepper for herself; two Bengal handkerchiefs, one pound of black tea and one pound of pepper for Mr. Snook. If the Spaniards had similar rules for the share of loot as had English and Jersey privateers, the cargo which this replaced must have posed problems for those who had to divide it into equal shares. Another letter written at this period to Mrs Linthorn bears messages for her husband, which confirm that he too had escaped from his captors.

Several letters are to Mr Matthew Mauger, a merchant of Poole and a connection by marriage, for whom Mrs Luce had been shopping: 'my wife hath bought a half piece of damask pearl colour and the best she could like in colour and goodness, for it is scarce at present in Jersey as they sell a great deal to the French. My wife hath been all round the town and could not get better to her liking'. Further letters to Matthew Mauger refer back to Luce's captivity and attest that Mr Fennell has also survived. There is a hint that Luce had fallen out with his owners, 'although I have been a servant good to them for nine years, our Poole voyage is not agreeable to them'.

In 1744 Edouard Luce appears as part owner of a *corsair*, for Jerseymen were now arming their vessels as privateers to counter attacks from the French and Spaniards engaged in the struggle for maritime supremacy. We learn that the *Industrie* had sunk at night and payment was due to those who had hauled her ashore, to the carpenters for repairs, and for drinks for the men who had relaunched her. She had been repaired in Madame Patriarche's yard, and indeed the merchants' wives often acted for their husbands in their absence, while many other competent women played their part in affairs. The Dauvergne sisters, aunts of Charles Robin, kept a ship-chandler's shop at St Aubin with their brother-in-law, Philippe Robin,[26] and Mrs de Vaumorel kept the accounts of her doctor husband.

There are many interesting names mentioned in the accounts. Mr Nicholas Ollivier is charged for ammunition bought in England for the sloop *Aurigny*, while Captain Denton appears as a shareholder in the corsair *Industrie*. His portrait still exists and was until recently in St Aubin's Hospital; for he and his wife left money for the establishment of a Poor House at St Brelade. He was also one of the founder members of St Aubin's church. Others whose names appear are Daniel Messervy of diary fame[27] and Elizabeth Orange, widow of Philippe Janvrin of Janvrin's tomb. More domestically Luce paid Peter Seale for the schooling of his ward, Jacques Vibert, and arranged for him to be apprenticed as a carpenter. He also settled the affairs of his widowed mother,[28] paying off arrears in *rentes* to various prominent merchants and landowners.

The prosperity of these merchants and their acquaintance with a wider, more sophisticated world is reflected in the development of domestic architecture. With the dawn of the 18th century the design of houses, while remaining essentially the same, became simpler and more symmetrical; the façade was made of ashlar, the windows were larger, spaced evenly and of equal size, and windows and doors no longer had chamfers. Inside the fireplace lintel was often of wood and gradually the floors became boarded over; the stairs too were of wood and within the house itself. The rooms became larger and loftier and often the house was double-piled[29] or additional rooms were built on the north, to make a four-roomed plan. These later houses are in less danger from modernisation, as their plan and proportions are entirely suited to modern living.

Although local houses have much in common with those found in Normandy and Brittany and indeed in Guernsey, Jersey's independence is evident here as elsewhere in some purely insular developments in details, so that a Jersey house is readily distinguishable from one in other regions. In the 18th century carved dates and initials became almost *de rigueur* and attained a marked degree of excellence, the digits being often raised, instead of incised. One feature which is most noticeable is the so-called marriage stone, of which many hundreds may be seen. They are usually on the south façade and consist of the initials of husband and wife, with a device of interlocked hearts and a date. This is not necessarily that of the building of the house, but may record any event of importance to the couple concerned. The stone in its fully developed form did not appear until the early 18th century and continued for about two hundred years, perhaps attaining its maximum popularity between about 1720 and 1880.

As the century advanced and the merchants prospered, the desire for new houses increased. An interesting glimpse of the situation occurs in a letter written in 1772 from Pierre Mauger in Jersey to a Mr Seale in London, who has just lost his eldest son and is thinking of selling land in Jersey. Mauger gives the current price of *rente foncière* and this piece of advice:

> You'll find nobody that will take the whole as the houses are old and a person who would settle there properly must be at the expense of building a new house, whereas if the houses were new it would encourage purchasers ... the best will be to sell by auction each field by itself, and in that case your attorney (presumably Mauger himself) can find a friend that will bid till it come to its value.

The accounts of Edouard Luce end in 1745 and the next entries in the book are by Edouard's son Jean, who became Constable of St Lawrence in 1795 and before that had used the book to keep records of men in the militia in his parish. They must have taken part in the Battle of Jersey. But before we reach that point in Jersey history there are further *troubles intestins* to be considered: *troubles* which reflect the complexity of the monetary system and the conflict between the old ways and the new.

Chapter Twenty-two

THE SIX-AU-SOU REVOLT, 1714-1739

Men seldom rebel against anything that does not deserve rebelling against.–Carlyle

GEORGE I's REIGN passed uneventfully in Jersey, but George II had hardly been three years on the throne when an explosion of popular fury convulsed the Island. The immediate cause of the uprising was the attempt by the States to reform the monetary system, but the pent up feelings expressed in the revolt had been simmering for years. *Vous vous êtes donné la peine de naître*; commenting on this bitter remark by Figaro to his seigneur, le comte Almaviva, Lytton Strachey wrote: 'In that sentence one can hear far off but distinct the flash and snap of the guillotine'.[1] Jersey's revolt was less sanguinary, but, in the protest against *les six-au-sou,* one is perhaps witnessing the bourgeonning of political parties, the Charlots and the Magots, which later developed into the Laurel and the Rose.[2]

With the growth of colonialism and the great merchant companies, power in England was gradually passing from those who owned land to those with money. The creation of the Bank of England and the Consolidated Funds date from this period, as indeed does the less successful South Sea Bubble. England, however, had greater reserves than France, where, as Louis XIV and his heirs exacted more and more in taxation, finances reached a parlous state.

The Jerseyman's only bank was up the chimney or in a *paûte* or *pouchette*.[3] This was a hiding-place in the depth of a wall about the size and length of a forearm in which was embedded a receptacle, usually a pottery jar; its position in the house was a family secret. For centuries Jersey had traded in French money: the *livre tournois*, the *sol* or *sou*, and the *denier*. Twelve *deniers* made one *sou* and 20 *sous* made one *livre*, but the *denier* was virtually out of circulation and none were minted from about the end of the 17th century.[4] The commonest coin in use was the *liard* (*le quart d'un sou*) worth three *deniers*, and Jersey was caught in a crisis of fluctuating values which has no exact parallel today. To talk in terms of a farthing or threepenny bit is misleading, for when Falle wrote in 1693 the *livre tournois* was worth roughly 1s. 6d. (7½p), the Order in Council of 1729 which provoked a riot quoted the English shilling as worth 14 *sous*, which would give 280 *sous* to the pound sterling, while in 1834, when the English monetary system was introduced,[5] the English pound was reckoned as being worth 520 *sous*. In making calculations one has also to take into account that the pound sterling has itself been devalued many times since the early 18th century.

At the time of the revolt, *livres* and *sous* in France still kept their intrinsic value against the pound sterling, but the smaller denominations in copper were gradually devalued, so that it soon took six *liards* to make a *sou* in St Malo, while only four were required in St Helier. Much of Jersey's trade was with France at this period and percipient merchants on both sides took advantage of the situation. The French insisted on being paid in *livres* and *sous* backed by their silver content, while paying the Jersey traders in *liards*; nor were the latter worried, as they stood to gain against the value of the *sou* when they took their *liards* back to the Island. The result was that Jersey was being drained of gold and silver and flooded with copper *liards*.

In 1701[6] the States decreed that no one should take out of the Island more than the value of thirty *livres tournois* in gold, silver or copper. In 1714, realising that foreigners were bringing in quantities in *liards* and very little in gold and silver, they varied their tactics and forbade the importation of more than sixty *sous* worth of *liards* at one time, on pain of confiscation of boats and coins with a further fine of 60 *livres tournois* for the ship's master; one third of this money to go to the Queen, one third to the poor and one third to the informer. However, smuggling of liards was too profitable to be stopped, and soon there was hardly a larger coin to be found in the Island.

In April 1720 the amount of *sous* and *liards* that could be exported was reduced to five *livres tournois* per person; this too was ineffective. By now the States, who had no regular income except the impôt being used to build St Aubin's harbour and rates levied at intervals for specific purposes, were finding it impossible to repay sums lent interest free by individuals for work on the harbour. In May 1720, to avoid the problems caused by the fluctuation in monetary values *dans le royaume voisin,* the States sent the greffier[7] to the Privy Council to ask permission to issue bank notes up to the value of fifty thousand *livres tournois* to be guaranteed by the expected revenue from the impôt. They did not realise that paper currency to maintain its value must be exchangeable for a metallic one.[8]

The scarcity of gold and silver remained, however, and in 1726[9] the States attacked the problem from another angle. They asked permission of the Privy Council to reduce the value of the *liard* in Jersey to one sixth of a *sol* or *sou* as in France with the intent of 'clearing the island of that trash the *liards*' and lowering the price of bills of exchange. Meetings of the States were held in secret, and for a time the people did not realise what was happening. Indeed nothing did happen for more than three years, as the Council was occupied with more urgent matters. In May 1729 an Order in Council arrived granting this permission, but allowing six months respite before the measure came into force.

As soon as it became known a howl of indignation arose. To many people it seemed a piece of brazen-faced robbery. The thrifty farmer suddenly found his hard-earned fortune reduced by a third. The poor man who owed a pound to a merchant or money-lender, unless, as was often impossible, he could pay within six months, would have to find in *liards*, since these were the only coins available, one third as much again as he had calculated. The cry was raised that it was a trick of the wealthy members of the States to rob the poor. Nor did the opposition come from the poor alone. Feeling grew so ferocious that the majority of the States took fright and in November 1729 sent François Marett, Constable of St Lawrence,[9] to the Privy Council with a petition asking that the order might be revoked. One influential group, however, was determined to prevent the repeal. Lieutenant-Bailiff Philippe Le Geyt,[10] nephew of the commentator on Jersey Law, Dean Payn, Jean Le Hardy, Attorney-General, and Jurat Dumaresq crossed to Westminster to oppose the petition and were successful. In July 1730 a second Order in Council commanded that the original Order be enforced, while granting another six months' respite.

At this stage a powerful group of 27 merchants drew up a petition urging the States to consult the Parish assemblies. They suggested that, had the States consulted them earlier, instead of presenting them with a *fait accompli*, the merchants might have applied themselves to finding a remedy to replace the Order, which, they prophesied, would bring about *la ruine totale de l'île*. It is instructive to study the list of signatories: some were of French origin, some based in London; they included Thomas Denton, benefactor of St Aubin, and Francis Bartlet, whose widow was to endow the General Hospital, and others whose descendants were to advertise their wares in the Magot papers at the end of the century. Jersey was already taking sides.

It is however doubtful whether the merchants would have been able to explain the complexities of the situation to the ordinary inhabitants. As one reads the learned dissertation of

Le Quesne in his *Constitutional History* or the more contemporary comments of *The Daily Advertiser* of January 1733,[11] one can but sympathise with the protesting mob. To quote the *Advertiser*:

> So of *livres*, everyone understood, according to the constant actual reception and use of the term in Jersey for these many years past ... that it signified the same thing as if they had said 80 *liards* if paid in copper ... a third more is now signified by the word *livre* or a *livre* of a third more value, a third more coin goes to it than has been understood, or used to signify, or has gone to it for these many years; for if I pay in *liards* I am to pay 120, when at the time of my making the agreement I was to pay but 80 *liards* ... It is a very confused method that this is effected by and which I believe was one reason it was not so well understood.

Le Quesne thought a century later that the Act and the Order in Council had been highly injudicious. The tinder was lit and flash-point reached.

On Saturday 29 August the Denonciateur began to publish the Order in the Market Square, when there broke out 'the greatest riot ever known in Jersey'.[12] Before he was halfway through, a mob of three hundred was breaking the windows of the Lieutenant-Bailiff's house (where de Gruchy's shop now stands)[13] and threatening to kill him and his brother-in-law, Jurat Dumaresq. But young Advocate Jean Dumaresq of Augrès, the leader of the opposition, arrived and pacified them, urging them to wait and see what happened when the States met on the Monday. Le Geyt then hurried to the home of the Lieutenant-Governor, Colonel George Howard,[14] and demanded protection, but the latter showed him scant sympathy, telling him 'the fault was his own and he was fallen into the pit he had digged'; but he gave him a guard of soldiers for his house.

On Sunday there were excited conferences in all the country churchyards after the evening sermon and plans were laid for a mass demonstration on the following morning. Early on Monday the church bells rang and the militia drummers marched round every parish calling all men from 18 to 70 to march to the town to destroy the *six-au-sols*, the name coined for those who wished to debase the currency. From west, north and east the march on the town began, angry men following the drums with cudgels, flails and pitchforks. Over five hundred came from St Ouen's alone. The States met hurriedly and passed an Act restoring the *liard* to its former value. But the people did not trust them. They burst open the doors of the Court House and rushed in crying, 'Death to the *six-au-sols*!' One old woman shrieked, 'We'll have their guts and I've brought the bag to put them in' .

The members of the deputation to the Council made a hurried exit. The Dean, François Payn, the Attorney-General and Jurat Dumaresq 'crawled under the benches of the Court and got out by the back door'. The Dean ran into a tavern, and, disguised in a borrowed greatcoat and the taverner's cap, jumped out of the rear window, ran up the Town Hill and escaped to Elizabeth Castle. The mob ransacked the tavern but found their quarry had fled. The Constable of St Lawrence, François Marett, against whom feeling was especially bitter, because he had gone to Westminster to secure the repeal of the Order, but had agreed to its re-enactment, seized a horse and galloped to the Castle. Le Geyt's son-in-law, Advocate Dauvergne, defied the rioters, shaking his whip and shouting: '*Mes garçons, ils sont à six-au-sou pour la vie*'. 'Whereupon one struck him across the legs, and another struck off his wig; upon which he took to his heels with part of the mob after him, some flinging sticks'. But he reached his father-in-law's house in safety.

Lieutenant-Bailiff Le Geyt and Lieutenant-Governor Howard left the Court House together, but Le Geyt found himself insulted on every side and even received a blow. The Lieutenant-Governor extended his arm to save him and likewise received a blow. He then advised Mr Le Geyt to run for his life. They both ran, Mr Le Geyt, on looking back, saw a man with a grappling iron about to strike, whereupon 'he mended his pace' and entered the Lieutenant-Governor's house in safety, where he remained till night. Next morning he and Jurat Dumaresq went to the

43 *Queen Victoria's visit on 2 September 1846, by J. Le Capelain.*

CELEBRATIONS IN THE ROYAL SQUARE

44 *'Our dear Channel Islands are also to be freed today', 8 May 1945. A sea of faces at the Liberation. (Photo:* Jersey Evening Post*)*

Castle, where they stayed three days until they could get a boat to take them to Guernsey. Before leaving Le Geyt wrote to Colonel Howard:

> Since Providence has delivered me in so marvellous a fashion from those who could so cruelly have taken my life ... I have come to the conclusion that it would be tempting a wise and divine Providence to expose my person and reputation any longer to such cruel dangers and indignities. Since I can no longer live in safety in the isle, I seek asylum elsewhere.

He added that, to enable the Governor and the States to restore and maintain order in the name of the King, he was entrusting the Bailiff's seal to his son and leaving the Mace at his house.[15]

The wider implications of this revolt are revealed in a petition presented to the States on Saturday, 5 September 1730, in which the inhabitants of the Island asked that the Acts passed on the previous Saturday be enrolled and stamped with the island seal and that various grievances against the seigneurs be redressed, a reduction made in fines and forfeitures and in the profits from the farming of the King's revenue. The petitioners threatened to ask the King for a Royal Commission to consider their grievances, if their requests are not granted.

Meanwhile Le Geyt and his colleagues had taken their side of the story to the Privy Council held in the presence of George II. The official report says that the King regarded the cancelling of the Order by the States as 'a high insult to his Royal Authority', and they were commanded to expunge the offending resolution from their minute book and to see that the Order was carried into immediate execution, 'as they will answer the contrary at their peril'. Four days later Governor Howard was recalled and Colonel Hargrave sent to replace him with four hundred soldiers who were quartered on the inhabitants of the town 'to their no small injury'.[16]

Unofficially we have an interesting commentary on these events in the letter-books and papers of François Marett, which allows us to glimpse the activities in exile of those who fled the mob.[17] In their petition to the Privy Council they describe how, in their passage to the Court, 'they went peaceably and quietly there without any threatening of the populace or clattering of their weapons'. They had not taken a military guard, as it would 'rather have enraged the mob than anything else'; however, after the sitting, word was brought that the mob was pulling down Mr Marett's house 'which was without the town'. On 7 April 1731, Marett sent news from London: 'Howard is turned out from government of our island, but ye Lords will not have it publick till their report is laid before His Majesty'. Later Marett informed his brother-in-law, Tapin, in Oxford, that Howard had been found guilty concerning the riots and it was hoped his dismissal would bring everything 'to good order'. On 19 April he mentioned the arrival of five Jurats who had sided with the people, but thought they had come too late: '*C'est après la mort le médecin*'. Finally on 22 April he wrote to his wife in Jersey that in Howard the people had lost a good friend, '*sa conduite a été extraordinaire en cette affaire*'. He also reported the arrival of 17 merchants from Jersey in support of Howard.

Meanwhile Marett himself was hoping to settle his claim for damages to his house, which he called '*la maison des Sablons*', so that he could return to Jersey. He had the support of the Lord President of the Council, of Lord Cobham, the absentee Governor, of Lord Carteret of Hawnes,[18] the absentee Bailiff, and of their respective Lieutenants, all of whom were out of London and preoccupied with the restoration of law and order in Jersey after the currency riots.

While Marett awaited the result of his personal application for redress he was not without other preoccupations: 'Mr Le Geyt and ye Lieut-Bailly propose to take a trip with me to Oxford and Somerford ... Mr Pipon is very well and is fully satisfied of my being impossible [*sic*] to meet you at Windsor being obliged to tend ye Treasury.' He visited Lord Carteret at Hawnes in Bedfordshire. He also dealt with merchants who were to sell stockings in Lisbon for his widowed mother-in-law Tapin, in what appears to have been an over-supplied market. As Constable of

St Lawrence, *absent de l'île*, he instructed Noë Le Cras in Jersey to bring down beeches for a mill-wheel–those near the roadside so that he could plant oaks. He reported to his wife that Madame Dauvergne had not been able to find her a bed of suitable size and suggested she had one made. He also asked his wife to proceed with plans for rebuilding. Noting what she had told him in a letter about the mood of the mob, he expressed his fears that he would still be under threat from his enemies when he returned to Jersey. He was finally able to assure his wife that '*Les Messieurs de la Thésorie*' [*sic*] had been ordered by a warrant signed by the King to pay him £400 sterling and 15 shillings to cover the damage to his house and the interruption to his affairs during his enforced absence from the Island as a witness.

In October 1732 Marett wrote to his cousin in Jersey to say that the Order in Council reinstating the Act had been sent to Southampton addressed to Mr Thomas Bandinel, who was to get it across to the Island at the first opportunity. The Council moved slowly; long before it arrived the opposition had won the day.

In April 1731 the Council had found Howard guilty of 'a great breach of duty in grossly neglecting to maintain His Majesty's Royal Authority and to support the Civil Government of the Island', and ordered him to be removed from his post. It also signified 'His Majesty's high displeasure at the undutiful and unprecedented proceedings' of those members of the States who had 'obstructed the execution of His Majesty's Orders'. But Jersey did not take these rebukes meekly. A minority of Jurats even ventured to vote against the publication of the new Order, and it was not until June 1731 that the Court ordered its translation into French and its proclamation in the parishes. That month Jeanne Poingdestre was arrested for saying: 'If they be so hardy as to publish the Order, the Town shall be destroyed'. When the Provost of St Martin tried to read the Order at the church door, 'he was beat, pulled by the hair, knocked down and abused, and the Order flung in the dirt and torn'.[19]

A definite opposition party was formed. Five of the Jurats came out openly on the popular side. They were Mons. Ph. Patriarche, Monsieur de Diélament (Michel Lemprière), l'Avocat du Roi (Jean Durell), Jean Dumaresq (of les Colombiers, St Mary) and le Dénonciateur Dumaresq. Then two of the *six-au-sol* Jurats died and at each election the opposition candidate was successful, the second being the young advocate Jean Dumaresq des Augrès. At his swearing in there was a great commotion. The Attorney-General Le Hardy pleaded that the election was null and void because the voters had been intimidated. There was not secret ballot, and everyone who voted for the *six-au-sou* candidate had a cross chalked on his back to expose him to 'the fury of the outrageous miltitude'. When this was over-ruled, he argued that the whole election was irregular, because an Order in Council of 1671 had been ignored.[20] This laid down that 'in the election of Jurats none shall vote but Masters of Familys only, who contribute to the Poor and to Publick taxes'. Little notice had ever been paid to this rule, and Jurats and Constables had continued to be elected by all the men of the parish. Le Hardy also challenged the right of two of the opposition Jurats to vote on this point, as they were Dumaresq's uncles. There was now uproar. 'The populace who filled the Court lost all sort of respect … and were guilty of laughing and loud acclamation.' The Lieutenant-Bailiff Le Geyt sent for the Lieutenant-Governor, Colonel Hargrave, and asked for protection. There was further acrimonious debate and at last, under protest from Le Geyt, young Dumaresq was sworn in. But, although it was usual on such occasions 'to resort to the Publick Dinner provided by the new sworn Jurat, this was omitted, there being very important business to be done'.

The opposition in the Royal Court now had seven Jurats against five, and they used their power to secure that all arrested rioters should be released on bail and never called up for trial. They had laid plans to secure a majority of the States also. They resurrected an old law that had fallen into disuse, that Constables held office for three years only. Constables who had been sitting in the States for 20 years without remission were forced to retire, and in the contests that followed only two *six-au-sou* Constables retained their seats. Court and States now passed into the control of the opposition.

The *liard* controversy was solved by ignoring the Order altogether, In some official documents amounts were quoted in what was called Order money (*livres d'ordre*); occasionally merchants used the term in their accounts but for general commercial purposes the Order remained a dead letter. Jersey continued to reckon four *liards* to the *sou* until the English monetary system was introduced a century later in 1834 by the passing of an Act of the States.[21]

The struggle now switched to another grievance that had all the time been simmering behind the money question. All except a few odd tithes were paid to the King, and the Receiver adopted the bad system of letting out the various parishes to speculators, who paid a lump sum down and made as much as they could for themselves out of their farmers. As tithes were paid in goods and not in cash this gave rise to endless disputes as to what was a fair tenth. The States had been so conscious of this that, when they heard that the mob was marching on the town, they had not only restored the value of the *liard*, but had also passed an Act that henceforth tithes would be paid at a fixed price instead of in kind.[22] This reform had been revoked when all the other Acts of that session had been wiped out.

The Island did not let the matter rest. All who undertook the collection of the tithe knew that they did so at their peril. The St Ouen's collector, John Payn, had his wall broken down, his oxen turned loose in his corn and about twenty trees 'peeled and spoilt'.[23] A week later his gates were broken and an epitaph on the death of a *six-au-sol* nailed to his front door. As soon as his wall was rebuilt, it was thrown down again, and a fortnight later a horse and a fat ox were shot. At St Brelade in July

> the mob publickly rose and assembled to the number of 200 persons and upward with clubs and staves and forced the under-farmers out of their houses and by force and violence robbed them of their leases and contracts for the tithes and tore and destroyed them before their faces.

A petition to the Council from Jean Le Hardy noted these events and added: 'So far has the malice of the multitude carried them beyond the bounds of common humanity that when Philippe Le Haguais' house was on fire the great numbers of people (who might have saved it) stood idly gaping on and publickly rejoicing that such misfortune befell a man who was for six-a-penny'. In August the Trinity collector, Charles Marett, a 'substantial inhabitant' of the parish, found six men peeling his fruit trees, and, while he was firing shots at these as they ran away, six more pulled down a rick of corn and scattered three hundred sheaves. He too found a paper on his gate threatening him with death, if he did not leave the tithe alone. As he took no notice of this, the cable of his eight-ton boat was cut and she was dashed to pieces on the rocks.

Le Geyt appealed to the Council against the seven Jurats in opposition, complaining that they had refused to punish rioters, to enforce the rule that only ratepayers who were heads of households could vote, and to sign the Act of the Court directing that the King's Order be published. The offenders were summoned before the Council in April 1734 and were declared to have 'incurred His Majesty's high displeasure and to have justly deserved to be removed from office'.[24] Nevertheless, as Jersey law required the presence of seven Jurats to make a Full Court, and as the Council had no desire for a new election until island tempers had cooled, only five were dismissed, including Advocate Dumaresq, and two were pardoned.

But the opposition was not yet beaten. The two pardoned Jurats declined to take their seats on the Bench, with the result that there was never a quorum to deal with important cases. So complete was the deadlock that in 1736 Mary Le Maistre and John Bishop, who had been in prison for three years for the supposed murder of their child, had to be released, because there seemed to be no hope of securing a Court to try them.[25] Moreover party spirit was undermining the Militia. At St Ouen a whole company refused to obey the orders of its colonel calling him to his face 'an old *six-au-sol*'.

Meanwhile in 1735 the Council had permitted the election of three new Jurats, and the Island by immense majorities returned the eldest sons of three of those who had been dismissed: they were Michel Lemprière, David Patriarche and Philip Le Geyt. But the purged Court refused to swear them in on the ground that no one could be a Jurat who was 'suspected of disaffection to the Crown'. So the matter had again to be referred to the Council, which was by this time getting tired of Jersey squabbles. Already in January 1731 the Council had complained that, because they were often uncertain as to whether all material relevant to an appeal had been laid before the Courts of the Islands, their Lordships had had great difficulty 'in determining which of such acts, deeds or instruments ought to be read on hearing such appeals'. They drew attention to an Order in Council made in the reign of Queen Elizabeth on 13 May 1572 'wherein there is a particular direction that no appeal be hereafter received without a copy as well of the sentence or judgment as also of the whole process of the cause closed together under the seal of the isle'. The Council in expressing its displeasure expected 'an exact and due obedience to be paid to the said Order for the future'; moreover the Court must understand

> by the words *the whole process* not only the plaintiff's declaration and all the other matters pleaded by any of the parties and the orders of the Court, but also the proofs either by depositions of witnesses or by deeds or instruments in writing which shall be admitted as evidence together with all determinations made by the Court for overruling or rejecting any matter offered in evidence by either party.

This did not deter succeeding generations from appealing to the Council on many issues. In 1737 the Council ordered that the three young Jurats be sworn in, and two years later, as the excitement died away, the normal system of filling vacancies on the Bench as they occurred was restored.[26]

However the *liard* controversy was not quickly forgotten. Twenty years later people were complaining to the Court that they had been insulted by being called *six-au-sols*, and in 1837 Durell, in his notes to the new edition of Falle's *History*, wrote: 'It became a term of reproach in some families to be called a *six-au-sou*, which has been continued down to our times'.[27]

Chapter Twenty-three

BUILDING FOR THE FUTURE

Tenure of houses and land amongst us is à fin d'héritage. *Hereby a man being perfectly master of what he possesses builds substantially, and does many things for a lasting improvement which one who holds only for a time has not encouragement to do.*–Falle, *An Account of the Island of Jersey*

ALTHOUGH UNREST was to continue until it exploded in the riot of 1769, the States were kept busy in the mid-18th century with other more constructive matters. Philippe Falle, on his delegation to England in 1692, had found much ignorance about Jersey and had written the first edition of his history to enlighten William III about this 'parcel of the dominion of the Crown',[1] which the King now possessed with his Stuart wife Mary. In 1729, now an old man, Falle wrote from his Hertfordshire rectory offering to the States two thousand volumes to form the nucleus of a public library.[2] He later donated *trois cents livres sterling* towards the cost of erecting a building to house them. In 1737 the foundation stone was laid in what is still called Library Place. For over twenty years there are constant references to the project in the Actes des États. The States accepted the offer from Falle's heirs to arrange the books, discussed shelving and the investment of the endowment, and elected a committee to draw up detailed rules about subscriptions, hours of opening, treatment of books, and behaviour within the new building: minutiae which in the 20th century might well have been delegated to specialists. This library, which acquired an additional storey in the early 19th century,[3] still stands and is now the office of the Departement de la Partie Publique.[4] Architecturally it is an interesting building, being one of the earliest in Jersey made of brick. It has simple Georgian lines. Inside there is a very fine staircase and the principal room on the first floor, which housed Falle's original gift, is large and impressive. When in 1866 it ceased to be the island library, the fine baroque marble plaque, dated 1736 and designed by Falle himself, was moved to a new building which in its turn is bursting at the seams and destined to be replaced in the near future. Such are the origins of the extensive library service we enjoy today.

Another legacy, which caused the States rather more trouble, was that of Marie Bartlet (née Mauger), widow of a St Aubin merchant who had obtained the right to farm the import duties and anchorage fees.[5] In 1741 she left 100 *livres tournois* to the poor of each parish (the gift is noted in the parish records of St Ouen and no doubt in others) and to the Island 50,000 *livres tournois* for the erection of a Poor house, with a further endowment for its upkeep—an attractively phonetic gift by the terms of her will:

> I bequathe to the Poore of Jersey on Honder livers Franche money to Iche Parishe to be distributed after my buriale: i give morear to the Poore of the Iland Fifteay thousent to beay a Reivenu to mantaigne the Poore that shall be Pouite in the House, wiche shall be Poore widows and Fatherlaise Childrane and Enchant Piple of the Illande, and shale alwaise be quipe Foule; and shale the saide House be built in St. tobins and everything be ordered as my Excrs hear after named and the Staites of the Iland shall judge Fitting'.

Her good friends were Philippe Le Geyt, Lieut-Bailiff, and James Pipon, Seigneur of Noirmont. The will was contested on many counts 'by reason of the wrong spelling thereof and the many disputes among her relations'. It was not until 1765 that building began, not at St Aubin, but on a plot of land 'on the sandhills of St Helier', the gift of Philippe Bandinel, Seigneur of Méléches. When completed the hospital was requisitioned as barracks for the army, partially destroyed by an explosion of gunpowder in 1783 and not finally allowed to fulfil its original purpose until after restoration by the British Governor and a temporary occupation by Russian troops. The present hospital, still in process of enlargement and no longer used for housing the poor and aged, replaces the original building, most of which was gutted by fire in 1859.

Ecclesiastically the Island grew somewhat calmer, but fear of invasion from France made refugees less welcome, even if they abjured the Catholic faith. In 1763 the States were asked to enforce an Order in Council forbidding any foreigner of the Roman Church to live in the Island or to marry a Jersey woman without the permission of the Governor. Even Protestants *de bonnes moeurs* might be asked for references, if they wished to settle in Jersey.[6] In 1736 a church was built at St Aubin, the first to be erected in the Island since the Reformation. This was the result of a petition or prayer to the Bishop of Winchester from the inhabitants of St Aubin, which, as Falle noted in his edition of 1734, had become 'a town of merchants and masters of ships'. They pointed out the distance they had to go to attend services at the parish church of St Brelade, and in 1716 were granted a licence to build a private proprietary chapel at St Aubin. Its erection was a splendid example of self help, as so many people contributed money, materials or labour. The square, barn-like building remained until 1892 when it was replaced by the present church. This is architecturally a very fine example of its period and includes a Burne-Jones window in the Lady Chapel.[7]

Acutely aware of the Island's dangerous proximity to France, the States were constantly exercised by the need for strong defences. In 1736 they decided that boulevards should be constructed on which to place the cannon supplied by the Board of Ordnance. Contractors were appointed for the various bays and parishes, and expected to complete the work within a year, while the Constables promised to underwrite the enterprise, the cost being divided proportionately between them.[8] In this role the Constables appear to have been acting as their English counterparts, for in England too

> the Constable was responsible for maintaining the parish armoury, which was normally lodged in the church, and for seeing that the local militia was fully recruited and equipped. Expenses were met out of a parish rate; but it was the Constable who made the necessary purchases and rendered an account to the Vestry (the Parish Assembly).

This adds weight to the comment made at a later date by François-Victor Hugo, son of the poet: '*Ainsi l'origine du connétable est tout anglais; l'organisation de la municipalité jersiaise est tout anglaise … A Jersey, l'État est normand, mais la commune est anglaise*'.

The work on the *boulevards* took longer than expected and in 1739 contractors were empowered to send before the Magistrate any men who refused to work for the agreed wage. In 1744 the road down to Bouley Bay was proving so formidable a task that other parishes were asked to provide 12 men each to help the inhabitants of Trinity.

In this same year detailed regulations were drawn up for the reform of the Militia. By 1750 the States were proposing to redeem their considerable debt by levying on the parishes a rate in *livres d'ordre*. The military establishment was increased by the presence of English regiments, and in 1761 the States had to take special measures to ensure that there were sufficient billets available, as the barracks provided by the Constable of St Helier, *aux frais de l'île*, were insufficient. There seemed no end to military requirements. In 1758 an Order in Council set out further proposals by the Board of Ordnance for the defences of the Island, noting that,

> whereas it has been this day humbly represented to His Majesty that the poverty of the inhabitants of the said island is such as to render them unable to finish at their expense the Lines [a connected series of fieldworks] upon St Helier's Hill, and the repairs of the several bays in the said island, His Majesty doth therefore hereby order that the said lines as likewise the repairs of the several bays, be carried on and completed by the Board of Ordnance and the necessary cannon and stores for them sent thither, as soon as they can be spared: and that the cistern in Elizabethan Castle be made secure from bombs.

The States had other more peaceful ploys which reveal a commendable civic pride. Already in the 17th century permission had to be sought from the States to build or alter houses around the market place. In 1669 Suzanne Dumaresq, Dame de La Haule, had obtained permission to build at her expense a Corn Market (*une Halle à Blé*) for the use of the Island in exchange for the right to build her own dwelling above it. This was achieved in 1672.[10] A large room in it was let for public meetings and here John Wesley preached in 1787. The building is now the premises of the United Club, the pillars of the old Corn Market being incorporated into offices on the ground floor.

In 1697 Jean Carter was allowed to build, next door to the property of M. Clement Chevalier, a direct descendant of the diarist, *une maison de hauteur et forme qui puisse être un ornement au marché publique* (this is now the 'Cosy Corner'). At the same time M. Chevalier asked permission to improve his house (now the Chamber of Commerce), and suggested that, as the cage, which had formerly been used for prisoners awaiting trial or escort to Mont Orgueil, was no longer needed since the erection of a prison in town, it should be replaced by a pedestal on six steps surmounted by a sundial. In 1701 Carter and Chevalier asked to be allowed to erect in front of their houses a canopy under which they would place a bench to be maintained at their expense for the benefit of the public.

Such bargains are not uncommon. In 1720 a M. Edouard Le Préveu, in exchange for certain concessions, undertook to build the suggested 'Tuscan' column in place of the cage, and provided elaborate details about its dimensions and suggested materials. Plans took time to come to fruition. In 1708 the heirs of Suzanne Dumaresq were allowed to enlarge the Halle à Blé and were enjoined to provide the public with measures to be used on Saturdays: *un caboteau, un demy caboteau* and *un sixtonnier.*[11] Well into the 20th century apples and potatoes were still sold by the *cabot.* The heirs were also to be responsible for the cleanliness of this section of the market.

In 1748, on the death of Le Préveu, Abraham Gosset took over his commission, but suggested that it would be more fitting to erect a statue in gilded lead of His Majesty, King George II. This is now known to have been the work of John Cheere, a sculptor who worked in partnership with his more famous brother Sir Henry.[12] It was completed to the satisfaction of the States in 1751 and enclosed in iron railings sent from London as a gift from the Lieutenant-Governor, Colonel William Deane.[13] These were considered to be 'not only a great ornament, but very necessary for the preservation of the statue'; it was not fear of vandalism that prompted this precaution, but Falle reminds us that

> there a market is kept every Saturday, more resembling a fair than an ordinary market, by reason of the great concourse of people resorting to it from the remotest parts of the island, not only to buy and sell, but to dispatch all sorts of business, or even purely to enjoy the conversation of their friends.

It has been said that the statue was erected in gratitude to the King for a gift of £200 'for carrying on the public works of our piers at St Helier and St Aubin'. The gift, however, was not received until 1752 after a favourable report from the Governor, Lieutenant-General Huske.[14] At all events the unveiling ceremony on 9 July 1751 was an occasion of great

45 *Léoville, St Ouen. Perhaps 15th century.*

TRADITIONAL DOMESTIC ARCHITECTURE

46 *Sous les Bois, Trinity, 1683.*

military and civic splendour culminating in the proclamation by the Deputy-Viscount 'that this statue is erected in honour of His Sacred Majesty King George the Second whom God long preserve to reign over us', followed by a signal from the top of the church to the castle, where a suitable salute was fired.[15] The Market Place was renamed Royal Square in honour of the King, but for many years was referred to as *le marchi* or *le vier marchi*. In the 1760s it was decided further to enhance the square by erecting a new Court House, which in its turn was replaced in the 19th century.[16]

At this period the Ecclesiastical Court was also busy inspecting the schools of St Mannelier and St Anastase. In 1745 it noted that no pupils were studying Latin, and made recommendations for the repair of the regents' houses.[17] Private owners continued to build new houses or to embellish old ones, and the States instructed the Constable of St Helier 'once and for all' to see that the streets of the town were kept clean; for the fear of plague was never far from their minds.[18]

The States indeed had many other preoccupations besides the buildings around the Square. There were paupers to be cared for and regulations to be made about the import and export of wool, meat and grain. They exhorted the Constables to find work for the poor, arranged for a guard boat to protect shipping lanes and enforced stringent regulations against plague. In 1733 and 1749 it raged in North Africa; in 1751 in the Levant. By now the islanders were trading far and wide and shipping provided their greatest source of wealth. No risks could be taken.

Many of the Jurats and Constables had shares in privateers. Their captains carried Letters of Marque which enabled them to bring prizes of considerable value to the Island. The building of a proper harbour at St Helier and further shelter at St Aubin was of paramount importance, and in January 1750, on the proposition of several merchants, the States decided to institute a lottery to provide the necessary funds.[19] Merchants who had been engaged in the 'sack' trade were now hoping for a foothold on the eastern seaboard of Canada, which fell into British hands in 1763 after the Treaty of Paris. Foremost among these was the firm of Robin, Pipon and Company for which the young Charles Robin was an agent in Arichat, on Cape Breton Island and later at Paspébiac on the Gaspé Peninsula. Although many other firms were engaged in the fishing trade, it was Charles Robin, who, by his perseverance and meticulous attention to detail, finally established the pattern of that trade by Jersey firms based in Canada, but with head offices in the Island, which was to last well into the 19th century and dominate the life of the 'coast' for over a hundred years.[20]

Charles Robin's diary, begun in 1767, gives a graphic picture of 18th-century Jerseymen pioneering in Nova Scotia and on the Gaspé Coast. Another Jerseyman of the period, Joshua Mauger, nephew of Matthew Mauger, merchant of Poole, rose to prominence as a distiller in Halifax, Nova Scotia, became agent-victualler for the British Navy, and finally, on his return to England, first agent-general for Nova Scotia, an elder brother of Trinity House and M.P. for Poole. A copy of the petition presented to the States in 1769 was sent to Mauger as a man of influence in high circles, and it is to him that indirectly we owe the building which houses the Jersey Museum at Pier Road. When Mauger died, he left his considerable fortune to his nephew, whose son Philip Nicolle, built an impressive town house to back on to his ship-building yard, the family having exchanged their business in knitted goods for a more profitable trade in Newfoundland cod.[21]

Jersey merchants continued to do business through agents in Southampton, Poole and other ports and the anglicisation of trade continued. In the papers of the Fiott family[22] we learn of one firm from a letter written by John Fiott to the guardian of Harriet Lee, the young lady he wished to marry. To an enquiry about his financial position he replied that he was working for the firm of de Gruchy and Le Breton, established as merchants in London.

> The house in which I am a partner is an old-established Jersey house. Henry Durell was chief of the house fifty years ago and was succeeded Mr de Gruchy. Our chief business consists in purchasing ships and goods, by orders of our different correspondents to be consigned as they direct, in making their insurances in ships and goods, in buying and selling stock for them and receiving their dividends. Our connections are with the principal people in Jersey, from which island by our family connections we have the chief of business. With several of our friends we take a share in their ships. Another branch of our business is with Norway.[23] We are connected with the chief House in that Kingdom, receiving all their cargoes of deals, masts etc. to the amount of £50,000 per annum. The Danish Ambassador now receives through our hands his yearly salary from the Court of Denmark. We have besides correspondents at Ostend, Hamburg etc., with whom we do business on commission. Our commission business alone (exclusive of the concerns we occasionally take in ships for our friends) has for these three years past amounted to £2,000 per annum; this year it has exceeded it.

We learn from the diaries of Charles Robin that he dealt with the firm of de Gruchy and Le Breton, and, on the death of de Gruchy, with Fiott himself.

It is not surprising that in 1768 with so much at stake the Jersey merchants should form a Chamber of Commerce, the oldest by a few months in the English-speaking world, to ensure in those dangerous days that their ships 'came home'. It is also significant that, although the title of the first book of minutes is in French: *Règlements des Armateurs de Jersey*, from the outset the actual minutes are written in English. The list of the original subscribing members, besides containing many Jersey names, includes some which at the time were of recent French origin, while the first president, George Rowcliffe, was an Englishman. Among the Jersey names we find Daniel Messervy, whose papers have provided us with much information about privateers,[24] Philip Lys of the *London Packet*, Thomas and James Pipon standing in for Messrs de Gruchy and Le Breton, Noë Le Cras, Brelade Janvrin and William Patriarche. The French include Simonet, de Vaumorel, Hemery, Villeneuve, Thoreau and Perrochon, whose initials, I.P. 1748, may still be seen high up on the façade of 16 Hill Street. Ships listed include the corsair *Charming Nancy*, subject of a famous quarrel,[25] and the *Hope* belonging to Philip Robin and mentioned as present in 1788 in the raid on Arichat by the American privateer, Paul Jones. Early on Jersey ships were given English names, a sign of the times.

The subscribing members of the new Chamber drew up regulations as a guide for their proceedings. They decided, in order to forward their purpose 'to the well-being of trade and to support and keep the merchants upon a respectable footing, in unity', to create a fund of threepence sterling per ton per annum 'to be raised upon the tonnage belonging to each respective member, the vessels to be measured by direction of the committee; condemned vessels for breaking up not included. The tonnage to be entered in ye book of the Chamber'. They were to assemble on the second Monday of every month 'to begin March, 1768, at Mr Lys at the King's Head there to meet at ten in the forenoon and to proceed to business by eleven at the farthest; everything determined by the then majority to be valid as if the whole had been present'. In February 1768 Mr James Hemery was elected secretary and Mr George Rowcliffe[26] president. Dinner was served at two for those attending the general meeting at a cost of 24 *sols* French currency.

From the outset the Chamber of Commerce found many matters for its agenda. The first ever item was a proposal 'to take steps for relieving the trade of the island from the persecutions carried on by Mr John Jas. Gruchy, receiver of the sixpences for the Greenwich

Hospital, to the great prejudice of every individual'. In 1696 the year in which the foundation stone was laid of Greenwich Hospital, an Act was passed under William and Mary which required the deduction of 6d. a month from the pay of all seamen in the Royal Navy and the Merchant Service towards the cost of maintaining the Hospital.[27] At first this did not apply to the Channel Islands, but in July 1731, 'with the advice of his Privy Council', George II ordered that the Act

> for the more effectual collecting in Great Britain, Ireland, and other parts of His Majesty's dominions, the duties granted for the support of the Royal Hospital of Greenwich be transmitted to the Royal Courts of Jersey and Guernsey, requiring them to register and publish the said Act and to cause the same to be carried into due execution.

Apprentices under eighteen and those 'in a boat taking fish brought fresh ashore' were exempt, but no others. Masters were empowered and required to detain

> 6d a month of lawful money of Great Britain or the value thereof in the money of the said islands ... and proportionately for a shorter time than a month ... out of the wages, shares or other profits ... a customs' officer or such person as he or they shall think fit to collect the same

was to be appointed. The money was used almost exclusively for naval pensioners or for the upkeep of buildings in England, so it is not surprising that this early form of compulsory contribution to 'social security' was unpopular in Jersey and the receiver accused of persecution. When the levy was abolished in England, the States, on the recommendation of a committee, passed a law setting up in 1835 *La Société de Bienfaisance pour la Marine Marchande de Jersey* now familiarly known as The Jersey Merchant Seamen's Benefit Society. The monthly contribution of 7½d. per month of service began on 1 July 1835 and ceased in 1895, but the Society still functions today with the help of legacies, and has never been subsidised by public funds. For well over a hundred years it has helped seamen in distress, their widows and orphans. The early records are now housed at La Société Jersiaise and are a mine of information on Jersey shipping captains and crews in the 19th century.

At the first meeting of the Chamber of Commerce in 1768 it was also suggested that approaches be made through Mr Dauvergne and Mr James Amice Lemprière, both living in England, to Lord Albemarle, Governor, and Lord Granville, Bailiff,[28] for their patronage. (Lemprière might well have been referred to as Jacques Amyas, for in this transition period French and English versions of Christian names were interchangeable. Similarly even today certain surnames like Le Feuvre and du Feu are pronounced differently in town and country.)

Members were particularly concerned with harbour facilities and they drew up a petition recommending that a quay be carried

> from the bank within the Town pier round the rocks to the point turning into *le havre aux Anglais* and returning the wall to the nearer bank as the only means of securing the said harbour. This would make a wharf absolutely requisite to the loading and unloading of vessels afloat which at present can only be done by turns and which from the great increase of trade is attended with great inconvenience.

In October 1768 the President suggested that a small cargo of barley be sent from France for the relief of the poor, a collection for this being made from the various 'societies' (a literal translation of the French word for 'company') and from members in due proportion. It was also suggested that a protest be made against the Navigation Act which might prevent their carrying goods to America without clearing through England. They requested 'that we might have liberty to carry out trade to Newfoundland and New England according as we have hitherto done'. Trade with the latter would soon be disrupted by the War of American Independence.

As time went on the Chamber became critical of reactionary States' members. Acting as a 'ginger' group, they often took matters into their own hands and direct to the Privy Council. It is significant that amid the political rivalries of the latter part of the 18th century, they were to prefer as their delegate to London another Jean Dumaresq (1749-1819),[29] champion of the popular party against Charles Lemprière, and would appear to have been more in sympathy with the Jeannot, or liberal party so soon to come into being. For the birth of the Jeannot (or Magot) and the Charlot parties we must revert to the *troubles intestins* so soon to surface in riot.

Chapter Twenty-four

THE DICTATORSHIP OF CHARLES LEMPRIÈRE, 1750-1781

The poor have come out of leading strings and cannot any longer be governed as children.– J. S. Mill

THE BAILIFFSHIP had at this time become hereditary in the de Carteret family by custom though not in law. Earl Granville, great-grandson of Sir George Carteret and one of the ablest Whig statesmen in Walpole's cabinet, now held this post. But for 60 years neither he nor his playboy son, who succeeded him, ever visited the Island.[1] So when, in November 1750, Charles Lemprière was appointed his Lieutenant, he became for all practical purposes Bailiff. During the 30 years that he held office the Governors also were absentees, and their Lieutenants were ineffective and constantly changing.[2] Of Colonel Ball, Lieutenant-Governor at the time of the revolt that was approaching, a contemporary writes: 'He possessed no more idea than an oyster, and like that inert animal he seldom opened his mouth but to take in fluids'.[3] So Lemprière had a free hand in the government of the Island.

His family had sided with the Parliamentarians and their traditions were democratic. His great-grandfather, Michel, had been Cromwell's Bailiff; his grandfather one of the five Jurats degraded for sedition. He himself had at first followed in their steps: 'Damnation to the Governor', was a popular toast, 'and success to honest Charles Lemprière'. But by temperament he was autocratic; when in power he found it saved trouble to rule as a dictator. His position was strong. The States at this time were entirely subservient to the Royal Court, which consisted of 12 equally autocratic Jurats who were far from sympathetic to the populace. Among them were his father, his father-in-law and a cousin. Soon two brothers-in-law were added to their number. In 1758 his brother, Philippe, became Attorney-General, and now the Lemprière faction was as strong as that of the de Carterets had been under Sir George. Entrenched behind this family phalanx, Charles Lemprière issued ordinances through his Court and through the same Court punished all who protested. But the people had not forgotten the *six-au-sou* riots, and the middle of the 18th century was a little late for totalitarianism.

There are many sources of information on the riots of 1769 and the events which led up to them. Some are patently biased, but a clear overall picture emerges. The first open resistance came from Nicholas Fiott, a sea-captain who had settled down as a merchant with nine vessels engaged in the Newfoundland trade.[4] First came personal squabbles. Fiott prosecuted the regent of St Mannelier for caning his nine-year-old son, and Lemprière dismissed the case. Fiott also bought some fields from Lemprière's wife, accepted an old measurement and found later that he had paid for four vergées too many. A privateer, the *Charming Nancy*, in which he had shares, was sold by the Lemprières without his consent. Soon the quarrel shifted to public ground.

During the Seven Years' War Lemprière had charge of the French prisoners and was castigated for the conditions which they had to endure. Shebbeare tells us that the windows of the prison were broken and the men fed twice a week on dried cod. Fiott visited the place and

47 *The college that bears the Queen's name, opened 29 September 1852, by Felix Benoist.*

VICTORIAN JERSEY

48 *John Folley, Mr. Poingdestre's 'very clever gardener', with the basket of fruit presented to Her Majesty on her arrival. An exceptionally early photograph.*

49 *Memorial pillar on Victoria Avenue to celebrate the Queen's Diamond Jubilee, 1897.*

found it disgraceful. The half-starved prisoners had been brutally treated and were sleeping on filthy straw. It emerged that they had been allowed no fresh straw for 36 days.

With half-a-dozen lawsuits on his hands, Fiott found difficulty in getting anyone to plead his cause, since all Advocates were appointed by the Lieutenant-Bailiff. Annoyed when Mauger, his lawyer, deserted him, he made some blunt remarks and was arrested for damaging Mauger's reputation. At his trial he objected to the presence on the Bench of four Jurats with whom he had quarrelled. He was told to put his reason in writing. He did this in such forthright language that he was ordered to make *amende honorable* by asking pardon on his knees of God, the King and the Bench. This he refused to do and was committed to prison. Now the resentment at the Lemprière tyranny first became manifest. A monster petition for Fiott's release was sent to the Privy Council signed by *principaux* (men who had the right to attend their Parish assembly and vote, a right determined by the amount of property they held in the parish, though this was often assessed to suit particular circumstances). In St Ouen only one name was missing, in St Helier ten. The Council ordered that bail be granted and Fiott's militia company welcomed him with a *feu de joie*. Wishing to keep an eye on his English lawsuits, Fiott decided to forfeit his bail and cross to Westminster. Lemprière thereupon proclaimed him a fugitive from justice, and he was unable to return to the Island for six years.

This was a rich man's quarrel and in the first round Lemprière seemed to have won; but now the people themselves began to intervene. A revolutionary spirit stirred once more. In 1767, when the supply of food in the Island was short, mysterious placards appeared on the walls to warn shipowners: 'Whoever shall directly or indirectly presume to take any cattle or other provisions on board for exportation, their vessels will be burnt, sunk, blown up or otherwise destroyed without distinction and themselves deemed as cannibals and treated as such'. That 'black dog Gilbert' (the Lieutenant-Governor) was informed that 'some of his friends will present him with an ounce of lead which will soon convert him into worm's meat'.[5] In 1768, to keep all available corn for local use, the States forbade its export; but next year the harvest improved and this Act was repealed. A furious outcry arose based not only on fear of starvation but on a darker suspicion. A rich man's favourite form of investment was in wheat *rentes* (the local form of mortgage raised on real property). He would lend a farmer money on condition that he received annually so many quarters of wheat, which were generally paid in kind but sometimes in money according to a fixed scale which varied with the market price of wheat. If the price fell, so did the rich man's income; thus dear bread meant prosperity to the capitalist and starvation for the poor.

Justly or unjustly the suspicion arose that the Lemprières were encouraging the export of corn to create a shortage and so increase the *rentes*. A mob of women raided a corn-ship in the harbour, forced the sailors to unload her, sold the corn on the quay but with due honesty paid the owners.[6] On 18 September 1769 the *Salisbury Journal* announced: 'There are great disturbances in Jersey on account of the exportation of corn'. On Thursday, 28 September, the northern parishes brought matters to a head. The men of St Martin, Trinity and St John marched to the town armed with stout sticks. Three hundred came from Trinity alone, and others joined them from St Saviour and St Lawrence.[7] Daniel Messervy, who left in his diary a vivid contemporary account of the riot, describes them as *la populallace*, artisans, day labourers and 'other common people', but he was a Jurat. It was evidently a planned rising, for they brought demands which included the reduction of the price of wheat to 20 *sols* a *cabot* and of the Crown tithes to 20 *sols* a vergée, the abolition of *champart* (the seigneur's right to every twelfth sheaf of corn or bundle of flax[8] and his right to enjoy for a year and a day the revenue from the estates of all who died without direct heirs (known as *l'année de jouissance*),[9] the limitation of the Rector's tithes and the tithe on apples, the banishment of all aliens, the removal of the Customs' House officers and the complete withdrawal of all charges against Fiott.[10]

The men forced their way into the Court House, where the *Assize d'Héritage* was sitting, threw the usher over the railings and banged the seats with their cudgels, uttering blood-curdling threats. 'I did not believe', wrote Charles Poingdestre, who was present, 'that any of the magistrates could escape with their lives.'[11] A letter in the papers of Pierre Mauger, Fiott's enemy, reports that

> the worse of them threatened their neighbours to pull their houses down if they did not come to town ... most everybody they pressed on their way ... and after the Court was sat, the most daring forced in the Court house with great sticks in a furious manner and threatened the Court for above five hours and till they had compelled them to make and publish several ridiculous acts.

Then they dispersed. However violent their actions, one can but sympathise today with their demands.

On Saturday the new Acts were proclaimed in the Market Place, and on Sunday after church in every churchyard except St Brelade. For three days the Island had apparently been quiet, though, according to Daniel Messervy, there was feverish activity behind the scenes, speeches in churches and coffee houses and the organisation of a petition which for townsmen was lodged with Pierre Symonet, son of a Frenchman and vendor of snuff in *La Grande Rue* (Broad Street) and ancestor of the Simonets who built Radier in Grouville.

Whether they had news of plans for another rising or whether this was a political ruse to arouse sympathy in England, no one can now say, but on Sunday evening Lemprière and the Jurats took refuge in Elizabeth Castle, a favourite resort for frightened officials, who felt safe there at least at high tide. Here they held a meeting of the States which sent the two Lemprières and two Jurats to report to the King. When the deputation entered the Council Chamber, they apologised somewhat theatrically for their bedraggled garments, explaining that they had no clothes but those in which they had escaped for their lives across the sands. In fact they had had three days between the riot and their flight. They drew a lurid picture of the mob ordering the King's laws to be erased from the Statute Book, and the magistrates forced to fly to the shelter of the castle walls. To the Council in England this must have appeared as barefaced anarchy against which the Crown must act, and they got all they desired: a declaration that the Acts passed under pressure were an insult to His Majesty's royal authority,[12] an offer of a reward of £100 sterling for any information that would lead to the arrest of the authors of the riot and the dispatch of five companies of the Royal Scots to restore order.

Their commander, Colonel Bentinck, a shrewd Dutchman,[13] soon discovered another side to the story. He found among Lemprière's opponents three Army officers, who had been placed on half pay at the end of the Seven Years' War: Moyse Corbet, Philippe Fall and Charles William Le Geyt,[14] who explained the cause of the unrest. By parading the Militia he was able to meet all the men of the Island. He visited every parish and invited those with a grievance to set it down in writing. This led to an exciting series of Parish assemblies held in the churches.

The real organisers of the revolt had kept successfully in the background. Fiott from his exile in England was thought to have a hand in it. Lemprière obviously did not know, or so high a reward would not have been offered for their discovery. Our chatty diarist, Daniel Messervy, kept open house for everyone, yet he was equally in the dark. But now one of them stepped out of the shadows. Thomas Jacques Gruchy had been elected churchwarden of Trinity five years before. He was a man of 60, a well-to-do farmer and Captain in the North regiment. At his Parish assembly he outlined a list of reforms of quite a moderate nature, but then he incautiously added amid thunderous huzzas: 'Should a third revolt unfortunately become necessary, a third of the inhabitants may be murdered or burnt in their homes'. For these words he was arrested.[15]

At the Town Assembly Corbet read a petition demanding reforms which he afterwards had printed in *Griefs de l'Isle de Jersey*.[16] This received hundreds of signatures, and he took it to England to present it to the Bailiff, the Governor, Parliament and the King. Meanwhile in the country parishes Le Geyt was organising an enormous petition to the Privy Council, asking for a Royal Commission to investigate the Island's complaints. He too crossed to Westminster to present it in person. The faith of the English authorities in Lemprière was seriously shaken as the lack of justice in his rule became clear.

Then came the heaviest bombardment of all. Le Geyt had married a daughter of John Shebbeare, the notorious pamphleteer,[17] who, in 1758, had stood in the pillory in England with an umbrella over his head, accused of libelling the Tories, but had been won over by them with a pension so that he might bespatter the Whigs with mud. Messervy records that in August 1770, '*le docteur Shebeare*' was with his wife on a visit to his father-in-law, Captain Le Geyt, then living in Captain Fiott's house in St Saviour: '*ledit Shebeare est un grand génie*'. Drawn into the struggle Shebbeare published, at Fiott's expense, his *Authentic Narrative of the Oppressions of the Islanders of Jersey*, and a stream of similar pamphlets, painting every misdeed of the Lemprières in the darkest possible colours. Philippe Lemprière bowed before the storm, resigned his post as Attorney-General and went to live in Devon, never to return. Charles stood his ground. He was rebuilding Rozel Manor and had no intention of abandoning his estates. He still had the Royal Court solidly behind him, a large majority in the States and all the well-to-do in the Island who had been alarmed at the revolt.[18]

Meanwhile Bentinck had received instructions from England that the Island must be pacified and necessary reforms introduced. In June 1770 he was made Lieutenant-Governor. His first step was to secure an amnesty for all concerned in the revolt. The prisoners were released and Fiott was at last allowed to return home. Then came three important reforms. By Order in Council the Royal Court was deprived of its ancient right to legislate and became merely a Court of Justice. The power to enact laws was confined solely to the States. This demarcation of the functions of the two assemblies is an important landmark in island history.

The practice of farming out the Crown revenues was forbidden. The Receiver was paid a fixed salary and had to hand over all that he collected, a rule which removed all temptation to demand more than was due. There were other reforms. Most important of all and for the first time in island history the laws of Jersey were collected in a printed code 'that everyone may know how to regulate his conduct and be no more obliged to live in continual dread of becoming liable to punishments for disobeying laws it was impossible for him to have knowledge of'. This was approved by the Privy Council and published in 1771. Known as 'the Code' it was frequently quoted in subsequent years, and when, in 1950/51, amid strong opposition, the Social Security Scheme was introduced, it was repeatedly invoked.[19]

Two more heavy blows were to fall on Lemprière's head. Bentinck secured the resignation of three aged and infirm Jurats: Charles Hilgrove, Daniel Messervy and Jacques Lemprière. The Order in Council declared His Majesty's 'gracious disposition to allow them the continuance during their lives of those privileges and distinctions which Jurats do now or may hereafter enjoy'. Three members of the opposition were elected with immense majorities: Daniel's cousin, Nicholas Messervy, the Denonciateur, Monsieur Charles Payn, Constable of St Ouen, and Monsieur David Patriarche of the Town. Daniel Messervy tells us that only the latter stood drinks, offered after church or at Mr Lys' tavern, to those who promised him a vote. This tavern was the venue of the newly-formed Chamber of Commerce and it may be significant that Messervy associated Rowcliffe, its first president, with the recent disturbances. At the customary swearing-in of the new Jurats in January 1771, the tradition of shaking hands was waived, and only Colonel Bentinck and Philippe de Carteret, the circumnavigator,[20] went to drink wine with them after the ceremony. Nevertheless a breach had been made in Lemprière's stronghold and worse was to come. When Bentinck was recalled in 1771, Moyse Corbet, the most irritating of all the agitators, was appointed Lieutenant-Governor.[21] But Lemprière still had a large number of supporters and was determined to fight his enemies to the bitter end.

A new opponent now appeared on the scene. In 1773 Jean Dumaresq, not to be confused with the earlier champion of the people during the *six-au-sou* riots, was sworn in as Advocate.[22] A brilliant young man, full of enthusiasm for the ideals of Liberty, Equality and Fraternity that were fermenting in France, he plunged into politics determined to smash Lemprière's government by a junta of Jurats. He claimed that the States should be purged of Rectors and Jurats to become a Chamber of Deputies, and that this assembly should be entrusted with the administration of the Island; he thus anticipated by nearly two centuries much of the constitutional reform of 1948.[23]

Between Dumaresq and Lemprière there was now war to the knife. Dumaresq, a born demagogue, a brilliant speaker, an untiring organiser, was quick to exploit to the uttermost every popular grievance. The Island became divided into two ferociously hostile parties, the Charlots, supporters of Charles Lemprière, and the Jeannots, followers of Jean Dumaresq, who later defiantly adopted the name, contemptuously given them by their opponents, of Magots or cheese-mites. De la Croix relates that a Charlot orator at one of their party banquets picked a mite out of the cheese and crashed it between his finger and thumb boasting: 'This is what we will do with Dumaresq's rabble'.[24] Dumaresq when he heard of it, is said to have replied: 'We may be maggots, but we shall make these seigneurs bite the dust'. Greatly hated by his political opponents, Dumaresq was loved by his followers and his large family. He was the first Liberal in the modern sense of the word, a man of personal integrity and an idealist who worked for the betterment of his fellow-islanders.

Every election was now fought with incredible ferocity. Neither side shrank from outrageously illegal actions, bribery, corruption, even the kidnapping of electors. Hostile voters might be seized from their beds and dumped for the day on the Ecréhous. Others would be made so drunk that they could not reach the poll. In 1776 Dumaresq secured election as Constable of St Peter. In the next few years more than half the parishes chose Magots for their Constables. As several of the Jurats and eight of the Rectors voted with them Dumaresq had, by 1781, a majority in the States, and the steadily increasing Magot vote at every election for Jurat showed that before long he would have a majority in the Court also. Pleasure at this state of affairs is reflected in the contemporary minutes of the Chamber of Commerce whose members, when blocked by opposition in the States, often appealed to the Privy Council. By 1785 Jean Dumaresq was being thanked for one of the many missions he undertook to plead the cause of island trade in London. The Chamber also expressed thanks to John Fiott and Paul Le Mesurier, merchants in London, the latter being a son of the hereditary governor of Alderney and later Lord Mayor of London.[25]

In 1781, a few months after the Battle of Jersey, Lemprière at last acknowledged defeat. He had crossed to England to resign his post in favour of his son, William Charles,[26] who, however, predeceased him. Charles eventually returned to Jersey and died at Rozel Manor in 1806.

While Magots and Charlots were squabbling, the world had not been standing still. In 1776 France began to send arms and money to help the Americans in their War of Independence and threat of invasion from France emphasised once more the need for coastal defence. Jersey's so called 'martello' towers began to appear at this period. In 1794 the Governor, General Conway, referred to a plan he had formed in 1779 to erect 'a number of towers of masonry with corresponding batteries in all the accessible parts of the coast, the whole number at first projected being thirty-two of which twenty-two have been built'. The name martello arises from Cape Mortella in Corsica, where a round coastal tower caused the defeat of British warships in 1794, 15 years after Conway's original plans had been drawn up.[27] These towers, of a design unique to Jersey and even differing slightly from that adopted in Guernsey, ring the south and east coasts and there is also one at Grève de Lecq; their architect has not been identified, but is likely to have been a man in the artillery stationed in the Island. True Martello towers were built later in the Napoleonic period from about 1810 onwards and are found on west, south and east coasts. Long before then Jersey was to be called upon to defend herself against the French.

Chapter Twenty-five

THE BATTLE OF JERSEY, 1781

Cet animal est très méchant. Quand on l'attaque, il se défend.–La Ménagerie

WHILE LEMPRIÈRE was in London, an alarming crisis suddenly arose in Jersey, aggravated by the Boston Tea Party and the War of American Independence. Jersey had long had links with the area around Boston and Massachusetts Bay and, when France in 1778 made a military alliance with the American rebels, islanders found their trade threatened by hostile vessels on both sides of the Atlantic.

England's reply to the Revolutionary alliance was to let loose the Jersey privateers on French shipping. During the wars of the Spanish and Austrian Succession privateering had become a major industry in Jersey. Scores of brigantines and cutters, armed with a few swivel guns, had prowled the Channel and the Bay of Biscay snapping up French traders. In a letter dated August 1755, written to Captain Dauvergne,[1] Daniel Messervy reported on 'the quantity of prizes and men taken by our privateers during the last war, the first amounting to about £60,000 sterling, the latter, I believe, to above 600 men'. The Seven Years' War was to bring even greater activity; but, when peace was proclaimed, the privateers had to return to normal commercial work. When news arrived that yet another French war had begun, there was a tremendous rush to obtain Letters of Marque.[2] The French commander in Cherbourg, General Dumouriez, wrote, in his observations on the attacks made on Jersey by the French in 1779 and 1781, that the two islands of Jersey and Guernsey were the despair of France at the beginning of every war, because of their very active privateering.[3] He noted that in the winter of 1777/8 'there were then in St Helier's roads more than 150 prizes, and in the island over 1500 seamen prisoners belonging to the said vessels'. Nor did Jerseymen confine their buccaneering to the sea. On 6 October 1778 the French newspaper, *La Gazette des deux Ponts*, reported that Jersey pirates had landed near Caen and carried off oxen, cows and sheep, all the curé's washing and two of his housekeepers who were washing elsewhere.[4] Such acts made reprisals inevitable.

Many plans for the capture of Jersey were discussed at the French Court. In 1779 permission was given to that gallant adventurer, the Prince of Nassau, who had sailed round the world with Bougainville, to raise a legion for this purpose. Corbet knew what was coming and sent all the prizes in St Aubin's Bay to England for safety. On 1 May the enemy was sighted and Corbet hurried to St Ouen with his Highlanders and the Militia. A portrait of him by Philippe Jean shows St Ouen's Bay in the background.[5] There he sat all day watching an absurd fiasco. As the tide was ebbing, the French warships refused to come close enough inshore to cover the landing with their guns. The captains of the transports would not take their ships within range of the Jersey cannon. After hours of frantic threats and arguments, the Prince was forced to sail back to St Malo, where five of his vessels were destroyed at anchor by a visit from the British fleet. Corbet was highly commended for the steps he had taken. The news of the impending attack had been reported to Admiral Arbuthnot, who took immediate action, although in the event his aid was not needed. However, the States were so grateful to him for his prompt response that they offered him a ceremonial sword worth 50 guineas '*comme un sincère, mais faible témoignage de la plus vive reconnaissance*'.[6]

But the danger was not over. A new adventurer hoped to succeed where Nassau failed. Le Chevalier de Luxembourg obtained permission to make a second attempt. He chose as his commander a dare-devil soldier of fortune, the Baron de Rullecourt. Luxembourg gathered a motley force of 950 men; some had enlisted for the previous raid, some were drafts from the Normandy militia, others were convicts released from chain-gangs on condition that they joined the Legion. While they were being drilled into shape, de Rullecourt crossed to Jersey in the guise of a grain smuggler to survey possible landing-places.

His secret was well kept. Even the Governor of Lower Normandy supposed his men to be the crew of a new privateer. Corbet's secret service had not the smallest inkling of their intentions. On 27 December 1780 they set sail from Granville, having learnt that during the Christmas festivities the Militia were inclined to neglect their duties; but the 29th found them off Chausey, where they waited in appalling conditions of cold, lacking shelter and food, detained by contrary winds. These did not shift until 5 January; but not a word of the impending danger reached Corbet. De Rullecourt had chosen La Rocque as his landing-place, the last spot where an invader might be expected, for the jagged reef of *le Banc de Vielet*[7] stretches out two miles to sea. But there is a channel between the rocks known to local fishermen, and he had as pilot one Journeaux, who had fled from the Island to escape the hangman's rope. At midnight his 26 boats sailed up the narrow passage. The nine militiamen, who should have been on guard, had been celebrating Twelfth Night, and the landing went undetected. So, leaving about 100 men at La Rocque and leading about 600 by inland lanes to avoid the guard-houses on the coast, he marched into the town before sunrise on 6 January 1781.[8]

The surprise was complete; but even so his one chance of success was bluff. His seven last boats had been unable to land their men, as the tide turned and they had to put out to sea. The 600 men he had with him was an absurd force with which to invade an island garrisoned by a thousand regulars and three thousand militiamen. But he nearly succeeded. Corbet was in bed when the news reached him and, before he could escape, the French were at his door. He was taken prisoner and de Rullecourt told him that the 600 troops in the Square were only his advance guard, that 4,000 others had occupied all important points in the Island, that 10,000 more were on the sea and would land before nightfall, that the Regulars at Grouville had surrendered and that he would burn the town, unless Corbet ordered all his remaining troops to lay down their arms immediately. Corbet was a St Helier man. Resistance seemed hopeless. After some hesitation he signed the order. De Rullecourt regarded his victory as complete. He sent invitations to the principal Jerseymen to dine with him that evening.

He was soon disillusioned. Captain Aylward, in command at Elizabeth Castle, ignored Corbet's order and his men opened fire on the French when they tried to cross the sands. Captain Mulcaster, taking up a typically British pose, returned the demand for a surrender, saying that he did not understand French. The Highlanders, who were billeted in the Hospital, withdrew to Gallows Hill, now called Westmount and previously known as *Le Mont Patibulaire* or *Le Mont ès Pendus*. Several companies of the Militia joined them there. Away in St Peter was Francis Peirson, a young major aged 24 in command of the 95th Foot, as his senior officers were all in England on Christmas leave. When he heard of the French landing, he at once beat to arms and marched to join the Highlanders on Gallows Hill. Here, including the Militia, about 1,600 had gathered. No one yet knew the strength of the enemy. The militia colonels placed themselves under the orders of this juvenile Major. But then a serious problem arose. Corbet's order to surrender arrived. Dare junior officers disobey their Commander-in-Chief?

Everything depended on this point. Was Corbet a free agent? Peirson sent his Adjutant[9] into the town under a flag of truce to discover. De Rullecourt then dispatched Corbet on parole to insist on obedience. Peirson told him bluntly that he and his forces meant to die rather than surrender and gave him 10 minutes to get back into the town. He proved himself a skilful tactician. The French were massed in the Royal Square, so Peirson sent some of his troops by a devious route to seize the Town Hill. Fort Regent was not yet built, and the Old Court buildings were sufficiently low for it to be possible to fire from the hill-top right into the Square. Peirson sent his main force up what is now Broad Street, while he himself led another party to the *Rue de Derrière*, which is now the King Street precinct, to burst into the Square by the opening now known as Peirson Place. The French were hopelessly outnumbered and the fight did not last ten minutes. They threw down their arms and the raid was over. But both Peirson and de Rullecourt were dead.

A simple stone in St Helier's churchyard bears the name de Rullecourt; the actual site of his grave is unknown. In the Town Church there is a memorial to the gallant Major and, near the chancel step, a gravestone inscribed with the one word 'Peirson'; a silent and eloquent testimony to this very brave young Englishman who earned the undying gratitude of Jersey. He is also commemorated in Copley's picture, *The Death of Major Peirson*, which hangs in the Tate Gallery at present and of which it is said every Jerseyman has a print hanging over his dining-room mantelpiece. When the original painting was put up for sale on the death of Copley's son, Lord Lyndhurst, the States attempted to buy it for the Island, but were outbidden by the National Gallery. Disappointed they commissioned a copy to be made by the artist, Holyoake, and this now hangs in the Royal Court.[10]

On Peirson's death James Corbet[11] took command of the 95th Regiment, while Major Moyse Corbet, now free once more, confined the prisoners in the Town Church and kept the troops under arms all night, waiting for the 10,000 men who were supposed to be coming from St Malo. He even dressed some in captured French uniforms to decoy the enemy ashore.

Meanwhile at La Rocque a rear-guard action, inspired by the patriotism of the Rector of St Martin, François Le Couteur,[12] had taken place.

> Monsieur Le Couteur brought down two cannon, which he had bought and furnished with ammunition at his own expense after the attack of the first of May, and having joined the Glasgows, he showed Captain Campbell where the French had landed, and urged him to attack them.

After some hesitation 'the Captain ordered his Grenadiers to charge the enemy with the bayonet, which they did, killing and wounding twenty, and taking the rest prisoners'. This action is commemorated on a memorial stone in Grouville churchyard.

On 23 January Moyse Corbet was arrested. His Court-martial at the Horse Guards lasted five days. On the whole his defence was accepted, that by signing the capitulation, which he knew his officers would disobey, he had saved the town, immobilised the enemy and given the scattered British units time to assemble. He was deprived of his Lieutenant-Governorship; but he was not otherwise punished. He was allowed to draw his pension until his death.

Despite further alarms and fears of invasion, Jersey was never again attacked by the French, and life behind the shore defences resumed its normal pattern. We are fortunate to have this recorded in a letter written on 13 July 1781 by James Playfair, chaplain to the 83rd Regiment stationed in Jersey. He describes the Island thus to his parents.[13]

> The island of Jersey is considerably larger than the island of Guernsey; it is some-thing of a square form, 8 miles one way and four the other; on account of the distance of one side of it from the other, I have not seen very much of the island. Our regiment is situated on the east end

50 *The Ile Agois eremetic settlement.*

ANCIENT SITES AND BUILDINGS

51 *The colombier at Diélament, a Seigneur's prerogative.*

52 *La Hougue Bie, prehistoric tomb and place of pilgrimage.*

> of it, opposite the coast of France. On a clear day I can see with my telescope the houses, trees and hedges on the coast, but I could never distinguish either man or beast. We have sometimes reports of intended invasions here, but as they always turn out to be false we never disturb ourselves about them. The face of both islands is very much the same, only there is more wood in Guernsey than in Jersey. This island, like Guernsey, is all divided into small enclosures, two or three acres of ground and all surrounded with fail dykes[14] or rather dykes of earth, which dykes are planted thick with trees, so that from the roads you can scarcely see thirty yards about you anywhere, and the only view that one can have of the island is from the tops of steeples, from which it appears like a forest so you see nothing but wood. More than one fourth of the inclosures of the island are planted with apple trees under which the cows feed. The apple trees furnish them with cider which is all their drink and the branches of the barren wood serve for fuel. There is nothing of what may be called agriculture carried on here. Every man lives in his few acres, which are generally his own, he labours them with his own hands and keeps a horse and two cows. And his wife manages the matters of the house, so that among the common sort there are no servants in Jersey. When a man dies his acres are divided among his children, and in the next generation they are subdivided. So that everybody has but little, yet everybody is above want.[15] They sometimes feed cattle but their chief animal food is pork. To feed cattle and swine they make use of parsnips, the root of which I am told grows to the bulk of one's thigh. Having trenched the ground with a spade they sow it with parsnips and beans mixed. When the beans are ripe, they pull them and apply them to the feeding of the swine; and after the beans are pulled they feed their cattle by putting them into the field to eat the straws of the parsnips, and after the straws are done they take out the shoots and give them to the swine. They likewise feed their swine on rotten apples; they sometimes give them sour milk and sometimes oats. Every man has a pig stye. The breed of cattle and swine is large and good, but the breed of horses is very bad. In all their carriages they have an ox between the trams. They have no flax here, but commonly sow a small quantity of hemp to make ropes of. They winnow their corn in a basket made in the form of a pearl shell, about two feet and a half in breadth, and four or five feet in length. They hold the broad edge to their breast, and throw up the corn in the air, which falls down again into the basket and the chaff flies away. I am told the women thresh the corn with two sticks fixed together with a string and that they grind the corn without drying it, which is the cause that the meal is very course [sic].
>
> I have enjoyed my health very well since I came to this island, and live very comfortably … When I came to Jersey there was no room for me in the barracks, and I took a room in the neighbourhood at half a crown a week; the Mess here is 9 shillings a week. In the morning and at night I live upon bread and milk. So that my expenses here are a great deal less than in Guernsey, and I am enabled to live much more at my ease.
>
> You need not be alarmed at any reports of our Regiment going abroad; the newspaper accounts are often false, as they mistake one Regiment for another. I hope now we shall stay all this winter here. I could live very well here, and I have no desire to go to an unhealthy climate and upon my present pay, it is impossible for me to go.

Many such letters must have been written from the Island from members of the regiments which were an important element in the social life of Jersey until the early years of the 20th century.

Chapter Twenty-six

THE MAGOT VICTORY, 1781-1793

Nothing is more common than for men to call loudly for a reformation, who, when it arrives, by no means like the severity of its impact.–Burke

CHARLES LEMPRIÈRE had grown weary of fighting a losing battle. During de Rullecourt's raid he was in London arranging to transfer his office to his son.[1] William Charles was even more anti-democratic than his father. His haughty manner is said to have won him the nickname of *Bec en l'air.* He informed the Privy Council that the government of the Island rested with the Royal Court, that the function of the States was merely to give advice when invited to do so, and that, although by the Code every new law required the States' acceptance, there was nothing to compel the Court to pass any law that the States might send up to them. He added:

> It is evident from the Constitution of the States that the Clergy and Constables, being originally called merely to advise the Court, could have no right to make motions properly so called, and therefore when they have anything to ask it was by way of Petition or Remonstrance like all other private persons.

Dumaresq, leader of the Magots, furiously denied this. To him the States were: 'An Assembly in which the whole legislative power of this country, under his Majesty in Council, resides'.[2]

The political struggle was now renewed with redoubled fury. Dumaresq had the support of two Jurats and a majority of Constables and Rectors, including the Dean. Six years before the French Revolution these zealous members of the States were protesting against the dictatorship of one man supported by a group of die-hard Jurats. The members of the States, who felt 'called forth to sacrifice the repose of a private life to the service of the State, without the least emolument', complained to the Council about

> the irregularities, the indecencies and disorder which prevail in the management of publick affairs in Your Majesty's island of Jersey to the great prejudice of the people in general and of the corporate body of the States in particular ... everything that is dear and precious to free-born subjects being now at the disposal and under the control of one man.

Lemprière invented a way of reducing to impotence the Magot majority in the States. Whenever they were about to pass a motion he disliked, he left the chair and so closed the session before any vote could be taken. A further complaint was sent to the Council:

> As the Lieutenant-Bailly has in some instances refused to put questions to the vote when regularly proposed and seconded, and in others has thought fit to break up the Assembly by his sudden departure, and in others a number of Jurats have thought proper to absent themselves wilfully, in consequence whereof the States have been disabled from acting when assembled.

However, in 1784 Jean Dumaresq had forged an even more potent weapon. Mathieu Alexandre[3] set up the first printing-press in Jersey and, financed by Dumaresq's brother, Philippe, he started a sixpenny monthly, *Le Magasin de l'Ile de Jersey.* It was outspokenly Magot. 'A neutral', it said in its opening number, 'is a vile creature who does not look you in the face.'[4] But in his tenth number

Alexandre overstepped the mark. In close imitation of Montesquieu and Voltaire, the French *philosophes*, he printed a letter from Mirza to his friend Zadig of Ispahan. This was a skit on an island called Yeseri and its rulers, who were feathering their nests at the expense of the people. Each of the black-hearted officials of Yeseri, or Jersey, could be easily identified. Lemprière arrested Alexandre for criminal libel and then took a subtle revenge. For two years he was constantly called up before the *Cour de Samedi* (not always on a Saturday) and on several occasions the case was adjourned *sine die*, he being on bail, as were many other cases being heard concurrently.[5] This killed *Le Magasin*.

However in 1786 Alexandre started Jersey's first newspaper, the three-sous weekly, *Gazette de l'Ile de Jersey*. This was a success and lived for 50 years. Its party spirit was incredible. It gave entirely one-sided accounts of the private meetings of the States (there had long been pressure from the democrats for more open government), and it harried Lemprière without mercy. For six years it was the only island newspaper, and this gave a very great advantage to Dumaresq and his party. In 1788 Lemprière complained to the King in Council of the

> incendiary harangues and publications of evil-disposed persons ... this venom is spread over the whole island and artfully directed at the feelings and passions of the multitude, by means of a printed weekly paper called the *Jersey Gazette* ... the inflammatory and artful insinuations are daily sounded in the ears of the undiscerning multitude against Your Majesty's civil government.

He claimed that it had become impractical to administer justice without risk of insurrection.[6]

Political feeling became more and more bitter as the ding-dong battle was waged in the States, in the *Gazette* and in the stream of petitions to the Council. Dumaresq was now the idol of his party. One Rector even quoted the text: 'There was a man sent from God whose name was John'.[7] The *Gazette* describes a dinner given him in 1787:

> A Tent was erected on the Town Hill and magnificently decorated to receive this patriot guest. Flags floated everywhere, and everything testified to the joy which the presence of Mr Dumaresq instilled into every heart. The interior was decked with branches of oak, emblems of that perseverance with which he upholds the People's cause.[8]

Two hundred people sat down, and after dinner Dumaresq was chaired through the town. The Charlots view of the demonstration is expressed in Lemprière's complaint to the Privy Council.

> A mob to the number of some thousands was invited and assembled by the firing of guns, and exhibited a scene of the greatest riot and disorder; in the evening the party, attended by the populace, paraded in the most tumultuous manner in the streets of St Helier wearing in their hats blue cockades with the inscription of "Dumaresq and Liberty"; the said Dumaresq being seated in a chair and carried in the midst of them upon their shoulders with colours flying and music playing; and we are sorry to observe that on this occasion two Jurats and several of the clergy and Constables were among the most active in the crowd.

In the face of this almost hysterical enthusiasm, the Charlots were powerless. Whenever a Jurat died, the Magot candidate was returned. The first to be elected after Lemprière's appointment had been his father's enemy, Nicholas Fiott, who was sworn in in October 1782. The spectre of earlier riots was never far from Lemprière's mind. In January 1788 he petitioned the Council, asserting that the minds of the people had been 'so much heated and enflamed as to make any steps we would take, not only unsafe to our person, but dangerous to the peace of the island and most likely productive of the same commotions which happened in the years 1729 and 1769'. In March 1788 the Magots retorted:

> Nor will the States of Jersey entertain the comfortless idea that upwards of twenty thousands of Your Majesty's British subjects whom they represent shall be doomed to perpetual vexations and troubles and shall be left to entail on their posterity the contentions of the present times.

By 1790 Dumaresq had a majority in the Court as well as in the States; and that year Lemprière died.[9]

Many other matters affecting the authority of the States came into question in this stormy period. Should a Constable in his absence be represented by his senior centenier, *le chef de police*? Should he consult his parishioners before voting in the States? Had that Assembly the right to levy taxes? Was there a danger to democracy in the suggestion that three stipendiary judges be appointed? In 1791, in an attempt to curb the power of the Court, Dumaresq drew up proposals for the re-introduction of trial by jury. The Council, however, did not favour this reform, and it was not until 1864 that jury service in its present form was introduced. Prior to this, if an accused person pleaded not guilty, the evidence of the witnesses was taken down in writing before the Inferior Number of the Royal Court, and at the close of the evidence a 'jury' of 13 men including members of the Honorary Police of the parish in which the offence was committed, was empanelled; this body was known as the *hommes d'enditement*. They did not hear the witnesses, but the evidence that had been taken down was read out to them. If the accused were found guilty, he could accept the verdict of the *enditement* or elect to be tried by the *grande enquête*.[10]

But these domestic problems were soon overshadowed by more important matters, as in 1789 the French Revolution was on our doorstep. Whatever party was in power, de Rullecourt's raid and near victory had made the States realise that money had to be raised for Guard Houses and Arsenals. So, to avoid taxing the parishes, the States in 1783 had had recourse to a lottery. Everything possible was done to stimulate interest. The draw was held in the Vestibule of the old Court House. Two boys in blue with red sashes drew the numbers out of the wheels. Two Jurats in their red robes registered the winning numbers. The *Gazette* of 24 January 1789 described the ceremony in detail and listed the winning numbers. But, as the novelty wore off, interest began to flag. In December 1792 it was suggested that sets of 50 tickets be allotted to be disposed of by individual members of the Chamber of Commerce, but in 1793 a large number of tickets remained unsold, and in 1794 so few were bought that the draw had to be cancelled.[11]

Meanwhile the French Revolution, coinciding with the moment of the Magot triumph, was before long to cool the Island's democratic fervour, with the fear that liberalism might easily turn to revolt. However the effect was not immediate. In 1788, in an open letter to the Bailiff of Guernsey, who had attacked the anti-Charlot party, the Rev. Thomas Sivret, doughty champion of the Magot cause, questioned the need for a public levy to finance defences against the French. His letter reveals that, even in the moment of supreme danger, doubts had been cast on the loyalty of the Magots by reason of their association with Moyse Corbet in the riots of 1769. 'Weakness', he wrote,

> rather than treason was the cause of the shameful capitulation of 6 January 1781 ... you accuse us of having surrendered the island to the enemy for having refused to allow a levy on the public in order to enable the Governor to fortify us against the French. I do not doubt that the Governor had cause for alarm, but I also know that then we were as we are now in a period of peaceful calm and tranquillity and that the members of the States who refused these contributions had the best reasons in the world to justify their conduct ... All the ports of France were open to us; our merchants went backwards and forwards daily.[12]

The *Gazette* welcomed the Revolution with eager applause. As late as 1792, even after the massacre had begun, it asked: 'What is a Jacobin?' (the left wing of the Revolution), and it replied:

> A Jacobin is an enlightened patriot, who stands on the peak of the high principle on which his wise politics are founded. He is a citizen of the world, to whom all men are brothers. Standing firm on this holy truth, he detests all tyrants and their satellites, whom he rightly regards as the scum of the earth.[13]

TIMELESSNESS

53 *Je n'en veux pas d'machinne mé.' 1980*

In Jersey the first result of the Revolution was the arrival of thousands of French aristocrats. They began to dribble in during 1790; but throughout 1791, 1792 and 1793 they poured in like a flood. No exact figures are available, but in 1795, when all Frenchmen of military age were enlisted for the Quiberon expedition,[14] some 3,500 were enrolled, and in addition there was a host of old men, women and children. Moreover in 1792, when all priests who would not take the oath of loyalty to the new constitution were expelled from France, 1,800 of them came to Jersey with three bishops (those of Bayeux, Tréguier and Dol) and before long the number was increased, according to L'Estourbillon,[15] to three thousand.

Jersey boatmen made a lot of money ferrying these exiles across; but this was a perilous occupation. One captain, settling his affairs in Jersey while waiting for the war to end so that he might rejoin his wife in Cape Breton, spoke of an offer made to him by friends who suggested that he should join with his brothers in unspecified work in France: 'having a neutral vessel belonging to this place and while the vessels are stopped here waiting for peace the voyage might be done ... but cannot say if I shall face it yet'.[16] The refugees themselves, priests and others, were hospitably received and well treated, so long as they did not attempt to convert the local population,[17] apart from some incidents when they complained that they were insulted and that stones were thrown through their windows. The States reported to the Lieutenant-Governor that many of them were wandering about fully armed. A secret arsenal of theirs was discovered with 1,000 muskets, collected for a raid on France. Moreover the Island which never had much margin in its food supply, grew alarmed lest it should run short of corn and coal. This, however, was eased by special supplies from England.[18]

The permanent result of this invasion was an increase in the size of the town. Until now it had been a tiny place, a huddle of small thatched houses, crowded inside the triangle formed by the present King Street and Queen Street precinct, Hill Street (la Rue des Trois Pigeons), Church Street (Rue Trousse Cotillon), Library Place and Broad Street. There was a bulge at Hue Street, Old Street and Dumaresq Street where a recent development has replaced the old granite houses with modern blocks of flats and offices built on plans approved for States' tenants by the Housing Committee. Eastward the town ended at Snow Hill (*la pompe du haut*) and westward at Charing Cross (*la pompe du bas*). But many of the *émigrés* had brought gold or jewels with them, and speculative builders began to run up houses in all directions, a prelude to the 19th-century growth of the town.[19]

An event that had results far beyond what was intended was an Act passed by the States in 1789. At that time Jersey cattle could be imported into England without restrictions, but French cattle had a pretty stiff import duty to pay. So the wily Normandy farmer discovered that, by sending his cows to Jersey, turning them loose in a field for a week and then sending them on to England, he could save quite a lot of money. The Island was being used as a staging post for French cows destined for England. This was glutting the English market and bringing down the price for everyone. So the States resolved that, 'whereas the fraudulent importation of cattle from France has become a most alarming matter', anyone introducing any cow, heifer, calf or bull from France should be fined 200 *livres* for each animal landed, with forfeiture of boat and tackle, and the beasts should be immediately slaughtered and distributed to the poor. This might seem a very ordinary Customs' Regulation but it laid the foundation of one of the Island's most remunerative trades. Till then Jersey cows had been a very mongrel breed; French, Dutch, Ayrshire, Friesian strains had often been imported. From the date of this Act, however, though it only mentions France, all foreign cattle have been excluded and Jersey has been given a chance to develop the famous breed that is characteristically its own. However this did not occur immediately, and it was not until the reforms advocated by Colonel (later Sir John) Le Couteur in the 1830s that the breed as we know it today began to emerge.[20]

While the elected or appointed representatives of the people were locked in political battle, the ordinary citizens were living through a period of rapid change and development. Personal diaries and letters, and particularly the advertising columns of the newspapers, help us to build up a picture of their occupations and leisure pursuits, the opportunities for emigration, the alarms and excursions of a troubled era.

The merchants and the wives of sea-captains advertise in *La Gazette* a variety of goods for sale. In 1790, from his *moulin à peinture* at St Aubin, François Jeune[21] offers at a fair price paints of all colours ground in oil, turpentine, Prussian blue and linseed oil. In 1787 and 1788 the firm of Bishop and Chevalier of St Helier have a wider range: West of England butter in barrels, bohea tea, Bristol bottles, sugar in loaves, Indian silk and cotton, Irish linen, Russian corduroy, hemp, velvet and iron, pipes of Dutch gin and grapes. By July 1790, with the threat of war ever present, they advertise elegant épaulettes in gold and silver, and militia uniforms at competitive prices. They also hire these out, as three years later we find that they are asking those who borrowed uniforms to return them. In October 1790 M. Legarat of St Aubin is selling fruit trees: he lists almost thirty different varieties of pear, as well as many kinds of apple, peach and apricot.

There is also much buying and selling of property and land, as builders and speculators take advantage of the rapid expansion of the town. In 1790 Mr Seaton offers for sale his house on the sand dunes in the area now known as Seaton Place. In 1787 he describes a large house built in what is now Hill Street. It had a courtyard, several cellars, a good pump, two gardens, while the land behind the cellar and one of the gardens ran up to the top of the Town Hill. The cellars of such houses were used for storing wine and later as vaults for local banks. As early as May 1789 we find that Messrs Chevalier and Bishop, tenants of Mr Seaton in Hill Street, are offering to remedy the shortage of coins of small denominations, particularly *liards*, by issuing two hundred pounds sterling in a new English coinage known as *monnoie d'Anglesey*, in which the large variety was worth a penny and the smaller a sou or halfpenny. The firm offered to act as guarantors for this issue. Charles Chevalier was later to be one of the founders of a Guernsey bank, Chevalier and de Jersey.

Sometimes in family papers we come across interesting details about the building of houses at this period. Le Clos Luce, situated in field 32 in St Peter, was erected in 1786. The total cost was 780 *livres tournois*, with small additional sums '*que ma mère a payé elle-même*'. One item was for 16 lbs of beef for cartage of wood and tiles, 12s for 100 bricks with 16s for cartage, and a sum of £78 7s. 6d. for M. du Bois and his colleagues as masons, £128 to Aaron de Ste Croix for 1600 tiles, 14s.6d. to M. Guillet for nails, £26 12s. for ironwork, £45 12s. for roofing by Jean Vautier, and other sums for paint, linseed oil, faggots for straw, and three pots of cider supplied when the gable walls were completed.[22]

Money was often short in those days, particularly when captains of ships suffered delay at sea. A letter written in August 1788 from the London firm of Paul Le Mesurier and Co. informs Mrs Anne Ingouville of Jersey that she must not be anxious if her husband appears to be overdue, as no vessels have as yet arrived from Cape Breton or Quebec. Meanwhile the firm promises to honour a drawing she had made on her husband's account to be later debited to him. He was Captain Philip Ingouville, great-uncle of Jersey's first V.C. and one of those who at this difficult period decided to seek a better life in the New World. In April 1789 he announced in *La Gazette* that he wished to thank his customers in Jersey and to inform them that he and his family would shortly be leaving for Cape Breton, where he hoped to employ Jersey labour, if there were any people prepared to entrust themselves to his care. In June he put his furniture up for sale together with his stock of building materials and lime. Later we learn from shipping news in the paper that not only has the recently built *Tupper* arrived safely at Ile Madame in Cape Breton in November of that year after a voyage of 33 days, but the *Kenton,* Captain Ingouville, has reached Sydney, also in Cape Breton. From Nova Scotian records we discover that Ingouville began to farm a thousand acres of land and employed 40 workers. He also built in 1790 the first sea-going vessel to be constructed in Sydney Harbour, where to this day a street is named after him in an area still known as the old ship-yard. Ingouville Place in St Helier commemorates the same family. Philip Ingouville's daughter, Anne, married a member of a prominent legal family in Nova Scotia, and her descendants have preserved for posterity an old contract which Ingouville took with him as the eldest of his line. This establishes him as a direct descendant of the first Ingouville recorded in the parish registers of St Saviour in 1603 and confirms that in 1625 this same Gilles Ingouville sold to Richard Dumaresq a field called Le Clos Daublin in the Parish of St Saviour, which he had earlier bought from Jean Mourant. Such is the continuity of Jersey family history in the Old World and the New.[23]

One of the letters preserved in Nova Scotia comes from a Renouf cousin in Jersey. It records that the winter of 1790 had been milder than had ever been known without a single frost, but provisions were so expensive that it was difficult to keep up with the cost of living. The letter came from a town-dweller who could not live off her own produce as in the country. Meanwhile in Sydney, Nova Scotia, pioneer conditions still prevailed, so ribbons were sent out by the *Kenton* — not grey as requested by Mrs Ingouville as it was out of fashion, but several yards of pink and blue, perhaps for the two small children, Philip and Nancy, after whom was named the first ship built in Sydney Harbour, the *Nancy*.

Some merchants were able to make money by selling valuables brought in by the rising tide of French *émigrés*. In April 1790 a Mr Gallichan advertised that he would shortly sell by auction at Madame Le Tubelin's lodging a great quantity of silver, including six pairs of candlesticks in silver, 30 pairs in silver-gilt and six coffee-pots.

There are opportunities for furthering one's education. We learn that in May 1789 Monsieur J. Lemprière's classical dictionary, *le Bibliotheca Classica*, is actually on sale at the Imprimerie at *10 livres 10 sous*. We read that on 4 July 1789 the Reverend Richard Valpy, Headmaster of Reading School, has arrived in the island, as has the Reverend Jean Dupré,[24] Headmaster of Berkhamsted School, accompanied by some of his pupils including the two sons of M. Hemery. Nearer home a number of private individuals, often of French or German nationality, offer coaching. In June 1789 M. Meinhard, a German master of the flute, advertises a grand concert to be held in *la Salle du Bal*, entry three *livres* per head. In 1792 a 'foreigner lately arrived in the island' proposes to teach elementary French, writing, vocal and instrumental music. Indeed the opportunities for music-making are many. In January 1794 le sieur Le Rond, *maître de musique du bataillon de St Hélier*, offers violin lessons, bass, flute, clarinet, bassoon etc., accompanies on the pianoforte, copies music, plays for dances and keeps a private school every Saturday for people from the country who wish to play an instrument. He lives with a Mr de la Haye, on the sand-hills at St Hélier (the area from Charing Cross to Westmount originally known as *les Mielles*[25]), and his wife takes in washing, mends cotton, silk and woollen stockings and is prepared to take on any sewing in linen.

For those who can afford them there are many leisure activities to be enjoyed. In June 1789, to celebrate the King's birthday, MM Matthews and Barnett of the 12th Regiment, MM Dumaresq of Gros-Puits and Jacques Pipon, fils, give a subscription dance for the ladies of the Island, while in November 1790 M. Angot opens *une chambre littéraire* to enable master-craftsmen and farmers to read English and French newspapers brought from London. In 1793 a M. Guyot suggests opening a subscription for *amateurs de botanique* to a *Botanicum Jerseycum* and a herbal to contain the names of all indigenous plants. It was to cost two guineas and was to be ordered from M. Angot. In 1793 the *Almanach* for 1794 is advertised at *8 sous pièce*. The library continues to serve the public, but readers are constantly reminded that fines will be imposed if books are not returned punctually.

The Committee of the Agricultural Society meets regularly, and in 1792 there is an opportunity to see a group of English actors performing *Duglas*, a tragedy in five acts, followed by a comedy translated from the French and entitled *Midnight Hour*, with singing in between the acts. The performance is billed for 6 p.m., tickets for the little gallery to be 3 *livres* 12 *sous*, for the front stalls 48 *sous* and for the back stalls 24 *sous*. Performances are thrice-weekly and tickets may be bought from M. G. Atkins, baker of King Street (the name is already anglicised) and from M. Lys in the Square of St Helier.

The pages of *La Gazette*, while obviously biased in favour of Magot supporters, are an endless source of interest to the social historian. For many generations, despite the appearance of many other newspapers, the word *gâzette* was ubiquitously applied in Jersey-Norman French to all such publications. Not only do we find local news in its pages. Indeed it is only since the competition of radio and television that world news has been relegated in local journalism to the back page. Throughout this period and the 19th century islanders were supplied with ample comment on international affairs. In *La Gazette* serious events in England, France and Jersey are given equal prominence. On 24 June 1789 a hurricane swept across the Island from south-west to north-east causing particular damage in St Peter and St Mary, carrying in its path the roof of M. de Carteret's house at les Augerez and depositing it two miles away: 43 apple trees were uprooted and several oaks. In 1793 comes news of the execution of Louis XVI: *L'infortuné Louis n'est plus: il a été décapité ce matin, à six heures à la Place Louis XV*. In June 1794 come reports of Admiral Howe's victory against the French fleet in an action off Cape Ushant, which history was to immortalise as 'the glorious first of June' and which drove the threatening enemy from our waters. News of the engagement reached Jersey from Guernsey whither three frigates had escaped with help from Captain (later Admiral) de Saumarez. But this is to anticipate events recorded in a later chapter. Already in 1789 tenders had been invited for the construction of batteries at Beauport and La Collette, where a tower was to be built. In 1793 a curfew was imposed by the Lieutenant-Governor on all foreigners of whatever denomination.[26] Yet another war with France was about to be declared.

Chapter Twenty-seven

PRELUDE TO THE NINETEENTH CENTURY

I look upon all the world as my parish.–John Wesley's Journal

IN THE FITFUL YEARS of peace after the Battle of Jersey, pioneer spirits were turning to the New World and laying the foundations of 19th-century Jersey.

The Treaty of Versailles, which, in 1783, ended temporarily the war with France, encouraged merchants to renew the contacts with Canada and Newfoundland, which had been disrupted by the American War of Independence. In 1778 Charles Robin had returned to Jersey after rebel privateers had seized two of his vessels off Paspébiac. He was present at the Battle of Jersey, but went back in 1783 to set up the new firm of Charles Robin and Company and to administer and increase the Canadian stations which had previously traded as Robin, Pipon and Company. In a memorandum to the Governor of Canada, prepared in 1787, he noted that many firms had had to give up business, among them Le Mesurier of Guernsey and Gaspé and Nicholas Fiott at Percé. Robin soldiered on and gradually built up connections around la Baie des Chaleurs, where he peopled its small towns and villages with immigrant Jerseymen.[1]

Janvrins also traded from Grande Grève, south of Gaspé, from the Magdalen islands and from Arichat, where, in 1794, John Janvrin was given the lease of an island off Ile Madame in Cape Breton, which to this day is known as Janvrin's Island.[2] Some merchants, including the Hemerys, traded from Labrador.[3] Other 19th-century firms have their roots in these pioneer days. In the 1830s two men, who had trained in Robin's methods, broke from the parent firm to set up rival establishments. One was John Le Boutillier, who had married the daughter of Charles Robin's nephew, Philip, and his French-Canadian wife. He entered politics and became a member of the Legislative Assembly for Bonaventure County and later for Gaspé, and is still remembered as 'the Honourable John'. Soon after his death in 1872 his firm was taken over by Charles Robin and Company. The other was William Fruing. He came of a family of English origin, but long settled in Jersey. His mother died when he was still a child and he was apprenticed to Charles Robin, who is thought to have been his guardian. He married an Alexandre of St Brelade and, with his brothers-in-law, formed the firm of William Fruing and Company, first at Pointe des Alexandres at Shippegan and later at many other stations along the Gaspé shore and in Labrador. In the early 1840s Fruing acquired the property of Frederick Janvrin at Grande Grève in Gaspé Bay. This firm continued to trade as William Fruing and Company until 1917, when it sold to Robin, Jones and Whitman.[4]

Meanwhile in Newfoundland, more permanent establishments were also being created at this time. Recent research shows that at first settlements were dispersed and sparsely populated, colonisation being discouraged by merchants in England. Of the settlers some 45 Channel Island families accounted for were outnumbered by those from the West Country. By 1763 about a third of the fish exported from Conception Bay was carried in Jersey vessels. However, the take-off period of growth of a permanent population was about 1780, and Jersey firms

54 *Marriage stone of Jean Lemprière and Anne Durell. A very early example of the heart motif on marriage stones.*

55 *Jean Janvrin's stone on the last arm of St Aubin's Harbour.*

HISTORY IN GRANITE:
RAISED, V-CUT AND INCISED

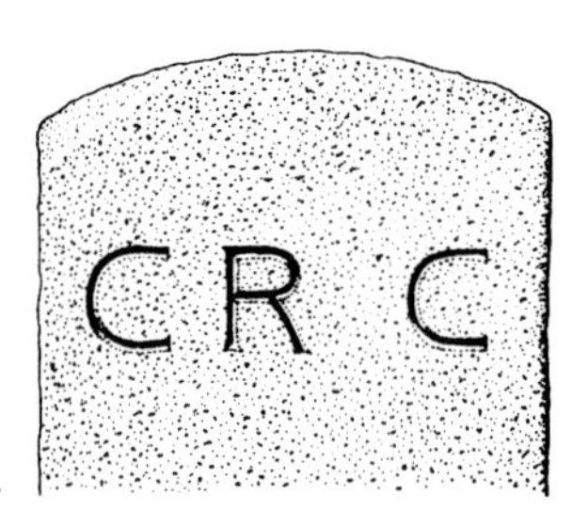

56 *Initials representing the firm of Charles Robin, Collas and Co. A stone at Percé.*

with resident staff were set up between 1783 and 1800. These included de Quetteville at Forteau in Labrador on the Belle Isle Strait, while a move was made from the crowded Avalon peninsula to the more southerly points of Fortune Bay, La Poële and St George's Bay. Falle was at Burin and Nicolle at Fortune Bay.[5]

The story of these firms is now part of Canadian history, but throughout the 19th century they had a profound influence on island life; for not only were Jerseymen employed on their vessels and encouraged to emigrate as managers, clerks, farmers and beachmasters, but in Jersey the firms were the mainstay of a flourishing shipbuilding industry.

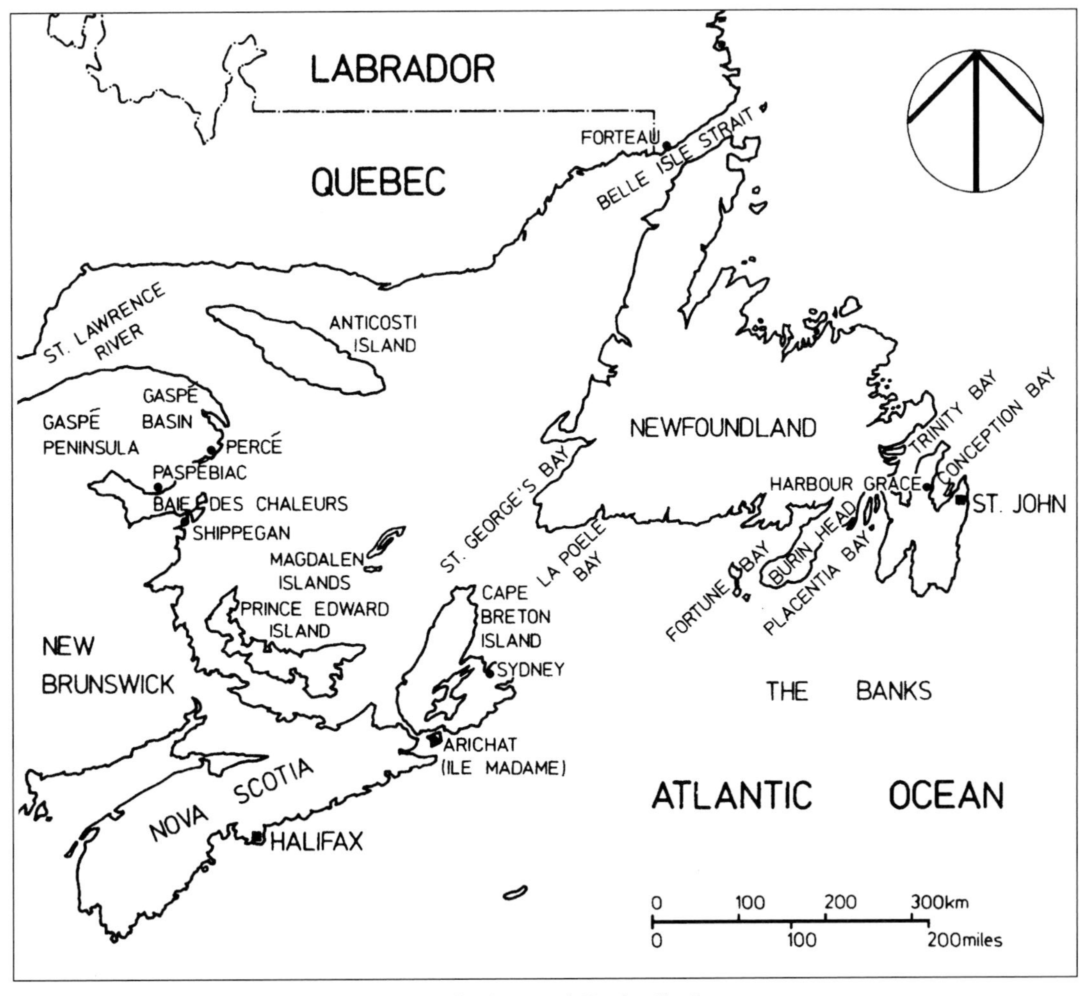

57 *The Gaspé and Newfoundland*

Jerseymen must have built smaller boats for coastal trading from very early times. In 1671 the Rolls of the Court record that two men were sued for payment of two pieces of wood: one of oak for a beam and one of ply-wood for a rudder. Repairs too must have been carried out on the Island, often in land running down to the sea from merchants' houses. In 1683 Richard de Carteret, Thos. Poingdestre, Jean Pipon and Jean Dorey were fined by the Constable of St Brelade for cluttering up with masts and other material the road which ran from their houses towards the Boulevard.[6] It is, however, uncertain whether any bigger vessels capable of crossing the Atlantic were built in Jersey in early days. It seems more likely that they were bought by merchants from shipyards in Southampton, St Malo or London.

In 1676 Abraham Balleine was sued for the cost of a ship and canvas by a merchant from St Malo. In a letter dated 1693 Philippe Pipon advises his father that he will get a better price for his ship, the *Pear Tree*, if he sells it in London,[7] and we have evidence from Jean Fiott that his firm in the City bought and sold ships for their clients in Jersey. In 1725 Moody Janvrin, almost certainly descended from Jersey stock, was apprenticed to a shipwright on the Hamble River and later built for the Navy at Bursledon, Buckler's Hard and Lepe.[8] We have already noted that some ships engaged in trade with Spain and America were built for Jersey owners in New England, where ship-building was carried on by early settlers from the latter part of the 17th century. Essex deeds record that in about 1700 Daniel Bacon, jun. of Salem, shipwright, was building a ship '54 feet by ye keel' for Captain John Balleine of Jersey, 'at present resident in Salem'. Schooners were also built at Marblehead in New Brunswick and in Nova Scotia.[9] In 1845 Francis Perrée bought from Edward Mabé of Malbaie, ship-builder, 'a certain vessel now laying on the stock of Malbaie (Gaspé) of about 160 tons old measurements to be launched and completed in a carpenter-like manner'.[10]

Many of the vessels immortalised in the 19th-century paintings against a backcloth of Vesuvius or Elizabeth Castle were built in shipyards at Paspébiac and Arichat. While owners and builders of vessels often commissioned Jersey marine artists, and particularly P. J. Ouless,[11] to record them on canvas, the masters in charge of them often bought likenesses of their ships in pairs, one in full sail and one in rough weather. They were painted in *gouache* in Naples and were often inscribed with the master's name. Highly prized, they adorned the walls of many Jersey homes.

Another frequent means of acquiring ships was through privateering. Early Customs' records in Jersey reveal the origin of many Jersey-owned vessels: the *Union*, Captain Hocquard, was a prize formerly called *Los Dos Amigos* and taken from the enemy 'of the Government of Great Britain'. The *Lottery*, owned by the brothers Janvrin, was also a prize taken by the 'private ship of war' the *Phoenix*, condemned in the High Court of Admiralty and later made free. The *Phoenix*, a Jersey-built ship, was one of the most famous of the privateers in Napoleonic days, particularly when captained by Peter Duval, whose descendants lived for many years on Bonaventure Island off Percé on the Gaspé Coast, where the cutlass he used is still on display. A stirring story of a more local voyage in the *Young Phoenix*, undertaken by Francis Janvrin and his daughter and son-in-law, Sir John Le Couteur, is told in *Victorian Voices*. Customs' records also note that the *Good Intent*, owned by Edward Le Feuvre and Philip Blampied, was built at Bursledon in 1788, the *Duke of Argyle*, master Joshua Le Masurier, at St John's Newfoundland, in 1794, and the *Oliver Blanchard*, owned by a consortium of Robins, Pipons and Janvrins, at Paspébiac in 1819.[12]

Jersey was not to be outdone. Perhaps the revolutionary mood of France threatened a repetition of the dangers encountered in American waters during the War of Independence, and Jersey felt the need for self sufficiency. On 6 June 1789 a notice appeared in *La Gazette* which heralded the great days of ship-building in Jersey: the *Tupper*, a vessel of 280 tons, which was being built near the entrance to St Peter's Valley, was to be launched on the following Monday on the high tide. Another slightly smaller ship would be finished by the end of the summer. M. Janvrin, who had ordered their construction, had bought most of the oak in St Lawrence and would have enough left to build another smaller vessel. *La Gazette* suggested that there was sufficient oak left at St Lawrence, ready for felling by reason of age, and in other well-wooded parishes, to build all the ships necessary for island trade. M. Janvrin and his partners 'had set the example'.

The choice of the name *Tupper* reveals an interesting link with the great merchant houses of Guernsey. *La Gazette* informs us that the vessel was so named as a compliment to M. (Elisha) Tupper of Guernsey, who for over forty years in peace and war had played a part in the commercial life of that island and who, in 1789, had an interest in 10 to 12 ships going from Jersey to Newfoundland. In his *History of Guernsey*, Elisha Tupper's grandson[13] gives an interesting account of Guernsey's trade in the 18th century, which differed in many respects from that of Jersey. Our neighbouring island had been an *entrepôt* for French goods, particularly brandies, captured by privateers, and had become, as it were, the bonded warehouse of British merchants. The end of the 18th century was a time of great prosperity for Guernsey merchants and a number of them took shares in Jersey vessels, particularly privateers. In 1812 the *Young Phoenix* of Jersey was registered as belonging to Francis, Philip and John Janvrin of Jersey and Carteret Priaulx, Daniel de Lisle and John Elisha Tupper of Guernsey. From this time on ship-yards sprang up on the south and east coast of Jersey, in St Aubin's Bay, at Havre-des-Pas and at Gorey, including those of Le Vesconte, Deslandes, Clarke, Allix and Le Huquet. Subsidiary firms gave work to sail-makers, coopers and blacksmiths. There were rope-walks at St Aubin and Havre-des-Pas.[14]

By the end of the 18th century there was less demand for stockings, but boots and shoes were exported to America. In 1794 Jean Métivier, '*cordonnier en bottes et souliers*' was advertising in *La Gazette* boots and shoes made by excellent workmen recently arrived from England for export by merchants to Newfoundland.[15] As trade with South America developed,[16] craftsmen were kept busy making, in wood imported from Honduras, the beautiful and massive mahogany furniture which still adorns so many Jersey homes. Island life was also much enriched by the continued presence of French refugee families, including silversmiths and clockmakers like the Amiraux and Poignands, or Quesnel,[17] who was also for a time librarian of the recently established Public Library. Madame Perrot, one of whose grandsons was to found *La Chronique* in 1814, was an early follower of John Wesley.[18] Indeed nowhere was the influence of Huguenots more evident than in the establishment of Methodism in Jersey.

The quotation which heads this chapter may seem presumptuous, yet the many strands of 17th- and 18th-century life, which had been woven into the pattern of Jersey history — French Protestants, British regiments, Newfoundland and West Country merchants, and the strong Calvinist tradition which still permeated the established church — were drawn together in the new movement which was to exert so strong an influence throughout the 19th century.

In 1765 Lawrence Coughlan had introduced Methodism to Carbonear and Harbour Grace in Newfoundland, annoying the merchants by upholding the rights of their servants. Under his influence Pierre Le Sueur, who had a small fishing station, and Jean Tentin, of Huguenot descent, returned to Jersey as converts and began to preach in 1775.[19] They were joined by others, including, in 1779, John Brown, a sea-captain and lay preacher from Poole, who, anxious to extend his ministry to Jersey, was offered a cellar by Le Sueur at his house, no 22 Hill Street. In 1783 a regiment arrived from Winchester which contained some Methodist soldiers. Finding that Sunday services were in French, they appealed to Wesley to send them an English lay preacher. A Lincolnshire squire, Brackenbury, was chosen and held services at the house of Philippe Perchard, no. 3 Royal Square. Later he obtained *la Chapelle des Pas* on the lower slopes of South Hill, a partly ruined medieval chapel then in private hands. In 1784 Jersey first appeared in the *Minutes of Conference* as a Methodist station, but was listed with America as part of the mission field. In 1787 John Wesley himself spent 10 days in Jersey, lodging at 15 Old Street in a house only recently demolished.[20]

Brackenbury was joined in his work by a Jersey layman, Jean de Quetteville, who carried Methodism to the country parishes and later to Guernsey and Alderney; for the missionary spirit was evident from the outset. Among others who joined the movement were Abraham John Bishop, son of a Dorset father and Jersey mother, and partner in the firm of Bishop, Chevalier and Bishop, who were merchants with trading links in many parts of the world, and Marie-Louise Carcaux, daughter of a sea-captain, Jean Carcaux, and his wife Judith Cartault, both of Huguenot descent, who married and converted François Jeune, grandfather of the future bishop of Peterborough.

St Aubin was the scene of early persecution. Adam Clarke, later to become a President of the Methodist Conference, was howled down when he preached in the open air. The Jeunes lent a shed at their home at Les Vaux in St Aubin and fitted it with a pulpit and benches.[21] Once, shots were fired through a window, on another the mob, toughened no doubt by experience on privateers, arrived with sticks, swords and forks to the sound of drums, fifes and trumpets.

Once, pulpit and benches were carried down to the harbour and tied to the shrouds of vessels; but the Jeunes persevered.

Meanwhile in St Helier, when la Chapelle des Pas proved inadequate and the States refused to pass a contract '*au nom de la société*', Abraham John Bishop purchased in his own name a house on what now forms the junction of Don Street and King Street. The contract, drawn up in December 1790, describes it as bordered by other properties with ground running back to a brook, le Grand Douet, which crossed the town, and beyond to a second brook, le Faux Bié, to a garden (or was it an orchard, the usual significance of *jardin* at this period?). This house was modified to form a chapel and was used until 1813, when a new chapel was built in Don Street.[22] The two brooks mentioned in the contract have exercised a strong influence on the contours of the town: the winding of some of the streets and the narrow lanes and gaps between buildings are often indications of their presence not far below the surface of St Helier.

Many denominations and institutions were to be represented in Jersey in the 18th and 19th centuries. We know that members of the Society of Friends were meeting in 1740 in the home of Jean François de Vaumorel, and in his diary Daniel Messervy mentions a Quaker named Nicolle. Then there was Jean Cavalier, a picturesque Lieutenant-Governor to Lord Cobham (1738-40) . A Frenchman of humble origins, he became a leader of the Calvinist *camisards* in the Cevennes and is mentioned by Voltaire in *Le siècle de Louis Quatorze* and by Stevenson in *Travels with a Donkey*. After fighting with the Protestant rebels against the armies of Louis XIV after the Revocation of the Edict of Nantes, Cavalier found his way to England where he joined the British Army and rose to the rank of general.[13] In January 1771 there was a meeting of Freemasons, who marched to the Town Church, led by a clergyman wearing his masonic apron under his robes as he preached on 'charity and union'. Messervy reports that the church was full of people '*pour voir une masquerade qui n'avait jamais paru dans cette île*'. The French Revolution brought Catholic priests and aristocrats to the Island, while two grandsons of Madame Perrot became ministers of the Independent Church and built a chapel, in meadow land in Halkett Place, which was opened in 1808.[23] However, despite these varied denominations, it was the Methodist congregations which came to predominate throughout the 19th century.

Over thirty chapels were built, sometimes two on one site, as the original ones became too small, and, in the spirit of John Wesley, who early realised the potential of these French-speaking zealots, many of the early Methodists travelled abroad.[24] Abraham John Bishop was sent first to Nova Scotia and New Brunswick and thence to Grenada in the Windward Islands, where there were many French-speaking slaves as well as an English population. Before he left for the mission field, Bishop made a will in which Jersey was remembered in bequests for 'continuing to the inhabitants of the Island of Jersey and adjoining islands or in France the benefit of publishing and preaching the Gospel', for supporting preachers who, by reason of infirmity or age, could no longer 'travel' (move from circuit to circuit as ministers), and to 'relieve the poor and the widows and children of soldiers in the Island of Jersey'. At a later date François Jeune and his wife also went to Grenada. Both Bishop and Jeune died in that island overcome by tropical disease. Other Channel Islanders, including Pierre Le Sueur and Philippe Tourgis, worked in France. This link with French Methodism was maintained over a long period, and, at a later date, Jersey missionaries were also to go to French-speaking West Africa. Like their military and merchant brothers from the late 18th century onwards, the Jersey pioneer Methodists were to make the world their parish.

Chapter Twenty-eight

FRANCE AGAIN THE ENEMY, 1793-1815

France, hast thou yet more blood to cast away?–Shakespeare, *King John*

THE UNEASY TRUCE ended on 1 February 1793, when France declared war on England, and Jersey again, as so often in the past, became the most dangerously exposed salient in the King's dominions.[1] The first alarm came in April, when 17 French warships were sighted heading for the island. The Militia fell in with great promptness. The Town regiment was ready for action 10 minutes after the alarm had sounded. But the fleet sailed by without attempting a landing. In 1794, however, the French Committee of Public Safety ordered the capture of the Channel Islands and sent an army of 20,000 to St Malo for the purpose. The proposed expedition was well planned. Jersey, Guernsey and Alderney were to be attacked simultaneously and it was intended that all the inhabitants should be disarmed and horses commandeered. All preparations were made in the utmost secrecy, with General Rossignol in command. A wealth of detail about the proposed action has survived, but we do not so far know why the attack never materialised, unless perhaps it was delayed so long that it was overtaken by the 'glorious first of June'.[2]

Philippe Fall, the anti-Lempriére petitioner (who had dropped the final 'e' in his name, though other members of his family retained it) was now Lieutenant-Governor, having been appointed when Corbet was removed;[3] but the Island's danger called for a more experienced soldier. In 1793 Colonel Craig, who had served with distinction throughout the American War, was sent as Commander-in-Chief. But in 1794 he was transferred to the staff of the army in the Netherlands, and the man who did most to save the Island during the next 10 years was Philippe Dauvergne. He was a Jerseyman, who, by an extraordinary quirk of fate, had become heir to the Principality of Bouillon in the Belgian Ardennes, one of the tiny independent principalities that were dotted about Europe before the Napoleonic upheaval.[4]

Dauvergne, while a young naval officer, had been taken prisoner by the French in the previous war, and the semi-senile Prince of Bouillon, for a variety of reasons, including the coincidence that his own name was Latour Dauvergne, had adopted him as a son and heir. The throne offered him was not yet vacant, and Dauvergne had returned to his naval duties. When war broke out again he was given a flotilla of gunboats to protect the Channel Islands.[5] He made Mont Orgueil his headquarters and his little squadron kept ceaseless watch on the invasion ports. However the safety of the islands was mainly due to his success in other fields.

The Republican government was unpopular in Brittany with its strong Catholic tradition. In 1793 armed bands of Bretons began to take to the woods, much as the Maquis did during the German Occupation. They were known as Chouans, taking their name from their leader, Jean Cottereau, whose nickname of *chat-huant* (tawny owl) led to his being generally known as Jean Chouan. Their secret call was the hoot of the *chouette* or screech owl.[6] The movement spread through the province and even into Normandy and was welcomed by Whitehall as one means of creating difficulties for the enemy. Dauvergne was ordered to keep these bands supplied with arms and ammunition. He organised an invisible corps known as *La Correspondance*, who wore no uniform, marched alone at night, were known only by nicknames and carried their lives in their hands: an extraordinary team to handle—prickly aristocrats, dogmatic priests, peasant women, smugglers and scoundrels. Through them he kept in touch with the hidden guerrilla bands and even with the open revolt that was seething in La Vendée. Smuggling arms ashore on well-patrolled cliffs was desperately dangerous work, but it was done night after night. For example in September 1794 Dauvergne received from the Tower of London 1,000 double-barrelled guns and 40,000 cartridges and, a fortnight later, a cargo of powder and sabres, all of which reached the insurgents safely, and there were other similar consignments. In June 1795 he sent £33,000 to the Breton Chouans, dividing it among three messengers. Frotté, the Chouan leader in Normandy, received £1,000 every month. All of this may seem to have little to do with Jersey; but, by keeping the Chouan rising blazing in the rear of the army at St Malo, Dauvergne saved the Island from invasion. A vast collection of letters referring to these events is preserved at the Public Record Office and in the British Library.[7]

In other ways too Mont Orgueil became a thorn in the enemy's side. It was the depot for a form of economic warfare. Bales of foreign *assignats* (bank notes) were sent to Dauvergne from England to be smuggled into France to destroy confidence in the Republican paper money. The Castle was also the centre of a highly efficient spy system. When Hoche was preparing his expedition against Ireland, the Admiralty received every month from Dauvergne detailed reports of all ships in Brest, their names, their captains, the number of their guns and men. In one letter he reported that Captain Le Feuvre, a Jerseyman, had sailed his schooner into most of the French ports collecting information, but that he could do so no more, as every harbourmaster had been warned to look out for him.[8]

In 1794 trouble began in the Militia. Drills were held every Sunday after morning service, but many militiamen were now Methodists, to whom Sunday drill was a desecration of the Sabbath. At first they merely absented themselves and paid the fine for non-attendance; but their absence affected the efficiency of the whole regiment, so the authorities began to send defaulters to prison. In May 1796, after three successive *défauts*, François Jeune was banished from the Island for three years.[9] In 1798 his son was imprisoned with other laymen, while two appointed ministers were also banished. The more the courts sentenced, the stronger grew the opposition. In October 1798 the States passed an Act banishing all militiamen who absented themselves from drill.[10] In August they had closed the Methodist meeting house at 22 King Street and forced the worshippers to gather in private houses, but, as the building was privately owned, it was reopened soon afterwards. The States' high-handed disregard for liberty of conscience was countered by an influential deputation to the Privy Council of leading English Methodists supported by William Wilberforce M.P. and accompanied by Pierre Le Sueur of Jersey. The petitioners protested that, while the Jersey Methodists were willing to be placed in the front of the battle on any day at any hour, they could not 'consistent with their views and sentiments, consent to learn the military exercises or merely go through the military evolutions on the Sabbath Day'. His Majesty in Council was pleased to disapprove the Act, and the Methodists were then permitted to do their drill on weekdays.[11]

Meanwhile another religious difficulty had arisen. Protestant Jersey was naturally alarmed at seeing the Island overrun with Roman Catholic priests. The Royal Court stipulated that, if they received hospitality and were allowed to open private oratories, no attempt must be made to convert the native population.[12] This condition was loyally observed by the majority.

One exception was Mathieu de Gruchy,[13] a young privateer who had been captured by the French, and, while a prisoner of war, had been ordained as a Roman Catholic priest. When all non-juring priests were expelled, he had returned home. As a Jerseyman and a landed proprietor, he did not consider himself bound by the bargain made by his fellow Catholics. His zeal in winning his neighbours to his faith soon brought him into trouble. A farmer from St Martin named Grandin, whose daughters he had converted, demanded to know why de Gruchy as a Jerseyman was not in the Militia, and had him arrested as a deserter. The Court refused to grant his exemption, so he appealed to the Privy Council and obtained a dispensation from military service. However the conversion of two more girls, Elizabeth and Susanne Pinel, in 1795, caused the Court to arrest the Bishop of Tréguier for not keeping his clergy in order. This threw the refugees into a panic and de Gruchy was hurried out of the Island. In 1795 he offered his services as a volunteer unpaid chaplain to 30 Irish soldiers in hospital in the garrison town of Southampton. He was then called back to France, and, while carrying dispatches to La Vendée, was caught by the Republicans and shot.

The Government now decided to make use of the thousands of refugees in England and Jersey. All of military age were formed into regiments who would be landed in Brittany with some of the English troops to help the Chouans. Difficulties arose in Jersey, as all the French belonged to the officer class and most wished to be colonels.[14] They refused to put on the red and white uniforms sent from London and declared that they would wear nothing but the regimentals of the former French army. It required much tact to smooth away the problems, but at last they were ready. On 18 June 1796 the Bishop of Bayeux blessed their colours on the sandhills near the hospital.[15] Fortunately for the persons concerned, the first of the vessels to leave Jersey arrived the day after the battle of Quiberon Bay. It had been a ghastly fiasco. The main expedition had landed on 3 July and Lazare Hoche, the ablest of the French Republican generals, had smashed it to pieces. Very few who took part in it escaped with their lives. The Jersey-based contingent, called *l'Expédition le Trésor*, after their leader, le Comte du Trésor, had among its personnel about twenty Norman priests; they all wanted to return to Jersey, but were persuaded that they could be of more use to the Royalist cause in France.[16]

While Dauvergne was stirring up trouble in France, the Republican Admiral at St Malo showed that two could play at that game. He landed agitators in Jersey, who made contact with the wilder spirits among the Magots. In 1795 the Constable of St Helier read to the States a 'Call to revolt' that had been posted about the town. A year later the Constable of St John produced a manifesto, written in most indifferent French, which was passing from hand to hand in his parish:

> Awake! Now is the time. Stamp out with just vengeance those who would ruin the poor. The poor of France, once oppressed as we are, have shown us what to do. Let us follow their example. France has exterminated her tyrants and is happy. Jurats who grow fat on the toil of the poor richly deserve death. Anyone who kills one of them deserves his country's thanks.

An offer of a reward of £500 failed to disclose the author. Two months later it was reported that 150 men had been meeting secretly at dead of night at St John. In December 1797 the Commander-in-Chief, Major-General Andrew Gordon, issued a proclamation suppressing unlawful assemblies, while an Act of the States confirmed that secret meetings were being held in many parts of the Island and seditious pamphlets circulating, inciting people to murder the Jurats and follow the example of France.[17] However this agitation never reached the point of open revolt.

In 1798 the French once more made serious preparations for invasion, and Régnier, one of de Rullecourt's officers, was commissioned to lead the expedition. This came to nothing. In the following year, however, Jersey had an invasion of a different kind. The Russians were now our allies. A Russian army, which had landed in Holland, had been beaten and hurriedly evacuated. They could not get back to their own land until the ice broke in the Baltic, and the Bill of Rights forbade the landing of foreign troops in England. The only refuge anyone could think of was the Channel Islands, and over 6,000 of them were quartered in Jersey. The officers charmed the local ladies with their balls and dinner parties; but the shaggy privates were not so popular. They had a strange craving for tallow candles and lamp oil, due, it is thought, to a dietary deficiency, so they bought or stole all they could lay hands on, with the result that most of the Island was plunged in darkness. They also proved to be expert burglars and were not averse to highway robbery. Jersey heaved a sigh of relief when, in June 1800, they were sent home. Nevertheless the official line taken was different, for, on 7 June 1800, the States recorded their appreciation of the conduct of the troops and letters of fulsome flattery were exchanged with the Russian commander, le Comte de Viomenil.[18]

During previous wars many Jerseymen had grown rich through privateering and even benevolent old ladies had invested their savings in shares in privateers; but in this war the French were more heavily armed and more skilfully convoyed. In the first two years Jersey lost two-thirds of her shipping and nearly 900 Jersey sailors found themselves in French prisons. The records of the Chamber of Commerce from 1793 onwards highlight the dangers of the period. In January 1793 they petitioned the Lords Commissioners of the Admiralty for a convoy, stating that 'a considerable number of vessels are annually fitted out from the island and employed in carrying on trade and the fisheries at Newfoundland, Labrador, Canada and Nova Scotia'. These would be ready by 15 March and they asked for the escorting vessel to come to Jersey to avoid delay and the dangers of the press gang.

> Such are the apprehensions of our seamen with respect to the Press that notwithstanding any protections that may be granted, I have not the least doubt of their refusing to embark and running away; which of course must entirely prevent the vessels from sailing and annihilate the trade;

so wrote one Thomas Hammond on behalf of the Chamber to their merchant representatives in London, Le Mesurier and Fiott. The fisheries were proving such an excellent training for the Royal Navy that men engaged in the trade were still officially exempt from impressment.

In 1794 the Chamber invited Captain Dauvergne to dine with them in recognition of his friendship to the trade and navigation of the Island. In 1795 they asked the Lieutenant-Governor, Philip Fall, for a larger allowance of coal from Swansea and Newcastle, free of duty, 'on account of the decrease of wood in this island', of the increase in the garrison and the presence of three or four thousand immigrants. They expressed to the States their fear that, if the Southampton boat was not exempted from the embargo on vessels leaving England, they would not receive flour, grain or other provisions. When the Channel Islands were asked to provide 348 able-bodied men for the Navy, they protested that already they had offered bounties to seamen to serve on the Atlantic ship of war, in the roads and on the flotilla of gunboats and other vessels under Captain Dauvergne, that some had voluntarily entered the Navy or been impressed, and, as a result of all this, only one Letter of Marque, carrying thirty men, was fitted out and but six vessels were equipped for Newfoundland wanting altogether fifty men, while the crew employed to navigate our coasters consisted of boys and old men. They added that, in time of peace, not half of those who yearly went to Newfoundland were seamen,

THE SECRET WIRELESS

58 *'If the real idea were to stop people from listening in, it has not achieved its end', by Edmund Blampied, from* Jersey in Jail, *1945.*

> the rest go as passengers for the purpose of carrying on the fishery on their own account during the summer and return at the latter end of autumn to cultivate their grounds, and from the mode of parting estates according to the laws of this island into small farms, there are but few who do not possess some small property in land.

They also stressed that every inhabitant from 16 to 65 served in the Militia, which, during a war, 'falls very severe on the inhabitants from the numerous guards they mount'. Any diminution of their number would be 'a subtraction from the strength and defence of the island'.

When, however, the States suggested expelling French *émigrés* and priests, the Chamber protested that the French brought considerable sums to the Island and helped the employment of the poorer classes. They drew up a table to show that, as a result of the influx, salaries and wages had increased more than prices. An insular note is sounded in a letter to Paul Le Mesurier in November 1795, suggesting that, if soap and candles were to be rationed, a definite quantity should be specified for each island, 'to prevent injurious competition'. Messrs Fiott, de Gruchy and Company were requested to wait on Lord Granville and Mr Pitt to put the case for the protection of the fisheries and their markets against French competition 'in the negotiations for peace which may be entered into with the French government'. So the requests and protests continued and were carried to London, often by Jean Dumaresq, but sometimes by a Janvrin or other president of the Chamber.[19]

Yet despite the dangers encountered when crossing the Atlantic, diaries and letters of the period show that the sea still had a great attraction for young Jerseymen. Jean Syvret,[20] in his reminiscences, tells how, despite the prospect of inheriting a farm and settling down in Jersey, he was ambitious to go to sea like many of his school friends. He joined a Janvrin privateer when he was 15 and paints a vivid picture of life aboard this armed vessel, as it cruised near the coast of Spain and the Cape Verde Islands, and describes the method by which prizes were shared between owners and crew. In the brief interval of peace after the Treaty of Amiens in March 1802, he made a conventional trip to Arichat and Gaspé in another Janvrin ship. He describes how, when war broke out again, many Jersey vessels were sent to Boston, Massachusetts, where Jersey had trading connections, to prevent captains and crew being captured while crossing the Atlantic. Syvret, however, elected to return to Jersey and, after joining another privateer, was taken prisoner by the French. After one successful escape, he was recaptured and remained in French hands for 10 years.

Another literary seaman, John Béchervaise,[21] sketches in the background of a typical seafaring family. His father had a 'genteel and competent income', £52 a year from Bank of England funds, a small house, 26 acres of land and his pay as master of a ship. John was educated at a boarding school in the centre of the Island and later in the Isle of Wight and Southampton. His mother had destined him for a counting-house, but he too felt the lure of the sea and wanted to visit his father, one of the captains sent to Boston for safety, who had not returned home for many years. Such were the dangers in crossing the Atlantic, that John's mother, fearing that her son of 11 might be captured by the enemy, sewed nine guineas in a ribbon and instructed him to stow it away in safety. From Béchervaise we learn about trading conditions in the fisheries and of a visit to Rio de Janeiro, where they landed to cooper up oil and to take on a cargo of hides, tallow and sugar. From him we learn too of the horrors of impressment and the rigours of life in the Navy, which he later joined, before the reforms which followed Nelson's victories.

A few years later, in 1809, Stead was writing his *Picture of Jersey*, one of the earliest works of the guide-book type. From it we glean much about conditions at this time. He confirms that our privateer vessels 'have proved a great annoyance to the trade of our Enemy and a Benefit to the Public'. He tells us that the *Rover Packet*, a Post-Office cutter, in which he sailed as a passenger, was fitted with carriage guns and small arms. He likens St Aubin's Bay to the bay of Naples, almost forty years before Queen Victoria was to make the same remark.

He was much impressed with the people, their courtesy, hospitality, cleanliness and virtue; he writes that the merchants have a very high reputation for honesty, and that most young people can write both French and English, though he observes, incorrectly, that Jersey-French is 'daily falling into disuse and discredit, and doubtless in a few years hence English will be the only prevailing language'. He remarks on the industry and dexterity of the women at knitting and tells us that 'private concerts are very frequent, for many of the natives are musicians'. He records the custom of assembling on the Castle Green at Mont Orgueil on 29 May to commemorate the Restoration of Charles II.

Stead found the cost of living very low, about half of what it was in any similar place in England, and he quotes figures to show that the balance of trade was £58,317 10s.8d. in Jersey's favour.

Writing soon after the arrival of General Don, of whom more anon, he was aware that military roads had already been projected by the Reverend François Le Couteur. He notes a signal station near Rozel Manor which 'communicates from Bouley Bay to Mont Orgueil'. He tells us that Elizabeth Castle mounted 'nearly one hundred pieces of cannon' and was 'almost completely bomb-proof'. He mentions that Hyde's house at the Castle,[22] *la Maison du Chancelier*, was then still standing. Plémont had lately been 'strongly fortified' and he noted 'numerous martello towers', possibly referring to the Jersey round towers like la Rocco, as well as to the true martello-type towers like Kempt, which were being built from 1804 onwards. He observed that Jerseymen are 'protected from the exercise of the Impress Act by an Order in Council'.

He paints a more glowing picture than Playfair of the country scene. Like so many later writers he extols the fertility of the soil, the beauty of the landscape, the quality and quantity of the crops, fish, flowers, honey, and fruit, pears in particular: chaumontels were selling at 5s. per 100, but fetching as much as 2s.6d. (about 12p) each in England. He recalls the felling in 1804 of a gigantic oak at Grouville churchyard, which gave 50 tons of timber and was sold by auction for £5 l0s. (one has constantly to remind oneself that money went further in those days). Camomile he reports as abundant, particularly in Bouley Bay.

Like Plees, a few years later, Stead speaks of the 'strata of pipe clay' in St Catherine's Bay, as being of use to the troops. He also refers to 'blocks of variegated marble susceptible to a fine polish, black with red and white veins' in St Ouen's Bay and to 'pure ochre' in roadside banks in St Brelade's Bay. This island paradise, which all writers of the period describe, where people tilled the land amid stone cottages, gardens and fields, yielding all the fruits of the earth, makes a pleasant contrast to the scenes of war being waged in neighbouring France, in the Atlantic and in the seas around Jersey.

To go back to the war situation: by 1801 it seems that stale-mate had been reached. England was weary of the struggle and Napoleon was anxious for peace. In the brief respite afforded by the Treaty of Amiens, Dauvergne had dashed to Paris. He realised that he had little chance of recovering the Duchy, which he had never been able to enjoy, but he hoped to claim Navarre. However, his Secret Service work was too well-known, and he was arrested and expelled from the country.[23]

Jersey was now getting on Napoleon's nerves. In articles in *le Moniteur*, his official organ, which were inspired and probably dictated by him, he constantly returns to the subject: 'The Government of his Britannic Majesty permits, nay authorizes, hundreds of brigands, assassins, fire-bugs, to find refuge in Jersey, whence they slip back to France to commit further crimes', or again, 'the monarchical Powers want to make Switzerland a second Jersey, to hatch plots, to hire traitors, to disseminate lies'; or one last example: 'No! France can tolerate no longer this nest of brigands and assassins. Europe must be purged of his vermin. Jersey is England's shame'.[24]

In May 1803 war was renewed and lasted for 12 more years. General Gordon, the Lieutenant-Governor, proposed to the States that the Island be placed under martial-law, which meant that the civil courts would be superseded by courts martial. The members were so taken aback that they adjourned for 24 hours, and, for the only time on record, met on a Sunday. A wave of fury swept through the Island when the news was known. Half the population thronged the Royal Square and its approaches. The proposal was rejected by 26 votes to 10 and the ten were not quickly forgiven. Dean Dupré found a whip and halter fastened to his front door, and three of the Rectors were burnt in effigy in their churchyards.[25]

A more permanent result of the new war was the fortification of the Town Hill. Before Fort Regent was built, this was an open common on which the townsfolk grazed their cattle. 'It affords', said Falle, 'a lovely walk with a most extended prospect on all sides.' In 1785 part of it was levelled as a parade ground for the Town regiment, and a dolmen, a miniature Stonehenge, was discovered under a mound. No one knew what to do with it, as it was proving an impediment to the military. Then it was remembered that Marshal Conway, the Governor, was interested in archaeology; so, making the best of both worlds, la Vingtaine de la Ville presented it to Marshal Conway,[26] who, in 1787, removed it in a barge and had it re-erected in his park near Henley, where it still stands.

The British Government, having decided to fortify the hill, bought it from la Vingtaine de la Ville by compulsory purchase. Its value was assessed by a *Vue de Justice* and the sale was registered in the Court in November 1804. At first nothing more elaborate was planned than a gigantic earthwork, and each parish supplied on separate days men to dig the trenches. One of the first things to be constructed was the powder magazine. The King's Birthday was on 4 June 1804. A great crowd had gathered on the Hill to see the royal standard hoisted and a royal salute fired. That evening Philippe Lys, the signals officer, noticed smoke pouring from the magazine. The soldiers fled for their lives, all but Private Penteney, who, with Lys and a carpenter named Touzel, burst open the door. Cannon in those days were fired with lengths of rope soaked in nitre, and a careless gunner had put back one of these 'matches' still smouldering into the magazine. It had set fire to a pile of 'matches' and had actually begun to char the barrels of gunpowder when the three men rushed in, heaved out the burning rope and extinguished the fire. If the explosion had taken place, it is probable that half the town would have been destroyed. The States rewarded each of them with a gold medal and 5,000 *livres* (about £300 sterling), and with a pension which has continued to be paid to their descendants up to the present time.[27]

In the following year the War Office decided to build, instead of an earthwork, a strong modern fortress, which could be held, if an enemy should land, until reinforcements arrived. The foundation stone was laid in 1806 and the work completed in 1814. Much of the credit for what was a very fine piece of defensive architecture must go to J. H. Humfrey R. E., the engineer in charge, who was perhaps inspired by the great French military engineer de Vauban. It was named Fort Regent after the Prince of Wales (later George IV), who was acting as Regent during his father's incapacity.

In 1806 General Don[28] became Lieutenant-Governor. He was a man of immense vigour, who was determined to keep the Island safe from invasion. He established a signalling system by which, if the French fleet left St Malo or any of the neighbouring ports, the news could be flashed from look-out ships to Mont Orgueil and thence to Grosnez, Sark and Guernsey, where a British fleet was stationed. He tested the system and proved that the news could reach St Peter Port a quarter of an hour after the enemy had sailed. A charming and minute printed booklet of signals was published 'by authority of His Excellency Lieutenant-General Don, Commander-in-Chief' and printed by P. Mourant, printer to the States.

General Don firmly disciplined the Militia, building drill sheds near the parish churches and appointing additional drill inspectors. Every bay and possible landing place was fortified. But Don's great achievement was road-making. When he arrived the only roads were narrow winding lanes, along which no one could move artillery or troops with speed. All contemporary writers comment on this. 'The roads of this island are, in general, very bad', wrote Captain Lyte, late of the 1st Garrison battalion, in 1808, 'and sunk so low that they act as drains to the adjoining fields, and in the winter are nearly impassable.'[29]

In 1815, Thomas Quayle, reporting to the Board of Agriculture on the state of the islands, wrote:

> The ancient communications in the island under the name of roads are numerous; but narrow, winding, and, in consequence of frequently branching off and crossing each other, very intricate. They are sunk below the level of the land, flanked each side by the enormous mounds usual in the island, which are crowded with trees over-canopying the road, and, in a rainy season, rendering it a real gutter ... they are much worn away and altogether bearing marks of great antiquity. To express anything very old, a Jerseyman says "vieux comme les Quémins".

The depth of the roads below the surrounding land was largely due to erosion, particularly on slopes as at Daisy Hill, Gorey. This erosion ceased when tarred surfaces were made. Quayle also notes another circumstance not unfamiliar to the 20th-century motorist: 'Two carts meeting each other could not pass; one or other must back till it reached the nearest field or gateway or some other recess to which it might retreat during the passage of the other' — to which Quayle adds the comment: 'To this little circumstance in their internal economy and the disputes which it engenders, may perhaps in part be attributed the remarkable proficiency of the Jersey populace in swearing'.

Don determined to remedy this state of affairs. It was no easy task. Carving new roads was not only costly, but it involved an enormous amount of interference with private property, cutting corners off fields, felling trees, even demolishing outhouses. His first road, from the town to Grouville, is said to have been held up by an old farmer who threatened to shoot the first man who removed a sod. Don himself, in full regimentals, took a spade and dug through the boundary bank, and the farmer did not fire. His next road was from St Ouen to Beaumont; his third from the town to La Haule. It is astounding to think that until 1810 the sands had been the only means of communication between St Helier and St Aubin, other than by boat, and both were governed by the tide, as no vehicle could pass at high water. Don persuaded Trinity Parish to make a new road to the town; but then trouble began. Someone conceived the idea that the new roads would expose the town to attack, that the winding lanes had been a protection against raids by the enemy. One Rector is said to have preached from the Text, 'The broad road leadeth to destruction'. When the Trinity Road reached the town boundary, the St Helier Parish Assembly forbade the making of the last section; but the States overrode the Assembly and the road was finished. In St Saviour Philippe Le Geyt raised the *Clameur de Haro* when, in September 1810, 'a party of soldiers under General Don entered a piece of land or orchard in the parish of St Saviour and began to dig and break up the same for the purpose, as they declared, of making a public road'. He protested to the Privy Council that he had wished to 'repress the invasion of his private property and to try the legality of this proceeding' by raising the *clameur*. The Royal Court had overruled him, but the Council admonished them for not holding a *Vue de Justice* 'for the payment of the fair appreciated value of that property before the individual was stripped of his freehold'.[39] In all 18 main roads were made with many connecting cross roads, and for this alone Don richly deserved his statue in the Parade.[31]

Another danger faced by Jersey in wartime is to run short of food. One would hardly have expected an infantry man like Don to take much interest in farming, but he made strenuous attempts to bring waste land under cultivation, and at Don Farm in the middle of les Quennevais (now a housing estate), he showed what could be done, growing good crops of peas, potatoes, rye and white clover on land that had hitherto been regarded as hopelessly barren.[32]

He had one failure. Like some of his predecessors he tried to alter the constitution of the Island. Local politics had now taken a new twist. The French Revolution had killed the Magot party. Jean Dumaresq had become Lieutenant-Bailiff in 1802, but he had been so appalled by the Reign of Terror and the fact that some of his party had begun to dabble in treason, that in office he had become almost as autocratic as Lemprière. The States, in spite of their Magot majority, passed Acts in 1796 and 1797 suppressing meetings 'tending to stir up the hate of the inhabitants against the constituted authorities'.[33]

A new democratic leader now came to the fore, Thomas Anley, a book-keeper in a butcher's shop, who had become Constable of St Helier.[34] Twice he had been fined for 'indecent reflections on the authorities', but, in December 1807, he was elected Jurat by the largest majority ever known. The Court, however, refused to swear him in on the ground that 'he had used words tending to vilify the constituted authorities and had rendered his loyalty suspect by speeches highly culpable'. His election so startled Don that he tried to change the method of appointing Jurats. He asked for a Royal Commission, which recommended that in future all Jurats should be selected by the States and Crown Officers; but the Privy Council refused to sanction this change. When, a few years later, Anley was re-elected, the Council insisted that he should be sworn in, and he became one of the leading members of the States.

All this time Dauvergne was tirelessly weaving plots with the French Royalists, the most ambitious being one to kidnap Napoleon and carry him off to England; but few were successful. His opponent was now the Emperor himself. Napoleon continued to be worried about Jersey. Many of the instructions to the secret police are in his own handwriting. His counter-measures checked Dauvergne at almost every point. In 1808 he trapped one of Dauvergne's most trusted agents, Prigent, a Frenchman who had made 184 journeys between France and Jersey. When captured, Prigent tried to save his life by filling folios with confessions, revealing the secret hiding-places, the letter-distributors, the peasants who had given him shelter, though every page meant death to those who had trusted him; and after all he was shot. When Napoleon took charge of operations, Dauvergne's Fifth Column had little chance of success.

When, in 1814, Napoleon was beaten and banished to Elba, Dauvergne hurried to Paris, where his right to his Principality was recognised by the new French King, and he was graciously received by Louis XVIII. The little State acclaimed him in name, his brother, and a leading nobleman of the Duchy, Baron de Vauthier, visited it and reported events to him. A quarter of a century's strenuous help given to the French Royalists deserved its reward, and his claim was supported by the Duke of Wellington, who was now Ambassador Extraordinary at the French Court. Officials were appointed and the tiny, white-uniformed army reconstituted. As Prince de Bouillon, Vicomte de Turenne, Duc d'Albert et de Château-Thierry, Comte d'Évreux et du Bas Armagnac, Baron de la Tour, pair (peer) de France and one of the reigning sovereigns of Europe, Dauvergne seemed firmly seated on his midget throne with the great wealth of his adoptive father to maintain his position.[35]

But Napoleon escaped from Elba. Everything was again in the melting pot. After Waterloo the Congress of Vienna was given the task of redrawing the map of Europe. Nine days before Waterloo the Congress had reported that they would consider the merits of various claimants, but Dauvergne's chances were slender. He briefed an expensive lawyer to press his claims, but the

Congress abolished the independence of Bouillon and made it part of the Netherlands. Two months later Dauvergne died suddenly in an obscure hotel in Westminster. It has sometimes been reported that he committed suicide, but this is unlikely to be true. We have the record of a contemporary letter, from Marie Le Couteur to her son, the future Sir John, in which she wrote:

> … the poor man, it is supposed that he could not survive the loss of his titles and supposed riches. Two days of illness have rid him of the cares and disappointments of life, the greatest part of which has been spent in the enjoyment of "imaginary" wealth and honours, now declared to be the property of another. If he has been happy in the pursuit, he is not to be pitied. He leaves few people to regret him.[36]

The costly litigation had ruined him and in Jersey alone he left debts of over £7,000. But the personal tragedy of his later years has tended to obscure his remarkable contribution to the English Secret Service, to the cause of the French *émigrés* and above all to his native Island. Jersey owed him a bigger debt than was ever acknowledged.

Chapter Twenty-nine

THE LAUREL AND THE ROSE, 1816-1838

The civil history of the island is replete with instances of how cordially the people, in their party disputes, have hated each other.–Le Quesne, *A Constitutional History of Jersey*

AS SOON AS the Napoleonic Wars were over, Jersey suffered from another violent attack of politics. Human nature being what it is, mankind everywhere tends to fall into two groups: those who are satisfied with things as they are and those who believe that they can and should be bettered. In Jersey differences, already evident in the 18th century, engendered extraordinarily bitter disputes. Tradition has it that St Ouen provided each party with an emblem and a name. At an election for Constable in August 1819, the Progressives or Magots wore a rose, while the Conservatives or Charlots sported a laurel leaf. Those badges quickly spread through the other parishes, while references to their use appeared in local newspapers. When *La Chronique* changed its format on 1 January 1825, a wreath of roses headed the leading article for the first time. In 1820 the Attorney-General, John William Dupré,[1] founded with five friends *Le Constitutionnel* as the organ of the Laurel party. Inglis[2] wrote in 1834:

> The whole inhabitants of Jersey are divided into two factions, calling themselves Laurel and Rose; which in their mutual animosity and extreme blindness resemble the Guelfs and Guibbelines of the Middle Ages ´... It is utterly impossible for anyone unacquainted with Jersey to form any idea of the length to which each party spirit is carried there. It not only taints the fountains of public justice, but enters into the most private relations of life ... Families of different parties do not mingle and even tradesmen are in a considerable degree affected in their custom by this distinction.

In 1842 *the Royal Channel Islands Almanach and Guide Book* endorsed this opinion:

> The natives themselves (alas for silly squabbling mankind!) are divided into two factions or parties — the 'Laurel', or high, and the 'Rose', or low party, who hate each other more bitterly than do rival actors or singers. They seldom intermarry, seldom salute each other in the public ways; and they, for the most part, carry their mutual animosities into every transaction of their lives, legislative, judicial, municipal and private.

It is said that gardens with laurel hedges still indicate where Laurel supporters lived, as no Rose man would allow that accursed shrub on his land, while the universality of green or pink paint on woodwork, so apparent until the early 20th century, is also thought to have signified the Rose or Laurel adherence. These comments by outsiders confirm what might otherwise be thought exaggerated reporting by partisan newspapers.

The election at St Ouen in 1819 had resulted in a defeat for the reigning Constable, Jean Arthur, by Philippe du Heaume, but the validity of this result was contested in the Court over a period of 17 years, during which time St Ouen was led by a succession of *chefs de police*. Finally, in November 1836, Monsieur du Heaume took his seat in the States.[3]

One other example of the bitterness of feeling must suffice. In 1821 there was an election for Jurat. It was not a specially exciting one, for no burning question was put before the electors. The candidate was George Bertram, the Rose, Philippe Durell.[4] It was then the custom for each party to hold a supper before an election. At St Lawrence the two suppers were on the same night. The Laurelites met in the drill shed, and, after Monsieur Dupré had spoken against their rivals and advocated the overthrow of the St Helier police, they attacked M. Rondel's inn near the church, smashed all the windows with stones and pelted the Rose guests as they left. At St John the inn where the Rose men were supping was raided by a mob armed with pikestaffs and cudgels, who wrecked the building inside and out, even destroying the staircase, injured the innkeeper and his wife and wounded many of the company. In the same parish attendance at militia drills had been slack and nothing had been said. Suddenly the defaulters were paraded and told that anyone who failed to vote for Bertram would be fined for every absence. In the town the police erected a gallows in the Parade on which they hanged Bertram in effigy.[5]

In those days there was no ballot. Votes had to be given audibly in the church porch at the close of the Sunday service. In St Martin the first man to vote Rose was belaboured with fists and umbrellas, and escaped leaving his coat-tails in his assailants' hands. The next two fared worse, for they had their coats torn off. The fourth was thrown to the ground and kicked. After that most of the Rose men refrained from voting. The figures for the parish were Bertram 232, Durell 11. Nevertheless, in the Island as a whole, Durell had a majority; but the Laurelites boasted that it would be 10 years before he could take his seat. They challenged the result on the ground that non-ratepayers had voted. This involved an almost endless enquiry. Each separate disputed vote was considered by the Court. This dragged on for two years; but the Laurel purse proved the longer. Durell could not keep up the struggle, and Bertram took his seat in March 1823.[6]

Contemporary writers have supplied us with interesting, non-political glimpses of the period. The old-fashions had not yet been entirely ousted by the new. Plees wrote in 1824: 'In the country, indeed, notwithstanding late innovations, we not infrequently meet the old farmer, with his large cocked hat and thin *queue à la française*'. Jurat Anley, until his death in 1827, wore a pigtail which he tied with a red bow, and Plees observed that among females 'the short jacket, or bed gown and coarse red petticoat still form a prevalent, though declining costume'.[7] Inglis in 1834 reported that everyone, even the gentry, spoke in what he rudely calls 'a barbarous dialect of French'. In the churches, the States and the Courts standard French was used, but in ordinary conversation it was 'looked upon as affectation'. 'Although', wrote Inglis, 'the English language be sufficiently comprehended for the purpose of intercourse, it is certainly not understood by many in its purity.'

Agriculture had as yet made little progress. Oxen might still be seen drawing the plough; but, in 1815, Quayle[8] mentioned that 'in drawing the great plough (*la grand' tchéthue*) two bullocks and six or eight horses are requisite'. This, the trench-plough, had been introduced to the Island in about 1765 and had the effect of reducing the number of ploughings in the fallowing season and increasing the weight of subsequent crops. It also reduced the labour force which had formerly trenched the land by hand. This plough was first used for root crops, particularly for the popular parsnip. The hoe was not generally used except for potatoes. The trade in earlies and the Royal Jersey Fluke were as yet undreamed of, but it is interesting to read Quayle on the growing of potatoes at this period:

> Though the root is comparatively of modern introduction, not having been admitted into ordinary field culture till within thirty years, though it has had to struggle with the favourite parsnip and does not agree with the application of the no less favourite article of improvement, sea-weed, in substance, yet the culture of potatoes is general and extending; their quality nowhere superior, and this is the only field product which is at present exported.

Inglis reported that in the four years 1828-1832 a total 134,341 tons of potatoes had been exported, an average of over 30,000 tons a year.

Despite earlier legislation to prohibit the importation of French cattle, the Jersey cow was still far from her later perfection. In 1830 Colonel Le Couteur called her 'the Meg Merrilies of the bovine race ... ungainly high-boned and ragged in form'.[9] It was largely through the energy of the Colonel that farmers were turning their attention to scientific breeding, with the result that England had begun to appreciate the milking qualities of the Jersey and was buying seven or eight hundred annually. The fawn colour, which we associate with the Jersey today, has been produced by selective breeding. In the 1830s there were white Jerseys, dark-brown Jerseys and black ones, commonly known as mulberry. It was found that the fawn-coloured cows sold best, so the best milkers and butter producers from their progency were kept, while other markings went to the butcher. Colonel le Couteur was the first to recognise that the choice of the bull was as important as that of the dam; his appreciation of selective breeding was far ahead of his time and earned him a Fellowship of the Royal Society. He was also allowed a stand at the Great Exhibition in 1851 to exhibit his varieties of wheat; there were 105 in all.

In August 1833 an announcement of a meeting appeared in *Le Constitutionnel*: 'on se propose d'établir à Jersey une Société pour l'amélioration des fermes et jardins ainsi que de la race de bétail'. As a result the Jersey (now Royal Jersey) Agricultural and Horticultural Society was founded and our forefathers set about breeding the compact, well-proportioned beast we know today; so very different from the ungainly creatures which illustrate Le Couteur's dissertation to the Royal Agricultural Society of England.

The Jersey with its soft and kindly eye, its long dark lashes, mealy muzzle, fine coat and delicate, somewhat deer-like limbs, often leads those who are unfamiliar with the breed to consider that it must be delicate and need cossetting. This is not so; it is a sturdy animal with an astonishing ability to withstand extremes of climate around the world without ill effect. Each cow, moreover, has a strongly individual character; there never was, in our particular island breed, what might be termed a 'cow-like' cow. It has a natural immunity to many diseases which is much envied by breeders from abroad. The value of the Jersey's rich milk, both in fat content and in S.N.F. (solids-not-fat), which are greater than in the milk of other breeds, has gained world-wide recognition.

In agriculture between 1793 and 1815 certain modifications had become necessary in the pattern of cultivation to meet, as in the Occupation, the requirements of a wartime situation; notably there had been an increasing and sometimes alarming shortage of grain. After 1815 changes in staple crops and experimentation once more became possible. These too were to benefit from the Society founded in 1833 and from the pioneer work of such men as Sir John Le Couteur and Colonel C.P. Le Cornu.[10]

In the 1830s cider was still the main source of the farmer's wealth. A quarter of the Island was given up to apples, and many farms in the eastern parishes grew little else. Every farm had its cider-press and, in 1839, 268,199 gallons were exported to England. An analysis of imports and exports at this period makes interesting reading.[11] Much of the island trade consisted in re-exporting goods imported from abroad. Foreign goods were excluded from the British colonies by a high tariff, but no duty was imposed on anything made in Jersey. The Island was thus able to import leather from France, duty-free, turn this into boots and shoes manufactured locally, and undersell all competitors on the other side of the Atlantic. This industry had taken the place of the stocking trade, a victim to the Industrial Revolution in England, but it in its turn disappeared with the sailing ship later in the 19th century.

Oyster fishing was another industry that now sprung into prominence.[12] Jerseymen had always known of the oyster-bed off Gorey. Oyster-shells are indeed found in the prehistoric

59 *A typical cow im 1800-1830 at the time of the foundation of the Agricultural Society.*

THE TRANSFORMATION OF MEG MERRILEES

60 *'Beauty' bred by Colonel Le Couteur in 1843.*

tomb at La Hougue Bie. In 1606, when the Governor claimed this bed as Crown property, the Royal Court decided that every islander had a right to dredge there. In 1755 the Court prohibited dredging during the months with an 'R' in them. For years this trade was confined to local fishermen; but early in the 19th century it attracted the attention of fishing companies in England. A Report in 1830 said 'Messrs Alston and Co., Messrs Martin and Co. and six or seven other firms at Sittingbourne, Faversham and other places in Kent employ upwards of 250 boats, each manned with sixmen'.[13] In addition there were 70 boats from Colchester and others from Portsmouth, Shoreham and Southampton. At lest 2,000 men were employed, and the oysters were brought ashore (305,670 bushels in 1834) and sorted and packed by hundreds of women and girls. To accommodate this new population rows of cottages were built at Gorey, and the States constructed the present pier to give shelter to the oyster fleet. In 1832 Gouray church was built to provide English services for the fishermen and their families.

Many of these were rough customers. They dredged the Grouville bed so recklessly (the average catch was 12,000 oysters per boat per day), that it rapidly became exhausted and they began to encroach on the French beds off Chausey. The French had never objected to occasional visits by Jersey fishermen, as there were oysters enough and for all; but when large commercial fleets arrived, they naturally ordered them off. In spite of warnings from the British Government[14] that they must not expect protection, the men continued to poach: this more than once led to fighting. On 23 March 1828 the *Sunday Times* reported:

> An unpleasant affair has taken place between the English fishers off the coast of Jersey and two French vessels of war, which has led to serious consequences, many lives having been lost ... About 300 sail of English vessels are engaged in oyster-fishing on the coast of Jersey, towards the French shore, and they have been repeatedly warned not to approach within a certain distance of the French shore. These warnings have been little attended to, and two French vessels captured and took into port an English boat. On this intelligence reaching Jersey, all the fishing smacks proceeded to the French coast, boarded the vessels of war, retook the English boat and brought her back in triumph to Jersey. But several of the boatmen lost their lives, and a considerable number were taken prisoner and are in irons.

A clash took place later with the island authorities. To assist the fishery the States had spent £4,000 in laying down new beds in Grouville Bay, but these had to be preserved until they were ripe for dredging. In April 1838, 120 boats set out for the forbidden beds. The Constable of St Martin followed in a rowing-boat, but the men merely jeered. Next morning he arrested the ringleaders. Four days later, however, the men raided the beds again. So the Constable appealed to the Lieutenant-Governor, who called out the garrison and the town militia. A couple of cannon-balls, dropped among the boats, brought them back to port, and 96 captains were arrested and fined. The poor Governor caught cold and died a few days later, perhaps of pneumonia.[15] By 1863 the export of oysters had declined very rapidly, only 3,148 tubs being sent away. It is interesting that, in the second half of the 20th century, this industry, together with the cultivation of mussels, has been revived in the same Royal Bay of Grouville, but with more up-to-date methods.

Less creditable, but more profitable, was the smuggling business, naïvely known as *La Fraude*. Large quantities of French spirits were imported by Jersey merchants and sold to smugglers to be run ashore in lonely English creeks; big profits could also be made by landing tobacco, not only in England but in France, where the manufacture of tobacco was confined to certain licensed companies as it was a state monopoly. In 1823 the British Customs' House records report:

> On 17 March a Cawsand boat took in at St Brelade's Bay upwards of 300 ankers of brandy. On 31 March a Plymouth cutter took in at the same place upwards of 600 tubs of brandy and geneva

> [gin]. On 10 June a cutter from East Looe took in the same place 690 casks of brandy, and during the same month a Cawsand boat took away a large cargo of spirits.

That year an advertisement appeared in the Jersey papers:[16]

> Whereas it has been represented to the Commissioners of His Majesty's Customs that Humphrey Oxenham, being out on duty about one o'clock of the morning of Thursday 19 June, saw a smuggling vessel in the offing and some carts on the beach, which were accompanied by upwards of forty smugglers, armed with bludgeons, who surrounded him, struck him a violent blow above his eyes, which knocked him down, and, whilst on the ground, beat him severely, until James Hudie, an extra boatman, came to the assistance of the said Humphrey Oxenham, on which the smugglers dispersed. The Commissioners offer a reward of £50 to any person or persons who shall discover or cause to be discovered any one or more of the said offenders, so that he may be apprehended ... and pay dues to Southampton upon conviction.

An English Customs' House had been finally established in Jersey in 1810 and was closed in December 1973. This smuggling trade went on merrily for years, as indeed it did from the opposite coasts of Devon and Cornwall. New dodges were constantly invented. In 1831 the Customs seized sacks of what looked like potatoes, but was really rolls of tobacco covered with a thin skin smeared with mud. In 1834 the smack *Rambler* of Jersey was arrested in Langstone Harbour with 141 casks of spirits concealed in a false bottom. One more example is enough: here is the confession of the master of the *Eliza*, one of Philippe Nicolle's brigs:

> On the morning of 8 June, instead of proceeding to St Germain, for which we had cleared, we went to Bonne Nuit and there took in 2½ tons of tobacco, spirits in casks, segars [*sic*] and snuff, which I have agreed to take to Wales at the rate of £50 per ton. We proceeded to Fishguard where we arrived on the fifth day and, running in about eleven that evening, assisted in conveying the goods to a store close by. We then went on to St Germain, took in 32 sheep and returned to Jersey. At 3 a.m. on 22 September I left St Helier's without clearance, proceeded to Grève de Lecq and took on board 5 tons of leaf tobacco and several bags of tea and cases of spirits. We reached Fishguard the night of the 25th and landed all safely.[17]

One thing that changed the tempo of life in Jersey was the coming of the steamers. The sailing cutters were always at the mercy of wind and weather. When Queen Anne died, it took 10 days for the news to reach Jersey, and then it came via Paris and St Malo. Ninety years later a Guernsey Jurat embarked at Southampton. He was becalmed at Cowes but, when a breeze sprang up, he was five times driven back to the Solent by a gale. It was three months before he landed at St Peter Port.[18] This was of course exceptional; but even in the best of weather no one who set sail for England could be sure when he would arrive. This meant that the delivery of mail and goods to the islands was also very uncertain.

Until 1794 there had been no official post-office in Jersey. Mail from the Islands was handed to merchants or coffee-house keepers, who gave it to the captain of the first available vessel sailing for England. He handed his bundles of letters to an agent, who passed it to the official postmaster. Merchant, agent and captain were each paid a penny, while the addressee paid postage calculated by distance. Between 1778 and 1783 the Postmaster-General had placed an ex-Dover armed packet, the *Express*, on the Southampton-Channel Islands run to keep communications open during hostilities. Later other commercial packets kept the service going; some were armed and carried passengers as well as mail. Finally in 1794 an official Post Office was set up in Jersey with Charles William Le Geyt as Jersey's first Postmaster. He made up the mail every day at his house, which was on the east side of Hue Street near the corner of Union Street,[19] and the official packet, the *Royal Charlotte*, later joined by other post-office cutters, sailed for Weymouth of an evening. This system of carrying mail by sailing boat lasted until the mid-1820s, when the greater efficiency of privately owned steamers forced the post-office to resort to steam as well.

The first paddle steamer to visit Jersey, and she came only once, was the *Medina.* Hired to bring a Colonel Fitzgerald and his family and furniture to Guernsey, she ran an excursion to Jersey on 11 June 1823, where she was welcomed by great crowds and by the militia band. In 1824 two rival companies established a weekly service, the *Ariadne*, 138 tons, sailing from Southampton, and the *Lord Beresford*, 155 tons, from Portsmouth and later from Southampton.[20] The advertisements for these sailings in the local press give interesting glimpses of how passengers and goods continued their journey on arrival at the English ports. The promoters of the *Ariadne* list the departure times of coaches for London and other cities, with one overnight coach leaving at 8 p.m. for London. The proprietors of the *Lord Beresford* provide a table of prices by which goods are conveyed by canal from London to Portsmouth by the London Fly Barge Company, light crates costing 3d. per foot, heavy crates ls.3d. per hundredweight. In 1831 the *Lord of the Isles* began running between Jersey and London. Then ensued an extraordinary battle of fares, each company striving to undercut the others. The original fare to England on all these lines was 30s.; the *Lady de Saumarez*, which had replaced the *Lord Beresford*, finally brought this down to three; whereupon the *Ariadne* advertised 'Fare, half-a-crown'.

There was also rivalry in the early 19th century between the private shipping companies and the Post Office. Faced with the competition of steam, the G.P.O., which had always granted concessions to commercial companies to carry mail, as well as having its own fleet of cutters from Weymouth, made arrangements for steam vessels to operate the official service. Three paddle-steamers undertook this: the *Watersprite* and the *Ivanhoe* in July 1827, the *Meteor* in April 1828. In 1837, owing to financial losses, the Government transferred the official packet service to the Admiralty. The *Watersprite* was renamed H.M.S. *Wildfire*, the *Flamer* which had replaced the *Meteor* (she had foundered in 1830) was renamed H.M.S. *Fearless* and the *Ivanhoe* was withdrawn from the Channel Island service. H.M.S. *Dasher* joined the service in 1838 and H.M.S. *Cuckoo* in 1839. In 1840 the railway reached Southampton and, under pressure from the islands, mail was allowed to travel by this route if endorsed 'To Southampton by private steamer'. This saved two days compared with Weymouth. Finally, faced with hopeless competition, the mail contract was transferred by the Post Office from the Admiralty to the South Western Steam Packet Company in 1845. The Weymouth and Channel Island Steam Packet Company was formed in 1857, backed by the Great Western Railway. In 1862 an Act of Parliament authorised the London and South Western Railway to own and operate ships. Rivalry and competition between Weymouth and Southampton mailboats was to last well into the 20th century, as they raced to be first to arrive in Guernsey to pick up passengers for Jersey, or cut across on very high tides between Elizabeth Castle and the shore to save time.

This fleet of competing steamers brought thousands of passengers to Jersey, many of whom came to stay. The Island now had to adjust itself to an enormous English invasion. Three-quarters of the newcomers were half-pay officers and their families. By 1840 there were said to be 5,000 English residents. They formed a separate colony and did not mix easily with French-speaking Jersey folk. One guide book says: 'The English society of Jersey is quite distinct from the native society. I do not say that they never mingle, but the intercourse is limited and infrequent';[21] another states: 'Between Jerseymen and the British there is little social intercourse'. Inglis agrees: 'There is not a perfectly cordial feeling between the natives and the residents' ... he also notes:

> One thing is very striking in the aspect of the street population of Jersey ... the extraordinary contrast exhibited between business and idleness ... The English residents have nothing to do. There is therefore the constant contrast between that portion of the population whose object,

> and I may even say, whose difficulty is to get quit of time, and that other portion, the native inhabitants namely, whose object is to make the most of it. The former is certainly the most difficult and the more laborious task.

However, perusal of the Le Couteur diaries and others of the period suggest considerable social intercourse at certain levels and belies these impressions.

This influx of educated people of reasonable income had a great effect on local architecture. Until about 1810 the standard Jersey house had remained relatively unchanged for about a century. Now there was a sudden need for superior houses in or near town for these newcomers, and also for local people who had made money in the fishing and shipping industries. So speculators appeared and built very fine houses and terraces of late Georgian and Regency styles, of which there are good examples in Almorah Crescent, Rouge Bouillon and Queen's Road. These houses owed nothing to Normandy, as had the early architecture of Jersey, and in appearance and proportions were such as could be found in prosperous towns in England. The windows were

61 *Amaryllis belladonna, the Jersey Lily.*

tall, rooms lofty, stairs broad, floors of parquet and, in many cases, doors of mahogany imported from South America. Bedroom space was often sacrificed to the impressiveness of the entrance and the grandeur of the reception rooms. The drawing-room was often on the first floor, and basements or semi-basements housed the kitchen quarters. The facades were plastered, and even when the actual walls were constructed of granite, it is doubtful if the surface was ever meant to be exposed. Whereas the stripping of plaster from the granite walls of a pre-1800 house is an improvement and a return to the original intention, it is questionable whether this is so with a 19th-century stucco house.

Noirmont and Avranches manors were built at this period and Rosel was remodelled and enlarged, but many more modest but substantial houses were erected all over the Island. So many of them bear date stones of this period that one cannot escape the impression of great prosperity, seeping down to the single storey cottage of two or three rooms: many of these have as good stonework as their superior neighbours and carry fine granite chimneys and beautifully wrought date stones. At the same time gardening became quite the fashion, and many houses of the period have laid out front gardens with lawn, borders and shrubs. The earliest of our fine camellias, imported from France, date from this time. Some have grown into veritable trees and are a joy to behold through late winter and spring. Diaries of the period speak of much activity in purchasing trees, shrubs and bulbs.[22]

Of other buildings, the mills were reconstructed many times, usually after fire, but on simple utilitarian lines; the Castles had no further alterations, though a notable defensive building was Fort Regent (1804), where granite was again used. All this time the town was growing by leaps and bounds. To give only a few examples: Burrard Street was opened in 1812 on land given by General Burrard, a Jerseyman who saw service in the American and Peninsular Wars and was Wellington's successor; Beresford Street, named after Jersey's last Governor, is mentioned in 1822. It had originally been laid out as a private road when the Market area was developed in 1800 as had Halkett Place, named after Sir Colin Halkett, Lieutenant-Governor to Lord Beresford and the first to reside in the present Government House. Waterloo Street was opened in 1825 and Bath Street, Belmont Road and Great Union Road are spoken of as 'recently opened' in 1827. In 1831 the streets were for the first time lighted by gas.[23]

New churches now became necessary. The first, St Paul's, had a stormy birth. Dean Dupré, Rector of St Helier, was a Laurel man, who could not keep politics out of his sermons. Part of his congregation belonged to the Rose party and they resented this so deeply that they planned to build a new church in which they could worship without annoyance. They obtained an Order in Council permitting them to build a new proprietary chapel, as had been done at St Aubin. But no clergyman welcomes the secession of half his congregation. Dupré resisted the registration of the Order, inhibited all local clergy from officiating in the building and held up the use of the chapel until his death in 1823.[24] Church construction in the 19th century tended to be Gothic (St James, a second proprietary chapel, was opened in 1829) or Classical Revival (All Saints opened in 1835 as a chapel of ease to the Town Church).

The Nonconformists, too, were building chapels. We have already mentioned the French Independent Church in Halkett Place, built by the brothers Perrot. In 1813 the Methodists built a new chapel in Don Street, later to be replaced by the splendid building in Halkett Place now known as Wesley-Grove Chapel. In 1827 they built another chapel for their English-speaking members in what is now Wesley Street. The Baptists opened the Albion Chapel in August 1819 and another in Ann Street; the Bible Christians (later United Methodists) opened a chapel in January 1826, known as Ebenezer but later as Great Union Road Chapel, and the Primitive Methodists in Aquila Road in July 1839. The Roman Catholics had their first small chapel, adapted from an upper room, in Castle Street and an Irish mission in Hue Street.[25] In St Helier the

Anglican church was no longer in sole possession of the field. This was also true in the country where a number of Methodist chapels were built in this period.

The problems and aspirations of those 19th-century builders are well-illustrated in the minutes of the meetings held by the trustees of the first chapel built for the English Methodists.[26] Early in 1827 a site was acquired from a Mr Benest, who owned land on both sides of the plot and had recently made a roadway to the west (now Wesley Street). Ironically, with the diversification of denominations, the style and title of George IV, which appear in the contract of purchase, proclaim him as 'Défenseur de la Foi et chef suprême sur la terre de l'Eglise Unie de l'Angleterre et d'Irlande'. In January 1827 the Leaders' Meeting had been asked to consider sources of money for carrying on the building. This they did in a manner characteristic of a period when notes of many kinds were in circulation, some guaranteed by the parishes,[27] others by private individuals. Having found a sponsor willing to sign his name as a security for the issuing of promissory notes of £1 each, payable on demand and not exceeding the sum of £1,000, they promised to keep him 'harmless from any demand either directly or indirectly on account of the said promissory notes'. The trustees themselves would stand surety.

When, in 1830, it seemed likely that the States would adopt English currency to replace the *livre tournois*, the trustees wrote to the President of the Methodist Conference in England. 'Apprehensive that should the law which as it stands enables them to keep their notes in circulation be repealed and so altered as to oblige them to recall their notes, they would not be able to go on without increasing the debt', they asked if they would be entitled to relief from the 'Chapel Fund' in case of need. In 1835 they changed the plate for issuing notes from 'one pound Jersey notes' into 'one pound British'.

The trustees included Nathaniel Westaway, a builder who died a rich man, and whose daughter, after a number of legal wrangles within the family, left money to found the Westaway Crèche, now replaced by buildings to accommodate hospital staff, and the Don Westaway, which provided a fund to assist '*les pauvres honteux*' (those who were too proud to ask for help from the Constables), and to buy clothing and books for Protestant, elementary (primary) school children.[28] Others among those first trustees were Henry Dart, a member of a well-known building family, and John Philipps, another builder, who gave his name to the road which runs parallel to Peter Street to the north, and who, at one point, was asked to look after and keep in order the road in Peter Street which led to the chapel, while Messrs Anthoine, Bisson and Guiton endeavoured to persuade the authorities to make the road public.

The Utility companies, as we know them today, were non-existent, so the trustees were required to sink a well and to construct at their expense a barrel drain along the east wall and to continue this in a straight line to the Faux Bié, the brook which ran through the town as an open drain until the reforms of Constable Le Sueur,[27] and which was recently exposed during demolition in Ann Street and Philipps Street. If the seller wished to use the drain, he was to reimburse half the cost: a wise precaution, as later his vinegar factory was to be the subject of a remonstrance in Court against the 'nuisance of Mr Benest's premises'.

Lighting also had its problems. In June 1828 M. Pequin was instructed to write for a number of 'Japanese and Liverpool Lamps, sconces and wicks', but in 1831 burners were ordered for lighting the chapel with gas. Mr Edge, the owner of the first gas-works in Jersey, who later sold his premises to the Jersey Gas Company,[30] was asked to place a gas-light over the entrance gate. A month later there was 'surprise and dismay' that Mr Edge had removed the branchers and burners belonging to the chapel without the consent of the trustees. By 1842 it was considered too expensive to bring gas to the two vestries, so candles were used.

Every detail of the work of construction is recorded. Masons are to be paid five shillings a day and carpenters four. Their apprentices are to receive one shilling and ninepence respectively.

Four-inch planks are to be used for the foundation of the building, 'the beams under the same to be three feet asunder in the cleat between'; the ceilings and walls are to be plastered with lime, 'the best that can be found in Captain Moore's quarry, to be used as it comes without sifting the clay'. There are enquiries to be made into the cost of a rail for the front of the 'singing gallery', and Mr Pinel, Superintendent of the Sunday School, is asked to provide green curtains to protect the children from the wind; they are placed at the back of the free seats so that pews can be let; in 1828 there is an unfortunate double-letting:

> The trustees do greatly lament the circumstances, yet conscience does forcibly dictate to them that the Miss Sinels have the greatest right to the pew in question and do sincerely hope that the Miss Smiths will not resent the unanimous decision of the trustees there present.

In 1829 the trustees agreed to let a room for the use of the Church Infant School for £15 a year, to be occupied except on Sundays and on six other days in the year reserved for meetings and to be given up 'cleaned and washed' by 5 p.m. on Saturday. In 1838 they acquired an organ and decided to sell their two bass viols. They waited on Mr Ollivier in order to make the best arrangement for playing the organ, and agreed that the lad appointed to blow the bellows should receive 'five shillings British per quarter'. It is indeed refreshing in these days of mass-production to find so much individualism and enterprise in this small band of trustees.

One great improvement to the Town was the making of the harbour. As late as 1786 ships coming to St Helier could find no shelter but a broken-down jetty near the inn called La Folie, which gave protection to a little creek among the rocks. When ships unloaded there, carts came along the sands at low tide to reach them. Most merchants landed their goods at St Aubin. In 1786 the Chamber of Commerce had urged the States to provide a proper harbour, and Smeaton, the famous engineer who built the Eddystone lighthouse (the one which now stands on Plymouth Hoe), was brought to Jersey. But the States turned down his plan on the advice of local sea-captains. They then decided to be their own engineer and in 1790 marched with the Mace at their head to lay the foundation stone. The old jetty was rebuilt and lengthened, and a breakwater 200 yards long constructed to shelter two little coves known as the French and English harbours. But then all further work was stopped by the war. From 1814 onwards the merchants themselves built le Quai des Marchands in front of what came to be known as Commercial Buildings, the ownership of which was largely in the hands of the fishing and shipping magnates. However the harbour was still inadequate. When the Duke of Gloucester, who was both nephew and son-in-law of the King, visited Jersey in 1817, it was low tide and he had to scramble ashore on all fours over rocks covered in seaweed, until he reached the beach, where the States and Militia were drawn up to welcome him, a royal entry that certainly lacked dignity.[31]

The next step in St Helier was to give access to the harbour from the western parishes by building a sea-wall and the Esplanade, where before there had been nothing but sand dunes. This was finished in 1832.[32] But shipping was increasing so rapidly that further extension became necessary, and in 1837 the States commissioned James Walker to draw plans for a new harbour.[33] It is from these plans that sprang the harbour and quays enclosed by the Victoria and Albert piers, their names symbolic of a thriving era in Jersey maritime history.

One of the features of this period was the number of newspapers that now sprang up like mushrooms. The old *Gazette* still survived, called contemptuously *la Grand-mère* by its enterprising rivals. In 1814 the *Chronique* was born followed by *le Constitutionnel*. After these organs of the Rose and Laurel parties, came *l'Impartial, le Jersiais, le Miroir* and *La Patrie*, all in French, but not, be it noted, in Jersey Norman French. As the number of English residents increased, no less than 10 weekly papers were published for their benefit, the *British Press*, the *Jersey Observer*, the *Jersey Loyalist*, the *Jersey and Foreign News*, the *Patriot*, the *Jersey Times,* the *Jerseyman*, the *Jersey Argus*, the *Jersey Herald* and the *Jersey Gazette*. No place of its size ever had so many newspapers.[34] 'On Saturday', says Inglis,

> when three of the French papers are published, one is seen in every market stall. The fishwoman, the butter-woman, has each her newspaper, and lays in for another week a stock of knowledge as to the affairs of Jersey. The circulation of the island papers is very considerable ... without exception these are the furious organs of party and are conducted with apparently the sole view of pleasing certain partisans. The acrimony, invective and personal abuse, which figure in their columns, extremely surprise a stranger who has been accustomed to the more gentlemanly tone of the English press.[35]

This is mildly put. Dickens' *Eatanswill Gazette* was a model of courtesy compared with most Jersey papers. The *Jersey Times* described the editor of the *Constitutionnel* as a 'spavined, glandered, broken-down, broken-winded, bedevilled, old pettifogger's hack', and the editor of the *British Press* as a 'mercenary, libeller and shuffling coward'[36] and added, 'Even the fellow Payn, his proprietor, stupid and contemptible as he is, must loathe the grovelling poltroon he hires to do his dirty work'. The French papers were just as scurrilous. The popularity of these newspapers indicates not only a high degree of literacy among the islanders, but a party spirit that was by no means dead.

Chapter Thirty

THE EARLY VICTORIANS, 1837-1872

Aidjous trejous et sachez y t'nir
Djieu vos aidra et vos f'ra arriver.
Banner in Jersey French displayed at the laying of the foundation stone of Elizabeth Castle breakwater.–La Chronique 29.8.1872

IN JERSEY, as in England, Victoria's long reign witnessed great changes. The first noteworthy local event was the minting of Jersey money. For centuries the island currency had been the *livre tournois*, the *sou* and the *liard* but in 1834 the States had adopted the English system of reckoning in pounds, shillings and pence. It was not easy to adjust the relative value of the two currencies. The riots of 1730 had shown the danger of deflating the value of the coins in the people's pockets. So, after long debate, it was decided that 520 *sous* should be the equivalent of the British Sovereign. But old customs die slowly, and as late as 1851 a howl of protest was raised when Abraham de Gruchy, founder of the now large department store, advertised that henceforth he would sell 'exclusively on British sterling'. To pay in pennies for goods marked in *livres* involved difficult feats of arithmetic, so, to ease the situation, the States obtained permission in September 1840 to issue pennies, halfpennies and farthings 'to the amount of one thousand pounds for the use of the island' and of a value more easily equated to the old system of reckoning. The new half penny and the *sou* were to be roughly of the same value, and, as 520 *sous* made a pound, it followed that thirteen pence made a shilling. So the new pennies were stamped '1/13th of a shilling' and it was not until 1876 that the English figure of '1/12th of a shilling' was adopted. In the early years of the 20th century French copper coins were still accepted as legal tender in Jersey.[1]

The change in currency must have puzzled the older residents, and in this context it is interesting to read the will of Jeanne Gruchy,[2] who, in 1843 at the age of 80, bequeathed 'to the most necessitous Poor of this Isle the sum of 1,728 silver *livres,* according to the ancient currency of France, that is to say 144 *livres* in one payment for the poor of each of the twelve parishes, to be distributed at the discretion of my executors'.

After some personal bequests, she left the residue of her estate equally between the 12 parishes, 'this money to be used for the purchase of land, the rent of which was to be given to the necessitous poor'. In 1860 the income derived from these fields amounted to £338. Most parishes put up commemorative stones bearing the words 'Don Gruchy' in the wall of the field so acquired, but there is much variation in the design of the stones, in the wording they carry and indeed in the number of fields purchased, some parishes having organised their buying of land more beneficially than others.

The great excitement of these early years was the young Queen's visit in 1846.[3] It lasted only three hours. She stepped ashore at eleven and was back on her yacht by two; but it stirred the Island to its core. Painters produced albums, poets composed odes, many of them painted on silk. The preparations were fantastic. Parishes through which the Queen could not possibly drive put up costly arches of welcome. St Ouen's had a magnificent one; Trinity erected four. At sunset on 2 September the yacht anchored in St Aubin's Bay. Rockets soared; bonfires blazed; Noirmont

62 *A Clos des Pauvres, Jeanne Gruchy stone at St John.*

ROADSIDE PRIDE IN GRANITE

63 *A parish boundary stone, St John–Trinity.*

was especially spectacular, for the whole hillside caught fire. Next morning, before the Queen landed with Prince Albert, M. Jean Poingdestre, Seigneur of le fief ès Poingdestres and living at Grainville, went aboard the Royal yacht

> in the company of his very clever gardener, Mr Folley ... and had the honour of presenting to Her Majesty a basket of fine fruit from his noble garden. The basket contained pineapples, figs, melons and grapes. The Queen was most graciously pleased to accept the timely and appropriate offering.[4]

When the Queen landed on the newly-completed South Pier, it was then and there renamed the Victoria Pier. A 'bevy of drawing-room beauties' in white scattered roses at her feet, as they sang the National Anthem, 'led on a concertina by Master Bridgeman'. A pavilion had been erected on the harbour, the materials 'furnished, gratis, by those old and respected firms, Messrs Gray, Godfray, Falle and Co., and Messrs Abraham de Gruchy and sons; the furniture, made by Mr Richard Le Gallais, the work executed by him in a masterly manner'.[5] After receiving addresses from the States and the Militia, the Queen drove through deliriously cheering crowds past la Hougue Bie (then surmounted by Prince's Tower), through the countryside and 'orchards without end' to Mont Orgueil and then back to her yacht. It would seem from an entry in her diary that the person who enjoyed the proceedings least was the Queen herself: 'The heat and glare made me so ill and giddy that I remained below the greater part of the afternoon'. However she did record the Royal weather: 'A splendid day. I never saw a more beautiful deep blue sea, quite like Naples; and Albert saw that this fine bay of St Aubin in which we lie, really is like Naples', while the contemporary account by Sir John le Couteur, her Militia A.D.C., who rode beside her carriage throughout her visit, shows her to have been lively and interested, asking him numerous questions as they drove through the countryside and climbed to the upper ramparts of Mont Orgueil.

The enthusiasm is easy to understand; though Charles II had come as a fugitive, and records of earlier Royal visits are difficult to authenticate, this was the first State visit of a monarch, and there was a mystique about royalty, undimmed by the impact of films and television. Illustrations in newspapers were rare, and the States commissioned Jean Le Capelain,[6] Jersey's brilliant water-colour painter, to produce a portfolio of views to remind her of her visit; these were engraved and later published as '*The Queen's Visit to Jersey*'. However, something more was demanded to perpetuate the memory of her visit. Three suggestions were put forward: a public walk lined with trees and with the Queen's statue in the centre, a lighthouse on the spot where she landed, and Laurens Baudains' old scheme for a college. At first the promenade was most popular, but General Touzel, the Receiver-General, worked untiringly for the college, and at last his project was carried in the Assembly of Governor, Bailiff and Jurats, by the Bailiff's casting vote.[7] The foundation stone was laid on a superb site east of the town on the Queen's birthday, 24 May 1850, and there in 1852 Victoria College was opened. It gradually replaced the two 15th-century grammar schools, and became a strong influence in island life, maintaining a high standard, academically and in athletics, under a series of distinguished headmasters. Other memorials to Queen Victoria were to follow. In 1890 her statue (now opposite the Grand Hotel) was unveiled on the Weighbridge; in 1897 her Diamond Jubilee was marked by the founding of the Victoria Cottage Homes in St Saviour, while in June 1897 the Boulevard Baudains, originally commemorating a Constable of St Helier, was renamed Victoria Avenue, an event marked by a granite pillar surmounted by a crown carved in this difficult material, which is an outstanding piece of craftsmanship.[8] Other streets and a crescent bear her name.

Meanwhile some of the new residents were planning an audacious attack on Jersey institutions. Many of the retired colonels, who had chosen Jersey for its mild climate and low taxation, were annoyed at finding the local laws different from those in force in Harrogate or Tunbridge Wells. They secured as spokesman Abraham Le Cras, 'born in Salisbury of a Jersey family', a man of tireless energy and a master of trenchant English.[9] Le Cras won his first victory in 1840 when he challenged the right of the States to naturalise aliens, which they had been doing for centuries. In the light of the Code of 1771, the Privy Council decided that no such privilege existed, and the States had to petition that all the certificates they had granted since that date be confirmed.[10]

Le Cras' erudition impressed laymen, though later the Royal Commissioners treated most of it as irrelevant antiquarianism. His backers enabled him to publish two weekly newspapers, the *Jersey and Guernsey News* and the *Patriot*, as well as an annual volume, the *Englishman's Almanac*. This gave him a three-decker pulpit from which to thunder at the States, the Royal Court and the Honorary Police. Against the last he was especially bitter and published a black list of all tradesmen who were members of it, so that English residents might boycott their shops.

In 1846 he determined to stir up Parliament to exercise its supposed rights. He persuaded John Roebuck, M.P. for Bath, to move in the House for a Parliamentary Committee to enquire into the Criminal Law of Jersey. The Government refused this, but promised a Royal Commission. Parliament's right to enquire was dubious, but the Queen's no one could dispute. The appointment of these Commissioners (Ellis and Bros) was a great triumph for Le Cras. 'I have made a compilation', he told them, 'of about 3,000 Orders in Council, and from 5,000 to 6,000 Acts of the Court.' From these researches he had evolved the sensational theory that Jersey's claim to Home Rule was 'founded on fraud and usurpation', that local officials had bamboozled innocent English Commissioners into recognising rights that were entirely bogus; that Parliament and the English Law Courts had precisely the same powers in Jersey that they had over the Isle of Wight. 'The States are not a Provincial Parliament but a Municipal Council' ... 'Their power is restricted to making by-laws for markets, pumps and taverns' ... 'The law-making power for Jersey rests with Parliament and nowhere else' ... 'The States have no more power to make laws for Jersey than I have'.

The Commissioners did not endorse all Le Cras' demands. 'It was urged upon us,' they said, 'to recommend measures which would stop little short of an absolute adoption of the English Law and the annexation of the island to an English circuit.' But they did advise the abolition of the Royal Court and its replacement by three Crown-appointed paid judges and the formation of a paid police force independent of the Parish Assemblies.[11]

For the next few years the Home Secretary, the Commons and the Privy Council were bombarded with Le Cras' petitions; but in 1850 he temporarily grew tired of the struggle. He dropped his newspapers, left Jersey, and went to live in England, declaring that 'there was no security for his life through the corruption of the police'. He had gained few Jersey supporters; but the two old parties were still clapperclawing angrily. Each now had a brilliant leader. Advocate François Godfray,[12] the Laurel spokesman and successively Constable of St Helier, St Martin and St Saviour, before being elected a deputy of the States, would beat down all opposition with whirling arms, a voice of thunder and tempestuous rhetoric. States and Court sometimes had to adjourn, because his paroxysms of rage made the conduct of business impossible. Once he followed the Bailiff out of Court and challenged him to a duel. Yet despite his furies, he was one of the most trusted men in the island.

The Rose leader, on the contrary, Advocate Pierre Le Sueur,[13] was cool and imperturbable, quiet and concise, and in argument almost diabolically clever. He succeeded Pierre Perrot, who had ousted Godfray as Constable of St Helier. He proved to be one of the best Constables the town has ever had. When he took office, its sanitary condition was appalling. Sewage from the better streets poured into open waterways. The poorer houses had no sanitation whatsoever. It is

64 *Victoria Pier,* c.*1900, showing the LSWR* Alberta.

THE AGE OF STEAM

65 *The Jersey Eastern Railway, with the engine* 'Calvados' *at Le Hocq cutting. Shrubs are being planted by driver F. Gallichan, fireman P. Cabot and others.*

interesting to note the comments of Dr. George Hooper, M.D., in his *Observations on the topography, climate and prevalent diseases on the Island of Jersey*. These were published in serial form in the *Guernsey and Jersey Magazine* of 1837.[14] Hooper speaks of the common diseases of malaria, dysentery and cholera, and offers suggestions

> for the efficient removal of an insidious source of disease ... the effluvia arising from the brooks which flow sluggishly near and even underneath many of the houses. These streams, if they deserve the name, are during the summer months partially dry, and have at all times too trifling a current to carry off a constant accumulation of decomposable matter, rich with the elements of deleterious exhalation.

He admits that, 'notwithstanding the many fertile sources of febrile miasma which exist in St Helier, fever is not proportionately more frequent than in other parts of the island', but adds, 'a very fertile source of disease, in this otherwise happy spot, arises from an excessive use of ardent spirits, the low price of which is attended by the double evil of increasing temptation and facilitating indulgence'. Beginning in 1845 Le Sueur carried out a complete and costly system of underground sewers, and, though the ratepayers grumbled at the cost, they kept him in office for 15 years, and, when he died, erected to his memory the obelisk in Broad Street.

In 1847 he had to face an extremely ugly crisis. In the 'hungry forties', wages remained pegged at two shillings a day, while the price of bread was rising weekly, and the workers began to threaten violence. In January several ship's-carpenters took away rudders from the grain ships *Greyhound* and *Zelia* to prevent them sailing with grain for England. These were returned after the States had promised to meet and discuss the crisis. On 1 February the Assembly decided to arrange for bread to be baked at the special price of 4 *sous la livre* for working men as against the normal price of 5 *sous*. The Constable of St Helier presented a petition from ship's-carpenters, blacksmiths and other workmen, and promised to find work on the new road to St Aubin, which had reached La Haule. However the price of bread continued to rise and in April the States decided to discontinue the baking of cheaper loaves. A notice to this effect, inserted in *La Chronique,* on 15 May, proved to be the last straw. On 17 May a large gang of hungry workers, who were constructing the final section of General Don's road at La Haule, downed tools and marched to the town, sweeping up on their way the men from Deslandes' ship-building yards near First Tower and those who were building the new Albert Pier. In the Square they were joined by crowds from all parts of the town, including the Havre-des-Pas shipwrights. Le Sueur and his centeniers tried to reason with them; but a cry was raised: 'To the Town Mill'.[15] The mill was situated in Grands Vaux below Steep Hill in the district known for many years as Town Mills. The property had belonged to a number of well-known men: Charles William Le Geyt, the first postmaster, François Valpy dit Janvrin, a prominent merchant and ship-owner, and François Jeune, father of the future Bishop of Peterborough. In 1835 Jeune had sold the property to Nicholas Le Quesne, whose family held it at the time of the bread riots. Part of the site is now owned by the Caesarean Lawn Tennis Club.

So the mob moved on towards Grands Vaux, shouting 'to Le Quesne's mills', or chanting:

> Cheaper bread or Pellier's head:
> Cheaper flour or Pellier's last hour.

Pellier was the miller at the time. While Le Sueur was enrolling Special Constables, Centenier Le Bailly met the crowd at the mill and argued with them. But the women egged them on; the doors were broken in, and two waggons were loaded with stolen flour. Le Sueur met these near Robin Hood Inn, as they were returning to the town, climbed into the first and challenged anyone to move it; the rioters slunk away. The second waggon was not recaptured without a fight; but the Lieutenant-Governor, Major-General James Reynett, sent troops and order was restored. The demonstration was effective. The States agreed to sell bread once more to the poor below cost price; the country Constables increased their scale of parish relief, and the rich, who had had a fright, subscribed over £700 to the Relief fund opened by Le Sueur. In this lean and hungry period many Jerseymen emigrated with their families to Canada and Australia.

In the same Year, 1847, work began on St Catherine's breakwater. Seven years before, by Royal petition, the States had warned the Government that the French were building powerful forts at Cherbourg, Granville and St Malo, and suggested that a Naval station might be set up on the north coast of Jersey. The Admiralty now decided to construct two, one at Alderney, the other in St Catherine's Bay, chosen after some debate in preference to Bouley Bay or Noirmont. Eight hundred workmen were brought from England and the present pier was run out; but the southern arm at Archirondel very soon came to a halt and remains today as a mere stump, a few yards east of the Jersey round tower. The reason for this was not made public. It was said that the French had protested that the stationing of a fleet within sight of their coast would be considered an unfriendly act. The truth was that the northern arm had encouraged silting, a possibility foreseen by the eminent hydrographer, Admiral Martin White, whose advice had gone unheeded. Moreover the introduction of steam had made a harbour of refuge less vital to Britain, and the Alderney pier was never completed. The lantern at the seaward end of St Catherine's was first lit in 1856, and finally, in 1876, the States accepted the pier as a gift from the British Government.[16] St Catherine's is now the home of a thriving yacht club.

The year 1848 was one of Revolutions, most of them unsuccessful, and Jersey became a home of refuge for Republicans and Socialists of many nations, among them Paul Harro Harring, a Dane, who died in Jersey in 1870. The first to arrive were the Poles. Then came Russians, Hungarians,[17] Italians and finally Frenchmen fleeing from the wrath of Louis Napoleon. In 1852 Victor Hugo arrived. Poet, dramatist, novelist and politician, he had stormed against Napoleon in the Assembly and raised barricades against him in the streets. He fled to Brussels with a price on his head, and, when Belgium expelled him, came to join his fellow *proscrits* in Jersey.[18]

Some of these refugees opened shops; others gave lessons in languages, fencing and phrenology, Hugo wrote *Les Châtiments*, poems which bitterly attack Louis Napoleon, Napoléon Le Petit, as he called him, and part of *Les Contemplations*, which express a quieter mood and include poems reflecting Jersey scenes. In the evenings, at Hugo's home at Marine Terrace, Grève d'Azette, the exiles dabbled in table-turning and the occult. The anniversary of every revolution was celebrated with an orgy of speech-making. Funerals became demonstrations. If a *proscrit* died, he was buried in the Independent Cemetery at St John, known as Macpela; the procession was led by the red flag, the whole colony of exiles marched behind the coffin, a Hungarian, a Pole, an Italian and a Frenchman holding the corners of the pall, while over the grave Hugo would deliver one of his orations.

The French section of the refugees published a weekly paper, *L'Homme*, and in 1855 this brought trouble. England and France were now Allies in the Crimean War, and Queen Victoria paid a visit to Napoleon III in Paris. To the *proscrits* Napoleon was a rattle snake with whom no decent person would associate. Three French Socialists in London published *An Open Letter to the Queen*: 'You have sacrificed your dignity as a Queen, your fastidiousness as a woman, your pride as an aristocrat, even your honour'; *L'Homme* reprinted this. Next day posters covered the walls: 'Have you seen *L'Homme*? It says your Queen has lost her honour. Will you allow the first lady of the land to be insulted with impunity?'. The Queen's Assembly Rooms,[19] the largest building in the town (now swallowed up by Ann Street Brewery), was crowded for an 'Indignation Meeting'. The offending newspaper was burnt on the platform, though a copy is now preserved at La Société Jersiaise. Next day the Lieutenant-Governor expelled the three editors from the Island.

Hugo had disapproved of the letter; but he, with 35 other *proscrits*, signed a protest against the banishment of their colleagues. As a result they too were ordered to leave Jersey. Hugo and his family went to Guernsey, where they remained for 14 years. They had a very rough crossing in the *Dispatch*, which is graphically described in *La Normandie Inconnue*, written by Hugo's son, François-Victor.[20]

Meanwhile a new constitutional struggle had begun. The Laurel party was now in control, and for years they had blocked even the most urgent reforms. At last the Privy Council lost patience and in 1852[21] issued three Orders in Council, establishing a Police Court, a Petty Debts Court and a Paid Police Force for the town. This obvious infringement of the Island's right to govern itself roused furious opposition. Rose and Laurel were for once united. The Royal Court refused to register these Orders and asked to be heard by Counsel. Seven thousand persons petitioned that the Orders might be withdrawn. At length, after 20 months' negotiations, a compromise was arranged. The Council revoked the Orders and the States passed Acts establishing almost all that the Council desired, but in so doing they asserted their right to initiate laws relating to the internal government of the Island.

Jersey now began to realise that further reforms must be introduced, if Home Rule was to survive. If the States were the Island Parliament, they could not continue to consist merely of three groups of officials: Jurats, Rectors and Constables, the latter elected for three years, the others appointed for life. Like other democratic Parliaments they must include elected representatives of the people. In 1856[22] they consented to add to their number 14 Deputies, one from each country parish and three from the town. The first election was held in 1857; but, if reformers hoped this would be a stepping-stone to big changes, they were disappointed. Three only of their candidates were successful. Most of the others returned were sturdy advocates of the *status quo*, and strongly conservative in their views.

In August 1859[23] the Queen paid the Island a second visit. This time there were no marquees and no triumphal arches, for no one knew she was coming. She had been worried by a controversy with her Cabinet, and Prince Albert persuaded her to take a sea-trip. The Lieutenant-Governor had had no warning of her plans until a telegraph official received a message from Cowes that the Royal yacht had left for Jersey. Even then it was assumed that there was no intention of landing. Next morning, however, when the yacht anchored in the roads, and the Deputy-Governor and the Bailiff rowed out to pay their respects, they returned with news that the Queen was coming ashore in half-an-hour. She had had the happy thought that she would like to visit the College to which she had given her name and of which she and successive sovereigns have been 'Visitor'. Then there was a hurry and scurry. A red carpet was hastily procured and a landau from Gregory's stables. Members of the State arrived much out of breath as the royal party landed. The Queen's welcome, as she rode through the town, was embarrassingly boisterous. There were no militiamen to line the route, and impulsive market-women pelted her with bouquets of flowers, so that the Centeniers had the greatest difficulty in getting her carriage through. The College too had been taken by surprise and no preparations made to receive her; indeed they have in their archives a letter of thanks for the address of welcome which had perforce to be composed and sent after her departure. The Queen arrived back at the pier ahead of time and had to wait half-an-hour for a boat to take her to her yacht, but Colonel Le Couteur, her A.D.C., saved the situation. He persuaded her to land again after tea quietly at St Aubin and took her in carriages, once more supplied by Gregory's stables, for a peaceful drive up St Peter's Valley and through the northern parishes to St Catherine, where her yacht picked her up.

This was a transient excitement, but the constitutional struggle was not yet over. Le Cras had returned to Jersey and resumed his stream of pamphlets: *The Origin and Power of the States, The Laws of Jersey and Some Abuses*, etc, etc, etc. In 1858 he sent a petition to the Commons demanding the abolition of the Royal Court and the appointment of the three paid judges suggested by the previous Commission, and also asked for a new Commission to enquire into the laws of Jersey, civil, municipal and ecclesiastical. He followed this up with a second petition, which was presented by George Hadfield, M.P. for Sheffield, who spoke scathingly of the jungle of incomprehensible laws in which Englishmen found themselves entangled, if they went to live in Jersey. The result was the Royal Commission of 1859-60. To this Le Cras presented a memorial of nearly two hundred pages, beginning with a request for the three judges and ending (curiously, as he was a Swedenborgian) with one for the establishment of a bishopric for the Channel Islands.[24]

The Commissioners reaffirmed their predecessors' advice that Crown-appointed Judges should replace the Jurats. The rabid party politics of those days certainly made it doubtful whether judges should be elected. Every Jurat owed his red robe to the fact that he was a party leader, and a Laurel Jurat might well be loth to be hard on a Laurel rascal, as Le Cras was quick to point out in his evidence. The States referred the Commissioners' report to the Parish Assemblies, and, when these turned it down, did nothing further. So Le Cras found a new ally in Serjeant Piggott, M.P. for Reading, who in 1861 introduced into the Commons 'a Bill to amend the constitution of the Court of Jersey'. In spite of the Government's declaration that, 'It is not the habit of this House to legislate on the internal concerns of Jersey', there was a long debate on the second reading, but at last the Bill was withdrawn. Le Cras was however irrepressible. Three years later in 1864 he got John Locke, M.P. for Southwark, to reintroduce Piggott's Bill, and this time it reached the Committee stage. The States then took a plebiscite on the question, 'Jurats or paid Judges?', and, though Le Cras and his committee worked their hardest to whip up voters, in the whole Island they secured only 189 votes. After this defeat Le Cras took little further part in public life.[25]

The Island was now showing further signs of progress. More fine terraces and individual houses appeared on the outskirts of the town, many of them splendid examples of the period. In or about 1864 Daniel Hamon put up a marriage stone on his new house, Beauvoir, at the top of Mont Cochon, with the date, his initials and those of his wife, Mary Jeanne Hamon. In this case the gable walls were to be three feet thick and the front and back walls two feet. The height of the rooms was to be 9 ft. 10 ins. with the windows 6 ft. 2 ins. by 3 ft. The corner stones and surrounds of doors and windows to be dressed in granite, with granite sills projecting ⅝ ins. to allow for the cement plaster. The mortar was to be one third lime, one third '*bonne rouge terre*' and one third gravel. Interior partitions were to be of best quality brick, and the roof in best slates, 22 ins. by 11 ins. fixed with zinc nails, well plastered inside with a lime and sand mixture, the apex of the roof to be in zinc or lead. Inside the first two coats of plaster were to be a mixture of lime, earth and sand, with a third coat of stucco. Hearths were to be of slate, those in the main parlour and the kitchen 18 ins. wide. The joists in the parlours to be '*rouge sap*' (probably the Baltic pine often seen in such houses) 7 ins. wide and 2½ ins. thick at 16 ins. centres; those of the bedrooms 8 ins. wide and 1½ ins. thick at 12 ins. centres, the wall plates to be 10½ ins. wide and 1¾ ins. thick, the rafters 8 ins. wide and 1½ ins. thick at 14 ins. centres; the gutter to be 10½ ins. wide and 4 ins. thick (which suggests a wooden gutter) and the cistern head 6 ins. wide and 3 ins. thick with six down pipes 2½ ins. in diameter. The sash-windows on the front of the house were to be glazed with good English glass and the rest with Bohemian glass. Floor boards of the main rooms were to be red wood and 1 in. thick and those of the bedrooms in white wood ⅞ in. thick. All doors, and considerable detail is given, were to have four panels and moulding. The staircase was to be in red wood with handrail, balusters, nosings and brackets in mahogany. All mouldings, architraves and other such details were to be in the latest fashion.[26]

Details for the building of La Pompe at St Mary in 1886 were rather similar. The builders were William Blampied and Alfred Le Sueur and it was modelled on Lansdowne (now Springland) at Millbrook, the granite being covered with the fashionable stucco. All wood was to be Baltic red pine, with the floor boards in deal and the detailing of the stairs, the 'side boards' to be fitted on each side of the fireplace in the back parlour and the seat of the water-closet were all to be in mahogany. Roof slates were of the type known as 'Bangor Countess' and the whole of the work on the house was to cost £820.[26]

Yet more churches and chapels were built in early Victorian times. St Matthew's was opened at Millbrook in July 1842, St Mark's in October 1844, Grove Place in October 1847, St Andrew's (on the Esplanade) in February 1854, the Presbyterian Church in April 1859, the Congregational Church in Victoria Street in July 1861 almost opposite the Swedenborgian Church opened in April 1849. The number of chapels of ease and the variety of denominations reflect to some extent the influx of English residents. The sailors were not forgotten. In April 1831 a chapel named Bethel had been opened on the harbour at St Helier for the use of seamen, and the original St Andrew's Church was built for the same purpose.[27]

In 1870 the Jersey Waterworks Company, as it was first known, made the old street pumps an anachronism, although many were still to be seen in the town in the early 20th century. In 1870 a railway company, which at this period was administered from the same office in Broad Street and under the same managing-director as the Water-works,[28] and known as the Jersey Railway Company (later the Jersey Railways and Tramways) opened the line between St Helier and St Aubin. In August 1884 a line was opened between St Aubin's Hospital, Mont les Vaux, and the Corbière quarries, and in August 1885 this was linked with St Aubin. The railway tunnel at St Aubin was opened in December 1898. In September 1872 the first turf was cut for the Jersey Eastern Railway, which was to run from St Helier to Gorey. The section from Green Street to Grouville was opened in August 1873 and then extended to Gorey Village. When the earlier cutting below Fort Regent had been extended, Snow Hill was linked with Green Street. It was almost twenty years before the final extension to Gorey Pier was opened in May 1891.[29]

In 1858 telegraphic communication with England was established, and in 1872 the States decided to build Corbière Lighthouse. It was lit for the first time in April 1874. In 1872 the foundation stone was laid for an ambitious enlargement of the harbour, whose arms were to embrace the area between La Collette and Elizabeth Castle. The existing harbour had two drawbacks: it was too small for the ever-increasing traffic and it could not be entered at low tide. When the Queen landed, the Prince Consort asked, perhaps remembering the unfortunate experience of the Queen's cousin,[30] 'Why do you Jerseymen build your harbours on dry land?'. But Jersey's exceptional tidal rise of up to 40 feet at spring tides made any harbour construction difficult, and the States were to be disappointed in this ambitious project.

The number of Jersey ships owned by Jersey firms had doubled in 30 years, thanks to the enormous growth in the cod-fishing industry. Side by side with the large firms of Robin, Fruing and le Boutillier, Falle and Nicolle, were many others bearing Jersey names, among them the brothers Perrée, who in 1851 sold their business to their agents in Gaspé, John and Elias Collas; also in Gaspé peninsula were Valpy and Le Bas, while in Newfoundland one finds Orange, Poingdestre, de Gruchy, Renouf, and Clément. Geographical names too such as Jerseyman Head, Jerseyman Rock, Jerseyman's Harbour and Jerseyman Island bear witness in modern charts to a Jersey presence in Fortune Bay and Placentia in Newfoundland, while the Anglican cemeteries in Gaspé are filled with the names of Jerseymen and their families, who lived and worked on the 'coast' in the 19th and early 20th centuries. A plaque in the cemetery of St George at Gaspé bears the inscription: 'They came on the sea from the Channel Islands of Guernsey and Jersey. Beside the sea they built homes, churches and schools, and from the sea they lived and by the sea they rest'. But the writing was on the wall for the great fishing firms even at the height of their prosperity. The long saga of Jersey's merchant adventurers was drawing to a close.[31]

Chapter Thirty-one

THE OLD ORDER CHANGETH, 1873-1900

On ne murmure pas contre la mer; chacun sçait que c'est un élément où l'inconstance règne: elle enrichit et ruine.–Le Geyt, *Du Varech*

IN 1870 the fleet numbered some 450 vessels and more accommodation was needed. This was why the States had advertised inviting engineers to submit plans for yet another enlargement of harbour facilities. Forty-two had been sent in and the Harbours Committee had chosen that of Sir John Coode.[1] This seemed a wise choice, for he was the most distinguished harbour-engineer of the century. His plan was to build a breakwater out from Elizabeth Castle (this part of the scheme still stands), with another pier threequarters of a mile long running out from La Collette to meet it. But, alas, although the first stone had been laid with such panache, with banners in Jersey French proclaiming that the present harbour (*Cauchies d'Aniet*) of 113 vergées was to be replaced by one of 855 vergées (*Cauchies d'Avenin*), their optimism was misplaced. The planners had not realised the strength of the waves that south-westerly gales send thundering in from the Atlantic. In December 1874 two hundred feet of the eastern pier were swept away. This was rebuilt; but next winter three hundred feet were destroyed. The following winter another great breach was made, and the States gave up the struggle.[2] They dropped the idea of enlarging the harbour and concentrated on dredging. The tumbled blocks of the eastern breakwater remained until 1970, when it was decided to reclaim the adjoining site, and, with more modern techniques, to build accommodation for storage tanks. The failure in 1874 had cost the States £160,000.

Pressure for more harbour space was soon to lessen. The coming of steam led to a decline in local ship-building. Schooners became obsolescent as iron ships and railways replaced the wooden sailing vessel. There was an increasing demand for fresh fish as Canada made a bid for the American market, where the recent Civil War had hindered trade. At a later period refrigeration was to make salting and drying unnecessary. These factors and the States' abortive expenditure on the harbour led to a series of financial crises in Jersey, in which, as so much money was tied up in one industry, many firms and families were ruined.

A proliferation of banking facilities is no new phenomenon in Jersey. In 1797 Hugh Godfray, a wine merchant, had founded what came to be known as the Old Bank. Then came the Commercial Bank of Janvrin, Durell, de Veulle and Company. In 1834 both these banks were drawing on de Lisle and Company of London, the de Lisles having a family connection with the Janvrins. The Jersey Banking Company also drew on London and was known locally as the States' Bank, because, although it was privately owned, its manager was also Treasurer of the States and banked with his own firm. In addition there were the Jersey Joint Stock Bank, a Methodist concern in which the chapels and most of their members kept their money, and two other joint stock banks; the Mercantile Union and the Channel Islands Bank.[3]

In addition to these banks, the parishes, la Vingtaine de la Ville and a number of private individuals issued their own notes. *A Guide to the Island of Jersey*, printed in 1834 as one of the many publications by A.J. Le Cras, states that 'all promissory notes are payable only in the island and its currency; some are guaranteed by personal security and others by the mortgage of houses and land at valuation to the Treasurer of the States. The three principal banks in the town draw bills on London and Paris'. Of the coinage he writes: 'It is supposed that from £50,000 to £60,000 in specie is circulated in the island comprising coin of the realm, States tokens, French crowns, Spanish dollars, franc and half franc pieces' . In 1813 and again in 1831 the States took measures by legislation to protect the public against abuses of the system, which had 'occasioned great inconvenience, loss and even fraud to the injury of the poor and uneducated inhabitants and the soldiers of the garrison'. A *règlement* of 1831 required every person wishing to issue paper money to seek the permission of the Court, to produce two sureties responsible for the amount to be put into circulation and to have an office in town where he must be in attendance every day from 10 to 4 to change his notes. If permission was granted, an Act of the Court was registered against the property of the applicant and his two sureties. However the notes of the Town Vingtaine and the parishes were exempted from the provisions of the Bill, and no one had cause to doubt the reliability of the six main banks.[4]

But in Jersey as in England the days of small privately owned banks were numbered; for the failure of an owner or firm could all too quickly swallow up the small amount of capital involved. In February 1873 the Mercantile Union Bank, the leading bank of the Island, suddenly closed its doors with liabilities of £300,000 and assets of £30,000. This affected not only the depositors; among members of the public £55,000 worth of its notes were in circulation and these in a moment became waste paper. Josué Le Bailly, the chairman, had been a man whom everyone respected. When elected as Jurat,[5] his majority had broken all previous records. Now it was proved that for years he had been robbing those who trusted him, and he was sentenced to five years' penal servitude.[6]

Four months later the Joint Stock Bank also suspended payment. Here there was no dishonesty, but the managers of this Methodist bank were arrested, then honourably acquitted. The auditor however said: 'The directors may be good farmers, but they were not good bankers. Those who conducted the affairs of this bank were not fitted for their office'.[7]

This second failure caused a run on other banks. Of the Union Bank *The British Press and Jersey Times* wrote: 'The approaches to the Bank were crowded. Persons with bundles of notes of all sizes clamoured for immediate change. People were standing on the window-sills, and one man jumped on the counter in his eagerness to possess hard cash'. Crowds even more unruly besieged the Savings Bank which had been founded in 1834.[8] But for the moment these other banks weathered the storm.

They were not all in a healthy state, however. The leading concern was now the Jersey Banking Company or 'States' Bank. On 11 January 1886 a notice appeared on the door: 'Unforeseen circumstances have compelled the bank to suspend payment'. Subsequent investigations showed that for years it had been insolvent and that Gosset, the States' Treasurer, had been gambling wildly with the funds. On 13 January, *La Nouvelle Chronique* published two dramatic leading articles on '*la catastrophe financière*'. It was sufficient shock to the Island to learn that Gosset could no longer honour the States' coupons, but worse was to come. On 12 January the firm of Charles Robin and Company had closed its doors and applied to the Royal Court for permission to meet its creditors for the purpose of making an arrangement to safeguard their interests as well as those of the Jersey Banking Company, as the interests of the two institutions were closely connected.

The second of the leading articles spoke of the firm as the largest, most important and oldest of the Jersey companies:

66 *La Rocco tower, built 1800, before restoration. (Photo:* Jersey Evening Post*)*

AREAS OF CONSERVATION

67 *Marram grass on the dunes at Les Mielles, La Rocco in the distance. (Photo: E.F. Guiton)*

> for more than a century the house of Messrs Robin and Company had advanced from success to success. If Providence had favoured them for many a long year with great prosperity, hundreds of ship's captains, thousands of sailors and fishermen, numerous clerks, indeed the better part of three generations of Jerseymen had borne witness, not only to the excellent care exercised by the administration of this great commercial house, but also to the numberless small amenities which employees had enjoyed as the fruits of their industry.

La Chronique painted a gloomy picture of the future:

> In the old Ordnance Yard at the harbour,[9] the seat of Robin's business, where once the sound of hammer and saw rang out in the vast warehouses and fish stores, where hundreds of men were employed throughout the long winter months, drying and stacking fish; the workshops where sails were mended, the offices which employed numberless clerks and book-keepers and dealt with voluminous correspondence, once the scene of animation and life, a great hive of industry, now there reigned the silence of death.

The reason for the closure of Robin's was that they had borrowed extensively from the Jersey Banking Company to help tide them over a bad season. When fishermen in Canada could not make money in the summer by selling their fish, they relied upon the merchants to advance funds or supplies to help them through the winter. So, although the firm was owner of extensive properties in Canada, beyond the jurisdiction of the Viscount, it could avoid disaster only by coming to some agreement with the Bank before the Judge-Commissioner. In time the owners promised to realise their assets, so that they could settle with their creditors and simultaneously help the affairs of another firm in similar difficulties; for Abraham de Gruchy and Company, owners of the long-established drapery firm, who had interests in banking and the fishing industry, had also been driven into bankruptcy.[10]

Fortunately the Court granted the application made by Robin and Company; for already, on hearing of the closure of the firm, the fishermen in Paspébiac had stormed the food stores and it had been necessary to call in Canadian troops to restore order. There was a precedent for this in the history of the Hudson's Bay Company. The position in Jersey was stabilised with the help of the surviving banks. The Hampshire Bank, which had earlier taken over the assets of the Jersey Joint Stock Bank and was now known as the Capital and Counties Bank, offered to advance to the States the amount due to their creditors. Two other solvent banks, the Channel Islands Bank and the Commercial Bank, also offered to assist the States and thus maintain the reputation of the local administration. On 31 March 1886 Gosset was sentenced to five years' penal servitude.

The year 1886 was a watershed in the history of Jersey banking and of the great fishing firms. On 1 April 1886 the Article of the Jersey Companies Act, which excluded the banks from the clause on limited liability, was repealed. Gradually the surviving banks were taken over by the large English Banking Companies. In 1877 the Channel Island Bank had taken over the Old Bank; these two were absorbed by the London and Midland Bank in 1897. In 1908 the Commercial Bank, once Janvrin and Durell and now, through marriage and inheritance, known as Robin Brothers, was taken over by Parr's Bank and in 1918 by the London, County and Westminster Bank. In 1918 the Capital and Counties Bank was absorbed by Lloyds. These three banks, their titles sometimes shortened, continued to function on the sites of the original Jersey banks. With the addition of Barclays in 1921 and the National Provincial in 1926, the 'big five' and the Jersey Trustees Savings Bank conducted most of the financial business of the Island until after the Second World War, when they were joined by many other banking firms.[11]

Mergers also took place in the fishing trade in Canada. In 1892 John and Elias Collas united with Charles Robin and Company to form the Charles Robin, Collas Company. Gradually the firm diversified its interests, shed some assets, acquired others, merged with a number of allied firms, moved the head office, from Jersey to Halifax, Nova Scotia, and became the firm of Robin, Jones and Whitman. Although the commercial links with Jersey were thus severed, men were still sailing to the Gaspé and Newfoundland to work for the fishery firms in the early years of the 20th century, and a link with relatives on the coast or in other parts of Canada is still maintained by many Jersey families.[12]

Jersey recovered with remarkable speed from the catastrophes of 1886, although the bank crashes were remembered for many years and induced some farmers to revert to the habit of hoarding money at home. Well-to-do English families in ever increasing numbers were settling and spending their money in the Island. They were attracted by the climate, the beauty, the pleasant social life and the good educational facilities. There were also great financial advantages. Jersey was almost the only place in the Queen's dominions that was free from taxes; for the income of the States was entirely raised by the duty on wines and spirits, the harbour dues, the taverners' licences and the letting of the market stalls. There was no direct taxation. In addition to the permanent residents, increasing numbers of summer tourists from England and France were finding their way to the Island. Newspaper advertisements and almanachs of the period show that many Jersey folk were adding to their income by taking lodgers, and new hotels were springing up. Already in 1866 the large Imperial Hotel (later Maison St Louis and now the Hotel de France) was in existence. In the 1880s were built many of the Victorian seaside terraced villas still to be seen at West Park and in the St Luke's district, their names often commemorating outposts of empire and British victories, a reminder of those who retired to Jersey and lived in these then quiet suburbs.

Farming, the backbone of the Island's life, was prospering as never before. Colonel Le Couteur's work in improving the breed of Jersey cows was now bearing fruit and bringing the farmer wealth undreamed of in days before the Herd Book. In 1860 Ansted reported[13] that 1,138 cows had been exported to England at an average price of £16 per head. Twenty years later prices up to £400 were common, and American buyers were known to have paid £1,000 for a cow, though this was a rare occurrence. In the 1880s a new gold mine was discovered. The old custom of the Big Plough (*la Grand 'tchéthue*), when farmers brought their horses to help a neighbour with his ploughing, had not yet died out, and Hugh de la Haye, a Mont Cochon farmer, was entertaining to supper those who had come to help him. He passed round the table as curiosities two huge potatoes that had been given him at a local store. These were cut into pieces at the supper table (one had 16 eyes) and next day were planted. In the spring they produced a large and exceptionally early crop, and the new potatoes, unlike the parent round potato, was kidney-shaped. De la Haye nursed these carefully until he had enough to trade with and then exhibited them in the window of *La Nouvelle Chronique*, where the owner of the paper, Charles Le Feuvre, named them the Royal Jersey Flukes. From this small beginning sprang the early potato trade which attained such huge proportions. In 1858 the Royal Jersey Agricultural Society had lamented that the export of potatoes had 'dwindled to a mere nominal item'. In 1891, 70,000 tons were exported and brought in to the growers nearly half a million pounds. In September 1892 de la Haye's fellow-farmers presented him with an illuminated address and a purse of gold as a mark of their appreciation.[14]

Banks might crash and harbour schemes fail, but into this fortunate Island money kept pouring. New public buildings were erected, including the Town Hall in 1872, the present Markets in 1882 (these were the scene of a great tea-party given to the children of island schools to celebrate the Golden Jubilee of Queen Victoria in 1887), the new Public Library in 1886 and the States' Chamber in 1887.[15]

XIX *Victoria Tower above St Catherine's Bay, 1837. Now the property of the National Trust for Jersey.*

WAR AND PEACE

XX *Fort Regent, built 1810. Now used as a leisure centre.*

XXI *Quétivel Mill, St Peter. First mentioned 1309. Restored by the National Trust in 1979, and now grinding corn. (Photo: David Fry)*

XXII *Cows grazing at Mont au Prêtre, St Helier.*

RURAL JERSEY

XXIII *Tomato fields at St Clement.*

JERSEY GARDENS
IN
SPRING AND AUTUMN

XXIV *A camellia tree in flower. Clairval, St Martin. (Photo: B. de Veulle)*

XXV *Jersey lilies at La Fontaine, St Brelade.*

XXVI *Le Coin, St Brelade, a Janvrin house built in 1763. (Photo: R. Long)*

STATELY HOMES AND GARDENS

XXVII *Waldegrave, Beaumont,* c.*1845. (Photo: P. Stevens)*

The Victorian period also witnessed a resurgence of Roman Catholicism, whose congregations, with the arrival of Irish labour for the building of the harbours, had soon outgrown the chapel in Castle Street and the Irish mission in Hue Street. In 1842 St Thomas' Chapel in New Street (later known as le Cercle St Thomas) was acquired from a group of Anabaptists. By 1870 this proved too small and a site was bought in Val Plaisant on which stands the present dramatically sited Church of St Thomas. It was opened in 1887 and consecrated in 1893. Meanwhile the Irish community had acquired a site in Vauxhall in 1841. Over a period of years and with much alteration and rebuilding has been created the present Church of St Mary and St Peter. A number of other Catholic churches have also been built in country parishes.

Anti-clerical laws in France towards the end of the 19th century led to the arrival of a number of teaching and nursing orders. In 1886 came the De La Salle brothers and in 1909 the sisters known as the Faithful Companions of Jesus. They founded the schools now known as the Beeches and the F.C.J. Convent in Val Plaisant (recently moved to Grainville). Other orders included the Little Sisters of the Poor, who came in 1886, and the Carmelites, the last of whom left Jersey in October 1945.

A familiar sight from 1880 until the Second World War was the 'crocodile' of Jesuit students from Maison St Louis. Already in 1828, when the French government had closed all Jesuit colleges, they had acquired from the Ingouville family, le clos de la Frégonnière, but had on several occasions been refused permission to build. In 1850 Jesuits were allowed back into France, but in 1880 came new anti-religious laws and they returned to Jersey. To their surprise they found that the Imperial Hotel had been built on their land and was for sale. As aliens they were not permitted to purchase the building in their own name, but did so with the help of the English province. With some additional building they converted the hotel into a college. Between 1880 and 1940 some 3,000 students spent three years of their training in Jersey, one of their most distinguished pupils being Teilhard de Chardin. In 1894 they installed an observatory for which they built a miniature 'Eiffel Tower', a familiar landmark until it was demolished in the snowy winter of 1929.

In 1881 a French Naval School settled in Jersey and in 1894 acquired the site of what is now Highlands College. After three years they were replaced by the College of Bon Secours run by the Jesuits. In 1923 the Brothers of Christian Education from Ploermel bought Highlands and set up a Training College. Finally in January 1973 the building was acquired by the States of Jersey to be used as a College of Further Education.[16]

Jersey owes much to this new influx of '*réfugiés de religion*': a number of fine schools, now grant-aided by the States, homes for the aged and infirm including The Limes and St Augustine's, which now form an integral part of the local welfare service, and considerable contributions to scholarship from members of the Jesuit community, notably Père Burdo and Père Rey, who were prominent members of La Société Jersiaise, specialising in archaeology and meteorology respectively.

The year 1880 saw the founding of the Jersey Ladies' College, now known as the Jersey College for Girls. Hitherto the education of women and girls had not been taken over-seriously. Public and Church elementary schools were open to girls as were the dame schools. Apprenticeships in dress-making and allied trades were available, and in the country girls were expected to help on the farms and prepare for marriage. Those of good family were taught by governesses or occasionally sent to school in England or France. In December 1879 *La Chronique* recorded that several '*lycéens et demoiselles en pension dans les environs de Granville*' had missed a boat on Christmas Eve but chartered another to ensure their arrival for the Christmas festivities '*à leur cher petit Jersey*'. *La Chronique* commended the young ladies and remarked that they were decidedly made of stern material: '*il y a de l'étoffe chez ces jeunes personnes*'. Timely provision for their education was already envisaged by a group of islanders.[17]

For some years a move had been made in England to provide for girls the same facilities as the boys enjoyed. In 1864 the Schools Enquiry Commission had found that 'the notion that women have minds as cultivable and as well worth cultivating as men's minds is still regarded by the ordinary British parent as an offensive, not to say revolutionary paradox'. In the 1870s colleges for women were established at the ancient universities, and in 1872 the Company later to be known as the Girls' Public Day School Trust was formed under the patronage of Princess Louise to provide a High School education for girls in London and other cities.[18] The idea of founding a similar school in Jersey was first discussed on 28 November 1879 at a special meeting called in the vestry of Grove Place Wesleyan Chapel. Under the chairmanship of the Reverend Nicolle it was decided to form a limited liability company to carry out the scheme.

In June 1880 an advertisement appeared in the *British Press and Jersey Times* stating that the College, under the patronage of Sir Robert Pipon Marett, Bailiff of Jersey, would open in September.

> It is designed to give to the daughters of residents and others, at an extremely moderate rate, an education of the highest order. Its promoters have long felt there is a pressing need for such an institution in Jersey ... The basis upon which the College is to be directed and governed is similar to that inaugurated by Her Royal Highness the Marchioness of Lorne and other High Schools sanctioned by the Endowed Schools Commission.

Subjects to be taught included Latin, German, Mathematics and branches of Physical Science. When appropriate, girls were prepared for Oxford and Cambridge Local Examinations and for Matriculation of London University. Special attention was to be given to the teaching of French, and arrangements were to be made for those who had studied in France to take the *Brévet de Capacité* in Paris. Within three years the Misses R. Hovey, E. Ahier and L. French[19] had achieved a notable distinction in the Matriculation Examination of London University. The subjects taken included Latin and Roman History, French, German, Arithmetic and Algebra, Geometry, English Language, English History and Geography, Natural Philosophy (Mechanics, Hydrostatics, Optics and Heat) and Chemistry — a formidable list. The *British Press and Jersey Times* of 12 July 1883 wrote of their achievement: 'When it is understood that a failure in any one subject means a failure in the whole examination, we think the College may be proud that in the third year of its existence each candidate sent up for this examination has been successful. We believe that they are the first ladies to have matriculated from Jersey'.

The College first assembled at Adelaide House in Roussel Street; this building was later taken over by the Jersey Modern School, one of the many privately-owned secondary schools for boys which flourished in the 19th and early 20th centuries, among them Oxenford House, Oakwood House, Harleston House and St James' Collegiate School, familiarly known as Parlett's.

In 1887 the Ladies' College acquired their present site (excluding the Mont Cantel property which was added as a Junior School between the wars), and in 1888 the new building was opened.[20] In its early days the school attracted boarders from many parts of the world and so helped to broaden the outlook of the Jersey girls, who attended as day girls or weekly boarders. At first both the Chairman and Secretary were Methodists, and Superintendent Ministers of the Wesleyan church were regularly members of the Council. In 1928 the school was purchased by the Church of England Schools' Trust, which also at the time administered Westonbirt, Canford and Stowe. In 1935 the States of Jersey took over the College, which by then had been renamed the Jersey College for Girls.

Among the earliest pupils was Lilian Mary Grandin, who was the first Jerseywoman to obtain a medical degree and who did pioneer work as a medical missionary in China.[21] Since her day more and more girls have gone on to university or other forms of further training, both from the College and from the other secondary schools for girls founded since 1880. The group of enlightened men, who met in that vestry a hundred years ago, would perhaps be gratified to learn that women now sit in the Juvenile Court, in the Royal Court as barristers and in the States as deputies and senators, while others practise medicine, dentistry and other professions, while playing the role of mother, grandmother and great-grandmother to the new generation, who enjoy all the educational facilities that the Island has to offer. In July 1980 the last male bastion was stormed with the election of Jersey's first woman Jurat, Dr Barbara Myles.

Towards the end of the 19th century three expensive lawsuits highlighted a tension between the Crown and island officials and had repercussions far beyond the comparative insignificance of the cases in question. A Frenchwoman was convicted at the Criminal Assizes, but found to be insane. In 1890 she received the Queen's pardon. This was sent to the Lieutenant-Governor, General Ewart, who ordered her release; but the Bailiff, Sir George Bertram, insisted that the pardon must first be registered in the Court. The General, however, went to the prison when the gaoler was out, overawed the turnkey, carried off the woman and put her on the boat for France. The States fought the matter out before the Privy Council at a cost of over £1,000, only to be told that 'A pardon by the Sovereign acts immediately and requires no further Act to make it effectual'.[22]

Before this matter was settled the so-called Prison Board Case was dominating the scene. At a meeting of the Prison Board the Bailiff was absent and the Lieutenant-Bailiff took the chair. But General Ewart claimed the right to preside, and, when the Lieutenant-Bailiff refused to move, he and the Crown Officers withdrew, taking the minute-book with them. The Privy Council then issued an Order, 'Whenever the Lieutenant-Governor is present, he shall preside'. The States, however, appealed to be heard before this Order was registered. The case lasted four years. Lord Haldane was briefed as the Island's leading Counsel. Five enormous volumes of evidence and precedents were printed, and at last the unpalatable Order was withdrawn; but this victory cost over £5,000.[23]

The States now seem to have suffered from a mania for litigation. In the midst of the Prison Board Case they started a third legal struggle, this time over a paltry £12. They had bought the property called Overdale, now part of the island Hospital system, for the erection of small-pox isolation huts. To extinguish the seigneurial rights they offered £36. But the Seigneur was the Crown,[24] and the Crown officials demanded £48. The States won their case, but their costs came to 50 times as much as the money they had saved.

The old party spirit was now almost dead, though in some country parishes it survived in parochial elections long after Victoria's reign, even churchwardens being selected on Rose and Laurel lines. But in the States, instead of disciplined parties, expected to vote *en bloc*, there were now strong personalities, who swayed one way or another the mass of the members. Those who grew up in the last years of the 19th century were to look back on these men as to a race of giants. Henry Durell (1845-1921), who in his long career was to serve the Island as Advocate, Deputy, Solicitor-General and Attorney-General,[25] had known them all. In his *mémoirs* he tells how, when he returned to the Island after a long absence and began to practise law, he found

> men of light and leading in every department of intellectual life, a powerful *bourgeoisie*, clustered mostly round the shipping and Newfoundland industries, and in every parish families of the gentleman-farmer type, taking an interest — an absorbing interest — in local affairs. In St Helier the trading and commercial classes were far above the average.

No doubt later generations will have a similar regard for those who steered the Island through the hazards of the Occupation and plotted the post-war course to prosperity; but there was surely something special about these Victorian Jerseymen. They were the last generation to have known the centuries-old pattern of Jersey life, unchanged by the advent of modern inventions. Durell blames the disappearance, as he saw it, of men of their calibre on the arrival of the fast tramp steamer, the absorption of local banks by English banking companies and the creation of limited liability companies which demanded combination and concentration as against individual enterprise.

On the Conservative side was Le Couteur Balleine, Rector of St Mary (1856-1879), who in his home would allow only Jersey French to be spoken to or by his children until they were six years old; of him Durell wrote, 'He was the best fighter I have known in our political arena giving and taking the severest blows with apparent unconcern'; and Jurat Josué Falle, an austere aristocrat, who could reduce fools to pulp with his sarcastic tongue; and Edouard Luce, Rector in turn of St John (1870-80), St Mary (1880-95) and St Saviour (1895-1912), who moved round with his broad smile from deputy to deputy, persuading each to vote in the way he desired.

The cause of Progress also had two giants: Philippe Baudains, Constable of St Helier, whose bronze bust may be seen in the Parade gardens, and Durell himself. A born orator, Baudains persuaded the States in 1891 to substitute the ballot box at elections for the old open voting. In his way Durell was as eloquent as Baudains, but whereas the Constable's orations were pulsing with stormy rhetoric, Durell, who was for 22 years one of the Town deputies, pleaded every case with cool, lawyer-like precision. The disappearance of the party system is illustrated by the fact that, though these men were both reformers, they were lifelong opponents, for Baudains drew his inspiration from free-thinking French radicals, his brother-in-law being one of the French *proscrits* and his nephew the radical French politician, Henri Franklin Bouillon, whereas Durell's rigidly religious ideals were those of Gladstonian Liberalism.

Apart from the Progressive Party, formed after the Second World War to expedite reform, and the Democratic Movement, party politics have not again reared their head. There have been efforts from time to time, but they have not been noticeably successful. Perhaps memories of the evils inseparable from the Rose and Laurel system remain in the back of the Jerseyman's mind. Now a member can stand for election to the States on personal record and, if elected, can speak and vote freely with no thought of a party whip to intimidate him. This is too small a community to absorb feelings of animosity engendered by party political strife.

Among the Victorian giants must surely be numbered some of the Bailiffs and Deans: John Hammond (1858-80), who died while presiding in Court, Sir Robert Pipon Marett (1880-84), father of Dr R. R. Marett, Rector of Exeter College, Oxford and a noted anthropologist, Sir George Bertram (1884-98) and Sir William Vernon (1899-1931); Dean François Jeune, who became Master of Pembroke College, Oxford, and Bishop of Peterborough, Dean William Corbet Le Breton (1850-88), father of Lillie Langtry, and Dean George Orange Balleine (1888-1906), father of the historian.[26]

Great changes had passed over the Island during the Queen's long reign. The population had increased from 36,000 to 52,000. A new language had become acclimatised. When Victoria came to the throne, everyone spoke Jersey Norman French, while most people understood and many spoke French. Gradually English was replacing both, although for many years French remained the language for all official proceedings. To this day the prayers in both the Court and the States are said in French, and members answer the roll call with the word '*présent*'. If they have failed to give prior notice of absence, they are said to be '*en défaut*'. Votes are recorded as '*pour*' or '*contre*'. These vestiges of ancient customs harm no one and are a living proof of the continuity of island institutions through the centuries.

In the last year of Queen Victoria's reign, in spite of furious opposition from diehards, the use of English was made optional in the States.[27] Old industries like knitting, oyster-fishing and cider-making for export had passed away. With the advent of steam the great fleet of Jersey-built and Jersey-owned brigantines and barques was fast disappearing and there was no longer any need to enlarge the harbour. When chemical manures were imported, the vraicing harvest ceased to be one of the great events of the year. But new and even more profitable industries had replaced the old, and, in spite of the swarm of retired and leisured people that had descended on the Island, the tough old strain of Jersey character remained little altered; on country farms and in merchants' offices typical Jerseymen abounded, whom no one would ever mistake for either English or Frenchmen.

Chapter Thirty-two

TWO WORLD WARS

The reasonable man adapts himself to the world; the unreasonable one persists in trying to adapt the world to himself. Therefore all progress depends on the unreasonable man.– Shaw

THE EARLY YEARS of the 20th century saw the birth of many institutions, some of which are still with us in the 1980s. A 'Battle of Flowers' was included in the fêtes which were held to celebrate the coronation of Edward VII[1] and proved so popular that, apart from the war years, it has been ever since an annual event, gradually becoming more spectacular and sophisticated. In May 1906 Samuel Falle,[2] who had already had a distinguished career in the Church in England, was appointed Rector of St Helier and Dean of Jersey. A vigorous and forthright man, he made an invaluable contribution to the religious and secular life of the Island. When, in 1919, the Enabling Bill in Parliament gave the Church of England a new constitution, which did not include the Channel Islands, Falle fought over a long period for the ancient rights of the island church to be preserved. In 1931 the Channel Islands Church Representation Measure, passed by the States,[3] brought the Jersey church into the main system with safeguards to ensure the Island's independence, the rights of the States and of the local Parish Assemblies. Dean Falle was also responsible, with similar safeguards, for the transfer of secular education in the Church schools to the control of the States. His broad churchmanship brought him into fruitful contact with men of other denominations, and, caring deeply for the welfare and education of fellow islanders, he helped to found the St Helier's Church Literary Society, the Jersey District Nursing Association and the Jersey Maternity and Infant Welfare Centre. In the 1920s he was Chairman of the Jersey Dispensary and in 1936 a founder member of the National Trust for Jersey. In 1908 the Jersey Eisteddfod was started at his suggestion and under his presidency. Meanwhile his son-in-law, Mr A. H. Worrall, was setting a similar high standard to boys at Victoria College as a much respected Headmaster.

Strangers to the islands are often puzzled by the differences in government, language and economic structure which distinguish Jersey from Guernsey, and it is true that, since the islands were divided into two bailiwicks with separate Governors centuries ago, they have pursued an independent course. A friendly but fiercely partisan rivalry exists between the two larger islands, and one of the major factors in maintaining a link has been the many sporting fixtures between the two, as exemplified by the annual Muratti matches in which Alderney also takes part. In 1905 a cup for inter-insular football was presented by a firm then making the brand of cigarettes known as Muratti and was won in April of that year by Guernsey. There were also many sporting fixtures between the schools of the islands.

As the century advanced, cooperation grew in other spheres. The Jersey Green Room Club, founded in the winter of 1909/10 as the Jersey Amateur Dramatic Society, was later to enter plays in the Guernsey Eisteddfod, while choirs and instrumentalists from Guernsey competed in Jersey. A number of commercial firms had branches in both islands and common interests of an international nature, such as the arrival of television and the question of entry to the Common

Market, were to draw the islands closer together as the century advanced. But long before this, the early, peaceful Edwardian days were to become a nostalgic memory.

At the outbreak of the First World War the British garrison was withdrawn and the Militia mobilised. Three hundred militiamen volunteered for foreign service; they were attached as a company to the Irish rifles and served at the Front until the war ended.[4] As time went on three thousand other Jerseymen joined the ranks and, when the Military Service Act came into force in March 1915, another three thousand were called up. So safe was Jersey considered that a Prisoner of War camp for 1,500 Germans was maintained at Blanches Banques. Large sums were raised for war charities and, when all was over, the States contributed to the cost of the war.[5] Jersey's Roll of Honour numbered 862 killed, among whom were 126 boys from Victoria College, including two who had won the Victoria Cross.[6] As in England, war memorials were erected in all the parishes and in many churches, and a local cenotaph was built in the Parade almost opposite the Town Hall.[7]

But despite the anxieties and sorrows of war, the loss of life and later the deaths in the great influenza epidemic of 1918, the Island itself had remained comparatively undisturbed. What was left of the Militia guarded the coast and telegraphic cables but no enemy came in sight. Occasionally an unfortunate cargo boat was sunk in the Channel; but letters and newspapers arrived regularly; there was no serious shortage of supplies; nothing was rationed except petrol and sugar,[8] and, in spite of the war, the first 40 years of the century were for the most part prosperous, peaceful and carefree. When peace came, the Militia was reduced to one regiment of 500 men, and, in 1928, when the British Government withdrew its financial contribution, this was further reduced, after prolonged debate, to an infantry company of 260, and service was made voluntary.[9]

During this whole period reforms were gradually introduced. In 1907 the number of Town Deputies was increased from three to six. In the same year elementary education was made free. It had been made compulsory in 1899[10] at a nominal charge, the so-called 'Ragged School' providing for those who could not pay the fee. The year 1919 saw three reforms. The old Jersey liquid measures were abolished and English ones adopted. A use was found for the endowments of the ancient grammar schools of St Mannelier and St Anastase, which had long outlived their usefulness. St Mannelier had lost its last pupil in 1860 and in 1863 St Anastase too was left without scholars. The funds were now used to establish scholarships at Victoria College for boys who had spent at least two years in island schools. In the same year women over thirty were given the vote.[11] In 1924 an Act of the States permitted women to sit in the States as Deputies. This was fiercely resisted by the diehards, but they need not have been alarmed, as it was four years before any woman offered herself as a candidate and then she was crushingly defeated.[12] It was twenty years more before the first woman deputy, Mrs Ivy Forster, was elected to the States. In 1925 the Married Women's Property Act abolished the injustice by which a wife's property passed to her husband at her marriage. In 1928 the States at last recognised that they could no longer pay their way without direct taxation and authorised an income tax 'not to exceed a shilling in the pound'. But for years this remained very moderate; when the Germans came in 1940 it was still only ninepence in the pound.[13]

A very welcome royal visit was made at this time by King George V and Queen Mary, and it was then that the arms now in use as parish badges were designed. They first appeared on the loyal address of welcome presented to Their Majesties. The designs were by A. G. Wright, then Art Master at Victoria College, in collaboration with N. V. L. Rybot who had a profound knowledge of heraldry. These designs have no foundation in antiquity but are widely used and are both attractive and distinctive.

In 1923 the burning question of the day was the Imperial Contribution. The British Government asked Jersey for a sum of £275,000 per annum towards the expenses of empire; a

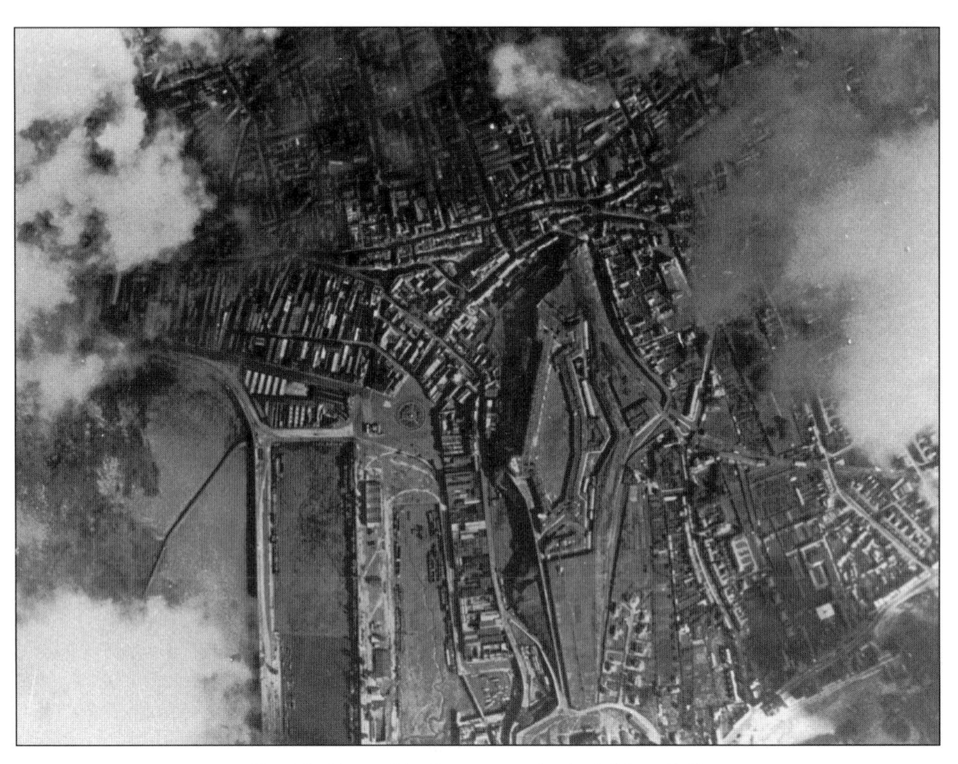

68 *The Fort and harbour as seen by the RAF in 1943.*

AIR RECONNAISSANCE

69 *La Mielle de Morville. A conservation area, 1980, showing Kempt Tower 1834. (Photo:* Jersey Evening Post*)*

vast sum of money at that time, and the States felt bound to refuse. Instead they offered a once only contribution of £300,000 towards the expenses of the war. Alexander Coutanche, who was then Solicitor-General, undertook the protracted negotiations which finally resulted in Jersey's offer being accepted. It was at this period that Lord Coutanche, as he was to become, forged and nurtured the close cooperation with the Home Office, which was noticeably absent before then. His account of these events shows that already the British Government was uneasy about the tax position of wealthy residents in Jersey.[14]

During the placid inter-war years enthusiastic work was carried on by La Société Jersiaise, the local archaeological and historical society, who also owned the Jersey Museum. From its inception in 1873 its members had produced a steady flow of scholarly publications concerning all aspects of island life; now, by strenuous digging, they were making spectacular discoveries which threw light on the Island's earliest history. Among their numerous finds were the cave or rock shelter at La Cotte, St Brelade, where perilous excavation brought to light thousands of relics of paleolithic man (the site has since been excavated by students from Cambridge University under the guidance of the late Professor MacBurney), a neolithic cemetery on Green Island or La Motte, and the dolmen at Les Monts, Grantez, a fine passage grave disclosed when a hummock at St Ouen was removed. Then in 1919 la Société made its biggest gamble: it bought the great mound known as La Hougue Bie. But it was rewarded, for a trench driven into it in 1924 revealed one of the finest megalithic tombs in Western Europe.[15]

New forms of transport now began to change the tempo of life. In 1899 Peter Falla, an old-established solicitor, astonished the town by appearing at the wheel of a new motor-car, a 3½-horse power Benz which travelled at five miles per hour. Others followed his example, including a stock-broker, who, in the 1920s, drove a vehicle powered by electricity and relatively silent. In 1910 a second-hand motor bus began to chug its way between St Helier and St Aubin to the amusement of contemptuous cabbies, whose horses with those of the farmers were still to be seen lining the pavements of the town, their heads buried in nose-bags of hay; but the bus was a portent of things to come. In the next few years a swarm of small proprietors put private buses on the roads, many of them known by humorous nicknames—the 'Orange Boxes', because they were painted yellow, or the 'Hallelujahs', because the owner belonged to the Salvation Army. Then an English company stepped in, the Devon Motor Transport, which soon had a fleet of buses running to every corner of the Island and known as the Jersey Motor Transport Company or briefly as the J.M.T. All this competition meant death for the railways. In 1929 the Eastern Railway died without a struggle; but the other line put up a gallant fight for existence. It substituted rail-cars for trains and started buses of its own to link its stations with places like St Brelade and Portelet. Faced with competition from the J.M.T. the Jersey Railways and Tramways bought the bus company in August 1928. The winter train service was dropped in 1932 and three years later the company ceased altogether to use rail-tracks and relied entirely on road transport. Later the western line from town to St Aubin was paved over, forming a pleasant esplanade along the edge of the foreshore; the Corbiére track became a tree-lined gravel path known as the 'Railway Walk' and much enjoyed by islanders and visitors alike. The more substantial station buildings have survived as dwelling houses or cafés, while the Terminus Hotel at St Aubin, once part of the station complex, makes an admirable Parish Hall for St Brelade.[16]

A more shattering innovation was air travel. Jersey had welcomed the first sea-planes in 1912, when the French Aero-Club organised a race from St Malo to Jersey and back. Seven sea-planes entered, of which two failed to rise, one turned back half way and four landed for half-an-hour in St Aubin's Bay to refuel, and then returned safely. So hazardous had this feat appeared, that a string of torpedo boats had patrolled the course to pick up those who fell. In 1925, however, sufficient progress had been made for Imperial Airways to start a service of flying-boats to Guernsey, some of which came on to Jersey, if passengers so desired. But this venture did not pay and was discontinued. In 1931 two young men began a bi-weekly service to Southampton; but this too proved a failure. In 1933, however, Jersey Airways commenced a daily service, landing on the sands at West Park. This was extremely inconvenient, as the timetable had to be altered daily to suit the tide. Nevertheless, in the first year, nearly 20,000 passengers were carried. When the States built St Peter's Airport, which was opened in March 1937, London became little more than an hour's journey from Jersey and the Island's links with England were immensely strengthened.[17]

Another important innovation was the introduction of a mains supply of electricity in 1924. This first came to Jersey through the enterprise of the Parish of St Helier, which granted a concession to Messrs Crompton and Company for the supply of electricity to the Town in that year, and they began to furnish it in July 1925. The concession remained with the parish until 1936, but there were complications, as its validity was queried. In 1936 the shareholders sold to the Electrical Supply Corporation Ltd, and in August 1936 the States purchased the whole of the ordinary shares of this company. Since then, although they have issued shares to the public, the States have retained overall control of the company and the supply has been extended to the whole Island.[18] During these inter-war years a generous benefactor was showering gifts on his native island. T. B. Davis[19] was a Jersey boy, who had made a fortune in South Africa. In memory of his son Howard, who had been killed in the First World War, he presented to the Island the Howard Davis experimental farm at Trinity, the Howard Davis Scholarships (originally intended to provide education and maintenance at school and university for boys from elementary schools who wished to take up appointments in the then British Empire), the Howard Hall at Victoria College, the Howard Davis Park at Plaisance and the *Howard D* life-boat. Few benefactors can have given more to their homeland. Other generous donors at this period were Sir Jesse Boot (later Lord Trent), founder of Boot's the Chemist, and his Jersey-born wife, née Florence Rowe, whose name is commemorated in the Florence Boot Estate and the F. B. Playing Fields at Grève d'Azette.

Another generous benefactor at this time was Miss Emilia Augusta Barreau. She had inherited £8,000 from her nephew, a talented water colourist, and decided to devote this sum to the building of an art gallery at the Museum of the Société Jersiaise at Pier Road as a suitable permanent memorial to her nephew, Arthur Hamptonne Barreau. This was opened in January 1925 by the then Bailiff, Sir William Venables Vernon, who was also at the time President of La Société. The gallery now houses its permanent collection. At intervals exhibitions are held of works by local artists, of which the most memorable was the one held in 1979 to commemorate the 150th anniversary of the birth of Sir John Millais, an *originaire* of Jersey.[20]

Between the wars farming continued to progress along lines already established in the early years of the century. England, America, Denmark and South Africa were competing for all the cows the Island could afford to part with. In 1910 over a thousand went to the United States alone, where the prices, we are told, were 'exceptionally high'. Tomatoes, with which a few farmers had begun experiments nine years before, brought in £72,000 in that same year. But potatoes still held the first place, more than half of the arable land being devoted to this crop, which in 1912 earned half a million pounds and in 1919 almost a million. These exports continued to increase steadily, but farming methods did not change very rapidly. Potatoes were still planted and dug by hand, though the tractor was gradually ousting the horse. The freshly-dug potatoes were then packed in hundredweight barrels and taken to town in the traditional horse and van, although by the mid-30s these were being replaced by the motor lorry. The load was then sold to one of the merchants waiting on the weighbridge, and the farmer would drive to the merchant's store, usually on the Esplanade, for packing and eventual shipping to the United Kingdom. The long queue of vans and then lorries, waiting their turn to sell for subsequent packing, was an outstanding feature of the potato season until the mid-50s.[21]

Cider was still made on many farms, and a considerable amount of grain was grown until the mid-50s. Originally, the threshing was done on the farm but, in later years neighbours would co-operate and take the grain to a threshing centre. Vraic was still collected by horse and cart, dried and spread on the land, the smallest and steepest cotil[22] being considered worth cultivating. One could still see cows being hand-milked in the fields and uncultivable cotils, now often rank and overgrown, were cropped by heifers.

But a tiny enemy was advancing. The Colorado beetle, first noticed by naturalists in 1855 in the Rocky Mountains, had slowly munched its way across America to the Atlantic and crossed to Bordeaux with the American troops; it had spread through France, appearing outside St Malo in 1936. In February the States lodged *au greffe* a proposition to introduce compulsory spraying of potatoes with an arsenate of lead mixture, and declaring the ports of St Malo, Granville and St Brieux 'infected areas as from April 4'. This high-handed treatment of French harbours was described as 'panicky legislation' by the opposition and unlikely to find favour with H.M. Government. Nevertheless on 12 March by 42 votes to two the States decided to impose compulsory spraying; the Constable and Deputy of St John alone voted '*contre*'. On 6 April a protest meeting was held by farmers in St Lawrence and St John, when it was decided to organise an island-wide petition. Other such meetings followed. On 25 April a leading article in *Les Chroniques* spoke of a grave crisis 'L'heure est grave ... cette résistance de nos cultivateurs possède la sympathie de la grande masse du public ... jamais de mémoire d'homme il n'a existé dans cette île un tel état d'esprit que celui qui règne actuellement parmi notre communauté'. On Monday 27 April, at a special sitting of the States, the Constable of St John[23] proposed an amendment to rescind the order. *The Evening Post* wrote: 'One of the most momentous sittings of the States was held today ... unprecedented scenes were witnessed outside the States' building, as several hundred farmers vainly tried to gain admission to the building.' Once more a decision was deferred by lodging *au greffe*. Finally on 11 May a resolution from the Constable of St John that there should be no spraying was adopted by 33 votes to 16 and the Committee of Agriculture resigned. The farmers gathered in the Square had won their battle. A young man, who had taken a prominent part in the opposition to compulsory spraying, addressed the assembled farmers on this occasion from the balcony of the United Club, his name Cyril Le Marquand, a name destined to become famous in the post-war political life of the Island.

Three years later there was a happy interlude which gave much pleasure to islanders, but which was to have a sad sequel. A destroyer was named H.M.S. *Jersey* (the sixth naval vessel to carry the name). She was launched by Mrs Coutanche, wife of the Bailiff, in 1938 and visited her island namesake in July 1939 just before the outbreak of war. There was at Springfield a ceremonial presentation of gifts subscribed for by enthusiastic islanders. She was not a lucky ship. In September she was in collision with another vessel, in December she was torpedoed with severe loss of life and in 1941 she was blown up by a mine and sank in Malta harbour, again with heavy loss of life.[24]

The outbreak of war in 1939 came as a rude shock to many islanders. At first everyone expected the experience of the previous war to be repeated. Tucked away safely behind the Fleet and the Maginot Line, Jersey, too insignificant to be bombed, was said to be 'the safest place on earth'. Excellent crops and high prices promised prosperity for the farmers, and, as late as March 1940, Jersey was advertised in the English papers as 'the ideal resort for wartime holidays this summer'. But the phoney war soon ended and there came the collapse of Belgium and the evacuation from Dunkirk. On 18 June the Germans entered Cherbourg. On the 22nd they captured St Malo, and on that day France surrendered. Jersey lay within range of the enemy's guns.[25]

After Dunkirk a British force had been sent to France to help stem the German advance. When the French surrendered, these troops had to be brought home without delay. Early on the 16th the Bailiff received orders that all available small craft must be sent at once to St Malo, and, with the help of the Harbourmaster and the Yacht Club, this was promptly done. For three days these craft were kept busy ferrying back soldiers, who rapidly dug themselves in. At first there was a plan to hold Jersey, at least until withdrawal from France was complete, and additional troops were sent from England for this purpose. The question of a compulsory evacuation of the civilian population was also considered. But the German thrust swerved aside towards Rennes, giving time for the last of the St Malo troops to embark for England. Whitehall then decided that the defence of the islands was impracticable.

On 1 September 1939 the Militia had been mobilised. The men had reported on the following morning to their respective arsenals for medical inspection and the drawing of arms and equipment. In the afternoon they assembled at the Town Arsenal and marched to Fort Regent, where they were quartered until June 1940. It was their commanding officer, Lieutenant-Colonel H. M. Vatcher, M.C., who, on duty on the night of 18/19 June, took the order for demilitarisation. Next morning he informed the Lieutenant-Governor, Major-General J. M. R. Harrison, who then announced to the States and the Island that he had been recalled, that the troops would be withdrawn and that the Island, now declared an 'open place', would be left undefended. He also informed the islanders that ships were on their way to evacuate to England any who wished to leave. Faced with the disbanding of his force, Colonel Vatcher asked the Lieutenant-Governor and the Bailiff for permission to leave the Island with his men. By an Act of the States passed on 20 June the battalion was disbanded and, although it had been raised solely for the defence of the island, its members to a man volunteered to go over to England to join the forces there. At 3 p.m. on 21 June 11 officers and 193 other ranks left for England on a potato ship, the *S.S. Hodder*: the first and last time that the Royal Militia of the Island of Jersey[26] left these shores as a complete unit.

Meanwhile Alexander Coutanche, the Bailiff, was sworn in as Civil Governor, at the request of the Home Office, with the invidious duty of surrendering the Island to the enemy and making the best terms he could for the inhabitants. Evacuation took different forms in the four islands. In Jersey it was left to the individual to decide for himself, in the light of his several responsibilities, whether to leave or to stay. Should he abandon his home and property and seek safety in England or should he remain to face the unknown perils of invasion? Should he volunteer for the armed forces in England or should he send his wife and children away and remain to help the Island as best he could? In round figures 10,000 left the Island and 41,000 remained. In Guernsey, possibly because the schools had been evacuated, a larger proportion chose to leave, making the ratio of invaders to residents higher in that island.

Some of the refugees stepped ashore in a strange land with only a single suit-case. But plans had been made to receive them. Many of the men of military age joined the forces as soon as possible, though as volunteers they sometimes had to wait months for their call-up. Of the rest the majority were billeted in the northern counties, particularly in Bolton and Glasgow. Smaller groups were settled in Swansea, Bath, Bristol, Bournemouth and Exeter. Until work was found, the British Government provided free board and lodging and 18 pence a week as pocket money. But Channel Islanders, who already lived in England, proved in a practical way their love for their native land by forming a highly efficient committee to care for exiles, while Channel Island Societies were formed in many parts of the country where exiles could meet and exchange news, often received through Red Cross messages or later via the camps for deportees.

Meanwhile in Jersey on 27 June German planes began to fly overhead. On the 28th they started machine gunning and dropping bombs, and a number of civilians were killed. For two more days they swooped over the chimney-pots to create an atmosphere of alarm. Then on 1 July they dropped an ultimatum ordering that large white crosses be painted on certain spots and white flags flown from every building. 'If these signs of peaceful surrender are not observed, heavy bombardment will follow.' That afternoon a German force arrived by plane, the Bailiff himself lowered the Union Jack at the Fort and drove to the airport, where, accompanied by the Crown Officers, he had the heart-breaking task of handing over the Island to the enemy.

For the next five years Jersey was under Nazi rule. Alexander Coutanche, later to be knighted and then created Baron Coutanche of Westminster and St Brelade, the first Jersey life peer, had a more difficult task than any Jerseyman before or since. He had to maintain a delicate balance between unnecessarily offending the invaders with consequent reprisals being inflicted on the inhabitants, and running the risk of being accused of collaboration. He also had to watch the steadily dwindling food supplies, particularly during the last few months of Occupation, and take what steps he could to remedy the serious situation without creating alarm.

The German Commandant took up residence in Government House. Troops were quartered in the large hotels and houses, at first only 2,000, but for the last four years 12,000 on average. Military police patrolled the streets and secret field police in plain clothes were ever watchful for hints of disaffection. The *Evening Post*, the local daily paper, was controlled by a German editorial staff, but was still available for the publication of notices and orders, the 'exchange and mart' columns being used by the islanders with commendable ingenuity. Troop commanders came and went, and to the average civilian they were mere names; but one man left his mark on the Island. Count Rudolf von Schmettow, a Silesian nobleman, descended from a long line of Generals and Field-Marshals, arrived as Commandant in Jersey in September 1940, was promoted in 1943 to be Commandant of the Channel Islands, and was removed only in the last hectic months, when Hitler's régime was tottering to its fall. Though he realised that the population was hostile to his rule, and though he sometimes had to enforce harsh orders that came from Berlin, all who had dealings with him found him courteous and considerate, and he probably saved Jersey from some of the evils which other occupied countries endured. The discipline of the troops remained unimpeachable almost to the end, and, though there were no doubt bad men among them, as in all conscript armies, there was little crime.

The story of the Occupation has been told by many pens. Here it can be sketched only in outline. It falls into three parts: the Occupation itself, the making of the fortress and the siege. For the first 11 months the Germans were settling in. Even before the enemy arrived, when surrender seemed to be inevitable, the States began to make plans to cope with the new conditions. They resigned many of their powers to eight sub-committees, to each of which was entrusted one essential department of the Island's life, and these were authorised to act promptly without consulting the States. The Germans allowed these committees to function, realising that it would be easier to deal with them than to set up machinery of their own; and for the next five years these eight little groups, confronted by wholly unfamiliar problems, and harassed by German demands, did their best to steer the ship through the storm. Their eight Presidents, with the Crown Officers and the Bailiff, formed a kind of Cabinet known as the Superior Council.

The most pressing problem was food. For years Jersey had specialised in agriculture for export and had imported from England all that it needed for its own use. Now that English supplies were cut off, there could be nothing for man or beast, except what the Island could grow. The Department of Agriculture had to revolutionise the whole system of farming. It ordered four-fifths of the potato land to be sown with corn and claimed the right to buy and distribute all the food that was grown. In order to grind the grain into flour, some derelict water-mills were repaired, among them Quetivel (this mill after years of post-war neglect was burnt down in 1969, but has recently been restored by the National Trust for Jersey and is being run as a working mill). Sugar-beet was planted to provide sugar, and the inhabitants found their own means of making *ersatz* coffee and tea, boiled sea-water to obtain salt and invented new dishes from their limited supplies.

But there were many things that Jersey could not produce. For these the only possible source of supply was France. The Department of Essential Commodities obtained permission from the Germans to establish a purchasing office at Granville; but the French, desperately short of supplies themselves, were not easy to persuade to spare anything for Jersey. Eventually, when the Germans, to use their own phrase, 'rectified the map of Europe' by placing the Channel Islands for many purposes under le Département de la Manche, they allowed Jersey the same meagre rations that they granted to Occupied France.

The Labour Department also had some hard nuts to crack. Nearly three thousand men and women had been thrown out of work by the closing down of hotels and offices and the lack of harbour traffic. Some way had to be found by which they could earn a living. The men were used to widen roads and to construct new ones, their main achievement being the fine Route du Nord along the northern cliffs. Here and on Noirmont Point there are commemorative stones to the memory of the men and women of Jersey who suffered in the Second World War. Later, when the fuel problem became urgent, and coal supplies were exhausted, they cut down trees and sawed them into logs. Without this work, everyone would have frozen and nothing could have been cooked. Before the end came 200,000 trees had been felled, a hideous but necessary sacrifice, but one which 30 years later has been mercifully erased by nature and by the efforts of such bodies as the Men of the Trees. A number of men were also employed, when leather could be obtained from France, in making boots with soles of Jersey beech. For the women a clothing factory was opened, which kept hundreds employed. Much skill was revealed in the creation of new garments from scraps of material, and the children in particular and in spite of shortages were noticeably well dressed.

All this required money, and the Finance Department was faced with a Herculean task. Not only had it to meet the bills of all other departments and help large numbers of English residents, whose pensions no longer reached them, but, by the terms of the Hague Convention, it had to pay the expenses of the Army of Occupation. At one time 16,000 troops were stationed in the Island and the number seldom fell below 10,000; their food, their light, their fuel, the wages of their huge civilian staffs, the constant structural alterations that they demanded in their billets, had to be paid for by the States, and, during the last year, when after D-Day the Island was cut off from the Continent, the pay of the soldiers too.

Income tax was raised to four shillings in the pound (and remains at that sum). Bank notes to the value of £55,000 were printed. But the position would have been impossible, if the banks had not agreed to advance the money needed. As little money could leave the Island, all that was paid out came back to the banks; so they were never short of cash. But by the end of the war, the States owed them almost six million pounds. However the banks gave help by refunding the interest which had accrued on loans to the Island government during the Occupation, and the British Government agreed to provide a capital sum for each island, provided that this gift of money was used solely to liquidate the debts owing to the banks, secondly the States were to ensure the strictest economy in plans for rehabilitation. The banks also accepted States' bonds to cover the balance of the Islands' debts. These generous gestures must have removed a load of anxiety from members of the Superior Council who had coped with the financial problems of the Occupation.

The position had been further complicated by the conflict between two currencies. The Germans flooded the Island with marks and pfennings, not true reichsmarks current in Germany, but reichskreditmarks, printed for use in occupied countries only, which were worth nothing but the paper on which they were printed. It is a well known law of political economy that bad money drives out good; so English coins began to disappear. Many were hoarded, some sent home by German soldiers as curios. The States' notes also vanished, though many must have been saved for the sake of the designs on the back, from drawings by Edmund Blampied, Jersey's most famous modern artist.[29] Soon for ordinary trading purposes nothing was left but marks. But Jersey stubbornly refused to think in anything but sterling. Goods were priced, accounts rendered, banking operations carried out in £.s.d., even though money used had to be marks and pfennigs; and it was no easy task to remember how many pfennigs went to the shilling at the frequently changing rate of exchange.

When the supply of British postage stamps was exhausted, the States printed stamps of their own for island or inter-island letters. One set was designed in 1941 by N. V. L. Rybot, a respected historian and heraldic expert, who displayed a puckish wit in his works. His set bore the Jersey arms and almost invisibly in the corners were the letters AA for Atrocious Adolf and BB for Bloody Benito. Throughout the Occupation there were many examples of island humour leavening adversity. Some of these are recorded in *Jersey in Jail*, published in 1945 by Horace Wyatt and Edmund Blampied, the artist responsible for Jersey's second issue of stamps in 1943. These depicted Jersey scenes and were printed in France.

The Education Department also had unaccustomed difficulties, and much credit must go to those teachers who remained in the Island and manned the schools for the children who had stayed on. Victoria College was commandeered for the *Reichs Arbeits Dienst*, a German Labour Service which was an intermediary service between that of the Hitler Youth and the German army itself. The College Boarding House became the headquarters of the Feldkommandantur.

The College for Girls became first a barracks and then a naval hospital. Pencils, ink, paper, books were unprocurable. Yet in spite of the shortage of teachers, the school-leaving age was raised to 15 to keep the children off the streets. Then came a peremptory command that every child must learn German, and, to avoid having Nazi teachers in schools, volunteers, who could give elementary lessons, were hastily gathered together; but neither teachers nor pupils showed any enthusiasm, and, in spite of special prizes offered by the Germans, little progress was made. Towards the end of the Occupation the children were in any case too hungry and too cold to attend to their lessons, and it was extremely hard for parents outside the town to get their children to school. Medical experts were, however, surprised at the end of the war to find that the health of the children of Jersey was better than had been anticipated; this was attributed to two causes, the shortage of sugar and the daily, if small, ration of full-cream milk, which the authorities had managed to preserve for all children of school age and under. There must be many today who are grateful for the grounding they were given in those difficult years, which enabled them to continue their studies and gain qualifications after the Liberation.

These small Departmental Committees of business men and farmers were confronted almost daily with problems that would have tested the wisdom of Solomon. Being human they made mistakes; but on the whole they did surprisingly well. They acted as a buffer between the Germans and the civil population and they pulled the Island through dangers that might easily have proved fatal. The Royal Court continued to administer both civil and criminal justice, still using the seal granted by Edward I to the Bailiff of the Island; and the States, though many of their functions had been surrendered to departments, were permitted to meet occasionally to pass the Budget. Prayers for the Royal family were allowed in Island churches, and some organists interpreted this as permission to play 'God save the King' for the congregation to sing as a final prayer before returning home.

The second stage in the Occupation began on 20 October 1941 with an order from Hitler, stating that England might for political reasons attempt to recover the islands; therefore they must be made an impregnable fortress (*eine unangreifbare Festung*) on the lines of the Western Wall. Labourers of many races began to pour in; first large numbers of French unemployed supplied by the Vichy government; then hundreds of Spanish Communists and Anarchists, who had been forced to flee their own land at the close of the Civil War; then Poles, Czechs, Belgians, Dutchmen. They were followed by 1,000 Russian prisoners of war, said to have come from a convict colony that the Germans had captured. Certainly they proved themselves expert thieves. Half-starved by their guards, they burrowed their way out at night under the barbed wire and soon created a reign of terror through the Islands. Householders found that their rations disappeared while they slept; newly planted potatoes were scooped out of the fields; one unfortunate farmer who disturbed a party of Russians in his fowl-house, was stabbed to death with their knives. Nevertheless their piteous condition aroused the sympathy of many islanders, and members of one family suffered deportation and the horrors of Belsen as a result of their helping one young Russian. Later came coloured men from North Africa, Algerian prisoners of war, Moroccans, Senegalese. No exact figures remain of the actual number of these labourers, but one of the German contractors alone had more than 7,000 on his pay-roll.

With their help Jersey became a fortress, which experts after its liberation described as 'the strongest in Europe; far more powerful than Heligoland'. Wherever a sandy beach made landing possible, the sands were studded with steel rails, each with an explosive charge. Then came high anti-tank walls of steel and reinforced concrete. Then a broad mine-field and masses of barbed wire. Then on the heights the guns. Guernsey had the four biggest, taken from a Russian battle-ship. These had a range of 37 miles and covered all the sea between the islands; but Jersey had big guns too. One at St Martin could reach France, and others at La Moye, les Quennevais and St Ouen were almost as powerful. In addition the Island was ringed with cunningly placed, camouflaged gun emplacements, to say nothing of the dummy houses, complete with flower-pots in the windows, which concealed medium guns or machine-gun nests. Six fortresses, carved out of solid rock and roofed with armour-plate, contained every housing amenity, including grand pianos. Mont Orgueil and Elizabeth Castles, long regarded as museum pieces,[30] were strengthened with concrete walls, crowned with fire-control towers, and brought up to date. Every field in which aircraft could land bristled with steel spikes. The old railway to the Corbière was relaid, and branches ran inland from this track across St Peter, St Mary and St John to Ronez quarries. Another line ran from l'Etacq round St Ouen's Bay; a third linked the town, via a tunnel under South Hill, with Gorey. A radar station was built at Les Landes, St Ouen (this is still standing), and telephone wires ran from the battle headquarters at Panigot, St Peter, to every point in the defence. For storing ammunition tunnels were driven deep into the rocky hills, and a huge underground hospital was made, after the invasion of Normandy, with 260 beds and several operation theatres, but it was never used. With justice the Germans called Jersey 'the mailed fist of the Western Wall'. A direct assault must have entailed enormous casualties. This was fully realised at Whitehall and so no attempt was made to recapture any of the islands, even after the Normandy landings. This is fortunate, because of the damage which would have resulted in such a small and, even at that time, thickly populated place. This was resented by many, both in and out of the Island, who felt that no effort was being made to save the only part of the British Isles in enemy hands. Reconnaissance photographs taken by the R.A.F. during the war reveal that the Government was well aware of the fortifications in the Island.

But what of the 40,000 inhabitants who had to live in this fortress? Their attitude can be summed up in two oft-repeated maxims: 'Only a fool kicks against the inevitable', and 'If you have to share a cage with a tiger, it is better not to twist its tail'. But in June 1942 an order was published that aroused deep resentment: All wireless sets were to be handed in. This was challenged for three reasons. The German ultimatum had solemnly guaranteed the property of peaceful inhabitants. The Hague Convention allowed the seizure of 'appliances adapted for the transmission of news'; but wireless sets only receive, and Frenchmen in Occupied France were allowed to retain their sets to the end. The Bailiff refused to countersign the order; but the German authorities in the Island declared that they could do nothing, as the confiscation was 'decreed by higher command'. Two brothers issued a cyclostyled pamphlet, *Bulletin of the British Patriots, No. 1*, which they dropped into letter-boxes at night: 'We have carried pacification to the point of seriously compromising our honour'. This infuriated the Germans, who seized 10 prominent islanders as hostages: after some days the authors of the pamphlet were discovered and the hostages released. Over 10,000 radios were handed in, the majority of which were sent to Germany, but a large number were hidden in lofts, up chimneys and even in the organ of a chapel. As the months passed, more than 700 clandestine sets were discovered by the Germans and their owners sent to prison; but still the news circulated surreptitiously throughout the Island.

A heavier blow was to follow. In September the Germans announced: 'By order of higher authorities the following British subjects will be transferred to Germany; all not born in the islands, together with their families'. Again the Bailiff protested vigorously, but was told that remonstrance was useless. The order came from Hitler's headquarters and had to be obeyed. The Superior Council then threatened to resign and to throw the whole responsibility for the Government of the Island on the Germans; but on second thoughts they decided to carry on their thankless task. At the first deportation, 1,186 were carried off; 140 followed later. As one of the boats left harbour a defiant deportee was heard to sing 'There'll always be an England'. The reason for the order appears to have been a form of reprisal against the British request that Germans living in Iran should be interned. The exiles went to three camps in southern Germany, where, apart from the boredom of life behind barbed wire, they were not ill-treated. Indeed, thanks to Red Cross parcels, they were better fed than they had been in Jersey and were able to send letters to England as did prisoners of war, as against the 25-word messages allowed to islanders through the Red Cross messages sent from Jersey. Nevertheless their deportation had caused great distress and indignation within the Island.

In Jersey meanwhile supplies were growing less and less. It was a sign of the times when one of the largest grocers in the town had nothing to put in his windows but pink toilet paper cut from sheets normally used for packing tomatoes. The butter ration came down to 2 oz a week, the meat to 4 oz, the bread to 4lb 4 oz, and everyone's waist-line grew slimmer. Naturally there was much grumbling, and the Superior Council was blamed for not compelling the Germans to make life more comfortable. The *Times* published a letter, written by a lady to her daughter and brought to England by a lad who managed to escape from Jersey, in which she said: 'The States are in a condition of complete jitters, and give way to the Germans in everything'. Whereas, in reality, a perpetual struggle was going on behind the scenes. Early in 1941 an order arrived that all church bells were to be sent to Germany; but on appeal to Paris this was withdrawn. Orders were frequently issued that only skimmed milk should be supplied to islanders, but these were so firmly resisted that at the end Jersey was the only occupied territory that was getting full cream, even Guernsey having been placed on 'skim'. In 1943 the R.A.F. sank off Noirmont a supply ship coming from France. Three days later, as a reprisal, the Germans knocked 20 per cent off the bread ration. The Bailiff at once expostulated that to take reprisals on civilians for a legitimate act of war was an unheard of breach of international law, and requested that his protest might be forwarded to the Swiss Ambassador in Berlin. The result was that the old ration was restored. A fierce tussle took place over an order that 250 skilled mechanics should be sent to France; but this was eventually revoked, and the Labour Department put up a large notice in their office calling attention to the fact that, by the Hague Convention, no one could be compelled to work for an occupying force. The number of German orders that the Court refused to register must by the end of the Occupation have amounted to several hundred; but of all this the Island knew little or nothing, for the German-controlled newspapers were not allowed to mention such matters. Lord Coutanche used to say in after years that his epitaph should be: 'I protested'.

Worse, however, was in store. On 6 June 1944, the allied armies landed on the Normandy beaches. Cherbourg was captured on 1 July, Coutances on the 28th, Granville on the 31st. Jersey listened to the sound of the guns and could see the smoke from the burning towns and villages, and hearts were filled with hope. On 17 August St Malo surrendered. Now all the opposite coast of France was in the hands of the allies; but for 10 months more the fortress of Jersey remained in German hands and Jerseymen endured the strange experience of being besieged by the British fleet. The ships kept out of range of the guns, but nothing could get in or out of the islands, the intention being to starve the garrison into surrender. This however meant starving the civil population as well. The salt ration, the sugar ration, the butter ration ceased. The bread ration was reduced to 2 lb a week, then to 1 lb; then it petered out altogether. The fuel supply also failed, as the half starved men of the Labour department no longer had the strength to saw. Gas and electricity failed, and candles were unobtainable; so from sunset to sunrise everyone had to grope in the dark. Water was only pumped at intervals.

In August 1944 the Bailiff had sent a long memorandum to the Germans giving the dates on which supplies of essential stocks would run out, adding:

> It is an undisputed maxim of International Law that a military power, which in time of war occupies any part of the inhabited territory of an adversary, is bound to provide for the maintenance of the lives of the civilian population. Sooner or later the clash of arms will cease, and the Powers will meet, not only to consider the means of an enduring peace, but also to pass judgment on the authorities, be they civil or military, upon whose conceptions of honour, justice and humanity the fate of occupied peoples and places has been temporarily determined. May the Insular Government be spared the duty of adding to the problems, which will face the Powers, an allegation that, by an unjustified prolongation of the siege of Jersey, the military representatives of the German Government unnecessarily endangered the health, and indeed the lives, of the people.

Meanwhile in England that ultra-patriotic Jerseyman, Lord Portsea (formerly Sir Bertram Falle),[31] had long been trying to lash the House of Lords into making efforts to send food to the islands. He had even offered to take a food ship across himself and run the risk of her being sunk. Finally they listened, and the two-fold prodding, of the British by Lord Portsea and the Germans by the Bailiff, at last had some effect. Arrangements were made by which the Red Cross was permitted to send twice a month a neutral ship loaded with food from Lisbon. On 30 December the *Vega* arrived with 750 tons of food parcels. No one who was in Jersey at that time will forget the opening of his first food parcel. Into the pattern of the paving stones of the Royal Square a workman set the word VEGA, unnoticed by the occupying force but recognised by a grateful population.

On 28 February 1945 the Islands received a new Commandant. The plot against his life had made Hitler doubtful of the loyalty of officers of the old aristocratic type, who had never been members of the Nazi party. Von Schmettow was suddenly removed from his command and replaced by Vice-Admiral Hueffmeier, a Nazi with a reputation for bull-dog determination. In a speech to his troops in the Forum cinema he said: 'The first duty of a fortress is not to be captured by the enemy. I mean to hold out here, here with you, till the victory is won'. And he had no intention of remaining on the defensive. Nine days after his appointment he organised a raid on Granville. The Americans were taken by surprise. Locks were destroyed; fires were started; six ships were sunk; German prisoners of war were freed and British and American prisoners captured, including a Lieutenant-Colonel.

But in May the end came. On the lst Hitler committed suicide. On the 8th his successor, Grand-Admiral Doenitz, ordered the surrender of all German sea, land and air forces. On the same day Churchill declared the war in Europe at an end, adding 'Our dear Channel Islands are to be freed today'. His speech was relayed by loud speakers to an immense crowd in the Royal Square, the Bailiff ran up the Union Jack on the Court House, and on almost every flagstaff in the Island other Union Jacks appeared. When the destroyers *Bulldog* and *Beagle* arrived off Guernsey to receive the surrender, Hueffmeier sent a curt message that, if they did not depart at once, he would regard their presence 'as an act of provocation'; and they had to steam out of gunshot. Next morning, however, he realised, or was made to realise by his officers, that further resistance was impossible, and he sent a Major-General out to sign the instrument of surrender. The *Beagle* than came to Jersey and received a tremendous welcome. In the afternoon British troops arrived and the Germans were disarmed.

After the First World War the islanders had been thrilled to welcome King George V and Queen Mary, with the Princess Mary, in the hot summer of 1921. Now on 7 June 1945 morale was wonderfully raised by a flying visit by King George VI and Queen Elizabeth, only a month after Liberation, a Royal act which was deeply appreciated. Hasty arrangements were made and the traditional Loyal Address was presented to His Majesty in the States' Chamber. The King also inspected a parade of representatives of all organised associations, drawn up in St Saviour's road, before flying on to Guernsey. In September the Queen presented a silver cross and candlesticks to St Helier's Parish Church as a thank-offering for the Liberation of the Island.

In the months immediately after the end of the war there remained much for the troops and civilian authorities to tackle; a fortress to be dismantled, supplies to be brought in, arrangements made for the return of evacuees and deportees. But on that first 'Liberation Day', 9 May 1945, which by a happy coincidence was also the Bailiff's birthday, one thought alone was in the minds of occupied and exiles alike. The long ordeal was over.

Chapter Thirty-three

THE AMAZING RECOVERY

We have a limited amount of space and much to fit into it.–Nos Iles

NO ONE WHO WATCHED the departure of the occupying force in 1945, or returned to the Island in the following months after enforced exile in England, could have foreseen what was to happen in the next 35 years of the 20th century. A group of these exiles, in 1944, published *Nos Iles*, a symposium on the Channel Islands, in which they set forth, often prophetically, though occasionally with undue pessimism, the post-war needs of the islands. These included secondary education for all, a further development of the tourist industry, an encouragement of the traditional forms of agriculture and greater cooperation between the islands in matters of mutual concern. There were no plans for new trades or industries, as they considered that the possibilities for these were very limited. Perhaps their most penetrating glimpse of the future was their insistence on the need for careful planning of land utilisation. But what they could not reasonably be expected to foresee was how quickly Jersey would recover from the austerities and tribulations of the Occupation, the tremendous growth of the economy and of the population that was to come, with all the political, social and environmental problems that this would create.

Throughout the Occupation there had inevitably been a good deal of cavilling. There were many who thought that they could have managed this or that better; and the Superior Council was never able to explain or defend its actions. In 1942 this muttering found an outlet in the Jersey Democratic Movement, which rather strangely the Germans fostered, granting paper for its publications, when no one else could get any. In a series of pamphlets it fanned discontent, doing all it could to undermine the authority of the Council. In 1944 it started *The Workers' Review*, which later became *The Jersey Democrat.* As soon as liberation came, this party organised a monster petition to the King asking for a Commission of Inquiry 'to report on all the activities of the Council and the States during the Occupation', and for a plebiscite to be taken 'to enable the people to vote for or against incorporation of Jersey with England as an English county', or 'in the event of the majority of the islanders voting against incorporation', for a Commission to establish 'a just, equitable and representative form of government'. By wheeling this petition about on barrows and waylaying everyone who came to town on market-days, the organisers managed to collect over 6,000 signatures; and they chalked the walls everywhere with the slogan, 'Out with the States'.

But soon it became evident that most of those who signed the petition were far from being supporters of the J.D.M. programme. They had put their names merely as a protest against some personal grievance. When the elections for Deputies for the States took place in December 1945, the J.D.M. put up 12 candidates, but only one of them was returned, most of the others being defeated by overwhelming majorities. But in spite of this it was recognised that the time had come for the Constitution to be overhauled. The changes were carried out in a truly democratic manner. Before the election the States had extended the franchise to all adult British subjects (hitherto it had been limited to men over twenty and women over thirty who paid rates or taxes on property above a given rental value).[1]

The new States immediately appointed a committee to draw up a scheme for the reform of the Assembly and invited the Royal Court also to consider what changes were desirable in its constitution. The Reform Committee's report was accepted by the States and submitted to the Privy Council, which commissioned five of its members, including the Home Secretary, Chuter Ede, to look into the matter on the spot. They spent a week in the Island hearing evidence and then drafted careful suggestions, which were sent back to the States. These were referred to parish meetings specially called for the purpose, at which 64 per cent voted in favour and 36 per cent against. The result of all this discussion was the two Reform Acts of 1948.[2]

These enacted that for the Royal Court Jurats in future should be elected, not by popular suffrage, but by an Electoral College composed of the Bailiff and Jurats, the States, and all Advocates and Solicitors of more than six years' standing; that normally Jurats must retire at the age of seventy, unless permitted by His Majesty in Council to serve until seventy-five; that in cases before the Court, the Bailiff should be sole judge of law and the Jurats of fact, except at the Assizes, when the Jurats' duty would be merely to determine the sentence. In civil cases also they would assess damages. In the States the Jurats would be replaced by 12 elected Senators 'who might be either men or women', four of whom would retire every three years; the Rectors would cease to have seats *ex officio*, though the Dean might attend and speak, but not vote: no change would be made in the position of the Constables, and the number of Deputies would be increased from 17 to 28, the Rectors' seats, other than the Dean's, going to the additional Deputies, giving six extra to the town, two more to St Saviour and three between the other rural parishes. Adjustments to the composition of the Court and States since these reforms have been of a minor character except in respect of the Jurats.

Wary of too hasty a change in their function, the States included in the 1948 Act the following clause:

> An elected member of the States, by reason of his membership of the States shall not be disqualified for being appointed Jurat and shall be entitled to enter upon and discharge his duties as Jurat without resigning his seat in the States ... provided that in the two years next following the coming into force of this law, the Royal Court and States shall appoint delegates to consider whether it is possible to ensure a complete separation of judicial and legislative functions without unduly depriving the Royal Court or the States of the services of a sufficient number of experienced persons to ensure the efficient discharge of the functions both of the Royal Court and of the States.

The last holder of both offices simultaneously was Lieutenant-Colonel J. J. Collas, D.S.O. However the increased work load in both Court and States after the war made the holding of joint office impossible for practical reasons. The 1948 Act also removed many of the disqualifications for the office of Jurat which had been in force over the years, though brewers and owners of licensed premises were still excluded, as the Jurats formed the Licensing Bench.

Another change in April 1947 was the transfer by *acte rapport*, under certain conditions, of the Crown revenues to the States, who undertook to pay the salary of the Lieutenant-Governor and for the upkeep of Government House.[3]

The States elected after these reforms included some who had served the Island throughout the Occupation and others who brought back from the mainland experience in many fields, a most healthy and advantageous mixture. Together they faced the challenge of a new age. Their first major task was the introduction of a scheme of social security in line with modern practice. Since the early 1930s the viability of a contributory old-age pension scheme had been explored; in 1937 a report, presented by Jurat G. F. B. de Gruchy, had been adopted, and in 1938 the law draftsmen were asked to prepare the necessary legislation. The War intervened, but by May 1949 Senator Philip Le Feuvre was able to present to the House a Bill for the introduction of a comprehensive contributory Social Assurance scheme embracing all classes and based on a weekly contribution paid by stamp. It was described by *The Evening Post*, which published it in full, as one of the biggest and most important Bills ever presented to the Assembly. But, when parochial meetings were held to consider its implications, it soon became evident that, while the town representatives, many of whom were employers of large labour forces, were solidly for the Bill, those who in the country employed foreign or seasonal labour, were almost equally solidly '*contre*'. In November 1949 the Bill was rejected in the States by 24 to 23 votes. This raised the vexed question as to whether a *chef de police*, in the absence of his Constable, a member of the committee presenting the Bill, should have the power, by voting '*contre*', so to affect the democratic process.

In May 1950 the Bill was again presented to the House and, after a debate of great intensity and lasting two and a half days, it was finally adopted. With the Law at last on the Statute Book, one might have assumed that Senator Le Feuvre's task was completed. However, as the appointed day for its implementation drew near, opposition, led by the Deputy for St Ouen, J. J. Le Marquand, once more grew militant. Deputies were urged to voice the opposition of their constituents, while an all-island petition was organised. Although members supporting the scheme were not forced to flee the Island or take refuge in Elizabeth Castle, as had the '*six au sou*' two hundred years before, those who maintained that it was unconstitutional to oppose a law democratically passed met with criticism and abuse, and one town deputy had to be rescued from the opposing mob when, at a meeting in the People's Park, he raised a hand in favour of the scheme.

On Friday 24 August 1951 the Deputy for St Ouen presented a *projet d'acte* and a petition 'to bring to the notice of the States our strong opposition to the Insular Insurance Law decreed to come into force on the appointed day, 10 September 1951'. This was debated at a special sitting of the States on 7 September in the presence of the Lieutenant-Governor. Private and public galleries were full, while a large crowd gathered in the Royal Square, including four countrymen bearing a coffin in which to bury once and for all the Insular Insurance Law. An amendment to defer the Appointed Day was nullified by the time-honoured procedure of lodging it *au greffe*, that is postponing it for a fortnight, by which time the law would have been in force. After renewed debate, Deputy Le Marquand's *projet d'acte* was defeated by 28 to 23 votes.

On the following Monday the Act came into force. But the story ends sadly for the man who had courageously steered a dream to reality. Senator Le Feuvre had served the Island well. He had been a member of the Labour Department under the presidency of Deputy Edward Le Quesne, which devised the idea of using surplus men for the construction of La Route du Nord, thus avoiding their having to work for the occupying forces. After the War he had been elected President of the Jersey Farmers' Union and had formed the Tomato Panel to set the industry back on its feet; but the last years of his life were darkened by the continued hostility of many of his fellow *campagnards*, who had opposed the insurance scheme at every stage.[4]

In other internal matters Jersey was quick to recover from the years of Occupation and, in the 1950s, made steady progress in many directions. Educational facilities were greatly expanded. In 1952 a state secondary school was founded at Hautlieu to supplement the work of Victoria College and a similar school for girls was opened at Rouge Bouillon. Some ten years later these were amalgamated to form one non-fee-paying grammar school at Hautlieu, while a secondary school for girls took over the buildings at Rouge Bouillon and St Helier boys moved to d'Hautrée. It was then decided to combine the two schools of St Helier Boys and St Helier Girls as a co-educational establishment. Comprehensive secondary schools were then built for the west of the Island at Les Quennevais and for the east at Le Rocquier, while some of the existing primary schools were modernised and new ones built. In 1973 the States acquired Highlands, the former Jesuit College, and provided additional opportunities for further and adult education.

There were also some important changes in the laws of the island; divorce was legalised in 1949, a Channel Island Court of Appeal was brought into operation in 1964, a Juvenile Court was created in 1969 by the Children's (Jersey) Law which came into force on 1 September 1970, and the first Assistant Magistrate was sworn in on 28 November 1969. The Police Court had been created in 1853.[5] At first there was no stipendiary magistrate and the Court was presided over by the Judge of the Petty Debts Court, who was one of the Jurats, named for that purpose by the Bailiff. In 1864 *la loi règlant la procédure criminelle* increased the duties of the Judge to such an extent that it was felt that a stipendiary magistrate should be appointed, and effect was given to this decision.[6] It is a sad fact that in 1979 it was found necessary to rent an auxiliary building[7] so that two Courts might sit simultaneously to cope with the disturbing rise in criminal and civil cases.

Public utilities were expanded to meet the needs of an ever growing and prosperous community: main drainage was gradually extended to the outlying parishes, new reservoirs and dams, and a desalination plant, which is costly to operate, have been provided by the Jersey New Waterworks Company; the Electricity Company harnessed the tides for cooling their generators at their new site at La Collette and the Gas Company installed a new production plant. But the oil crisis of the late '70s brought a sharp reminder that gas and electricity in the Island were both dependent on a steady supply from the oilfields of the world. The tourist slogan 'Sunny Jersey' took on an added connotation as solar panels became increasingly popular.

Hospital services were increased and diversified, and more homes created for the old and infirm. A new ecumenical spirit, fostered by the Jersey Council of Churches, drew together the various denominations and inspired the creation of community centres in many of the parishes. Although some of the churches and chapels, built with such zeal in the 19th century, became redundant, a number of them were converted into successful centres for youth work. Community life and village development were also encouraged by the parish authorities.

Although much of this development was financed from public funds, Jersey continued to enjoy the fruits of voluntary service. The Welfare Board of St Helier and the Constables of the country parishes continued in harness with the Social Security Department to care for the needs of the poor and aged. Centeniers still worked in conjunction with the paid police, although a change was made in that the latter, who previously could operate outside St Helier only at the request of the parish police who were voluntary, were now able to operate independently throughout the Island, a change necessitated by the increase in criminal offences.

In 1966 the last of the feudal dues was abolished, that of the *Année de Jouissance*, by which the seigneur of a fief received the income for a year and a day from the land of a tenant who had died without direct heirs. However the picturesque ceremony of the *Assize d'Héritage*, at which the seigneurs who owe '*Suite de Cour*' attend yearly in the Royal Court and answer when the names of their fiefs are called, has been retained. The seigneurs, too, pay homage to the Queen when she visits the Island, and time-honoured customs are observed such as the presentation of two mallard on a silver dish by the Seigneur of Trinity.

So, if a Rip Van Winkle of the early 19th century were to return in the post-war period, he would still find some familiar features in the life of the Island. He would not be unduly disturbed by the increasing number of yachts, for he had lived in an age of sail, nor by the increasing numbers of horses, for he had never known the internal combustion engine; but two features of island life would surely intrigue and perhaps disturb him: the near monopoly enjoyed by one newspaper, The *Jersey Evening Post*, and the lack of any military establishment. Both may be attributed to some extent to the enormous increase in air traffic.

Once it became possible to receive the London dailies at breakfast time, there was no longer a need for a morning paper. *The Morning News*, which had not been published during the Occupation, was revived for a while, but finally ceased to appear in July 1950. With an ever decreasing circulation among French readers, *Les Chroniques* published its last edition in December 1959. From 1962 onwards television gradually became available from English and French channels and in colour from 1976, while the creation of Channel Television, with local colour in 1977, brought local news and other matters of local interest, not least the hustings, into one's own home.

The forts and other defences and the two Castles, which had been handed over to the Island by the British Government,[8] were converted into museums, cafés, sports halls and private dwellings. The Militia no longer existed. It had become plain in 1940 that, with modern methods of warfare, the islands could not be defended without great destruction of life and property. On 14 February 1946 the War Office wrote to the Lieutenant-Governor, Sir Edward Grasett, advising and ordering the disbanding of the battalion which had fought with the Hampshires during the war, noting that 'the battalion has given splendid service in whatever rôle it has been called to perform'. So the Jersey Militia was disbanded, and at the same time it was decided not to send Jerseymen to do National Service in England. The loss of the centuries-old force was sadly deplored by many of the older generation. On 10 January 1954 the colours of the Royal Militia of the Island of Jersey were laid up in the Town Church in the presence of the Dean. The Lieutenant-Governor and Colonel Vatcher read the lessons at the service. So ended the history of a force that had been in existence for the defence of the Island in one form or another at least since the reign of Edward III.[9]

The post-war period also produced an interesting chapter of events and some crucial decisions concerning the external relations of the islands. In 1953 a drama of historic importance to Jersey was played out on the international stage. An unresolved dispute as to the ownership of the off-shore islets and reefs known as the Minquiers and Ecréhous had been taken by France and Great Britain to the International Court at the Hague. A vast amount of material, gathered by local experts in these fields from medieval documents, parish records and geological evidence, was presented to the Court by Jersey's Attorney-General, Cecil Harrison (later to become Bailiff), and, after 26 public sessions, the Court ruled that sovereignty over the islets belonged to Great Britain. This judgment did not affect earlier agreements, redefined in 1951, which gave equal rights of fishing to French and British nationals in the areas of the Ecréhous and Minquiers 'between the limit of three miles calculated from low-water mark on the coast of the island of Jersey and the limit within which exclusive right of fishing is reserved to French nationals by the 1839 Convention'. Thus an age-old link was confirmed in areas which had seen much clandestine cooperation in earlier centuries.[10]

As the Queen, through her Privy Council, is ultimately responsible for the safety of her subjects in the islands, it is clear that she has an interest in ensuring that law and order are maintained; but constitutionally it is generally recognised that Jersey may legislate, and does so in a responsible manner, for her internal affairs, subject to permanent laws being approved by the Queen in Council. (An exception is made in the case of amendments to the Tourism and Licensing laws, where the States have power to amend these by regulations, provided that, if the original law has to be re-enacted, the new law is sent to the Council for approval.) The normal channel of communication between the Insular Authorities and Her Majesty in Council is the Home Office through a special department responsible for Channel Island affairs, while the Home Secretary, as a Privy Councillor, replies on behalf of the Queen in Council to questions in Parliament which relate to island affairs.

In international matters, while the United Kingdom had generally taken responsibility for the Channel Islands and the Isle of Man, binding them by treaties and agreements entered into by the United Kingdom, the complexities of the post-war period, with a multiplicity of international reciprocal agreements on matters like social security and the employment of foreign labour, brought with them a redefinition of the islands' position. This was set out in 1950[11] by the then Foreign Secretary, Ernest Bevin …

> His Majesty's Government have come to the conclusion that it would be more consistent with the constitutional position of these islands to regard them for international purposes as not forming part of the United Kingdom of Great Britain and Northern Ireland. Accordingly, any treaty or international agreement to which His Majesty's Government in the United Kingdom may become a party after this date ... will not be considered as applying to the Channel Islands ... unless they are expressly included. For the purpose of any treaty or international agreement to which His Majesty's Government may become a party hereafter, the Channel Islands and the Isle of Man will, unless the contrary is expressly stated in each case, be included among the territories for whose international relations His Majesty's Government are responsible.

The Constitutional position of the Island was being brought into question on two separate issues, which proved to be closely connected: the question of entry into the Common Market or European Economic Community, and the Crowther Commission on the Constitution. In January 1967 the States appointed a Committee, under the chairmanship of Senator Ralph Vibert, to consult with her Majesty's Government 'on all matters relating to the Government's application to join the E.E.C'. In May 1967 a letter, sent by Sir Philip Allen of the Home Office to the island authorities, assumed that, if the application of the United Kingdom for entry to the Common Market were successful, the islands, because of Article 227/4 of the terms of the Treaty of Rome, would automatically follow. In Jersey, however, it was quickly realised that full membership would cause serious problems, not least in the administration, if all the statutes enacted in Brussels had to be registered and enforced in the Island (in one year there had been over three thousand), and this external source of legislation, of unlimited potential in scale and subject, could threaten our basic right to manage our internal affairs. On the other hand, non-entry would put us outside the tariff wall and so remove the age-old immunities we had enjoyed in our trade with Great Britain.

In November 1967 the States debated the report of the Common Market Committee and, by a unanimous vote, accepted its recommendation that the Bailiff be requested to inform Her Majesty's Government that, in the event of the United Kingdom entering the European Economic Community, it was the wish of the Island that Jersey should remain outside the Community, but that it should be included within the Common External Tariff, or failing that, that the Island should retain its ancient right to export its goods into the United Kingdom free of duty. The Government was asked to take all necessary steps to ensure that the wish of the Island was achieved.[12]

While negotiations were in progress, the British Government, in February 1969, set up a Commission on the Constitution under the chairmanship of Lord Crowther, to consider

> having regard to developments in local government organisation and in the administrative and other relationships between the various parts of the United Kingdom, what changes, in the interests of prosperity and good government, are desirable in those functions or otherwise in present constitutional and economic relationships.

Despite the peculiar status of the Isle of Man and the Channel Islands; they too were included in the terms of reference. In April 1970 the Commission sat in Jersey. They invited and received written submissions and also held a public enquiry at the Town Hall. Lord Crowther, in considering possible entry into the Common Market, admitted that the difficulty of drawing a line between international and domestic affairs was a new problem posed by the Treaty of Rome. The Bailiff, Sir Robert Le Masurier, in outlining the position of the Island, claimed that the ability to exercise control of internal affairs was stated by right and custom, and he submitted that the Island had developed a sense of responsibility and a capacity to govern itself. Other submissions were made on behalf of the States, the Jersey Constitutional Association, the Jersey Democratic Association, the Transport and General Workers' Union and other interested parties.[13]

A wide range of opinion was expressed. Experts in Constitutional Law and Economics spoke on behalf of those who had sought their advice. States representatives favoured an Act of Parliament to define the constitutional position of the island, the Jersey Democratic Association wished for integration with the United Kingdom, the Jersey Constitutional Association proposed that the Judicial Committee of the Privy Council be asked for a ruling on the status of the Island, basing their request on a statement by Le Quesne in his *Constitutional History of Jersey*:

> Now with regard to Acts of Parliament affecting the Channel Islands, there are a few circumstances not to be forgotten. The islands are not represented in Parliament; they do not derive their laws or their constitution from Parliament; they belong to the Crown, but do not form part of the realm of England. They are not a portion of the United Kingdom.

The resultant Kilbrandon-Crowther Report,[14] published in 1973, admitted that 'an authoritative pronouncement on aspects of the existing constitutional relationships which are in dispute could be made only in a court of law', but concluded that 'so long as the United Kingdom Government remains responsible for the international relations of the islands and for their good government, it must have powers in the last resort to intervene in any island matter in the exercise of those responsibilities'. However they did not find it possible to define these powers with the precision needed for inclusion in a statute.

Meanwhile negotiations continued for Great Britain's entry into the Common Market and, in October 1970, a delegation, led by the Deputy-Bailiff, Frank Ereaut, and Senator Vibert, president of what had then become the Constitution and Common Market Committee, known as the 'Con-Com', met Mr Geoffrey Rippon, who was negotiating Britain's entry, and other Home Office officials. Negotiations took time, and many fears were expressed as to the possible erosion of the Island's independence. When, in July 1971, the E.E.C. rejected Britain's application for the Channel Islands and the Isle of Man to be granted association under Article 238 of the Treaty of Rome, the Constitutional Associations of Jersey and Guernsey organised a petition to the Queen. It was clear that acceptance of the islands' special status could not be made a pre-condition for the United Kingdom's terms of entry. The case for remaining within the tariff wall, but not applying for full membership, was strengthened when Guernsey and the Isle of Man agreed to make common cause with Jersey. The Foreign Office promised that, in the period between acceptance in July 1971 and the signing of the Treaty of Accession in the following December, the case for the islands would again be put forward.

New proposals, accepted by the Commission, were put before the States on 16 November 1971, Mr Geoffrey Rippon addressed the States on the 19th, on the 23rd the Con-Com Committee recommended to the States acceptance of the E.E.C. terms, and on 15 December the States approved by 51 votes to 1 (Senator J. J. Le Marquand) the proposition to accept the terms negotiated for the Island's links with the E.E.C. These were implemented in a Protocol to the Treaty of Accession and allowed the islands free movement of goods within the Community, while stipulating that conditions of employment in the islands must be the same for nationals of any member country including Great Britain. It was hoped that cattle would be an agreed exception to the free movement of goods and livestock, in view of the importance of preserving the purity of the island strain, with its disease free record.

In the economic sphere the post-war period has seen a remarkable growth in the level of business reflected in a significant growth in the resident population, an increase in the affluence of the Island's inhabitants and the range and scale of public services provided, leading to a loss of open space to residential and commercial development. Over this period there have also been significant changes in the relative importance of the Island's main sources of wealth and employment.

In the 1950s and 1960s the tourism industry was the mainstay of the economy, supported by agriculture and by a growing number of new wealthy immigrants drawn to the Island by the attractive tax structure. At the end of the 1960s it is estimated that the expenditure of tourists accounted directly and indirectly for over 50 per cent of the Island's national income, the expenditure of those residents reliant on investment income from abroad accounted for nearly 25 per cent, agriculture accounted for 10 per cent and the relatively 'young' finance industry less than 10 per cent with those manufacturing goods for export accounting for the remaining 5 per cent. The 1970s, 1980s and the early part of the 1990s saw a dramatic change with the extension of the Islands role as an international finance centre. At the same time growing competition from other holiday resorts in Europe for tourists from the United Kingdom, upon which market the Island's tourism industry has continued to depend for over 80 per cent of its customers, put the tourism industry under increasing pressure. In the mid-1990s it is the finance industry which dominates the economic scene accounting for some 55 per cent of the national income. Tourism's relative position has declined to 25 per cent and those reliant on investment income abroad account for less than 15 per cent. Agriculture has slipped to 5 per cent but, as with the tourism industry, this decline in the relative position expressed in percentage terms is due more to the growth of the finance industry than to any real decline in the size of the traditional industries. Those manufacturing goods for export account for less than 2 per cent.

Agriculture, an essential element in the Island's life for centuries past, has declined with the development of tourism, the arrival of wealthy immigrants and of merchant banks and the introduction on a modest scale of light industry. But, in spite of escalating costs of labour, freight, cattle foods, fertilisers and oil for heating green-houses, agriculture is still of immense importance to Jersey, if not so much for economic reasons, though the world's population must be fed, as for the rural atmosphere it engenders, on which the Island depends so much for its charm and character. In the country parishes the farmers are still essentially the custodians of that most cherished of island institutions, the honorary system of parochial police and officials.

Conservative by nature, the farmers have met the challenge of change. In the 1970s, although the industry remained to some extent dependent on the potato and tomato, outdoor tomatoes largely gave way to glasshouse culture, and crops such as cauliflowers, lettuce, courgettes, melons, parsley and flowers have been added to the farmers' and growers' repertoire, while it is now more economical to spread chemical manures than to collect seaweed. Similarly the importance of *bannelais* has decreased. This is the term used for road sweepings, which in most parishes are collected in piles, the onus to collect them being on the proprietor of the adjoining field. In some cases they are collected by the parish and auctioned. Before the advent of motor traffic they were composed of leaves and horse manure and so of agricultural value. They were usually collected by elderly men 'on the parish', that is in receipt of parish relief, or by others who would have been unemployed without the work found for them by the parish. The provision of Social Security has resulted in younger men being employed at current rates of pay. Though landowners are less interested in *bannelais*, indeed it has been thought to spread eel-worm from one field to another, the collection and sale by parish authorities still operates.

Although most work on farms is mechanised, with perishable catch crops it has been necessary for over a century to introduce seasonal foreign labour. Traditionally this was supplied from Brittany, but in recent years Portuguese and Irish workers have largely replaced the Bretons, who were once a familiar and picturesque sight in town on a Saturday, when the women wore their attractive regional head-dresses. Another feature still seen in the 1920s, but long since a mere memory, was the butter-women in the market, selling farm butter with its distinctive markings and often wrapped in a cabbage leaf. The Jersey Milk Marketing Board, delivering cardboard packs of milk on motorised trolleys, has replaced the local milkman pouring his creamy milk from a traditional Jersey milk can into a pint measure at one's door.

As economic factors put up the cost of milk production, it is important that a high standard of conformation and performance is maintained in the Island as in the animals for export. As early as 1949 the South African Jersey Society proposed that a meeting be convened in Jersey of all Jersey Breed Societies in the world to discuss matters of mutual interest such as milk recording, lactation periods and points awarded at shows. Ten countries accepted the invitation of the Royal Jersey Agricultural Society to implement this idea, and the World Jersey Cattle Bureau came into being. Since then conferences have been held in Canada, Britain, South Africa, U.S.A., Denmark and Australia. In May 1979, to mark the 30th anniversary of its formation, the Bureau held its conference in Jersey.

The theme of this conference was the 'Rôle of the Jersey in the Future'. Having regard to the food shortage in the developing world, particularly of protein, it was thought that the Jersey cow, a small animal able to walk long distances to forage, and to survive extremes of heat and cold, still capable of economic milk production, could make a useful contribution in alleviating this problem which was likely to become more and more acute unless active steps are taken to remedy the situation.

Meanwhile changes in the cattle industry within the Island have taken place. High freight charges have led to a decline in the export trade, although there is still a demand for Jerseys in many parts of the world. Herds today are much larger than they were, and the days are over when a farmer kept several cows as part of a mixed farming enterprise. One seldom sees a tethered cow, for many now graze dehorned within electric fences. Cattle shows, however, are still held annually in the parishes and for the Island by the Royal Jersey Agricultural Society. Their Spring show, held in May 1979, reached a very high standard, there being a record of over 500 entries which much impressed the visitors from overseas.

Potato root eel-worm, already mentioned,[15] became a serious menace soon after the war, perhaps aggravated by a tomato crop being planted after potatoes, as both plants belong to the same family, *solanaceae*. The best cure for this pest is diversification of crops, which may also be forced on the farmer for economic reasons. In more recent years Jersey has not escaped the virulent form of Dutch elm disease which, as in England, threatens to change the landscape, as the elm was probably the commonest of all local trees, both in hedgerows and in woods and gardens. The States embarked on an energetic policy of felling and burning the infected wood *in situ* or at Les Landes in an effort to slow down the disastrous effect of the disease, even if it cannot be entirely eliminated. It is hoped that replanting, particularly in country hedgerows, will take the form of indigenous trees such as holly, hazel and above all hawthorn, so familiar a sight in Jersey at least since the 17th century.[16] It has the advantage of having pretty, scented flowers in spring and red berries in autumn, as well as being stock-proof and far more effective than an electric fence.

Tourism began in the Island in a modest way with the coming of the steamship in the early 19th century, and in the 20th the aeroplane has added enormously to the annual flood of visitors: 243,000 landed in Jersey in 1950, 620,000 in 1965 and a phenomenal 1,507,000 in 1990. Of this number approximately half were visitors staying in the Island in hotels or guest houses, the rest being day excursionists, mainly from the continent. Those who are rash enough to brave the crowds in St Helier in the peak summer months will not be surprised to learn that an estimated £70 million a year was spent in the islands by tourists in 1977, a financial *bonanza* which, in spite of the nuisance suffered by local residents and the increased hazard of rabies entering the Island from France, Jersey could ill afford to turn away. Altogether the direct and indirect contribution from tourism and the conference industry was estimated to account for about a third of the Island's tax revenues.

Without doubt the most dramatic influence on the Island's economy since 1960 has been the growth of the finance industry and the Island's growing reputation as an international offshore finance centre of world renown.

Until 1960 the development of banking in Jersey was largely a response to the requirements of those living and doing business in the Island, although this did not mean that the Island had not proved attractive to non-residents looking for a refuge for their assets. In the 1920s the British Government was so concerned at the use of Jersey by UK residents that, following meetings in London, the States agreed not to allow British residents to form Jersey companies to avoid UK tax, an embargo that remained until the early 1970s through the inclusion in the memorandum and articles of association of a Jersey company of what became known as the Bailiff's Clause. In 1940 large quantities of foreign securities held in the Island on behalf of non-residents were shipped to the United Kingdom in advance of the occupation of the Island by German forces.

Bank deposits which totalled £2 million in 1903 and £9 million in 1939 had shown modest growth in real terms by 1960 when deposits totalled £40 million. By then, however, the world was changing and with the granting of independence to many former British Colonies many UK ex-patriates sought a safe refuge for their funds. Jersey offered the fiscal and political stability for which they were looking. To take advantage of this source of money it was necessary to repeal the provision in the Code of 1771 that interest rates should be limited to a maximum of five per cent.[17] This the then President of the Finance and Economics Committee, Senator Cyril Le Marquand, achieved in 1962. By the end of that same year the first of the merchant banks had established themselves in the Island. Within ten years 25 banks and other deposit taking institutions had been established and the total deposits held in the Island had increased to approximately £0.5 billion.

Since 1960 the finance industry has come a long way. During that time it has made an enormous contribution to the Island's tax revenues, to employment opportunities and to many other aspects of Island life. The industry has also expanded the range of services provided and markets served in addition to enjoying a period of remarkable growth. By September 1996, there were 78 deposit-taking institutions holding deposits of £91.6 billion, more than 300 mutual managing assets of £31.9 billion, 25 legal firms, some 50 accountancy businesses, including the top six international firms of accountants, over 20 insurance companies and more than 200 trust companies. Including industrial trust assets the total funds managed in Jersey in 1996 exceeded £200 billion. There were also over 30,000 Jersey companies. This is all a far cry from the position of the Island in 1960.

The finance industry in 1996 accounted for some 20 per cent of the Island's work force and each year provides many good job opportunities for school leavers and graduates. The profits of the finance industry covering banks, fund managers, trust and company administrators, lawyers etc. in 1996 were estimated to account for over 45 per cent of the total income tax yield and, if employees in the finance industry are included, the industry accounted for over half of the Island's revenue from income tax.

Jersey's success as an international offshore finance centre has depended and continues to depend on a process of change and new initiatives. A good example of this process was the introduction in January 1993 of the international business company which opened up the new areas of business for the finance industry. The international business company was developed for use by non-resident companies and individuals and offers the opportunity to pay two per cent or less on international profits. By the end of 1996 over 100 international business companies had been established with owners from countries as far apart as Switzerland, United States, Middle East, France, South Africa and the Netherlands.

Deposit taking and collective investment funds activities remain strong features of the finance industry. However, the diversification of the industry continues. From the early days when the emphasis was very much on deposit taking and trust and company administration, the industry has widened and deepened the nature of its activities and global custody, treasury operations, security issues, captive insurance and employment benefit and a host of other banking, investment, insurance, accounting and legal services are now provided.

Through the strength of the finance industry the island was able to come through the recession in the United Kingdom, and Europe generally, in the early 1990s without the need to increase the tax burden to maintain a balanced budget and without incurring any public debt. At the same time the States built up reserves equal to one year's tax income, and maintained a high level of investment in essential public services. An unemployment rate of less than one per cent, and a standard rate of income tax of 20 per cent which has remained unchanged since 1940, are other examples of the relative strength of the Island's economy for which the finance industry must take most of the credit. The industry, however, not only makes a considerable contribution to the island's economic welfare. Through its international role it has made a significant contribution to the flow of funds to the City of London and to the capital markets of the European Union.

But prosperity brought in its wake pressures of many kinds, all of them stemming ultimately from over-population. In the 1960s the number of inhabitants, which had remained at around 60,000 for a considerable number of years, took a significant leap forward. Many factors were involved. Between 1960 and 1970 there was an increase of births over deaths, accounting for a rise of some 300 a year, but more significant was the increase in immigration.

This demand sprang from a number of causes. The 'wealthy' immigrant was attracted, as in the 19th century, by the mild climate, pleasant social life and other amenities, but above all by low taxation and absence of death duties. So-called 'essential employees' had to be imported from the mainland to fill technical and managerial posts for which local people lacked the qualifications, by the newly established and rapidly expanding financial institutions, and, on a smaller scale, by the firms starting up in business in the new industrial estates. A similar demand for imported technical staff arose as the Civil Service, the health service and the other public services were expanded to meet the needs of a growing and increasingly affluent population. At a lower level in the labour market the boom in tourism gave rise to a demand for hotel workers, many of them now Portuguese. The building industry, greatly expanded to deal with the demand for housing, office accommodation and the renovation of hotels, likewise found itself unable to fill its needs from the limited pool of local labour. In short, the expanding economy created more jobs than could possibly be filled locally, with the unavoidable result of increased immigration. One advantage has been that until recently there has not been an unemployment problem of any magnitude in Jersey. Restrictions and recession have led to a reappearance of training schemes within the Island, so that more posts may be filled by local people.

As the inevitable result of over-population the environment too began to suffer. As the price of houses rose, there was a temptation for a farmer to sell his house and land. This resulted in the creation by wealthy purchasers of some beautiful homes and gardens, which have enhanced the landscape, but in a dearth of farm dwellings and agricultural land. As the price of houses soared, it became imperative that the States provide adequate cheap housing for the local buyer; the result was a growing number of housing estates, blocks of flats and village developments, thus increasing the urban spill into the countryside. The airport too was constantly enlarged, making it one of the busiest in the British Isles. A tunnel was built under Fort Regent to carry east-west traffic and by-pass the town. The Fort itself has become a recreational centre, its indoor swimming pool being particularly popular. The scheme was brought into being by a handsome bequest from the late Sir John Wardlaw Milne, who saw the need for indoor facilities to be

CELEBRATION

70 *The Liberation Sculpture, by Philip Jackson, unveiled by H.R.H. The Prince of Wales, 9 May 1995, in Liberation Square, St Helier.*

provided for tourists in bad weather, and for sporting activities for residents. Financially it has proved a burden and has absorbed the profits from the States Lottery established in 1966. The scheme has aroused much criticism, but has also provided a venue for several outstanding events. The Swimarathon, organised by the Lions Club for local charities, has more than once found its way into the *Guinness Book of Records*, and has helped immeasurably in cooperation with the Jersey Swimming Club[18] young swimmers in their training, a number of whom have completed the cross-Channel swim in recent years. The Gloucester Hall, a very large area roofed within the parade ground, has staged some outstanding concerts and other events including in 1980 the 25th anniversary concert of the Jersey Festival Choir, which over the years has performed a number of major musical works in collaboration with students of the Royal Academy of Music. Indeed such performances give the lie to the myth that Jersey is a cultural desert. There can be few places of comparable size which offer so much varied entertainment in music, drama and the arts.

Over-population and affluence produce the concomitant problem of excessive waste matter and its disposal. Surplus rubble has been used on a reclamation site at La Collette to increase harbour facilities and among other things to produce a storage area for fuel supplies. But by the 1960s it was already beginning to be realised that 'enough was enough', and that such pressures were spoiling just what visitors and residents wished to enjoy.

In 1962 the Natural Beauties Committee of the States (formerly *la Comité des Beautés Naturelles*) changed its name to the Island Development Committee, and this new body was charged with the task of implementing the 'Barratt Plan', the first comprehensive scheme the Island had had for protecting its beauty spots and its agricultural heritage from the threat of over-building. But the I.D.C. was attacking the symptoms, not the disease. A further alteration of its name in 1996 to Planning and Environment Committee reflected a change in the Committee's emphasis from a passive to a more active rôle in both urban and rural conservation.

In 1968 an Immigration Working Party was appointed to report on all the implications of containing and curbing immigration, and to consider the desirability of imposing some sort of control. This Committee, under the presidency of Deputy Philip de Veulle, reported in March 1973 and recommended various ways in which immigration might be curbed, with the object of insuring that 'the annual average net rate of immigration should be such that by 1995 the population would not exceed 80,000'.

The ball was then passed to the newly-created Policy Advisory Committee, under the presidency of the late Senator Cyril Le Marquand, and, on their recommendation in 1973 and 1974, some important steps were taken by the States to regulate immigration. A Regulation of Undertakings and Development Law was enacted, which gave the States power to control the number of businesses that might be established in the Island; a Housing Law was approved to regulate the number of 'wealthy immigrants' and 'essential employees' coming into the Island and to make sure that the needs of the local people for housing would be given priority.[19] As a result of the application of these two measures, immigration, which was running at an average net rate of 710 during the 10 years 1961-1971, has been cut down in recent years to 420. Even so the environmental pressure has continued to mount. In 1979 a newly constituted Policy Advisory Committee under Sir Robert Marett, a Deputy of St Brelade, recommended to the States that this last figure should be halved, and in future the net rate of immigration should not exceed 250.

Thus, as the years have gone by, the once independent islanders have been forced to accept, in their own best interests, wider and wider measures of control in areas which our ancestors would have considered sacrosanct. Ironically a predominantly conservative government has been forced to impose socialistic controls affecting land-owners and businessmen alike; indeed in one way or another, virtually every class of the population.

Even so the main problems are with us still: how to ensure adequate housing, sufficient water, facilities for the disposal of rubbish (perhaps the most pressing of all), and flowing traffic without spoiling the Island. We need to find a means to conserve for the summer water that runs away in winter for lack of storage space, yet the infilling of yet more valleys is strongly opposed. In high summer traffic congestion is acute, aggravated by the arrival of drive-on drive-off ferries. Immigration controls, however strict, will not make these problems go away, but at least they should prevent them from becoming much worse.

So much for what the island government has done. But the spirit of voluntary service, which was always such a strong feature of Jersey life, is by no means dead, and in many fields supplements what the various States' committees are trying to do in order to protect the environment. In this context it must not be forgotten that by 1980 the majority of States' members were themselves serving the Island in a voluntary capacity. In 1968 Marguerite Filleul, among her other benefactions, left almost a quarter of a million pounds to the National Trust for Jersey, which was founded in 1936 and, since the Occupation, has done much to preserve the beauty and traditions of the Jersey countryside. Charitable Trusts have made their contribution, notably the Benjamin Meaker Trust which, among its many benefactions, has enabled Jersey, through the National Trust, to preserve as a natural habitat La Mare au Seigneur at St Ouen, where a bird sanctuary is operated by La Société Jersiaise. It has also contributed generously to the extension, opened in 1980, which commemorates the centenary in 1973 of La Société, and to the Jersey Wildlife Preservation Trust. Founded at Augrès Manor by Gerald Durrell, it is dedicated mainly to the saving of endangered species — a venture in conservation which has carried the name of Jersey to many parts of the world, as have the stamps of the Jersey Post Office, which became an independent institution in 1969, having up till then formed an integral part of the British Post Office. The Jersey branch of the Men of the Trees has played its part in preserving and enhancing the landscape, while a committee composed of members of the States and representative outside bodies is presently engaged on a project for the rehabilitation of St Ouen's Bay, an area of unique interest, which was gradually becoming degraded by neglect and poor types of building, an area important not least because of the dune system which is among the 10 largest such systems in the British Isles and the fourth richest in higher plants.[20] In 1978 the States appointed a Conservation Officer, a post which, by the mid-1990s, had been expanded into an Environmental Adviser, a Director of Conservation and a States Ecologist. These were supported by considerable staff and resources, as the Island was carried inexorably forward on a tide of conservation policies that was by then flowing around almost every developed nation.

Another Trust, the Clarkson Foundation, has done much to encourage literature and the arts in the Island, and since the Occupation vast sums of money have been raised in the Island for charitable purposes by groups and for causes too numerous to mention. Help has also been given by the States to developing countries in the 'third world', both through financial aid and by the encouragement of groups of volunteers sent out to help in practical ways, as for example in the building of hospital units in Kenya. As in earlier centuries, benefactors, both of English and Jersey descent, have given large sums of money for the Island causes. Some two hundred years after Mrs Marie Bartlet had bequeathed money for the building of a hospital, Anne Alice Rayner, who had come to live in Jersey between the wars, left a considerable fortune for the erection of a nurses' home, for the creation of exhibitions at Victoria College and for a fund to be used for the relief of needy persons of either sex of the professional classes residing in Jersey.[21]

As the end of the century approaches, it is encouraging to find that islanders are still concerned for the preservation of their heritage. The parishes have been listing the treasures that remain: old houses, well-trodden by-ways, ancient stones and trees. The traditional language of Jersey has been preserved in the dictionary compiled by Dr Frank Le Maistre and by the many activities sponsored by the Don Balleine Trust and by L'Assembliée d'Jèrriais. Local artists continue to record our changing scenery, while an ever-growing number of books and typescripts on many aspects of island life flow from the hand of Jersey authors, many of them members of La Société Jersiaise. A hundred and twenty-five years after its foundation they are carrying on a tradition set by earlier members and epitomised in a leader in *La Nouvelle Chronique* of 10 October 1888:

> Sans tambour, ni trompette, sans bruit, sans faste, sans affiches et sans réclames, La Société Jersiaise poursuit sa marche digne et régulière. Elle a jeté ses fondements sur la large base de l'histoire, et sur cette base elle est occupée à élever un édifice littéraire, qui devra se soutenir après que la brique et le granit même seront redevenus poussière.

In 1950 Mr Balleine concluded his history with a quotation from John Oxenham, a writer known to Channel Islanders by his novels set in Sark:

> The world is in the melting-pot
> What was is passing away;
> And what will remain when it cools again,
> No man may safely say.

These words, a warning to the writer on contemporary events, are equally true today. As the world enters a period of recession and western Europe argues over fishing rights, will the Common Market survive its growing pains? Will increasing inflation and an ever-ageing population erode the Beveridge-Le Feuvre schemes for Social Security? Will Jersey, as so often in the past, have to change its pattern of life and find new sources of income to maintain its population? Judgment lies in the future. But those whose families have lived in the Island for centuries and those who, over the years, have come to share the rich heritage of Jersey, will realise that an inheritance nurtured for over a thousand years is not lightly to be laid aside.

A quotation, chosen to preface their symposium by the compilers of '*Nos Iles*', writing in exile in 1944, makes a fitting postscript to this latest chapter in our island history:

> Tel est le petit pays qui nous est cher, qui a été cher à nos pères depuis tant de siècles et que nous vous prions de chérir pour l'amour d'eux, pour l'amour de nous et pour votre propre bien. On ne perd rien à l'idée d'être venu de peuple dont on est fier. On s'en respecte de plus.
>
> Pendant près de sept cents ans, isolés dans la mer, nous avons tenu notre place au soleil, avec des lois, des coutumes, une langue, le tout bien à nous. Prenons soin de les garder et de les passer intactes à ceux qui viendront après nous.

BIBLIOGRAPHY

Source Books on Jersey

Cartulaire de Jersey, Guernsey, et les autres Iles Normandes (a reprint of all documents relating to the islands in the Archives of the Départment de la Manche: 1025-1698). Société Jersiaise, 1919.

Jersey Prison Board Case: Memorandum prepared for the Privy Council by W. H. V. Vernon and H. Sutton (The Appendix contains many documents that touch on the Constitution of the Island from 1130). Eyre & Spottiswoode, 1893.

Documents Historiques relatifs aux Iles de la Manche tirés des archives conservées dans le Public Record Office 1199-1244. Société Jersiaise 1879.

E. Rotulis Litterarum Clausarum Excerpta ad Insulas Normanniae Spectantia 1205-1327. Société Jersiaise 1893.

Ancient Petitions of the Chancery and Exchequer 1290-1454. Société Jersiaise 1902.

Rolls of the Assizes held in the Channel Islands 1309. Société Jersiaise 1905.

Extentes for 1274, 1331, 1528, 1607, 1668, and 1749. All published by Société Jersiaise.

Rapport des Commissaires de Henri VIII 1515. Société Jersiaise 1878.

Actes des Etats 1524-1800. Société Jersiaise.

Ordres du Conseil enregistrés à Jersey 1536-1867. Jersey. Printed for the States.

Discipline ecclésiastique dans iles de la Manche de 1576 à 1597: ed. by G. E. Lee. Guernsey 1885

Chroniques de Jersey 1585 (Edition published by A. Mourant. Jersey 1858).

Chroniques du Bon Duc Louis de Bourbon. J. Cabaret d'Orville (giving an eye-witness' account of du Guesclin's raid). Paris

Journal de Jean Chevalier 1643-51. Société Jersiaise 1906.

The Lyar Confounded. Wm. Prynne. London 1645.

Pseudo Mastix, the Lyar's Whip. Michel Lemprière and others. London 1646.

A Survey of the Channel Islands. Peter Heylin. London 1656.

Caesarea or a Discourse of the Island of Jersey. Jean Poingdestre 1682. Société Jersiaise 1889.

A Survey of the Island of Jersey. P. Dumaresq 1685. Société Jersiaise 1935.

An account of the Island of Jersey. Ph. Falle, 1st edition 1694: 2nd edition 1734: edition with notes by E. Durell 1837.

Journal de Daniel Messervy 1769-72. Société Jersiaise 1896.

A Code of Laws for the Isalnd of Jersey. 1771.

Collection of Petitions relative to Political Differences 1779-88. Jersey 1788.

Proceedings in the Trial of Moses Corbet. London 1781.

Many references to Jersey will be found in Rymer's *Foedora* 1066-1383. and in the Calendars of State Papers, specially in the volume 'Domestic Series 1625-49 Addenda'.

Some Modern Books Concerning Jersey

Ahier, Philip, *Stories of Jersey's seacoasts and seamen* (Huddersfield). In 3 parts.

Balleine, G. R., *The Bailiwick of Jersey* (Hodder and Stoughton, 1951, Revised 1970)

Balleine, G. R., *A Biographical Dictionary of Jersey* (Staples Press, 1948).

Balleine, G.R., The Tragedy of Philippe d'Auvergne (Phillimore, 1973).

Balleine, G. R., *All for the King* (Société Jersiaise, 1976).

Bisson, Sidney, *Jersey, Our Island* (Batchworth Press, 1950)

Bois, F. de l., *The Parish Church of St Saviour, Jersey* (Phillimore, 1976).

Bois, F. de L., *Walks for motorists* (Frederick Warne, 1979).

Brett, C. E. B., *Buildings in the town and parish of St Helier* (Ulster Architectural Heritage Society for the National Trust for Jersey, 1977).

Cottrill, D. J., *Victoria College, Jersey* (Phillimore, 1977).

Cruickshank, C., *The German Occupation of the Channel Islands* (Trustees of the Imperial War Museum, 1975).

Davies, William, *Fort Regent* (Published privately, 1971).

de Gruchy, G. F. B., *Medieval Land Tenures* (Bigwood Ltd., States Printers, 1957).

de la Croix, J., *La Ville de St Helier* (Jersey, 1845).

de la Croix, J., *Jersey, ses antiquites, ses institutions, son histoire* (Jersey, 1859).

de la Croix, J., *Les Etats* (Jersey, 1847).

de Veulle, P. M., *Le Gouvernment particulier de Jersey* (Société Jersiaise, 1974).

Dobson, R., *The Birds of the Channel Islands* (Staples Press, 1952).

Dupont, Gustave, *Histoire du Cotentin et de ses Iles* (Caen, 1870).

Durell, Rev. E., *A Picturesque and historical Guide to the Island of Jersey* (1847).

Eagleston, A. J., *The Channel Islands under Tudor Government 1485-1642* (Cambridge University Press, 1949).

Evans, Joan, *The Unconquered Knight. A translation of de Gamez' El Vitorial* (London, 1928).

Falle, Raymound, *The Royal Court House of the Island of Jersey.*

Falle, Raymound, *A Brief history of the States of Jersey and the States chamber.*

Falle, Raymond, *The States of Jersey Libraries* (The States of Jersey, 1965, 1968, 1971).

Havet, J., *Série Chronologique des Gardiens et Seigneurs des Iles Normandes de 1198-1461* (Paris, 1876).

Hawkes, Jacquetta, *The Archaeology of the Channel Islands*, Vol. II, Jersey (Société Jersiaise, 1937).

Hoskins, S. E., *Charles II in the Channel Islands* (London, 1854).

Inglis, H.D., *The Channel Islands* (1838).

L'Amy, J. H., *Jersey Folklore* (Jersey, 1927. Reprinted).

Le Couteur, F., *Apercu sur le cidre* (Jersey, 1806).

Le Feuvre, George, *Jérri jadis* (Don Balleine Trust, 1973).

Le Maistre, Dr. F., *Dictionnaire Jersiais Français* (Don Balleine Trust, 1966).

Le Maistre, Dr. F., *English-Jersey Language vocabulary*, in conjunction with A. Carré and P. M. de Veulle (Don Balleine).

Lemprière, R., *Portrait of the Channel Islands* (Robert Hale, 1970).

Lemprière, *History of the Channel Islands* (Robert Hale, 1974)

Lemprière, R., *Customs, ceremonies and traditions of the Channel Islands* (Robert Hale, 1976).

Lemprière, R., *Buildings and memorials of the Channel Islands* (Robert Hale, 1980).

Le Patourel, J. H., *The medieval administration of the Channel Islands 1199-1399* (Oxford University Press, 1937).

Le Quesne, C., *A Constitutional History of Jersey* (Jersey, 1856).

Le Sueur, Frances, *A Natural History of Jersey* (Phillimore, 1976).

Marett, R. R., *A Jerseyman at Oxford* (Oxford 1941)

Mayne, R. H., *Old Channel Islands Silver, its makers and marks* (Jersey, 1969).

Mayne, R. H., *Mailships of the Channel Islands* (Picton Publishing, 1971).

Mayne, R.H., *Jersey Through the Lens* (with Joan Stevens) (Phillimore, 1975).

Millais, Geoffroy, *Sir John Everett Millais* (Academy Editions, 1979).

Moignard, I. G., *A History of Jersey's Lifeboats* (Jersey, 1975).

Mollet, R., *A Chronology of Jersey* (Société Jersiaise, 1954).

Moore, R. D., *Methodism in the Channel Islands* (London 1952).

Nicolle, E. T., *Mont Orgueil Castle* (Jersey, 1921).

Nicolle, E. T., *The Town of St Helier* (Société Jersiaise, 1931).

Payne, J.B., *An Armorial of Jersey* (London, 1859).

Perrot, M., *La Surprise de Jersey en 1781* (Paris, 1929).

Pocock, H. R. S., *The Memoirs of Lord Coutanche* (Phillimore, 1975).

Porter, H. R., *Lillie Langtry* (Société Jersiaise, 1973).

Quayle, T., *General View of the agriculture of Jersey* (1815).

Ragg, Rev. A., *A Popular History of Jersey* (1895).

Rybot, N. V. L., *Gorey Castle Jersey* (Official Guide).

Rybot, N. V. L., *Elizabeth Castle Jersey* (Official Guide).

Saunders, A. C., *Jean Chevalier and his times* (Jersey, 1936).

Saunders, A. C., *Jersey in the 17th, 18th and 19th centuries* (1930-1931).

Schickler., *Les Eglises du Refuge en Angleterre* (Paris, 1892).

Sinel, L., *The German Occupation of Jersey. A diary* (Jersey, 1946).

Shepard, H. G., *One hundred years of the Royal Jersey Agricultural and Horticultural Society* (Jersey, 1933).

Stead, J., *A Picture of Jersey* (1809).

Stevens, C. G., *A Corpus of Jersey Toponymy, dictionary and maps* (1975). Further Typescripts in Société Jersiaise library.

Stevens, Joan, *Old Jersey Houses*, Vol. I (Jersey, 1965; Reprint by Phillimore, 1980).

Stevens, Joan, *Old Jersey Houses*, Vol. II (Phillimore, 1977).

Stevens, Joan, *A Short History of Jersey* (Société Jersiaise, 1972).

Tessier Yandell, J., *H.M.S. Jersey 1654-1976* (Société Jersiaise, 1977).

Turk, M. G., *The Quiet Adventurers in America* (Detroit, 1975).

Turk, M. G., *The Quiet Adventurers in Canada* (Detroit, 1979).

Wood, A. and M., *Islands in Danger* (Evans Brothers, London, 1955).

Woolmer, S. C. and Arkwright, C. H., *Pewter in the Channel Islands* (Edinburgh, 1973).

A great many relevant articles may be found in the *Annual Bulletins* of La Société Jersiaise, from 1873. Further material may be found in the reports and transactions of La Société Guernesiaise, the *Occasional Publications* of The Jersey Society in London and the *Bulletins* of L'Assembliée d'Jèrriais.

SOURCES AND CROSS-REFERENCES

We are indebted to Mrs Margaret Finlaison, the late Professor McBurney and Doctor Arthur Mourant for considerable help in updating the information contained in chapters one and two.

ABSJ	Annual Bulletin of the Société Jersiaise
AE	Actes des Etats
AP	Ancient Petitions
AR	Assize Roll
BDJ	*Biographical Dictionary of Jersey* by G. R. Balleine
Cart.	Cartulaire des Iles
Chev.	Diary of Jean Chevalier
Chron.	*Chroniques de Jersey* (Mourant, 1858)
Chron.	*La Chronique* (19th-century newspaper)
DM	Diary of Daniel Messervy
DNB	*Dictionary of National Biography*
Doc.Hist.	Documents Historiques
EP	*Jersey Evening Post*
LC	Lettres Closes
MOC	*Mont Orgueil Castle* by E.T. Nicolle
OC	Orders in Council
OJH	*Old Jersey Houses*, Vols I and II
OP	Occasional Papers
PBC	Prison Board Case
PC	Privy Council
PRO	Public Record Office
R of C	Rolls of Royal Court
RTSG	Report & Transactions of La Société Guernesiaise
SJL	Société Jersiaise Library
SP	State Papers

Notes to Chapter One

1. ABSJ VII (1912), pp.209-245.
2. *ibid.*, VII (1911), pp.112-120.
3. *ibid.*, IX (1920), pp.109-117, X (1923), p.57, XIV (1946), pp.238-252.
4. *ibid.*, XIV (1946), p.242.

5/6. *ibid.*, VII (1911), pp.112-120.

7. *ibid.*, VII (1911), pp.69-74.
8. *ibid.*, I (1883), pp.385-396; De la Croix, *Jersey:ses Antiquités*, I, p.22; Jacquetta Hawkes, *Archaeology in the Channel Islands*, II, pp.25-28.
9. ABSJ XII (1933), p.178.
10. *ibid.*, XXII (1978), p.160.
11. *ibid.*, IX (1922), p.332; X (1924), p.211; XII (1933), p.218.
12. *ibid.*, X (1924), pp.179-229.
13. See ch.28, p.228.
14. ABSJ III (1890), xiii; VII (1912), pp.247-254.
15. *ibid.*, XXII (1977), pp.18, 19.
16. Caesar, *De Bello Gallico*, IV and VI; Dupont, *Histoire du Contentin*, I; Dillon and Chadwick, *The Celtic Realms*, p.6 *et seq.*
17. ABSJ XVII (1959), pp.259-264.
18. Mac Cullock, *The Celtic and Scandinavian Religions*; Dillon and Chadwick, *op.cit.*, ch.7.
19. *ibid.*, p.8 (Strabo IV, trans. by J. J. Tierney).
20. There is no evidence that men from Scythia reached western Europe, but at this time the word Scythian appears to have been a synonym for Hun. Procopius (see ch.2, p.12) in Anecdota 18, pp.20-21, says that the yearly invasion of the Balkan provinces by the

Huns caused a 'Scythian wilderness', Tηv Σκνθων ερημιαv, a reference back to the desolation caused by the old time Scyths of many centuries before, as we used the word 'Turk' when referring to the Sallee pirates (see ch.21, p. 174).

Notes to Chapter Two

1. ABSJ XXII (1979), pp. 281-285.
2. *ibid.*, XXII (1979), pp.322-327.
3. *ibid.*, XIV (1941), pp.311, 312.
4. Camden, *Britannica*, ed.1587.
5. RTSG XVII (1962), p.352.
6. Mac Culloch, *op. cit.*
7. ABSJ XV (1949), pp.21-100; XV (1950), pp.165-238.
8. F. Le Maistre, *Dictionnaire Jersiais-Français.*
9. The name first appears in a letter of Sidonius Apollinaris, Bishop of Auvergne (Dillon and Chadwick. *op. cit.*, p.80).
10. See ch.3, p.23.
11. Dr. Ian Short, *Anglo-Norman Text Society*; Canon Doble, *Laudate*, XXIII, p.79, *et seq.*, June 1945.
12. But see *Revue du département de la Manche*, tome XXI, fasc. 82, April 1979.
13. ABSJ XXI (1973), pp.174-179.
14. *ibid.*, III (1893), pp.243-250.
15. BDJ, p.637; Isherwood, *Jersey Catholic Record*, June 1972.
16. Joan Stevens and Jean Arthur, *The Parish Church of St Mary, Jersey.*
17. Dillon and Chadwick, *op. cit.*, p.176.
18. Pégot-Ogier, *Histoire des Iles de la Manche*, p.44, ch.3 *passim*; Toustan de Billy, *Histoire Ecclésiastique du Diocése de Coutances*, I, ch.4, p.36, *et seq.*
19. Bois, *A Constitutional History of Jersey*, p.45.
20. At St Ouen they are known as *cueillettes.*
21. ABSJ XXI (1973), p.174; *Chronique de Fontenelle.*
22. Du Cleuziou, *La Bretagne*, ch.6, p.206 *et seq.*
23. De Gruchy, *Medieval Land Tenures*, p.205 *et seq.*; Dupont, *op. cit.*, I, p.165.
24. Wace, *Roman de Rou*, lines 424, 425.

Notes to Chapter Three

1. Dupont, *op. cit.*, I, p.121 *et seq.*
2. Published by the Société Jersiaise (1918-1924).
3. Dupont, *op. cit.*, I, p.150 *et seq.*; Toustan de Billy, *op. cit.*, I, ch.4, p.36 *et seq.*
4. Joan Stevens, *Old Jersey Houses II* (map of fiefs as end paper).
5. de Gruchy, *op. cit.*, pp.179-196.
6. Wartburg, *Evolution et Structure de la Langur Française*, ch.2.
7. Le Quesne, *A Constitutional History of Jersey*, p.38; Le Geyt, *Manuscripts* (published by the States, 1841), I, p.29; R.E. Latham, *Revised Mediaeval Word List*, p.221.
8. See chapter 16, p.138.
9. OJH I, plates XIX-XXII.
10. Cartulaire (published by La Société), p.372 (charter 20.4.1042).
11. ABSJ XXII (1978), pp.163-175.
12. OJH I, p.139; OJH II, p.27.
13. Cart., p.372, no.291 (charters circa 1028-1031, copied in 1667).
14. *ibid.*, p.410 (charter signed by William as Duke, not as King, mentions a gift of a carucate of land (the fief de l'Abbesse de Caen in Trinity) and a water-mill (Ponterrin in Trinity) with half the tithes of six parish churches in Jersey. The gift was to the first abbesse of Holy Trinity, Caen.). See also *Rolls of the Assizes*, 1309, pp.80-82.
15. Wace, *op. cit.*, lines 7897-7950.
16. Cart., no.35 (Cal of documents français 747).
17. *ibid.*, pp.50, 51 and BDJ, p.116.
18. Dupont, *op. cit.*, I, pp.190, 263.
19. *ibid.*, I, p.320; Cart., pp.50, 51 (donation in 1125, ratification by Philippe in 1135).
20. The source of this picturesque phrase has not been found. For an early portrait of Henry II see Dupont *op. cit.*, I, pp.384-390, which includes a description by Pierre de Blois, secretary and chaplain to Henry II.
21. Cart., p.307, no.228 (dated 1185).
22. *Journal de Jean Chevalier*, p.958.
23. Cart., p.320, no.327 (charter of Henry II, *c.*1186).
24. ABSJ XIII (1936), p.46.
25. Pluquet, *Roman de Rou,* I, vii, et seq.; Wace, *op. cit.*, line 16547.
26. ABSJ IX (1919), pp.18-44.
27. Cart., p.417, no.327 (charter of John, 7.1.1200); Assize Roll, 1309, p.319.
28. Cart., p.419, no.328 (charter dated 1203); ABSJ XII (1933), pp.185-192.
29. Dupont, *op. cit.*, I, 455; see also OP, 13, p.25 in SJL; PRO Charter Roll I, John m, 28.
30. Assize Roll, 1309, p.12.
31. RTSG XIX (1976), p.569.

Notes Chapter Four

1. Falle, *An Account of the Island of Jersey*, ed. Durell (1837), pp.37, 38.
2. Bois, *op. cit.*, p.16; Le Quesne, *op. cit.*, p.58; OC, 15.7.1813, *Report of Royal Commissioners* (1860), p.IV, para. 2; PRO, *Chancery Inquisition Post Mortem,*

32 Henry III, no.6 (dated 11.9.1248).
3. J.P. Ahier, *Tableaux Historiques*, p.181; Le Quesne, *op. cit.*, pp.58-61.
4. *Lettres Closes*, p.11, no.37; Henry III anno 2e, p.1, memb.11 (13.2.1217/18); *ibid.,* p.13, no.40 and p.14, no.44.
5. de la Croix, *op. cit.*, II, p.149 *et seq.*
6. E.T. Nicolle, *Mont Orgueil Castle,* p.3 and Patent Rolls (14.11.1212); see also ch.7, p59.
7. Lettres Closes, p.60, no.179 (Henry III anno 23,24.8.1295); *Cartulaire*, p.2 (1333), from Archives de la Manche.
8. ABSJ III (1893), pp.173-190; Lacroix, *France in the Middle Ages*; Le Patourel, *Mediaeval Administration in the Channel Isles*, p.113; De Gruchy, *op. cit.*, p.151; Colin Platt, *Mediaeval Southampton*, p.55; Walter Mundy, *Romney Marsh.*
9. ABSJ II (1895), pp.35-41; Grandison was Warden 1275-1294 and 1297-1328.
10. See ch.7, p.59; ch.8, p.69; ch.30, p.251; ch.33, p.279.
11. RTSG XIX (1976), p.569 *et seq.*
12. But see J.P. Ahier, *op. cit.*, p.180, footnote 2.
13. Le Quesne, *op. cit.*, p.55; Ewen and de Carteret, *The Fief of Sark*, p.21.
14. or 1214; See *Revue de la Manche*, Tome 20, p.197 (July 1978).
15. LC, 9.13 (Henry III 9.2.1222/3).
16. ABSJ X (1926), pp.237-258; See ch.24, p.197; ch.33, p.281.
17. e.g. Gombrette in St John for which records exist.
18. LC, p.15 (Henry III, 21.10.1224, 9.1.1224/5, 28.1.1225/6.).
19. *ibid.*, p.30 (Henry III, 25.4.1234); AR, 1299, 1309, p.226.
20. LC, p.30 (Henry III, 11.9.1247); AP, p.8, no.13674 (1294-97); Roles Gascons, 2113 (15.10.1247); See OP, 13, p.8 in SJL.
21. Charles Stevens; MSS on de Carteret family.
22. AP, p.31, no.12834 (1321); p.47, nos 8295, 8296 (1328); pp.60-62, nos. E 822, 2648, 5884; ABSJ II (1885), p.45.
23. Bois, *op. cit.*, p.20, 5/3; Le Patourel, *op. cit.*, p.89.
24. AP, p.5, no.8719 (*c.*1294); LC p.57 (Edw. I, 24.8.1294).
25. LC, pp.15, 18, 22, 23 (Henry III 1224/5 *passim* and 13.3.1234/5); E.T. Nicolle, *Mont Orgueil Castle*, p.7.
26. PRO, Assize Roll, no.1158 anno 1299; Typescript by C.G. Stevens in SJL.
27. See ch.5, p.39; ch.26, p.209.
28. John Gillingham, *Richard the Lionheart* (1978), pp.70, 71.
29. Preface to Assize Roll, no.1309, p.vi.
30. *ibid.*, p.233.
31. *ibid.*, p.73; Falle, *op. cit.*, p.157; Possibly Roger Malcael, Richard I's vice chancellor and seal bearer, drowned in Cyprus, April 1191; see J. Gillingham, *op. cit.*, p.164.
32. BDJ, p.265; AR 1309, pp.318, 319, 322, 323; LC, pp.76 (Ed. I, 10.4.1305), 79 (Ed. II, 3.4.1309), 80 (Ed. II. 15.5.1309); Unless otherwise stated further examples are from the Assize Roll of 1309.
33. This occurred in Guernsey. See AR, 1309, p.183.
34. See ch.19, p.160; ch. 22 *passim*; ch.30, p.244.
35. Cart., p.321 (March 1212), taken from copy in Archives de la Manche dated 2.1.1471.
36. ABSJ XII (1932), p.17; *ibid.*, XIV (1943), pp.139-148.
37. AP, p.35 (*c.*1327).
38. Local land measurement, app. 2,150 English sq. yds; 2¼ Jersey vergées make one English acre or 40 Jersey perch.
39. Le Quesne, *op. cit.*, pp.65-67.
40. AP, pp.48, 49 (1328/29).

Notes to Chapter Five

1. AR, 1309, p.viii (footnote); Dupont, *op. cit.*, II, pp.245-248; Havet, *Cours Royales* XXIV-XXVI, pp.228-231; *Commissioners Criminal Report for Guernsey* (1848), p.310; *Ancient Petitions*, p.63 (footnote); *Placita Corona* 5 Ed. III, *Placita coronae coram Roberto de Scardeburgh.*
2. PRO; AR, no.1160 anno 1309, p.viii, re 1331 and 1333.
3. The Commissioners were Robert de Norton and Guillaume de la Rue; PRO, Assize Roll no.1166; ABSJ I (1876), p.25; SJL typescript translation into English by C.G. Stevens completed 1980 by H. Coutanche.
4. ABSJ III (1891), p.11; XI (1928), p.69; Le Patourel, *op. cit.*, p.73 *et seq.*
5. See also ABSJ III (1891), pp.23, 31; MOC, p.13.
6. AP, pp.67-69 (12.4.1338/9); ABSJ III (1891), p.14.
7. BDJ, p.191; AP, p.70 (1341 Ed. III).
8. Leland (Bodleian, MS, *c.*1540).
9. MOC, p.16 (footnote).
10. ABSJ XI (1928), pp.60, 61; Rymer, *Foedera*, II, pt.II, p.1167.
11. AP, pp.74, 75 (*c.*1342).
12. *ibid.*, p.74, no.12212 (1342).
13. BDJ, pp.137, 187.
14. Cart., p.460 (Archives of Warwick Castle 5.5.1343).
15. PRO, Originalia Roll, 24 Ed. II, m.2; OP, II p.58, in SJL; Abbot Gasquet, *The Black Death of 1348-9* (pub.1900).
16. ABSJ IX (1919), pp.60-62; Cal. Close Rolls 31

Edw. III, m.9, p.372, m.8, p.374 (25.8.1357), m.4, p.384, but see Tupper, *History of Guernsey*, ch.VI.
17. Falle, *op. cit.*, p.47 (footnote), (*Role de Tractat. Pacis Franc*, 34, Ed.III, m.10).
18. ABSJ V (1902), p.85; BDJ, pp.114, 432.
19. *ibid.*, XI (1928), pp.82, 83; MOC, p.19.
20. Froissart, II, ch.31; de la Croix, *op.cit.*, II, p.399.
21. MOC, p.167 (Camb. Uni. MSS Dd III, 53, p.170).
22. *ibid.*, p.20 (*Rot. Franc.*, 47 Edward III, MS 29).
23. *ibid.*, p.20 *et seq.*
24. *ibid.*, p.169.
25. *ibid.*, p.170 (*Rot. Franc.*, 47 Ed. III, m.10).
26. Rymer, *Foedera*, III, pt.II, p.997.
27. MOC, p.171 (Camb. MSS, Dd iii, 53 fol.163).
28. Accounts of Thomas de Appleby (1374-7), PRO, Foreign accounts, Ric. II; RTGS VII (1914), pp.154-158.

Notes to Chapter Six

1. Dupont, *op. cit.*, II, p.451.
2. DNB; BDJ, p.223; MOC, p.24; PRO, Early Chancery Rolls; Patent Rolls Ed.III, 12.12.1376 and Close Rolls Ed.III, 1374-1377; French Rolls, 10, Ric.II, m.15, letter of pardon 16.1.1388; see also OP 20 in SJL.
3. Dupont, *op. cit.*, II, p.471 *et seq.*
4. *ibid.*, II, p.494.
5. DNB; *Rotuli Parliamentorum* iii, p.382.
6. BDJ, p.111.
7. PRO, *Rot. Franc.*, Chancery, I Henry IV, m. 7, no. 8.
8. Dupont, *op. cit.*, II, p.494.
9. Doc.Hist., p.16; Lettres patentes, An.5 de Henry III, p.1, m.6; ABSJ II (1886), pp.131, 132.
10. Dupont, *op. cit.*, II, p.497; MOC, p.25.
11. *ibid.*, II, pp.450, 451.
12. ABSJ X (1923), pp.32-46, *Le Victorial*, Diaz de Gomez, trans. into French by de Circourt and de Puymaigre, pub. Paris, 1867; see also *The Unconquered Knight*, Joan Evans, London, 1928; MOC, pp.25-27; Archives Nationales X, 1a 54, fol.166.
13. Possibly Jacquot de Vinchellez. See ABSJ V (1903), p.101.
14. ABSJ XII (1935), pp. 503-520, XXII (1979), pp.284-285; Poingdestre, *Caesarea*, pub.1682, p.10.
15. Philippa, daughter of John of Gaunt.
16. Shakespeare, *Henry IV*, pt II, Act IV, sc.4.
17. See *Alien Priories*, Nichols, pub.1779; Dr. A.J. Taylor (personal correspondence).
18. Cart., no.192, p.272, letter from Louis XI of France written from Tours to 'baillis du Cotentin et de l'île de Jersey.' (13.12.1461).
19. J.P. L'Amy, *Jersey Folk Lore*, pub.1927.
20. Cal. Pat. Rolls, Edw. I, memb. 26; but see original roll where the words Sancte Marie de Castro do not appear. St Mary, Castel, is in Guernsey.
21. ABSJ VIII (1915), p.8. No successor to de Marchia is quoted for 50 years; perhaps this indicates the constantly changing fortunes of war.
22. Cart., pp.244, 249, 253, 261, 263, 265; showing that St-Sauveur-le-Vicomte acquired tithes on this and other churches from 1100 to *c.*1400.
23. Dupont, *op. cit.*, II, pp.519, 526.
24. *ibid.*, II, p.527.
25. ABSJ IX (1919), p.67; Dupont, *op. cit.*, II, p.528 *et seq.*
26. Dupont *op. cit.*, II, p.509.
27. ABSJ V (1905), p.329; but see Bois, *The Parish Church of St Saviour Jersey*, pp.19, 20; OP 13, p.69 in SJL (E.T.N. quotes Ellis, *History of the Antiquities of the Borough and Town of Weymouth*, p.133, pub.1829).
28. ABSJ VIII (1917), pp.302, 303.
29. See ch.4, p.35.
30. Lt. Col. R. Gardner Wharton, *Parish Churches of Jersey* (1920); ABSJ XXII (1978), pp.163-173; Local church guides.
31. MOC, pp.2, 3; see also ch.7, p.58.
32. Dupont, *op. cit.*, II, p.554 *et seq.*, 609 *et seq.*
33. Du Fresne de Beaucour, *Histoire de Charles VII*, Tome V, p.53.
34. Cart. no.245, p.329 (1462).
35. Pat. Rolls, 22.7.1452 and 3.7.1456.
36. AP, p.89 (1454); Paston MSS, B.Museum, Vol.I, p.289.

Notes to Chapter Seven

1. RTSG VI (1910), p.222; MOC, pp.28-30; Havet, *Gardiens et Gouverneurs de Jersey*, pp.37, 38.
2. ABSJ IX (1919), pp.71-73; BDJ, p.218.
3. ABSJ IX (1920), pp.168-188; MOC, p.29; de Viriville, *Histoire de Charles VII*, vol.III, p.463.
4. Rybot, *Gorey Castle*, p.65.
5. ABSJ VI (1906), p.108 (proceedings of Royal Commissioners of 1531).
6. ABSJ X (1924), pp.150, 151; BDJ, p.218.
7. *ibid.*, XIII (1936), pp.37-61 (Eagleston on *Chroniques*).
8. Cart., pp.326, 327, no.244 (anno 1461).
9. ABSJ VI (1907), pp.210, 211; *ibid.*, IV (1897), pp.26, 27; Cart., pp.272, 273, no.192 (3.12.1461).
10. ABSJ X (1924), p.104.
11. *ibid.*, VII (1912), pp.187-192; MS, no.1392 de la Bibliothèque de Grenoble, Tome III, folios 387 *et seq.*; MOC, pp.32-34; PBC, App. Crown Case, p.163, no.76.
12. Le Quesne, *op. cit.*, pp.123, 565 (note XXVI); see also ch.11, p.92.

13. Coysh and Toms, *Guernsey through the Lens*, no.29 (1978).
14. ABSJ XXII (1977), pp. 95-97.
15. A genealogy of the Le Hardy family to the present time includes Hardy, the novelist, Hardy of Trafalgar fame, three admirals and Jacqueline du Pré, the cellist.
16. See ch.29, pp.234, 236.
17. Andrieux Vieulchastel.
18. Transcribed by Mr D.J. Shone.
19. St Ouen's Manor MS copy of a Latin text: *Divers documents relatifs à Jersey et Guernsey*, states that he was killed.
20. MOC, p.32 (article V of Maulevrier's Ordonnances).
21. Chron. IV, 'his pond' is La Mare au Seigneur (St Ouen's Pond). A stone in the manor grounds records the discovery of the horse's bones in 1901.
22. There is no evidence to suggest that Harliston was a knight.
23. Chron. V.
24. A resinous powder used for colouring medicines.
25. MOC, pp.35, 36; ABSJ IX (1920), pp.184-188; Bibliothèque nationale MSS franç, 26092 no.764.
26. MOC, p.35; PRO Pat. Roll 8, Edw. IV memb. 3 (28.1.1468/9).
27. De Gruchy, *Mediaeval Land Tenures,* p.140 (footnote); AR, 1309, p.29; de la Croix, *op. cit.*, I, p.137; ABSJ X (1927), p.299.
28. de la Croix, op. cit., II, p.101.
29. S.W. Bisson, *Jersey Chantry Certificate*, p.5.
30. Bois, *The Parish Church of St Saviour, Jersey*, p.61, *et seq.*; BDJ, p.325.
31. A *Vidimus* dated 1536 reaffirms the Bull and reiterates the papal fulminations in all their fury; MS in SJL. See also *Revue de la Manche,* Tome 20, p.197 (July 1978); Vatican registers, Vol. DCLXXII, fol.406.
32. PRO, Pat. Rolls 4 Eliz; Bois, *Const. Hist*, pp.119, 120, 141-143; AE, 25.3.1595, 10.4.1595.

Notes to Chapter Eight

1. He had also a claim through his descent from John of Gaunt whose great-granddaughter was Margaret Beauchamp, Henry's mother.
2. Memorial inside west door of Abbey; BDJ, p.398.
3. Chron. VLI.
4. MOC, p.108.
5. ABSJ XXII (1978), p.134.
6. *ibid.*, II (1886), pp.109-111; de la Croix, *op. cit.*, III, p.249.
7. Son of the Duke of Clarence and Isabella Neville.
8. BDJ, p.614.
9. MOC, p.38 and footnotes.
10. Chron. IX; BDJ, p.161.
11. Durham, 1494; Winchester, 1501.
12. *ibid.*, p.398, Chron. IX (Clement Le Hardy).
13. Cal. of Pat. Rolls, Henry VII, 5.11.1503, for other grants to Baker see Pat. Rolls Henry VII, 10.6.1486, 28.2.1486/7, 28.2.1504/5.
14. Bois, *op. cit.*, p.21, 5/9.
15. MOC, p.15; Lemprière, *Customs and Ceremonies of the Channel Islands*, p.132.
16. Colin Platt, *Mediaeval Southampton*, pt.IV, pp.139, 176-7, 185 and App.I, p.254.
17. MOC, p.92.
18. PRO and Bishop Langton's register at Winchester. Lambeth Palace Library MS 585, p.779. Final annexation 1568, see ch.9, p.81.
19. ABSJ VIII (1916), p.99.
20. BDJ, pp.224, 512.
21. Probably Anastasius who taught the monks of Mont-St-Michel and Cluny.
22. See ch.32, p.265.
23. de la Croix, *op.cit.*, III, pp.265, 335.
24. ABSJ XIII (1936), pp.44-55, Chron XV.
25. MSS, La Haule Manor.
26. OJH, I, p.154 (Jurat Payn's House, Grouville Court); de la Croix, *op. cit.*, III, p.265.
27. BDJ, p.141; Le Quesne, *op. cit.*, p.135.
28. ABSJ VI (1906), pp.87-110.
29. Le Geyt, *op. cit.*, IV, p.374.
30. See ch.4, p.32; ch.33, p.279.
31. AE, 18.9.1526 (C 2 folio 158).
32. MSS, La Haule Manor.
33. R of C, 25.9.1540; See OP 12, E.T.N.
34. AE, 16.1.1541/2; Bois, *op. cit.*, p.152, 9/3.
35. *ibid.*, 25.2.1545/6.

Notes to Chapter Nine

1. BDJ, p.226, DNB and many MSS in La Haule Manor.
2. Lecanu, *Histoire du Diocèse de Coutances*, I, ch.XX.
3. ABSJ X (1925), pp.186-190, 196-200; BDJ, p.466.
4. *ibid.*, III (1893), p.225; XX (1970), pp.159-161.
5. D'Aubigné, *Histoire de la Réformation*, II, bk.IX, p.219 *et seq.*
6. *ibid.*, II, bk.XII, p.495, *et seq.*; Smiles, *The Huguenots* I, p.17.
7. Lelièvre, *Histoire du Méthodisme dans les Iles de la Manche*, ch.II.
8. S.W. Bisson, *op. cit.*, p.7.
9. de la Croix, *op. cit.*, I, p.169 *et seq.*
10. La Haule MSS nos.176, 197 (16 cent.).
11. Stead, *A picture of Jersey*, p.140.

12. ABSJ XIV (1947), pp.333-339. This is now at the foot of Beaumont Hill.
13. La Haule MS no.179c, dated 1546.
14. MS in possession of Constable of St Martin.
15. See BDJ, p.689, re procureur du bien public (public trustee).
16. See ch.19, p.160; ch.24, p.197.
17. La Haule MS no 267 (16 cent.).
18. S.W. Bisson, *op. cit.*, p.5.
19. *ibid.*, p.7; ABSJ X (1927), pp.325-326; AE, 1549 (7.11.1549); Le Patourel, *C.I. under Tudor Gov.* p.36; Chron., ch.XXIV.
20. Chron., ch.XXVI.
21. C.G. Stevens, *Jersey Place names* (typescript SJL), p.215.
22. AE, 21.8.1548, 5.10.1549; Schickler, *Les Eglises du Refuge en Angleterre*, II, p.366.
23. ABSJ IV (1901), p.375; BDJ, p.662; AE, 8.10.1551.
24. OC, Ed.VI, 15.4.1550.
25. OC, 19.4.1550.
26. ABSJ XIV (1948), pp.367-375.
27. Cal. Pat. Rolls, Ed.VI, 25.4.1550; de la Croix III, pp.367, 368.
28. E.T. Nicolle, *The Town of St Helier*, pp.26, 27.
29. OJH I, p.58 *et seq.*
30. Chron., XXVI; F. de Schickler, *op. cit.*, II, p.367.
31. Chron., XXVIII.
32. Foxe's *Book of Martyrs*, Book XI (pub.1563).
33. Chron., XXVII.
34. BDJ, p.19; Act of Royal Court 27.6.1555; Le Quesne, *op. cit.*, pp.570, 571.
35. Le Maistre MSS in SJL.

Notes to Chapter Ten

The source for much of this chapter is Schickler. We have cited some, but not all, references to this source.

1. Pub. Basle, 1536.
2. Chron., XXXVII.
3. BDJ, p.516; ABSJ XI (1930), pp.247-249; Chron., XXXI; AE 8.3.1560/1.
4. SP Dom., Add. Eliz. 12.12.1559.
5. SP Dom., Eliz. LXXXIII
6. Hatfield MS.
7. MOC, pp.49, 54, 128; de la Croix, *op. cit.*, I, p.241; OC 25.4.1550.
8. Toustain de Bailly, *op. cit.*, III, p.138.
9. SP Dom. Eliz. 7.8.1565; Falle, *op. cit.* p.195.
10. Schickler, *op. cit.*, II, pp.371-373; Dupont, *op. cit.* III, p.441 (d'après le Recueil de Havilland).
11. See ch.8, p.67.
12. Schickler, *op. cit.*, II, pp.377, 378.
13. Recueil des Lois, Probate (Jersey) Law, 28.1.1949, reg. 19.2.49.
14. SP, Add. Eliz., XXVII 49 (29.10.1580).
15. *ibid.* (2.10.1568, 13.12.1568); Schickler, *op. cit.*, I, p.215; ABSJ VII (1913), p.280; *Histoire du Protestantisme Français*, LXXXI, p.82.
16. Ewen and de Carteret, *op. cit.*, pp.28, 29.
17. BDJ, p.48.
18. Chron., XXXVIII.
19. Schickler, II, p.390; DNB (under Sir Isaac Wake).
20. Le Quesne, *op. cit.*, pp.157-159.
21. Chron. XLII.
22. ABSJ XVI (1954), pp.195-199.
23. de la Croix, *op. cit.*, III, pp.365, 395.
24. Schickler, *op. cit.*, *passim*; OJH, II, ch.2, p.7; Rolls of Court, June 1563, Sept. 1588, 6.9.1589, 11.10.1589, Sept. 1599.
25. Lemprière, *op. cit.*, pp.154, 163.
26. ABSJ IV (1899), p.249; R of C, Oct. 1619.
27. *ibid.*, XIII (1939), pp.379-398; R of C, Dec. 1585, Dec. 1599, Oct. 1608.
28. AE, 17.12.1593.
29. ASBJ V (1903), pp.136, 137; BDJ, p.32.
30. Now the site of a reservoir.
31. MSS in SJL and information from Trustees of Don Baudains. Note: the top membrane of the Letters Patent, granted and sealed 13.9.1611, is now framed in the Bailiff's Chambers.
32. ABSJ III (1893), p.191 and XXII (1978), pp.187-189 re *trésor.*

Notes to Chapter Eleven

1. ABSJ XII (1934), pp.261-270.
2. Pouliot, *La Grande Aventure de Jacques Cartier*, p.52, (ii) (the list of the crew is preserved in the archives of St. Malo); Le Maistre MSS in SJL, II, pp.35, 36.
3. Rolls of Court.
4. St Ouen's Parish records.
5. Chev., pp.271, 272.
6. ABSJ IV (1900), pp.325-332; Port Books of Southampton; *Southampton in 1620* (Mayflower exhibition), p.41, no.87.
7. *The Third Book of Remembrance of Southampton* (1574-1602), II, p.96.
8. *Registre de l'Eglise Wallonne de Southampton.*
9. James Norbury, *Traditional Knitting Patterns* (Batsford).
10. British Library, Letter of Robert Wynkfielde to Lord Burleigh.
11. SP Dom. Eliz., Dec(?) 1596.
12. ABSJ XXI (1975), pp.359-362.
13. AE, 21.4.1608; See also R of C, 23.10.1607; Le Quesne, *op. cit.*, pp.285-288; Falle, *op. cit.* pp.122,

123, 362 (note 73).

14. Sark, MSS, Vol III, no.405 of copy in SJL.
15. Southampton Record Society, *Examinations and Depositions*, I, pp.92-96.
16. ABSJ XVIII (1961), pp.103-106; XXII (1978), pp.220, 221; MS in SJL by the late Capt. John Tessier-Yandell.
17. BDJ, pp.651-668; see also *The Poulets of Hinton St George*.
18. ABSJ I (1883), pp.385-396; *Gazette*, 28.4.1787.
19. SP, Eliz. Add. 13.7.1591, 12.3.1591/2.
20. PC to Governor 10.9.1593; MOC, pp.60, 61; see also ch.9, p.77.
21. Ralegh to Sir Robert Cecil, 15.10.1600. Information from Sir John Summerson re Byson.
22. AE, 20.9.1600, 3.7.1602, 24.7.1602.
23. Information from P. Bisson.
24. Philip Ahier, *The Governorship of Sir Walter Ralegh*, p.4.
25. Ralegh to Sir Robert Cecil, 15.10.1600.
26. ABSJ IX (1919), pp.102-106; Ahier, *op. cit.*, pp.138-143; Le Quesne, *op. cit.*, p.215; G.M. Trevelyan, *England under the Stuarts*, pp.104, 105.
27. OC 8.8.1603; see Falle op. cit., p.199; PBC vol. II, p.275 *et seq.*
28. Schickler *op. cit.*, II, p.175.
29. BDJ p.493; Schickler, *op. cit.*, II, pp.475-477; ABSJ VII (1912), p.140.
30. AE 3.5.1617; SP Dom. James I, 6.3.1609/10; see also ch.12.
31. OC 15.6.1618; Le Quesne *op. cit.*, p.171.
32. MSS nos. 470, 744, Lambeth Palace Library.
33. Chev., p.980.
34. BDJ 616; SP James I, Add. 31.1.1620/1; Le Quesne, *op. cit.*, p.578, note XLII; ABSJ IX (1919), p.4; SP Dom., Feb 1619/20, 17.1.1622/3; re Stallenge see DNB and *Jersey Society in London*, 25.4.1949.
35. Falle, *op. cit.*, pp.245-262, App.XII.
36. SP Dom. James I, Add. 15.4.1622; ABSJ II (1889), p.462 (5); Schickler, *op. cit.*, II, p.469; SP Dom., Ch.I, 1628 (p.324).
37. Chev., pp.860, 861; ABSJ VII (1910), pp.35-46.
38. Heylin, *Survey of Guernsey and Jersey*, pub.1656; Bk.VI, ch.V, pp.311, 312.
39. Eagleston, *The Channel Islands under Tudor Government*, p.140; PBC II, p.350, No.140.

Notes to Chapter Twelve

Many of the documents referred to in this chapter are reproduced in full in the Prison Board Case Vol.II, pp.293-356.

1. BDJ p.317; ABSJ IV (1898), p.99, pp.125-138 (1901), p.378; OC 5.9.1605, 5.8.1607; AE 5.8.1607; SP Dom., Add James I, 26.5.1606, 1.9.1616.
2. ABSJ IV (1898), p.125 (footnote); OJH, II, p.170.
3. Le Geyt, *op. cit.*, IV, p.55.
4. SP, July 1616.
5. In early records the titles of Warden and Governor are much confused.
6. SP, 18.3.1616/7 (footnote), 22.5.1616.
7. *ibid.*, 26.4.1616, 21.2.1617/18, 3.5.1617, 28.5.1617, 24.6.1617; Calendar of State Papers, pp.564, 565; Falle, *op. cit.*, pp. 403-407; Le Quesne, *op. cit.*, pp.269-280 (The original of the Commissioners' Report is in the PRO.).
8. BDJ, p.477.
9. J. Poingdestre, *Caesarea*, p.20; Jersey Society in London, 4.5.1962.
10. La Haule MSS.
11. BDJ, p.317; SP Dom, Add. James I, 27.3.1620, 15.4.1620, 16.4.1620, 21.4.1620, 15.3.1623/4; OC 27.9.1621.
12. PBC, II, pp.344-345 (nos. 137, 138); Rolls of Court, 17.8.1621.
13. ABSJ IV (1898), pp.134-138; Le Geyt, *op. cit.*, IV, p.60; OC, 13.1.1623/4; R of C, 27.3.1624.

Notes to Chapter Thirteen

1. Sir Edward Conway, later Lord President of the Council.
2. His reply to Crown Officers. See BDJ, pp.155, 164.
3. Rybot, *Eliz. Castle*, pp.38, 39.
4. ABSJ II (1889), pp.464 (15), 477 (77).
5. *ibid.*, XIII (1937), pp.192, 246; Trevelyan *op. cit.*, pp.130, 131.
6. SP, Dom., Ch.I, 21.11.1627, 11.12.1627, 13.12.1627.
7. ABSJ II (1889), p.464 (17); SP Dom., Ch.I, 15.3.1628/9.
8. ABSJ V (1905), pp.371, 372 (19.5.1627); II (1889), p.479, item 80.
9. St Aubin's Fort is in St Brelade; SP 8.7.1630.
10. ABSJ XII (1935), pp.453-484; XIV (1941), pp.76-84; XX (1972), pp.361-378.
11. *ibid.*, II (1889), pp.466-468 (38), 474 (65), 488 (112).
12. *ibid.*, XIV (1941), p.79; XII (1935), p.456; Frances Le Sueur, *A Natural History of Jersey*, p.116.
13. Le Maistre, *Dictionnaire*, p.138.
14. ABSJ XIV (1941), pp.80, 81.
15. Heylin, *op. cit.*, VI, ch.1, p.302; see also ch.19, p.159.
16. ABSJ VI (1906), pp.115-117.
17. See. ch.10, p.86.
18. AE, 8.4.1662; Le Quesne, *op. cit.*, pp.397, 398; see ch.18, p.154.
19. See ch.8, p.68; ch.23, p.191.

20. BDJ, pp.210, 616; see note 7 above.
21. ABSJ II (1889), p.486, item 102; SP Dom., Ch.I Add. 27.9.1629.
22. BDJ, p.334; Pat. Roll, ch.1, pt. 8, no.10 (17.6.1633); Le Quesne, *op. cit.*, p.177; Falle, *op. cit.*, pp.215, 216; Cottrill, *Victoria College, Jersey*, ch.1 and pp.17, 18; OP 13, p.63 in SJL.
23. DNB; MOC, pp.71, 72; SP Dom., Ch.I; Prynne, *Mount Orgueil or Divine and Profitable Meditations …* (London 1641); see also *Pseudo Mastix*.
24. ABSJ V (1903), p.103 and BDJ, p.167, reveal uncertainty as to who was Receiver-General; see also ABSJ II (1888), p.316.
25. BDJ, p.623.
26. Prynne, *The Lyar Confounded*; see Pamphlets 70, p.151 in SJL.
27. Copy in SJL; BDJ, p.423.
28. Pamphlets 70 in SJL and ABSJ II (1888), pp.309 *et seq.*
29. BDJ, p.234, Henri Dumaresq (1614-1654).
30. Chev., pp.6, 7; Le Quesne, *op. cit.*, p.303 *et seq.*
31. Chev., p.83, Acte de la Cour 7.10.1643.
32. OC, 5.5.1642.
33. ABSJ (1889), p.489 (114).

Notes to Chapter Fourteen

1. The original diary in manuscript is in the Library of La Société Jersiaise. The full French version was published by La Société in 1906 and is well indexed. A typescript version in English is in the SJL. It is possible to confirm many of the events recorded by Chevalier from other contemporary documents. See also BDJ p.77.
2. Osborne papers quoted by Hoskins in *Charles II in the Channel Islands*, II, pp.18-24.
3. Brevint, *op. cit.*, IV, p.19.
4. ABSJ II (1888), p.330 (*Pseudo-Mastix*).
5. BDJ, pp.42, 134, 234, 423, 626.
6. ABSJ II (1888), p.329 (letter signed by Pym and Hampden).
7. BDJ, p.54; Chev., pp.3, 4; Balleine, *All for the King*, ch.2; SP Dom. and Clarendon Papers *passim*.
8. SP Dom., Ch.I, 16.2.1642/3; ABSJ II (1888), pp.328, 329; Chev., p.10, 25.
9. ABSJ II (1888), *Pseudo-Mastix*, pp.323, 331-333. Chev., pp.12-19.
10. ABSJ IX (1922), pp.301, 303 (Jean fils Laurens, Dénonciateur).
11. *ibid.*, II (1888), pp.353, 354.
12. Chev., pp.23-27.
13. Daughter of Sir Francis Dowse of Nether Wallop, Hampshire.
14. Chev., pp.14, 15, 20 *et seq.*
15. BDJ, p.312.
16. Tupper, *Chronicles of Castle Cornet*, p.66 (Sir Philippe to Sir Peter Osborne); Chev, pp.15, 18.
17. Probably Le Douet Le Gallais, but see Chev., p.19 (footnote).
18. See ABSJ V (1905), pp.364, 365.
19. Now Broad Street.
20. Chev., pp.27-48 *passim*.
21. *ibid.*, p.49 *et seq.*
22. *ibid.*, pp. 56, 133; BDJ, p.173.
23. *ibid.*, p.13 (footnote), pp.64, 65.
24. *ibid.*, pp.58-62; DNB.
25. *ibid.*, pp.62, 63.
26. *ibid.*, pp.79, 80.
27. *ibid.*, p.81.
28. *ibid.*, p.77.
29. BDJ, p.175; MOC, pp.74-76.
30. Chev., p.985.
31. *ibid.*, pp.101-103.
32. *ibid.*, p.83; AE, 7.10.1643.
33. *ibid.*, pp.134, 152-156.
34. *ibid.*, pp.93-102; Balleine, *op. cit.*, pp.54, 55; BDJ, p.341; ABSJ VIII (1916), pp.86-88.
35. Chev., pp.101-109; BDJ, p.626.

Notes to Chapter Fifteen

1. AE, 24.11.1643.
2. Grampus is a form of whale, see ABSJ XIII (1939), p.359.
3. OJH II, p.65.
4. See ch.18, p.152.
5. Chev., p.175 (16.6.1645), *All for the King*, pp.54, 55.
6. ABSJ XXII (1978), p.130; Hoskins, *op. cit.*, II, p.67, Carteret to Osborne.
7. *All for the King*, p.30; ABSJ IV (1901), pp.380-383.
8. BDJ, pp.25, 616; Chev., pp.152-155.
9. AE, 24.4.1645, 5.3.1645/6.
10. Chev., pp.166-182, *All for the King*, p.34; Tupper, *Castle Cornet*, pp.125-127.
11. ABSJ X (1927), pp.316-324; Hoskins, *op. cit.*, I, p.250.
12. MS copy in SJL (18.5.1647); *All for the King*, p.34.
13. BDJ, pp.42, 341; AE, 21.3.1643/4.
14. Esther de la Planche.
15. BDJ, p.495; ABSJ II (1889), pp.477, 478 (78).
16. Thomas fils Michel, Jurat 1617-1645. He had bought Les Augrès in 1616, selling it and the mill to Elie Dumaresq in 1643; see Reg. Pub., folio 313.
17. Constable of St Mary 1652-1655.
18. Chev., pp.222-223 and footnote.
19. Published by the Société Jersiaise in 1886.

20. *All for the King*, pp.40-42; Clarendon Papers Bk.VIII, pp.441, 494.
21. Chev., pp.286-336.
22. One of the Commissioners, see note 9.
23. BDJ, p.23.
24. Hoskins, *op. cit.*, II, pp.138-142; Chev, pp.332, 454 (Maison Michelle Guerdain).
25. *All for the King*, pp.46, 48; DNB; Clarendon Bk. X, pp.350-384; Chev., pp.336-340.

Notes to Chapter Sixteen

1. Chev., pp.414, 749.
2. *ibid.*, p.514.
3. *Calendar of Clarendon Papers*, 15.11.1646; *All for the King*, pp.58-60.
4. BDJ, pp.234, 306, 423.
5. AE, 26.3.1647; Chev., pp.424, 429-431.
6. Clarendon Papers, 3.4.1647 at Castle Eliz.
7. Clarendon, *History of the Great Rebellion*, XI, pp.29 *et seq.*, 118.
8. A preserve made from apples and cider, see Lemprière, *Customs Ceremonies and Traditions of the Channel Islands*, pp.152, 153.
9. AE, 3.12.1646; Chev., pp.403, 404.
10. ABSJ XIX (1965), pp.84, 85; The de Carteret arms are now at the Museum, presented by the Maretts of La Haule; Chev., p.593.
11. ABSJ XIII (1939), pp.379-398; see also ch.10 page 86.
12. Clarendon, *op. cit.*, VI, pp.186-197 (6.12.1647); Chev., pp.522, 523.
13. Laurens Hamptonne; BDJ, p.312; ABSJ XV (1952), pp.431, 432.
14. Admiral Robert Blake (1598-1657); DNB.
15. Clarendon, *op. cit.*, XII, *passim.*
16. Chev., pp.705-767; Collins, *History of the de Carteret family* (1756), says it was then in Herr van Alderhelm's cabinet of curiosities at Leipzig. He was quoting Brown, p.172.
17. Chev., p.774.
18. ABSJ III (1896), pp.424-428 and footnote p.427 (7); Chev., pp.714, 715.
19. ABSJ XIII (1937), p.217.
20. The Jersey Attorney-General was Helier de Carteret; see DNB for Sir Edward Herbert (1591-1657), A-G of Charles II.
21. Sir E. Nicholas to Marquis of Ormonde, Jersey 16-26.10.1649.
22. John, first Lord Byron, see DNB.
23. DNB; *Clarendon Papers* II, p.32.
24. Captain Smith (1579-1613). This was not the present New Jersey which lies much further to the north; Chev., pp. 766, 799.
25. DNB; ABSJ (1938), pp.319-322.
26. AE, 21.9.1649.
27. Chev., pp.814, 848.
28. *ibid.*, p.870.
29. Chev., pp.667, 670; Hoskins, *op. cit.*, p.107; Whitelock, *Memorials.*
30. Part of the dune system overlooking St Ouen's Bay.
31. *All for the King*, pp.91, 92; *Clarendon Papers.*
32. Chev., pp.945 *et seq.*; ABSJ XIII (1937), pp.224 *et seq.*
33. La Pulente at the southern end of St Ouen's Bay.
34. For articles of capitulation see MOC, p.79.
35. No proof of Hollar's stay in the Island has been found other than the signature on the engravings.
36. BDJ, p.460.
37. Anne, wife of 1. Thomas Seale and 2. Jean Nicolle, and Rachel, wife of Clement Le Montais.
38. *All for the King*, pp.99, 100.

Notes to Chapter Seventeen

Note: The *Diary* of Jean Chevalier ends in 1651.

1. Chev., pp.948, 949.
2. *ibid.*, pp.954-956; *Clarendon Papers.*
3. PC Doléances and OC, 27.8.1669.
4. Hoskins, *op. cit.*, II, app., pp.395-400.
5. Firkin: a small cask; tod: about 28 lbs.
6. BDJ, p.475.
7. *ibid.*, p.174; Compounding: a monetary payment to settle a case.
8. *ibid.*, p.155; ABSJ II (1888), pp.470, 471 (49); Chev, pp.650, 651.
9. Hoskins, I, *op. cit.* II, app. I.
10. This is an important fact.
11. ABSJ VII (1914), pp.393-394.
12. BDJ, p.307.
13. DNB; ABSJ IV (1901), p.383.
14. OC, 27.9.1655.
15. OC, 28.2.1654/5; Le Quesne, *op. cit.*, p.342.
16. BDJ, p.175.
17. Falle, *op. cit.*, notes page 304.
18. See Pamphlets 70 in SJL (*Articles of impeachment exhibited against Col. Robert Gibbons and Cap. Richard Yeardley*); see ch.15, p.122, re Gallie.
19. Pamphlets 70 in SJL, Col. Martin's reply from Council of State 22.10.1652.
20. See ch.28, p.224.
21. *Articles of Impeachment, passim.*
22. Extremists who believed Christ was about to establish a Fifth Monarchy, which would suppress all previous monarchies.
23. DNB; Chev, pp.754, 761; Hoskins, *op. cit.*, II, p.391.
24. Aaron Stocall, see BDJ, p.576.

25. BDJ, p.469.
26. ABSJ IV (1901), pp.383, 384.
27/28. The diarist has not yet been identified. Balleine mentions a de la Rocque MS, de la Croix a Le Geyt MS, and some isolated extracts attached to Chevalier's diary dated 1660.
29. ABSJ VIII (1917), p.271; Acte de la Cour, 11.8.1660.
30. de la Croix, *Ville de St Hélier*, p.92; the source of the quotation is not given. See, however, Baptismal Register, St Martin 23.4.1661

Notes to Chapter Eighteen

1. See also ABSJ III (1890), pp.1-10.
2. Chev, p.252.
3. BDJ, p.54; *All for the King*, Ch.II; Pepys' *Diary, passim.*
4. *Hudson's Bay Company - A Brief History* (1934).
5. BDJ, pp.129, 131.
6. OP, 26 in SJL; Foote and Wilson, *The Viking Achievement*, pp.382, 383; *The Times*, 16.1.1980; ABSJ (1934), 243-246.
7. ABSJ IX (1919), pp.3, 4.
8. Poingdestre, *Lois et Coutumes de Jersey* in SJL.
9. de Gruchy *op. cit.*, pp.116, 117; see also ch.28 p.229. Traces are still found of a *chemin de moulin* at St Saviour and a *chemin des morts* (used for carrying the coffin from a house to the church) at St Brelade.
10. See ch.28 p.229.
11. MS in SJL.
12. The *livres de perchage* in Guernsey are a form of *extente*, still in use recently, in which are entered in vergées and perches measurements of property held on various fiefs.
13. Overton offended Cromwell by joining the Levellers. The death of the regicides is recorded in the *livres de la Cour de Cattel* or in the register of St Saviour's Church; see also SP 13.2.1668/9.
14. See footnote to AE 13.10.1660.
15. ABSJ XII (1932), pp.152-155.
16. OC, July 1660; AE, 23.11.1661, 9.4.1663/4; BDJ, pp.383, 625.
17. R. of C. and Rolls of Ecclesiastical Court.
18. DNB; BDJ, p.460; Le Quesne, *op. cit.*, p.597, note XLIX, Letter of Edward Nicholas for King, 6.10.1662.
19. BDJ, p.423; ABSJ VIII (1917), pp.271, 272; AE, 11.8.1660.
20. Petitions to Council 1660-1669 *passim.* particularly 27.8.1669; PRO Calendar of Committee for Compounding 28.4.1650, 2.1.1650/1, 22.6.1652, June 1660 re Jean Pipon.
21. SP Dom., Ch.II, 26.12.1665 and 1666 *passim.*
22. DNB; AE, 16.4.1661, 13.1.1665/6; SP Dom, 1665/6, pp.110-119; Falle, *op. cit.*, p.398 notes 126,127; Army lists, 26.12.1665.
23. AE, 15.3.1677/88; SP Dom., 25.12.1665, 30.6.1666, 11.10.1666, *inter alia.*
24. ABSJ XIV (1948), pp.382-385. This refers to the sketch of St Aubin's bay with ships dated *c.*1545.
25. BDJ, pp.92, 245; see also ch.19, pp.158, 159.
26. AE, 24.7.1669, 3.12.1673.
27. ABSJ XV (1949), pp.131 *et seq.*; OJH I, p.189; SP, 4.12.1675.
28. AE, 20.2.1670/1, 19.5.1679.
29. Market Street.
30. AE, 8.2.1790, petitions dated 7.12.1789.
31. See ch.23, p.193; ch29, p.242; ch30, p.246; ch31, p.254.
32. AE, 17th and 18th centuries *passim*; SP Dom., 2.2.1694/5.
33. Rolls of Court (samedi), 30.8.1688; Le Geyt, *op. cit.*; J.K. Clark, California Institute of Technology.
34. Parish records of St Ouen; AE, 3.12.1646, 25.9.1666.
35. *Southampton Book of Examinations and Depositions II*, pp.96, 97.
36. AE, 15.3.1670/1; ABSJ XIII (1939), pp.399-404.
37. Turk, *The Quiet Adventurers in America*; Church registers at St Ouen.
38. Information from New England Records via Mrs Nielsen.
39. BDJ, p.353 and Pipon MSS in SJL.
40. AE, 5.3.1677/8; PC Colonial Papers, 8.1.1672/3, 10.3. 1676/7, 31.5.1676, 5.12.1677, 14.12.1677; PRO entries in Port Books.

Notes to Chapter Nineteen

1. SP Dom., Ch.II, 18.1.1678/9, 21.1.1678/9, 2.2.1678/9.
2. Pepys, *op. cit.*, 14.8.1665.
3. AE, 5.3.1645/6, 27.2.1665/6.
4. AE, 24.7.1669, 12.1.1670/1 ('le haut mur' mentioned as the site was in the La Motte Street area); Cottrill, *op. cit.*; Falle, *op. cit.*, pp.214-217, 451-453, note 219; Le Quesne, *op. cit.*, pp.177-179.
5. DNB; AE, 3.7.1679 *et seq.*
6. ABSJ IV (1891), pp.71-74; BDJ, p.131.
7. MOC, pp.84-88.
8. AE, 7.11.1681.
9. See papers of P. Mauger in SJL.
10. ABSJ IV (1901), pp.386-389.
11. *London Gazette*, March 1685; Saunders, *Jersey in the 17th century*, p.216.
12. BDJ, pp.245, 273, 552.
13. Falle, *op. cit.*, pp.363-365, notes 75, 76; Le Quesne,

op. cit., pp.33-36.
14. Falle, *op. cit.*, pp.125, 126.
15. Le Quesne's *Constitutional History* was published in 1856.
16. ABSJ XVII (1960), pp.343, 344.
17. Lavisse, *Histoire de France*, VII; Richard Mayne, *Old Channel Islands Silver.*
18. Rolls of Ecc. Court 1663-1698; ABSJ II (1888), pp.205-220.
19. OC, 4.8.1680; AE, 19.3.1680/1.
20. AE, 12.1.1685/6, 11.11.1686, 4.2.1693/4; ABSJ XIX (1965), pp.61-70.
21. J.S. Clarke, *Life of James II*, II; Falle (1st ed. p.44).
22. Chev, pp.321, 457, 556, also the date of the restoration of Charles II, 29.5.1660.
23. AE 20.11.1688.
24. SP, 30.5.1689 and Dec. 1693.
25. R. of C., 2.1.1668/9; OC, 26.2.1688/9; SP, 30.5.1689.
26. BDJ, p.392.
27. AE, 2.4.1689.

Notes to Chapter Twenty

1. This is thought to have been first published in Bordeaux in 1647; See ch.7, p.62; Poingdestre, *Caesarea*, p.64.
2. AE, 5.3.1677/8, 3.5.1689.
3. Lord Teignmouth, *The Smugglers.*
4. SP Dom., 19.3.1690/1.
5. ABSJ IV (1901), p.388.
6. SP Dom., Aug. 1691, Dec. 1693.
7. DNB; SP, 4.6.1798 (re house at St Saviour) and 25.1.1703/4.
8. OC, 9.5.1710.
9. SP, 7.6.1691, 30.7.1691; OC, 10.3.1691/2.
10. AE, 31.1.1677/8, 24.3.1687/88.
11. La Haule Manor MSS.
12. OJH II, p.5; Chron., 11.12.1819.
14. A new prison was opened at La Moye on 27.2.1975.
15. ABSJ II (1887), pp.192-198; Trevelyan, *op. cit.*, p.439; holograph MS Archiepiscopal Library Lambeth no. 929.35.
16. ABSJ IV (1898), pp.105-108; (1901), pp.386-391.
17. BDJ, p.541 and Pipon MSS in SJL.
18. Letters of Ph. Pipon 12.7.1691 in SJL; OC, 26.6.1706, 10.5.1707.
19. SP, Wm. and Mary 1691.
20. BDJ, p.541; OC, 18.10.1711.
21. R of C, 24.3.1704/5, OC, 31.12.1702 and 3.8.1704.
22. OP 2 in SJL.
23. R of C, 9.7.1705, 20.4.1706
24. BDJ, pp.69, 122, 539.
25. Syvret documents *inter alia.*
26. BDJ, p.370; R of C, 25.2.1699/70.
27. OC, 23.3.1703/4.
28. PC, 4.7.1704; SP, June 1703; R of C, 20.11.1703.
29. PC, 23.2.1703/4, 15.6.1704; *Chronique*, 2.5.1868.
30. Copy in SJL.
31. See ch.8, p,66; ch.33, p.279.

Notes to Chapter Twenty-one

1. Pipon MSS in SJL.
2. *All for the King*, App., p.177.
3. Pipon letters in SJL.
4. New England records (from Mrs Nielsen, a descendant of Janvrin).
5. BDJ, p.328.
6. Original copy in SJL.
7. MSS in SJL.
8. BDJ, p.285 and Fiott papers in SJL; Dr. R. Ommer.
9. Innis, *The Codfisheries*, p.19.
10. Brevint, *op. cit.*, I, p.76.
11. See ch.22, *passim.*
12. Papers of P.Mauger in SJL.
13. Letter of Daniel Messervy from Bath dated 8.5.1758; SP Dom., Add. James I re Maret 'at the Baths'.
14. ABSJ VI (1906), pp.48-51.
15. *All for the King,* pp.12-15.
16. AE, 26.1.1712/13.
17. ABSJ XI (1928), pp.107-117.
18. See ch.23, p.191; ch.27, p.215.
19. MSS in SJL.
20. ABSJ XI (1928), pp.111, 112.
21. MSS in possession of Jurat Max Lucas.
22. Probably son of Jacques Lemprière (see BDJ, p.416).
23. A term for stale fish, often reserved for slaves in W. Indies.
24. ABSJ VI (1908), pp.261, 262; VIII (1907), p.204.
25. Probably a connection by marriage of Edouard Luce.
26. Robin papers in SJL; see also ABSJ VI (1907), pp.156-171; Mrs de Vaumorel, née Constance Charlotte Le Hardy.
27. BDJ, pp.213, 328, 490; see also ch.24, *passim.*
28. Marie de Veulle.
29. OJH II, p.62, para.4.

Notes to Chapter Twenty-two

1. Lytton Strachey, *Landmarks in French literature.*
2. See ch.29; Trevelyan, *op. cit.*, p.441.
3. F. Le Maistre, *op. cit.*; OJH I, p.82.
4. Information from Mr Raymond Falle.
5. See ch.30, p.244.

6. AE, 3.10.1701, 1.7.1714, 9.4.1720.
7. Deputé Jean Dumaresq; AE, 3.5.1720.
8. Le Quesne, *op.cit.*, pp.406-424.
9. ABSJ VI (1908), pp.261, 262; AE, 19.7.1726, 9.8.1729.
10. MSS in SJL; BDJ, 30, 213; see also ch.21, petition 25.7.1730.
11. Copy in SJL.
12. ABSJ III (1892), pp.155-162; III (1895), pp.307-339.
13. See *Gazette*, 17.3.1827.
14. ABSJ V (1903), pp.158-162; IV (1901), p.392.
15. *ibid.*, III (1886), pp.161, 162.
16. P. Mauger, letter in SJL, 7.4.1731.
17. Papers and letters of François Marett in SJL.
18. The country home of Lord Carteret (it is now a school in Hertfordshire).
19. ABSJ III (1895), p.321; OC (petitions 11.4.1734); R of C.
20. OC, 19.5.1671; AE 27.7.1671; Le Quesne, *op. cit.*, pp.382-386.
21. AE, 18.9.1834; see ch.30, p.244.
22. ABSJ III (1895), p.309.
23. *ibid.*, pp.326-331.
24. OC, 1.4.1734.
25. MSS in SJL riot (4.6.1736).
26. OC, 1.8.1732, 1.4.1734, 21.7.1736, 30,5.1740; R of C 12.9.1735.
27. Le Quesne, *op. cit.*, p.420; Falle, *op. cit.*, pp.457, 458, note 231.

Notes to Chapter Twenty-three

1. Falle, *op. cit.*, p.106.
2. AE, 6.10.1729, 13.4.1730, 10.2.1736/7, 14.5.1737, 28.6.1737, 29.1.1741/2; ABSJ XIII (1937), pp.259-274; de la Croix, *La Ville de St Hélier*, pp.116-119.
3. de la Croix, *op. cit.*, p.118.
4. A department serving the Crown Officers.
5. BDJ, p.30; de la Croix, *op. cit.*, pp.21-25; Balleine, *The Bailiwick of Jersey*, p.34.
6. AE, 5.2.1763.
7. ABSJ XIII (1937), pp.131-141; XXII (1979), pp.301-309; Balleine, *op. cit.*, p.75.
8. AE, 23.3.1735/6.
9. Information from F. de L. Bois; François-Victor Hugo, *La Normandie Inconnue*, p.138.
10. AE, 25.8.1668, 4.6.1672, 15.5.1744, 24.8.1761; Lelièvre, *Histoire du Méthodisme dans les Iles de la Manche*, p.257; Wesley's *Journal*, 28.8.1787.
11. ABSJ V (1902), pp. 44-56; AE, 22.3.1697/8, 3.10.1701, 14.6.1708, 21.12.1720 (this refers to an extra piece of land adjoining la Halle on which the United Club now has its entrance in Church Street).
12. AE, 2.6.1750, 26.7.1751, 16.9.1751; Susan Legouix, Article in *the Connoisseur* on John Cheere's statue of George II.
13. ABSJ V (1901), pp.8, 9.
14. AE, 26.7.1751, 16.9.1751, 18.11.1751.
15. MSS in SJL.
16. Nicolle, *The Town of St Helier*, pp.34-37; AE, 12.3.1768; Raymond Falle, *The Royal Court House of the Island of Jersey.*
17. Rolls of the Ecclesiastical Court, 20.6.1745.
18. AE, 9.7.1733, 10.7.1749, 2.10.1751.
19. AE, 11.1.1749/50.
20. BDJ, p.563; ABSJ VI (1907), pp.156-164; XI (1929), pp.169-182; XXI (1976), pp.469-476; MS diary in SJL.
21. Namier and Brooks, *History of Parliament*, pp.267-271; Daniel Messervy, *Diary*, p.32; ABSJ XIX (1966), pp.131, 132.
22. Fiott papers in SJL.
23. The trading connection between Jersey and the Baltic dates back for a considerable period.
24. Minutes of the Chamber of Commerce (Réglements des Armateurs).
25. ABSJ XIII (1939), pp.407-412; *Authentic Narrative of the Oppressions of the Islanders of Jersey*, II, pp.174-295; BDJ, p.285; see ch.24, p.195.
26. Rowcliffe appears to have had a rope-walk, one of two at La Corderie, Green Street; see also Messervy *op. cit.*, p.39.
27. OC, 1.7.1731; ABSJ XIX (1965), pp.75-83.
28. BDJ, p.69.
29. BDJ, p. 240.

Notes to Chapter Twenty-four

1. BDJ, pp.69, 76.
2. ABSJ IV (1898), pp.108-110.
3. *ibid.*, V (1902), pp.10, 11; *Authentic Narrative*, II, p.121.
4. BDJ, p.285; Fiott papers in SJL; *Authentic Narrative*, II, pp.174-295; *Diary* of Daniel Messervy, p.70 (12.6.1771).
5. OP 15 in SJL contains relevant documents; see also AE, 28.11.1767.
6. *Salisbury Journal* 6.11.1769; DM, App.9, pp.96, 97.
7. BDJ, p.490; DM, p.3 (28.9.1769).
8. Champart was exacted on certain fields only, these being *terres champartières*.
9. See ch.4, p.30; ch.33, p.281.
10. DM, app.3, 4, pp.83-89.
11. *Assize d'Heritage*: a ceremonial meeting of the Full

Court held once a year, at which all seigneurs, who owe *suite de cour*, attend to do homage, and advocates renew their oath. See OJH II, p.13; Charles Poingdestre MS in SJL; Pierre Mauger MS in SJL.

12. PC, Lord Weymouth to Mr Lemprière, 24.10.1769; AE 1.11.1769.
13. DNB; *Authentic Narrative*, ch.VI; DM, pp.11, 12; AE, 7.7.1770.
14. BDJ, pp.80, 269, 391; DM, pp.22, 23, 49, 57.
15. DM, pp.13, 17, app.81-83, 88, 89; *Authentic Narrative*, II, pp.286, 287.
16. DM, app.3, pp.83-87.
17. DNB; DM, p.57.
18. BDJ, pp.410, 431.
19. Le Quesne, *op. cit.*, pp.426-429; AE, 6.9.1770; Code of 1771; see also ch.33.
20. BDJ, p.181; DM, p.63.
21. ABSJ V (1902), p.12 and footnote; DM, p.66.
22. BDJ, p.240; Stevens, *Victorian Voices*, *passim*.
23. See ch.33.
24. de la Croix, *La Ville de St Helier*, p.161.
25. Minutes of Chamber of Commerce; RTSG XV (1951), pp.145-153.
26. BDJ, p.447.
27. ABSJ XX (1971), p.289.

Notes to Chapter Twenty-five

For a more detailed account see Richard Mayne, *The Battle of Jersey*, published 1980.

1. D. Messervy MSS in SJL.
2. See ch.15, p.119; ch.16, p.135; ch.28, p.224.
3. ABSJ VI (1909), pp.457-460.
4. Brachet, *La Dernière Expédition contre Jersey*, p.73.
5. This portrait is in the Museum of La Société Jersiaise; BDJ, p.329.
6. AE, 20.3.1782; This sword is now in the Metropolitan Museum of Art in New York.
7. Vielet is an older spelling for le Banc de Violet marked on modern charts.
8. Plaques have been placed at Fort Henry and St Helier to mark the bi-centenary of the Battle.
9. Adjutant Harrison is a central figure in Copley's painting of 'The Death of Major Peirson'.
10. ABSJ XXII (1980), pp.407-417.
11. Evidence suggests he was the son of Moyse Corbet.
12. BDJ, p.374; ABSJ XVII (1957), pp.65-73.
13. ABSJ XXII (1978), pp.213, 214.
14. A wall built of turfs.
15. For detail on the laws of inheritance see Le Quesne, *op. cit.*, pp.228-291.

Notes to Chapter Twenty-six

1. OC, 18.5.1781.
2. OC, 22.12.1783.
3. BDJ, pp.11, 251.
4. *Magasin de l'Ile de Jersey*, October 1784, July 1785.
5. Rolls of Court 11.10.1785 *et seq.*
6. Lieut.-Bailiff's petition to King in Council, 24.1.1788.
7. *Gazette*, quoted by Thomas Sivret, BDJ, p.574.
8. *ibid.*, 16.6.1787.
9. PC, 24.1.1788. A collection of the several petitions etc. relevant to political differences 1779-1788 is in SJL.
10. AE, 5.11.1792.
11. *ibid.*, 16.9.1788, 21.3.1789, 5.5.1794; *Gazette*, 24.1.1789.
12. Copy of letter in SJL.
13. *Gazette* 13.10.1792.
14. See ch.28, p.223.
15. L'Estourbillon, *Les Familles Françaises à Jersey pendant La Révolution* (pub. Nantes, 1886).
16. Ingouville letters, Beaton Institute, Nova Scotia.
17. L'Estourbillon, *op. cit.*, p.185; *Revue de la Manche*, Tome 19 (1977), pp.179, 185.
18. AE, 1.11.1788; 12.11.1790; 1.2.1796; 30.6.1796.
19. E.T. Nicolle, *The Town of St Hélier*, p.75; de la Croix, *La Ville de St Hélier*, pp.119-122; see also *Gazette* for notices of property transactions.
20. AE, 8.8.1781; see also ch.29, p.234; ch.31, p.258; ch.32, p.268; ch.33, p.286.
21. BDJ, p.334; unless otherwise stated examples are from *La Gazette*.
22. OJH II, p.82 and La Haule Manor MSS.
23. Ingouville papers (Anne *née* Martin); Turk, *The Quiet Adventurers in Canada*, p.281; and Beaton Institute, Nova Scotia.
24. BDJ, pp.257, 420, 591.
25. Sandhills.
26. AE, 15.5.1793.

Notes to Chapter Twenty-seven

1. BDJ, p.563; ABSJ XI (1929), pp.169-182; XXI (1976), pp.469-476; George Le Feuvre (George d'la Forge), *Jérri Jadis*, p.120 *et seq.*
2. Beaton Institute, Sydney, Nova Scotia.
3. *Gazette*, 28.2.1789.
4. Information from G.H. Pimm, descendant of Le Boutillier family, and from Provincial Archives in New Brunswick, M. Fidèle Thériault, M. Donat Robichaud and Memorial University of Newfoundland, Maritime History Group; local

parish registers.

5. Innis, *op. cit.*, pp.403, 404.
6. Rolls of the Court, April 1676, 22.5.1676 *inter alia.*
7. Pipon MSS in SJL.
8. *Mariners Mirror*, Feb. 1963, p.114; Southampton church registers.
9. Parker, *Sails of the Maritimes*; ABSJ XIII (1939), p.399.
10. MSS in SJL.
11. BDJ, p.521.
12. English Customs Records; J. Stevens, *Victorian Voices*, pp.62, 63.
13. Ferdinand Brock Tupper, Guernsey historian.
14. ABSJ XVIII (1962), pp.229-235.
15. *Gazette*, 8.2.1794.
16. Jersey vessels carried fish to the Catholic countries of South America and the Mediterranean and returned with mixed cargoes.
17. R. Mayne, *Old Channel Islands Silver.*
18. BDJ, p.530; Lelièvre, *op. cit.*, p.164.
19. Lelièvre, *op. cit.*, II, ch.1 *passim.*
20. *ibid.*, II, ch.VI *passim.*
21. *ibid.*, III, ch.1.
22. *ibid.*, III, ch.III.
23. C.A.R. du Feu, MSS in SJL; DM, pp.22, 67; Cavalier, *Memoirs of the Wars of the Cevennes*, pub.1727.
24. Lelièvre, III, ch.VII; John Parker, *A Church in the Sun* (Grenada).

Notes to Chapter Twenty-eight

1. Ch. of Com, 9.2.1793; *Gazette*, 27.4. 1793.
2. ABSJ XX (1972), pp.388-390.
3. *ibid.*, V (1902), pp.14, 15; DNB.
4. BDJ, p.92; Balleine, *The Tragedy of Philippe d'Auvergne*, *passim.*
5. AE, 10.6.1794.
6. Michel de R, *Jean Chouan et la Chouannerie*, pub.1889.
7. Documents in PRO and British Library.
8. Bouillon to Huskisson, Jersey, 17.4.1797.
9. Lelièvre, *op. cit.*, III, Ch.II; Rolls of Court, 2.4.1796, 7.5.1796.
10. AE, 24.3.1798, 28.7.1798, 18.10.1798; Lelièvre, *op. cit.*, p.367.
11. OC, 12.12.1797; AE, 28.1.1799, 27.7.1799.
12. Hettier, *Relations de la Normandie avec les Iles pendant l'Emigration* (Caen 1885), p.89; OC, 25.1.1794.
13. BDJ, p.201; OJH, II, p.153; *La Patrie*, 25.1.1851, 1.2.1851.
14. War Office, Bouillon to Dundas, 16.3.1796; Bouillon to Jersey Royalists, 14.5.1796; Hettier, *op. cit.*, pp.166-169.
15. *Gazette*, 18.6.1796, 25.6.1796.
16. *Revue de la Manche*, July 1975, p.177; Oct. 1977, p.179.
17. AE, 23.10.1795, 1.10.1796, 16.2.1797; *Gazette*, 17.12.1796.
18. ABSJ VII (1914), pp.416-424; AE, 7.6.1800.
19. Minutes of Chamber of Commerce, *passim.*
20. BDJ, p.578.
21. Béchervaise, *Thirty-six Years of a Seafaring Life*, pub.1839.
22. See ch.16, p.127.
23. Renier Chalon, *Le Dernier Duc de Bouillon*; Balleine, *op. cit.*, ch.12.
24. Balleine, *op. cit.*, p.118.
25. ABSJ V (1902), pp.16-18.
26. de la Croix, *op. cit.*, pp.47-49; see ch.1, p.5; William Davies, *Fort Regent.*
27. BDJ, p.465; de la Croix, *op. cit.*, pp.56-59.
28. BDJ, p.631; MSS in SJL.
29. Thomas Lyte, *A Sketch of History*, p.281.
30. OC, 8.6.1816.
31. Commissioned 1872, unveiled 29.10.1885.
32. Quayle, *op. cit.*, pp.70-73.
33. AE, 10.12.1796, 10.5.1797.
34. BDJ, p.14.
35. Hettier, *op. cit.*
36. *All for the King*, ch.15, 16; *Victorian Voices*, p.25.

Notes to Chapter Twenty-nine

1. BDJ, p.258.
2. Inglis, *The Channel Islands* (1834).
3. ABSJ VII (1910), pp.32, 33; *Chronique*, 4.9.1819.
4. *ibid.*, VIII (1918), pp.347, 348; BDJ, p.38.
5. *Chron.*, 14.7.1821, 21.7.1821, 28.7.1821.
6. *Constitutionnel*, 28.7.1821; Rolls of Court, 28.7.1821.
7. BDJ, p.14; Plees, *op. cit.*, p.84.
8. ABSJ XIX (1968), pp.315-318; Quayle, *op. cit.*, p.64.
9. Le Couteur, *Royal Agricultural Society of England*, Vol.V, pt.1; *Victorian Voices*, ch.16.
10. BDJ, pp.368, 379; *One Hundred Years of the R.J.A. and H.S.* (1933).
11. ABSJ XV (1952), pp.439-443; Inglis, *op. cit.*
12. ABSJ XII (1935), pp.407-412.
13. *ibid.*, XII (1934), p.291 (footnote); Report from Mr George Louis, Post Office Surveyor, dated 23.4.1830.
14. OC, 12.7.1841; AE, 11.4.1838; R of C, 21.4.1838.
15. ABSJ V (1902), p.25; Jersey Society in London, 13.11.1934.
16. *Constitutionnel*, 10.7.1823.
17. English Customs' House Records, now in England.
18. Tupper, *History of Guernsey*, pp.375, 444.

19. BDJ, p.391; R.Mayne, *Mail-ships of the Channel Islands.*
20. *Chronique*, 3.4.1824, 15.5.1824.
21. *Queen of the Isles*, 1840; Inglis *op. cit.*; *Royal Channel Islands Almanack and Complete Guide Book*, 1842.
22. Brett, *Buildings in the Town and Parish of St Helier*, OJH II; Le Couteur Diaries; B. de Veulle in *Bulletin of the International Camellia Society*, 1979, 1980.
23. Davies. *op. cit. passim*; see ch.33, pp.288, 290; de la Croix, *Ville de St H.*, p.40; E.T. Nicolle, *op. cit.*, p.75; ABSJ V (1902), pp.22-24; *Gazette*, 21.3.1812; BDJ, p.50; for the general development of town see de la Croix and Nicolle *passim.*
24. BDJ, p.254; OC, 10.2.1810; Ecc. Court, 5.3.1818; Royal Court, 31.3.1819; de la Croix, *op. cit.*, p164.
25. de la Croix, *op. cit.*, pp.165-168; Isherwood, *Jersey Catholic Record*; *Chronique* (opening dates), 3.1.1813, 29.8.1819, 7.1.1826, 3.1.1827, 1.11.1829, 28.6.1835, foundation stone of Aquila Road 9.7.1839.
26. Minutes of the Trustees' Meetings, Methodist Archives, Jersey.
27. See ch.31, p.254.
28. BDJ, p.611.
29. *ibid.*, p.451.
30. de la Croix, *op. cit.*, p.150; Harbour first lit 2.11.1831.
31. See ch.30, p.253; see also Saunders, *Jersey in the 18th and 19th Centuries*; de la Croix, *op. cit.*, 122 *et seq.*; Ch. of Comm., 14.3.1786; OJH, II, p.181; ABSJ XXI (1975), pp.313-316; *Chron.*, 27.9.1817.
32. Foundation stone 2.11.1829; work completed 4 p.m. 24.8.1832.
33. AE, 18.10.1836, 29.5.1837; foundation stone 29.9.1841.
34. For dates of first publication see *A Chronology of Jersey*.
35. Inglis, *op. cit.*, pp.172, 176.
36. *Jersey Times,* 24.3.1837, 24.10.1837.

Notes to Chapter Thirty

1. AE, 1.10.1834; OC, 11.9.1840; Pamphlets 33 in SJL; *Observations on the Currency of the Island of Jersey 1845* printed by Coutanche, late Gosset, 20 Queen Street and 33 Hill Street; BDJ, p.196.
2. BDJ, p.305.
3. Helsham, *A Reminiscence of Queen Victoria's Visit to Jersey*; *A Royal Souvenir of the Queen of England's visit to Jersey* (printed by Gosset); *Victorian Voices*, ch.12; Pamphlets 23, 38; a number of poems, some on silk, in SJL; local papers.
4. ABSJ XX (1969), pp.57, 58; *Jersey Times*, 3.9.1846.
5. Founders of firms still in existence.
6. BDJ, p.367; Le Capelain, *Royal Jersey Album*, 1847; *Chron.*, 10.7.1847.
7. Cottrill, *Victoria College Jersey*, pp.3-7.
8. Pamphlets 92 in SJL, *Rapport du Comité chargé de considérer le meilleur moyen de célébrer le Jubilé de la Reine Victoria.*
9. BDJ, p.385; Evidence to Royal Commission (Ellis and Bros) 1860.
10. OC, 21.8. 1841.
11. All the quotations may be found in the Report of the Commissioners to Parliament in 1861.
12. BDJ, p.290; ABSJ V (1905), pp.327, 328, 335; VI (1906), p.146; OC, 15.5.1833, 20.5.1833.
13. BDJ, p.451; ABSJ V (1905), p.328.
14. *Guernsey and Jersey Magazine*, Vol. IV, July 1837, pp.113-117, 182-186.
15. Local newspapers, 1847, *passim.*
16. ABSJ XXI (1973), pp.166-173; XXII (1979), pp.286-298.
17. ABSJ XXII (1978), pp.176-180; *The French Empire and the Poles*, printed in Jersey, 1853.
18. Maurois, *Olympio ou la Vie de Victor Hugo.*
19. *Chronique*, 17.10.1855 *et seq.*; 1,500 people reported as present at protest meeting.
20. François-Victor Hugo, *op. cit.*, pp.12-20.
21. OC, 11.2.1852, 20.12.1853 (enterinée Jan. 1854).
22. AE, 29.12.1856, 3.1.1857.
23. *Chron.*, 13.8.1859; *Victorian Voices*, pp.150, 151.
24. Commissioners 1859, 1860 were Sir John Awdry, Sir Richard Jebb and the Earl of Devon.
25. BDJ, p.385.
26. Information from H. Coutanche and Jean Arthur.
27. See *Chronique* and other papers for opening dates: 19.7.1842, 13.10.1844, 10.10.1847, 8.4.1849, 25.2.1855, 3.4.1859, 18.7.1861.
28. Hills, *Historical Directory* 1874; 13.7.1870, replaced by Jersey New Waterworks Co. in 1882.
29. For details see ch.32 note 16.
30. See ch.29.
31. See Almanachs of the period; *Newfoundland and Labrador Pilot*, pub. by Hydrographer of the Navy; see also article in *Guernsey Press* on Gaspé 5.12.1979.

Notes to Chapter Thirty-one

1. AE, 31.3.1871.
2. AE, 31.1.1877, 23.6.1877; *Chron.*, 29.8.1872, 2.12.1874, 12.12.1874, 13.11.1875, 6.12.1876, 13.12.1876, 6.1.1877.
3. Contemporary Almanachs; RTSG XIV (1949), *Banking in the C.I.*; S.J. Le Rossignol, *Banking and Political Events in Jersey* (1915).
4. OC, 5.7.1813, 24.5.1832; AE, 31.12.1831.

5. Jurat, 1856-1873; *Chron.*, 28.5.1856.
6. Criminal Assizes, 12.5.1873; *Chron.*, 14.5.1873.
7. *Chron.*, 5.11.1873, 10.1.1874, 17.1.1874.
8. *British Press and Jersey Times*, 4.7.1873 and other contemporary accounts.
9. *Nouvelle Chronique*, 13.1.1886.
10. Le Rossignol, *op. cit.*, p.16 and local newspapers.
11. *ibid.*, pp.18-22; *Evening Post*, 29.9.1962, re centenary of Lloyds Bank in Jersey.
12. Much research continues to be undertaken in Canada and Jersey on the history of these firms.
13. Ansted, *The Channel Islands* (1862), p.510.
14. BDJ, p.209; *Les Chroniques*, 24.9.1892.
15. *Weekly Express*, 25.6.1887; dates of opening: 3.1.1872, 1.12.1886, 21.6.1887.
16. Isherwood, *op. cit.*
17. *Chron.*, 27.12.1879; *Brit. Press and Jersey Times*, 30.6.1880.
18. *G.P.D.S.T. 1872-1972, A Centenary Review.*
19. Rosa Hovey became Headmistress of Penrhos College, Colwyn Bay and has an Oxford Scholarship named after her. Emily Ahier was Jersey's first woman graduate. Louie French taught at the college and later accompanied her medical missionary husband, Dr. A. Morley, to China.
20. *Nouvelle Chronique*, 30.6.1888, 28.7.1888, 8.9.1888, 15.9.1888.
21. BDJ, p.304.
22. *PC Jersey in re Regis of Royal Warrant, 1890.*
23. This is fully documented in the 5 volumes reporting the Prison Board Case. These are also a valuable source for students of Jersey's Constitutional history.
24. Overdale bought from Thomas Godfray, 30.3.1889; OC, 15.7.1893.
25. Jersey Society in London, Occasional Publications, VIII, H.E. le V. dit Durell, *The Men whom I have known*; see also BDJ, pp.34, 45, 271, 458.
26. BDJ, pp.20, 38, 309, 334, 366, 483, 598.
27. AE, 8.2.1900.

Notes to Chapter Thirty-two

1. *Nouv. Chron.*, 9.8.1902, 13.8.1902.
2. BDJ, p.279.
3. *Rec. des Lois*, 8.7.1931, 12.12.1931, 16.12.1912.
4. *Nouv. Chron.*, 19.9.1914, 30.9.1914, 20.2.1915, 2.3.1915, 6.3.1915, POW camp, 20.3.1915; *EP*, 2.3.1915.
5. See ch.32, pp.265, 267.
6. Lieut. W.A. McCrae Bruce; Capt. A.M.C. McReady-Diarmid.
7. Unveiled 11.11.1923.
8. Cargo boat, *inter alia*, wrecked 10.10.1916; from the outbreak of war Mr F.J. Bois, Deputy for St Saviour, undertook to negotiate from his office regulations for rationing or controlling scarce commodities such as coal. He also obtained for the Island supplies of cattle food and manure, and arranged for the marketing of potatoes and their transport. On 15 January 1921, islanders presented him with a silver salver and candlesticks in gratitude for his work in negotiating with the British authorities as his contribution to the war effort; *Chron.*, 19.1.1921; *EP*, 17.1.1921.
   The Defence of the Realm Act, 8.9.1914, with later amendments, was extended to Jersey and breaches such as the hoarding of petrol were dealt with under this heading. *Chroniques,* 12.2.1916-18.3.1916.
9. *EP*, 10.7.1928, 22.9.1928.
10. *Rec. des Lois*, 14.7.1899
11. *ibid.*, 1.1.1919, 19.6.1919, 12.7.1919.
12. *ibid.*, 12.4.1924; *EP*, 11.12.1928 (Mrs Trachy).
13. *ibid.*, 10.4.1928.
14. Pocock, *The Memoirs of Lord Coutanche*, pp.62-67.
15. See ch.1, *passim*; ABSJ VII (1913), pp.289-305, 315-325.
16. Bonsor, *The Jersey Railway*, *The Jersey Eastern Railway*; Ginns and Osborne, *Transport in Jersey.*
17. Opened 10.3.1937, see *EP.*
18. The Chairman of the Board is always a member of the States.
19. BDJ, p.103.
20. *ibid.*, p.29; ABSJ X (1926), p.xxv.
21. Information from Jurat H. Perrée.
22. A sloping but usually cultivable field.
23. John Le Masurier; local newspapers Feb-May, 1936.
24. John Tessier-Yandell, *HMS Jersey*, 1654-1976.
25. G.R. Balleine's account of the Occupation and immediate post-war period is that of an eye-witness who lived through the events described and knew the Jerseymen in office.
26. ABSJ XV (1951), pp.317-328; the right to use the prefix Royal was granted on the 50th anniversary of the Battle of Jersey.
27. See Bibliography.
28. J. Stevens, *Le Moulin de Quetivel.*
29. ABSJ XIX (1967), p.178.
30. The usufruct of Mont Orgueil was handed to the States by the British Government 28.6.1907 and that of Elizabeth Castle, 21.5.1923.
31. Son of Josué Falle; BDJ, p.271.

Notes to Chapter Thirty-three

1. Paragraphs 2 and 3 are from the last chapter written by Balleine and thus a contemporary

account of the immediate post-war period; Franchise Law, 5.10.1948.
2. *Recueil des Lois*, 2.6.1948, 5.10.1948.
3. *Acte rapport*; see *EP*, 18.3.1947, implemented 1.4.1947.
4. The debates are fully recorded in the local press 1949-1951.
5. *Rec. des Lois*, 29.12.1853, 25.11.1949, 20.1.1964.
6. *ibid.*, 1.3.1864.
7. At present the Perrot Hall, Victoria Street.
8. See p.274.
9. ABSJ XV (1951), pp.317-328; XVI (1956), pp.365-372.
10. *The Minquiers and Ecréhos Case, France/United Kingdom. Judgment of 17 November, 1953*; copy in SJL.
11. *Report and Recommendations of the Special Committee of the States appointed to consult with H.M.'s Government on all matters relating to the Government's Application to join the European Economic Community*, pp.48, 49.
12. The debate is reported fully in the *EP*.
13. *ibid.*; see also Heyting, *The Constitutional Relationship between Jersey and the United Kingdom* (1977).
14. Lord Crowther died before the report was completed and was replaced as chairman by Lord Kilbrandon.
15. See page 285.
16. Poingdestre, *Caesarea.*
17. Code of 1771 Amendment (Jersey) Law, reg. 22.10.1962.
18. Lottery: Gambling Law, 26.3.1966, first draw August 1966; Swimming Club founded, 9.10.1865.
19. Rec. des Lois, 12.6.1973, 24.10.1973, 26.3.1974.
20. ABSJ XXI (1975), pp.381-391; (1976), pp.505-516; Frances Le Sueur, *op. cit.*, pp.15, 25.
21. Died 7 May 1948.

INDEX

Note: In earlier documents there is considerable variation in the spelling of surnames, and Christian names may be spelt in French or English. This accounts for some apparent discrepancies in the index.

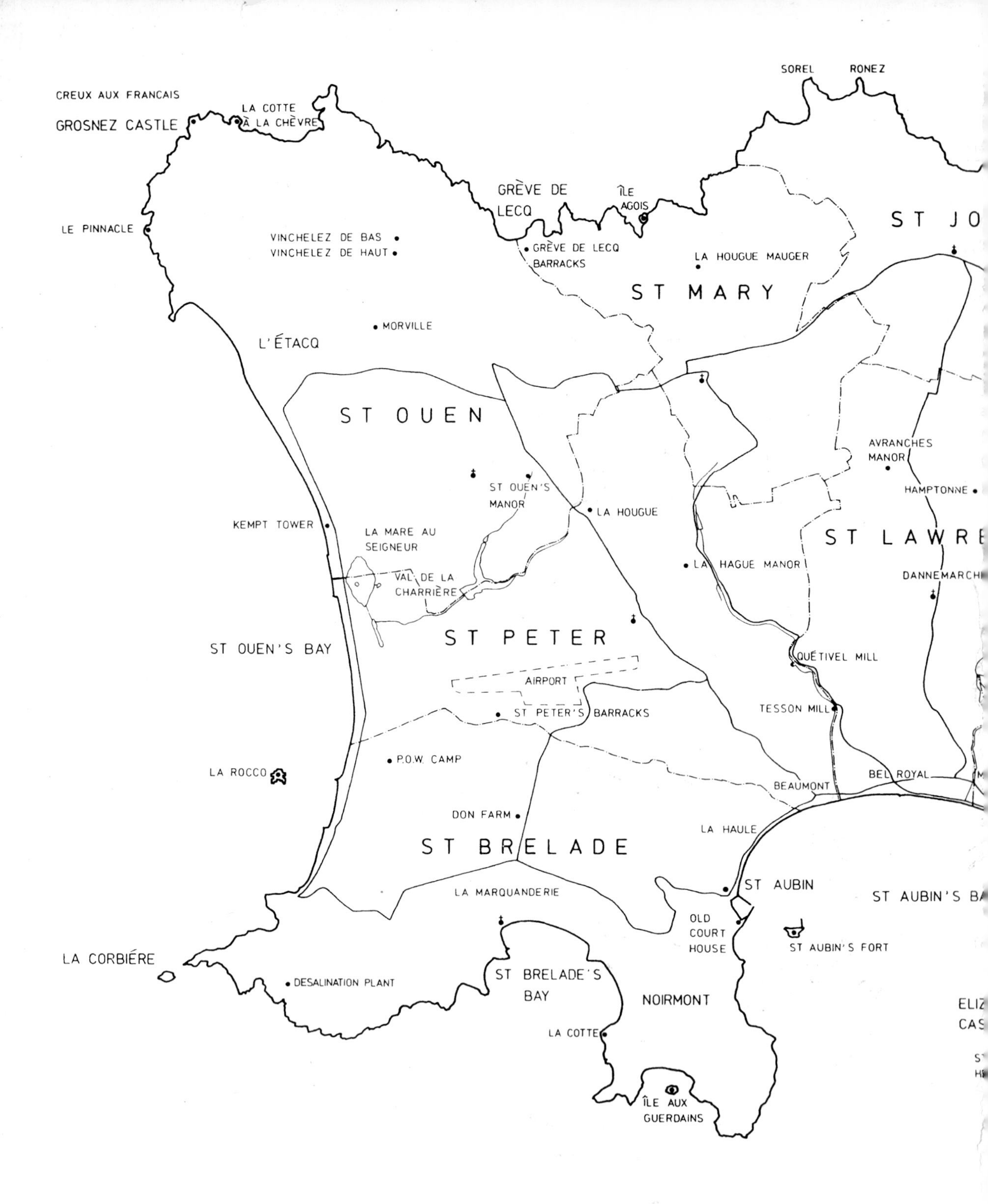
CREUX AUX FRANCAIS
GROSNEZ CASTLE
LA COTTE À LA CHÈVRE
SOREL
RONEZ
LE PINNACLE
VINCHELEZ DE BAS
VINCHELEZ DE HAUT
GRÈVE DE LECQ
ÎLE AGOIS
GRÈVE DE LECQ BARRACKS
LA HOUGUE MAUGER
ST MARY
L'ÉTACQ
MORVILLE
ST OUEN
AVRANCHES MANOR
HAMPTONNE
ST OUEN'S MANOR
LA HOUGUE
KEMPT TOWER
LA MARE AU SEIGNEUR
VAL DE LA CHARRIÈRE
LA HAGUE MANOR
ST PETER
ST OUEN'S BAY
QUÉTIVEL MILL
AIRPORT
TESSON MILL
ST PETER'S BARRACKS
P.O.W. CAMP
LA ROCCO
BEL ROYAL
BEAUMONT
DON FARM
LA HAULE
ST BRELADE
ST AUBIN
LA MARQUANDERIE
OLD COURT HOUSE
ST AUBIN'S FORT
LA CORBIÉRE
DESALINATION PLANT
ST BRELADE'S BAY
NOIRMONT
LA COTTE
ÎLE AUX GUERDAINS